Ambient Intelligence Techniques

Ambient Intelligence Techniques

Edited by
Prince McCurdy

www.willfordpress.com

Published by Willford Press,
118-35 Queens Blvd., Suite 400,
Forest Hills, NY 11375, USA

ISBN: 978-1-68285-340-5

Cataloging-in-Publication Data

Ambient intelligence techniques / edited by Prince McCurdy.
    p. cm.
Includes bibliographical references and index.
ISBN 978-1-68285-340-5
1. Ambient intelligence. 2. Artificial intelligence--Data processing. 3. Cognitive radio networks.
4. Wireless sensor networks. I. McCurdy, Prince.
QA76.9.A48 A64 2017
004.019--dc23

For information on all Willford Press publications
visit our website at www.willfordpress.com

Printed in the United States of America.

Contents

Preface

Ambient Intelligence is a futuristic technological approach to carry out complex tasks. It will play a crucial role in the fields of telecommunications, electronics, etc. Ambient systems are built with the help of advanced technologies such as context-aware systems, adaptive systems, etc. The ever growing need of advanced technology is the reason that has fueled the research in the field of ambient intelligence in recent times. This book includes a detailed explanation of the various concepts and applications of this field. It elucidates new techniques and their applications in a multidisciplinary approach. The extensive content of this book provides the readers with a thorough understanding of the subject.

This book has been the outcome of endless efforts put in by authors and researchers on various issues and topics within the field. The book is a comprehensive collection of significant researches that are addressed in a variety of chapters. It will surely enhance the knowledge of the field among readers across the globe.

It gives us an immense pleasure to thank our researchers and authors for their efforts to submit their piece of writing before the deadlines. Finally in the end, I would like to thank my family and colleagues who have been a great source of inspiration and support.

Editor

A Virtual Environment based Serious Game to Support Health Education

Tiago Gomes[1], Tiago Abade[1], José Creissac Campos[1], Michael D. Harrison[2], José Luís Silva[3,*]

[1]Departamento de Informática/Universidade do Minho & HASLab/INESC TEC, Braga, Portugal
[2]Newcastle University & Queen Mary University of London, UK
[3]Madeira-ITI, Universidade da Madeira, Funchal, Portugal

Abstract

APEX was developed as a framework for ubiquitous computing (ubicomp) prototyping through virtual environments. In this paper the framework is used as a platform for developing a serious game designed to instruct and to inform. The paper describes the Asthma game, a game aimed at raising awareness among children of asthma triggers in the home. It is designed to stimulate a healthier life-style for those with asthma and respiratory problems. The game was developed as the gamification of a checklist for the home environment of asthma patients.

Keywords: Human Factors, Design, Health Education, Serious Games, Asthma, Virtual Environments

1. Introduction

Serious games support playing to learn. Games can be used to promote training, education, health, public policies and strategic communication as well as to provide pleasure [1–3]. This paper is concerned with the possibility of promoting health education through computer-based serious games.

The paper describes a first person game that addresses the problems faced by children with asthma. Asthma is a chronic disease and specific procedures prevent the emergence of crises. The goal of the game is to convey knowledge about these procedures, focusing children at elementary school level. The game was designed as the gamification [4] of a checklist used to evaluate the living conditions of asthma sufferers.

First person games typically involve control of an avatar that is placed inside a 3D virtual world. The paper illustrates the use of a framework called APEX, that is designed to prototype ubicomp environments [5], to support the rapid development of serious games. Ubicomp environments provide personalized services to users within physical spaces through the integration of environmental information using sensors. APEX supports the creation of virtual environments (using a 3-D application server) and the definition of behaviors within them, and can be used to develop games within these environments.

The paper extends work originally presented in [6], providing a more detailed description of the rationale behind the game's design. It also describes an evaluation of the first version of the game and proposals for design improvement.

2. Related work

A substantial research literature is concerned with exploring how best to design serious games for health education and training. An extensive review of the general area of video games in health care can be found in [7]. This review spans education and training to therapeutic applications of games. The more specific topic of immersive 3-D environments in healthcare education is also reviewed in [8].

3-D application servers, that can be used to develop the kind of immersive 3-D game that is the focus of the paper, have also been explored in other work. Boulos provides an overview of the use of Second Life [9]. Two of their conclusions are: (1) that educators need to *think out of the box* when using this type of environment,

*Corresponding author. Email: jose.l.silva@m-iti.org

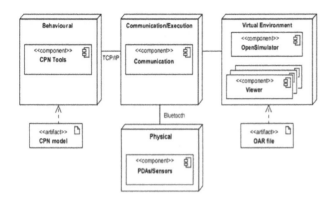

Figure 1. APEX Architecture

avoiding a replication of the class room context inside the virtual environment, and (2) that research is still needed to make 3-D virtual worlds more accessible and to improve the efficiency and effectiveness of their use for learning and teaching. The present paper addresses these two issues. Gamification provides a means of making environments more engaging than a simple replication of the physical world. APEX provides a flexible means to develop such games.

3. The APEX framework

APEX (rApid Prototyping for user EXperience) [5] is a framework for the rapid prototyping of ubicomp environments, enabling their simulation and analysis in the early stages of development. The platform consists of a number of components providing support for prototyping at different levels. There are four main components (see logical architecture in Figure 1).

(1) The behavioral component (top left in the figure) is responsible for managing the behavior of the prototype. It is based on CPN Tools[1] and uses Coloured Petri Nets (CPN) [10] to describe the behavior of the virtual environment in response to user actions and context changes.

(2) The virtual environment component (top right) is responsible for managing the physical appearance and layout of the prototype. It is based on OpenSimulator[2], a multi-platform and multi-user virtual environment simulator.

(3) The communication/execution component (top middle) and (4) the physical component (bottom middle) are responsible for coordinating the communication between all components and for communication with external devices, respectively. These components form an OpenSimulator module.

The platform supports different types of evaluation of the prototypes using these components. The models of the behavioral component can be analyzed. The developed prototype can be used to evaluate user experience experimentally.

This paper describes how APEX was used to create a virtual environment that incorporates a serious game (cf. [11]). The aim of the proposed game is to convey information about asthma and how best to prevent asthma attacks.

4. Asthma

Asthma is a chronic inflammatory disease of the respiratory tract characterized by variable and recurring symptoms, reversible airflow obstruction, and bronchospasm. The most common symptoms include wheezing, coughing and shortness of breath [12].

Asthma attacks can arise for a number of reasons. The most common reasons are drug intake while eating or taking medication, and inhaling substances such as pollen, smoke, animal dander or dust. Many of the substances that cause asthma attacks derive from the presence of mites. These substances are often present in the home. Upholstery, curtains and clothes often harbor large communities of mites.

There are several procedures that prevent the causes of asthma attacks, but these procedures are not always known by asthma sufferers. Parents, and especially children, need support to identify what triggers asthma so that they can take appropriate action. Government and non-government organizations have developed checklists that aim to provide such support. The EPA[3] Asthma Home Environment Checklist [13] is one example. The checklist covers six allergens and irritants (Dust Mites, Pests, Warm-blooded Pets, Mold, Secondhand Smoke and Nitrogen Dioxide), as well as mentioning a generic class of chemical irritants. For each allergen/irritant the checklist identifies triggers as well as typical locations where it can be found. The checklist contains 23 questions divided into two categories distinguishing Home interior and Room interior. Each question is associated with action that can be taken.

Examples of Home interior questions include "Does anyone smoke in the home or car", "Is the patient's asthma worse when around warm-blooded pets?" and "Are there air conditioning window units?".

Examples of Room interior questions include: "What does the patient sleep on?", "Are stuffed toys present?" and "What window coverings are present?"

An illustration of action steps proposed by the checklist relating to warm-blooded pets is the following:

---

[1]CPN Tools: http://cpntools.org (last visited: 29/11/2013)
[2]Opensimulator: http://opensimulator.org/ (last visited: 29/11/2013)

[3]The United States Environmental Protection Agency.

Figure 2. The Asthma game's house (outside view)

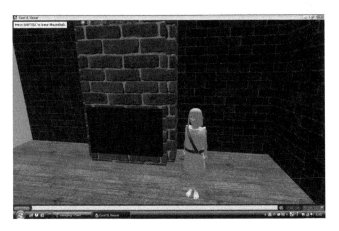

Figure 3. A fire place in the house

- If possible, remove the pet from the home or keep the pet outside.

- If this is not possible, keep the pet out of the patient's sleeping area and off the furniture.

Checklists, however, are not the best way to help children learn how to avoid asthma attacks. The EPA checklist was originally designed for home care visitors, rather than children or parents. The aim of the game is to convey the information contained in the EPA checklist more attractively to parents and children. As a result it is to be hoped that quality of life will be improved and dependency on home care visits reduced.

5. Design of the Asthma Game

The APEX platform was used to develop a 3D immersive environment that aims to allow players to connect the information provided in the checklist to their daily lives. A more technical description of how APEX was used to build the game is provided in [14]. Here the focus of the discussion is on how the game was derived from the EPA checklist.

Since the checklist offers information about the interior of homes, the game was set in a house (see Figure 2). The house used (derived from a model of the Aware Home at the Georgia Institute of Technology [15]) is a two storey building containing rooms and areas typically found in a home.

The first version of the game addresses six of the allergens and irritants identified in the EPA checklist: Dust Mites, Warm-Blooded Pets, Mold, Nitrogen Dioxide, chemical irritants and second hand smoke. Pests were not addressed. One or more situations were created that represented the presence of the allergen/irritant in question, providing a potential asthma trigger.

Nine situations covered the first five of these allergens/irritants.

1. Domestic pets were placed inside the house, more specifically in a bedroom. This was done to illustrate the second question in the checklist ("Is the patient's asthma worse when around warm-blooded pets?").

2. Laundry was littered around some of the floor areas, thereby offering threat of Dust Mites. While this feature did not relate directly to the checklist, it was considered relevant given the target group for the game.

3. A fireplace was created in the house (see Figure 3) that would generate Nitrogen Dioxide. This feature illustrated the checklist item: "Are supplemental heating sources used?".

4. Stuffed toys were provided, particularly in the bedroom. This was another situation relating to Dust Mites and addressed the checklist question: "Are stuffed toys present?".

5. Some of the walls in the house had accumulated mold. Relevant checklist questions here were: "Is there evidence of water damage, moisture, or leaks (such as damp carpet or leaky plumbing)?" and "Do you see or smell mold or mildew (such as in the bathroom on tub, shower, walls, or windows)?".

6. Curtains were used in the house, again relating to Dust Mites and the question:"What window coverings are present?".

7. Blankets were provided on beds, again relating to Dust Mites, and to the question "What types of bedding does the patient use?".

8. Cleansing products were placed in easily accessible places, for example the bathroom (see Figure 4). This related to the question "Is the patient's asthma worse when around chemicals or products

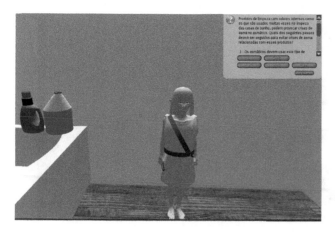

Figure 4. Cleansing products in the bathroom

with strong odors (such as cleaners, paints, adhesives, pesticides, air fresheners, or cosmetics)?".

9. Carpets were provided on the floor. This occurrence further related to dust mites and the question:"What type of floor covering is present?".

No explicit situation was created for second hand smoke. However, as explained below, this allergen's presence was addressed outside the house.

A quiz game was conceived to convey information about actions relating to these situations. A Non-Player Character (NPC) was placed next to each trigger (see Figures 3 and 4). These characters were designed to provide relevant information about "their" allergen/irritant. They were also designed to ask players relevant questions about how to act to avoid asthma attacks. A further NPC was placed at the entrance of the house to deal with the secondhand smoke allergen, dealing generically with this situation.

Each player controls an avatar in the virtual world (see Figure 2). They can interact with NPCs by approaching and explicitly *touching* them (allowing interaction with the object in the virtual environment). Players can also see and interact with each other (e.g. by exchanging messages). Each player is allowed to continue to answer a question until the right answer is found. For each correct answer, the player gets a word which, at the end of the game, can be used to form a sentence about asthma. This is intended as an incentive for players to attempt to answer all the questions. After answering the questions, the player is notified that the game has ended, and of how many wrong answers were given. If playing competitively, the first player to correctly answer all questions wins.

As far as is possible the phrasing of the questions is similar to that of the EPA checklist. However, some adaptations were made to accommodate the age range of the target audience for the game. As an illustration the question relating to cleansing products,

see item 8 above, was expressed as (translated from the original Portuguese formulation used in the game and illustrated in Figure 4):

- "Cleansing products with intense odors, such as those often used in the cleaning of toilets, can cause asthma attacks. Which of the following steps should be followed to prevent asthma attacks related to these products?"

The NPC puts forward four possible answers to choose from. Correct answers capture action steps listed in the checklist. Wrong answers correspond to actions that go against what is recommended. Because the checklist offers more than one action step for each question, it is possible that more than one correct answer can be provided by a player. The correct answers must therefore be chosen from a set of alternatives.

For example, take the case of chemicals and products with strong odors (specific examples are cleansing products) the checklist proposes the following action steps:

- "Limit patient's exposure as much as possible by minimizing product use, using products only when patient is not present, or trying alternative products."

- "If products are used, carefully follow manufacturer's instructions on the label and make sure the area is well ventilated."

This was *translated* into the following four possible answers/actions:

1. Asthmatics should use this type of product

2. The use of these products should be avoided or minimized, if possible replacing them with other products

3. If their use is unavoidable, they should be used when the asthmatic person is not in the house

4. This type of product is never harmful for asthmatics

The player must then identify the correct answers from this set of alternatives.

6. User Study

A usability study was designed to assess the acceptability of the game as well as its potential as a means of learning about asthma. Participants in the study were aged 9 and 10 years, attending the fourth year of primary school. All participants were already in possession of a personal computer[4] with enough features and

---

[4]Intel Classmate-based laptop computers.

capabilities to run the game. Their machines were pre-installed with the software needed to play the game (the Cool VL Viewer[5]).

Initially, a study had been planned to compare a group of children playing the game with a group attending a *regular* lesson about Asthma. When discussing the study with the teaching staff, however, two concerns were raised. Only half of the children would play the game. It was felt that this would be unfair to the other half, and could make them feel less motivated. At the same time it was felt that comparing the game against a particular teacher would not necessarily represent traditional teaching practice in general.

It was therefore decided to evaluate the children's perception of what they had learned, an indirect measure of evaluating the game that follows the approach taken in [16, 17] for example.

18 children (11 boys and 7 girls) were chosen to play. The study took place in a classroom. None of the children had previous experience of 3D application servers (e.g. Second Life[6]). Twelve children stated that they had played computer games before (this information was obtained through a questionnaire – see below). The session began with instructions designed to enable all participants to use the platform without problems. They were allowed time to familiarize with the Cool VL Viewer and the virtual environment. The participants were given a minimum of 30 minutes to complete the Asthma game. During this period they were observed by three evaluators. Their teacher was also present.

The children were asked to answer questions as requested by the NPCs when *touching* them. The game finished when all questions were correctly answered by the player. Wrong answers were counted and the results presented at the end. At that point, using the words won by each right answer, the player should be able to form the sentence about asthma.

Apart from two computers that had initial problems accessing the APEX server, all users were quickly engaged in the game. Their engagement was of two types. Some children actually played the game, trying to answer the questions. A majority, however, became more interested in exploring the virtual environment and interacting with other players through it. This interaction could be observed both as chatting within the virtual environment, and pushing or running into other avatars. Some children complained of not being able to play the game as a result of this type of interference.

Exploration of the virtual environment progressed through stages. Initially, players realized they could walk into the water surrounding the island where the house was set and could explore the seabed. Then they realized that they could activate a flight mode and fly around in the environment (a particularly popular activity). These two features were the main distractions. They caused a few players to lose their way so that they required help to return to the island and the house. At a later stage, a reduced number of players realized they could manipulate the virtual environment by creating (later also deleting) objects.

In consequence, while reaction to the game was positive, some of available features of the virtual environment contributed to distraction from the purpose of the game.

After playing the game, each player completed a 3-point Likert scale questionnaire[7] describing their experience. The data collected helped complement and extend the analysis derived from observation. Results show that players enjoyed the game. For example, 16 out of 18 players found the game fun to play, and 12 found it easy to play. None gave negative replies to these questions. In terms of perception of what the children had learnt, despite the observed distractions during game play, the results were positive (with the mode of all questions being the Yes reply). 12 children felt the game had helped them to know more about the disease and to be able to help others. 14 felt they now knew what to do at home to prevent respiratory problems (one child gave a negative answer to this question), and all felt motivated to apply what they had learnt.

In summary, results indicate that the game can help in conveying information about asthma, but some improvements were needed to guarantee that players stay focussed on the game's objectives.

7. Game redesign

A second version of the game was developed to overcome some of the problems with the first version. This new version preserves the rules and mechanics of the game. Changes were mainly concerned with the set up of the virtual environment.

A transparent barrier was placed between land and water, and the flight mode was disabled. These limitations made it possible to prevent both entry into water and distraction caused by the flight functionality. Since a significant number of players lost time changing the environment, the functionalities that enabled construction and editing of the environment were disabled. The chat functionality was not disabled as it was felt that some degree of interaction between players is useful.

---

[5]Cool VL Viewer: http://sldev.free.fr/ (last visited: 29/12/2013)
[6]Second Life: http://secondlife.com/ (last visited: 29/12/2013)

[7]Available at: http://ivy.di.uminho.pt/apex

At this stage we are preparing a second study with the new version of the game. Preliminary results indicate that the new configuration of the virtual environment succeeded in focussing players on the game. A number of preliminary test subjects have been able to complete the game successfully.

8. Conclusions and future work

Serious Games combine learning with entertainment. As part of the APEX project an approach was developed to enable the rapid development of prototypes of ubicomp environments. This paper describes how the environment was used for the development of a serious game that addresses the problems faced by children with asthma.

The goal of the game is to impart knowledge about how to act when faced with factors that might cause asthma attacks. The game was designed as a gamification of the EPA Asthma Home Environment Checklist. Action steps in the checklist were transformed into answers to questions that addressed the items in the checklist. The game does not cover all aspects of the checklist (it would become too long). However the advantage of using APEX is that new versions can be created quickly that address further different aspects of the checklist.

To validate the concept, a user study was conducted. This study revealed that the game (its virtual environment) succeeded in capturing the attention of children. Additionally, it showed that children felt they had learnt about the disease while having fun playing the game. However, the study also showed that there is a need to restrict what avatars can do in the environment, to better focus the players on the goals of the game. Several features of Opensimulator were new to children and may explain the distraction. A second version of the game was developed that avoids the problematic features of the virtual environment. Preliminary results based on evaluation of the new version are positive, indicating that this version succeeds in focusing the players' attention.

In conclusion, while virtual environments prove engaging for activities of this kind, there is a need to configure them appropriately to ensure adherance to the objectives of the game. The development of both versions of the game demonstrate that the APEX framework is a feasible and flexible approach to the rapid development of serious games.

Acknowledgements

This work was carried out in the context of the APEX project, funded by ERDF - European Regional Development Fund through the COMPETE Programme (operational programme for competitiveness) and by National Funds through the FCT - Fundação para a Ciência e a Tecnologia (Portuguese Foundation for Science and Technology) within project FCOMP-01-0124-FEDER-015095.

References

[1] Abt, C.C. (1970) *Serious games* (The Viking Press).

[2] Zyda, M. (2005) From visual simulation to virtual reality to games. *IEEE Computer* 38(9): 25–32.

[3] Mouaheb, H., Fahli, A., Moussetad, M. and Eljamali, S. (2012) The serious game: What educational benefits? *Procedia - Social and Behavioral Sciences* 46: 5502 – 5508.

[4] Marczewski, A. (2013) *Gamification: A Simple Introduction*, 2nd ed.

[5] Silva, J.L., Ribeiro, O.R., Fernandes, J.M., Campos, J.C. and Harrison, M.D. (2010) The APEX framework: prototyping of ubiquitous environments based on petri nets. In *Human-Centred Software Engineering* (Springer), *Lecture Notes in Computer Science* 6409: 6–21.

[6] Gomes, T., Abade, T., Harrison, M., Silva, J. and Campos, J. (2013) Developing serious games with the APEX framework. In *Proc. Wksp. Ubiquitous games and gamification for promoting behavior change and wellbeing*: 37–40.

[7] Kato, P.M. (2010) Video games in health care: Closing the gap. *Review of General Psychology* 14(2): 113–121.

[8] Hansen, M.M. (2008) Versatile, immersive, creative and dynamic virtual 3-D healthcare learning environments: A review of the literature. *Journal of Medical Internet Research* 10(3): e26.

[9] Boulos, M., Hetherington, L. and Wheeler, S. (2007) Second life: an overview of the potential of 3-D virtual worlds in medical and health education. *Health Information & Libraries Journal* 24(4): 233–245.

[10] Jensen, K. and Kristensen, L.M. (2009) *Coloured Petri Nets* (Springer).

[11] de Freitas, S. (2008) *Serious Virtual Worlds: a scoping study*. Tech. Rep. 480, JISC.

[12] Akinbami, L.J. and Schoendorf, K.C. (2002) Trends in childhood asthma: Prevalence, health care utilization, and mortality. *Pediatrics* 110(2): 315–322.

[13] EPA, U. (2004), Asthma Home Environment Checklist, United States Environmental Protection Agency.

[14] Gomes, T., Abade, T., Campos, J., Harrison, M. and Silva, J. (2014) Rapid development of first person serious games using the apex platform: The asthma game. In *ACM SAC 2014*. Accepted.

[15] Kientz, J.A., Patel, S.N., Jones, B., Price, E., Mynatt, E.D. and Abowd, G.D. (2008) The Georgia Tech aware home. In *CHI '08 Extended Abstracts* (ACM): 3675–3680.

[16] Mendonça, C., Sousa, N., Soares, P., Varajão, I. and Oliveira, J. (2012) The role of motion interaction in learning mathematical tasks in a computer game. In *Proc. 5th Intl. Conf. of Education, Research and Innovation (ICERI 2012)* (IATED): 1370–1376.

[17] Fernandes, A., Sousa, N., Soares, P., Noy, D., Varajão, I. and Oliveira, J. (2013) Type of task in a mathematical skills videogame affects children's perception of learning and amusement. In *Proc. 7th Intl. Technology, Education and Development Conf. (INTED 2013)* (IATED): 515–522.

On Movement of Emergency Services amidst Urban Traffic

Manoj Bode[1], Shashi Shekhar Jha[1], Shivashankar B. Nair[1,*]

[1] Department of Computer Science & Engineering,
Indian Institute of Technology Guwahati,
Guwahati-781039, Assam, INDIA

Abstract

Managing traffic in urban areas is a complex affair. The same becomes more challenging when one needs to take into account the prioritized movement of emergency vehicles along with the normal flow of traffic. Although, mechanisms have been proposed to model intelligent traffic management systems, a concentrated effort to facilitate the movement of emergency services amongst urban traffic is yet to be formalized. This paper proposes a distributed multi-agent based mechanism to create partial green corridors for the movement of emergency service vehicles such as ambulances, fire brigade and police vans, amidst urban traffic. The proposed approach makes use of a digital network of traffic signal nodes equipped with traffic sensors and an agent framework to autonomously extend, maintain and manage *partial green corridors* for such emergency vehicles. The approach was emulated using *Tartarus*, an agent framework over a LAN. The results gathered under varying traffic conditions and also several emergency vehicles, validate the performance of this approach and its effects on the movement of normal traffic. Comparisons with the *non-prioritized* and *full green corridor* approaches indicate that the proposed *partial corridor* approach outperforms the rest.

Keywords: Intelligent Traffic Management, Emergency Services, Mobile Agents, Multi-agent systems, Distributed Intelligence, Tartarus, Emulation

1. Introduction

The ever increasing number of motorized vehicles has made commuting in urban areas an agonizing predicament. With the growth of cities and also the standards of living, management of such traffic has become a challenging task. Increase in traffic creates congestions especially at junctions which ultimately translate to delays in reaching respective destinations. Although such delays may be tolerated normally, the same become a serious impediment in case of an emergency. The delay in the movement of *emergency services* such as ambulances, fire brigade and police vehicles amidst Urban Traffic can result in loss of lives and property. The movement of such emergency services thus needs to be prioritized over the flow of normal traffic. This calls for an effective mechanism to facilitate free flow passage of emergency services in heavy traffic scenarios.

The most common method used to ensure a path for an emergency vehicle on the road is the use of a siren. This is a reactive mechanism which only caters to a local change in the traffic scenario within the immediate vicinity of the moving emergency vehicle. Although this mechanism is easy to implement, it does not guarantee a congestion free route. One naïve, effective and yet proactive mechanism to ensure a free flow of such emergency services is to create a *full green corridor* along the complete route of an emergency vehicle. A *full green corridor* essentially means blocking all other traffic that are orthogonal to the route of the emergency vehicle until its passage. The method has an adverse impact on the flow of adjoining traffic. In case of multiple emergency services moving in different directions, the task of making *full green corridors* for all such vehicles

* Corresponding author. Email: sbnair@iitg.ernet.in

translates to a multi-objective optimization problem. Hence, a mechanism for the movement of emergency services which is proactive and has least effect on the adjoining traffic forms the need of the day.

With advent of the digital era, advanced devices and smarter gadgets are being used to manage traffic in urban spaces. Cities are becoming smarter; using sensor networks to analyze traffic conditions and make quick and smart decisions on-the-go. State-of-art traffic management systems [17] use various approaches to manage traffic within the city. These approaches can be broadly classified into *centralized* and *distributed* approaches [20]. In a centralized approach, sensors collect local traffic information and send them to a central server. This information is used by the server to carry out massive computations to eventually manage the traffic. This approach calls for sophisticated infrastructure with high speed computational capability and bandwidth. The approach also implies a single point of failure. Further, making centralized decisions can be time consuming and may not be feasible in real-time scenarios.

Infrastructure of a traffic scenario is by nature distributed with a large number of concurrent and asynchronous processes and events occurring simultaneously. A distributed approach to manage traffic in urban areas thus seems more appropriate to realize a better traffic management system. Researchers have used multi-agent systems [9] to model the traffic management infrastructure effectively. These systems inherently provide enhanced features such as autonomy, adaptability, asynchronous processing, localized decisions, etc. which make them an ideal candidate for realizing distributed infrastructures. Although quite a few multi-agent based mechanisms have been proposed in the literature [5], to the best of our knowledge there seems to be no focussed work towards prioritizing the movement of emergency services within a traffic management system.

In this paper, we propose a multi-agent based mechanism to facilitate the movement of emergency services amidst urban traffic. The proposed mechanism creates partial green corridors *en route* the emergency vehicles with minimum impact on the movement of adjoining traffic. Extensions to our previous work [2] using a detailed and formal model of the proposed approach along with exhaustive experimentation and results have also been described.

The next section provides a background on the available multi-agent based approaches for traffic management. In succeeding sections, we describe the proposed approach for the movement of emergency services and its related dynamics. Further sections discuss the emulation experiments and the results obtained. The last section concludes the paper citing scope for future work.

2. Multi-agent based approaches for Traffic Management

Multi-agent technology, due to its inherent distributed characteristics, provides a natural solution to the highly distributed and dynamically changing traffic management and control scenarios. In [5], the authors have discussed the application of agents to different modes of transport by road, rail and air. They emphasize the power of agent based systems to regulate and improve the performance of traffic and transportation systems. Weyns et al. [19] present an agent-based approach using delegate multi-agent systems for anticipatory vehicle routing to avoid traffic congestions. They extend their approach in [6] with an environment-centric coordination model. In their approach, individual vehicles dispatch lightweight mobile agents for exploring alternate routes to find the shortest path to the destination, based on current traffic conditions. They further use intention agents to confirm the intended travel route on the road infrastructure. This information is used by the situated agents to estimate the future traffic so that they can alter the route of the approaching vehicles. In [15], the author proposes an intelligent travelling assistant based on a distributed model. They use personal agents for each individual traveller to communicate with the driver and the system to provide optimal advice to the former and update stored traffic information in the system. Katwijk and Koningsbruggen [18] present an agent-based model for the coordination of traffic-control and management of instruments. They modeled the traffic instruments as individual intelligent agents to tune their actions at a local level. They demonstrate that traffic management instruments can coordinate their actions to attain a common goal at the network-level using agent based concepts. Balaji et al. [1] attempt to exploit the advantages of evolutionary techniques for traffic management operations and congestion avoidance in Intelligent Transportation Systems. They propose a multi-agent based real-time centralized evolutionary optimization technique for urban traffic management using an evolutionary strategy for the control of traffic signals. Chen et al. [4] have proposed a model to integrate mobile agent technology with multi-agent systems. They have designed a model to enhance the ability of traffic management systems to deal with the uncertainty in dynamic environment. They use a system which facilitates mobility of agents (mobile agents) within a network called Mobile-C [3] to design an agent-based real-time traffic detection and management system. They argue that the use of mobile agents allows the deployment of new control algorithms and operations on-the-fly to respond to unforeseen events and conditions in urban traffic scenarios.

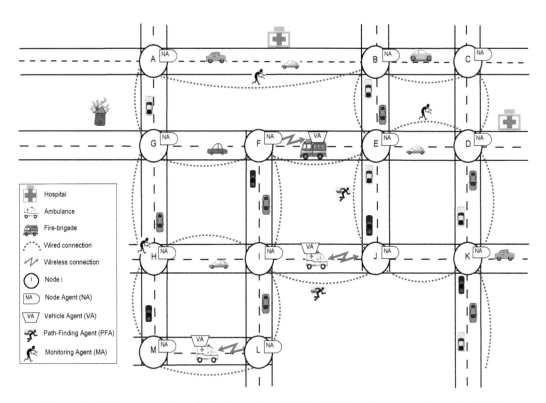

Figure 1. A Conceptual view of the Agent based Digital Traffic Infrastructure Network (DTIN)

The agent based traffic management and control approaches discussed so far focus on the city traffic as a whole. They seem to ignore the manner of movement of emergency services amidst general traffic. Handling the seamless flow of such emergency services constitutes a vital requirement in urban traffic. Discovering, managing and maintaining a *partial green corridor* towards the destination for such high priority services is mandatory in today's ever increasing traffic scenarios. In this paper, we present a concerted effort to prioritize the movement of emergency services within the general traffic flow using a mobile agent based multi-agent mechanism.

Mobile agents [8] have been used as an effective tool to realize various distributed applications. Their features such as autonomy, social ability and adaptability [8] along with the capability to migrate to other nodes of a network, carry their execution state and code and also clone provide for all the necessary characteristics of an intelligent distributed mechanism. Due to such features, mobile agents have a wide range of applications ranging from network management, electronic commerce, energy efficiency and metering, wireless sensors, grid computing, distributed data mining, human tracking, security, e-learning, etc. [13]. Martin-Campillo et al. [10] use mobile agents to collect medical data about patients related to allergies and infectious diseases in a mass emergency case, asynchronously. This avoids delay in deciding treatment once the patient reaches the

hospital. Pan et al. [14] have used mobile agents to contact hospitals for emergency services for elderly people. These agents carry the health information of patients to notify an ambulance about necessary medicines and equipment required. In the proposed approach, mobile agents are used to disseminate the traffic information along with the creation of *partial green corridors*.

3. Generating Partial Green Corridors

The proposed multi-agent based approach uses a Digital Traffic Infrastructure Network (DTIN) constituting an Internet of Things (IoT) of traffic signals and sensors [7]. Figure 1 shows the conceptual DTIN. An agent framework that supports all agent related functionalities such as autonomy, mobility, cloning, asynchronous executions, etc. forms a crucial part of the DTIN. In addition, the DTIN consists of the following components:

1. *Nodes*: Traffic signals connected using wired links are called *Nodes*. Each node comprises an agent framework, the traffic signal, traffic sensors and a digital banner.

2. *Node Agents (NA)*: The DTIN consists of a set of *Node Agents*. These agents are the static agents situated at every node within the DTIN. They gather local traffic information from traffic sensors and also control their respective traffic signals and the digital banner.

3. *Vehicle Agents (VA)*: Every emergency vehicle is equipped with hardware running the agent framework. Hence, every emergency vehicle hosts a static agent called *Vehicle Agent*.

4. *Monitoring Agents (MA)*: This set of mobile agents within the DTIN is responsible for acquiring and updating the flow of traffic information at the nodes. They move around in the network, collect information regarding the quantum of traffic and provide the same to all the nodes within the DTIN.

5. *Path-Finding Agents (PFA)*: These mobile agents are spawned by the *VA*s. They migrate within the DTIN to construct and ensure a partial green corridor along the shortest path with least traffic load, leading towards the destination of the emergency vehicle.

The node to node communication within the DTIN is assumed to be wired whereas the communication between a *VA* and an *NA* is wireless.

3.1. Dynamics of the Monitoring Agents (MA)

In the proposed approach, as every *NA* has local traffic information (Tm_{local}), the *MA* constructs a traffic flow map (Ψ) using this information. The information within Ψ comprises the location of nodes', their current traffic inflow and outflow, traffic load, timestamps, etc. Figure 2 shows a conceptual view of Ψ. An *MA* carries Ψ as its payload and migrates within the DTIN to update the same at all the nodes. As a result, every node within the DTIN contains a copy of Ψ termed Ψ_{local}. As there may be more than one *MA* within the DTIN, the Ψ_{local} can be updated by different *MA*s at different times. Whenever an *MA* arrives at a node within the DTIN, it communicates with the *NA* at that node to collect the latest Tm_{local} and Ψ_{local}. The *MA* then updates its Ψ with the new information received from Tm_{local} and Ψ_{local}. In addition, it also updates the Ψ_{local} available with the *NA*. Algorithm 1 depicts the working of the *MA* within the DTIN. Hence, all the *NA*s contain the information about the overall traffic conditions of the DTIN. The total number of *MA*s required within the DTIN depends on the size of the DTIN and the frequency of updates needed at the nodes.

Due to the inherent flexibility of the agent framework, this approach is readily scalable. Hence, if new nodes are added to the DTIN, the *MA* automatically updates their information at other nodes without any reconfiguration cost. The same is true if some nodes crash or are removed from the DTIN. Even multiple *MA*s can communicate within a node to share their information with each other. This can hasten the exchange of information on any sudden change in the traffic flow such as an accident within the DTIN.

Node	GPS Coordinates <lat, long>	Neighbouring Nodes (NN)	Distance to NN (in KM)	Traffic load towards NN	Timestamp HH:MM:SS
A	26.0000° N, 91.0000° E	B	8	3	12:01:02
		G	3	2	12:02:26
B	26.0000° N, 91.0481° E	A	8	4	12:01:02
		C	4	2	11:59:34
		E	5	6	12:01:53
C	26.0000° N, 91.0730° E	B	4	2	12:01:22
		D	2	1	12:02:17
⋮	⋮	⋮	⋮	⋮	⋮

Figure 2. A sample Traffic flow map (Ψ)

Algorithm 1: Monitoring Agent (*MA*)

---

1 **while** *true* **do**
2 $\quad$ $Tm_{local} \leftarrow$ get local traffic information;
3 $\quad$ $\Psi_{local} \leftarrow$ get local traffic flow map;
4 $\quad$ update Ψ with Tm_{local};
5 $\quad$ **foreach** Tm_i *collected from node* $i \in \Psi$ **do**
6 $\quad\quad$ **if** *exists* $local\_Tm_i \in \Psi_{local}$ **then**
7 $\quad\quad\quad$ **if** *timestamp_Tm_i* > *local_timestamp_Tm_i* **then**
8 $\quad\quad\quad\quad$ update Tm_i to Ψ_{local};
9 $\quad\quad\quad$ **end**
10 $\quad\quad$ **else**
11 $\quad\quad\quad$ update $local\_Tm_i$ to Ψ;
12 $\quad\quad$ **end**
13 $\quad\quad$ **end**
14 $\quad\quad$ **else**
15 $\quad\quad\quad$ add Tm_i to Ψ_{local};
16 $\quad\quad$ **end**
17 $\quad$ **end**
18 $\quad$ set node as visited;
19 $\quad$ move to next node;
20 **end**

3.2. Dynamics of the Path-Finding Agent (PFA)

As soon as an emergency vehicle decides a destination, the *VA* situated within this vehicle communicates with an *NA* in its vicinity. The *VA* then spawns a *PFA* with the knowledge of the destination location into the DTIN. The *PFA* uses the Ψ_{local} available with the *NA* at that node and constructs the shortest and least crowded path from that node to the destination. The algorithm used by the *PFA* for the construction of such a path is provided by the system administrator. Such algorithms may depend upon the type of emergency vehicle or the complexity of the DTIN.

After calculating the path, the *PFA* informs the subsequent nodes within a distance λ (partial window) along the intended path about the arrival of the emergency vehicle. Hence, λ decides the length of the *partial green corridor*. The *PFA* then moves from the starting node (where it calculated the path) along the next η nodes thus traveling a distance d. If $d < \lambda$ then it

---

Algorithm 2: Path-Finding Agent (*PFA*) algorithm

Input: η - Minimum number of nodes in *partial green corridor*;
λ - Partial window;

1 **while** *local node ≠ destination node* **do**
2   **if** *Path R = null* **then**
3 | calculate path *R*;
4   **end**
5   **if** *not alerted about arrival of emergency vehicle* **then**
6 | alert local node;
7 | add local node to corridor node list;
8   **end**
9   **if** *number of nodes in corridor < η OR corridor length < λ* **then**
10 | move to next node from path list *R*;
11   **end**
12   **else**
13   **if** *change in traffic detected* **then**
14 | recalculate path R_{new} from local node;
15 | modify corridor from local node with R_{new};
16   **end**
17   **else**
18   **if** *emergency vehicle passed local node* **then**
19 | extend corridor forward from last node in corridor list;
20   **end**
21   **else**
22 | move to next node in corridor node list;
23   **end**
24   **end**
25   **end**
26 **end**

---

moves forward to the next node along the path to extend the *partial green corridor*. Once $d \geq \lambda$, then the *PFA* ceases further migration and commences monitoring for possible road jams, sudden blockages, etc. along the stretch of the corridor to ensure that it remains green. Since the *MA* continuously updates the current traffic at all nodes, if the *PFA* finds some blockage or increase in traffic load at a node within the *partial green corridor*, it recalculates the path from that node and modifies the *partial green corridor* accordingly.

The *NA* after receiving the information of the approaching emergency vehicle from the *PFA*, starts broadcasting the route to be taken by the vehicle. The *NA* controls the traffic signals so as to make a *green corridor* for the incoming emergency vehicle. It displays this message on a digital banner at the node along the route thereby alerting nearby traffic. Once the emergency vehicle comes in the vicinity of the *NA*, the *VA* within, receives the intended path from it and informs the *NA* about its transit from that location. Once the *NA* receives this information from the *VA*, it changes traffic signal state and allows other vehicles to move on. Once the *PFA* patrolling along the *partial green corridor* receives the information about the passage of the emergency vehicle along the node, it extends the corridor further. Algorithm 2 portrays the working of the *PFA*.

For illustration, consider an emergency vehicle such as an ambulance shown in Figure 1 which is in the vicinity of node *L*. Assume the destination of the ambulance is node *D* which is near to the hospital. The *VA* on the ambulance releases a *PFA* into the DTIN via node *L* using the wireless connection. The *PFA* calculates the route to the node *D* using the Ψ_{local} with the *NA* on node *L*. The *PFA* finds a route *R* viz. $L \to I \to J \to K \to D$. It first moves a distance *d* up to node *J* (initial $\eta = 3$) to alert these nodes about the approaching ambulance. If the $d \geq \lambda$, the *PFA* then starts moving to and fro along $L \to I \to J$ nodes in that order to ensure a *partial green corridor* along these nodes. While oscillating, it checks for any sudden change in traffic conditions using the Ψ_{local} available at each of these nodes. Once the ambulance passes node *L*, the *PFA* moves forward from *J* to the subsequent nodes till the λ and η conditions are satisfied. Suppose the ambulance crosses node *L* and the traffic in between node *J* and node *K* increases suddenly, the *PFA* then recalculates the path from node *J* to the destination node *D*. Suppose the new path from *J* is $J \to E \to D$, the *PFA* now starts alerting nodes on this new path. The *PFA* expands the *partial green corridor* to *E* and then moves to and fro to monitor the traffic in the path $I \to J \to E$.

4. Implementation

To implement the proposed approach for creating multiple *partial green corridors*, we emulated the same using the SWI-Prolog based agent framework nicknamed *Tartarus* developed at the Robotics Lab. of the Department of Computer Science and Engineering, Indian Institute of Technology Guwahati, India. *Tartarus* provides all agent based functionalities such as mobility, autonomy, cloning, asynchronous execution and payload carrying capability. *Tartarus* is an advanced version of *Typhon* [11] with enhanced payload carrying capability, thread based execution support and lower hop times. It has been developed over open source SWI-Prolog and can run on heterogeneous systems including Windows, Linux and embedded systems like the *Raspberry Pi* and

Intel's Galileo. *Tartarus* also has an interface to control LEGO® MINDSTORM® NXT robots. These make *Tartarus* suitable for realizing applications based on an Internet of Things (IoT) or Cyber Physical Systems (CPS).

An instantiation of *Tartarus* can emulate a node in a network. Such instantiations can be created on either a single computer or different computers to form various overlay network topologies. For our emulation experiments, we created a 500-node *Tartarus* based network over a LAN. These nodes were connected to each other in a grid topology. Thus, the *Tartarus* based grid network emulated the proposed DTIN. The distances between a pair of nodes within the emulated DTIN was initialized randomly. In addition, the traffic flowing within the DTIN was also initialized randomly during the creation of the network. Vehicles (mobile agents) within the DTIN move from different sources to different destinations. The NA constituted the static agent on each *Tartarus* instantiation. The MA used the *conscientious migration strategy* [12] to migrate from one node to another. The *conscientious migration strategy* evenly distributes the frequency of visits of the MA at all the nodes. In the current implementation, the movement of emergency vehicles as also the rest of the traffic was emulated using mobile agents.

We equipped the *PFA* with an A^* [16] based algorithm to calculate plausible routes to the destination using the Ψs available with the NAs. Evidently there can be k different paths to reach a destination. To minimize the search space, we have used a heuristic approach. For calculating a path R to destination D from a node n, the *PFA* evaluates all possible routes and selects the one with minimum time to traverse. Hence, R is chosen as per Equation 1.

$$R = \min_{\forall i \in k}(\xi(i) + \rho(i)) \tag{1}$$

where $\xi(i)$ is the estimated time to travel from a node n to the next node i. $\rho(i)$ is the heuristic to calculate the expected time of traversal from node i to the destination D.

The heuristic function, $\rho(.)$, is calculated as the Euclidean distance between the immediate neighbour nodes and the destination D based on their GPS locations multiplied by the average traffic load within the DTIN. For instance, suppose the emergency vehicle has to move from a node I to the destination node S, and node I has 3 routes leading to nodes J, K and L along the paths to S. As per the current traffic estimates at node I, suppose it takes $\xi(J)$, $\xi(K)$ and $\xi(L)$ units of time to reach the nodes J, K and L respectively from the node I. Let τ be the average time to travel a unit distance within the DTIN and $\alpha(;)$ be the function which returns the distance between two nodes based on GPS coordinates

then,

$$R = min\{\xi(J) + \rho(J), \xi(K) + \rho(K), \xi(L) + \rho(L)\}$$

where,

$$\rho(j) = \alpha(j, S)\tau$$

5. Results and Discussions

Experiments were performed by varying the number of emergency vehicles and the traffic conditions. Along with the proposed *partial corridor* approach, two more approaches were considered for the experimentation viz.

- *Full corridor approach*: In this approach, the *PFA* finds the complete path to the destination and alerts all nodes on that path to create a *full green corridor*. Other vehicles crossing the *green corridor* are forced to wait till the emergency vehicle passes that node.

- *Normal approach*: In this approach, no method is used for alerting the traffic in advance for the movement of emergency vehicle. Hence, the emergency vehicle moves just like any other vehicle in the traffic in a *non-prioritized* manner.

Experiments were performed under different traffic loads. The traffic load is a numeric quantity which signifies the delay overhead in traveling the distance between two nodes within the DTIN. A higher numeric value denotes a higher traffic load and vice-versa. Each experiment was carried out at least 5 times, with different initializations to discard any stochastic effects. The graphs have been plotted by taking the average of the readings gathered from multiple experiments.

The graphs in Figure 3 show the average time required for the emergency vehicles to reach their respective destinations (*reaching time*) with varying traffic loads ranging from 3 to 12 and number of emergency vehicles ranging from 1 to 15 within the 500-node DTIN. The *reaching time* is defined as the time taken by a vehicle to reach its destination from its starting location. The number of other vehicles that constituted the general traffic in this case was 50. As can be observed, the *reaching time* is least in case of the proposed *partial corridor* and the *full corridor* based approaches. It is always high in case of the *normal* approach and increases with increase in traffic load. The graphs clearly depict that the proposed approach is at par with the *full corridor* based approach facilitating a seamless movement of emergency vehicles. Further, the performance of the proposed approach does not deteriorate with increasing traffic load and number of emergency vehicles.

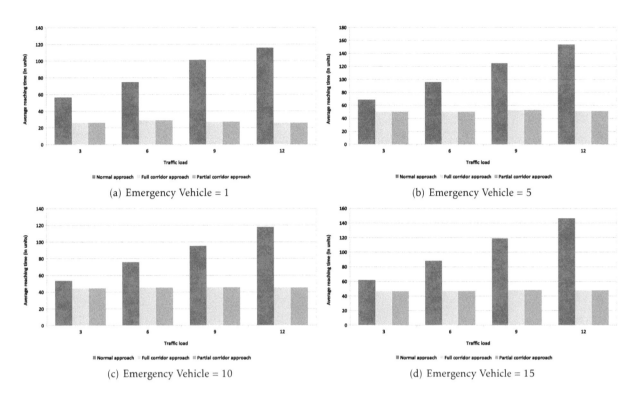

Figure 3. The average *reaching time* for varying number of emergency vehicles under different traffic loads in case of *Normal, Full Corridor* and the proposed *Partial Corridor* based approaches

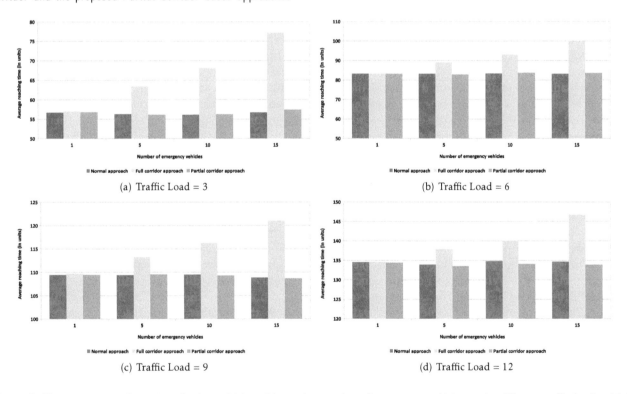

Figure 4. The average *reaching time* of other vehicles with varying number of emergency vehicles under different traffic loads with 50 other vehicles within a 500-node DTIN

The graphs in Figure 4 depict the *reaching times* of other vehicles in case of multiple emergency vehicles moving towards different destinations, under different traffic loads. It can be observed that the *reaching times*

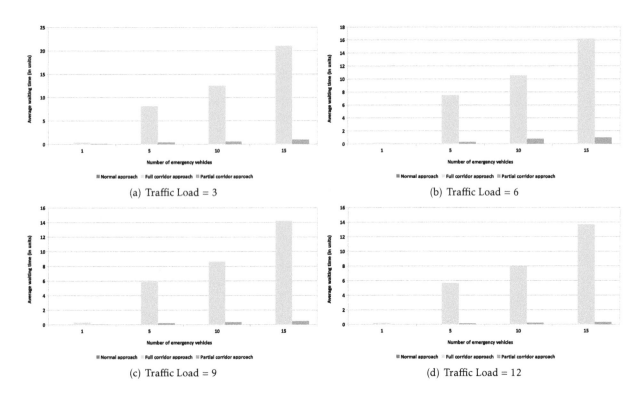

Figure 5. The average *waiting time* of other vehicles with varying number of emergency vehicles under different traffic loads with 50 other vehicles within the 500-node DTIN

of the other vehicles are almost same for all the three approaches (*Normal*, *Full corridor* and *Partial Corridor*) when there is only one emergency vehicle for all the cases of traffic loads. The point to be noted is that as the number of emergency vehicles increases, the *reaching times* of the rest of the vehicles increase for the *full corridor* approach. This is due to the fact that multiple emergency vehicles block large portions of the traffic flow hindering their hassle free passage. Further, the *reaching times* of the other vehicles in case of the *normal* and *partial corridor* approaches are similar. This shows that the use of the proposed *partial green corridor* based approach has least impact on the movement of the adjoining traffic flow.

The graphs in Figure 5 show the average *waiting times* of the other vehicles with varying number of emergency vehicles under different traffic loads. The *waiting time* of a vehicle is defined as the total time a vehicle has to wait whenever it has to cross *green corridors* within the DTIN. The graphs depict the usefulness of the proposed *partial green corridor* approach. While the waiting times of the other vehicles are always high in case of the *full corridor* based approach, the same is very low in case of the *partial corridor* approach. Apparently, the *waiting times* in case of the *normal* approach will be zero as there is no distinction or priority given to the emergency service vehicles.

It may also be seen that when the traffic load is low (equal to 3 in Figure 5(a)) the *waiting times* for the *full*

corridor approach is higher than those in cases when this load is high (compared to Figure 5(b) and 5(c)). This is contrary to the general intuitive deduction that as the traffic load increases the *waiting times* also increase. When the traffic loads are low the other vehicles reach the *green corridor* in lesser times making them wait a longer time till the emergency vehicle clears the *corridor*, thereby increasing their *waiting times*.

Hence, the proposed approached not only prioritizes the movement of emergency vehicles by significantly reducing their *reaching times* (as shown in Figure 3), it also causes least impact on the movement of the normal traffic as shown in the graphs in Figures 4 and 5. Further, one can also observe that the proposed *partial green corridor* based approach shows similar performances across different traffic loads in all the graphs reported in the Figures 3, 4 and 5. Even, increasing the number of emergency vehicles does not affect the *reaching* and *waiting* times of the other vehicles as shown in graphs in Figures 4 and 5. Similar performances were observed when the number of other vehicles were increased to 60 and 70 in case of 5 emergency vehicles under different traffic loads. Since, these results do not aid in portraying any new information, the same have not been depicted here.

Figure 6 shows the variation of *waiting times* on part of other vehicles with increasing corridor lengths, λ. It can be seen that these times keep progressively increasing with λ and eventually peak when the

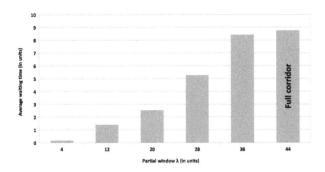

Figure 6. Comparative graph of *waiting times* for other vehicles with increasing corridor length, λ

complete path from the source to the destination is made the *green corridor* (*full corridor* approach) at $\lambda = 44$ units. The graph provides insights into the manner in which one may determine the value of λ which may be based on the gravity of the emergency situation. The value of λ thus provides an indication of the impact on the *waiting times* of the other vehicles due to the creation of *green corridors*.

6. Conclusions and Future work

Traffic management in urban spaces has become a crucial part of an urban infrastructure due to the ever increasing inflow of affordable motor vehicles. The problems in traffic management can be addressed by evolving intelligent and smart solutions. Although many mechanisms have been proposed to model an intelligent traffic management system, most of them do not segregate traffic based on the priority or need. Thus, a concentrated effort to facilitate the seamless movement of *emergency services* with minimal effect on the adjoining traffic flow amidst urban traffic is grossly missing. This paper proposes a multi-agent based approach to create and manage *partial green corridors* for prioritizing the movement of *emergency services* within urban traffic with minimal effect on the movement of normal traffic. The proposed approach has been implemented using *Tartarus*, an agent framework. Various emulation experiments, with varying number of emergency vehicles and traffic loads were performed. The results validate that the proposed approach allows the movement of the emergency services with minimum delays and causes least impact on the flow of adjoining vehicles.

In future, we endeavour to enhance this approach by using real traffic data and sensory information such as traffic speeds, the length and number of parallel lanes and their capacities, speed limits, traffic regulations, etc. There is also a need to look into the priorities of different emergency vehicles so that they can be segregated based on their current requirements and importance. The proposed *partial green corridor* based

approach is completely distributed and autonomous with no human intervention. A human in the loop is however a major requirement so that at times of need some aspects of the agent based system could be overruled. A hierarchical system could thus be the best suited one wherein, at the top level there are humans who are centrally monitoring the overall DTIN by periodically collecting data from all the nodes while at the bottom, the proposed agent based *partial green corridor* approach carries out operations autonomously. Such a hierarchical system not only enhances the control of the complete system but also provisions to alter or prioritize decisions on-the-go which may not be possible with a completely automated system. Evidently, the *Tartarus* agent framework can be used to create such hierarchical systems. In addition, the traffic load considered for experimentation does not change while the vehicles move within the DTIN. Dynamically changing the traffic load, while the vehicles are moving within the DTIN, can provide more insights on how the proposed approach tackles dynamically evolving scenarios.

Acknowledgements

The first and second authors would like to acknowledge the Ministry of Human Resource Development, Govt. of India for providing support during the work reported in this paper. The second author would also like to acknowledge Tata Consultancy Services, India for rendering support under their TCS RSP scheme.

References

[1] BALAJI, P., SACHDEVA, G., SRINIVASAN, D. and THAM, C.K. (2007) Multi-agent System based Urban Traffic Management. In *IEEE Congress on Evolutionary Computation*: 1740–1747. doi:10.1109/CEC.2007.4424683.

[2] BODE, M., JHA, S.S. and NAIR, S.B. (2014) A mobile agent based autonomous partial green corridor discovery and maintenance mechanism for emergency services amidst urban traffic. In *Proceedings of the First International Conference on IoT in Urban Space* (ICST (Institute for Computer Sciences, Social-Informatics and Telecommunications Engineering)): 13–18.

[3] CHEN, B., CHENG, H.H. and PALEN, J. (2006) Mobile-c: a mobile agent platform for mobile c/c++ agents. *Software: Practice and Experience* **36**(15): 1711–1733.

[4] CHEN, B., CHENG, H.H. and PALEN, J. (2009) Integrating mobile agent technology with multi-agent systems for distributed traffic detection and management systems. *Transportation Research Part C: Emerging Technologies* **17**(1): 1 – 10. doi:http://dx.doi.org/10.1016/j.trc.2008.04.003, URL http://www.sciencedirect.com/science/article/pii/S0968090X08000314.

[5] CHEN, B. and CHENG, H. (2010) A Review of the Applications of Agent Technology in Traffic and Transportation Systems. *IEEE Transactions on*

Intelligent Transportation Systems **11**(2): 485–497. doi:10.1109/TITS.2010.2048313.

[6] CLAES, R., HOLVOET, T. and WEYNS, D. (2011) A Decentralized Approach for Anticipatory Vehicle Routing Using Delegate Multiagent Systems. *IEEE Transactions on Intelligent Transportation Systems* **12**(2): 364–373. doi:10.1109/TITS.2011.2105867.

[7] GODFREY, W.W., JHA, S.S. and NAIR, S.B. (2013) On a Mobile Agent Framework for an Internet of Things. In *International Conference on Communication Systems and Network Technologies*: 345–350. doi:10.1109/CSNT.2013.79.

[8] HARRISON, C.G., CHESS, D.M. and KERSHENBAUM, A. (1995) *Mobile Agents: Are they a good idea?* (IBM TJ Watson Research Center Yorktown Heights, New York).

[9] HORLING, B. and LESSER, V. (2004) A survey of multi-agent organizational paradigms. *The Knowledge Engineering Review* **19**: 281–316. doi:10.1017/S0269888905000317, URL http://journals.cambridge.org/article_S0269888905000317.

[10] MARTÍN-CAMPILLO, A., MARTÍ, R., ROBLES, S. and MARTÍNEZ-GARCÍA, C. (2009) Mobile agents for critical medical information retrieving from the emergency scene. In *7th International Conference on Practical Applications of Agents and Multi-Agent Systems (PAAMS 2009)* (Springer): 30–39.

[11] MATANI, J. and NAIR, S.B. (2011) Typhon - A Mobile Agents Framework for Real World Emulation in Prolog. In *Multi-disciplinary Trends in Artificial Intelligence* (Springer Berlin Heidelberg), *Lecture Notes in Computer Science* **7080**, 261–273.

[12] MINAR, N., KRAMER, K. and MAES, P. (1999) Cooperating Mobile Agents for Dynamic Network Routing. In HAYZELDEN, A. and BIGHAM, J. [eds.] *Software Agents for Future Communication Systems* (Springer Berlin Heidelberg), 287–304. doi:10.1007/978-3-642-58418-3_12, URL http://dx.doi.org/10.1007/978-3-642-58418-3_12.

[13] OUTTAGARTS, A. (2009) Mobile Agent-based Applications : A Survey. *International Journal of Computer Science and Network Security* **9**: 331–339.

[14] PAN, J.I., YUNG, C.J., LIANG, C.C. and LAI, L.F. (2007) An intelligent homecare emergency service system for elder falling. In *World Congress on Medical Physics and Biomedical Engineering 2006* (Springer): 424–428.

[15] ROTHKRANTZ, L.J.M. (2009) Dynamic Routing Using the Network of Car Drivers. In *Proceedings of the 2009 Euro American Conference on Telematics and Information Systems: New Opportunities to Increase Digital Citizenship*, EATIS '09 (ACM): 11:1–11:8. doi:10.1145/1551722.1551733, URL http://doi.acm.org/10.1145/1551722.1551733.

[16] RUSSELL, S. and NORVIG, P. (2010) *Artificial Intelligence: A Modern Approach*, Prentice Hall series in artificial intelligence (Prentice Hall), 3rd ed.

[17] VAA, T. (2007) Intelligent transport systems and effects on road traffic accidents: state of the art. *IET Intelligent Transport Systems* **1**: 81–88(7). URL http://digital-library.theiet.org/content/journals/10.1049/iet-its_20060081.

[18] VAN KATWIJK, R. and VAN KONINGSBRUGGEN, P. (2002) Coordination of traffic management instruments using agent technology. *Transportation Research Part C: Emerging Technologies* **10**(5 - 6): 455 – 471. doi:http://dx.doi.org/10.1016/S0968-090X(02)00034-7, URL http://www.sciencedirect.com/science/article/pii/S0968090X02000347.

[19] WEYNS, D., HOLVOET, T. and HELLEBOOGH, A. (2007) Anticipatory Vehicle Routing using Delegate Multi-Agent Systems. In *IEEE Intelligent Transportation Systems Conference*: 87–93. doi:10.1109/ITSC.2007.4357809.

[20] WUNDERLICH, K., KAUFMAN, D. and SMITH, R. (2000) Link travel time prediction for decentralized route guidance architectures. *IEEE Transactions on Intelligent Transportation Systems* **1**(1): 4–14. doi:10.1109/6979.869017.

Detecting Multi-Channel Wireless Microphone User Emulation Attacks in White Space with Noise

Dan Shan, Kai Zeng *, Weidong Xiang, Paul Richardson

4901 Evergreen Rd, Dearborn, MI, USA, 48092

Abstract

Cognitive radio networks (CRNs) are susceptible to primary user emulation (PUE) attacks. Conventional PUE attack detection approaches consider television broadcasting as the primary user. In this work, however, we study a special kind of PUE attack named wireless microphone user emulation (WMUE) attack. Existing work on WMUE attack detection deals with single channel senario. Although multi-channel WM (MCWM) systems are common, detecting WMUE attacks under a multi-channel setting in noisy environments has not been well studied. In this work, we propose a novel multi-channel WMUE attack detection scheme which operates in low signal-to-noise ratio (SNR) environments with low computational complexity, thanks to the first 1.5-bit FM demodulator whose outputs are represented by only 0, 1 and -1. Experimental results show that, the proposed scheme can effectively detect multi-channel WMUE attacks within 0.25 second when SNR is lower than 6 dB.

Keywords: CRN, WMUE, MCWM, FM demodulator

1. Introduction

Cognitive radio (CR) enables secondary users (SUs) to share the spectrum temporarily unused by primary users (PUs). To open the door for this new technique and enhance the spectrum efficiency, regulators in many countries have issued permission for radio frequency (RF) transmissions for license-exempt users on part of television (TV) bands, known as white space. The wireless devices that are carried by SUs and operate on white space are called white space devices (WSDs).

WSDs perform spectrum sensing on white space to avoid collisions to the signals from PUs (incumbent signals), mainly including TV signals and wireless microphone (WM) signals. Many spectrum sensing techniques are proposed to detect these two types of incumbent signals [3, 8, 12, 16, 20]. When PUs emerge, SUs are required to evacuate from the spectrum in order to avoid interference to PUs. Exploiting this policy adversely, an attacker may block all SUs within an area by emulating the signal of a certain PU. This kind of attack is named primary user emulation (PUE) attack [4].

Over the years, tremendous efforts have been expended in the area of PUE attack detection. By evaluating the received signal's coverage area, one can differentiate between the signal from a PUE attacker and the real TV signal [4, 22]. However, these detection techniques do not apply to the attack that emulates WM signals (named WM user emulation attack, or WMUE attack), because WM signals may be transmitted from anywhere. Moreover, WMUE attacks may be launched on a frequency band where no WM system has ever worked on; as a result, one cannot detect these attacks by comparing their channel-specific features with the features contained in real WM signals [14]. In short, detecting a WMUE attack is not easy, while launching a WMUE attack is as simple as building a cheap FM modulator.

Existing work detects WMUE attacks in a single-channel system by comparing the FM signal with the audio signal acquired simultaneously [5]. Since a WMUE attacker wants to abuse the white space and meanwhile hide himself, he is not willing to generate any audio signals correlated with the FM signal(s) he transmits, and this fact leads to low similarity between the FM signal and audio signal around the WM system.

---

*Corresponding author. Email: kzeng@umich.edu

Although multi-channel WM (MCWM) systems are are common, PUE attacks in these systems are rarely studied, leaving several open challenges. Firstly, multiple WM users in the same MCWM system may speak simultaneously. This situation frequently happens; for examples, multiple performers sing a song at the same time on a stage, or several invited speakers on a conference are having a heated discussion with many overlapped talks. Then the audio signals on different channels interfere each other, and the relationship between the mixed audio signal and the FM signals on multiple audio channels become more complicate. Secondly, the audio signal and FM signals are further contaminated by both acoustic noises and RF noises (we use the term "noise" to represent both thermal noise and interferences coming from other systems, but not including interferences coming from other audio channels in the same MCWM system). Thirdly, some WSDs have only one receiver branch and may monitor the FM signal only on one audio channel. As a result, RF signals on different audio channels may not be observed simultaneously.

An intuitive idea to solve these challenges is to check the cross-correlation between a demodulated FM signal and the audio signal acquired simultaneously. Since a WM user's speech is uncorrelated with noises and other users' speeches, interferences from other channels and noises can be resisted by a cross-correlator effectively. However, two issues remain: (1) this solution requires a FM demodulator which only works in high signal-to-noise ratio (SNR) conditions; (2) a cross-correlator conducts massive multiplications and has very high computation complexity. These issues are tackled by a major contribution in this work: a 1.5-bit FM receiver, which maps the FM signal to a piece of acoustic signal whose amplitude is represented by 0, 1 or -1. This is not only the first 1.5-bit FM receiver, but also the first FM receiver that works effectively when SNR is as low as -3 dB. This novelty not only lowers the complexity and SNR requirement of a FM demodulation, but also significantly reduces the complexity of a cross-correlator, since massive multiplications are eliminated by the simple coefficients 0 and ± 1. The 1.5-bit FM receiver results in a cross-correlator with three-level quantization, which is the optimal quantization that processes the least information with the given quantization error [7].

We evaluate the performance of the proposed 1.5-bit FM demodulator by simulations, and evaluate the performance of the whole detection scheme in a real-world testing environment, which includes an off-the-shelf MCWM system and a WSD prototype. Based on the waveforms acquired in this real-world testing environment, we derive the detection rate β and false alarm rate α of the proposed detection scheme. Experiment results show that, the proposed scheme requires only -3 to 0 dB SNR when two audio channels are used, and requires about 5-6 dB SNR when four audio channels are used, with the performance that $\beta > 0.9$ and $\alpha < 0.1$. The detection time is as low as a quarter second.

Our contributions are summarized as follows:

- We propose a cross-correlation based WMUE attack detection scheme with the ability to resist noises and interferences in MCWM systems;

- We propose the first 1.5-bit FM demodulator which enjoys low complexity and simplifies the cross-correlator, and evaluate its performance by both theoretical analysis and computer based simulations;

- We design a hardware based prototype and validate the performance of the proposed detection scheme in a real-world environment.

Throughout the paper, "acoustical signal" and "audio signal" are synonymous. We use the terms "wireless channel" and "acoustic channel" to represent the channels experienced by RF signal and sound, respectively. All SNR's in this work are measured over the effective bandwidth of a FM signal which is at the level of 50 KHz, while those in some other works are measured over the entire 6MHz TV band [3, 8, 20]. The -3 dB SNR in this work is equivalent to -23.4 dB in those works, and is close to the limitation of those FM signal detection schemes.

2. Related Works

Various methods are proposed to detect PUE attacks. Among them, localization based methods draw much attention, with the basic principle that the location of some incumbent signal transmitters, for example, the TV towers, are preknown and hard to be emulated. By localizing the transmitter using received signal strength (RSS), one can differentiate between legitimate users and PUE attackers [4, 22]. Alternatively, PUE attacks may be detected through the fact that, the channel characteristics at different users are different and hard to be altered [6, 14]. Although this method is able to differentiate between different users, it cannot tell which user is the attacker. In other words, additional information about the legitimate user, like location or channel state information (CSI), are also required. All these methods cannot detect WMUE attacks, since both the locations and CSIs of MCWM users are hard to acquire.

The algorithm proposed in [5] detects the WMUE attacks by correlating the acoustic signal with the RF signal acquired simultaneously, and this principle is also adopted in this work. However, the work in [5] only considers the single-channel WM system, while this work covers both single-channel and multi-channel cases.

Authors in [2] propose a cooperative spectrum sensing scheme that maximizes the detection rate when PUE attacks exist. Moreover, a frequency hopping strategy is proposed in [13] to combat with PUE attacks under a game-theoretic model. These works are devoted to alleviating PUE attacks, rather than detecting PUE attacks.

Several all-digital FM receivers are proposed in [11, 15, 19], and all of them ignore noises. A FM receiver that works when SNR is as low as -3 dB is not found in the literature. Moreover, no 1.5-bit FM demodulator is found in the existing literature to detect WMUE attacks. In this work, a low-precision FM demodulator can significantly reduce the computation complexity, and is studied for the first time.

The design of multiplierless cross-correlators is discussed in [21], while design considerations and performance evaluation for the complex cross-correlator with three-level quantization are presented in [7]. These works guide us to the idea of 1.5-bit data precision; however, the main focus of this work is to detect PUE attacks, while the multiplierless cross-correlators is only part of the whole scheme.

Some preliminary results of this work are presented in [18]. In this paper, we add more technical details and evaluate the performance of the proposed FM demodulator in noisy environments through both theoretical analysis and simulations. Moreover, detecting threshold of the proposed WMUE attack detector is also discussed.

3. System Model

3.1. System Setup

A MCWM system is surrounded by a set of WSDs, as shown in figure 1. This MCWM system is composed of M audio transmitters (WMs) where $M \geq 1$, one MCWM receiver and one loudspeaker. The audio signals acquired by different WMs are modulated on different wireless channels, and are all received by the MCWM receiver and mixed together. We denote the audio signal and FM signal at the mth WM as $a_m(t)$ and $s_m(t)$, respectively. Then the audio signal output $a^T(t)$ at the MCWM receiver equals to $\sum_{m=1}^{M} a_m(t)$, which is further amplified by the loudspeaker and overcast all acoustic signals generated by WM users. The WSD is able to acquire (some of) the FM signals $s_m(t)$, as well as acoustic signal $a(t)$ which contains $a^T(t)$, its reverberations and acoustic noises. The central frequency of $s_m(t)$ is denoted as f_m.

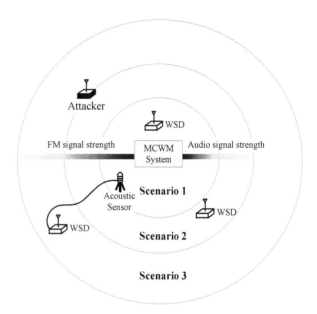

Figure 1. The system model and three scenarios considered in this paper. Scenarios differ from each other in the qualities of FM signals and acoustic signals.

According to [3], the FM signal can be modelled by

$$s_m(t) = A_C \cos \left[2\pi f_m t + 2\pi \Delta f \int_0^t a_m(t) dt + \theta \right] \quad (1)$$

where A_C and Δf control the amplitude and bandwidth of this FM signal, respectively, and θ represents a random phase with uniform distribution over $[0, 2\pi]$.

We consider that the quality of acoustic signal $a(t)$ drops much faster than the qualities of $s_m(t)$, when the propagation distance d increases. The reasons are twofold. Firstly, acoustic signals are more easily being blocked by obstacles like buildings, compared with FM signals operating on very high frequency (VHF) and ultra high frequency (UHF) bands. According to the measurement results in [9], FM signals may have more than 30 dB SNR when $d = 500$m, while effective ranges of the acoustic signals from most MCWM systems are less than 100m. Secondly, the sources of RF interference are much less than the sources of acoustic interferences, since different wireless systems operate on different frequency bands, while many types of acoustic interferences collide with human speeches in both time-domain and frequency-domain.

According to the propagation models above, we define three operating scenarios:

- *Scenario 1*: $d < 20m$, so both $s_m(t)$ and $a(t)$ are noise-free;

- *Scenario 2*: $20m < d < 200m$, so $s_m(t)$ is noise-free, but $a(t)$ is noisy;

- *Scenario 3*: $d > 200m$, so $s_m(t)$ is noisy, but high-quality $a(t)$ is acquired by the sensor close to the

MCWM system and sent to the WSD through infrastructure.

These three scenarios are also illustrated in figure 1. Our proposed WMUE attack detection algorithm covers all these three scenarios. For each scenario, we will focus on one WSD in the following analysis.

We assume that the power of $s_m(t)$ is above the noise floor at each WSD in all scenarios, so that f_m can be estimated by the WSD [8]. Since f_m can only be a multiple of 25 kHz [10], the WSD is able to adjust its estimates on f_m according to this rule. As a result, the WSD knows exact values of f_m for $m = 1, ..., M$.

3.2. Attacker Model

An attacker emulates the MCWM system by transmitting FM signals on one or multiple channels used by the legitimate MCWM system. These emulated FM signals and the FM signals transmitted by WMs are indistinguishable in terms of the modulation scheme and transmission power.

The attacker is not willing to convert the demodulated FM signal to audio signal and send it to the loudspeaker, since such audio signal would be very strange and expose the attacker directly, unless the original data transmitted by the attacker is just a piece of analogue audio signal (the exceptional case). Therefore, we consider that the attacker does not generate any audio signal, or generates audio signal that is not correlated to the FM signal. We consider that the "attacker" in the exceptional case is actually a legitimate WM system which may use the spectrum legally. We assume that the attacker has the ability to sense the spectrum and avoids collisions with existing MCWM systems. Therefore, there is one and only one source of $s_m(t)$.

3.3. The Detection Problem

The detection problem we study here is defined as the task to identify the source (either the MCWM system or the attacker) of $s_m(t)$, given a set of $a(t)$ and $s_m(t)$. It can be modelled as a hypothesis test:

- H_0: $s_m(t)$ is generated by the MCWM system;

- H_1: $s_m(t)$ is generated by the WMUE attacker.

H_0 and H_1 are called null hypothesis and alternative hypothesis, respectively.

4. The WMUE Attack Detection Scheme

The proposed WMUE attack detection scheme is based on the principle that, the acoustic signal and FM signals coming from the MCWM system correlate to each other, while those coming from the WMUE attacker do not. Then by evaluating the cross-correlation between the demodulated FM signal on a specific wireless channel

and the acoustic signal, one can distinguish between a MCWM user and a WMUE attacker.

Basic procedures of the proposed scheme are shown in figure 2. The WSD first searches any FM-like signal on the frequency band interested. Once detecting a signal, it records the RF signal $s_m(t)$ and acoustic signal $a(t)$ simultaneously. Then it down-converts $s_m(t)$ to an intermediate frequency (IF) signal $s_m^{(IF)}(t)$, and feeds the latter one into a low-complexity FM demodulator. In other words, a superheterodyne receiver is considered here. Finally, the scheme computes the peak value X of the cross-correlation between the demodulated signal Y_n and the down-sampled acoustic signal A_n. X is close to 1 if $s_m(t)$ is transmitted from the MCWM system, and close to 0 if not. The same operations are repeated for other channels interested.

The cross-correlator suffers from very high computation complexity. To solve this problem, we first notice that reducing the data precision reduces the complexity of cross-correlator dramatically, but only degrades the performance slightly [7]. Consider the operation $\sum_n Y_n A_n$ required in the cross-correlator shown in figure 2; if Y_n equals to either 1 or -1, all the multiplications are unnecessary. Moreover, if $Y_n = 0$ at some points, the number of additions is also reduced. Motivated by these facts, we represent Y_n by only 0, 1 and -1. In other words, we propose a 1.5-bit FM demodulator with input $s_m^{(IF)}(t)$ and output Y_n, and show the relationship between the original audio signal $a_m(t)$ and the desired output Y_n in figure 3. This simplified FM demodulator in turn simplifies the cross-correlator significantly.

We introduce the 1.5-bit FM demodulator in subsection 4.2, and discuss its performance in noisy environments in subsection 4.3. Audio signal processing and the cross-correlator are introduced in subsections 4.4 and 4.5, respectively. Finally, the WMUE attack detector is given in subsection 4.6.

4.1. Preliminaries

We first analyse the properties of IF signal $s_m^{(IF)}(t)$ with central frequency f_I:

$$s_m^{(IF)}(t) = A_C \cos\left[2\pi f_I t + 2\pi \Delta f \int_0^t a_m(t) dt + \theta\right]. \quad (2)$$

For most superheterodyne receivers,

$$f_I > 2f_{max} \quad (3)$$

and

$$f_I > 2\Delta f a_{max} \quad (4)$$

where f_{max} and a_{max} denote the maximum frequency and maximum amplitude of $a_m(t)$, respectively. Then

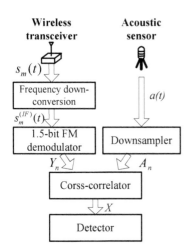

Figure 2. Basic procedures of the proposed WMUE attack detection scheme.

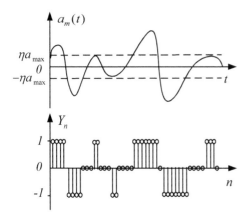

Figure 3. The relationship between $a_m(t)$ and the desired output Y_n of a 1.5-bit FM demodulator, where $-\eta$ and η are two decision thresholds.

we define T as a number that satisfies

$$2f_{max} \leq 1/T < f_I \tag{5}$$

and get the following observations.

Observation 1:

$$\left| \int_{nT}^{(n+1)T} s_m^{(IF)}(t)e^{j2\pi g_k t}dt \right| \approx A_C T \text{sinc}((g_k - f_{t_0})T) \tag{6}$$

where

$$f_{t_0} := f_I + \Delta f a_m(t_0) \tag{7}$$

$$|g_k - f_{t_0}| \leq 1/(2T) \tag{8}$$

and $\text{sinc}(x) := \sin(\pi x)/(\pi x)$.

Proof. Define $\theta_1 := 2\pi\Delta f \int_0^{t_0} a_m(t)dt$ and $\theta_2 := 2\pi\Delta f a_m(t_0)t_0$. From (2) we have

$$s_m^{(IF)}(t) = A_C \cos\left[2\pi f_I t + 2\pi\Delta f \int_{t_0}^{t} a_m(t)dt + \theta_1 + \theta\right]$$
$$\approx A_C \cos\left[2\pi f_{t_0} t + \theta'\right] \tag{9}$$

where $\theta' := \theta_1 - \theta_2 + \theta$.

The approximation in (9) is due to the reason that, $1/T \geq 2f_{max}$ according to (5), $a_m(t)$ shows limited change during $[t_0, t]$, and $\int_{t_0}^{t} a_m(t)dt \approx a_m(t_0)(t - t_0)$. Then we get

$$\int_{t_0}^{t_0+T} s_m^{(IF)}(t)e^{j2\pi g t}dt$$
$$\approx \int_{t_0}^{t_0+T} A_C \cos\left[2\pi f_{t_0} t + \theta'\right]e^{j2\pi g t}dt$$
$$= \frac{A_C}{2}\left[\underbrace{\int_{t_0}^{t_0+T} e^{j2\pi(g+f_{t_0})t+j\theta'}dt}_{d_1} + \underbrace{\int_{t_0}^{t_0+T} e^{j2\pi(g-f_{t_0})t-j\theta'}dt}_{d_2}\right] \tag{10}$$

The integrands in d_1 and d_2 are two periodical functions with frequencies $g + f_{t_0}$ and $g - f_{t_0}$. According to (5) (7) and (8), $g + f_{t_0} \approx 2f_I > 2/T \geq 4|g - f_{t_0}|$. As a result, d_1 is much smaller than d_2. By ignoring d_1, (10) becomes

$$\int_{t_0}^{t_0+T} s_m^{(IF)}(t)e^{j2\pi g t}dt$$
$$\approx \frac{A_C}{2}\int_{t_0}^{t_0+T} e^{j2\pi(g-f_{t_0})t-j\theta'}dt \tag{11}$$
$$= \frac{A_C}{2}e^{-j\theta''}(e^{j2\pi(g-f_{t_0})T} - 1)/(j2\pi(g - f_{t_0}))$$

where $\theta'' := \theta' - 2\pi(g - f_{t_0})t_0$.

Then from (11) we have

$$\left| \int_{nT}^{(n+1)T} s_m^{(IF)}(t)e^{j2\pi g_k t}dt \right|$$
$$\approx \left| \frac{A_C}{2}e^{-j\theta''}(e^{j2\pi(g-f_{t_0})T} - 1)/j2\pi(g - f_{t_0}) \right| \tag{12}$$
$$= A_C(1 - \cos(2\pi T(g - f_{t_0})))/(4\pi^2(g - f_{t_0})^2)$$
$$= A_C T \text{sinc}((g_k - f_{t_0})T)$$

$\square$

Observation 2: If $|g_1 - f_{nT}| \leq |g_2 - f_{nT}| \leq 1/(2T)$, $S_{m,n}^{(1)} \geq S_{m,n}^{(2)}$ where $S_{m,n}^{(k)} := \left| \int_{nT}^{(n+1)T} s_m^{(IF)}(t)e^{j2\pi g_k t}dt \right|$ and $f_{nT} := f_I + \Delta f a_m(nT)$.

Proof. It is easily shown that $S_{m,n}^k$ equals to the left part of (6) when $t_0 = nT$. According to *Observation 1*, $S_{m,n}^{(k)}$ is a monotonically decreasing function with respective to $|g - f_{nT}|$ during $[0, 1/(2T)]$. Therefore, *Observation 2* holds.

$\square$

Since we focus on the mth audio channel here, we drop the index m in $S_{m,n}^{(k)}$ if doing this would not cause misunderstanding.

4.2. The 1.5-bit FM Demodulator

Definition: A demodulator with output $Y_{m,n}$ is the 1.5-bit FM demodulator of the IF signal $s_m^{(IF)}(t)$ defined in (2) if and only if

$$Y_{m,n} = \begin{cases} -1, & a_m(nT) < -\eta a_{max} \\ 0, & -\eta a_{max} \leq a_m(nT) < \eta a_{max} \\ 1, & others \end{cases} \tag{13}$$

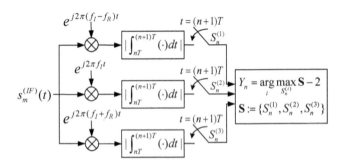

Figure 4. The proposed 1.5-bit FM demodulator.

Figure 5. The proposed 1.5-bit FM demodulator can be interpreted as a sampler for the audio signal $a_m(t)$ with sampling frequency $F_s = 1/T$ followed by a three-level quantizer.

where $n = 0, 1, \ldots$, while $-\eta$ and η are two decision thresholds with $0 < \eta < 1$.

Figure 3 shows the relationship between $a_m(t)$ and the desired output of this 1.5-bit FM demodulator. The thresholds $-\eta$ and η should guarantee that $Y_{m,n}$ equals to 0, 1 or -1 with equal probabilities, so that the amount of information contained in $Y_{m,n}$ is maximized. For example, if the amplitude of $a_m(t)$ is evenly distributed over $[0, a_{max}]$, $\eta = 0.5$.

Proposision 1: The demodulator shown in figure 4 with output $Y_n = \arg\max_{i} \mathbf{S_n} - 2$ is the 1.5-bit FM demodulator defined in *Definition*, where $\mathbf{S_n} := \{S_n^{(1)}, S_n^{(2)}, S_n^{(3)}\}$, $g_1 = f_I - f_R$, $g_2 = f_I$, $g_3 = f_I + f_R$, $f_R = 2\eta a_{max}\Delta f$, and

$$|g_k - f_{nT}| \leq 1/(2T) \tag{14}$$

where $k = 1, 2, 3$.

Proof. When $a_m(nT) < -\eta a_{max}$,

$$
\begin{aligned}
&|g_1 - f_{nT}| \\
&= |f_R + \Delta f a_m(nT)| \\
&= |2\eta a_{max}\Delta f + \Delta f a_m(nT)| \\
&< |\Delta f a_m(nT)| \\
&= |g_2 - f_{nT}| \\
&\leq 1/(2T)
\end{aligned}
\tag{15}
$$

and it is easily shown that $|g_1 - f_{nT}| < |g_3 - f_{nT}| \leq 1/(2T)$. Then according to *Observation* 2, $S_n^{(1)} > S_n^{(2)}$ and $S_n^{(1)} > S_n^{(3)}$. As a result, $\arg\max_{i} \mathbf{S_n} = 1$ and $Y_n = -1$.

By the same way, one can verify that $Y_n = 0$ when $-\eta a_{max} \leq a_m(nT) < \eta a_{max}$, and $Y_n = 1$ when $a_m(nT) \geq \eta a_{max}$.   □

The 1.5-bit FM demodulator proposed in figure 4 borrows the design of matched-filter [23]; however, their basic principles are different. In our system, the local signals fed into the multipliers, $e^{j2\pi f_I t}$ and $e^{j2\pi(f_I \pm f_R)t}$, do not necessarily match any pieces of the FM signal transmitted. Instead, our system is designed such that the integrators generate larger outputs when

these local signals match the present signal better. Then by searching the largest outputs from three integrators, the demodulator determines the best value (0, 1 or -1) for Y_n.

This 1.5-bit FM demodulator can also be interpreted as a sampler for the normalized audio signal $\tilde{a}_m(t)$ with sampling frequency $F_s = 1/T$ followed by a three-level quantizer, as shown in figure 5. After normalization, we assume that the average power of $\tilde{a}_{max}(t)$ equals to 1. This FM demodulator may also operate in digital domain, if the input $s_m^{IF}(t)$ is sampled with sampling rate G_s. It is easily shown that, basic principle of this demodulator still holds in digital domain, while the only change is to replace the integrators in figure 4 by adders.

By adopting integrators, the proposed 1.5-bit FM demodulator is able to work in low-SNR environments with low computation complexity. On the other hand, conventional digital FM demodulators [11, 15, 19] either suffer from high complexity or require high SNR.

4.3. Performance of the FM demodulator in Noisy Environments

We define the noisy IF signal fed into the FM demodulator as $\widehat{s}_m^{(IF)}(t)$, which is modelled as

$$\widehat{s}_m^{(IF)}(t) = s_m^{(IF)}(t) + w_m(t) \tag{16}$$

where $w_m(t)$ is the additive white Gaussian noise (AWGN) with power σ_m^2 at the mth wireless channel. Then according to figure 4, output of the ith integrator is given by

$$
\begin{aligned}
S_n^{(i)} &= |\int_{nT}^{(n+1)T} (s_m^{(IF)}(t) + w_m(t))e^{j2\pi g_i t}dt| \\
&= |\rho_n^{(i)}e^{j\phi_i} + \int_{nT}^{(n+1)T} w_m(t)e^{j2\pi g_i t}dt|
\end{aligned}
\tag{17}
$$

where

$$\rho_n^{(i)} := A_C T \mathrm{sinc}((g_k - f_{t_{nT}})T) \tag{18}$$

according to *Observation* 1, and ϕ_i denotes the angle of the complex value in (11) when $g = g_i$.

Let $N_m := \int_{t_0}^{t_0+T} w_m(t)e^{j2\pi g_i t}dt$ represent the random part in (17). One can easily verify that N_m is a random variable which follows complex normal distribution with mean value 0 and variance $\sigma_m^2 T$. As a result, $S_n^{(i)}$ in (17) follows Rician distribution whose probability

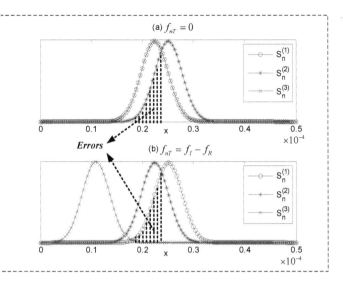

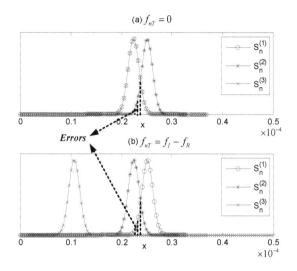

Figure 6. The PDF curves for $S_n^{(1)}$, $S_n^{(2)}$ and $S_n^{(3)}$ with (a) $f_{nT} = f_I$ and (b) $f_{nT} = f_I - f_R$, respectively, and $\gamma = 0$ dB.

Figure 7. The PDF curves for $S_n^{(1)}$, $S_n^{(2)}$ and $S_n^{(3)}$ with (a) $f_{nT} = f_I$ and (b) $f_{nT} = f_I - f_R$, respectively, and $\gamma = 8$ dB.

density function (PDF) is given by [1]

$$p_i(x) = \begin{cases} \dfrac{x}{\sigma_m^2 T} e^{-\frac{x^2 + \left(\rho_n^{(i)}\right)^2}{2\sigma_m^2 T}} I_0\left(\dfrac{x\rho_n^{(i)}}{\sigma_m^2 T}\right), & x \geq 0 \\ 0, & x < 0 \end{cases} \quad (19)$$

where $\rho_n^{(i)}$ follows the same definition as in (18), and $I_0(x)$ is the modified Bessel function of the first kind with order zero.

Similar to the bit-error-rate (BER) performance in digital communication systems [1], performance of the proposed 1.5-bit FM demodulator is closely related to the ratio γ defined by $\gamma := \rho_n^2/(\sigma_m^2 T)$, which is proportional to $A_C^2 T/\sigma_m^2$ according to (18). Note that A_C^2/σ_m^2 just equals to (twice of) the SNR of $s_m(t)$. As a result, larger SNR leads to larger γ and better anti-noise ability.

Larger T also leads to larger γ. However, T is also restricted by (5) and (14), while larger T makes both *Observation* 1 and *Observation* 2 less accurate and may increase demodulation error (we call it modelling error). In practice, the optimal value of T may not strictly satisfy both (5) and (14) due to the trade-off between γ and modelling error. We will derive the optimal value of T by simulations in subsection 5.1.

PDF's of $S_n^{(1)}$, $S_n^{(2)}$ and $S_n^{(3)}$ are plotted in figure 6, with $A_C = 1$, $f_I = 50$ kHz, $f_R = 5$ kHz, $T = 50\mu s$ and $\gamma = 0$ dB. When $f_{nT} = f_I$ as shown in figure 6.a, $S_n^{(2)}$ has the best chance to be the largest one among $\{S_n^{(1)}, S_n^{(2)}, S_n^{(3)}\}$; as a result, Y_n tends to be 0, which is correct. When $f_{nT} = f_I - f_R$ as shown in figure 6.b, $S_n^{(2)}$ is most likely the largest one, and Y_n tends to be -1. The shaded area denotes the chance of decoding error. When γ is changed to 8 dB and other conditions keep unchanged,

as shown in figure 7, the shaded areas become smaller compared with those in figure 6, and the demodulation performance is better.

Although a closed-form expression on the "BER" of this demodulator can be derived from PDF's, we note that this expression is valid only when this demodulator operates in analog domain. Performance of this FM demodulator operating in digital domain is affected by the sampling rate F_s, and we will show the normalized mean square error (NMSE) performance of this demodulator under the sampling rate adopted by the real-world experiments in subsection 5.1.

4.4. Audio Signal Processing

We model the acoustic signal $a(t)$ arriving at the WSD under H_0 as

$$a(t)|H_0 = a^{(T)}(t) \otimes h(t) = \sum_{j=1}^{J} h_j a^{(T)}(t - t_j) + z(t) \quad (20)$$

where $h(t) := \sum_{j=1}^{J} h_j \delta(t - t_j)$ represents the impulse response of the acoustic channel between loudspeaker and WSD, and $z(t)$ denotes audio noises.

In practice, acoustic signal travels slower than RF signal. To address this issue, we define the time $t = 0$ as the time when FM signal is detected by the WSD. Accordingly, all t_j's in the acoustic channel model $h(t)$ incorporate propagation delay of the acoustic signal. As an example, if there is line-of-sight with distance D between audio amplifier and WSD, $t_0 = D/v$ where v denotes the speed of sound in the air, while propagation delay of FM signal is much smaller than t_0 and has been ignored.

At the WSD side, $a(t)$ is sampled by the acoustic sensor at a high sampling rate (for example, 44.1 kHz). In order to match this acoustic signal with the FM demodulator output, we resample this acoustic signal at the rate $1/T$, which equals to the sampling rate of Y_n. Since $1/T = 10$ kHz is good enough to capture human voices, we consider this operation as a downsampler as shown in figure 2. Moreover, this downsampler features a lowpass filter with stop-band $1/T$ to resist out-of-band noises.

Denote the downsampled acoustic signal as A_n, which is obtained by

$$A_n|H_0 = a^{(T)}(t) \otimes h(t) \otimes h_s(t) + z_L(t) \tag{21}$$

where $h_s(t) := \sum \delta(t - nT)$ serves as the sampling function, and $z_L(t)$ denotes the lowpass-filtered noises. We combine the sampling operation with the acoustic channel response, and define

$$d(nT) := h(t) \otimes h_s(t) := \sum_{l=1}^{L} d_l \delta(nT - t_l T) + Z_n \tag{22}$$

where t_l is a non-negative integer, and Z_n denotes the samples of noises. Combining (21) and (22), we get

$$
\begin{aligned}
A_n|H_0 &= \sum_{m=1}^{M} a_m(t) \otimes \sum_{l=1}^{L} d_l \delta(nT - t_l T) \\
&= \sum_{m=1}^{M} \sum_{l=1}^{L} d_l a_m(nT - t_l T) + Z_n.
\end{aligned} \tag{23}
$$

On the flip side, A_n under H_1 is modelled by

$$A_n|H_1 = Z_n' \tag{24}$$

which incorporates both audio noise and possible audio signal generated by the attacker. We denote the average powers of Z_n and Z_n' as P_Z and P_Z', respectively. When the attacker emulates both audio signal and FM signals, $P_Z' > P_Z$, whereas $P_Z' = P_Z$ if the attacker only emulates FM signals.

4.5. The Cross-correlator

In this subsection, we will set up the connection between the audio samples A_n and the FM demodulator outputs Y_n under three scenarios defined in subsection 3.1.

Scenario 1. We first look at the simplest scenario (scenario 1) in which both audio noises and RF noises are ignored.

According to (13) and (23), both A_n and Y_n are functions of $a_m(t)$ under H_0. Moreover, the relationship between Y_n and $a_m(t)$ can be simplified by the interpretation given in figure 5:

$$Y_{m,n} = \frac{a_m(nT)}{\sqrt{P_a^{(m)}}} + Q_{m,n} \tag{25}$$

where $P_a^{(m)}$ denotes the average power of $a_m(t)$, and $Q_{m,n}$ denotes the quantization error at $t = nT$. Then from (23) and (25), we get

$$
\begin{aligned}
&Corr(A_n|H_0, Y_{m,n}, p) \\
&:= \frac{1}{P_{m,p}} \sum_{n=0}^{W-1} (A_n|H_0) Y_{m,n-p} \\
&= \begin{cases} \frac{1}{P_{m,p}}(C_{m,p}^{(0)} + C_{m,p}^{(1)} + C_{m,p}^{(2)}), p = t_l \\ \frac{1}{P_{m,p}}(C_{m,p}^{(2)} + C_{m,p}^{(3)}), others \end{cases}
\end{aligned} \tag{26}
$$

where

$$P_{m,p} := \sqrt{\left(\sum_{n=0}^{W-1} (A_n)^2\right)\left(\sum_{n=0}^{W-1} (Y_{m,n-p})^2\right)} \tag{27}$$

$$C_{m,p}^{(0)} := \frac{d_l}{\sqrt{P_a^{(m)}}} \sum_{n=0}^{W-1} |a_m(n - t_l)|^2 \tag{28}$$

$$C_{m,p}^{(1)} := \frac{1}{\sqrt{P_a^{(m)}}} \sum_{n=0}^{W-1} \sum_{\substack{m',l', \\ |m-m'|+|l-l'|\neq 0}} a_{m'}(n - t_{l'}) a_m(n - t_l) \tag{29}$$

$$C_{m,p}^{(2)} := \sum_{n=0}^{W-1} \sum_{m=1}^{M} \sum_{l=1}^{L} d_l a_m(n - t_l) Q_{m,n} + \sum_{n=0}^{W-1} Z_n Y_{n-p} \tag{30}$$

$$C_{m,p}^{(3)} := \frac{1}{\sqrt{P_a^{(m)}}} \sum_{n=0}^{W-1} \sum_{m'=1}^{M} \sum_{l'=1}^{L} d_l a_{m'}(n - t_{l'}) a_m(n - p). \tag{31}$$

and W determines the window size of this cross-correlator.

Similarly, $Corr(A_n|H_1, Y_{m,n}, p)$ is obtained by setting $a_m(t) = 0$ for $m = 1, ..., M$ in (26):

$$Corr(A_n|H_1, Y_{m,n}, p) = \frac{1}{P_{m,p}} \sum_{n=0}^{W-1} Z_n' Y_{m,n-p}. \tag{32}$$

The audio noises Z_n and Z_n' and quantification error Q_n are considered as uncorrelated to Y_n and $a_m(t)$, respectively. As a result, $Corr(A_n|H_1, Y_{m,n}, p)$ is close to 0. On the flip side, due to the existence of $C_{m,p}^{(0)}$ given in (28), $Corr(A_n|H_0, Y_{m,n}, p)$ always contains some values that are much larger than 0 (but smaller than 1). If audio signals $a_m(t)$ on different channels are correlated with each other, $Corr(A_n|H_0, Y_{m,n}, p)$ is even larger because of $C_{m,p}^{(1)}$ given in (29). In any case, $Corr(A_n|H_0, Y_{m,n}, p)$ is expected to exceed $Corr(A_n|H_1, Y_{m,n}, p)$ when $p = t_l$.

Finally, we design the output X of the cross-correlator as

$$X = \max_{p=0,...,\tau_{\max}} \{Corr(A_n, Y_{m,n}, p)\} \tag{33}$$

where $\tau_{\max}$ represents the maximum delay spread of the audio channel divided by T (and rounded to the nearest integer if necessary). Equation (33) searches the peak value X of the cross-correlation between demodulated FM signal and down-sampled audio signal within the time window $[0, \tau_{\max}]$, and $X|H_0$ is expected to exceed $X|H_1$. This searching process synchronizes the demodulated FM signal $Y_{m,n}$ with the strongest (sampled) path in A_n.

Scenario 2 and Scenario 3. *Scenario 2 differs from Scenario 1 only in that*, the audio signal $a(t)$ has poor quality, or in other words, Z_n has larger amplitude. As a result, all the analysis in *Scenario 1* directly applies to *Scenario 2*.

Scenario 3 differs from *Scenario 1* only in that, $s_m(t)$ has poor quality. As a result, $Y_{m,n}$ is contaminated by both quantification error and noises. For simplicity, we merge the the quantification error into noises, and let $Q_{m,n}$ represent both. As a result, all the analysis in *Scenario 1* still applies to *Scenario 3*. The value of $Corr(A_n|H_1, Y_{m,n}, p)$ increases when the amplitude of Z_n or $Q_{m,n}$ increases. As a result, the window size W of the cross-correlator in *Scenario 2* and *Scenario 3* should be larger than the window size adopted in *Scenario 1*. However, larger window size also leads to longer detection time which equals to TW, and there is a trade-off between the detection performance and computation complexity. We will discuss this issue in section 5.

4.6. The Detector

According to the analysis in subsection 4.5, $X|H_0$ is expected to be greater than $X|H_1$ under all three scenarios. Then the proposed WMUE attack detector is given as follows:

The Detector: a WMUE attack is detected if and only if $X < X_0$, where X_0 is the detection threshold.

To determine the detection threshold X_0, we first ignore the quantification error $Q_{m,n}$, and assume that audio signals at different audio channels are uncorrelated and have same average power P_R measured at the WSD. Then the first term in (23) (the power of the mixed audio signal at the WSD) has the average power MP_R, $C_{m,p}^{(1)} = 0$ and $C_{m,p}^{(2)} = \sum_{n=0}^{W-1} Z_n Y_{n-p}$. It is easily shown that $P_{m,p} \propto W\sqrt{MP_R + P_Z}$, $C_{m,p}^{(0)} \propto W\sqrt{P_R}$, and $C_{m,p}^{(2)} \propto \sqrt{WP_Z}$, where P_Z denotes the average power of Z_n. Then we get

$$X|H_0 \propto \frac{W\sqrt{P_R} + \sqrt{WP_Z}}{W\sqrt{MP_R + P_Z}} \tag{34}$$

and

$$X|H_1 \propto 1/\sqrt{W}. \tag{35}$$

When W is large, $X|H_1$ approaches 0 and $X|H_0$ approaches $\sqrt{P_R}/\sqrt{MP_R + P_Z}$. The detection threshold

X_0 equals to $\frac{1}{2}\sqrt{P_R}/\sqrt{MP_R + P_Z}$ accordingly, which only needs the second-order statistics of audio signal and background noise. X_0 may be further simplified as $1/2\sqrt{M}$ when P_Z is small compared with P_R.

When audio signals on different channels are correlated, $X|H_0$ increases while $X|H_1$ keeps unchanged. With the same detection threshold derived above, detection rate will be enhanced, while the false alarm rate is not affected.

4.7. Discussions

With the models (23) and (24), it seems that WMUE attacks can be detected simply by energy detection. However, such detection method is vulnerable if the attacker emulates audio signal in order to increase the audio noise floor. On the flip side, the proposed scheme always works as long as the emulated audio signal is uncorrelated to the FM signal.

In order to get X, $Corr(A_n, Y_{m,n}, p)$ needs to be calculated for $\tau_{max} + 1$ times with different values of p. In the definition of $Corr(A_n, Y_{m,n}, p)$ given in (26), the calculation of $\sum_{n=0}^{W-1} (A_n|H_0) Y_{m,n-p}$ requires only additions, because $Y_{m,n}$ only takes the values of 0 and ± 1. Moreover, the normalization factor $\frac{1}{P_{m,p}}$ can be derived iteratively [17], and takes only one multiplication and one square root operation per update, only except for the first update (when $p = 0$). The 1.5-bit FM demodulator requires only three analogue multipliers and three integrators if operating at analogue domain, and takes three multiplications and three additions per sample if operating at digital domain. As a result, the whole detection scheme enjoys low computation complexity.

5. Experiments

Performance of the proposed WMUE attack detection scheme is determined by the performances of the 1.5-bit FM demodulator and the cross-correlator. We first conduct computer-based simulations to evaluate the NMSE performance of the FM demodulator, then prototype the whole scheme and conduct real-world experiments to evaluate detection rate and detection time.

5.1. Performance of the FM demodulator

Performance of the FM demodulator is quantified by NMSE, which is defined as

$$NMSE := \frac{\sum_{n=0}^{N_{All}-1} \left(Y_{m,n}^{(1)} - Y_{m,n}^{(2)}\right)^2}{\sum_{n=0}^{N_{All}-1} \left(Y_{m,n}^{(1)}\right)^2} \tag{36}$$

where $Y_{m,n}^{(1)}$ denotes the outputs of the ideal FM-demodulator defined in (13), $Y_{m,n}^{(2)}$ denotes the outputs from the proposed FM-demodulator shown in figure 4, and N_{All} represents the length of both outputs. In this definition, we have excluded the quantization error, since the task of this demodulator is not to recover the original audio signal $a_m(t)$, but to provide valid coefficients for the cross-correlator.

The NMSE performances are derived from computer based simulations, with $\Delta f = 5$kHz, $f_I = 10$ kHz, $\eta = 0.5$ and $N_{All} = 500$. The audio signal $a_m(t)$ is read from an audio file which records a piece of human voice, with $a_{max} \approx 1$ (a little smaller than 1). Moreover, the IF signal $s_m^{IF}(t)$ is sampled at $G_s = 50$ kHz, which is the same sampling rate that will be used in our real-world testing, and the FM demodulator operates at digital domain.

The sampling interval T is considered as an important design parameter, since larger T leads to larger γ as discussed in subsection 4.3, but also reduces the sampling rate of $Y_{m,n}$ and may cause aliasing. Moreover, SNR of the FM signal, which equals to $A^2/(2\sigma_m^2)$, is also an important factor of NMSE.

We plot NMSEs of the FM-demodulator as a function of SNR in figure 8, when T equals to 0.1, 0.25, 0.5 and 1 ms, respectively. It is shown that the setting $T = 0.5$ms leads to the best performance in most cases, and is adopted in the following testing. The corresponding optimal sampling rate F_s^* is 2 kHz, which just satisfies (5) with the fact that the most energy in human voice concentrates in the frequency band below 1 kHz. On the flip side, F_s^* is smaller than the value required by (14) which equals to 10 kHz, since smaller sampling rate leads to longer integration window and better anti-noise ability, which compensates for the increased modelling error.

5.2. The Prototype

We prototype the proposed WMUE attack detection scheme by a commercial MCWM system and a self-designed WSD in a 12m × 7m room, as shown in figure 9. A commercial MCWM system and a WSD prototype are set up in a 12m × 7m room. The MCWM system contains an 8-channel WM receiver manufactured by Pyle Audio Inc. with model number PDWM8400, a 40W loudspeaker, and eight WMs. The carrier frequencies of these 8 channels are within the range of 170-240 MHz, which falls into VHF band. The WSD prototype is composed of two function blocks: (1) audio signal acquisition and (2) RF signal acquisition. An acoustic sensor connected to a laptop with sampling rate $F_s =$ 44.1 kHz takes response of audio signal acquisition, while RF signal acquisition is realized by a multi-channel oscilloscope and two RF branches, which is

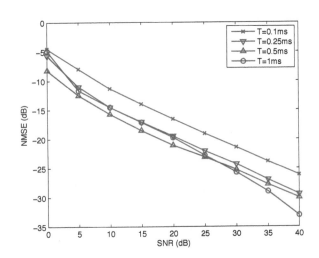

Figure 8. NMSE of the proposed 1.5-bit FM demodulator when T equals to 0.1, 0.25, 0.5 and 1 ms, respectively.

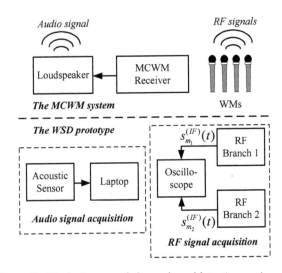

Figure 9. Block diagram of the real-world testing environment.

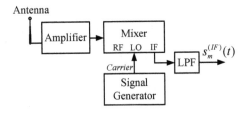

Figure 10. Block diagram of one RF branch.

capable to capture RF signals on two wireless channels simultaneously.

The two RF branches in figure 9 share the same design as shown in figure 10, which is mainly a frequency down-conversion circuit realized by a level-7 mixer. A signal generator serves as the local oscillator. Moreover, the wireless signal is amplified by an amplifier at RF and filtered by a LPF at IF. Both the

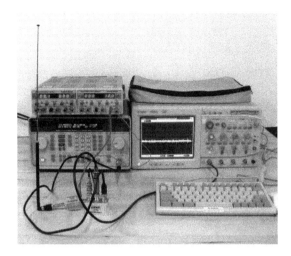

Figure 11. Photo of the WSD prototype.

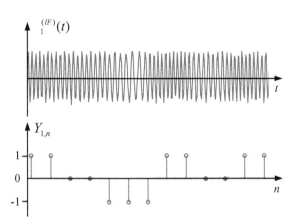

Figure 12. Waveform pieces of the IF signal and demodulator output acquired in the testing.

image in the mixer's IF output and the out-of-band interferences are also rejected by the LPF; therefore, we do not apply any RF filter here. The IF signals $s_{m_1}^{(IF)}(t)$ and $s_{m_2}^{(IF)}(t)$ coming from two RF branches are recorded by the multi-channel oscilloscope with sampling rate $F_a = 50$ kHz and $f_I = 10$ kHz. Figure 11 shows the picture of the WSD prototype.

5.3. Testing Method

We consider such a WMUE attacker who replaces the speaker of a commercial WM system with an earphone and uses the modified system as his personal wireless phone. This attacker is very similar to a legitimate WM user and hard to be detected. As a result, the WM user is emulated by the MCWM system with loudspeaker turned on, while the WMUE attacker is emulated by the same MCWM system with loudspeaker turned off. Meanwhile, we define detection rate β as the rate that the WMUE attack is detected when the loudspeaker is turned off, and define false alarm rate α as the rate that the WMUE attack is detected when the loudspeaker is turned on.

For each scenario described in section 3.1, we test two cases that (1) two wireless channels or (2) four wireless channels are used simultaneously; we will use the terms "two channels" and "four channels" to represent these two test cases, respectively. The FM demodulator operates in digital domain with $t = n'T'$ where $T' = 20$ μs and $n' = 0, 1, ...$ We set $\tau_{max} = 200$, since the maximum delay spread of the acoustic channel experienced in our experiments does not exceed 0.1 s. Two RF branches are designed to emulate some WSDs with multiple antennae; the waveforms acquired by two RF branches are considered as two independent samples, upon which our detection scheme are executed twice and the results are averaged. We set $\eta = 0.5$ in both cases and all scenarios.

Performance of the proposed WMUE attack detection scheme in *Scenario 1* is evaluated by the original waveforms acquired in the experiments, with about 30 samples for each test case. For the other two scenarios, we add random noises to either the acoustic signal (in *Scenario 2*) or IF signals (in *Scenario 3*) with certain SNR.

5.4. Testing Results

A snapshot of the waveform pieces of $s_1^{(IF)}(t)$ and $Y_{1,n}$ derived in the experiments is plot in figure 12. The IF signal $s_1^{(IF)}(t)$ is close to a sine wave but with varying frequency; its amplitude is not constant due to the limited over-sampling rate (which equals to 5 according to the settings in subsection 5.2). The demodulator output $Y_{1,n}$ equals to 1 when the instant frequency of $s_1^{(IF)}(t)$ is high, while equals to −1 when the instant frequency of $s_1^{(IF)}(t)$ is low.

Next, we evaluate the relationship between detection rate β and detection time TW in three scenarios with the simpler case of two channels, as shown in figure 13. Both the SNR of the audio signal in *Scenario 2* and the SNR of the IF signals in *Scenario 3* are set to 3 dB, and the false alarm rate α in all curves are kept below 0.1. The proposed scheme achieves good performance in all scenarios when the detection time is no less than 0.25 s, or $W >= 500$. We focus on the case of $W = 500$ in the following experiments.

Finally, the performances in *Scenario 2* and *Scenario 3* under different SNR conditions are further evaluated by receiver operating characteristic (ROC), which represents detection rate β versus false alarm rate α. In *Scenario 2*, the proposed detection scheme achieves the performance $\alpha < 0.1$ and $\beta > 0.9$ (named good performance) when SNR is higher than -3 dB and 6 dB in the cases of two channels and four channels, respectively, as shown in figure 14. In *Scenario 3*, the SNRs required to achieve good performance in the two

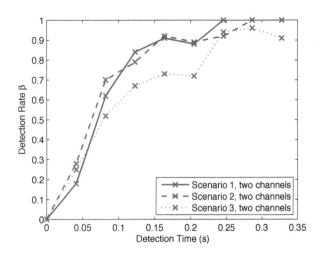

Figure 13. Detection rate versus detection time in three scenarios in the cases of two channels and four channels, respectively.

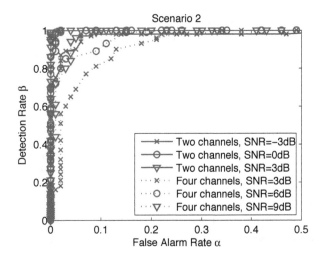

Figure 14. ROC curves in *Scenario 2* under different SNR conditions in the cases of two channels and four channels, respectively.

cases are 0 dB and 5 dB, respectively, as shown in figure 15.

These testing results validate that, the proposed scheme perform well in both noiseless environments and noisy environments.

6. Conclusions

In this paper, we propose a novel and simple algorithm to detect WMUE attacks imposed on MCWM systems in noisy environments. To the best of our knowledge, this is the first work that considers the MCWM systems. The cross-correlation between demodulated FM signal and the acoustic signal acquired simultaneously provides an effective way to detect WMUE attacks, and show good ability to resist noises/interferences. Moreover,

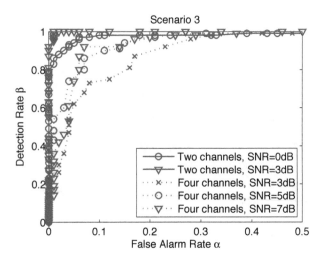

Figure 15. ROC curves in *Scenario 3* under different SNR conditions in the cases of two channels and four channels, respectively.

computation complexity of the cross-correlator can be significantly reduced by the proposed 1.5-bit FM demodulator. The optimal sampling rate of the FM demodulator is 2 kHz according to the simulation results.

We set up a MCWM system and design a WSD prototype for performance evaluation. Hardware based experiments show that, the proposed algorithm is able to detect WMUE attacks within 0.25 s in all scenarios when two or four wireless channels are used simultaneously, with detection rate $\beta > 0.9$ and false alarm rate $\alpha < 0.1$. The minimum and maximum SNRs required to achieve such performance in various conditions equal to -3 dB and 6 dB, respectively.

We conclude that, both the 1.5-bit FM demodulator and the WMUE attack detection algorithm achieve good performances in noisy environments. Performance of the proposed scheme may be further enhanced by multiple antenna or collaborative sensing techniques, which are considered as our future works.

Acknowledgement. This material is based upon work partially supported by the US National Science Foundation CAREER award under Grant Number (CNS-1149500).

References

[1] *Communication Systems and Techniques.* New York: McGraw-Hill, 1966.

[2] C. Chen, H. Cheng, and Y.-D. Yao. Cooperative spectrum sensing in cognitive radio networks in the presence of the primary user emulation attack. *IEEE Transactions on Wireless Communications*, 10(7):2135–2141, 2007 July.

[3] H.-S. Chen and W. Gao. Spectrum sensing for tv white space in north america. *IEEE Journal on Selected Areas in Communications*, 29(2):316–326, Feb. 2011.

[4] R. Chen, J.-M. Park, and J. Reed. Defense against primary user emulation attacks in cognitive radio networks. *IEEE Journal on Selected Areas in Communications*, 26(1):25–37, Jan. 2008.

[5] S. Chen, K. Zeng, and P. Mohapatra. Hearing is believing: Detecting wireless microphone emulation attack in white space. *IEEE Transactions on Mobile Computing*, 12(3):401–411, 2013.

[6] Z. Chen, T. Cooklev, C. Chen, and C. P. Raez. Modeling primary user emulation attacks and defenses in cognitive radio networks. In *Proc. Performance Comput. Commun. Conf. (IPCCC)*, 2009.

[7] L. R. D'Addario, A. R. Thompson, F. R. Schwab, and J. Granlund. Complex cross correlators with three-level quantization design tolerances. *Radio Science*, 19:931–945, May-June 1984.

[8] H. S. Dhillon, J.-O. Jeong, D. Datla, M. Benonis, R. M. Buehrer, and J. H. Reed. A sub-space method to detect multiple wireless microphone signals in tv band white space. *Analog Integr Circ Sig Process*, (69):297âĂŞ306, Sep. 2011.

[9] T. Erpek, M. McHenry, and A. Stirling. Dynamic spectrum access operational parameters with wireless microphones. *IEEE Communications Magazine*, 49(3):38–45, Mar. 2011.

[10] FCC. Fm broadcast translator stations and fm broadcast booster stations, 47 cfr part 74.

[11] J. Garodnick, J. Greco, and D. Schilling. Theory of operation and design of an all-digital fm discriminator. *IEEE Transactions on Communications*, 20(6):1159–1165, 1972 Dec.

[12] S. Kim, J. Lee, H. Wang, and D. Hong. Sensing performance of energy detector with correlated multiple antennas. *Signal Processing Letters, IEEE*, 18(8):671–674, Aug. 2009.

[13] H. Li and Z. Han. Dogfight in spectrum: Combating primary user emulation attacks in cognitive radio systems, part i: Known channel statistics. *IEEE Transactions on Wireless Communications*, 9(11):3566–3577, 2010 Nov.

[14] N. Nguyen, R. Zheng, and Z. Han. On identifying primary user emulation attacks in cognitive radio systems using nonparametric bayesian classification. *IEEE Transactions on Signal Processing*, 60(3):1432–1445, March 2012.

[15] A. Saha and B. Mazumder. A digital phase-locked loop for generating frequency discriminating codes and frequency multiplication. *Proceedings of the IEEE*, 69(4):472–473, 1981 April.

[16] A. Sahai, N. Hoven, and R. Tandra. Some fundamental limits in cognitive radio. In *Proc Allerton Conf Commun Control Comput*, 2004.

[17] D. Schmidl, T.M.; Cox. Robust frequency and timing synchronization for ofdm. *IEEE Transactions on Communications*, 45(12):1613–1621, Dec. 1997.

[18] D. Shan, K. Zeng, P. Richardson, and W. Xiang. Detecting multi-channel wireless microphone user emulation attacks in white space with noise. In *The 8th International Conference on Cognitive Radio Oriented Wireless Networks (CROWNCOM 2013)*, 2013.

[19] B.-S. Song and I. S. Lee. A digital fm demodulator for fm, tv, and wireless. *Circuits and Systems II: Analog and Digital Signal Processing, IEEE Transactions on*, 42(12):821–825, 1995 Dec.

[20] S. Xu, S. Xu, and H. Wang. Svd based sensing of a wireless microphone signal in cognitive radio networks. In *Int. Conf. on Computational Science (ICCS)*, 2008.

[21] K.-W. Yip, Y.-C. Wu, and T.-S. Ng. Design of multiplierless correlators for timing synchronization in ieee 802.11a wireless lans. *IEEE Transactions on Consumer Electronics*, 49(1):107–114, 2003 Feb.

[22] Z. Yuan, D. Niyato, H. Li, J. B. Song, and Z. Han. Defeating primary user emulation attacks using belief propagation in cognitive radio networks. *IEEE Journal on Selected Areas in Communications*, 30(10):1850–1860, Nov. 2012.

[23] L. Zadeh and J. Ragazzini. Optimum filters for the detection of signals in noise. *Proceedings of the IRE*, 40(10):1223–1231, Oct. 1952.

4

A Reputation-based Distributed District Scheduling Algorithm for Smart Grids

D. Borra[1,*], M. Iori[2], C. Borean[2], F. Fagnani[1]

[1]Dipartimento di Scienze Matematiche, Politecnico di Torino, Italy
[2]Swarm Joint Open Lab, Telecom Italia, Italy

Abstract

In this paper we develop and test a distributed algorithm providing Energy Consumption Schedules (ECS) in smart grids for a residential district. The goal is to achieve a given aggregate load profile. The NP-hard constrained optimization problem reduces to a distributed unconstrained formulation by means of Lagrangian Relaxation technique, and a meta-heuristic algorithm based on a Quantum inspired Particle Swarm with Lévy flights. A centralized iterative reputation-reward mechanism is proposed for end-users to cooperate to avoid power peaks and reduce global overload, based on random distributions simulating human behaviors and penalties on the effective ECS differing from the suggested ECS. Numerical results show the protocols effectiveness.

Keywords: Distributed Algorithms, Autonomous Demand Response management, Energy Consumption Scheduling, Smart Power Grids, Reputation algorithm

1. Introduction

The balance between demand and supply plays a leading role in smart grids applications and modern technologies aim to develop energy optimization algorithms able to provide efficient residential district dispatchment. Distributed optimization methods in power systems play a leading role, due to distributed energy generation and demand, renewables such as photovoltaic resources, storage devices, with changes in real time. A large literature has been devoted to decentralized versions of optimization algorithms applied to power systems, see, e.g., [15], due to distributed energy generation and demand, renewables such as photovoltaic resources, storage devices, with changes in real time. Multi-agent planning, as in [11], is often formulated as a combinatorial optimization problem: each agent has its own objectives, resources, constraints, and at the same time it has to share and compete for global resources and constraints. Moreover, new roles in the energy market are emerging, such as energy aggregators as intermediate between energy utilities and home users,

managing uncertainties due to variable customer actions, metereology and electricity prices. Given the huge number of agents, the optimization problem is often computationally intractable in a centralized fashion, and given the time-varying cost and constraints in energy demand-response (DR) problems, a fast single-agent planning algorithm is appealing. In this paper, as in [6], customers are incentivized to move their loads in off-peak hours despite their individual needs through marginal costs, using reputation scores as feedback. In [6] a cooperative game reduces peak-to-average ratio of the aggregate load and the Nash equilibria are reached using centralized information, whereas our approach is completely distributed. Evolutionary Game theory and Reinforcement Learning techniques have been applied to swarm intelligence problems, as in [1, 5, 12, 14].

Starting from a similar approach, we aim to modify humans behaviors of single houses in the district to follow a given global load curve. Our focus is on energy distribution to a residential district, according to the European Project INTrEPID [9].

In this scenery, the district global load is sensed by power meters, and using non-intrusive load-monitoring techniques (NILM, as in [8]) or smart

---

*Corresponding author. Email: domenica.borra@polito.it

plugs, the disaggregated data are available, turning the "blind" system to a decentralized smart grid [2]. A centralized unit senses local loads, and communicates with agents through smart-phone app or similar devices proposing day-ahead optimal Energy Consumption Schedules (ECS). Agents may accept the suggested ECS or not, according to individual needs.

The objectives of our district scheduler are threefold:

1. Following a load profile: act on the system so that the cumulated district load profile can follow a given load profile;

2. Solving distributed optimization problems: perform energy optimization of the IoT (Internet of Things) devices (e.g. smart connected appliances) by distributing computational power on different energy boxes ("swarm energy management");

3. Humans in the loop management: leveraging on "humans" to "close the loop" for no-IoT devices at home, by providing suggestions to them and tuning the system behavior accordingly.

From a concrete point of view, see the European Project INTrEPID [9], the challenges in the real world are (1) guide cumulated energy consumption for the residential district, (2) schedule smart appliances in a scalable way, and (3) work with the legacy system.

Our contribution is twofold. First, we provide a mathematical formalization of the optimization problem, decoupling the global constraint through Lagrangian relaxation as in [10], see Section 2. Second, in Section 3 we design optimal ECS in a distributed fashion at two levels: at the agent level applying meta heuristic optimization techniques as QPSOL (Quantum Particle Swarm with Levy's Flights) described in [3], in order to get feasible optimal suggested ECS; at the district level a reputation-reward mechanism provides incentives for users leading to an emerging cooperative behavior. Section 4 describes the numerical results: user habits have been analyzed to simulate user behaviors, based on diffusion of appliances and daily cycles for each appliance. Finally, we draw the conclusions of our study in Section 5.

2. Model Description

Consider a district with N users, each i-th agent has n_i appliances that are schedulable, like washing machine (WM), dish washer (DW) and tumbler dryer (TD). Refrigerator load is also included as background profile. The state of the multi-agent system is given by $\boldsymbol{x} = (x_1, \ldots, x_N)$, i.e., a vector of schedules that each user has to execute daily in a given time slot, and x_i is defined by the start times of all the n_i appliances of user i and their type (WM, DW, TD) with well-known load profiles. More precisely $x_i \in [0, 24]^{n_i}$ and x is the global vector

containing all start times of all users. Due to energy and time constraints, the goal to find a global optimum of the constrained optimization problem, called *primal problem*:

$$\min_{\boldsymbol{x}=(x_1,\ldots,x_N)} \sum_{i=1}^{N} f_i(x_i) \quad \text{s.t.}$$
$$\sum_{i=1}^{N} g_i(x_i) = a, \tag{1}$$
$$h_i(x_i) \leq b_i, i = 1, \ldots, N$$

where $a, b_i \in \mathbb{R}$ and the cost function $\sum_i f_i$ is a sum of weighted norms of three factors: overload, energy cost and tardiness of the current state $\boldsymbol{x}$. The first constraint is the only coupling object: g_i denotes the peak profile of each user and the global load of the district must attain a given curve $a = a(t)$ depending on time. All the functions f_i, g_i, h_i implicitly depend on time (they span a day), discretized in minutes or hours. The inequalities involving h_i are local time and energy (usually 3 kW) constraints of each user. The Lagrange function is

$$\mathcal{L}(\boldsymbol{x}, \mu, \lambda_i) = \sum_{i=1}^{N} [f_i(x_i) + \lambda_i(b_i - h_i(x_i))] + \mu(g_i(x_i) - a) \tag{2}$$

where $\lambda_i \geq 0, \mu$ are called *Lagrange multipliers*. Since λ_i can be computed locally, the Lagrange multiplier of our interest is μ, associated to the only coupling constraint. From now on, we neglect the local constraints as they can be included directly in the cost functions f_i. As detailed in [4], the corresponding relaxed *dual problem* becomes unconstrained:

$$\max_{\mu} \min_{\boldsymbol{x}=(x_1,\ldots,x_N)} \mathcal{L}(\boldsymbol{x}, \mu). \tag{3}$$

The standard algorithm is as follows: given an initial estimate of μ, each user computes its best ECS x_i^* such that

$$\boldsymbol{x}^* = \arg\min_{\boldsymbol{x}} \mathcal{L}(\boldsymbol{x}, \mu). \tag{4}$$

Then, $\boldsymbol{x}^*$ is sent to the central unit, and a subgradient of $\min_{\boldsymbol{x}} \mathcal{L}(\boldsymbol{x}, \mu)$ as function of μ is available. The central unit computes and sends to agents at iteration k:

$$\mu^{(k)} = \mu^{(k-1)} + \alpha^{(k-1)} \left(\sum_i g_i(x_i^*) - a \right), \tag{5}$$

where $\alpha^{(k-1)}$ is the step length of the gradient descent algorithm. Since the Lagrange multiplier μ can be interpreted as the energy price, in order to decentralize the given dual problem., we split $\mu = \sum_{i=1}^{N} \mu_i$. A distributed algorithm that can be applied acts as the previous one with the only difference: agent i solves the optimization problem

$$\min_{x_i} f_i(x_i) + \mu_i \left(N g_i(x_i) - a \right), \tag{6}$$

where $Ng_i(x_i) - a$ approximates the global overload $\sum_j g_j(x_j) - a$. The only computational effort of the central unit is the gradient descent step for μ. The latter optimization problem is solved by means of the population-based metaheuristic method QPSOL, see [3], that reduces a NP-hard combinatorial optimization problem to an adaptive algorithm requiring limited computational power.

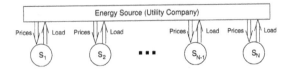

Figure 1. The panel displays the communication connections in network model, whereas the computation of the optimization problem is distributed among the agents $S_1, \ldots, S_N$ and the central unit has only to provide a computationally cheap step of gradient descent, as in Eq. (5).

The underlying idea is to split the optimization algorithm on 2 time scales: (1) the micro-scale concerns the improvement along the day of the day-ahead proposed ECS; (2) the macro-scale involves the reputation-reward mechanisms of the agents, described below, and their collective behavior.

3. Swarm Simulator Description

This simulation studies energy distribution to a city district managing its total daily power consumption without power peaks and achieving a given aggregate load curve. Users should follow utility suggestions and receive incentives according to their flexibility. This simulation aims to analyze ways to distribute reward and loads to obtain the best total power curve, considering human behaviors and dynamics. Initially users behave according to some random habits, but they modify their flexibility to perform suggested schedules and asymptotically the multi-agent system stabilizes: in order to encourage users to continue working together, individual credits are spread throughout the possible range. The reward and reputation mechanism explained in what follows aims to give benefits to the most flexible users, in terms of economical awards, e.g. discounts on the flat energy tariffs. Every day users compute local best ECS in a distributed way, according to their needs and utility constraints, as described in Section 2. In this Section we focus on the reputation mechanism defining the emerging learning process. Consider best ECS as daily input data. Agents actions define local effective ECS. Two indices evaluate end-users behaviors:

1. reputation depending on start times of effective ECS;

2. reward depending on the distance between best and effective (both local and global) load.

Reputation definition. Each agent may accept or decline n_i suggestions, with n_i number of appliances. Denote by x_i^* the best (sub-)optimal ECS found for Eq. 6 at the end of each day, and denote by $\hat{x}_i$ the effective ECS decided by user i. Formally, the reputation of user i along the day is

$$r_i = 1 - \frac{|x_i^* - \hat{x}_i|}{n_i} \in [0,1], \qquad (7)$$

, where $|\cdot|$ denotes the distance between the best and effective i-th ECS in terms of start times of appliances, i.e., reputation decreases as violation rate gets high.

Reward definition. The reward is defined in terms of credits: each agent may earn up to 24 credits each day, comparing hourly the best (b) and effective (e) two quantities: global load and local load. Formally the credits of user i at hour h is defined as

$$c_{ih} = 1 - \frac{|\text{glob\_load}_\text{b} - \text{glob\_load}_\text{e}|}{\text{glob\_load}_\text{b} + \text{glob\_load}_\text{e}} - \frac{|\text{loc\_load}_\text{b} - \text{loc\_load}_\text{e}|}{\text{loc\_load}_\text{b} + \text{loc\_load}_\text{e}}. \qquad (8)$$

At the end of each day, credits $c_i \in [0,1]$ are renormalized and create rank lists.

Behavior and learning process modeling. Each agent acts based on his own behavior profile, shaped according to

1. favorite start times to schedule appliances;

2. relevance given to reward and reputation by means of the weight parameter $\alpha_i \in [0,1]$, to define reaction to feedback;

3. natural predisposition to follow advice, to set the violation probability, defined by standard deviation σ_i of a Gaussian distribution.

Best ECS for utility are denoted by the start times vector x_i^* and actions are samples from Gaussian distributions

$$\hat{x}_i \sim \mathcal{N}(x_i^*, \sigma_i^2), \qquad (9)$$

with mean given by x_i^* and standard deviation σ_i representing flexibility. i.e. how much the performed start times are far from the suggested ones. At each iteration, the normal random variable $\hat{x}_i$ representing effective start times for all appliances of user i is sampled, and it will be statistically close to the best schedule x_i^* as the standard deviation σ_i is tending to zero. Profiles are modeled according to σ_i that is initially sampled uniformly in a given interval $[\sigma_1, \sigma_2]$. For large σ_i agents tend to selfish behaviors and do not accept suggested ECS. Another learning parameter is the weight $\alpha_i \in [0,1]$ each agent gives to reward and reputation as feedback,

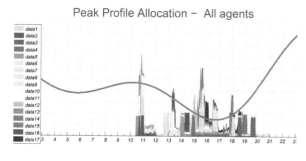

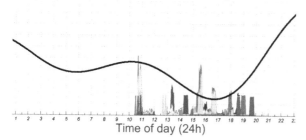

Time of day (24h)

Figure 2. The peak (upper plot) and mean (lower plot) power load (Watts) of a 5 agents neighborhood is displayed at the first of the distributed algorithm proposed in Section 2. The red (black) curve represents the district global load we aim to attain. It has to be compared with the result at the last iteration displayed in Fig. 3. All agents are flexible during 10 am-9 pm.

i.e., after each observation period user i evaluates the linear combination of its mean reputation $\bar{r}_i$ and its mean reward

$$\bar{c}_i : q_i = \alpha_i \bar{r}_i + (1 - \alpha_i)\bar{c}_i. \qquad (10)$$

Given the *satisfaction threshold* ϵ (in numerical experiments $\epsilon = 0.6$), if $q_i > \epsilon$, agent i is satisfied and there is a certain probability that relaxes decreasing its standard deviation σ_i, otherwise it increases according to a fixed discrete random distribution. In conclusion, behavior of agent i is defined by the Gaussian probability density function $f = f(x_i^*, \sigma_i, \alpha_i)$. At each feedback iteration the behavior parameter σ_i is updated. Houses with best and worse reputations and rewards are listed as another daily feedback, and emerging collective beahvior is described in Section 4.2.

4. Numerical Results

4.1. Micro-scale simulation

In this numerical experiments, using MATLAB software we run the simulator for small residential neighborhoods, i.e., $N = 5, N = 10$ agents and through QPSOL and Lagrangian relaxation described in Section 2, few iterations are sufficient to get a significant reduction of the global overload, as shown in Fig. 2. The output of

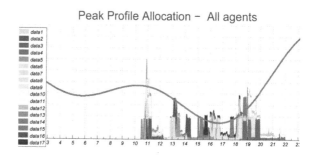

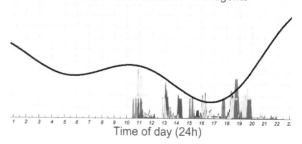

Time of day (24h)

Figure 3. The peak (upper plot) and mean (lower plot) power load (Watts) of a 5 agents neighborhood is displayed at the last iteration ($t = 10$) of the distributed algorithm proposed in Section 2. The red (black) curve represents the district global load we aim to attain. All agents are flexible during 10 am-9 pm.

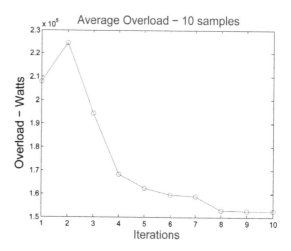

Figure 4. The panel displays the average overload (over 10 samples), i.e., the distance between best and effective global load, as function of algorithm iterations.

such distributed algorithm are the daily suggested ECS, and the macro-scale simulator deals with the learning process acting on human decisions for ECS. In what follows we describe in detail the proposed algorithm on the micro-scale, i.e. performing during the day on the micro-time scale.

State of the system:

- ECS of all users is a vector $\boldsymbol{x} = (x_1, \ldots, x_N)$;

- Lagrange multipliers, i.e. energy prices of all users $\mu_i, i = 1, \ldots, N$.

Input:

- Cost function $f = \sum_{i=1}^{N} f_i$ depending on overload, energy cost and tardiness;

- Constraint functions $g_i, i = 1, \ldots, N$ denoting the peak profile of each user, leading to the global constraint displayed in Eq. (1); constraint function $h_i, i = 1, \ldots, N$;

- Global mean load profile $a = a(t)$ and local peak load profile $b_i = b_i(t), i = 1, \ldots, N$ depending on time;

- Gradient descent step $\alpha \in (0, 1)$;

At each iteration k:

- Each agent $i = 1, \ldots, N$ solve the optimization problem

$$\min_{x_i} f_i(x_i) + \mu_i \left(N g_i(x_i) - a \right),$$

by means of a methaeuristic algorithm QPSOL, see [3] for further details;

- Each agent sends its estimate x_i^* to the central unit;

- The central unit update the global Lagrange multiplier μ as

$$\mu^{(k)} = \mu^{(k-1)} + \alpha^{(k-1)} \left(\sum_i g_i(x_i^*) - a \right),$$

where $\alpha^{(k-1)} = \alpha/(k-1)$ is the gradient descent step, decreasing as the iteration is large. Then, the central unit updates the local energy prices, i.e. Lagrande multipliers such that $\sum_i \mu_i = \mu$, as follows

$$\mu_i^{(k)} = F(\mu^{(k)}, x_i^*)$$

where F is a function decreasing with the load of agent i with ECS x_i^*. An example for F is a line $F(\mu^{(k)}) = 1 - \mu^{(k)}$, where $\mu^{(k)}$ actually depends on x_i^*.

Output:

- Each agent knows its daily optimal ECS $x_i^*(\infty)$;

- The central unit knows the final Lagrange multipliers $\mu_i(\infty)$ and the approximated global optimal state $\boldsymbol{x}^*(\infty) = (x_1^*(\infty), \ldots, x_N^*(\infty))$ solving the NP-had constrained optimization problem displayed in Eq. (1).

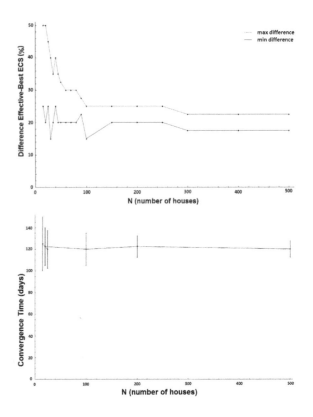

Figure 5. The upper plot shows the maximum (blue) and minimum (red) difference in percentage (converging to 20%) between best and effective total load varying the number of houses from 15 to 500. The plot below refers to necessary time to the district to reach a stable state $(3 - 6$ months$)$ and a stable difference between the two loads, compared to the number of houses from 15 to 500.

4.2. Macro-scale simulation

Software used for the development of macro-scale simulation is GAMA-platform [7], an agent-based, spatially explicit, modeling and simulation platform. Models are written in the GAML agent-oriented language, so that each house is considered to be an agent. We consider a district composed by $N = 100$ houses and a scheduled annual load for each resident about $1200 - 1400 \, kWh$.

Each agent at the beginning of the day will decide which and how many appliances would like to program. All houses compute the best load profile and decide to follow it or not. At the end of this process they send to central unit their data so that it can assess their behavior and spread credits.

Appliances are distributed according to the following percentages: 99% of houses have a WM, 70% have a DW and 30% have a TD. There are also some differences between user habits and families. These are modeled varying the maximum number of possible daily cycles for each appliance. In particular 40% of residents will use every appliance no more than once a day, 50% no more than twice and 10% no more than three times a day. Some exceptions are considered. Some users have also the ability to generate energy with solar panels, but they cannot share it with their neighbors.

Each agent acts based on his own behavior profile. This is shaped according to user reaction to the following different topics:

- Favorite times to schedule appliances: three time areas are identified as favorite and are shared with different probability. These regions are late afternoon, early morning and middle hours of the day.

- Relevance given to reward and reputation:agents can perceive feedback in several ways, in particular someone could give more importance to reputation, someone else to reward and other one could consider equally significant these two parameters.

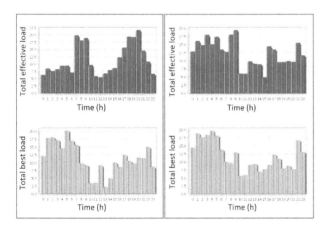

Figure 6. The charts are two examples of the values assumed by the total effective load (red) and the total best load (green) in the different hours of the day. The plot on the left represents the situation when the simulation starts, while in the right one the situation is stabilized.

- Natural predisposition to follow advice: there are three possibilities also in this case and agents are splint according on their tendency to take an active part in the multi-agent distributed system. Some users are interested in satisfy utility demands, other instead prefer not to schedule their appliances and finally some other try to balance these two trends.

Profiles are spread according to certain probability distributions and there is a little probability that agents change a specific profile during simulation. Moreover this classification is not so hard and some exceptions are taken into account.

Every day agents receive suggestions on load coming from the central unit and they are rewarded based on how they follow these advices. The purpose of the implemented optimization is to reduce the difference between the cumulative effective ECS and the cumulative best one. During simulation users learn to follow suggestions, in line with their behavior profile. The learning process depends on relevance that they give to reward and reputation. If they decide to not take the advice, they will schedule appliances in their "favorite times".

The energy utility awards prizes according on behaviour of agents and on credits that each user obtained in a fixed period. During the day time each agent can gain a maximum of 24 credits, one for hour. At any time, credits depends both on individual behavior and cumulative conduct. Rewards are redistributed according to rank list to encourage users to continue working together and following advice. Who does not consider the suggestions is doubly penalized, while virtuous people are rewarded even further. In this way concentrations of agents with the same score are avoided. Agent reputation is defined by rate of advice violation and run in range $[0, 1]$. Violation rate changes depending

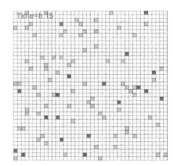

Figure 7. The picture displays houses in a district using the software Gama. The red houses are the ones with effective ECS slightly different from the suggested ECS, whereas the green houses are the more reliable and energy efficient. The used software allows a dynamic visualization as the iterations of the algorithm run.

on how they move from suggestion and increases with the hours difference between appliance best scheduling and effective scheduling.

Residents received periodic feedback on their conduct:

- Mean reputation in these days (from the previous feedback) in relation to best reputation. In fact reputation is a parameter for comparison with the other agents.

- Mean reward obtained in these days.

In simulations the time between a feedback and the following one is set to one week. This feedback can influence user behavior and system evolution. Outcomes show that this development tends to reach stable mean values of violation and reward and so system finds a balance, after a lot of days.

The system evolution stabilizes in the presence of perturbative phenomena on the input parameters, i.e., differences between effective and best ECS. Using default value of parameters we can reach a mean percentage difference (over the best load) between the best total load and the effective total load converges to 20% as in Fig. 5 (upper plot).

Varying the number of houses, the difference between effective and best load profile stabilizes starting from 100 houses in the district, as shown in Fig. 5 (the bottom chart). From numerical simulations with our setting ($N = 100$ houses), convergence time varies between 3 and 6 months. Reported values are the average over 10 simulations with the same number N of homes. Variance is greater if we consider few houses, while stabilization time increases with N.

In what follows, we describe in detail the algorithm iterations we propose on the macro-scale, i.e. perfoming along days and stabilizing after weeks or months.

Input:

- The number of appliances of each agent $n_i, i = 1, \ldots, N$;

- The initial reputation of each agent $r_i \in [0,1], i = 1, \ldots, N$;

- The initial reward of each agent i for every time slot (hour) h, i.e. $c_{ih} \in \{0,1\}, i = 1, \ldots, N, h = 1, \ldots, 24$;

- Weight parameter $\alpha_i \in [0,1]$ that is the relevance each agent gives to reward and reputation to define its reaction to feedback,

- Standard deviation $\sigma_i, i = 1, \ldots, N$ for Gaussian distribution $\mathcal{N}(0, \sigma_i)$ modeling predisposition to follow advice. Such value is initially sampled from a Uniform distribution in a preset range $\sigma_i \in [\sigma_1, \sigma_2]$;

- Behavior satisfaction threshold ϵ (in numerical experiments we choose e.g. $\epsilon = 0.6$). It is a weight that defines a tradeoff between the reputation and the reward, thus it is a real value in (0,1). For any other value in (0,1) there is no significant change in the results.

At each day/iteration k:

- Each agent decides how many appliances to program, between 1 and n_i;

- Each agent computes the best load profile based on the suggestions received from utility $x_i^{*(k)}$ (see micro-scale algorithm);

- Each agent decides to follows the suggestion or not, performing the effective schedule $\hat{x}_i^{(k)}$. Its decision

is based on its behavior characteristics:

$$\hat{x}_i^{(k)} \sim \mathcal{N}(x_i^{*(k)}, \sigma_i)$$

- reputation and rewards are updated and are given to agents as feedback

$$r_i^{(k)} = 1 - \frac{|x_i^{*(k)} - \hat{x}_i^{(k)}|}{n_i} \in [0,1]$$

$$c_{ih}^{(k)} = 1 - \frac{|\text{glob\_load}_b - \text{glob\_load}_e|}{\text{glob\_load}_b + \text{glob\_load}_e} - \frac{|\text{loc\_load}_b - \text{loc\_load}_e|}{\text{loc\_load}_b + \text{loc\_load}_e}.$$

and the total credits can be at most 24 and then they are normalized in $[0,1]$, defined as $\bar{c}_i = \sum_h c_{ih}/|\sum_h c_{ih}|$;

- each agent reacts evaluating

$$q_i^{(k)} = \alpha_i \bar{r}_i^{(k)} + (1 - \alpha_i)\bar{c}_i^{(k)}.$$

If $q_i > \epsilon$, agent i is satisfied and relaxes decreasing its standard deviation $\sigma_i^{(k)}$, otherwise it increases, i.e.

$$\sigma_i^{(k)} = F(\sigma_i^{(k-1)}, q_i^{(k)}).$$

Output:

- Asymptotic rewards and reputations $\bar{c}_i(\infty), r_i(\infty), i = 1, \ldots, N$;

- Global load attained by the residential district depending on effective schedules ECS $\hat{x} = (\hat{x}_1, \ldots, \hat{x}_N)$, approaching the optimal suggested ECS $x^* = (x_1^*, \ldots, x_N^*)$.

5. Conclusions

In this paper we provide a mathematical model and a simulator of an energy distribution system applied to a residential district. Once end-users compute local optima in a distributed way, human decisions are modeled and a reputation-reward mechanism is performed on large numbers. Numerical results prove the efficiency of our algorithm: on the macroscale with few houses (150) the difference between best and effective ECS converges to 20%, and with an average time of 3 months the district stabilizes. Moreover, the approach will be verified on the field with real devices and application in the INTrEPID project pilot.

Future research may be devoted to apply Lagrangian Relaxation methods also to the macro time-scale, updating individual energy prices each day, as a function of the difference between best and effective ECS. Another advance is to develop asynchronous versions of the proposed algorithms adapting optimal ECS to asynchronous end-users decisions. Finally, a further extended model we are going to study aims to to recover who is not cooperative: few residents, who are not usual to comply with the advice, are free to plan their load as they prefer, but they will have penalties in place of awards. On the contrary, the rest of users will have to compensate for the total load receiving a higher reward. This more adaptive system aims to attain the global load curve more precisely, considering and involving agents habits and schedules predictions.

Acknowledgments. Authours would like to thank Ennio Grasso for the scientific hints on the mathematical modeling and numerical implementation. The project has been partly funded by INTrEPID EU FP 7 project [9], grant n. 317983.

References

[1] Baharlouei, Z.; Hashemi, M.; Narimani, H.; Mohsenian-Rad, H.: Achieving optimality and fairness in autonomous demand response: benchmarks and billing mechanisms, IEEE Transactions on Smart Grid, 4(2), pp.968–975, (2013)

[2] Borean, C.; Ricci, A.; Merlonghi, G.: Energyhome: a user-centric energy management system, Metering International 3, pp. 52, (2011)

[3] Borean, C.; Grasso, E.: QPSOL: quantum particle swarm optimization with Levys flight, ICCGI 2014, Seville, Spain, (2014)

[4] Boyd, S.; Vandenberghe, L.: Convex optimization, Cambridge University Press, (2004)

[5] Campos-Nanez, E.; Garcia, A.; Li, C.: A game-theoretic approach to efficient power management in sensor networks, Operat. Res., 56(3), pp. 552, (2008)

[6] Caron, S.; Kesidis, G.: Incentive-based energy consumption scheduling algorithms for the smart grid, IEEE International Conference on Smart Grid Communications (SmartGridComm), pp.391–396, (2010)

[7] GAMA-platform, https://code.google.com/p/gama-platform/

[8] Hart, G. W.: Nonintrusive appliance load monitoring, Proceedings of the IEEE 80 (12): 1870, (1992)

[9] INTrEPID, FP7-ICT project, http://www.fp7-intrepid.eu/

[10] Jhi-Young Joo; Ilic, M.D.: Multi-layered optimization of demand resources using Lagrange dual decomposition, IEEE Transactions on Smart Grid, 4(4), pp.2081–2088, (2013)

[11] Krause, J., et al.: A survey of swarm algorithms applied to discrete optimization problems, Swarm Intelligence and Bio-inspired Computation: Theory and Applications. Elsevier Science & Technology Books, pp. 169–191, (2013)

[12] Liyan J.; Lang T.: Day ahead dynamic pricing for demand response in dynamic environments, IEEE Conference on Decision and Control (CDC), pp. 5608–5613, (2013)

[13] Pinyol, I.; Sabater-Mir, J.: Computational trust and reputation models for open multi-agent systems: a review, Artificial Intelligence Review, 40(1), pp. 1–25 (2013)

[14] Tuyls, K.; Nowe, A.: Evolutionary game theory and multi-agent reinforcement learning, The Knowledge Engineering Review, 20(01), pp. 63-90, (2005)

[15] Vinyals, M., et al.: Coalitional energy purchasing in the smart grid, IEEE International on Energy Conference and Exhibition, pp. 848–853, (2012)

5

High-level Programming and Symbolic Reasoning on IoT Resource Constrained Devices

Salvatore Gaglio [1,2], Giuseppe Lo Re[2], Gloria Martorella [2], Daniele Peri[2,*]

[1]ICAR CNR, Viale delle Scienze, Ed. 11, 90128 Palermo, Italy
[2]DICGIM University of Palermo, Viale delle Scienze, Ed. 6, 90128 Palermo, Italy

Abstract

While the vision of Internet of Things (IoT) is rather inspiring, its practical implementation remains challenging. Conventional programming approaches prove unsuitable to provide IoT resource constrained devices with the distributed processing capabilities required to implement intelligent, autonomic, and self-organizing behaviors. In our previous work, we had already proposed an alternative programming methodology for such systems that is characterized by high-level programming and symbolic expressions evaluation, and developed a lightweight middleware to support it. Our approach allows for interactive programming of deployed nodes, and it is based on the simple but e ective paradigm of executable code exchange among nodes. In this paper, we show how our methodology can be used to provide IoT resource constrained devices with reasoning abilities by implementing a Fuzzy Logic symbolic extension on deployed nodes at runtime.

Keywords: High-level programming, Resource constrained devices, Knowledge Representation, Fuzzy Logic.

1. Introduction

According to the Internet of Thing (IoT) vision [1], all kinds of devices, although computationally limited, might be used to interact with people or to manage information concerning the individuals themselves [2]. Besides reactive responses on input changes, the whole network may exhibit more advanced behaviors resulting from reasoning processes carried out on the individual nodes or emerging from local interactions. However, nodes' constraints leave the system designers many challenges to face, especially when distributed applications are considered [3]. Conventional programming methodologies often prove inappropriate on resource constrained IoT devices, especially when knowledge must be treated with a high level representation or changes of the application goals may be required after the network has been deployed [4]. Moreover, the implementation of intelligent mechanisms, as well as

symbolic reasoning, through rigid layered architectures, reveals impracticable on resource constrained devices such as those commonly used in Wireless Sensor Networks (WSNs). Often this issue is faced through the adoption of an intelligent centralized system that uses WSNs as static sensory tools [5]. Indeed, integration of WSN devices in the IoT seems quite natural and desirable, provided that the aforementioned issues be addressed. In our previous work [6, 7], we introduced an alternative programming methodology, along with a lightweight middleware, based on high-level programming and executable code exchange among WSN nodes. The contribution of this paper consists in the extension of the methodology to include symbolic reasoning even on IoT resource constrained devices. The remainder of the paper is organized as follows. In Section 2 we describe the key concepts of our methodology and the symbolic model we adopted. In Section 3, we extend the symbolic approach characterizing our programming environment with Fuzzy Logic, and in Section 4 we show an application to make the nodes reason about their position with respect to thermal zones of the deployment area. Finally, Section 5 discuss the adopted

---

*Corresponding author. Email: daniele.peri@unipa.it

solution in terms of efficiency, while 6 reports our conclusions.

2. Key Concepts of the Development Methodology

Mainstream praxis to program embedded devices consists in cross-compilation of specialized application code together with a general purpose operating system. The resulting object code is then uploaded to the on-board permanent storage. Instead, our methodology is based on high-level executable code exchange between nodes. This mechanism, while abstracted, is implemented at a very low level avoiding the burden of a complex and thick software layer between the hardware and the application code. Indeed, a Forth environment runs on the hardware providing the core functionalities of an operating system, including a command line interface (CLI). This also allows for interactive development, which is a peculiar feature of our methodology that can be used even to reprogram deployed nodes. This way, nodes can be made expand their capabilities by exchanging pieces of code among themselves in real time. The CLI is accessible through either a microcontroller's Universal Asynchronous Receiver-Transmitter (UART) or the on-board radio [6]. The Forth environment is inherently provided with an interpreter and a compiler. Both can be easily extended by defining new *words* stored in the *dictionary*. Being Forth a stack-based language, words use the stack for parameters passing. A command, or an entire program, is thus just a sequence words.

The acquisition of sensory data is already supported as we have previously extended the dictionary with the words to manage the sensor-MicroController Unit (MCU) interface, to enable the Analog to Digital Converter (ADC) and to leave the sensory reading on the stack. For instance, the program to measure the temperature is just the word temperature, whereas sensing the ambient light is achieved by executing the single word luminosity. Although the code is concise but expressive, the execution of these words involves the reading from the ADC and the return of the raw data on the stack. The description of a task in natural language and its implementation can be thus made very similar.

Our programming environment is composed of some nodes wirelessly deployed and a wired node that behaves as a bridge to send user inputs to the network. In previous work [7], we introduced the syntactic construct that implements executable code exchange among nodes:

$$\text{tell: } \langle code \rangle \text{ :tell}$$

in which $\langle code \rangle$ is a sequence of words, sent as character strings, to be remotely interpreted by the receiver node. The address of the destination node is left on the top

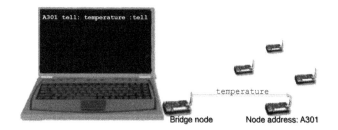

Figure 1. Executable code exchange to make a node sense the temperature quantity. To tell a node to locally perform temperature measurements, the user can interact with the bridge node interpreter by typing on its shell the sequence of words to exchange symbolic programs. The destination node address —the hexadecimal value A301 in the example— is expressed as a 16-bit value according to the IEEE802.15.4 short addressing mode. The word temperature is the symbolic program that is copied in the outgoing frame payload, sent as character string to be remotely interpreted.

of the stack. A numeric as well as a string value, can be taken at runtime from the top of the stack and inserted in the outgoing packet when special markers, such as ~ for numbers and ~s for strings are encountered.

Therefore, the exchange of code promotes distributed computations since a node that is not equipped with temperature and light sensors can tell another to measure the temperature or ambient light just by executing the construct tell: $\langle code \rangle$:tell and including the symbolic program for the measurement as follows:

$$\text{tell: temperature :tell}$$

or it can be typed at the CLI of the bridge node, as in Figure 1.

Due to their internal limitations, sensor nodes are mostly confine to perceive environmental conditions in WSN applications. This is not expected to change in the IoT context, yet in the following section we show how using a suitable programming approach even small sensors can be provided with symbolic reasoning abilities.

3. Distributed Processing and Symbolic Reasoning

In our programming environment, purely reactive behaviors can be easily implemented on the remote nodes by sending them the sequence of words to be executed if certain conditions are met. Let us consider the following command given through the CLI of the bridge node:

```
bcst tell: close-to-window? [if]
    red led on [then] :tell
```

This command broadcasts –the word `bcst` leaves the reserved address for the purpose on the stack– the code between the `tell:` and `:tell` words. Once received, each node executes the word `close-to-window?` to evaluate if it is close to the window and, if so turns the red LED on. The word `close-to-window?`, already in the dictionary, performs temperature and luminosity measurements and checks if both sensory readings are above a predefine threshold. As it can be noticed, the code is quite understandable, although all the words operate just above the hardware level by setting ports or enabling the ADCs to read temperature and light exposure. This code, as well as those in the rest of the paper, has been used on Iris Mote nodes equipped with the MTS400 sensor board to acquire data about temperature and light exposure. For the sake of showing how it is possible to incorporate in our middleware new abstractions to support intelligent applications here we introduce a Fuzzy Logic extension. Fuzzy Logic has the peculiarity to be appropriate to implement approximate reasoning in several contexts as well as for machine learning purposes [8]. We adopted a classic Forth Fuzzy Logic implementation [9] that we modifie to make it run on the Harvard architecture AVR microcontroller used in the Iris Mote platform. Finally, we also enriched the original implementation with the possibility to exchange fuzzy definition and evaluation among nodes.

The wordset to enable high-level fuzzy reasoning on IoT resource constrained devices is provided in Table 1 and allows for the creation of fuzzy input/output variables, for the definitio of the related membership functions, for fuzzific tion, for rule evaluation and for defuzzific tion processes.

Differently from [9], to create a new fuzzy variable we included the word `fvar` to be used according to the following syntax:

$$\text{<}min\_val\text{>} \quad \text{<}max\_val\text{>} \quad \text{fvar} \quad \text{<}name\text{>}$$

where <min_val> and <max_val> represent the defini tion domain of the fuzzy variable and <name> is the name associated with the new variable. Differently from <min_val> and <max_val> values that are expected to be on the stack, the variable name is provided at runtime. When this construct is executed by the node interpreter, a new entry named <name> is created in the dictionary, which is located in Flash memory, while a fi e cells structure is allocated in RAM. As illustrated in Figure 2, a fuzzy variable can be thought of as a sequence of fie ds. The Forth code to create this structure is self-explanatory:

```
begin-structure fv
    field: fv.crisp
    field: fv.link
    field: fv.low
```

Table 1. Words defined in the dictionary to implement fuzzy reasoning according to [9].

Word	Description
slope	Compute the slope given two points of a side
set-slope	Set the left and right slope in the appropriate membership fields
&	Fuzzy AND
|	Fuzzy OR
~	Fuzzy NOT
=>	Fuzzy implication
fuzzify	Given a crisp value and a membership, assign a membership value for it
apply	Apply the crisp input to the specified fuzzy input variable
output	Create an output fuzzy variable
singleton	Define a singleton output function
rules	Evaluate rules
conclude	Defuzzify and leave the crisp output on top of the stack

```
    field: fv.high
    field: xt
end-structure
```

Once the word `fvar` is executed, a generic `fv` structure is instantiated and <min_val> and <max_val> values are stored in the `fv.low` and `fv.high` fie ds. The firs fie d stores the crisp input value, and it is followed by a link fie d, i.e. the membership function list associated with that fuzzy variable. The following two fie ds contain the validity range, i.e. the minimum value and the maximum value allowed for the crisp input. Finally, as we want to allow the nodes to reason about sensory data, the last fie d contains the address of the word to perform the measurement of the physical quantity associated with that variable.

Let us defin two fuzzy variables, `temp` and `lightexp`. The last fie d of `temp` stores the address of the word `temperature`, while the address of the word `luminosity` is the last fie d of `lightexp`. The words `luminosity` and `temperature` have been already introduced in the previous section.

Similarly, to create a membership function, the word `member` expects on the stack four control points which determine the shape of the membership function and its name is provided at runtime according to the following syntax:

$$\text{<}bottom\text{-}left\text{>} \quad \text{<}top\text{-}left\text{>} \quad \text{<}top\text{-}right\text{>} \quad \text{<}bottom\text{-}right\text{>}$$
$$\text{member} \quad \text{<}name\text{>}$$

As a fuzzy variable, also a membership function is a generic structure composed of several fie ds:

```
begin-structure membership
    field: fval
```

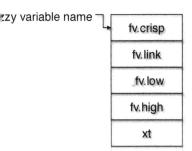

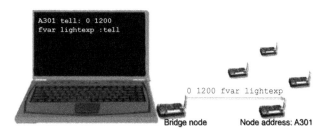

Figure 2. The definition of a fuzzy variable include a new entry in the Flash memory word dictionary and allocates five contiguous cells in RAM as a sequence of fields. The first cell stores the crisp input value, while the link field contains the address of the first defined membership function related to the fuzzy variable. The following two cells store the validity range, while the last one stores the execution token (*xt*), i.e. the address of the word to sense the physical quantity associated with the fuzzy variable. Once the fuzzy variable name is used, the address of the first field is fetched on top of stack.

```
field: link
field: lm
field: lt
field: rt
field: rm
field: ls
field: rs
end-structure
```

The firs fie d contains the truth value resulting after the fuzzific tion process, while the second fie d stores the address of the next membership function. Essen tiall y, a fuzzy variable and its membership functions are implemen ted as linked list. Membership functions are trapezoidal and theref ore four con trol poin ts are stored in the appropria te four successiv e fie ds, left-most (*lm*), left-top (*lt*), right-top (*rt*), and right-most (*rm*). Finall y, tw o further memory cells are required to store the left sl ope (*ls*) and the right sl ope (*rs*) of both sides. When the firs membership function is defined the fuzzy variable link fie d stores the address of the newl y crea ted membership function. As the word member is executed, the four con trol poin ts on top of stack are stored in the appropria te fie ds of the membership structure al ong with the left and right slopes. Figure 4 shows the code to defin the fuzzy variable rela ted to light exposure named lightexp and the rela ted membership functions according to the words described previousl y.

Moving on with the initial exam ple in which a node evalua tes its proximity to a window, in place of two crisp variables, the fuzzy variables temp and lightexp

Figure 3. Similarly to Figure 1, the executable code exchange mechanism allows to define fuzzy variables and their related membership functions on already deployed nodes. To remotely define the fuzzy variable lightexp, the code to be remotely executed must be enclosed between tell: and :tell and typed at the CLI of the bridge node that sends the executable code to the destination node. The remote node receives the sequence of words 0 1200 fvar lightexp and locally interprets it.

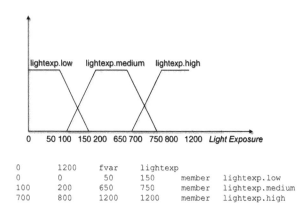

```
0        1200     fvar     lightexp
0        0        50       150       member   lightexp.low
100      200      650      750       member   lightexp.medium
700      800      1200     1200      member   lightexp.high
```

Figure 4. Fuzzy sets associated with the fuzzy variable lightexp. On the right side, the code to define the fuzzy variable lightexp and its membership functions. The definition domain, corresponding to the raw readings values interval [0,1200], is given before the word fvar, while the word member defines each of the three trapezoidal membership functions by using four control points (bottom-left, top-left, top-right, and bottom-right).

can be easil y define on depl oyed nodes provided that the symbolic progr am is placed betw een tell: and :tell as indica ted in Figure 3.

The represen ta tion of a fuzzy variable and its membership functions in memory is provided in Figure 5.

A node can be made measure light exposure, and fuzzify it with the code:

```
lightexp measure apply
```

The word measure fetches the xt fie d of the fuzzy variable that precedes it and executes the associa ted

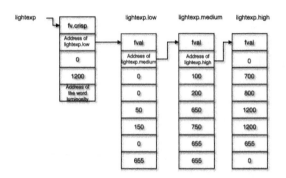

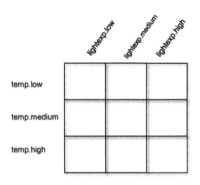

Figure 5. Memory representation of the fuzzy variable `lightexp` and its related membership functions after the code shown in Figure 4 is executed. The implementation refers to linked structures. Each link field stores the address of the next defined membership function. A link field that is equal to zero indicates the last membership function concerning that variable. It is worth noticing that the slope values are "scaled" to 65535 since this is the maximum number that can be expressed with 16-bits.

Figure 6. The execution of `temp lightexp 2 classification thermal-zone` creates the word `thermal-zone` that is bound to the two fuzzy variables. A 9 cells sized memory area is allocated as `temp` and `lightexp` have both three linguistic variables associated. In essence, each of these cells identifies a thermal-zone, a membership class according to which the node classifies itself. This area stores all the possible combinations for the rule evaluation process and aggregation.

code. In detail, when the word `measure` is interpreted, the word address, which is stored in the xt fie d, is executed. Then, the word `luminosity` is executed and the sensory reading is left on top of the stack. This value is trea ted as crisp input by the word `apply`. As its name sug gests, the word `apply` applies the crisp input to all the membership functions ref erring to `lightexp` and stores the fuzzy truth value in the corresponden t `fval` fie d. Basicall y this word scans the linked list and fuzzifie the sensory reading for each membership function.

To access the truth value resul ting from the fuzzific tion process the code:

```
lightexp.low @
```

pushes onto the stack the truth value by using the buil t-in word @ (*fetch*). Rather than through a threshol ding process, a device can establish if it is close to the window through the evalua tion of fuzzy rules in the form:

```
temp.high @ lightexp.high @ & => close-to-window
```

where `temp.high` and `lightexp.high` are membership functions of the fuzzy input variable `temp` and `lightexp` respectiv ely, and `close-to-window` is one of the linguistic labels associa ted to the output variable. Similar ly to the case of the threshol ding process, if both the tem per ature and the light exposure lev els are high a node can infer to be under sunlight , and thus close to the window .

4. Inferring the Node Distribution according to Thermal Zones

Let us suppose we intend to make the depl oyed nodes able to discov er their distribution with respect to thermal zones of an en vironmen t lighted by some windows exposed to direct sunlight , and lam ps. Each node assesses in turn the thermal zone it bel ongs to, and makes the others aw are of this infor ma tion. We define the syn tactic construct `classification` to make the nodes able to classify according to an arbitr ary number of fuzzy variables. With the previousl y define input variables `temp` and `lightexp` the code:

```
temp lightexp 2 classification thermal-zone
```

crea tes the new word `thermal-zone`, which is bound to the two fuzzy variables `temp` and `lightexp` as illustr ated in Figure 6.

When the new word `thermal-zone` is executed, it measures the tem per ature and luminosity , fuzzifie the crisp inputs and evalua tes the rules by storing the firin strength for each rule, indica ting the degree to which the rule ma tches the inputs. The rule gener ation process considers all the possible combina tions of all the membership functions, -i.e. in this case, the set of all ordered pairs (a,b) where a and b are linguistic terms associa ted respectiv ely with `temp` and `lightexp`. When handling few variables, this does not cause excessiv e memory occupa tion. It offers instead the adv antag e of considering a fine-g ained classific tion based on all the n-tuples, that in this case, are all valid. How ev er, optimiza tion methods for the red uction

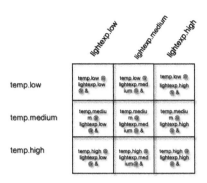

Figure 7. The rule generation involves the evaluation of all the possible combinations of the truth values of each membership function. Finally, the rule aggregation process consists in scanning the table to return the cell index storing the rule with the maximum strength. This index represents the class the node belongs to.

of a large scale rule base may be required in real-time fuzzy systems [10–12]. When needed, the table is traversed to compute the membership grade of the output by aggregating all rules. The rule with the maximum strength is taken as the output membership class (Figure 7). This way, each node is able to classify itself into one of the thermal zones. To support more sophisticated behaviors, it is possible to exploit the mechanism of code exchange among nodes to trigger the process of neighbor discovery in order to keep track of their classific tion into thermal-zones.

For this purpose, it is necessary to defin the table nodes-distribution to contain the number of nodes for each thermal zone (Figure ĩeffig:thermal classific tion). To trigger the whole classific tion process, the word classification-start can be sent to already deployed nodes through the executable code exchange paradigm. For instance, each device starts the timer and can transmit once, after waiting (word on-timer) for a time that is function of its unique ID. When its time is elapsed, the word classification-spread is executed, the node classifie itself into a thermal zone and then broadcasts the class it belongs to, together with the code to make the others update the whole distribution. The Forth code required for the entire process is the following:

```
: local-update
nodes-distribution update ;

: spread
dup local-update
bcst [tell:] ~ local-update [:tell] ;

: classification-spread
thermal-zone spread ;
```

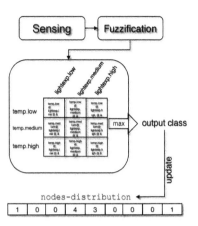

Figure 8. The word "thermal-zones" operates by sensing the temperature and light. Both sensory readings are treated as crisp input and fuzzified according to the membership functions of lightexp and temp. The rule generation considers all the pairs of truth values related to linguistic variables bound to different fuzzy variables. This is justified by the fact that each combination represents a different thermal zone identified by distinct temperature and light conditions. Indeed, the index of the cell storing the maximum value represents the thermal zone the node belongs to. The cell correspondent to the output class is incremented in nodes-distribution in order to allow each node to assess the distribution of the others.

```
: classification-start
start-timer
on-timer ['] classification-spread ;
```

in which the word spread creates a message with the code to make the other devices update locally the nodes-distribution. At the end of the update process, each node holds the current nodes distribution in terms of thermal zones, as such:

```
Class 1 2 3 4 5 6 7 8 9
    # 5 1 0 0 0 0 0 1 1
```

Five nodes belongs to class 1, one node to class 2 and so on. Each node knows the number of nodes in the network and their position, without any centralized computation. Once some nodes are moved from their position to another, and the process is triggered again, each node is able to detect the new distribution.

Moreover, the analysis of the nodes distribution may lead a node to classify itself as an outlier, to trigger self-diagnosis operations, and even to take specifi actions, by reasoning about the whole network configu ation and its membership thermal zone. The interactivity granted by our approach permits the programmer to communicate with the network through the serial shell of the bridge node. For instance, the programmer can tell the nodes belonging to class 8 to turn their red LED on:

```
bcst tell: thermal-zone 8 class? [if]
   red led on [then] :tell ;
```

5. Experimental Results

Because of the limitations in terms of available resources, the implementation of symbolic reasoning on resource constrained devices must be particularly efficient. Our approach makes IoT applications to be developed on real devices provided with an environment running at close contact with the hardware. This prevents the presence of further intermediate layers between the hardware and software applications, increasing efficiency. Moreover, as already widely discussed, although running on the hardware, the symbolic computation allows to treat knowledge with a high degree of expressiveness. Differently from mainstream approaches, distributed computation is made inexpensive due to the fact that both high and low level executable code can be exchanged. The inclusion of reasoning mechanisms on resource constrained devices is particularly efficient as it occupies only 6 bytes of RAM and 863 bytes of Flash memory. The fuzzy word-set consists of 31 words. The application allowing the classific tion into thermal zones is quite compact since it consists of only 20 words and occupies 560 bytes of RAM and 825 bytes of Flash memory.

6. Conclusions

In this paper, we showed how distributed symbolic reasoning can be implemented on resource constrained IoT devices by exploiting executable code exchange. Our contribution aims to fil the lack in the absence of programming paradigms enabling a vast adoption of IoT in everyday life. The possibility to exchange executable code makes the system adaptive and autonomous, since each node can evolve on the basis of real time inputs, in terms of both data and executable code, from other nodes and from the user. We showed how abstractions and symbolic expression evaluation can be efficiently incorporated into a programming model for such networks by exploiting both interpretation and compilation of code. As an example, we described the syntactic constructs that can be define to make the nodes aware of their position with respect to a subdivision of the environment into thermal zones. Our methodology reveals suitable for implementing more advanced behaviors on IoT devices since symbolic reasoning is performed even on inexpensive, and resource constrained microcontrollers.

References

[1] ATZORI, L., IERA, A. and MORABITO, G. (2010) The Internet of Things: A Survey. *Computer Networks* **54**(15): 2787 – 2805. doi:http://dx.doi.org/10.1016/j.comnet.2010.05.010 .

[2] GUO, B., ZHANG, D., YU, Z., LIANG, Y., WANG, Z. and ZHOU, X. (2013) From the Internet of Things to Embedded Intelligence. *World Wide Web* **16**(4): 399–420. doi:10.1007/s11280-012-0188- y.

[3] MARTORELLA, G., PERI, D. and TOSCANO, E. (2014) Hardware and Software Platforms for Distributed Computing on Resource Constrained Devices. In GAGLIO, S. and LO RE, G. [eds.] *Advances onto the Internet of Things* (Springer International Publishing), *Advances in Intelligent Systems and Computing* **260**, 121–133. doi:10.1007/978-3-319-03992-3_9 .

[4] KORTUEM, G., KAWSAR, F., FITTON, D. and SUNDRAMOORTHY, V. (2010) Smart Objects as Building Blocks for the Internet of Things. *Internet Computing, IEEE* **14**(1): 44–51. doi:10.1109/MIC.2009.143 .

[5] DE PAOLA, A., ORTOLANI, M., LO RE, G., ANASTASI, G. and DAS, S.K. (2014) Intelligent Management Systems for Energy Efficiency in Buildings: A Survey. *ACM Comput. Surv.* **47**(1): 13:1–13:38.

[6] GAGLIO, S., LO RE, G., MARTORELLA, G. and PERI, D. (2014) A Fast and Interactive Approach to Application Development on Wireless Sensor and Actuator Networks. In *Emerging Technology and Factory Automation (ETFA), 2014 IEEE*: 1–8. doi:10.1109/ETFA.2014.7005179 .

[7] GAGLIO, S., RE, G.L., MARTORELLA, G. and PERI, D. (2014) A Lightweight Middleware Platform for Distributed Computing on Wireless Sensor Networks. *Procedia Computer Science* **32**(0): 908 – 913. doi:http://dx.doi.org/10.1016/j.procs.2014.05.510 , URL http://www.sciencedirect.com/science/article/pii/S1877050914007108. The 5th International Conference on Ambient Systems, Networks and Technologies (ANT-2014), the 4th International Conference on Sustainable Energy Information Technology (SEIT-2014).

[8] NAVARA, M. and PERI, D. (2004) Automatic Generation of Fuzzy Rules and its Applications in Medical Diagnosis. In *Proc. 10th Int. Conf. Information Processing and Management of Uncertainty, Perugia, Italy*, **1**: 657–663.

[9] VANNORMAN, R. (1997) Fuzzy Forth. *Forth Dimensions* **18**: 6–13.

[10] DE PAOLA, A., LO RE, G. and PELLEGRINO, A. (2014) A Fuzzy Adaptive Controller for an Ambient Intelligence Scenario. In GAGLIO, S. and LO RE, G. [eds.] *Advances onto the Internet of Things* (Springer International Publishing), *Advances in Intelligent Systems and Computing* **260**, 47–59.

[11] JIN, Y. (2000) Fuzzy Modeling of High-dimensional Systems: Complexity Reduction and Interpretability Improvement. *Fuzzy Systems, IEEE Transactions on* **8**(2): 212–221. doi:10.1109/91.842154 .

[12] YAM, Y., BARANYI, P. and YANG, C.T. (1999) Reduction of Fuzzy Rule Base via Singular Value Decomposition. *Fuzzy Systems, IEEE Transactions on* **7**(2): 120–132. doi:10.1109/91.755394 .

6

Towards an Applied Gamification Model for Tracking, Managing, & Encouraging Sustainable Travel Behaviours

Simon Wells[1,*], Henri Kotkanen[2], Michael Schlafli[1], Silvia Gabrielli[3], Judith Masthoff[1], Antti Jylhä[2], Paula Forbes[1]

[1]University of Aberdeen, Computing Science, Meston building, Meston Walk, Aberdeen, AB24 3UE, UK
[2]University of Helsinki, Department of Computer Science, P.O. 68 (Gustaf HÃđllstrÃűmin katu 2b), FI-00014 University of Helsinki, Finland
[3]CREATE-NET - Via alla Cascata 56/D Povo - 38123 Trento - Italy

Abstract

In this paper we introduce a gamification model for encouraging sustainable multi-modal urban travel in modern European cities. Our aim is to provide a mechanism that encourages users to reflect on their current travel behaviours and to engage in more environmentally friendly activities that lead to the formation of sustainable, long-term travel behaviours. To achieve this our users track their own behaviours, set goals, manage their progress towards those goals, and respond to challenges. Our approach uses a point accumulation and level achievement metaphor to abstract from the underlying specifics of individual behaviours and goals to allow an extensible and flexible platform for behaviour management. We present our model within the context of the SUPERHUB project and platform.

Keywords: gamification, sustainable mobility, behaviour change

1. Introduction

In the SUPERHUB project we integrate multi-modal travel planning, journey resourcing and ticket purchasing with behaviour change mechanisms that encourage our users to not only find sustainable transportation options in their city but to use them also [2].

Our goal is to support our users in the formation of sustainable, long-term behaviours that are commensurate with solutions to problems in the domain of environmentally friendly travel. For example, weaning committed car drivers away from their heavy use of cars in the city center and encouraging them to use either individually sustainable travel modes such as bicycles or more sustainable mass transit modes such as buses and trams.

We achieve this by building a game-based model which "gamifies" the normal interactions and tasks related to sustainable travel behaviours. Gamification extends the core functionality of SUPERHUB, which is built around a capable multi-modal journey planner supplemented by personalisation features, behaviour

change mechanisms [3] and strategies for managing user behaviour [4].

In the remainder of this paper we present and discuss our Points Accumulation Gamification Model (PAG-M), explore how this model is applied to the challenges presented by the SUPERHUB project and demonstrate a specific application within the sustainable transport domain using the SUPERHUB platform as an exemplar. Subsequently, we discuss some challenges associated with this approach such as bootstrapping the system to a sustainable level of functionality and managing behaviour change in the longer term. Finally we draw some conclusions and indicate some directions in which the current work will develop.

2. Background

Gamification is the application of game-oriented design approaches and or game-inspired mechanics to otherwise non-game contexts. For example, taking familiar elements from games, such as points scoring as a method for measuring achievement, and applying it in a context that would not normally be associated with play, such as travelling sustainably within an urban environment. There are two core approaches to gamifying an interaction; the first is to metrify existing

*Corresponding author. Email: simon.wells@abdn.ac.uk

tasks and the other is to modify existing tasks with additional game-mechanics or elements of play.

Metrifying existing tasks involves incorporating a measure of attainment upon which a concept of goal directed movement is predicated. Metrics are allocated to standard, existing tasks within the problem domain which are then associated with values whose accumulation leads to either reward or sanction for either the user or some related set of the users social graph, as a result of their performance in relation to to the metrics. In this approach the domain task remains the same but is supplemented with gamified metrics that enable the user to gain feedback about their performance and achievements. This approach can also be made social by enabling users to compare their own achievements against the achievements of others, e.g. using leaderboards. This can introduce a competitive element for users acting within the domain and is a relatively straightforward approach as it does not require the core task to be modified in order to play the game. The aim of playing this kind of game is can be summarised as "attaining the highest score". However, in order to do so, and dependent upon the associated points model, the user may have to change the way that they complete their chosen tasks, or even perform different tasks entirely to accumulate the greatest reward. By balancing the accumulation of points against the available tasks, the users original behaviour may change in line with outcomes planned by the game designers, hence this approach provides a strong link between gamification and behaviour management techniques.

Modifying or extending existing core tasks to incorporate some element of play is a reliable way to transform the process of completing a mundane task into something that can be more fun to do. By carefully balancing which tasks are gamified with those tasks that aren't, the interaction can be designed to favour particular behaviours. Both metrified and modified tasks can be combined to provide further flexibility in the design of an engaging and persuasive platform. By incorporating these kinds of features, gamification aims to increase both long and short term user uptake and acceptance whilst simulataneously making the system both fun and engaging. It is this target that SUPERHUB is aiming for, an engaging and rewarding behaviour change experience.

3. The Gamification Model (PAG-M)

In this section we discuss elements of the Points Accumulation Gamification model (PAG-M) which underpins the gamified aspects of travel using SUPERHUB and relate this to the sustainable travel problem domain. In the remainder of this section we introduce and discuss points accumulation, levels, badges, and challenges. Points are the most basic gamification element within this model, on which are built a number of more complex constructs enabling goal-oriented behaviour, engagement, and social interaction to be facilliated and managed at different levels of complexity in order to provide a more richer environment for exploring behaviour change.

In PAG-M, users accumulate points for engaging in behaviours that the system deems to be positive, and, in the abstract model but not presently in SUPERHUB, there is the potential to remove points when a negative behaviour is measured. When a user engages in a given behaviour a number of points can be allocated according to the specific behaviour concerned. Points can be allocated either directly, to the user who performed the behaviour, or indirectly, for example to a group of users other than the performing user but who are in some way related to the performing user, e.g a peer-group that have an existing and declared relationship with the user that is otherwise captured by the system. The number of points allocated can be either fixed for all users or variable depending upon segmentation factors associated with individual users. For example, giving a larger award to a car user for taking a cycle journey than to a regular cyclist might be more likely to encourage a change towards a sustainable behaviour, whereas for the regular cyclist the reward is more of a 'behaviour maintenance' allocation.

Rather than merely accumulating an increasing but otherwise undifferentiated number of points, users can 'level-up'; their accumulation of points is translated into discrete levels that enable broad comparison of attainment according to levels. The transition between levels can occur in a number of ways such as with fixed and discrete transitions at predefined scores or with personalised levels calculated on a per-user basis. It should be noted however that if individual scores are set then it becomes difficult to directly compare the performance of individual users which might have repercussions if the system is subsequently deployed in a more social context. The scores required to trigger a level transition can be either fixed or variable, for example, the level could increase every time the user reached a score of 1000 points. Alternatively, the score could be a linearly, or otherwise, increasing amount, making progress slower as participants reached higher levels. However, such an approach might require additional incentives, such as opportunities to earn large numbers of points, so as to avoid the users participation level from dropping as a consequence. In determining a points based mechanism for gamifying interactions, such factors must be taken into account to balance the needs of novice users who are just beginning to develop new behaviours from those of more experienced users who are maintaining habits.

In non-computational contexts, badges are used to communicate and to signify status. It is the status role that is most commonly exploited when badges are deployed within gamified interactions. Badges can indicate that a user has achieved a particular level of success either by achieving particular goals or by accumulating sufficient points to achieve a defined status. Badges can thus play a social role, signifying to other users the status and achievements of the badged user, whilst also playing a more private role to users, as a kind of virtual reward. This can satisfy the need to aquire and collect, and can play an important role in facililtating greater user engagement as well as inter-user competition.

Challenges capture the idea of setting a particular goal, the achievement of which will earn a larger number of points, and whose solution is not necessarily straightforward, e.g. the goal in a challenge can be a higher-level, more complex achievement, such as reducing your personal carbon footprint, however there are a variety of tasks that can be performed to achieve this. This enable the basic 'complete tasks to earn points' interaction to be made more interesting and "challenging" for the user. By offering the user the opportunity to formulate solutions to challenges for themselves the aim is to facilitate greater engagement and greater satisfaction. Challenges can be of several types; those set by the system and directed at either individuals or groups of users, those set by users and directed towards others, and those set by users for themselves. This offers the opportunity to provide socially oriented, almost competitive, challenge interactions, as well as a personalised, individual, private, self-improvement interactions.

The MDA framework of game design [5] describes how games are composed from three elements: Mechanics, Dynamics, and Aesthetics. Mechanics define the parts of the game, for example the pieces, tokens, boards, or gamespace. Dynamics define how the pieces are placed, arranged, and moved in relation to one another. Aesthetics define the feelings that the composition of mechanics and dynamics engenders in the players. PAG-M is therefore situated across these levels, operating at both the mechanical and dynamic layers, and ultimately designed to affect the aesthetics of the interaction. The aim of applying PAG-M within SUPER-HUB is to engender real, lasting change, and an element of that is to create an emotional response in SUPERHUB users.

Given the widespread and well understood use of points and levels as a way to mark progress within games and competition in popular culture, one might pose the question: why is it necessary to cover similar ground in detail now? In answer to this, we suggest that such an approach gives us a reference point from which to build our solution within the sustainable travel problem domain, and enables us to fix the terminology with which we describe our solution. A second reason for taking this two-fold approach, developing a higher-level abstract model of points based gamification and a low-level, concrete implementation, is to enable the construction of more generally applicable gamification support in software tools that are designed to tackle societal problems both on a large scale and in a repeatable, and robust way. Finally, the recent CHI workshop "Designing Gamification" [1] identified that whilst gamification has recently become a popular technique in both HCI and the wider software industry, there is still little knowledge about the effective design of such systems whether as an additional layer to extant software or the wholesale design of new gamified systems from the ground up. We aim to tackle this issue by developing a core model that captures the essential elements of our approach to gamification and which can be extended to a range of problem domains either incorporated within existing systems or as the basis for new systems.

4. Applying PAG-M Within SUPERHUB

In this section we make concrete those specific aspects of the higher-level model, introduced in the previous section, by describing how the abstract notions of points and levels are instantiated within the SUPERHUB platform. In this way we distinguish between the flexible, higher-level model described earlier which necessarily has wider scope and capabilities and the narrower and more specific utilisation and implementation within SUPERHUB.

From a motivational perspective, in SUPERHUB we aim to encourage two factors. Firstly increased usage of the SUPERHUB apps, and secondly, increased frequency and choice of sustainable travel behaviours. We prioritise usage of SUPERHUB as our first factor because the core mission of the platform is to facilitate sustainable urban travel. Hence we assume that ceteris paribus increased SUPERHUB usage will lead to increasingly sustainable travel amongst SUPERHUB users.

New users join SUPERHUB at level one with a score of zero points. Subsequently, as the user accumulates an increasing number of points, they progress to higher levels. This gives the user an indication of their progress over time. Points can be collected for performing tasks and the range of available points varies depending upon the particular task that is performed. For example, there are low-level maintenance tasks that enable smooth running of the system, for example, fine-tuning the recommender component which provides personalised travel recommendations, requires that the user provide feedback about historical recommendations. Similarly, personalisation of challenges and measurement of key performance indicators for the entire system are based upon knowing more about the user and therefore require more complete profile completion. Some of these tasks are one-off occurrences, for example, completing the basic profile, whereas other tasks are recurrent, for example, asking the user to rate a set of points of interest associated with a given journey plan in order to fine-tune the recommender. In both of these cases, increasingly accurate functionality of the system is based upon the user performing tasks which attract small numbers of points.

An early design decision that was made during the gamification design process was to award small numbers of points for lots of common tasks that an active user of SUPERHUB might perform, for example, planning and selecting a journey, rating a complete journey, rating individual POIs within a journey in relation to their interest to the user, and reporting disruptive events could attract a lower number of points rewards. These are regularly recurring interactions that any user of SUPERHUB might commonly be expected to perform. The idea here is merely to encourage increased use of SUPERHUB so, just by using the system, users are accumulating points and can see that they are progressing. By taking this approach we are also able to tackle one of our bootstrap problems, specifically, a knowledge bottleneck associated with the fact that some of the functional components of the system both work better in general and work more accurately for individual users when there is more information in total and more information about individuals. In SUPERHUB larger amounts of points are awarded for successfully completing tasks associated with sustainable travel. For example, given a set of alternative journey plans which include a range of different, multi-modal, travel options and which are ranked in terms of their CO_2 emissions, a user could be awarded more points for selecting and completing a journey that has lower emissions than one that has higher emissions.

Within SUPERHUB, we only allow points to accumulate, users cannot lose points. This decision reflects the idea that whilst a traveller can aim to be environmentally sustainable in everything they do they cannot always control all aspects of the journeys that they make and such users should not be penalised for those journeys that they make that are outwith their control. Because SUPERHUB aims to support all travellers within a city, whether travelling for business, leisure, tourism, or any other reason, and some of those travellers may make journeys, for example business journeys by taxi, that run counter to their personal travel preferences it is better to reward the more sustainable journeys than to punish the less sustainable.

SUPERHUB also supports self-organised challenges which enable a user to pursue a higher level goal. Goal-based challenges are built atop the basic points and level mechanisms and enable users to set for themselves a personalised goal that they wish to satisfy and the successful completion of which will earn them points. The platform currently support 3 types of challenge which relate directly to the users CO_2 emissions, the money that they spend on their travel, and the calories burnt in travelling. Whilst it would be ideal if all users were motivated primarily by environmental concerns, and hence would compete in CO_2 reduction challenges, we recognise that many users have other priorities, for example, many users would prefer to save money, over concerns about either the environment or the amount of exercise that they took. However, whilst reduction of CO_2 emissions aligns directly with moving people to more sustainable travel options, a saving money goal can do the same. Generally, those transport modes that are individual and motorised are more expensive than either mass-transit or non-motorised modes, for example, the cost of taking a taxi is generally far in excess of the cost of taking a bus or tram. Therefore a goal of saving money on travel costs can align with a change of behaviour from taking taxis to using mass-transit, in which case there is a consequent CO_2 savings as the carbon burden, although larger in total for mass-transit, is amortised over a greater number of travellers. Similarly, a goal of burning more calories, which might be set by users who are primarily motivated to get more exercise or to increase their health, can also align with increasingly sustainable transport. Walking and cycling are both active travel modes which will increase the amount of calories spent whilst simultaneously reducing a users CO_2 emissions. In this way we support approaches that are directed at those users who are primarily motivated by issues of sustainability and which directly affect the environment, whilst also supporting users who are not motivated in the same way, but by satisfying the users other motivations, we can indirectly help the environment.

By using a range of techniques, incorporating points and levels, and building a challenge platform atop of them we have developed a scalable system that supports motivated travellers who want to increase the sustainability of their travel behaviours, whilst also supporting other users whose motivations may be differently oriented but who can be exposed to and encouraged to act sustainably through less direct means. In this way we reinforce the primary goal of SUPERHUB which is to foster, to facilitate, and to support sustainable travel behaviours whilst acknowledging that in the real world, people have a range of motivations and these are not always aligned with environmental sustainability goals.

5. Implementation Within SUPERHUB & Example Challenge Usage

The SUPERHUB platform has a distributed, component-oriented architecture which supports multi-modal journey planning and resourcing, personalised recommendations, and behaviour change for environmentally sustainable travel. There are also a range of supplementary functionalities, such as crowd-sourced disruptive event reporting, social media and transport data-feed scanning, open-streetmap tile servers, and address autocompletion that aim to make the user experience more self-contained, more comprehensive, and more accurate.

For challenges we make use of the supplementary data about each individual journey plan that is provided by the planner as well as the challenges set by the user within their account. When a user searches for a journey, they are presented with a range of possible multi-modal routes and for each one total CO_2 emissions, duration, cost, length, effort and satisfaction values are calculated as indicated in Figure 1. These are used as the basis for determining how a given journey contributes to the users current challenge.

The challenge process is as follows; the user accesses their SUPERHUB account and navigates to the goals functionality. The user is presented with options to set challenges relating to money, calories, or emissions. In this paper we use the emissions challenge as an exemplar but the other goals work in a similar fashion so emissions are representative.

The users can (without having to participate in a challenge) view their previous journeys, provided they've been planned with SUPERHUB, as well as visualise different aspects (CO_2 emissions, calories burned etc.) of individual past journeys or aggregated over freely specifiable periods of time. Also retrievable from the usage data stored in the platform are all other plans offered to the user, but which were ultimately discarded for the favor of the one journey plan which suited the user best at the time of planning.

For each user, using the data described above, it's possible to calculate overall indices for each aspect/criterion representing how much of that criterion they tolerated in relation to the worst case. For example, if over the course of their entire SUPERHUB history, a user could have emitted 20kg of CO_2 by choosing a car every time, but instead chose journeys which caused only 10kg of CO_2 emissions, their CO_2 index would be 50%. See Figure 2 for clarification.

The challenges are designed to reward improvement compared to a user's behavioural history. In other words, challenges are short time frames (in the current application arbitrarily set to a week, constrained by the length of the trial period) in which the user must try to choose journeys resulting in a better relative score than

their entire travel history. This way, even heavy car users can complete a challenge with success if they set a target of e.g. 80%, allowing them to still take about four out of five of their journeys with a car (caveat: previous is true if all journeys they take are the same length - the lengths of the trips obviously affect the score). Naturally, the better the target score, the more points will be awarded on success.

To mitigate exploits of the system, the user is limited to only having one active challenge per criterion at a time. Also, a minimum of 5 journeys must be planned and taken (as recognized by the activity tracker of the Android app) in order to complete a challenge as illustrated in Figure 3.

We plan to include feedback during journey planning to help remind the user to keep in mind their ongoing challenges and how the journeys they take affect the outcomes. When the user plans a journey and saves a plan, the backend updates the values and state of any ongoing challenges the user might have. Finally, users are given visual feedback as to the status of their current challenge as indicated in Figure 4 for a failing challenge and Figure 5 for a successful challenge.

By taking this approach, and making challenges the main way to accumulate large numbers of points, we aim to build a system in which users are active in choosing to perform behaviours that are commensurate with their goals, and are offered many system supported opportunities to be introspective with respect to their travel behaviours.

6. Supporting Longer Term Behaviour Change

Behaviour modification, and the ensuing formation of new habits, is a difficult task to achieve and manage. This requires not only that the users current habits are modified, but also that their new habits are sustained, perhaps indefinitely. Over a longer timescale, the parameters of what might be considered an acceptable habit may change. For example, within SUPERHUB the mobility of a user, and therefore the appropriate range of desirable and sustainable travel behaviours particular to that user, may change over time as a function of many parameters, including but not limited to health, social status, family status, and age. As a result the system must be sufficiently flexible to enable either new, or modified, habits to be targeted. During deployment, it is expected that the balance of points available on a per task basis must be adjusted in order to manage both user expectations and user performance. As a result we envisage that management and balancing of a points based system is a long term task that must extend across the lifetime of the system's deployment.

Furthermore, habits must be formed by many users of the system in order to have a measurable effect at the city-wide level. To target many people for behaviour

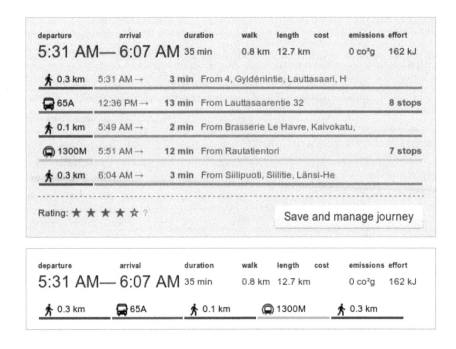

Figure 1. Example output from the multi-modal journey planner indicating the various parameters that are calculated for each journey and which are subsequenty utilised by the challenge functionality.

change requires the adoption of flexible techniques that can be modified to apply to users as individuals, with their own beliefs, goals, and pre-existing patterns of behaviour. What is an effective behavioural intervention for one user may not be as effective for the next, hence we must treat each user as an individual and personalise their experience of, and interaction with, the system.

Therefore we require a system that is both flexible, enabling it to target a wide, perhaps even dynamic, range of habits, and personalisable, enabling interventions, goals, and challenges to be targeted to the characteristics of individual users. Furthermore the system should support usage over the longer-term, providing feedback and a sense of progress to ensure that the experience does not become stale and so that users do not abandon the system as a result.

7. Bootstrapping The System

One aspect of creating and deploying a new system that can be problematic is bootstrapping the system to a sustainable level of usage. Social systems require a sufficient number of users for any social mechanisms to function correctly. If aspects of the systems functionality require a minimum number of users, for example, to provide activity data from which statistical baselines can be calculated, then for the system to function correctly, users must be attracted and retained. One solution to this problem, which aligns neatly with the point accumulation strategy, is to disburse real world rewards to users based upon their interaction with the system. Essentially, SUPERHUB allows users to redeem their points in exchange for items of real world value such as reduced fares on public transport and discounts on cycle sharing schemes.

Adoption of these approaches leads to a number of new challenges associated with ensuring that gamesmanship does not bankrupt the system and that user behaviour is directed toward desirable outcomes rather than merely towards those outcomes that accumulate the most rewards. This suggests that an ongoing adjustment of goals, triggers, and outcomes during deployment may be necessary whilst also taking steps to avoid a potential arms race with those users who might seek to exploit loopholes in the game rules.

8. Conclusions & Further Work

In this paper we have presented aspects of the model of points accumulation used in SUPERHUB. We have also described the goal-based behaviour management system that it underpins and explored the benefits of taking this approach. The SUPERHUB platform will be deployed in a second round of large-scale trials during Summer 2014 and results from this will be used to gauge the efficacy of the current system and to inform any subsequent development and refinement. We do however already have a range of directions that we would like to take the work in.

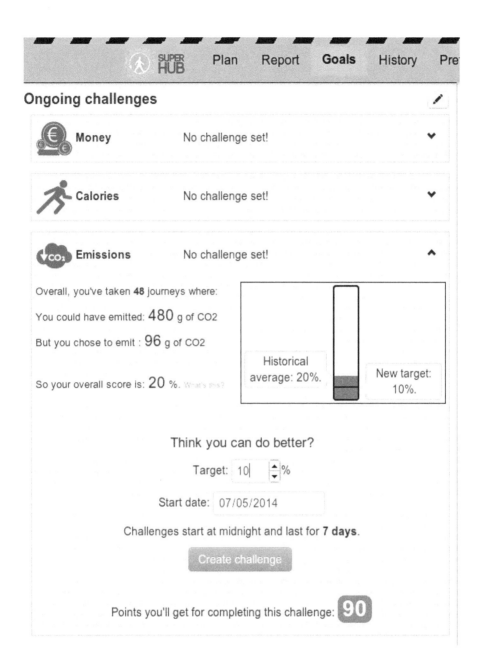

Figure 2. Challenge setting screen. User is shown the i) number of journeys they've taken, ii) amount of CO2 they could have emitted, iii) amount of CO2 they emitted by choice of journey plan, and iv) their resulting overall score/index. A bar/visual representation is also shown. As the users adjust the target for their challenge, the points promised for a successful completion is updated.

For longer term deployments of a goal-oriented challenge system efficient management and support tools are required. These would enable new challenge types to be defined, for the points allocation to be refined, and for the available real-world rewards to be altered and changed at run-time. Extending this idea further, machine learning tools could be deployed to support the recognition of new challenge types and to identify trends in point accumulation across the cohort of users. This would support the human-based management of the system with solid big data analysis leading, ideally, to a more robust, accurate and flexible system that can scale to very large numbers of users. Such an approach, utilising automated support tools of this type would prove invaluable, and would enable SUPERHUB to be deployed on a truly large scale. Additionally, by considering a more comprehensive set of points related behaviour management tactics we can ensure that the gamification approach taken in SUPERHUB can be adjusted to fit a wider range of problem domains.

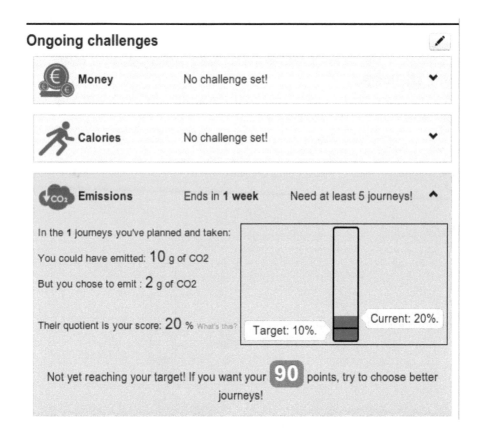

Figure 3. Illustrating the requirement to complete a minimum number of journey in order to not 'game' the system.

In the current system all points accumulation is a completely individual affair. An individual user is the only recipient of points allocated as a result of their own behaviours. However it would be interesting to investigate how rewarding members of a subset of a persons social graph, based upon that personâĂŹs behaviour, subsequently affects the perceived value of the reward. We would hope that for some users, such altruistic behaviour with the aim of increasing or maximising social gain is more important than individual gain. Therefore there is a rich thread of altruistic rewards that could be explored within SUPERHUB as we increase the amount of social functionality.

Finally, we aim to deploy similar gamification models in subsequent projects in other problem domains in order to gauge the general efficacy of this kind of approach. Our goal is to produce successful, repeatable behavioural interventions and behaviour change support tools which are generally applicable to societal problems and that can be incorporated into a wide range of domains, tools, and software platforms.

Acknowledgement. This work has been supported by the FP7 IP Project SUPERHUB No. 289067.

References

[1] S. Deterding, S. Bjork, E. N. Lennart, D. Dixon, and E. Lawley. Designing gamification: Creating gameful and playful experiences. In *Designing Gamification: Creating Gameful and Playful Experiences at the ACM SIG-CHI Conference on Human Factors in Computing Systems (CHI 2013)*, 2013.

[2] P. J. Forbes, S. Wells, J. Masthoff, and H. Nguyen. Superhub: Integrating behaviour change theories into a sustainable urban-mobility platform. In *Using Technology to Facilitate Behaviour Change and Support Healthy, Sustainable Living at BCS HCI 2012*, 2012.

[3] S. Gabrielli, R. Maimone, P. Forbes, J. Masthoff, S. Wells, L. Primerano, G. Bo, M. Pompa, and L. Haverinen. Co-designing motivational features for sustainable urban mobility. In *ACM SIG-CHI Conference on Human Factors in Computing Systems (CHI 2013)*, 2013.

[4] S. Gabrielli, R. Maimone, P. Forbes, and S. Wells. Exploring change strategies for sustainable urban mobility. In *Designing Social Media for Change at the ACM SIG-CHI Conference on Human Factors in Computing Systems (CHI 2013)*, 2013.

[5] G. Zichermann and C. Cunningham. *Gamification by Design*. O'Reilly Media, Inc. 1005 Gravenstein Highway North, Sebastopol, CA 95472., 2011.

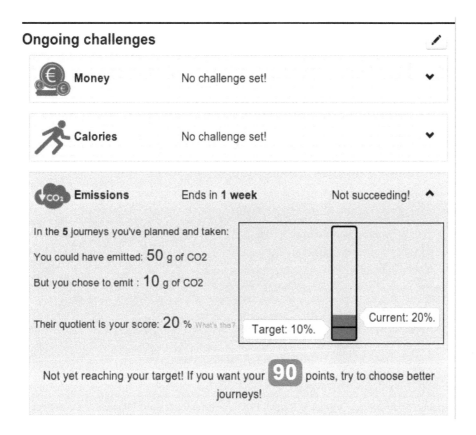

Figure 4. This figure illustrates the challenge screen that is displayed to the user when they are failing a challenge.

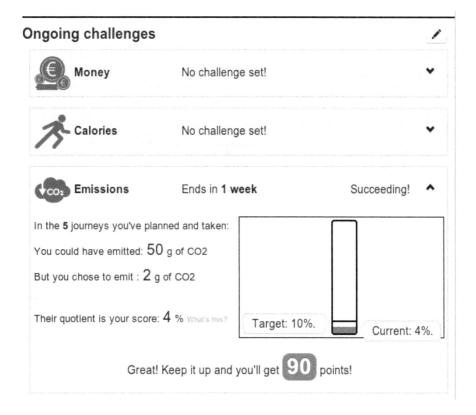

Figure 5. This figure illustrates the challenge screen that is displayed to the user when they are succeeding in a challenge.

7

A Hardware Prototype of a Flexible Spectrum Sensing Node for Smart Sensing Networks *

Ahmed Elsokary[1,*], Peter Lohmiller[1], Václav Valenta[1] and Hermann Schumacher[1]

[1]Ulm University, Institute of Electron Devices and Circuits, Albert-Einstein-Allee 45, 89081 Ulm, Germany.

Abstract

In this paper we present a prototype for a spectrum sensing node for a cognitive radio sensing network. Our prototype consists of a custom down-conversion front-end with an RF input frequency range from 300 MHz to 3 GHz and a Power Spectral Density (PSD) estimation algorithm implemented on a Virtex-6 Field Programmable Gate Array (FPGA). The base-band processing part is capable of calculating the PSD for a bandwidth upto 245.76 MHz achieving a resolution of 60 kHz and an online variable averaging functionality with a maximum of 32767 averages. We show the arithmetic optimization techniques used for the PSD evaluation to optimize FPGA resource usage. Real time performance and calculation of the PSD for real world signals in the GSM downlink, DECT and the UHF DVB-T bands are demonstrated.

Keywords: Spectrum Sensing, Multiband, Cognitive Radio, FPGA Implementation, Hardware Prototype, Periodogram, PSD, FFT

1. Introduction

Cognitive Radio (CR) is an appealing concept for solving the spectrum resource scarcity problem caused by the current static allocation of frequency bands [2][3]. In this context, the Primary User (PU) is the licensed user with priority to use a frequency channel. A Secondary User (SU) is a cognitive user who can reuse frequency white spaces that are channels unused by PUs. Once a PU transmission is detected, the SU must leave the used frequency band immediately to avoid interference. A key requirement for the CR concept is a reliable spectrum sensing [4] with the aim of robust PU detection.

Multiband spectrum sensing deals with the detection of multiple white spaces simultaneously. The main advantage is the quick detection of PUs and offering multiple opportunities to the SU. An important decision metric for multiband detection is the Power Spectral Density (PSD), that describes the average density of the power distribution within the detection bandwidth.

This paper deals with design, implementation and experimental deployment of a spectrum sensing node prototype. The future goal is the hardware implementation of a multiband distributed spectrum sensing network, where cooperative detection takes place between all nodes. Each node contains a flexible front-end and a bank of sensing algorithms for decision evaluation. The realized sensing node in this paper consists of a customized RF front-end and a PSD evaluation implemented on a Field Programmable Gate Array (FPGA). The system diagram is shown in Fig. 1.

The main goal is the optimization of the sensing speed and the evaluation in practical scenarios. Our prototype shows a sensitivity of -107 dBm and a bandwidth of 245.76 MHz with a frequency resolution of 60 kHz. Economic use of target FPGA resources was achieved through optimization of arithmetic and memory operations. The RF front-end covers an RF input frequency range from 300 MHz up to 3 GHz. The flexibility in the hardware prototype is achieved through the reconfiguration of parameters such as averaging and windowing in real time, and a tunable external local oscillator to select the target frequency

---

*This paper is an extended version of a manuscript presented at the 10th International Conference on Cognitive Radio Oriented Wireless Networks (CROWNCOM), 2015 [1] where section 3 was modified to include arithmetic precision selection. Implementation results on a lower cost FPGA family were appended to section 4.

* Corresponding author. Email: ahmed.elsokary@uni-ulm.de

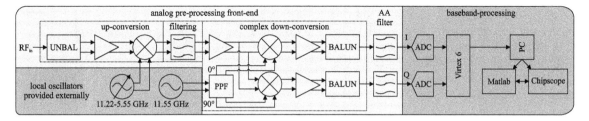

Figure 1. Frontend connected to the base–band processing.

band during operation. The prototype is tested and verified in realistic scenarios.

2. PSD Evaluation

The PSD is evaluated by averaging over several periodograms. This reduces the estimation error as more averages are taken [5]. The periodogram is the squared magnitude of the Discrete Fourier Transform (DFT) of the received signal. The L-point DFT of a discrete time domain vector x of length L is calculated as follows:

$$X_k = \sum_{n=0}^{L-1} x(n) \frac{-j2\pi nk}{L}, k = 0, 1, ..., L-1. \quad (1)$$

A window function is used to reduce spectral leakage, on the other hand it degrades the frequency resolution. Different window functions that offer different trades between resolution and leakage reduction are available [6]. In this paper, we use the Blackman window as it offers the highest sidelobe suppression. The modified periodogram calculation becomes

$$X_k = \sum_{n=0}^{L-1} w(n) \cdot x(n) \frac{-j2\pi nk}{L}, k = 0, 1, ..., L-1, \quad (2)$$

where w is the window function of size L.

The PSD is estimated by

$$\hat{P} = \frac{1}{N_{avg}} \sum_{m=0}^{N_{avg}-1} |\hat{X}|_m^2, \quad (3)$$

where

$$|\hat{X}|_m^2 = Re\{\hat{X}_m\}^2 + Im\{\hat{X}_m\}^2, \quad (4)$$

$$\hat{X} = \{X_0, X_1, X_2, ...X_{L-1}\}. $$

This is a special case of the Welch estimator described in [5] where there is no overlap between the time domain signals used to calculate the averaged periodograms.

3. Implementation Methodology

This section discusses the implementation of the PSD evaluation on the FPGA and the performed optimization to operate at the target clock frequency while choosing the precision to achieve a high sensitivity. In this section, D refers to the complex data path between the consecutive arithmetic blocks. F denotes complex signals that get stored in a First In First Out (FIFO) memory. Complex in this context implies the concatenation of the real and imaginary parts of the signal. Each block is enabled by a 1-bit signal en, it issues a signal $valid$ when it starts to stream its output into the following block. L refers to the Fast Fourier Transform (FFT) size and N_{avg} refers to the number of calculated spectral averages. A delay of m clock cycles is denoted by z^{-m}.

3.1. Main Building Blocks

A block diagram of the calculation is shown in Fig. 2. The DFT is practically realized using the FFT. A window function is applied to the FFT to reduce spectral leakage. The FFT is followed by magnitude evaluation and reordering that performs the bit reversed indexing of the FFT output to show the PSD in natural order of the frequency bins. This is followed by averaging of the calculated PSD for a user selected number of averages. The implementation is done in VHDL with generic parameters for each module for PSD calculation. This enables manual optimization and achieving an improved performance on the FPGA. Xilinx ISE 14.5 was used for synthesis and bit file generation for the FPGA.

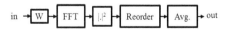

Figure 2. Block diagram for PSD evaluation.

3.2. Fast Fourier Transform

An FFT was designed based on the radix-2^2 architecture. The radix-2^2 algorithm introduced in [7] offers a simple butterfly structure similar to the radix-2 algorithm and a low number of multipliers similar to the radix-4. This technique was used in our design to conserve area and reduce complexity. Single-path Delay Feedback (SDF) architecture is used to reduce the control complexity and memory requirements. The implementation methodology in [8] was used for the FFT implementation, where we use arithmetic optimization and extended pipelining to increase clock frequency. Fig. 3 shows the block diagram of the FFT.

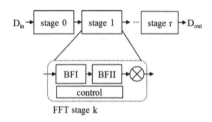

Figure 3. Block diagram of the FFT unit.

It consists of consecutive stages where each stage comprises two butterfly calculation units (BFI, BFII) and a complex multiplier to carry out the twiddle factor multiplications. Twiddle factors are the complex factors multiplied by the input samples in the DFT calculation. The number of stages r is equal to $\lceil \log_4 L \rceil$. The last stage does not contain a multiplier and contains only one butterfly (BFI) when the FFT length is an odd power of 2. When the length is an even power of 2, it contains both BFI and BFII.

Butterfly Unit. The difference between the two butterfly units is the BFII multiplication by $-j$ which is carried by multiplexers to swap the real and imaginary parts. The structure of BFII is shown in Fig. 4. The selection lines to the multiplexers from the control unit choose the samples that are multiplied by $-j$.

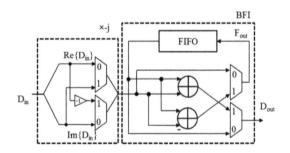

Figure 4. Butterfly unit BFII.

Twiddle Factor Multiplication. The twiddle factors were pre-calculated and stored in ROMs on the FPGA. A MATLAB script was written to write the ROM initialization file for a generic FFT length and precision. The method for the pre-calculation was mentioned in [8]. Each stage k has a ROM of size $N/2^{2k}$. The implemented complex multiplier for that purpose is shown in Fig. 5. The complex multiplier was fully

pipelined to achieve a minimum critical path delay. The real multipliers need three pipeline levels.

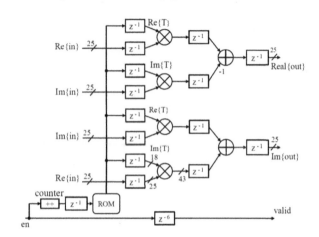

Figure 5. Twiddle factor multiplier implementation.

3.3. Reordering Unit

The reordering unit was designed according to the methodology shown in [9]. The design uses consecutive stages each with a memory feedback for reordering. It achieves a lower clock cycle delay than direct reordering schemes that use simple storing in a RAM and manipulating the read address.

3.4. Magnitude Evaluation Unit

This unit was realized by two multipliers and an adder, for performing addition of the squared real and imaginary parts of the calculated FFT according to Eq. (4).

3.5. Averaging Unit

An array accumulator was designed to perform the spectral averaging while streaming the input PSD frames continuously. The control structure is shown in Fig. 6. The first counter of size $\log_2 L$ counts the output PSD points. The second counter of size $\log_2 N_{avg,max}$ counts the number of accumulations. Resetting the FIFO is accomplished by adding 0 to the incoming frame to replace the current stored accumulation value.

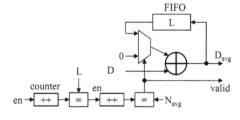

Figure 6. Implementation of the averaging unit.

The critical path delay introduced by the large adder was reduced using a conventional technique described in [10]. It is achieved by replicating the feedback path into two partial accumulators and pipelining them through the carry bit. It was used in our design where the registers in the partial accumulators were extended to FIFO buffers in the feedback, where each FIFO stores half of the bits of the accumulated PSD frame. In Fig. 7, an example of the structure for a 4-bit accumulator is given.

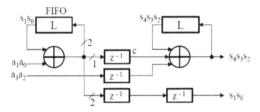

Figure 7. Pipelined averaging to reduce the adder critical path delay.

3.6. Arithmetic Operations

In the baseband subsystem, a dual channel 14-bit ADC [11] was used for data conversion. This finite accuracy introduces quantization noise to the system. In order to optimize the FPGA utilization of the PSD evaluation, truncation of the internal calculations was performed. The internal FFT bit size had to be selected to have minimal degradation regarding sensitivity and quantization noise while using the available FPGA resources optimally. The magnitude evaluation and averaging were done at full precision to conserve the sensitivity.

The software model of the implemented FFT was used to evaluate the necessary number of bits to accommodate the full dynamic range of the used ADC while using truncation of the internal calculations to optimize the FPGA utilization.

The slot noise test (used to evaluate the Xilinx FFT IP-core in [12]) was performed on the fixed point software model of the system to verify the effect of the arithmetic format used for our FFT. In the slot noise test, a time domain signal is generated that has non-zero values over all of its spectral components except for a small number of consecutive bins called the slot. This procedure is shown in Fig. 8. Ideally, performing the FFT on this input signal should yield a zero for the slot bins [12]. However, due to the effect of ADC quantization as well as the high peak to average ratio of such signals, noise appears in the slot band.

This test is used to determine the number of bits necessary so as to not further degrade the performance after the ADC quantization. The result for the test using different bit size configurations is shown in

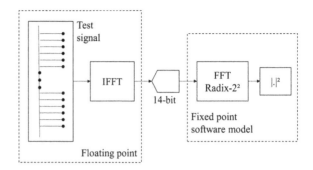

Figure 8. Slot noise test procedure – the bit size for the fixed-point FFT is increased until no further performance gain is noticeable in the calculated power spectrum.

Fig. 9. We notice that the performance is worse for the 18 bit internal bit size, which degrades the slot noise by approx. 25 dB. The degradation is reduced by increasing the FFT bit size. The performance of the 25 bit internal bit size is similar to that of a floating point FFT for a 14 bit ADC, and no significant improvement could be achieved by further increasing the internal FFT bit size for the same number of ADC bits. Therefore, a 25-bit accuracy was chosen for the FFT calculations.

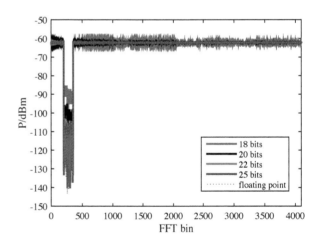

Figure 9. Slot noise test for various internal FFT bit size configurations, 14-bit ADC, power normalized to a 50Ω input resistance, slot size = 150 bins. A size of 25 bits for the FFT internal calculations achieves the least slot noise compared to a floating point implementation. Magnitude evaluation and averaging are implemented with full precision to avoid any performance degradation.

A test that uses a single tone input with an amplitude equal to the ADC full scale of 2Vpp is done to determine the effect on the quantization noise floor. The result is shown in Fig. 10. We notice no significant degradation of the noise floor due to the additional quantization by the FFT calculations. The input signal for the floating point and the fixed point models is quantized by 14-bits to model the quantization effect of the ADC.

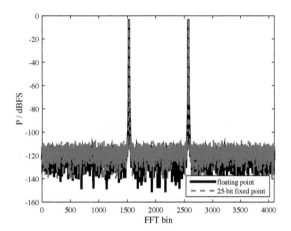

Figure 10. Software model test on a single tone, 14-bit ADC. The power is normalized to the ADC full scale, Blackman window is used. Two peaks are visible corresponding to the frequency of the real valued input single tone. The quantization noise floor is dominated by the ADC. No significant degradation due to the finite precision arithmetic is visible.

The arithmetic operations were optimized by exploiting the upper bounds for the expected intermediate calculations for the economic use of the arithmetic resources. The fixed point format [13] was used for the representation of the signal values. The notation $Q(1, i, f)$ refers to a fixed point format where the number is a signed number and i bits are assigned to the integer part and f bits to the fractional part.

Fig.[11-13] show the format used for the window function, butterfly additions and twiddle factor multiplications, respectively. The operator $tr(n)$ refers to the truncation of n Least Significant Bits (LSBs). A division by 2 to avoid overflow was realized by a shift-right after the butterfly addition. The multipliers on the target FPGA operate on 25×18 bit operands [14]. Therefore, a bit size of 25 bits was chosen for each of the real and imaginary parts of D to use an optimum number of multipliers achieving the desired sensitivity.

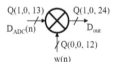

Figure 11. Number format for the window function multiplication.

Fig. 14 shows the format used for the squaring and accumulation operations. $sxt(n)$ refers to sign extension by n bits. No truncation is performed to preserve the sensitivity. Therefore, the implemented accumulator needs a sign extension by $\log_2(N_{avg,max} + 1)$ bits to avoid overflow.

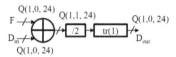

Figure 12. Number format for the butterfly additions.

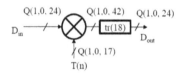

Figure 13. Number format for the twiddle factor multiplication.

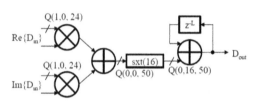

Figure 14. Number format for magnitude evaluation and accumulation.

3.7. Memory Optimization

To realize large depth FIFO buffers in the data path, the buffer implementation was optimized to achieve a low routing delay on the FPGA. As using a large number of slice registers results in high routing path delay, RAM resources were used instead. The idea was mentioned in [15] as a RAM based shift register.

For each buffer, a Dual Port RAM (DPRAM) was used with custom manipulation of the read and write address for the two ports to realize a FIFO functionality. A read before write scheme was used for the RAM implementation. Fig. 15 shows the control scheme for the addresses for the two RAM ports, where d is the desired FIFO depth.

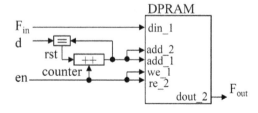

Figure 15. Realization of a FIFO memory using RAM

4. Sensing Node

4.1. Analog Front-end

As shown in Fig. 1, the front-end used in this work is based on an up/down-heterodyne architecture. It is capable of converting an input RF frequency range from

300 MHz to 3 GHz into the base-band. The dedicated front-end relies on external local oscillator sources and provides a base-band bandwidth of 100 MHz per I and Q channel. A detailed description of the analog front-end is given in [16]. For all the real world tests, a discone omni-directional antenna (frequency range 300 MHz to 3 GHz) was connected to the front-end. The front-end is followed by a dual channel Analog to Digital Converter (ADC) on the FMC150 evaluation board that provides the digital input of I and Q channels for the Virtex-6 FPGA.

4.2. Base-band Processing

The block diagram of the base-band processing for the implemented prototype is shown in Fig. 16. The Chipscope software communicates with the Integrated Logic Analyzer (ILA) [17] and Virtual Input Output (VIO) [18] Xilinx cores. A software interface was written to control Chipscope from MATLAB to update VIO with the user options for averaging and windowing, and to visualize the output in real time.

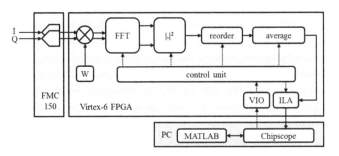

Figure 16. Block diagram for base-band processing for the sensing node.

The communication speed between the FPGA and the PC was the bottleneck for the update rate (approx. 1 s) to the PC due to the JTAG interface used by Chipscope. However, this only affects the data display update rate and not the calculation speed, as some calculated data has to be discarded to cope with the limited communication buffer size. In a real system, the communication between the sensing nodes can be implemented with a higher data throughput than JTAG to assist decision making speed.

4.3. Overview of the Hardware Results

The detection performance is shown in Table 1. The target clock frequency is 245.76 MHz to operate in streaming mode from the ADC. For the FFT size of 4096, the Place And Route (PAR) process estimated a maximum clock frequency of 262 MHz for the used Virtex-6 FPGA.

The FPGA resource utilization is shown in Table 2. The low usage of the DSP48E1 slices is a result of the

Table 1. Detection performance

Parameter	Value
f_s	245.76 MHz
Resolution	60 kHz
FFT size	4096
Calculation time /clock cycle	$10204 + 4096 \times Navg$
$f_{clk,max}$ (PAR.)	262 MHz

performed arithmetic optimization. The RAM resources were used to realize the ROM units used for storing the twiddle factors, and to realize large delays in the data path for optimum performance. The RAM resources used for buffering the output data to the PC are not shown. In Table 3, the resource utilization and the maximum frequency are shown for implementation on the lower cost Artix-7 FPGA. The achievable clock frequency is 220 MHz. The design uses a higher portion of the Artix-7 FPGA since it has lower resources. This shows that the design is suitable for implementation on a lower cost platform. However, the ADC sampling frequency would have to be reduced by 30 MHz which would impact the baseband detection bandwidth.

Table 2. Design FPGA resource utilization (map results)

Resource	Number used	Utilization(%) XC6VLX240T-1
DSP48E1 slices	26	3.3
RAM36K	25	6
RAM18K	15	1
Logic Slices	1496	4

Table 3. FPGA resource utilization and clock frequency for the low cost Artix-7 FPGA

Result	Value (XC7A100T-1)
DSP48E1 slices	26 (10%)
RAM36K	27(20%)
RAM16K	13(4%)
Logic slices	1520 (15%)
$f_{clk,max}$ (PAR.)	220 MHz

4.4. Comparison with Other Prototypes

Comparison with two other published platforms that use an FPGA based calculation of the PSD for spectrum sensing is shown in Table 4. Our design achieves superior performance regarding sensing bandwidth and calculation time. In [19], an extra overhead for using a soft processor core for control on the Spartan-6 FPGA and streaming from a low frequency ADC could have affected the detection time. Compared to [20], the use of custom arithmetic units and memory functions in this work helped to achieve a higher performance.

Table 4. Comparison with existing platforms

Platform	fclk (MHz)	bandwidth (MHz)	resolution (kHz)	calculation time(ms)
This work	245.76	245.76	60	$0.042 + 0.017N_{avg}$
[19]	12.8	12.8	25	$0.54(N_{avg}=10)$
[20]	125	62.5	122	N/A

5. Real Time Testing

5.1. Detection of DVB-T Signals

The detector was tested in the UHF digital TV band for a bandwidth of 245.76 MHz around a central frequency of 580 MHz. The TV signals in the received bandwidth can clearly be observed as shown in Fig. 17.

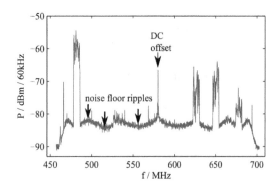

Figure 17. PSD output from the FPGA based PSD calculation. A ripple in the noise floor is observed. The calculation is performed using 100 averages.

This measurement is done for $N_{avg} = 100$. A ripple in the noise floor can be noticed due to the frequency response of the front-end. This ripple was calibrated by disconnecting the antenna, recording the PSD for 32767 averages and dividing the calculated PSDs by the corresponding noise power for each bin.

The result of that calibration is shown in Fig. 18. The three 8 MHz wideband signals at carrier frequencies 482 MHz, 626 MHz and 650 MHz are the DVB-T channels 22, 40 and 43 respectively which are received in the city of Ulm [21]. Image signals due to IQ mismatch can be also seen at 18 dB below the corresponding signal powers. Digital calibration to compensate the IQ mismatch is a remaining future task.

5.2. Detection of Signals in the Band from 1788 to 2033 MHz

To assess the detection speed, the prototype was tested in the frequency range 1788 to 2033 MHz which

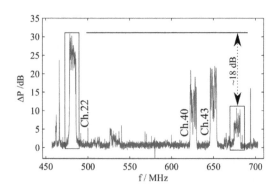

Figure 18. Calibrated PSD output to achieve a flat noise floor. The calculation is performed using 100 averages. Three TV channels can be observed at 482 MHz, 626 MHz and 650 MHz with their corresponding image signals, with 18 dB image suppression.

contains two known signals which apply frequency hopping; Global System for Mobile communication (GSM) downlink and Digital Enhanced Cordless Telecommunications (DECT) signals.

GSM downlink signals apply frequency hopping with time slots equal to 576.9 μs according to [22]. DECT phone signals in the band from 1880 to 1900 MHz have 5 ms frames [23]. Fig. 19 shows the spectrogram that is displayed real time from the FPGA calculation.

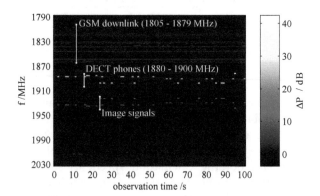

Figure 19. Spectrogram for the band from 1788 to 2033 MHz for a duration 100 seconds. The update rate is 1 PSD measurement /s. GSM downlink signals can be observed as well as frequency hopping of DECT phone signals. Images of DECT phone signals appear due to IQ mismatch

The detection time here is 1.76 ms for $N_{avg} = 100$. The frequency hopping of DECT signals can be distinguished more clearly than GSM downlink signals which exhibit faster changes. Image signals from high power DECT signals can also be seen approx. 18 dB below the corresponding signal powers.

5.3. Sensitivity

To assess the sensitivity, a sinusoidal signal with adjustable power is connected to the RF front-end's input. The central frequency was set to 580 MHz. The signal is generated at 600 MHz. It mimics a narrowband low power carrier in the TV band. By taking 32000 spectral averages, the lower bound for detection was -107 dBm. The result is shown in Fig. 20. We can clearly distinguish two peaks, at 580 MHz and 600 MHz respectively. The peak at 580 MHz is due to the DC offset of the ADC.

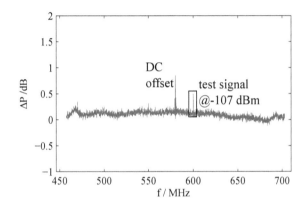

Figure 20. Sensitivity test on a sinusoidal signal with input power -107 dBm and $f = 600$ MHz. N_{avg} is set to 32000.

The IEEE 802.22 standard for Wireless Regional Area Networks (WRAN) requires a sensitivity of -107 dBm for a signal within a 200 kHz bandwidth [24]. As the PSD is calculated at a resolution bandwidth of 60 kHz, the system needs to be sensitive to a -112 dBm sinusoidal signal to meet the standard for microphone signals. The sensitivity is limited so far by the fairly high noise figure of the front-end [16], which is due to an unexpected reduced gain in the up-conversion stage as well as due to the losses introduced through the realization into a single module. A future re-design, including a low loss input BALUN as well as a re-design of the high-IF filter is expected to further improve the sensitivity of the system by lowering the front-end noise figure.

6. Conclusion and Future Work

In this paper, the design, implementation and real time testing of a sensing node that calculates the PSD are shown. A MATLAB based interface controls the FPGA design and displays the calculated PSD in real-time. The flexibility of the node is demonstrated for spectrum sensing in different frequency bands with different averaging options. The RF front-end down-converts signals in the range of 300 MHz to 3 GHz to baseband. The achieved baseband detection bandwidth is 245.76 MHz, with a frequency resolution of 60 kHz.

The internal bit size for the PSD calculation is selected to optimize FPGA usage while having a minimal effect of the finite precision arithmetic operations on the detection performance. The detection is tested on UHF TV signals, GSM downlink signals and DECT phone signals. A sensitivity test is performed and the node was able to detect signals at -107 dBm. Future work includes digital IQ mismatch compensation that is needed to cancel the image signals that appear during testing. Moreover, the noise figure of the front-end needs to be lowered in order to achieve a higher sensitivity. More integration is targeted by incorporating the local oscillators in the front-end chip, and implementation of wideband frequency sweeping over the full range of the front-end RF bandwidth. The next step is the decision implementation on FPGA and the deployment of several sensing nodes for evaluation of detection algorithms in collaborative sensing scenarios.

Acknowledgment

This project is partially funded by the German Research Foundation (DFG) under grant no. VA941/1-1.

References

[1] ELSOKARY, A., LOHMILLER, P., VALENTA, V. and SCHUMACHER, H. (2015) A Hardware Prototype of a Flexible Spectrum Sensing Node for Smart Sensing Networks. In *Cognitive Radio Oriented Wireless Networks* (Springer International Publishing), *Lecture Notes of the Institute for Computer Sciences, Social Informatics and Telecommunications Engineering* **156**, 391–404. doi:10.1007/978-3-319-24540-9_32.

[2] SHIN, K.G., KIM, H., MIN, A.W. and KUMAR, A. (2010) Cognitive Radios for Dynamic Spectrum Access: From Concept to Reality. *IEEE Wireless Communications Magazine, vol. 17* .

[3] VALENTA, V., MARŠÁLEK, R., BAUDOIN, G., VILLEGAS, M., SUAREZ, M. and ROBERT, F. (2010) Survey on Spectrum Utilization in Europe: Measurements, Analyses and Observations. In *Fifth International Conference on Cognitive Radio Oriented Wireless Networks and Communications (CROWNCOM)*.

[4] YÜCEK, T. and ARSLAN, H. (2009) A Survey of Spectrum Sensing Algorithms for Cognitive Radio Applications. *IEEE Communications Surveys & Tutorials, vol. 11* .

[5] MANOLAKIS, D.G., INGLE, V.K. and KOGON, S.M. (2000) *Statistical and Adaptive Signal Processing: Spectral Estimation, Signal Modeling, Adaptive Filtering and Array Processing* (McGraw Hill).

[6] HARRIS, F.J. (1978) On the Use of Windows for Harmonic Analysis with Discrete Fourier Transform. *Proceedings of the IEEE, vol. 66* .

[7] HE, S. and TORKELSON, M. (1996) A New Approach to Pipeline FFT Processor. In *IEEE Parallel Processing Symposium*.

[8] CORTÉS, A., VÉLEZ, I., ZALBIDE, I., IRIZAR, A. and SEVILLANO, J.F. (2008) An FFT Core for DVB-T/DVB-H Receivers. *VLSI Design* Doi:10.1155/2008/610420, Hindawi Publishing Corporation.

[9] GARRIDO, M., GRAJAL, J. and GUSTAFSSON, O. (2011) Optimum Circuits for Bit Reversal. *IEEE Transactions on Circuits and Systems II: Express Briefs* .

[10] CHAPPELL, M. and McEwan, A. (2004) A Low Power High Speed Accumulator for DDFS Applications. In *IEEE International Symposium on Circuits and Systems ISCAS*.

[11] 4DSP LLC., USA (2010) *FMC150 User Manual*.

[12] Xilinx, Inc. (2015) *Fast Fourier Transform v9.0 LogiCORE IP Product Guide*.

[13] PARHAMI, B. (2010) *Computer Arithmetic: Algorithms and Hardware Designs* (Oxford University Press).

[14] Xilinx, Inc. (2011) *Virtex-6 FPGA DSP48E1 Slice User Guide*.

[15] ALFKE, P. (2008) Creative Uses of Block RAM. *White Paper: Virtex and Spartan FPGA Families, Xilinx* .

[16] LOHMILLER, P., ELSOKARY, A., CHARTIER, S. and SCHU-MACHER, H. (2013) Towards a Broaband Front-end for Cooperative Spectrum Sensing Networks. In *European Microwave Conference (EuMC)*.

[17] Xilinx, Inc. (2011) *LogiCORE IP ChipScope Pro Integrated Logic Analyzer (ILA)(v1.04a)*.

[18] Xilinx, Inc. (2011) *LogiCORE IP ChipScope Pro Virtual Input/Output (VIO) (v1.04a)*.

[19] RIESS, S., BRENDEL, J. and FISCHER, G. (2013) Model-based Implementation for the Calculation of Power Spectral Density in an FPGA System. In *7th International Conference on Signal Processing and Communication Systems (ICSPCS)*.

[20] POVALAČ, K., MARŠÁLEK, R., BAUDOIN, G. and ŠRÁMEK, P. (2010) Real-time Implementation of Periodogram Based Spectrum Sensing Detector in TV Bands. In *20th International Conference Radioelektronika (RADIOELEKTRON-IKA)*.

[21] SÜDWESTRUNDFUNK (2009) Das Programmangebot in Baden-Württemberg.

[22] ETSI (1998) *Digital cellular telecommunications system (Phase 2+) Physical layer on the radio path: General description*. Tech. rep.

[23] ETSI (2013) *Digital Enhanced Cordless Telecommunications (DECT) - TR103089 V1.1.1*. Tech. rep.

[24] STEVENSON, C.R., CORDEIRO, C., SOFER, E. and CHOUINARD, G. (2005) Functional requirements for the 802.22 WRAN standard. *IEEE 802.22-05/0007r46* .

8

Hypernetworks based Radio Spectrum Profiling in Cognitive Radio Networks

Shah Nawaz Khan[1,*], Andreas Mitschele-Thiel[1]

[1]Integrated Communication Systems Group,
Technische Universität Ilmenau,
P.O. Box 100 565, Ilmenau 98693, Thüringen, Germany

Abstract

This paper presents a novel concept of active radio spectrum profiling for Cognitive Radio (CR) networks using evolutionary hypernetworks. Spectrum profiling enables cognitive radio nodes to abstract and predict usable spectrum opportunities in pre-defined Primary Users (PU) channels. The PU channels are actively monitored through spectrum sensing and the resulting binary time series are used for channel abstraction and prediction. An overlay spectrum sharing approach is assumed in this paper and the evolutionary hypernetworks are used for the realization of the radio spectrum profiling concept. The abstracted information not only facilitates the optimization of channel selection and mobility, but also improves the quality of service for the secondary user applications. This paper presents the main concepts, their application to CR ad hoc networks, and an analysis of its impact on the CR network performance.

Keywords: Channel prediction, Cognitive radio, Spectrum profiling

1. Introduction

Radio spectrum is a very valuable but scarce resource, especially when considering the overall picture of the existing wireless communication systems. However, this resource has not been utilized in the most efficient way which has resulted in spectrum scarcity and under-utilization problems. The main cause for these problems is considered to be the fixed radio spectrum allocation strategies employed by the spectrum allocation authorities across the world. Realization of these problems have resulted in the formulation of opportunistic and dynamic spectrum access concepts which are generally discussed in conjunction with the Cognitive Radio (CR) networks. CR networks are assumed to be able to identify and utilize the spectrum opportunities provided by the existing wireless networks, the so called Primary User (PU) networks. In the existing literature, the spectrum sensing is considered to be the *Eyes and Ears* of a CR node through which it can facilitate the two most important tasks of identify spectrum opportunities and avoiding interference with the PUs. These tasks are generally considered to be interrelated as quick and accurate spectrum sensing can facilitate both

function of a CR node. However, these two tasks have very different timing requirements which makes the use of spectrum sensing results impractical for both these tasks. Identifying spectrum holes requires the monitoring of the spectrum for a sufficiently longer period of time whereas interference avoidance with PUs should be instantaneous requiring immediate reaction to a sensing result. Spectrum sensing is also the enabler for the physical and link layer protocols which have stringent time constraints. In the traditional 802.11 family of protocols for example, the basic channel access tasks are in the scale of microseconds. If a similar functionality is assumed of CR MAC protocols, the spectrum sensing should be equally fast and accurate. We can summarize that for avoiding interference with PUs, the reliability and time-efficiency of spectrum sensing is very important. However, for identifying spectrum opportunities such primitive spectrum sensing results are not sufficient. There needs to be an abstraction process that can characterize spectrum holes from the primitive spectrum sensing results. Furthermore, the identified spectrum holes must be quantified to determine whether they can fulfill the SU applications' requirements. This serves as the basis for the proposed *Hypernetworks based Active Radio Spectrum Profiling* concept which aims to characterize the spectrum according to the application

*Corresponding author: shah-nawaz.khan@tu-ilmenau.de

requirements of the CR nodes. This concept is specially important for CR ad hoc networks which heavily rely on spectrum sensing and have no infrastructural support. The contributions of this paper in this outlined context can be summarized as follows:

- Introduction of a new *active radio spectrum profiling* concept for PU channels characterization,

- Application of *Evolutionary Hypernetworks* algorithm for the active radio spectrum profiling,

- Presentation of a new channel state prediction algorithm based on hypernetworks that can tolerate miss detection and false alarms of spectrum sensing algorithms and

- Analysis of CR ad hoc network performance with the new hypernetworks based active radio spectrum profiling concept.

The rest of the paper is organized as follows. Section 2 addresses the related work on spectrum characterization and channel prediction. An introduction to Hypernetworks is given in Section 3 before the details of the proposed evolutionary hypernetworks based spectrum profiling in Section 4. Simulation results are provided in Section 5 and the paper is concluded with a summary and future work in Section 6.

2. Related Work

To the best of our knowledge, the proposed hypernetworks based spectrum profiling concept is novel in the CR networks context. However, a number of research articles addressing channel prediction, channel recommendation and secondary access can be considered as related work since the hypernetworks based spectrum profiling aims to achieve similar objectives. Prediction techniques in CR networks have been applied for of PU activity and channel behavior prediction. The authors in [1] survey the main approaches applied in the literature for channel prediction in CR context. They overview the main approaches and classify them based on the prediction techniques used including Hidden Markov Models (HMM), Multilayer Perceptron Neural Networks, Bayesian Inference, Autoregressive Model, and Moving Average based prediction. As the results of channel prediction can be applied to the optimization of different CR functions, no comparative analysis of these techniques has been presented. The application of HMM to predict the basic state transitions involved in ON/OFF PU channel usage model can be found in many articles. The authors in [2] present a binary time series approach to spectrum prediction in CR networks. They apply HMM to predict the next state(s) of the channel based on the historic data. They essentially predict the next values of spectrum sensing and relate

them to spectrum holes. The authors in [3] also apply HMM based prediction technique for multi-step-ahead prediction. They aim to avoid interference with PUs based on the results of the prediction. They measure the level of interference caused by CR network and propose to keep it to a predefined level. Similar technique is used by authors in [4] to evaluate the radio resource availability in 802.11 networks scenario and apply multi-step-ahead prediction derived through an auto-regression (AR) Model. They apply their technique to 802.11 network data traffic by measuring the radio resource availability through Network Allocation Vector (NAV). HMM based approach has also been used by authors in [5] to predict exponentially distributed PU activity over radio spectrum. For most of the HMM based approaches, the activities of the channel are modeled under Markovian assumptions. The authors in [6] however, present temporal spectrum sharing scheme based on PU activity prediction that considers bursty PU traffic whose characteristics are not captured effectively by Markovian process. They propose to adapt the SU transmission power levels that can be adapted to any source traffic model of PUs. The benefits of PU activity prediction have been shown to optimize different functions of a CR node specifically those related to the spectrum management and dynamic spectrum access. The authors in [7] show the application of fast discovery of spectrum opportunity in multichannel context to CR performance optimization. They propose an adaptive sensing period optimization algorithm together with an optimal channel-sequencing algorithm. This allows a CR node to find spectrum opportunities from a number of available channels efficiently without loosing significant spectrum opportunities provided by the considered radio spectrum. They also show that the channel discovery delay can be reduced to less than half a second with an optimized channel sensing and sequencing approach. The same prediction algorithm has been applied for proactive channel access in [8] in order to vacate a channel before the PU arrives. They essentially apply the results from [7] to a different optimization objective. The information about channels derived through spectrum sensing has also been considered for CR optimization outside the context of channel prediction. The authors in [9] present a channel recommendation framework in which distributed CR nodes complement each other's channel access by recommending a successfully used channel. They derive the inspiration from customer reviews system associated with major online retail systems. The same idea has been optimized in [10] where the authors formulate the problem as an average reward based Markov decision process. They compare the performance of a dynamic spectrum access system using the adaptive recommendation system with a static channel recommendation system and show a performance benefit of upto 15%.

The existing literature on channel characterization and prediction generally assumes the spectrum sensing to be 100 percent accurate. This assumption is made in order to have a realistic representation of PUs communication in a binary time series. However, it is well known that even the most sophisticated spectrum sensing algorithms are prone to miss-detections and false alarms. This renders the algorithms that predict next state(s) of binary time series prone to lower performance when considered in a realistic CR network scenario. Another assumption that is explicitly made or implied in literature is that zero bits in the binary time series represent spectrum holes for secondary access. Based on the discussion in Section 1, this assumption does not hold true in most realistic scenarios. If the spectrum sensing results are collected in the scale of microseconds, a single zero bit loses its significance for overall spectrum hole representation. However, the same bit will have a very high importance for the channel selection and interference prevention with PUs. The proposed active spectrum profiling concept does not rely on such assumptions and instead, applies an abstraction process that is mostly independent of the accuracy and time scale of spectrum sensing results.

3. Hypernetworks

Hypernetworks is a relatively new research domain and a candidate architecture for cognitive learning and memory [11]. It is a graphical model that can abstract both low and high levels of interactions among elements of a dataset. Hypernetworks are an extension of the hypergraphs. A hypergraph is an undirected graph G, the edges of which can connect any number of non-null vertices. Formally, a hypergraph $G = \{X, E\}$, where $X = \{X_1, X_2, ...X_n\}$ is the set of elements of the dataset, $E = \{E_1, E_2, ...E_m\}$ is the set of edges and $E_i = \{x_{i_1}, x_{i_2}, ..., x_{i_k}\}$ represents the elements of the edge E_i. The edges E_i of a hypergraph are referred to as *Hyperedges*. Each hyperedge which is synonymous to a non-empty set, encapsulates some primitive relation in the dataset X. The number of elements k encapsulated in a hyperedge representing its cardinality, is referred to as a k-hyperedge. Figure 1-A shows an example hypergraph having five elements (X1-X5) and three hyperedges (E1-E3). In hypergraphs, each hyperedge encapsulate an association in the primitive dataset and is unique.

Hypernetworks are a generalization of the hypergraphs in which we assign a particular weight to the hyperedges. Graphically, this weight is represented by the width of the hyperedges in the hypernetworks. The more stronger a relation is in the dataset, the larger the width of the hyperedge. Formally, a hypernetwork is a triple $H = (X, E, W)$ where X represent the set of vertices or elements of the data set, E represents the

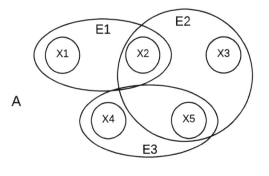

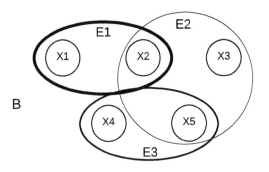

Figure 1. Hypergraph (A) and Hypernetwork (B) with five vertices and three edges

set of hyperedges, and W represents the set of weights associated with each hyperedge showing its strength in the dataset. The cardinality (number of enclosed elements) of a hyperedge is referred to as the order of that hyperedge. Figure 1-B shows a hypernetwork that is synonymous to the hypergraph in figure 1-A. The elements of a hyperedge are generally ordered. A hypernetwork can also be represented through a corresponding incidence matrix. The incidence matrix corresponding to the hypernetwork in Figure 1-B is given below.

$$\begin{array}{c c c c c c c} & w & X1 & X2 & X3 & X4 & X5 \\ E1 & \begin{pmatrix} 10 & 1 & 1 & & & \\ E2 & 2 & & 1 & 1 & & 1 \\ E3 & 5 & & & & 1 & 1 \end{pmatrix} \end{array}$$

The first column w in the incidence matrix represents the associated weight of the hyperedges in a hypernetwork. This weight can be in any appropriate form of a numerical representation. The exact value of the weight assigned to a particular hyperedge is determined by the weight function used in the hypernetwork development and learning process. In general, the weight of a hyperedge is increased proportional to the order of the hyperedge. Hyperedges with a smaller order tend to have a higher weight as they represent information that is very general/redundant in the actual dataset.

An important aspect of the hypernetworks is their complexity which can increase very rapidly depending upon the base of the dataset elements and the minimum and maximum order of the hyperedges. From a given dataset $D = \{x^{(n)}\}_{n=1}^N$ of N example patterns, the hypernetwork represents the probability of generating the dataset D as:

$$P(D|W) = \prod_{n=1}^{N} P(x^{(n)}|W) \qquad (1)$$

The W term in Equation 1 represents both the weight of the hyperedge and its structure. With a mixed order of the hyperedges, both low and high level features of the dataset can be encapsulated into the memory of the hypernetwork. The varying order of the hyperedges allows hypernetworks to keep a large number of random memory fragments $x_{i_1}^{(n)} x_{i_2}^{(n)} ... x_{i_k}^{(n)}$ to estimate the probability of any particular fragment. The probability of an individual fragment or pattern can be given as [11]:

$$P(x^{(n)}|W) = \frac{1}{Z(W)} \exp\left[\sum_{k=1}^{K} \frac{1}{C(k)} \times \sum_{i_1,i_2,...i_k} w_{i_1,i_2,...i_k}^{(k)} x_{i_1}^{(n)} x_{i_2}^{(n)} ... x_{i_k}^{(n)} \right] \qquad (2)$$

where $Z(W)$ is a normalizing term and $C(k)$ is the number of possible hyperedges of order k. The number of possible patterns or fragments grows exponentially and therefore an evolutionary approach of selection, replacement, and reinforcement towards finding an appropriate ensemble of hyperedges can be applied to collect information of complex datasets. Readers are encouraged to follow [11] for a deeper understanding of the hypernetworks based memory and cognition concept. Related work on hypernetworks have demonstrated their ability to predict future states from previous observations as well as its ability to mimic artificial intelligence [12–14]. Hypernetworks have also been compared to other approaches of learning and prediction and the results have shown the hypernetworks to be comparable in overall achievable results [15].

4. Hypernetworks based Spectrum Profiling

We coin the term *Radio Spectrum Profiling* as the process of abstracting usable channel information from primitive spectrum sensing that is performed by all the CR nodes in a network. This abstracted information is then used to optimize the performance of the CR nodes in terms of their channel access and handovers. Moreover, the spectrum profiling enables the CR network to develop a distributed network support architecture in which all the nodes maintain information about their local radio environment and

can share it with other peers [16]. Hypernetworks are well suited to the realization of the radio spectrum profiling concept introduced in this paper for the CR networks. We apply the hypernetworks based algorithm for the abstraction and prediction of spectrum holes from primitive spectrum sensing data which are given in the form of binary time series. Hypernetworks can achieve these objectives by keeping many fragments of the PU channel activity patterns in the hyperedges of different order which is determined based on the requirements of secondary user applications. Each hyperedge encapsulates a pattern of interest in the dataset for a specific secondary user application requirements. For example a hyperedge H_1 can encapsulate the pattern of interest for an application App_1. The encapsulated pattern consists of two parts i.e. the input part and the predicted output part. The total elements of the hyperedge $H_1 = input + output$. Encapsulating the inputs and outputs within the same hyperedge makes the prediction straightforward once the input pattern is matched. Over the course of the hypernetwork learning and evolution, the hyperedges are either reinforced or discarded based on their relevance in the original dataset. The underlying assumption for all prediction based CR research is that the events observed through spectrum sensing are repeated probabilistically and therefore intelligent decisions can be made based on their prediction. This assumption holds true for most of the activities of PUs operating in different frequency bands. However, these patterns have different time-scales over which they occur which can be captured by a varying order of the hyperedges. In general, the higher the correlation between training and testing dataset, the better the performance of the prediction algorithms in terms of accuracy. We shall now explain the main steps of the hypernetworks based spectrum profiling concept.

4.1. Hypernetwork Initialization

We apply the hypernetworks based learning approach to spectrum sensing results that can be collected over time by each CR node in the network. For simplicity, we shall explain the hypernetworks based spectrum profiling for a single CR node. The hypernetwork initialization/creation process is depicted in Fig. 2. The primitive input to the hypernetworks based spectrum profiling is the output of the spectrum sensing module in a CR node. We assume that all CR nodes are capable of detecting the PU activity with sufficient accuracy and timing constraints. From the basic binary time series of the spectrum sensing data, with an acceptable level of miss-detection and false-alarm errors, the hypernetwork first abstracts the patterns of interest for the SU applications. A pattern in essence is a variable sequence of bits (2 or more) in the provided

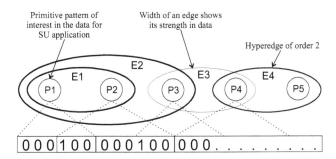

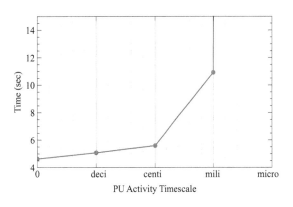

Figure 2. Hypernetwork with 4 hyperedges and 5 patterns

Figure 3. Throughput achieved over 2 GSM channels with varying time-scales of PU activity

binary time-series data. These patterns are selected based on the minimum requirements of the secondary user applications. The requirements of applications are diverse and can be represented in many forms such as in terms of reliability, throughput, security and etc. In this paper, these requirements are represented by the amount of channel access time the SU applications need to send their data over an opportunistically accessed PU channel. This approach is valid as many application require different throughput from the channel to function properly e.g. an email application and a high definition video stream have throughput requirements that are poles apart. This implies that the extracted patterns from the dataset represent variable lengths of spectrum holes and PU transmissions. Therefore, in our CR context, the patterns are essentially variable-length sequences of zeros implying the durations of no PU channel activity and ones implying busy channel states. The use of the variable length patterns enables the hypernetworks to be able to abstract and predict different durations of the PU activities on a channel.

The fundamental reason for deriving the patterns from the binary time series is to ensure that the hypernetworks are trained on the datasets that are usable for opportunistic spectrum access. Assuming that miss-detections and false-alarms are not sequentially redundant, each pattern can neglect some incorrect bits in the overall pattern by replacement. In Fig. 2 for example, pattern P1 can ignore the existence of the bit '1' in the sequence and treat the whole pattern as a sequence of zeros. Ignoring the existence of such sparse *erroneous bits* has to be based on a clear understanding of how the PU activity is represented in the binary time series. If the spectrum sensing is assumed to be fast enough to detect the smallest levels of PU channels access, then it is easier to differentiate such erroneous bits from the real PU activity patterns in the dataset. Another reason to ignore the significance of the individual bits in the binary time series is that these bits are not the actual representation of the spectrum holes on a PU channel. In order to avoid all possible interference instances with the PU network, the spectrum sensing has to work on a very minute time-scale in order to detect the smallest

levels of the PU channel access. With such a reduced time-scale of the spectrum sensing, the usefulness of detected idle instances of the PU channel also reduces. This aspect is highlighted in Fig. 3 which shows the time required to opportunistically transmit 1MB of data over two GSM channels having fixed PU duty cycles of 70 and 40 percent respectively. The x-axis shows the same duty cycle mapped on to different time scales. When the PUs are off (point 0 on x-axis), the time required to transmit the 1MB data is approximately 4.6 seconds, an indication of the maximum throughput achievable on a 200Khz GSM channel in the simulated network. When the PUs are active and operate at varying time-scales, the time required to send the same data increases considerably, an indication of reduced throughput. When the PU provides spectrum access opportunity in the order of a few milliseconds, the time required to send the data increases to infinity which is an indication of zero throughput as no secondary user connection can be established in such a short channel idle phase. From this result it is clear that a spectrum opportunity provided in the scale of microseconds is not suitable for any secondary application. Although the result from figure 3 it is a self-evident observation for such durations of spectrum holes, it signifies that the channel differentiation and prediction should not be based directly on the spectrum sensing results and justifies the utilization of the proposed patterns which aim to abstract application-specific spectrum opportunities from these sensing results.

An opposite argument to this proposal could be that the spectrum sensing duration can be increased to a point at which the binary time series becomes representative of the spectrum opportunities but this creates two problems. Firstly, the time scale at which the physical and link layer protocols operate (micro-seconds in existing networks) requires the spectrum sensing to be equally fast. Otherwise, the CR nodes cannot avoid interference with the PU networks. Secondly, the decision of accessing a spectrum hole must be taken at the very beginning of that opportunity and not after a long observation. In PU channels with heavy traffic, the spectrum opportunities for the CR nodes may require very quick access and mobility in order to avoid interference. The transformation of the binary time series into a sequence of patterns for the hypernetworks avoids both these problems without compromising on the interference constraints. The creation of the patterns also serve to smooth out the effects of miss-detection and false alarms which may be caused by the deficiencies of the spectrum sensing mechanism itself or because of the temporal variations of the RF spectrum. Another benefit of the extraction of the patterns from the binary time series is the reduction of the complexity of the hypernetworks. As stated before, the complexity of the hypernetworks can grow exponentially and working on a reduced set of patterns keeps this complexity under manageable bounds. This in theory, should also reduce the hardware and energy requirements as well. Furthermore, as different applications require different channel access guarantees, the patterns derived from the binary time series can be a representation of these requirements and can classify the PU channels based on these requirements.

The binary time series is transformed into a sequence of application-specific patterns which serve as the basic input to the hypernetworks. From this sequence of patterns, the hypernetwork randomly creates hyper-edges of the specified order. The hypernetwork in Fig. 2 for example, has four hyperedges formed from five basic patterns. The total number of possible hyper-edges in a hypernetwork depends upon the specified minimum and maximum order of the hyperedges and and this number grows exponentially. The maximum number of possible hyperedges are therefore equal to $\sum_{O=min}^{max}(Tp)^O$ where T_p represents the total number of the primitive patterns abstracted from the dataset and O represents the order of hyperedge. The patterns encapsulated inside a hyperedge are ordered based on their abstraction from the spectrum sensing data. In other words, each hyperedge encapsulates a sequence of observations on a predefined channel. The hyperedge creation process is undertaken using random sampling of the pattern sequences. The parameters that control the complexity of the hypernetworks are the *min* and *max* order of the hyperedges. If *min* = *max* then a fix order hypernetwork is created where each hyperedge encapsulates the same number of sequential patterns. If *min* ≠ *max* then a mixed order hypernetwork is created where small order hyperedges encapsulate small memory fragments and higher order hyperedges encapsulate larger, more specific channel activity information. The initial weight of a hyperedge is set to the same value i.e.

1, unless otherwise specified at the time of initialization. Explicit initial weights can be assigned to certain types of hyperedges in order to emphasize the importance of that particular relationship in the dataset. For example, a hyperedge encapsulating the patterns associated with PU connection and transmission phases can be assigned a higher weight in the hypernetwork. The process of the creation of a hypernetwork from a series of abstracted patterns is given in the pseudo-code in Algorithm 1.

From the given pattern series D, generate a hypernetwork H with vertices, edges and weights V, E, W using specified order $K_{min} - K_{max}$, and the number of hyperedges I per history window h;

$H = (V, E, W) = null$;
Initialize N as sizeOf(D);
Initialize I as the sampling rate;

for $i = 0; i < N; i++$ **do**
    /* select the history window from the dataset */
    $h \leftarrow D[i...sizeOf(h)]$;
    /* select the last element as current tag */
    $tag = lastElement(h)$;
    for $(j = 1; j<I; j++)$ **do**
        $E' \leftarrow null$;
        /* Select an order for E' based on the selected distribution */ ;
        $O = distribute(K_{min}...K_{max})$;
        for $k = 0; k<O; k++$ **do**
            $v' \leftarrow h[random(1, sizeof(h - 1))]$;
            $E' \leftarrow E' \bigcup v'$;
        end
        /* sort the elements in order */
        $E' \leftarrow sort(E')$;
        /* Assign the tag */
        $E' \leftarrow E' \bigcup tag$;
        /* Assign the initial weight to the newly created hyperedge */
        $W \leftarrow W'$;
        /* Update the E and W sets with new information */
        $E \leftarrow E \bigcup E'$;
        $W \leftarrow W \bigcup W'$;
    end
end
$H \leftarrow \{V, E, W\}$;

Algorithm 1: Hypernetwork creation process

4.2. Hypernetworks Learning Process

The hypernetwork learning is an iterative process through which it evolves and assigns different weights to the abstracted hyperedges. This process implies that the assigned weights are a representation of the relative frequency of the patterns in the dataset. The number of iterations is also a parameter of the learning algorithm and can be set at the beginning of the learning process. In the classical hypernetworks, the set of randomly sampled hyperedges remain alive throughout the lifetime of the learning process. An evolutionary approach is more suited to more complex hypernetworks where the addition of new hyperedges as well as the removal of the weak/old hyperedges is allowed. In our approach, on every iteration j, a new hyperedge E' of order $k \in \{min, max\}$ is created from the patterns in the dataset. Since the new hyperedge is created from the same patterns pool, the encapsulated elements can be matched to the previously sampled hyperedges. The weight of the matched hyperedge w_E is updated by a reward function for the next iteration $j + 1$:

$$w_E^{j+1} = w_E^j + \delta(E, E') \qquad (3)$$

where δ is a reward function. We utilize the same approach for the reward function as is used in [15] which bases the reward on the order of a hyperedge. The reward function bases its weight adjustment on the last element of the hyperedge which we refer to as the *tag* t_E of a hyperedge. The tag of the hyperedge is important as it is used for the prediction of the channel patterns when given an input from the spectrum sensing module. We consider the last pattern of the hyperedge as the tag of the hyperedge but in principle, the tag can be a combination of more that a single pattern. If E matches E' along with their respective tags, the reward is equal to the order of E which is added to the previous weight of the hyperedge. If the tags do not match, a penalty is imposed instead which is equal to the negative of the order of E. Formally,

$$\delta(E, E')$$
$$= \begin{cases} k, & \forall_i \in [1, k'], \exists_j \in [1, k] : e_i' = e_j \wedge t_E = t_E' \\ -k, & \forall_i \in [1, k'], \exists_j \in [1, k] : e_i = e_j \wedge t_E \neq t_E' \\ 0, & otherwise \end{cases}$$
$$(4)$$

where E is a k order hyperedge with tag t_E, and E' is the new hyperedge with tag t_E'. In the classical hypernetworks which do not utilize the evolutionary functions of replacement and weakening of the hyperedges, the number of randomly sampled hyperedges is usually kept very high in order to cover most of the search space from the dataset. The initial abstraction of binary time series into patterns of interest allows to keep this complexity under bounds. Furthermore, we employ the Data-driven Evolutionary Training approach [15] to optimize the learning process. When a newly generated hyperedge from the pattern pool is not matched with any of the existing sampled

hyperedges, one of the smallest weight hyperedge is replaced with the newly created hyperedge from the dataset. This allows for a continuous exploration of search space while keeping the hypernetwork information relevant to desired objectives. If the newly added information is relevant, its weight will increase in future iterations otherwise it will be discarded through the evolutionary process. To summarize, hyperedges encapsulate different levels of secondary channel access opportunities through different ordered hyperedges. During the evolutionary learning process, the relevant information in the hyperedges is reinforced that can serve to characterize channels and optimize CR node spectrum management functions.

4.3. Hypernetworks based Prediction

Once the hypernetwork is trained over the patterns pool, the desired information is reflected in the developed structure of the hypernetwork and the forecasting process is very straightforward. The most frequent patterns in the dataset are reflected in the weights of their respective hyperedges. The patterns that are least frequent in the dataset have very weak hyperedges i.e. with a small weight. The structure of the hypernetwork also represents the different parameters set for the initialization and training i.e. $min - max$ order of the hyperedges, evolution and iterations. When a new pattern extracted from spectrum sensing data is given as input to the trained hypernetwork it is first matched to the candidate hyperedges.

During the CR node operation, it actively monitors the current state of a channel and classifies it into the predefined patterns. These patterns are given as real-time input to the trained hypernetwork. The input pattern is always a subset of the patterns encapsulated inside the hyperedges of the hypernetwork. The hypernetwork structure can forecast the probability of next pattern in the dataset based on the strength of the matched hyperedge. For example, the real-time patterns may match five hyperedges in the hypernetwork. If there is a different tag associated with these matched hyperedges, the weights of these matched hyperedges is considered for the final prediction. The correct prediction of a future pattern is of higher significance to a CR application than the prediction of spectrum sensing results considered in many related literature. If the tag of the hyperedge is a representation of the absence of PU for a specific time frame, the channel access can be initialized by a CR transmitter. The drawback of the current hypernetwork structure however, is that it can only abstract one channel at a time, unless multiple channels are sensed simultaneously and their state represented with a single bit. This may be possible through a wide-band spectrum

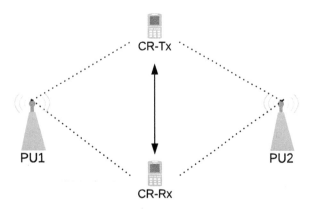

Figure 4. Simulated network scenario

sensor which can classify the channels' states from a single sensing iteration.

5. Simulation Analysis

In order to analyze the effectiveness of the hypernetworks based spectrum profiling in a CR networks, we carried out system level simulations using crSimulator platform [17]. This platform provides an detailed architecture of the CR nodes as well as PU nodes with adaptable activity patterns and duty cycles. As the CR ad hoc networks have to rely on spectrum sensing more than infrastructure-based networks, we simulated ad hoc connections under the influence of different primary users. Since a multi-hop CR ad hoc network can be considered as an extension of many single-hop links, we analyze the effect of the hypernetwork based spectrum profiling on a single multi-channel CR link. The evaluated network scenario is presented in Fig. 4 where two CR nodes attempt to use two PU channels (GSM specification) opportunistically. It should be noted however, that the selection of the GSM channels specification for the evaluation over any other spectrum band is of little significance for the proposed spectrum profiling. The important aspect is the representation of accurate channel state based on the PU activity profiles and the existence of secondary access opportunities. Representation of realistic PU activity profiles is an active area of research in itself as it is very difficult to have a generalized model for different locations and spectrum bands. From the numerous spectrum measurement campaigns, it has been observed that the PU activity can scale from completely free channels such as in the TV broadcast bands in remote locations, to 100% utilization of the spectrum such as in UMTS downlink or WiFi bands depending upon time and location [18]. In literature, two extremes can be found for the PU activity modeling which are using a fixed pattern with predefined duty cycles and a fully stochastic behavior with different random distributions. The actual PU activity distribution in any particular location can be

Table 1. Hypernetwork parameter settings

Parameter	Value
Order *min*	3
Order *max*	6
Patterns *max*	3
Reward function	δ
PU Activity	Variable Duty Cycle (30-75%)
Dataset size	100

Table 2. Successful forecasts

Setup	Avg Order	Success Rate
EHN(3,6)δ	4.4	74%
EHN(3,5)δ	4	71%
EHN(3,4)δ	3.4	71%
EHN(3,3)δ	3	68%

assumed to lie somewhere in the middle of these two extremes. In order to evaluate the performance of the hypernetworks based spectrum profiling, we employ the binary (ON/OFF) model for PU activity with time varying duty-cycles (30 to 70%) during the course of simulation time [19].

5.1. Successful forecasts

Table 1 shows the settings used for the formation and the training of the hypernetworks. The spectrum sensing results are abstracted into three distinct patterns based on the requirements of two different secondary user applications. The first two patterns abstract two distinct spectrum access opportunities in time-domain while the third pattern represents a busy channel state. With these three basic patterns, any binary time series data of spectrum sensing can be abstracted and fed into a hypernetwork structure representing different sequences of channel busy and idle states. This process essentially transforms the binary data into time series of the three primitive patterns. The association among these patterns is learned by the hypernetwork through the iterative evolution process described in the previous section. Table 2 gives the results of the forecasting process. The notation $EHN(3,6)\delta$ denotes an evolutionary hypernetwork with $min - max$ order of 3-6 of the hyperedges and a reward function of δ. The success rates shown for the different order hypernetworks are for the test cases where similarity between training patterns and and the test patterns was upto 60% only. If certain patterns of activity on PU channels repeat to a higher degree, the success rates of hypernetworks

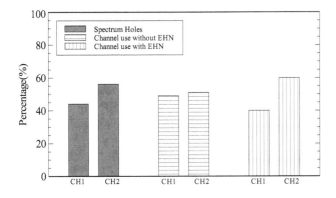

Figure 5. Percentage of spectrum opportunities on two PU channels and their opportunistic usage

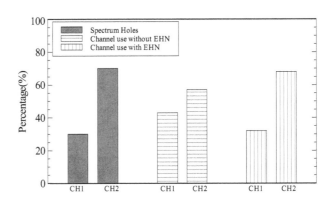

Figure 6. Secondary channel access with clear differentiation between channels

also increase proportionally. The success rates achieved through hypernetworks based channel state forecasting are significant and can potentially be optimized further by using more sophisticated approaches to the hypernetwork training and evolution process.

5.2. Channels characterization

The hypernetworks based spectrum profiling can characterize the available channels based on the application requirements. To test this, a time variant duty cycle between 60 to 70% was applied to the network scenario of Fig. 4 where each PU (PU1, PU2 in Fig. 4) followed its independent time-scale of transmission. In such a scenario, without spectrum profiling, the CR nodes will attempt to access both PU channels with equal probability and random access. With hypernetworks based spectrum profiling however, the CR nodes check for the probability of the next pattern in the channel and try to access that channel which has a predicted pattern of interest in the forecast. This effect is shown in Fig. 5 which shows the distribution of spectrum opportunities during the simulation on both PU channels and their utilization by CR nodes. The hypernetworks based profiling enables CR nodes to access the suitable channel (CH2) more frequently. This result shows that CR network performance can be optimized by differentiating among channels that generally look to provide similar spectrum access opportunities. The performance benefit increase even more when there is a clear difference between the channels as shown in Fig. 6. This performance improvement can also be seen in the number of channel handovers performed by CR network during the simulation and the achieved throughput as shown in Fig. 7. For the analysis of the impact on handovers, we assumed that the channel switching does not incur considerable time overhead. In real scenarios however,

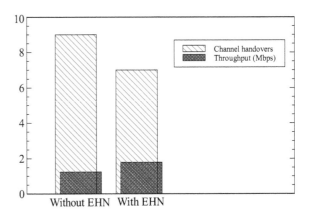

Figure 7. Achieved throughput and performed handovers

performing spectrum handovers will require some pre-agreement, about back-up channels through control message exchange, or through certain policies which may incur considerable time costs. Figure 8 shows the impact of the CR transmission on the PU transmission in terms of packet collisions per MB of data transmitted over the CR link. In our simulated network, a packet collision occurs whenever the CR nodes transmit a data packet simultaneously to the simulated PU nodes. This may happen when the PU nodes start transmission while the CR nodes were utilizing a spectrum hole on the licensed channel. It should be pointed out here, that the probability of creating zero interference with the PU nodes may be impossible for the CR network which utilizes the spectrum holes in an overlay manner. No matter how fast is the spectrum sensing of the CR nodes, it cannot guarantee that the PUs will not be switching to transmit state during the accessing of the spectrum holes. For the analysis of the impact of the spectrum profiling on the interference with PU nodes, we compared the hypernetworks based profiling with the channel recommendation scheme presented in [10] and a random channel access scheme.

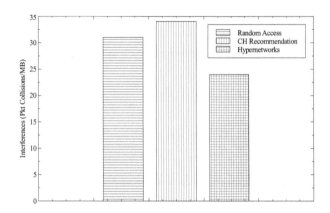

Figure 8. Collision instances with PU transmission

In the channel recommendation scheme, the CR nodes prioritizes the channel for access that was successfully used for the previous transmission. The random access scheme utilizes a uniform random distribution for the selection of the PU channel. In all three approaches, a reactive spectrum mobility approach was used for vacating a channel in response to the PU appearance. As can be seen in figure 8, the hypernetworks based spectrum profiling reduces the number of collision instances considerably when compared to the other two approaches. We acknowledge that the representation of the impact on the interference levels through packet collisions is not very representative and should be shown through SNR values. This shortcoming however does not invalidate the result shown in figure 8 as we expect a similar level of improvement when simulated on a signal level simulator.

6. Conclusion and Future Work

In this paper we presented a novel radio spectrum profiling framework that is based on the evolutionary hypernetworks. The hypernetworks can effectively capture and abstract the patterns of interest from the primitive spectrum sensing data and enable the characterization of the the available PU channels based on secondary users' application requirements which are represented through different ordered hyperedges. It was shown that spectrum holes can be identified from primitive binary time series of spectrum sensing results and utilized for differentiating among the available channels for spectrum management. In contrast to other channel prediction techniques e.g. those based on Hidden Markov Models, the hypernetworks do not require the spectrum sensing data to be 100 percent accurate and can reliably forecast the future channel states. Hypernetworks are suited to identifying spectrum opportunities for different types of applications. The implicit data smoothing through formation of patterns in the primitive sensing

data also serves to mitigate the effect of minor channel fluctuations in RF environment. Currently, a hypernetwork learns from a single dataset which implies that only one channel/band can be abstracted and multiple instances are required for multiple channels. A future extension this proposal could be to analyze a cross-channel pattern creation process for a single hypernetwork especially for adjacent frequency channels. This paper provided the analysis of hypernetworks for a single link CR network where the environment was similar for both the transmitter and the receiver nodes. However, in a distributed ad hoc network, disagreements about channel states among network peers will happen because one node may be affected by PU more than the other. This problem can be addressed through a consensus approach and is the subject of further investigations in future.

Acknowledgement.   This work is being carried out within the scope of the International Graduate School on Mobile Communications (Mobicom) at Ilmenau University of Technology, supported by the German Research Foundation (GRK1487) and the Carl Zeiss Foundation, Germany.The authors would like to further acknowledge Dr. Elena Bautu at Ovidius University, Constanta Romania, for her guidance, help and support.

References

[1] X. Xing, T. Jing, W. Cheng, Y. Huo, and X. Cheng, "Spectrum prediction in cognitive radio networks," *Wireless Communications*, IEEE, vol. 20, no. 2, pp. 90–96, 2013.

[2] S. Yarkan and H. Arslan, "Binary time series approach to spectrum prediction for cognitive radio," in *Vehicular Technology Conference*, IEEE 66th, 2007, pp. 1563–1567.

[3] R. Min, D. Qu, Y. Cao, and G. Zhong, "Interference avoidance based on multi-step-ahead prediction for cognitive radio," in *Communication Systems, 11th IEEE Singapore International Conference on*, 2008, pp. 227–231.

[4] S. Kaneko, S. Nomoto, T. Ueda, S. Nomura, and K. Takeuchi, "Predicting radio resource availability in cognitive radio - an experimental examination," in *Cognitive Radio Oriented Wireless Networks and Communications, 3rd International Conference on*, 2008, pp. 1–6.

[5] C.-H. Liu, W. Gabran, and D. Cabric, "Prediction of exponentially distributed primary user traffic for dynamic spectrum access," in *Global Communications Conference (GLOBECOM)*, IEEE, 2012, pp. 1441–1446.

[6] K. W. Sung, S.-L. Kim, and J. Zander, "Temporal spectrum sharing based on primary user activity prediction," *Wireless Communications, IEEE Transactions on*, vol. 9, no. 12, pp. 3848–3855, 2010.

[7] H. Kim and K. Shin, "Efficient discovery of spectrum opportunities with mac-layer sensing in cognitive radio networks," *Mobile Computing, IEEE Transactions on*, vol. 7, no. 5, pp. 533–545, 2008.

[8] L. Yang, L. Cao, and H. Zheng, "Proactive channel access in dynamic spectrum networks," *Physical Communication*, vol. 1, no. 2, pp. 103 – 111, 2008.

[9] X. Chen, J. Huang, and H. Li, "Adaptive channel recommendation for dynamic spectrum access," in *IEEE Symposium on New Frontiers in Dynamic Spectrum Access Networks (DySPAN)*, May 2011.

[10] H. Li, "Customer reviews in spectrum: Recommendation system in cognitive radio networks," in *New Frontiers in Dynamic Spectrum, IEEE Symposium on*, april 2010, pp. 1–9.

[11] B.-T. Zhang, "Hypernetworks: A molecular evolutionary architecture for cognitive learning and memory," *Computational Intelligence Magazine, IEEE*, vol. 3, no. 3, pp. 49–63, 2008.

[12] J.-K. Kim and B.-T. Zhang, "Evolving hypernetworks for pattern classification," in *Evolutionary Computation, IEEE Congress on*, 2007, pp. 1856–1862.

[13] H.-W. Kim, B.-H. Kim, and B.-T. Zhang, "Evolutionary hypernetworks for learning to generate music from examples," in *Fuzzy Systems, IEEE International Conference on*, 2009, pp. 47–52.

[14] S. Kim, S.-J. Kim, and B.-T. Zhang, "Evolving hypernetwork classifiers for microrna expression profile analysis," in *Evolutionary Computation, IEEE Congress on*, 2007, pp. 313–319.

[15] E. Bautu, S. Kim, A. Bautu, H. Luchian, and B.-T. Zhang, "Evolving hypernetwork models of binary time series for forecasting price movements on stock markets," in *Evolutionary Computation, IEEE Congress on*, 2009, pp. 166–173.

[16] S. N. Khan, M. A. Kalil, and A. Mitschele-Thiel, "Distributed resource map: A database-driven network support architecture for cognitive radio ad hoc networks," in *Ultra Modern Telecommunications and Control Systems and Workshops (ICUMT), 4th International Congress on*, 2012, pp. 188–194.

[17] S. Khan, M. A. Kalil, and A. Mitschele-Thiel, "crsimulator: A discrete simulation model for cognitive radio ad hoc networks in omnet++," in *Wireless and Mobile Networking Conference (WMNC), 6th Joint IFIP*, 2013, pp. 1–7.

[18] L. Stabellini, "Quantifying and modeling spectrum opportunities in a real wireless environment," in *Wireless Communications and Networking Conference (WCNC), IEEE*, 2010, pp. 1–6.

[19] M. Lopez-Benitez and F. Casadevall, "Empirical time-dimension model of spectrum use based on a discrete-time markov chain with deterministic and stochastic duty cycle models," *Vehicular Technology, IEEE Transactions on*, vol. 60, no. 6, pp. 2519–2533, 2011.

9

Power Minimization through Packet Retention in Cognitive Radio Sensor Networks under Interference and Delay Constraints: An Optimal Stopping Approach

Amr Y. Elnakeeb[1,*], Hany M. Elsayed [1], Mohamed M. Khairy [1]

[1]Department of Electronics and Electrical Communications, Faculty of Engineering, Cairo University, Egypt

Abstract

The aim of this article is twofold: First, we study the problem of packets retention in a queue with the aim of minimizing transmission power in delay-tolerant applications. The problem is classified as an optimal stopping problem. The optimal stopping rule has been derived as well. Optimal number of released packets is determined in each round through an Integer Linear Programming (ILP) optimization problem. This transmission paradigm is tested via simulations in an interference-free environment leading to a significant reduction in transmission power (at least 55%). Second, we address the problem of applying the scheme of packets retention through the Optimal Stopping Policy (OSP) to underlay Cognitive Radio Sensor Networks (CRSNs) where strict interference threshold does exist. Simulations proved that our scheme outperforms traditional transmission method as far as dropped packet rate and Average Power per Transmitted Packet (APTP) are concerned.

Keywords: cognitive radio, sensor network, optimal stopping rule

1. Introduction

Due to the wide proliferation of mobile communication, there is an inevitable rapid growth in mobile traffic leading to the problem of spectrum scarcity. However, many spectrum studies showed that huge part of the spectrum is underutilized. This, consequently, led to the concept of Cognitive Radio (CR) [1] which received a great attention to alleviate the spectrum scarcity problem. It enables unlicensed users to communicate over the licensed bands assigned for the licensed users through one of two modes. First: Spectrum Sharing (SS), or underlay, where CR Secondary Users (SU) can operate on same bands licensed for PU provided that sufficient interference thresholds to PU are strictly maintained. Second: Opportunistic Spectrum Access (OSA), or overlay, where SU can dynamically exploit spectrum holes when PU are inactive [2]. Wireless

Sensor Networks (WSN) have gained a great attention as a research area [3]. Due to the hardness of rechargeability of these networks, they have limited energy budget and hence a limited lifetime. Therefore, a considerable amount of research work has been exerted to mitigate the problem of energy limitation in WSN. Accordingly, energy minimization and lifetime maximization of WSN have been investigated in many research papers [4–7]. CRSN is a research trend that enables WSN to work in cognitive way. The essence of CRSN, its basic design principles, different architectures, applications, advantages and shortcomings have been well introduced in [8]. In this article, we are concerned about energy minimization through formulation of an optimal stopping problem and finding out its stopping rule. Optimal stopping is concerned with the problem of taking a specific action at specific time based on sequentially observed previous states so as for maximizing the payoff, or minimizing the cost, or both. With the optimal stopping problem, there always exists an optimal stopping rule, where the decision is taken based on it. This type of problems usually arises in areas of statistics, where the action is taken with the aim of testing an hypothesis or estimating a parameter. Considering seminal and recent work, optimal stopping theory has been applied to opportunistic scheduling [9] and spectrum sensing [10],[11], but not to power minimization; which is the problem we will consider in this context. In[9], the authors studied optimal transmission scheduling policies in cognitive radio networks. They proposed a cooperative scheme that improves the primary network performance and allows secondary nodes to access the licensed spectrum in order to cooperate. In [10], the authors studied joint channel sensing and probing scheme and they proved that this scheme can achieve significant throughput gains over the conventional mechanism that uses sensing alone. However, in [11], authors studied the problem of optimizing the channel sensing parameters in the presence of sensing errors. They proposed suboptimal solutions that significantly reduce the complexity and maintain a near-optimal throughput. In this article we apply the optimal stopping policy to the problem of power minimization in underlay cognitive radio sensor networks under interference and delay constraints. The rest of this article is organized as follows. Power minimization through packets retention via the optimal stopping approach is studied in Section 2, where the problem is formulated and the stopping policy is derived as well. In Section 3, the power minimization problem derived in Section 2 is extended to CRSN where interference threshold to PU does exist. Evaluating our performance is conducted through a simulation study which proves that our scheme through packets retention via OSP performs better than traditional transmission method as far as APTP and successful packet reception are concerned. Finally, Section 4 concludes the article.

2. Power Optimization through Optimal Stopping Policy

2.1. Problem Formulation and Stopping Rule Derivation

In this article, we focus on the problem of minimizing transmission power of nodes of any network through packet retention in a queue. Each node observes its power status round by round. Based on the observation sequence, it decides whether it sends its packet(s) instantaneously or further keeps it/them in the queue. To minimize the transmission power, each node makes the decision based on the result of comparing the instantaneous cost and the expected cost of future observations. The instantaneous cost is represented by the instantaneous power consumed if the packet

is transmitted instantly. It depends directly on the instantaneous channel quality at this round for the observed nodes. On the other hand, the expected cost of future observations is the expected power the node will consume if it keeps the packet for more rounds taking into consideration how many packets are already existing in the queue. Consequently, this issue can be formulated as a sequential decision problem and can be investigated by applying the optimal stopping theory.

We are following the communication model presented in [4], the total power consumption consists of two components: power consumption of the amplifiers P_{PA} which depends on transmission power P_t with the relation

$$P_{PA} = (1 + \alpha)P_t. \tag{1}$$

where $\alpha = \dfrac{\xi}{\eta} - 1$ with η the drain efficiency of the power amplifier and ξ the peak-to-average power ratio(PAR), which depends on the modulation scheme and the associated constellation size. Transmission power P_t is given by the link-budget relationship, when the channel experiences a square-law path loss

$$P_t = \overline{E_b} \times \frac{R_b(4\pi d)^2}{G_t G_r \lambda^2} M_l N_f. \tag{2}$$

where $\overline{E_b}$ is the required energy per bit for a given BER requirement, R_b is the bit rate of the RF system, d is the transmission distance. G_t and G_r are the antenna gain of the transmitter and the receiver respectively, λ is the carrier wavelength, M_l is the link margin compensating the hardware process variations and other additive background noise or interference, N_f is the receiver noise figure defined as $N_f = \dfrac{N_r}{N_0}$ with N_0 the single-sided thermal noise power spectral density (PSD) at room temperature and N_r is the PSD of the total effective noise at the receiver input.

The other term in the total power consumption is the circuit power P_c. Finally, this gives the total energy consumption per bit as

$$E_{bt} = \frac{P_{PA} + P_c}{R_b}. \tag{3}$$

The instantaneous required BER per-packet, assuming BPSK modulation scheme is used, is also given by

$$\overline{P_b} = Q(\sqrt{2\gamma_b}) = e^{-\gamma_b} = e^{-\frac{\overline{E_b}|H|^2}{N_0}} \tag{4}$$

where $|H|^2$ is the instantaneous squared magnitude of the channel. Substituting from (4) into (2), and rearranging, we get the transmission power per node as follows

$$P_t = -ln(2\overline{P_b}) \times \frac{N_0}{|H|^2} \times \frac{R_b(4\pi d)^2}{G_t G_r \lambda^2} M_l N_f \qquad (5)$$

Hence, and without loss of generality, we will consider only transmission power in our analysis as circuit power is, more or less, a constant that depends on the circuitry.

From now on, Q is defined as the queue size (Maximum number of packets could be kept) for each node in the network, and k is defined as the number of packets in the queue at round i. We intend to solve the stopping problem discussed above to minimize the cost represented by power by deriving an optimal rule that decides when to stop waiting for next rounds and transmit the packet(s) in the current round. Denote by $X_i^{(k)}$ the minimum cost the node can achieve at round i when k packets are in the queue.

$$X_i^{(k)} = min\{P_{t_i}^k, E\{min(P_{t_{i+1}}^{k+1}, P_{t_{i+2}}^{k+2}, ..., P_{t_{i+Q-k}}^{Q})\}\} \qquad (6)$$

where $P_{t_i}^k$ represents the instantaneous cost in round i (after the ith observation) when k packets are already existing in the queue. Also, $E\{min(P_{t_{i+1}}^{k+1}, P_{t_{i+2}}^{k+2}, ..., P_{t_{i+Q-k}}^{Q})\}$ represents the expected cost resulted by proceeding to keep the packet for next rounds till the queue is full. Inside the expectation operator, the minimum power scenario for keeping packets has to be chosen. To calculate $E\{min(P_{t_{i+1}}^{k+1}, P_{t_{i+2}}^{k+2}, ..., P_{t_{i+Q-k}}^{Q})\}$, we make the following mathematical analysis:

$$E\{min(P_{t_{i+1}}^{k+1}, P_{t_{i+2}}^{k+2}, ..., P_{t_{i+Q-k}}^{Q})\} =$$

$$E\{\frac{1}{max(\frac{1}{P_{t_{i+1}}^{k+1}}, \frac{1}{P_{t_{i+2}}^{k+2}}, ..., \frac{1}{P_{t_{i+Q-k}}^{Q}})}\} \qquad (7)$$

Furthermore, since the function inside the expectation operator of (7) is a convex one ($f(x) = \frac{1}{x}$ is a convex function) [12], Jensen's inequality can be applied:

$$\frac{E\{\frac{1}{max(\frac{1}{P_{t_{i+1}}^{k+1}}, \frac{1}{P_{t_{i+2}}^{k+2}}, ..., \frac{1}{P_{t_{i+Q-k}}^{Q}})}\}}{\frac{1}{E\{max(\frac{1}{P_{t_{i+1}}^{k+1}}, \frac{1}{P_{t_{i+2}}^{k+2}}, ..., \frac{1}{P_{t_{i+Q-k}}^{Q}})\}}} \geq \qquad (8)$$

We will consider the lower bound of (8). Consequently, the aim now is to get

$E\{max(\frac{1}{P_{t_{i+1}}^{k+1}}, \frac{1}{P_{t_{i+2}}^{k+2}}, ..., \frac{1}{P_{t_{i+Q-k}}^{Q}})\}$. For simplicity, we denote it by V_i^k.

According to (5), and extending for k to-be-transmitted packets, $P_{t_i}^k = \frac{C \times k}{|H_i|^2}$, where C is a constant equals to $-ln(2\overline{P_b}) \times N_0 \times \frac{R_b(4\pi d)^2}{G_t G_r \lambda^2} M_l N_f$. Similarly, $P_{t_{i+1}}^{k+1} = \frac{C \times (k+1)}{|H_{i+1}|^2}$, $P_{t_{i+2}}^{k+2} = \frac{C \times (k+2)}{|H_{i+2}|^2}$, and so on for all i and any k.

Then,

$$V_i^k = E\{max(\frac{1}{P_{t_{i+1}}^{k+1}}, \frac{1}{P_{t_{i+2}}^{k+2}}, ..., \frac{1}{P_{t_{i+Q-k}}^{Q}})\}$$
$$= \frac{1}{C} \times E\{max(\frac{|H_{i+1}|^2}{k+1}, \frac{|H_{i+2}|^2}{k+2}, ..., \frac{|H_{i+Q-k}|^2}{Q})\} \qquad (9)$$

Since all transmission channels $|H_i|^2$, for all i, are assumed to be Rayleigh-fading channels, any $|H|^2$ is exponentially distributed.

Rewritting (9):

$$V_i^k = E\{max(\frac{1}{P_{t_{i+1}}^{k+1}}, \frac{1}{P_{t_{i+2}}^{k+2}}, ..., \frac{1}{P_{t_{i+Q-k}}^{Q}})\}$$
$$= \frac{1}{C} \times E\{max(X_{i+1}^{k+1}, X_{i+2}^{k+2}, ..., X_{i+Q-k}^{Q})\} \qquad (10)$$

Where X's are set of exponentially random variables. Let $F_X(x)$ be the Cumulative Density Function (CDF) of the variables X_i^k.

$$F_X(x) = 1 - e^{-\lambda x} \qquad (11)$$

Let $F_q(v_i^k)$ be the Cumulative Density Function (CDF) of V_i^k. For Independent and Identically Distributed (iid) X's, $F_q(v_i^k)$ is simply given by:

$$F_q(v_i^k) = P[(x_{i+1}^{k+1} < v) \cap (x_{i+2}^{k+2} < v)..... \cap (x_{i+Q-k}^{Q} < v)]$$
$$= \prod_{n=k(i)+1}^{Q} (1 - e^{-\lambda_n x}) \qquad (12)$$

Where $\lambda_n = n \times \lambda$ with λ the rate of the exponential distribution (assumed to be 1) and $k(i)$ is number of packets kept in the queue at round i.

Then,

$$V_i^k = \int_0^\infty [1 - \prod_{n=k(i)+1}^{Q} (1 - e^{-\lambda_n x})]dx = \frac{Q+1-k(i)}{Q+1} \qquad (13)$$

Going backward from equations (8) to (6) with the known value of V_i^k, (6) can be rewritten as

$$X_i^{(k)} = min\{P_{t_i}^k, \frac{1}{C} \times \frac{Q+1-k(i)}{Q+1}\} \qquad (14)$$

Clearly from (14), the optimal stopping rule results in a threshold-comparison problem that compares the instantaneous transmission power with the minimum expected transmission power if the packet is kept in the queue. Also, it is clear that the stopping rule takes into consideration how many packets are already existing in the queue, denoted by k, besides the packet that has to be transmitted at this round. For instance, Tables 1 shows the values of the thresholds for queue size 3.

Table 1. THRESHOLDS FOR Q=3

Q=3	Threshold × C
$k(i) = 0$	$\frac{4}{4} = 1$
$k(i) = 1$	$\frac{4}{3} = 1.333$
$k(i) = 2$	$\frac{4}{2} = 2$
$k(i) = 3$	$\frac{4}{1} = 4$

Accordingly, for a queue of size Q, thresholds according to kept packets $k = 1, 2, ..., Q$ are given by

$$\frac{1}{C} \times \{\frac{Q+1}{Q+1}, \frac{Q+1}{Q}, \frac{Q+1}{Q-1}, \frac{Q+1}{Q-2}, \frac{Q+1}{Q-3}, ..., Q+1\}$$

2.2. Queue Releasing

In this subsection we intend to optimize the releasing paradigm of the queue. That is, how many packets should be released in any round so as to minimize transmission power. If the number of packets already existing in the queue is k and one packet comes at this round, the node has the option of releasing all of the $k + 1$ packets, or releasing k packets and keeping one, or releasing $k - 1$ packets and keeping two, and so on till reaching the scenario of releasing no packets and keeping all of the $k + 1$ packets. Hence the available scenarios for transmission at round i can be mathematically written as follows:

$(k + 1) \times P_{t_i}$

$k \times P_{t_i} + E\{\min(P_{t_{i,1}}, P_{t_{i,2}}, ..., P_{t_{i,Q}})\}$

$(k - 1) \times P_{t_i} + E\{\min(P_{t_{i,2}}, P_{t_{i,3}}, ..., P_{t_{i,Q}})\}$

.....

.....

.....

$0 \times P_{t_i} + E\{P_{t_{i,Q}}\}$

Where the second portion in any term of the above represents the expected transmission power if the packet(s) is/are kept till the queue is full. Actually, the second portion can be easily obtained from second portion of (14) for any value of Q and $k(i)$. Accordingly, we formulate an ILP optimization problem to choose the minimum transmission power scenario of all

scenarios discussed above.

$$\text{Minimize}_{x} \quad \sum_{j=0}^{k+1} x_j[(k + 1 - j)P_{t_i} + E\{\min(P_{t_{i,j}}, P_{t_{i,j+1}}, ..., P_{t_{i,Q}})\}]$$

$$\text{subject to} \quad \sum_{j=0}^{k+1} x_j = 1,$$

$$x_j = \{0, 1\}, \text{ for all } j.$$

Where x represents on-off states that enables only one scenario from the available ones. ILP is NP-complete problem. Hence, there is no known polynomial algorithm which can solve the problem optimally. Optimal solution is still eluding researchers and a huge research effort has been exerted to find optimal solution for such problems either by heuristic algorithms [13, 14] or by relaxation of the last constraint ($x_j = \{0, 1\}$, for all j) [15]. We will follow [15], where the authors proposed a Linear Programming with Sequential Fixing (LPSF) algorithm that relaxes the last constraint. In this case, the formulation becomes a Linear Programming (LP) problem that is solvable in polynomial time. The algorithm is as follows:

i) Relaxing $x_j = \{0, 1\}$, for all j to take any continuous value between 0 and 1, and the problem is solved as a LP one. The solution to this LP problem is an upper bound on the optimal solution to our problem.

ii) Among all x_j, for all j, the largest one is picked up and denoted, for ease of identification, by x_k. x_k is set to 1. As a result, all x_h for $h \neq k$ is set to 0.

iii) A feasibility check is conducted on the resulting LP problem. An empty feasible region means that the first fixing in this iteration isn't correct. So, x_k is reset to 0 in a new LP and other x_h for $h \neq k$ become variables again.

iv) At this point, either LP problem constructed with $x_k = 1$ or with $x_k = 0$ has a feasible solution.

v) A new iteration starts following the same process above. The process is repeated until all x_j are set to either 0 or 1. We evaluate the performance of our proposed optimal stopping scheme for power minimization by conducting extensive simulation study. Simulations are conducted for one node, and averaged over 100000 times. We assume transmission and interfering channels are constant for one packet transmission. We assume Channel State Information (CSI) of channels and distances from the node to the destination Base Station (BS) are well known at the BS where the decision is taken. We consider network parameters given in Table 2, in accordance with [4].

Fig. 1 shows the amount of saved power through the policy of packet retention. The amount of saving starts with 55% for $Q = 1$ and increases monotonically for larger queue sizes. It is clear that power profile

Table 2. SIMULATION PARAMETERS

Parameter	Value
$G_t G_r$	10 dB
η	0.35
f_c	15 MHz
$\overline{p_b}$	10^{-3}
M_l	10 dB
N_f	10 dB

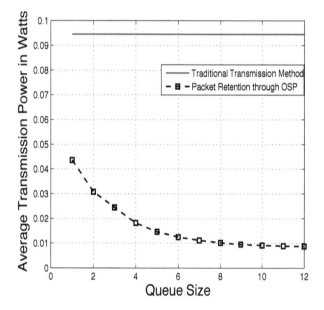

Figure 1. Power Saving through OSP.

is constant for traditional transmission method (No queue), however through packet retention scheme power decreases as queue size increases. That's because as queue size increases, there are more chances for the nodes to keep the packets in the queue expecting for better channel conditions in next rounds.

3. Applying OSP to CRSN under Interference and Delay Constraints

3.1. Problem Formulation and Simulations

In the previous section, we discussed the problem of power minimization in any network through OSP in an interference-free environment. However, inducing the work of OSP to CRSN will have some effects considering transmission power and dropped packets rate. We assume underlay CRSN where SU are transmitting on the same bands licensed for PU as long as strict interference thresholds are well maintained. We formulate a knapsack optimization that chooses the minimum transmission power scenario for the CRSN

and takes interference induced to PU into account. As mentioned earlier, we are dealing with delay-tolerant applications; though, we added to this formulation a delay constraint to show its effect. Denoting D_m^k as the delay which packet m undergoes when k packets are in the queue. D_m^k is updated within each round i based on how many rounds packet m has been kept in the queue till releasing. We assume for simplicity one SU interferes with one PU. The interfering channel from the SU to the PU is denoted by h_i^k (The interfering channel at round i when k packet are already in the queue), and it is assumed to be Rayleigh-fading channel as well as the transmission channel H mentioned previously. The new problem is formulated as follows:

$$\text{Minimize}_{x} \quad \sum_{j=0}^{k+1} x_j [(k + 1 - j) P_{t_i} + E\{\min(P_{t_{i,j}}, P_{t_{i,j+1}}, \ldots, P_{t_{i,Q}})\}]$$

$$\text{subject to} \quad \sum_{j=0}^{k+1} x_j (k + 1 - j) P_{t_i} \times |h_i^k|^2 < I$$

$$D_m^k \leq D_{max}, \quad \text{for each round } i,$$

$$\sum_{j=0}^{k+1} x_j = 1,$$

$$x_j = \{0, 1\}, \quad \text{for all } j.$$

Where I is a strict interference threshold that must not be exceeded by the SU transmission, and D_{max} is the maximum delay that could be tolerated for each packet m. This problem is a knapsack optimization problem. Knapsack problem is a decision problem that is well known in combinatorial optimization. The knapsack problem is known, as ILP, to be NP-complete. We will use the same algorithm discussed in Section 2 to solve it. We measure the performance of our scheme in terms of dropped packet rate and power saving. For convenience, a packet is considered dropped if its resulted interference exceeds the interference threshold I. Fig. 2 shows dropped packet rate percentage in case of traditional transmission method as well as transmission through OSP versus various interference threshold. We chose, without loss of generality, $Q = 8$. It is obvious that there is a significant decrease in the dropped packet rate through using OSP than using traditional method. In traditional transmission method, a packet is considered dropped if the resulted interference form its transmission exceeds the interference threshold instantaneously. However through the OSP, it can be kept in the queue expecting better interfering-channel conditions.

There is also an interesting point considering the comparison between traditional transmission method and transmission through OSP. In traditional

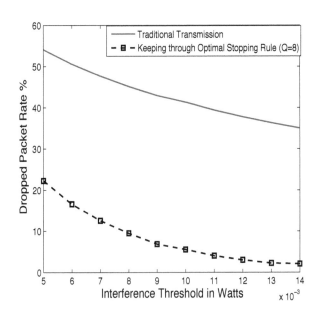

Figure 2. Dropped Packet Rate in Traditional Transmission Method versus transmission through OSP with Q=8.

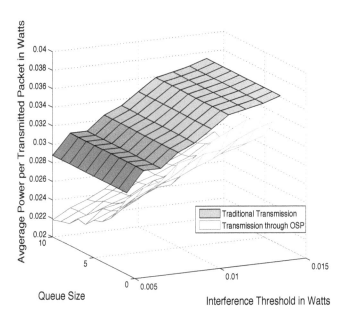

Figure 3. APTP through traditional transmission method and OSP versus Queue Size and Interference Threshold.

transmission method, there are more dropped packets, and hence less power is consumed. However, in transmission through OSP, there are less dropped packets and more consumed power. To discriminate one scheme from the other, we consider the term Average Power per Transmitted Packet (APTP) which is defined as average consumed power divided by successfully received packets. APTP is the factor that makes one scheme outperforms the other. As shown in Fig. 3, in both transmission schemes, APTP increases as I increases because less packets are dropped and more power is consumed. However, transmission through OSP outperforms traditional method as it has less consumed power for any I. Traditional transmission method isn't affected by the queue size (Constant curves for the same Q). On the other hand, as Q increases, APTP decreases in transmission through OSP. Improvement in APTP swings from 4% (small Q size ($Q=1$)) to 23% (large Q size ($Q=10$)). Improvement for other queue sizes are in-between.

3.2. Effect of Queue Size and Maximum Permissible Delay

As mentioned earlier, our transmission scheme is suitable for delay-tolerant applications such as mine reconnaissance, undersea explorations, environmental monitoring, and ocean sampling. In such applications power saving is an important issue as well as successful packet reception, and end to end delay isn't much important and could be afforded [16]. But, for convenience, we study the effect of both Q and D_{max} simultaneously on the consequent average delay. Fig. 4

shows average consequent delay per packet resulting from transmission through OSP when either one of the parameters Q or D_{max} is fixed, while the other is changing. It is clear that the average consequent delay is dominated by the fixed parameter of both. For instance, in Fig. 4.a, as Q increases, average consequent delay increases till $Q = 5$ which is the value of D_{max}, and then it starts to saturate. The same occurs in Fig. 4.b with fixing Q, and changing D_{max}. This phenomenon happens due to assuming, in our model, that packets are released according to their arrival in a First In First Out (FIFO) fashion. Hence, the smaller parameter dominates the effect on average consequent delay. Consequently, it is better to choose $Q = D_{max}$ to avoid the dominance of one parameter over the other on the average consequent delay.

3.3. Extension to a complete network of N nodes

In previous subsection, we discussed applying OSP to CRSN. However, this discussion was, for simplicity, for one node. Here, in this section, we are going to extend this work to a complete CRSN of N nodes. We, by here, formulate two problems; one for the traditional transmission method, and the other one for the OSP, and, by then, we are going to compare them which other in terms of power saving and dropped packets rate. In the traditional transmission method, as a matter of fact, it is required to minimize transmission power in the CRSN and to maximize number of nodes supported for transmission. In other words, hopefully; all nodes transmit their packets, but as the interference threshold to the PU does exist, only some of them will be able to

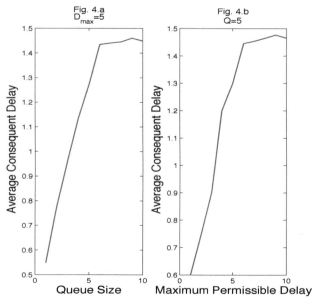

Figure 4. Effect of Queue Size and Maximum Permissible Delay Parameters on Average Consequent Delay.

transmit; and those will be chosen so as to minimize the total transmission power in the network. It is a multi-objective optimization problem. On one hand, the number of supported nodes has to be maximized. On the other hand, the total transmission power has to be minimized. Given a BER requirement for the CRSN transmissions and interference threshold that hasn't to be exceeded by the CRSN transmissions, the objective to maximize the number of supported nodes, on one plane, is as follows:

$$\underset{x}{\text{Maximize}} \sum_{i=1}^{N} x_i \qquad (15)$$

and the objective to minimize the total transmission power, on another plane, is as follows:

$$\underset{x}{\text{Minimize}} \sum_{i=1}^{N} x_i P_i \qquad (16)$$

Combining them together leads to a multi-objective optimization problem, each problem is solved separately and normalized to its maximum/minimum. So, the multi-objective formulation will be as follows:

$$\underset{x}{\text{Maximize}} \quad \sum_{i=1}^{N} \frac{x_i}{N} - \frac{x_i P_i}{P_{min}}$$

$$\text{subject to} \quad \textbf{C1:} \sum_{i=1}^{N} x_i I_{i_{PU}} \le I,$$

$$\textbf{C2:} \; x_i = \{0,1\}, \; \forall i \in N$$

Where,

C1: guarantees that the interference to the primary user base station doesn't exceed a predefined value I by secondary users transmissions. Where $I_{i_{PU}} = P_i \times |h_i|^2$

C2: guarantees that any x is 0 or 1.

The previous optimization problem represents the conventional transmission paradigm that we will compare with the OSP technique that will be discussed by then.

This problem is classified as ILP problem. The LPSF algorithm, as mentioned earlier, will be used for solving it.

On the other hand, for the transmission through he OSP: Each node is equipped with a single queue Q. The optimization problem of the total power minimization in this network through OSP is formulated as follows:

$$\underset{x}{\text{Minimize}} \quad \sum_{j=0}^{k+1} \sum_{n=1}^{N} x_j^n [(k+1-j)P_{t_i}^n$$
$$+ E\{\min(P_{t_{i,j}}^n, P_{t_{i,j+1}}^n, \dots, P_{t_{i,Q}}^n)\}]$$

$$\text{subject to} \quad \sum_{j=0}^{k+1} \sum_{n=1}^{N} x_j^n (k+1-j) P_{t_i}^n \times |h_{i,k}^n|^2 < I,$$

$$D_{m,k}^n \le D_{max}, \quad \text{for each round } i,$$

$$\sum_{j=0}^{k+1} x_j^n = 1, \; \forall n \in N,$$

$$x_j^n = \{0,1\}, \; \forall j, \forall n \in N.$$

Where x_j^n is the on-off state of node n of the set N, $P_{t_i}^n$ represents the instantaneous power cost of node n at round i, and the second term in the optimization problem represents the expected cost of each node, $D_{m,k}^n$ represents the delay which packet m undergoes when k packets are in the queue of node n, and $h_{i,k}^n$ represents the interfering channel from the SU number n to the PU (The interfering channel of node n at round i when k packet are already in its queue), and it is assumed to be Rayleigh-fading channel. The above problem is classified as Knapsack optimization problem. The LPSF algorithm, as discussed earlier, will be used for solving it as well.

Fig. 5 and Fig. 6 show power profile and dropped packets rate in traditional transmission method and transmission through OSP versus queue size. Clearly, the amount of dropped packets rate through OSP transmission is much less than that of the traditional transmission method, and it decreases monotonically with increasing the queue size. That's because each node can keep its packets in its queue hoping for better conditions. Therefore, the amount of power per transmitted packet is much more in the OSP because more packets are successfully transmitted in this case.

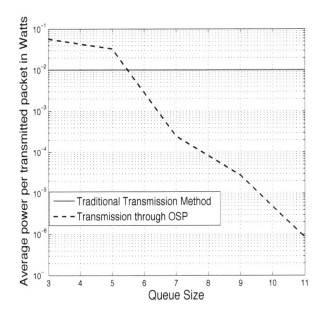

Figure 5. Power Saving through OSP for N=5.

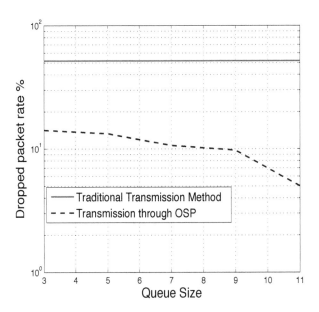

Figure 6. Dropped packets rate for N=5.

However, for large queue sizes, the power saving through OSP outperforms that of the traditional case, because with large queue sizes, the nodes have more flexibility to wait for better channel conditions because of the large queue size, and hence more opportunities.

4. Conclusion

We studied the power minimization problem through OSP fro delay-tolerant applications. Applying optimal stopping theory to packet retention and deriving the optimal stopping rule was the core of the work. We

deduced that this transmission scheme outperforms traditional transmission method as far as power minimization is concerned. Also, it was shown that the improvement is overly significant; it reaches 55% for small queue sizes and increases monotonically as queue size increases.

We also extended the work of packet retention through OSP to CRSN where interference threshold to PU must not be exceeded by SU transmissions. Moreover, we studied the effect of queue size as well as the maximum permissible delay for a packet on the average consequent delay. Simulations were conducted in terms of dropped packet rate, APTP, and consequent delay. Finally, the work was extended to a whole network of size N rather than one node.

Acknowledgment

This publication was made possible by NPRP grant # [5-250-2-087] from the Qatar National Research Fund (a member of Qatar Foundation). The statements made herein are solely the responsibility of the author

References

[1] J. Mitola and J. Maguire, G.Q., "Cognitive radio: making software radios more personal," *Personal Communications, IEEE*, vol. 6, no. 4, pp. 13–18, 1999.

[2] R. Zhang and Y.-C. Liang, "Investigation on multiuser diversity in spectrum sharing based cognitive radio networks," *Communications Letters, IEEE*, vol. 14, no. 2, pp. 133–135, 2010.

[3] I. Akyildiz, W. Su, Y. Sankarasubramaniam, and E. Cayirci, "A survey on sensor networks," *Communications Magazine, IEEE*, vol. 40, no. 8, pp. 102–114, 2002.

[4] S. Cui, A. Goldsmith, and A. Bahai, "Energy-efficiency of MIMO and cooperative MIMO techniques in sensor networks," *Selected Areas in Communications, IEEE Journal on*, vol. 22, no. 6, pp. 1089–1098, 2004.

[5] W. Farjow, A. Chehri, H. Mouftah, and X. Fernando, "An energy-efficient routing protocol for wireless sensor networks through nonlinear optimization," in *Wireless Communications in Unusual and Confined Areas (ICWCUCA), 2012 International Conference on*, pp. 1–4, Aug 2012.

[6] Y. Chen and Q. Zhao, "On the lifetime of wireless sensor networks," *Communications Letters, IEEE*, vol. 9, pp. 976–978, Nov 2005.

[7] Y. unxia Chen and Q. Zhao, "Maximizing the lifetime of sensor network using local information on channel state and residual energy," in *Information Processing in Sensor Networks, 2005. IPSN 2005. Fourth International Symposium on*, March 2005.

[8] O. Akan, O. Karli, and O. Ergul, "Cognitive radio sensor networks," *Network, IEEE*, vol. 23, no. 4, pp. 34–40, 2009.

[9] D. Zheng, W. Ge, and J. Zhang, "Distributed opportunistic scheduling for ad hoc networks with random access: An optimal stopping approach,"

Information Theory, IEEE Transactions on, vol. 55, pp. 205–222, Jan 2009.

[10] T. Shu and M. Krunz, "Throughput-efficient sequential channel sensing and probing in cognitive radio networks under sensing errors," pp. 37–48, Sep 2009.

[11] A. Ewaisha, A. Sultan, and T. ElBatt, "Optimization of channel sensing time and order for cognitive radios," in *Wireless Communications and Networking Conference (WCNC), 2011 IEEE,* pp. 1414–1419, March 2011.

[12] M. Shashi, W. Shouyang, and L. K. Keung, "Generalized convexity and vector optimization," vol. 90, 2009.

[13] X. Xiao-hua, W. An-bao, and N. Ai-bing, "Notice of retraction competitive decision algorithm for 0-1 multiple knapsack problem," in *Education Technology and Computer Science (ETCS), 2010 Second International*

Workshop on, vol. 1, pp. 252–255, March 2010.

[14] M. Islam and M. Akbar, "Heuristic algorithm of the multiple-choice multidimensional knapsack problem (MMKP) for cluster computing," in *Computers and Information Technology, 2009. ICCIT '09. 12th International Conference on,* pp. 157–161, Dec 2009.

[15] T. Shu and M. Krunz, "Exploiting microscopic spectrum opportunities in cognitive radio networks via coordinated channel access," *Mobile Computing, IEEE Transactions on,* vol. 9, pp. 1522–1534, Nov 2010.

[16] M. Keshtgary, R. Mohammadi, M. Mahmoudi, and M. R. Mansouri, "Article: Energy consumption estimation in cluster based underwater wireless sensor networks using m/m/1 queuing model," *International Journal of Computer Applications,* vol. 43, pp. 6–10, April 2012.

10

Energy/bandwidth-Saving Cooperative Spectrum Sensing for Two-hop WRAN

Ming-Tuo Zhou[1,†], Chunyi Song[2,†], Chin Sean Sum[3], Hiroshi Harada[4]

[1]Smart Wireless Laboratory, NICT Singapore Representative Office, 20 Science Park Road, #01-09A/10 TeleTech Park, Singapore 117674
[2]Institute of Marine Information Science and Engineering, Zhejiang University, China
[3]Wi-SUN Alliance
[4]Graduate School of Informatics, Kyoto University, Japan

Abstract

A two-hop wireless regional area network (WRAN) providing monitoring services operating in Television White Space (TVWS), i.e., IEEE P802.22b, may employ a great number of subscriber customer-premises equipments (S-CPEs) possibly without mains power supply, leading to requirement of cost-effective and power-saving design. This paper proposes a framework of cooperative spectrum sensing (CSS) and an energy/bandwidth saving CSS scheme to P802.22b. In each round of sensing, S-CPEs with SNRs lower than a predefined threshold are excluded from reporting sensing results. Numerical results show that the fused missed-detection probability and false alarm probability could remain meeting sensing requirements, and the overall fused error probability changes very little. With 10 S-CPEs, it is possible to save more than 40% of the energy/bandwidth on a Rayleigh channel. The principle proposed can apply to other advanced sensing technologies capable of detecting primary signals with low average SNR.

Keywords: TV White Space, Cognitive radio, IEEE 802.22, Wireless Regional Access Network, Cooperative Spectrum Sensing, Energy saving

1. Introduction

With the explosive growth of broadband wireless users and services, the current spectrum for wireless communications becomes more and more congested. Fortunately, to explore Television White Space (TVWS) – the unused TV channels at certain time in certain geographic area – may alleviate the problem. IEEE 802.22 is one of the current efforts to utilize TVWS for services in regional area. The 802.22 working group has developed IEEE Std 802.22-2011 for regional broadband services and now is working on IEEE P802.22b for regional monitoring and metering, etc [1, 2].

Unlike 802.22-2011 that employs cellular network topology, P802.22b incorporates two-hop relay by which a great number (e.g., tens to hundreds) of subscriber customer-premises equipments (S-CPEs) may connect to a relay CPE (R-CPE) and then a multi-hop base station (MR-BS). IEEE P802.22b S-CPEs require cost-effective and energy/bandwidth-saving designs due to the big volume and the fact that they may not be mains powered.

On the other hand, following regulatory requirement, periodic quiet periods (QPs) are reserved in P802.22b frames where an S-CPE can perform spectrum sensing to detect the presence of the primary users (PUs). The current P802.22b employs individual spectrum sensing technologies, of which some require high-capability processors and therefore lead to high-cost S-CPEs [1].

★Chunyi Song, Chin Sean Sum, and Hiroshi Harada were with the Smart Wireless Laboratory of National Institute of Information and Communications Technology (NICT) when they contributed to this work.
*Email: zhou.mingtuo@ieee.org;   cysong@zju.edu.cn; sum@wi-sun.org; harada@nict.go.jp
†Corresponding author.

For the goal of low-cost and simple design of S-CPEs, we propose cooperative spectrum sensing (CSS) for IEEE P802.22b. With CSS, many nodes sense the spectrum at same time and report individual result to a fusion center (FC). The FC compounds the received individual results and makes the final sensing decision. Compared to sensing by a single node, the sensing performance can be improved due to space diversity of the radio signal [7, 8]. It is therefore at each S-CPE, relatively lower sensing performance is required and then lower-cost processor can be used. In the proposed scheme, as shown in Fig. 1, a number of S-CPEs associated with a R-CPE perform CSS and report results to the R-CPE. The R-CPE acts as an FC and it reports the fused result to the MR-BS it associates with. If a fused result reported by a R-CPE is the presence of the PU, the MR-BS needs to request the R-CPE and the associated S-CPEs to stop transmissions immediately.

Moreover, in order to save energy and bandwidth for a P802.22b system that employs a great number of S-CPEs that may be powered by batteries, we propose only the S-CPEs with detected primary signal-to-noise ratio (SNR) higher than a threshold to report the sensing results to a R-CPE. An SNR threshold is stored at each S-CPEs for comparison to the detected SNR locally. Numerical results show that with the proposed partial reporting scheme, the energy/bandwidth can be saved while the sensing performance can be maintained. The saved energy/bandwidth increases with the number of S-CPEs. The principle of the proposal applies to other spectrum sensing technologies although energy detection is considered here for simplicity.

In the literatures [3]-[12], researches of energy/bandwidth-saving for CSS incorporating energy detection focus on two approaches: (1) to reduce energy for individual spectrum sensing; (2) to reduce energy for reporting individual sensing result to an FC. In [9], Chien *et al.* proposed a partial spectrum sensing technology to save energy for spectrum sensing. In [10], the spectrum sensors are divided into subsets and scheduled to cooperatively sense the spectrum in an optimized sequence so that the overall energy consumption is minimized. [3] and [4] demonstrated that the overall energy for CSS can be saved when only an optimal number of SUs participate CSS and each SU employs optimized sensing time. In [12], Zhang *et al.* studied the optimal fusion rule and optimized the number of SUs performing CSS. Compared to other proposals, the energy/bandwidth-saving scheme of this study requires no global comparison of the primary SNR thus extra energy and spectrum can be saved.

This paper is organized as follows. Following the introduction, we introduce P802.22b in section 2. Then we present the proposed cooperative scheme for P802.22b in section 3. CSS with energy/bandwidth-saving is proposed and analyzed in section 4. Numerical

results are presented in section 5 and the paper is concluded by section 6.

2. IEEE P802.22b and Spectrum Sensing

There are various broadband services and monitoring applications in context of wireless regional area networks where 802.22-2011 device may not able to serve. The regional services include real-time and near real-time monitoring, emergency broadband services, remote medical diagnose, etc, where a great number of subscriber terminals with simpler design and lower cost are needed but are not supported by 802.22-2011. For this consideration, IEEE P802.22b is to amend IEEE Std 802.22-2011 by introducing new class CPEs, i.e., R-CPEs and S-CPEs. An S-CPE is of lower capability, for example, lower transmission power, lower antenna height, and lower-gain/cost amplifier, etc. Thus the effective communication distance for an S-CPE is not likely to be tens of kilometers, but is of 1 to 2 kilometers. A R-CPE is a 802.22-2011 CPE supporting advanced functions such as relay, multiple-input multiple out (MIMO) and channel bounding, etc. The supported communication distance of a R-CPE is of tens of kilometers. Correspondingly, an MR-BS supports advanced functions like relay, MIMO and channel bounding, etc. As shown in Fig. 1, in P802.22b, the data traffic between the S-CPEs and an MR-BS is relayed by the R-CPEs.

The general frame structure of P802.22b is shown in Fig. 2, where both downstream (DS) subframe and upstream (US) subframe are divided into access zone and relay zone. As shown in the figure, a contention window in both access and relay zone of a US subframe is allocated for ranging, bandwidth request,

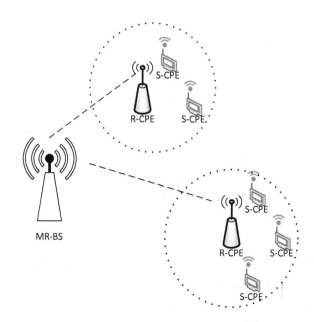

Figure 1. IEEE P802.22b network structure.

and urgent coexistence situation (UCS) notification. A UCS Notification window can be scheduled in this time period for urgent reporting detection of primary transmissions.

Following 802.22-2011, periodic Quiet Periods (QPs) are scheduled along the frames for incumbent detection by spectrum sensing in P802.22b. It has been designed that across a P802.22b network, QPs at all stations are synchronized. In a P802.22b system, a fraction of the S-CPEs/R-CPEs can be instructed to sense the spectrum and if the presence of PUs are detected, it needs to be reported to an MR-BS as soon as possible.

In current P802.22b, an S-CPE has two possible ways to report the detected results. For an S-CPE with upstream bandwidth allocation, it sets the UCS flag in the generic MAC header for reporting to a MR-BS. For an S-CPE without upstream bandwidth allocation, it needs to report in the UCS Notification window using contention or code-division multiplexing access (CDMA).

3. Cooperative Spectrum Sensing for P802.22b

3.1. Proposal of CSS

The big volume of S-CPEs under a R-CPE imposes requirement of simplicity and low-cost design for an S-CPE. To meet this requirement, we propose CSS framework for P802.22b. It is well known that by CSS, the overall sensing performance can be improved and then the requirement of individual sensing performance can be relaxed. Therefore, an S-CPE may employ a simpler and low-cost sensing component thus the total cost can be saved.

With the proposed CSS, under a R-CPE, a number of S-CPEs are instructed to sense the spectrum cooperatively. After a QP during which spectrum sensing is performed, an S-CPE reports to a R-CPE if the presence of PU is detected at its location. If an S-CPE has upstream bandwidth, it reports by setting the UCS flag of the generic MAC header, otherwise, it reports the PU presence in the UCS notification window. The

R-CPE acts as a fusion center and it reports to an MR-BS if the fused result is PU transmission is present. For simplicity, energy detection and OR-fusion rule are assumed. The energy/bandwidth-saving CSS proposed in this study is not limited to energy detection. If other advanced spectrum sensing method is applied at all S-CPEs, it is also possible to apply the CSS scheme proposed for P802.22b here.

3.2. System Model and Assumptions

Referring to the network structure shown in Fig. 1, it assumes that under a R-CPE, N S-CPEs are instructed to sense spectrum during any QP. Among the N S-CPEs, $g \cdot N$ S-CPEs have been allocated upstream bandwidth, and $(1 - g) \cdot N$ S-CPEs have no upstream bandwidth, where $0 \leq g \leq 1$. If an S-CPE detects the presence of PU during a QP, then it reports the detected result to the R-CPE immediately, otherwise it does not report. As required by P802.22b [1], if a R-CPE receives a report from an S-CPE, then it assumes that the S-CPE has detected the presence of PU, otherwise it assumes that the S-CPE has detected no presence of PU.

For presentation simplicity, the S-CPEs with upstream bandwidth are called Group-1 S-CPEs and the S-CPEs without upstream bandwidth are called Group-2 S-CPEs, since their reporting mechanisms are different. For Group-1 S-CPEs, it assumes that all S-CPEs can report successfully as they have upstream bandwidth. For Group-2 S-CPEs, contention/CDMA reporting method is used and in case there are two or more S-CPEs to report, an S-CPE may fail to report due to conflicts. Clearly, when more Group-2 S-CPEs report in an UCS Notification window, the success probability will be lower. It is difficult to precisely describe the relationship between the success reporting probability and the number of the reporting S-CPEs mathematically due to the complexity. In this study, we assume the success reporting probability is substantially modeled by following equation

$$p_t(X) = \begin{cases} 1, & X = 1, \\ e^{-X}, & X = 2, 3, \ldots \end{cases}, \qquad (1)$$

where X is the number of Group-2 S-CPEs reporting in same UCS Notification window.

If a Group-2 S-CPE detects the presence of PU but it fails in reporting, then based on the P802.22b reporting mechanism, a R-CPE shall assume that S-CPE has not detected the presence of PU.

We assume that the detected instantaneous signal-to-noise ratio (SNR) of the primary signal at each S-CPE varies with time due to channel fading, and the averaged SNR $\bar{\gamma}$ at all S-CPEs under a R-CPE are equal since the path loss exponent of the P802.22b scenarios is general low and the distance between the S-CPEs of a local cell is in range of 1 to 2 kilometers, which is

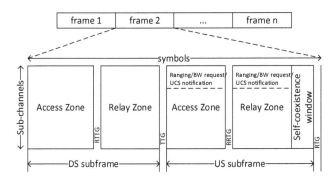

Figure 2. IEEE P802.22b general frame structure.

generally much shorter than the distance to a primary transmitter (usually a TV tower).

Let p_d and p_f stand for the local detection probability and false alarm probability at an S-CPE, respectively. For fading channel, p_d and p_f are averaged over the primary SNR.

High detection probability and low false alarm probability are required by P802.22b for effective protection of PUs and utilization of TVWS, respectively. Without loss of generality, for the proposed CSS scheme to P802.22b, we propose that at a R-CPE, the fused detection probability Q_d should be higher than 90% and the fused false alarm probability Q_f should be lower than 10%. The fused missed-detection probability, i.e., Q_m $(=1-Q_d)$ therefore should be less than 10%.

3.3. Fused Miss-detection Probability

The fused missed-detection probability at a R-CPE is given by $Q_m = Q_{m_1} \cdot Q_{m_2}$, where Q_{m_1} is fused missed-detection probability of the Group-1 S-CPEs and Q_{m_2} is fused missed-detection probability of the Group-2 S-CPEs.

Let H_1 stands for the assumption that PUs are present during sensing, and H_0 stands for the counterpart, i.e., no PU is present.

With assumption of H_1, we have

$$Q_{m_1} = (1 - p_d)^{gN}, \qquad (2)$$

and

$$Q_{m_2} = (1 - p_d)^{(1-g)N} + \sum_{K=2}^{(1-g)N} \left\{ \binom{(1-g)N}{K} \times \right. \\ \left. \{p_d \left[1 - p_t(K)\right]\}^K (1 - p_d)^{[(1-g)N-K]} \right\} \qquad (3)$$

where K is the number of Group-2 S-CPEs detected H_1. In Eq. (3), the first term corresponds to scenario when none of the Group-2 S-CPEs has detected the presence of the primary signal, for the second term, there are K Group-2 S-CPEs have detected PU signal, however, none of them succeeded to report to the R-CPE due to conflicts. Note K is in range of $[2, (1 - g)N]$. When only one S-CPE detects PU signal, it can report to a R-CPE successfully since there is no competitors.

3.4. Fused False Alarm Probability

The fused false alarm probability at a R-CPE is given by $Q_f = 1 - \left(1 - Q_{f_1}\right) \cdot \left(1 - Q_{f_2}\right)$, where Q_{f_1} is fused false alarm probability of the Group-1 S-CPEs and Q_{f_2} is fused false alarm probability of the Group-2 S-CPEs.

With assumption of H_0, we have

$$Q_{f_1} = 1 - \left(1 - p_f\right)^{gN}, \qquad (4)$$

and

$$Q_{f_2} = 1 - \left(1 - p_f\right)^{(1-g)N} - \sum_{L=2}^{(1-g)N} \left\{ \binom{(1-g)N}{L} \times \right. \\ \left. \{p_f \left[1 - p_t(L)\right]\}^L \left(1 - p_f\right)^{(1-g)N-L} \right\}, \qquad (5)$$

where L is the number of Group-2 S-CPEs detected H_1 (false alarm). In Eq. (5), the second term corresponds to none of the Group-2 S-CPEs falsely detects the presence of the primary signal (false alarm). And for the third term, there are L Group-2 S-CPEs have detected the primary signal falsely, however, all of them failed to report due to conflicts. Note that if only one Group-2 S-CPE detects the primary signal falsely, i.e., $L = 1$, then it can report to a R-CPE successfully since no competitor.

3.5. Fused Error Probability

The fused error probability at a R-CPE is given by

$$Q_e = P_1 Q_m + P_0 Q_f, \qquad (6)$$

where P_1 is the probability of H_1 and P_0 is probability of H_0. Clearly, when Q_m $(= 1 - Q_d)$ and Q_f is lower than 10%, Q_e should be less than 10%.

4. Energy/Bandwidth-saving CSS for P802.22b

The main mechanism of the proposed energy/bandwidth-saving CSS for P802.22b is to exclude the S-CPEs with ignorable contribution to the sensing performance from reporting their sensing results. By this way, power can be saved and conflicts in reporting sensing results to R-CPEs can be reduced.

4.1. Energy Detection

With spectrum sensing method of energy detection, an S-CPE collects energy during sensing window and the collected energy is compared to a predefined energy threshold. If the collected energy is bigger, it decides H_1, otherwise, it decides H_0. The local false alarm probability and missed-detection probability are given, respectively, by [13]

$$p_{f,i} = \Pr\{E_i > \lambda_i | H_0\} = \Gamma(u, \lambda_i/2)/\Gamma(u), \qquad (7)$$

$$p_{d,i} = \Pr\{E_i > \lambda_i | H_1\} = Q_u\left(\sqrt{2\gamma_i}, \sqrt{\lambda_i}\right), \qquad (8)$$

where E_i, λ_i, and γ_i are the collected energy, the energy threshold, and the detected instantaneous SNR at the ith S-CPE, respectively; u is the sensing time-bandwidth product and is assumed an integer for simplicity. $\Gamma(\cdot)$ and $\Gamma(u, x)$ are the complete and incomplete gamma function, respectively; $Q_u(a, x)$ is the generalized Marcum Q-function.

We assume that all S-CPEs have same energy threshold, i.e., $\lambda_i = \lambda$, then all S-CPEs have equal false

$$Q_{m_2}^* = \sum_{I=0}^{(1-g)N} \binom{(1-g)N}{I} (p_d \hat{p})^I (1-p_d)^{[(1-g)N-I]}$$
$$+ \sum_{M=2}^{(1-g)N} \binom{(1-g)N}{M} \{p_d(1-\hat{p})[1-p_t(M)]\}^M \left\{ \sum_{I=0}^{(1-g)N-M} \binom{(1-g)N-M}{I} (p_d \hat{p})^I (1-p_d)^{[(1-g)N-M-I]} \right\}, \tag{9}$$

$$Q_{f_2}^* = 1 - \sum_{J=0}^{(1-g)N} \binom{(1-g)N}{J} \left(p_f \hat{p}\right)^J \left(1-p_f\right)^{[(1-g)N-J]}$$
$$- \sum_{L=2}^{(1-g)N} \binom{(1-g)N}{L} \{p_f(1-\hat{p})[1-p_t(L)]\}^L \left\{ \sum_{J=0}^{(1-g)N-L} \binom{(1-g)N-L}{J} \left(p_f \hat{p}\right)^J \left(1-p_f\right)^{[(1-g)N-L-J]} \right\}. \tag{10}$$

alarm probability, i.e., p_f. For fading channel, the averaged detection probability, i.e., p_d is given by $p_d = \int_0^\infty Q_u(\sqrt{2x}, \sqrt{\lambda}) f_\gamma(x) dx$, where $f_\gamma(\cdot)$ is probability density function of the primary SNR (γ).

4.2. Proposed Energy/Bandwidth-saving CSS

Since at each round of spectrum sensing, the detection probability $p_{d,i}$ is increasing function of the instantaneous primary SNR, it is possible to exclude S-CPEs that have relatively low instantaneous SNR from reporting their results to a R-CPE, in condition that the deteriorated fused detection probability still meets the sensing requirement. Estimation of SNR at a receiver has been reported in [14, 15]. By excluding such S-CPEs to report results if they detect H_1, it also helps to reduce the fused false alarm probability and increase the success reporting probability. By doing so, energy consumption and bandwidth can be saved in a P802.22b system.

We propose to set a SNR threshold γ_T, and if a Group-2 S-CPE detects an instantaneous SNR smaller than γ_T, in this round of sensing, it does not report to a R-CPE even it has detected H_1. By this way, the S-CPEs that are excluded from reporting their results can save energy and bandwidth consumption in this round of spectrum sensing. However, this is not so meaningful to Group-1 S-CPEs since they have been granted bandwith and will be likely to transmit packages, no matter they set the 1-bit UCS flag in the generic MAC header to report the detection of PU signal or not.

In other studies, it is found that optimal CSS performance can be achieved if only letting nodes with high-enough SNRs report results for final fusion [4]. However, to select the nodes with 'high-enough SNRs', global comparison is needed. The scheme proposed in this section requires only local comparison to γ_T and no global comparison is needed thus it may save more energy and bandwidth.

Let $\hat{p} = \int_0^{\gamma_T} f_\gamma(x) dx$ stands for the probability that a detected instantaneous SNR is less than the SNR threshold, then the fused missed-detection probability of Group-2 S-CPEs and fused false alarm probability of Group-2 S-CPEs at a R-CPE are given by Eq. (9) and Eq. (10), respectively. In Eq. (9), I is the number of the Group-2 S-CPEs without upstream bandwidth having detected H_1 (under assumption of PU transmission) but the detected SNRs are less than γ_T so that the S-CPEs haven't reported the results to a R-CPE. M is the number of the Group-2 S-CPEs without upper bandwith having detected H_1 (under assumption of PU transmission) and the detected SNRs are higher than γ_T but all failed in reporting the results to a R-CPE due to competition and then the PU transmission is missed. Similarly, in Eq. (10), J is the number of Group-2 S-CPEs without upper bandwidth having falsely detected PU transmission (under assumption of NO PU transmission) but the detected SNRs are less than γ_T so that the S-CPEs haven't reported the results to a R-CPE. And L is the number of Group-2 S-CPEs without upper bandwidth having detected H_1 (under assumption of NO PU transmission) and the detected SNRs are higher than γ_T but all failed in reporting the results to a R-CPE due to competition therefore the PU transmission is not falsely detected.

With the proposed energy/bandwidth-saving CSS, the fused missed-detection probability and false alarm probability at a R-CPE are given by $Q_m^* = Q_{m_1} \cdot Q_{m_2}^*$ and $Q_f^* = 1 - (1-Q_{f_1}) \cdot (1-Q_{f_2}^*)$, respectively. The error probability at a R-CPE becomes $Q_e^* = P_1 Q_m^* + P_0 Q_f^*$.

Setting a high SNR threshold allows more energy saved, however, it leads to higher Q_m^*. Following the requirement of P802.22b system, Q_m^* and Q_f^* should be less than 10%, then γ_T^* can be found by solving following equation numerically

$$\gamma_T^* = \arg_{\gamma_T} \max\left(Q_m^*, Q_f^*\right), \quad Q_m^* \leq 0.1, \quad Q_f^* \leq 0.1. \tag{11}$$

The maximum overall normalized saved energy/bandwidth is then given by $(1-g)\hat{p}^*$, where $\hat{p}^* = \int_0^{\gamma_T^*} f_\gamma(x) dx$.

4.3. Number of Group–2 Reporting S-CPEs

With the proposed energy/bandwidth-saving CSS, in case a Group-2 S-CPE having detected PU transmission during a QP, only when its detected instantaneous SNR is higher than a predefined SNR threshold it reports the sensing result to a R-CPE. Therefore, usually only part Group-2 S-CPEs report sensing results. Based on above analysis, the probability that there are S Group-2 S-CPEs reporting sensing results under assumptions with and without PU transmission are given by Eq. (12) and Eq. (13), respectively, and the overall probability is given by Eq. (14), where $0 \leq S \leq N$.

$$
\Pr(X = S|H_1) = \binom{(1-g)N}{S} \{p_d(1-\hat{p})\}^S
$$
$$
\times \left\{ \sum_{0}^{(1-g)N-S} \binom{(1-g)N-S}{K} (p_d\hat{p})^K (1-p_d)^{(1-g)N-S-K} \right\}
$$
$$
(12)
$$

$$
\Pr(X = S|H_0) = \binom{(1-g)N}{S} \{p_f(1-\hat{p})\}^S
$$
$$
\times \left\{ \sum_{0}^{(1-g)N-S} \binom{(1-g)N-S}{L} (p_f\hat{p})^L (1-p_f)^{(1-g)N-S-L} \right\}
$$
$$
(13)
$$

$$
\Pr(X = S) = P_1 \cdot \Pr(X = S|H_1) + P_0 \cdot \Pr(X = S|H_0).
$$
$$
(14)
$$

5. Numerical results

Figure 3 and Figure 4 show the overall probability of S Group-2 S-CPEs reporting sensing results to a R-CPE as function of SNR threshold (γ_T) with parameter g of 0.2 and 0.6, respectively. $g = 0.2$ (or 0.6) means that there are 20% (or 60%) of the S-CPEs participating sensing have been allocated upstream bandwidth. A higher g means more Group-1 S-CPEs and less Group-2 S-CPEs. Rayleigh fading channel with an average SNR ($\bar{\gamma}$) of 10 dB is assumed, and the channel is assumed being occupied by the primary users over 80% of the time, i.e., $P_1 = 0.8$ and $P_0 = 0.2$. u is set to 10. At each S-CPE, the energy threshold λ is set to a value with which the fused error probability is minimized. As shown in the two figures, in most cases, only a small part (zero, one or two) of Group-2 S-CPEs report sensing results, indicating most of Group-2 S-CPEs usually keep silent, especially when there is a larger SNR threshold or a higher g.

Figure 5 shows the normalized saved energy/bandwidth as function of the SNR threshold when the energy/bandwidth-saving scheme is applied. g is set to 0.2, 0.4 and 0.6, and $P_1 = 0.8$ and $P_0 = 0.2$.

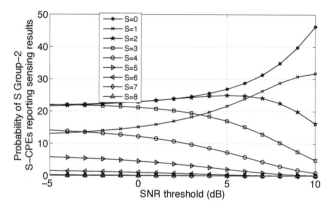

Figure 3. The probability of S Group-2 S-CPEs reporting sensing results as function of the SNR threshold (γ_T) (dB). Rayleigh fading channel with $\bar{\gamma}$ of 10 dB, $N = 10$, $g = 0.2$.

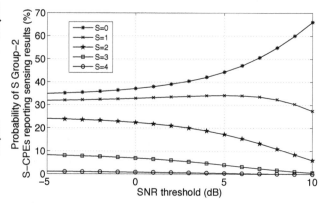

Figure 4. The probability of S Group-2 S-CPEs reporting sensing results as function of the SNR threshold (γ_T) (dB). Rayleigh fading channel with $\bar{\gamma}$ of 10 dB, $N = 10$, $g = 0.6$.

Rayleigh fading channel with average SNR of 10 dB is assumed. It can be seen that the saved energy/bandwidth increases rapidly with the SNR threshold. In case of $g = 0.2$, when γ_T equals to 8.5 dB, more than 40% of energy/bandwidth can be saved, while for γ_T above 10 dB, more than 50% of energy/bandwidth can be saved. For a higher g (0.4 or 0.6) less energy/bandwidth is saved owning to that more Group-1 S-CPEs will report sensing results if detecting PU transmission, no matter the detected instantaneous SNR is higher or lower than the SNR threshold.

Figure 6 and Figure 7 show the fused miss-detection probability (Q_m and Q_m^*) and the fused false alarm probability (Q_f and Q_f^*) at a R-CPE as function of the threshold of SNR (γ_T) with parameter g of 0.2 and 0.6, respectively. Other parameters setting are same as above while N is set to 10 and 20 for comparison. As shown in the figures, Q_m and Q_f keep unchange with γ_T since all Group-2 S-CPEs detecting H_1 need to report when the proposed energy/bandwidth saving CSS is not

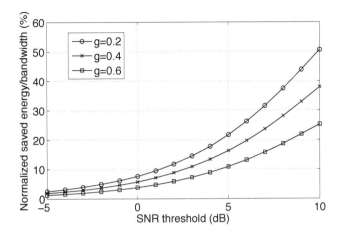

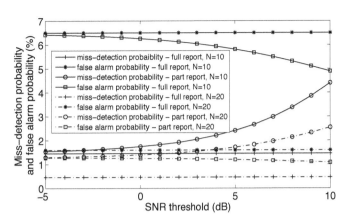

Figure 5. Normalized saved energy/bandwidth as function of the instantaneous SNR threshold. Rayleigh fading channel with $\bar{\gamma}$ of 10 dB, $N = 10$.

Figure 7. Fused miss-detection probability and fused false alarm probability at a R-CPE as function of the SNR threshold. Rayleigh fading channel with $\bar{\gamma}$ of 10dB. ($g = 0.6$)

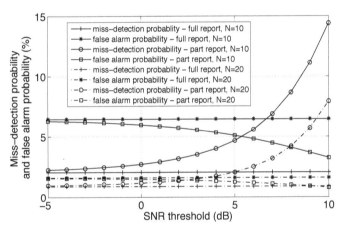

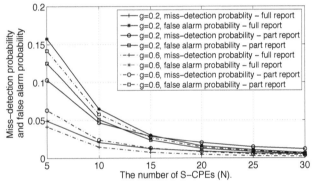

Figure 8. Fused miss-detection probability and fused false alarm probability at a R-CPE as function of the number of S-CPEs. Rayleigh fading channel with $\bar{\gamma}$ of 10 dB, $\gamma_T = 5$ dB.

Figure 6. Fused miss-detection probability and fused false alarm probability at a R-CPE as function of the SNR threshold. Rayleigh fading channel with $\bar{\gamma}$ of 10dB. ($g = 0.2$)

applied. As observed, the fused false alarm probability after enery/bandwidth-saving CSS is applied (Q_f^*) decreases with the SNR threshold (γ_T) since less Group-2 S-CPEs detecting H_1 report sensing results to a R-CPE, while the fused miss-detection probability increases with the SNR threshold because of the same reason. Comparison between $N = 10$ and $N = 20$ indicates that the proposed enery/bandwidth-saving CSS follows the usual rule of OR cooperative sensing that with more sensing S-CPEs, better sensing performance, i.e., lower Q_m^* and Q_f^*, can be achieved. In case of $g = 0.2$, for $N = 10$, when the SNR threshold γ_T is higher than 8.5 dB, Q_m^* becomes higher than 10%, meaning that the allowed maximum SNR threshold (γ_T^*) for $N = 10$ is about 8.5 dB. For $N = 20$, γ_T^* is higher than 10 dB. When $g = 0.6$, better performance can be achieved for both Q_m^* and Q_f^* indicating that more Group-1 S-CPEs leads to better sensing performance.

Figure 8 shows the fused miss-detection probability (Q_m and Q_m^*) and the fused false alarm probability (Q_f and Q_f^*) at a R-CPE as function of the number of the S-CPEs (N). Clearly, when the number of the S-CPEs increases, the spectrum sensing performance becomes better. When N equals to 10, Q_m, Q_m^*, Q_f and Q_f^* are all lower than 10%, meaning that the CSS approach meets the requirement of 802.22 system in both cases with and without applying the energy/bandwidth-saving scheme. $\gamma_T = 5$ dB leads to saving about 22% energy/bandwidth. Figure 9 shows the fused overall error probability (P_e and P_e^*) as function of the S-CPE number. From Figure 8, when the energy/bandwidth-saving SCC scheme is applied for a given N, the false alarm probability becomes lower and the miss-detection probability becomes higher, as result, the fused error probability changes very little (see Figure 9).

Figure 10 shows the maximum allowed SNR threshold (γ_T^*) as function of the average SNR ($\bar{\gamma}$). Condition of finding γ_T^* is $max\{Q_m^*, Q_f^*\} \leq 10\%$ as

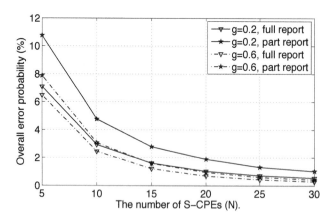

Figure 9. Fused overall error probability at a R-CPE as function of the number of S-CPEs. Rayleigh fading channel with $\bar{\gamma}$ of 10 dB, γ_T=5 dB.

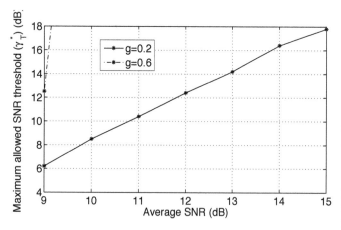

Figure 10. Maximum allowed SNR threshold (γ_T^*) as function of the average SNR ($\bar{\gamma}$). Rayleigh fading channel, $N = 10$.

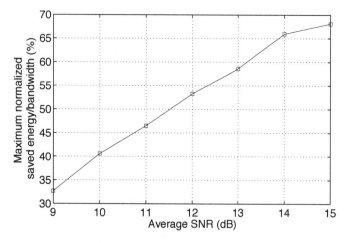

Figure 11. Maximum normalized saved energy/bandwidth as function of the average SNR ($\bar{\gamma}$). Rayleigh fading channel, $N = 10$, $g = 0.2$.

required by P802.22b. It is observed that for a Rayleigh fading channel with higher average SNR, higher γ_T^*

is allowed meaning more energy/bandwidth can be saved. This is confirmed by Figure 11 which shows the maximum normalized saved energy/bandwidth as function of the average SNR ($\bar{\gamma}$). When $\bar{\gamma} = 15$, γ_T^* can be set as 18 dB and about 68% energy/bandwidth can be saved for $g = 0.2$. Fog $g = 0.6$, i.e., 60% of S-CPEs are Group-1 S-CPEs with upstream bandwidth, in most cases ($\bar{\gamma} > 9$ dB), the Group-1 S-CPEs can meet spectrum sensing requirement of $max\{Q_m^*, Q_f^*\} \leq$ 10%, therefore, it may require no Group-2 S-CPEs to participate spectrum sensing, indicating that for a channel with good SNR and high g, all Group-2 S-CPEs may not sense spectrum so more energy can be saved.

6. Discussion and Conclusion

Due to the performance limitation of energy detection in complex condition, the assumed average SNR is relatively high. The required SNR for target performance could be decreased by applying other advanced sensing technologies, for example, feature detection used in [16, 17] can detect PU signal with low SNR of around -20 dB.

In conclusion, IEEE P802.22b engages two-hop network structure which each R-CPE connecting with an MR-BS and a great number of S-CPEs requiring low-cost and power/bandwidth-saving designs; in this study an energy/bandwidth saving CSS scheme is proposed for P802.22b to meet the design requirement of the S-CPEs while still maintain the sensing performance. With the proposed scheme, when an S-CPE without upstream bandwidth detects the presence of PU, it reports to a R-CPE only if the detected SNR is above a pre-defined SNR threshold. Numerical results show that with the proposed CSS, the fused miss-detection probability becomes higher and the fused false alarm probability becomes lower, while the overall error probability changes very little. It is possible to save more than 40% to 50% energy/bandwidth when 10 or 20 S-CPEs are instructed to sense a fading channel. Although energy detection is considered in this study for simplicity in analysis, the proposed principle may be applied to other sensing technologies with higher performance.

References

[1] IEEE Standard for Information Technology-Telecommunications and information exchange between systems Wireless Regional Area Networks (WRAN)àłSpecific requirements, Part 22: Cognitive Wireless RAN Medium Access Control (MAC) and Physical Layer (PHY) Specifications: Policies and Procedures for Operation in the TV Bands, IEEE Std 802.22-2011, IEEE-SA Standards Board, 2011

[2] PAR of the IEEE PP802.22b - Amendment to the IEEE Std-802.22-2011(TM): Enhancements for

Broadband Services and Monitoring Applications, http://www.ieee802.org/22/p802.22b_PAR_Approved.pdf

[3] H.N. Pham, Y. Zhang, P.E. Engelstad, T. Skeie, and F. Eliassen, "Energy minimization approach for optimal cooperative spectrum sensing in sensor-aided cognitive radio networks", WICON 2010, pp.1-9, Singapore, Mar 2010

[4] E. Peh and Y.C. Liang, "Optimization for cooperative sensing in cognitive radio networks", IEEE WCNC 2007, pp. 27-32, Hong Kong, Mar 2007

[5] F.D. Fadel, Mohamed-Slim Alouini, and K.S. Marvin, "On the energy detection of unknown signals over fading channels", IEEE ICC'03, pp. 3575 - 3579, vol.5, Anchorage, AK, USA, May 2003

[6] T. Yücek and H. Arslan, "A survey of spectrum sensing algorithms for cognitive radio applications", IEEE Commun. Surveys & Tutorials, vol. 11, no. 1, first quater 2009, pp.116-130

[7] K.B. Letaief and W. Zhang, "Cooperative communications for cognitive radio networks", Proceeding of the IEEE, Vol. 97, No. 5, May 2009

[8] Y. Zhang, J. Xiang, X. Qin, and G. E. Øien, "Optimal sensing cooperation for spectrum sharing in cognitive radio networks", European Wireless 2009, pp. 216-221, Denmark, May 2009

[9] W.-B. Chien, C.-K. Yang, and Y.-H. Huang, "Energy-saving cooperative spectrum sesning processor for cognitive radio system", IEEE Trans. Circuits Syst. I, Reg. papers, vol. 58, no. 4, Apr 2011, pp.711-723

[10] R. Deng, J. Chen, C. Yuen, P. Cheng, and Y. Sun, "Energy-efficient cooperative spectrum sensing by optimal scheduling in sensor-aided cognitive radio networks",

IEEE Trans. Veh. Technol., vol. 61, No. 2, Feb 2012, pp. 716-725

[11] M. Najimi, A. Ebrahimzadeh, S.M. H. Andargoli, and A. Fallahi, "A novel method for energy-efficient cooperative spectrum sensing in cognitive sensor networks", IST'2012, pp. 255-260, Tehran, Nov 2012

[12] W. Zhang, R.K. Mallik,and K.B. Letaief, "Optimization of cooperative spectrum sensing with energy detection in cognitive radio networks", IEEE Tran. Wireless Commun., Vol. 8, No. 12, pp. 5761-5766, Dec 2009

[13] H. Tang, "Some physical layer issues of wide-band cognitive radio systems", IEEE Dyspan 2005, pp. 151-159, USA, Nov 2005

[14] A. Wiesel, J. Goldberg, and Hagit Messer-Yaron, "SNR Estimation in Time-Varying Fading Channels", IEEE Tran. Commun., Vol. 54, No. 5, pp. 841-848, May 2006

[15] David R. Pauluzzi and Norman C. Beaulieu, "A Comparison of SNR Estimation Techniques for the AWGN Channel", IEEE Tran. Commun., Vol. 48, No. 10, pp. 1681-1691, Oct 2000

[16] Chunyi Song and Hiroshi Harada, "Proposal and Hardware Implementation of a Partial Bandwidth Based Feature Detection Method for Sensing under Adjacent Channel Interference," IEEE Transactions on Wireless Communications, Vol.12, Issue 11, pp.5444-5453, Nov. 2013

[17] Chunyi Song, Matsumura Takeshi and Hiroshi Harada,"A Prototype of TV White Space Spectrum Sensing and Power Measurement," IEICE Trans. on Communications, VOL.E97-B, NO.2, pp 314-325, Feb. 2014

11

Group-Based Museum Audio Dramas for Well-Being

Charles Callaway[1,*] and Oliviero Stock[2]

[1]TrentoRISE, via Sommarive, 20, Povo (TN) 38100, Italy
[2]FBK-irst, via Sommarive, 18, Povo (TN) 38100, Italy

Abstract

Well-being in a small group can be tied to how much its members interact. Small group tours are social occasions, and the discussion that ensues has been shown by ethnographers to be important for a more enriching experience. Increasing conversation can thus be seen as a way to improve social and psychological well-being. We present DramaTric, a mobile presentation system that delivers hour-long dramas to groups in museums. DramaTric gets sensor data from its environment and analyzes group behavior to deliver dynamically adapted dramatic scenes designed to stimulate conversation. Each scene contains slight differences in the story, leading visitors to understand their own drama only by talking with other group members. We describe an experiment with a full-scale drama to test if switching from presenting a drama with one technique to another results in more conversation. This shows that by using adaptive techniques we can modify social behavior, which can in turn promote well-being.

Keywords: Groups, cultural heritage, mobile and ubiquitous systems, ambient sensors and systems, drama.

1. Introduction

Improvements in the well-being of social groups can be gauged socially, emotionally and psychologically. But for implemented real-time mobile systems, such improvements must be measured quantitatively in order to have an impact on the system's adaptive responses to ongoing group behavior. In cultural heritage settings, such as museums and art galleries, social groups are accustomed to interacting via conversation. In fact, social groups are the dominant means of museum attendance [10], and conversation has been shown to be important in whether groups in such settings experience more positive visits [9]. We thus see adapations by the system as a purposeful way to increase conversation, and thus the well-being of groups touring cultural heritage sites.

Additionally, the deployment of audio guides in the last two decades has been characterized by fact-based exhibit descriptions and the semi-isolation of group members whose audio guides are not aware of each other. Such implementations can lead to a decrease in engagement on the part of group members which is an important factor in how much conversation takes place. A different approach to increasing engagement and thus conversation is to use presentations that evoke emotion, such as performed narrative like drama or film [2].

We created the DramaTric system (Drama Tension Release by Inducing Conversation) which uses a novel group-oriented approach integrating sensors and analysis of the resulting sensor data into a coordinated narrative system for mobile devices (specifically, smartphones and tablets as presentation devices) in a museum instrumented for ambient intelligence. DramaTric is based on adaptive narration, where by adaptivity we mean using observed and inferred characteristics of group behavior to choose when and which drama-based presentation to show, as well as how to link successive dramatic scenes together. DramaTric allows a group of visitors to move freely around a museum along any path they choose, and produces a larger drama by stitching together smaller drama segments and ensuring a coherent narrative regardless of that path. Sensors both in the museum and worn by the visitors allow DramaTric to know (a) where individual group members are, (b) objective characteristics such as proximity between members, speaker, and length of conversational turns, and (c)

*Corresponding author. Email: ccallawa@gmail.com

inferrable characteristics, such as who is the group leader, or how much time they spend near each other.

The specific method we use to increase conversation involves presenting slightly varied narratives for different individuals or subgroups of a small group while they are listening to the same dramatic scene. We purposefully create these variations by allowing some visitors to hear parts of the narration that others do not. We thus create conditions where visitors can only understand each drama segment by filling in the details that their fellows lack, resulting in subsequent conversation. Below we describe this methodology in further detail, followed by a description of the hardware, architecture, and adaptivity mechanism, and the description of an experiment in an actual museum that shows narrative variations can lead to significant differences in the amount of conversation immediately after the conclusion of each audio drama. We thus show that it is possible to increase conversation within a group, lending support to the hypothesis for increasing group well-being.

2. Narrative Variations and Drama Presentation

The methodology we have created for promoting interaction, and especially conversation, is to give group members dramatic presentations with a particular type of unresolved narrative tension that forces them to talk to each other to relieve that tension. We use the term tension to indicate that the visitor listening to the audio drama is engaged in the museum experience and hears a drama where certain information critical to understanding the narrative is removed in a *coordinated way*, or that it is different from what other group members hear. Group members will then notice that this content in our dramatic narrative variations is incomplete [3], and then act on this by questioning or discussing with their fellow group members, actively leading to a more general conversation ranging from the themes showcased in the museum to those themes in their daily lives. In other words, we want to purposefully increase narrative tension in the audio dramas heard by members of a small group, and let the natural curiosity inspired by that narrative tension spur the resolution of that tension, *i.e.*, by finding the missing narrative information that completes the story.

As our specific mechanism, we present slightly different audio dramas to different group members by selectively withholding information from some members of a group but not others. Thus person A hears something important that person B doesn't, and vice versa. We connect narrative variations to increased conversation by purposefully writing the dramas and manipulating the audio in such a way that each scene is missing one of the key points that narratively completes that scene. By carefully structuring these "information gaps", each person can be given content that their fellow group members require in order for them to completely understand the events in their own scene. We have developed three specific techniques to provide for this narrative content variation:

- *Telephone*: A one-sided conversation style where the audio of only one character can be heard as if talking via telephone. Pauses, music or sound effects are inserted when the other character, whom we can't hear, is speaking.

- *Audio blurring*: This technique "overlays" the dialogue at selected points with some source of ambient noise (*e.g.*, seagulls screaming, children yelling, the sound of waves or wind, etc.). The dialogue at these key points is thus rendered unintelligible. However, the group members can still tell that the characters are conversing, as the volume of the interference is just below the volume of the dialogue.

- *Point of View Change*: When there is a social conflict between two or more characters, we can allow each character to present their own viewpoint without interference. We thus have two or more monologues instead of a dialogue that reflects the point of view of specific characters, while other group members hear the point of view of a different character.

Museums typically consist of a large number of exhibits organized thematically in a number of different exhibit halls. Visitors can choose which route to take between the halls, skipping some exhibits entirely and exploring the others in whatever order they prefer. A principal difficulty is thus to maintain coherence regardless of which order the drama segments are heard, and even if some dramas are completly skipped. In our approach, we present a series of short, self-contained dramas for visitors in front of certain major exhibits or important locations, where the specific technique of narrative variation is based on adaptivity criteria described below. We found that when our drama tour was fully completed, an overall drama across 5 exhibit halls and consisting of 14 individual short audio dramas required between 35 and 55 minutes.

We utilized 4 distinct types of audio drama, each with its own role in maintaining the story arc and tension:

- Fixed drama segments: 30-second to 2-minute-long self-contained dramas that are standardized for every visitor. These function to set up the drama (introduction and initial development) and to bring the drama to a conclusion.

- Primary drama segments: 1- to 2-minute-long self-contained dramas with a cast of characters and an identifiable plot, written for a particular exhibit. Immediately after the completion of a primary drama segment, there is a 1-minute observation period of the behavior of the group members, and the results of that observation are used to adaptively select a set of linking segments and a technique (described below) to employ for the next primary drama segment.

- Secondary drama segments: 1-minute long dramas without narrative variations and not followed by an observation period. They serve to introduce the visitors to a new exhibit hall, artifacts of lesser importance, or to new characters who will play a role in later dramatic presentations.
- Linking segments: Because each drama segment is independent and the order they are played in is determined by the path visitors take through the museum, the end of one dramatic presentations may not match up coherently to the start of the second without some means of tying the scenes together. We thus use multiple *linking* segments, lasting about 10 seconds each, between the drama segments to provide continuity and to help the visitors perceive that the system is reacting adaptively to their behavior.

Because high quality acting and production values are critical to believability and engagement, our drama segments are not currently generated automatically, but instead are written by dramatists and recorded by voice actors with drama experience. To reinforce to the group members that they are seeing a drama rather than hearing about dry scientific facts, we import familiar expectations from drama and theatre, such as the bell chimes used to warn of the start of the next performance, animations of red curtains opening and closing on the display screen before and after a performance, and occasionally, applause at the conclusion of the audio drama. Figure 1 shows red curtains opening at the beginning of the presentation; the phone also vibrates at this point to gain attention, but then once the drama has begun, only the audio is active so that the visitor is not distracted.

3. System and Interface

DRAMATRIC presents audio dramas to small groups of museum visitors using smartphones or tablets as the presentation device (each has a color screen, earphones, WiFi, and various internal sensors such as a compass). Each device communicates with the other devices in the group and with a coordinating server [8], and receives updates once per second for position, orientation, proximity and voice information coming from all the sensor devices belonging to the group. Position is determined by instrumenting the museum with downward-facing WiFi beacons in the ceiling above, while proximity, orientation and voice level are determined by a small neck-worn device. When this device is within range of a beacon, that beacon's code is included in the device's sensor stream and is forwarded to the server and thus other group presentation devices via existing WiFi routers in the museum.

Knowing visitor position is necessary to initiate the proper drama at the right time, while visitor proximity enables the system to determine the degree of group cohesion. Individual voice activity detection is also important for inferring group conversation, and since the mobile nodes' microphones are pointed upwards towards the wearer's mouth, the difference in intensity of the audio signal between two mobile nodes in close proximity can help determine that conversation is occurring, and its characteristics: who is talking to whom, the length of conversational turns, and who talks most or least. Further inference allows us to assess the effectiveness of any given narrative variation techniques by looking at how much conversation occurred immediately afterwards.

When visitors are walking around the museum and not hearing a presentation, a map of the museum is displayed along with a picture of what they should be seeing around them (Figure 1, left). The visitor's current location on the map is updated whenever the underlying positioning system locks on to them. Once the group arrives at a position with a presentation, the map disappears, the curtains open, and a static drama scene is shown while the audio drama plays.

While group members listen to their audio channel, on their own phone's screen they see a set of images representing the main and supporting characters speaking in that drama, along with information about who or what they and the other group members are hearing. For instance, if visitors Antonio and Emily are listening to a scene on a ship, Emily might be listening to the ship's carpenter while seeing a large picture of the carpenter with a message saying "You are hearing the Carpenter", next to a small picture of the captain with a message under it saying "Antonio is hearing the Captain", while Antonio sees the version appropriate for him. The screen's graphics are deliberately kept simple to enable visitors to quickly understand there are hearing variations, and to allow visitors to spend more time looking at the artifacts or interacting with each other rather than staring at their smartphones.

Visitors hear self-contained drama segments that are combined adaptively and dynamically, and the next variation technique can be algorithmically determined based on sensor data. Our baseline algorithm sums up the voice level readings during a 1-minute "observation period" after drama presentations. If this average is above a threshold we assume that the current technique is working and retain it for the next drama; otherwise it switches technique to see if a new one will increase conversation after the next presentation.

Figure 1. DRAMATRIC graphic interface: museum map, start of a drama, and variations for different visitors.

To our knowledge research of group activity has rarely emphasized the mobile aspect. One of the closest works is by Kim and colleagues [7], who used a portable device called the "sociometric badge" to monitor speaking activity and other social signals in a team. Their work does not involve precise positioning and their aim is mainly meant to give feedback to individuals about overall group behavior via a graphical representation of the group behavior on a private display. However, their goal was very different: through reflection on their individual behavior, as represented on the display, participants were shown to better respect speech turns and to reduce overlap when talking. Other localization approaches have been used in specific situations and can be costly [12], or have been based on readily available technology like GPS and are thus more suited for outdoor use [5].

4. Technique Switch Museum Experiment

We wanted to explore the space of potential adaptivity functions by looking at a Technique Switch hypothesis: that changing from one variation technique to another in successive audio drama scenes will have an impact on the amount and/or quality of conversation. Specifically, we chose to test two dramas using the telephone technique, then either continuing with the same technique (Condition 1) or changing to the Blurring technique in the third drama (Condition 2). This allowed us to test the consequences of changing technique with an eye toward exploring what types of adaptivity might be successful.

Changing the narrative technique is per se a very dynamic element of the system, representing a true point of adaptivity. It may for instance help keep visitors' attention high or add to the general level of curiosity, but it may also have unforeseen consequences, such as causing too much confusion. While a variety of

selection algorithms may be used in a final deployment, for this experiment we purposefully started with what corresponds to a naïve hypothesis, namely that if the system determines that a given technique is no longer successful with this group, then it would change to another technique. The Technique Switch hypothesis we chose reflects this simplicity: does switching variation technique at a single point lead to more conversation immediately after that switch?

Before each pair arrived, the system was initialized and the microphone signal was synchronized to the system's sensor data. Each pair was assigned to one of two conditions, either hearing a drama with the telephone technique at all three primary drama positions (Condition 1), or hearing the telephone technique twice followed by the Blurring technique for the third position (Condition 2). Our reason for not switching technique immediately after the first position was to minimize bias stemming from the "surprise" of hearing different audio for the first time (this did in fact occur, with a 6% increase between the first two audio dramas that used the same technique). We did not specifically control for story quality effects, and we allowed pairs to choose their own path and then checked post-hoc for balance.

Subjects were either native or very fluent English speakers, recruited via posters placed around the University of Haifa campus where the Hecht Museum is located, and were paid 50 shekels each (about $10) for their participation. 29 subjects were between 18 and 30 years old, 8 subjects between 30 and 45, and 3 were older than 45. There were 17 women and 23 men, and 17 of the pairs described their relationship as being friends (1 as classmates, 2 as a couple). The subjects were reasonably balanced across the two conditions for a number of criteria: age, gender, native language, time

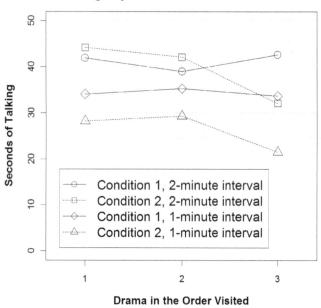

Figure 2. Talking change by condition.

of day of their tour, relationship, the order of exhibits visited, and the last exhibit visited.

After the subjects arrived and gave their consent for participation and data collection, they were shown how to use the device, and how to find their way to the beacon positions using the map on the device. They were explicitly told that they could go through the rooms in any order, that they might not hear everything the characters are saying, and that they might not hear the same thing as each other.

For the experiment 20 pairs of subjects walked through the museum listening to the dramas at each position with a smartphone equipped with earphones. They were given brief training, showing them how to use the device, and how to find their way to the beacon positions using the included map. To determine how much each pair talked, as well as the content of their conversations after the experimental manipulation, we attached a small digital voice recorder to the mobile node worn around their necks.

The resulting experiment data are 20 pairs of audio files, each about 1 hour, and the associated system events (such as initiating playback of an audio drama). Because a prior formative experiment [4] had shown that some subjects talked to each other about the ongoing audio drama while it was still playing (and thus presumably talked less during the observation interval immediately afterwards) we extracted 2 minutes of audio data per drama per pair: from 1 minute before the beginning of the observation

interval through the end of the 1-minute interval. We sent the resulting 2-minute audio files for professional transcription, with later in-house correction where possible. Some subjects who were near-native English speakers spoke in Hebrew, so we translated those portions of their transcripts into English.

The data thus consists of 6,840 total seconds of audio (19 pairs x 3 dramas x 2 minutes), for a total of 951 annotated turns. The average pair talked for 120.8 out of 360 seconds (33.6%, SD=50.7sec) and had 50 turns (SD=24.5). In condition 1, the average pair talked for 122.3 seconds (SD=26.5) with 47 turns (SD=18.0), while in condition 2 the average pair talked for 118.9 seconds (SD=67.2) with 52.5 turns (SD=29.9). Thus conversations in condition 2 showed significantly more variation in length and number of turns than those in condition 1. Frequent overlapping of turns was seen for the most talkative pairs, and only a few of the least talkative pairs had a dominant speaker, as measured by time but not turns. The longest utterance was 25 seconds and the longest dialogue was 36 turns.

To confirm the Technique Switch hypothesis, we needed to look at how much subject pairs talked to each other immediately after hearing the audio drama. We thus measured the amount of talking in 1-second intervals over the 1-minute period in terms of total elapsed time, conversational turns and semantic annotations. The results show that pairs in Condition 2 talk slightly more in the first two dramas, but immediately after in drama 3 there is a striking change: pairs in Condition 1 talk significantly more $\chi^2(1, 1476) = 11.8, p < 0.001$ than in Condition 2 (Figure 2). Thus the general hypothesis was confirmed: switching techniques had a significant impact on the amount of conversation immediately after the switch. Because conversation also occurred while the audio drama was still playing, we also examined the 2-minute period centered at the end of the drama, but there was no change: the amount of talking was still significantly lower after switching technique in the third primary drama segment (32.1 seconds for Condition 2 compared to 42.56 seconds for Condition 1, or a 24.6% decrease, $\chi^2(1, 1476) = 21.2, p < 0.001$). Thus we can confirm that adaptive manipulations can have a significant impact on the amount of group conversation.

We also conducted a semantic conversation analysis of the tours using the following annotation scheme:
1: Silence – No conversation occurs in the interval.
2: Indecipherable – Whispering, or face turned away.
3: Irrelevant – Unrelated to the museum/experiment.
4: Experiment – Talk about the experiment itself.
5: Technique – Discussion about narrative variations.
6: Content – Discussion about the museum exhibits.

As can be seen in Table 1, most conversation is devoted to talking about museum themes, followed by talking about the experiment itself (which decreases

Table 1. Content-categorized talking by condition, with proportion of category given total available time.

	D1-2	D1-3	D1-4	D1-5	D1-6		D2-2	D2-3	D2-4	D2-5	D2-6		D3-2	D3-3	D3-4	D3-5	D3-6
TOTAL	23	72	266	156	301		24	136	151	65	396		35	74	179	57	360
Cond 1	6	46	120	55	151		9	63	44	47	188		24	46	73	32	209
Cond 2	17	26	148	101	150		15	73	107	18	208		11	28	106	25	151
C1 %	0.3%	2.0%	5.2%	2.4%	6.6%		0.4%	2.7%	1.9%	2.0%	8.2%		1.0%	2.0%	3.2%	1.4%	9.1%
C2 %	0.7%	1.1%	6.4%	4.4%	6.5%		0.7%	3.2%	4.7%	0.8%	9.1%		0.5%	1.2%	4.6%	1.1%	6.6%

after the first drama as the pairs become accustomed to the hardware and the procedure). The table shows this data grouped by drama position number (which is variable as each pair chose their own path) where a given drama m and semantic code n is labeled D$m - n$. Indecipherable talk and talk about unrelated themes remains minimal as the pairs proceed through the museum, providing evidence that pairs were engaged with the audio drama tour. As before, contentful discussion in condition 1 increases, while in condition 2 it rises then falls after the adaptive change in technique.

5. Conclusions and Future Work

We have described the DramaTric system that presents audio dramas for small groups in cultural heritage settings for the purpose of increasing group conversation, which ethnographs have shown leads to more enriching cultural experiences. DramaTric uses museum sensor data such as current visitor position to adaptively modify the audio dramas. Using specific techniques to create narrative variations that different group members hear, we intentionally try to manipulate conversation (and thus social interaction) as a reaction to those variations. We created audio dramas for the Hecht Museum at the University of Haifa, and conducted a full-scale experiment that successfully determined that changing the narrative variation technique could in fact lead to observable differences in group behavior, namely the amount of conversation immediately after an adaptive action. This should lead to specific proposals for promoting social and psychological well-being by changing group dynamics in positive ways.

We are currently extending DramaTric to support remote participation where a family tours the museum while a relative, an elderly shut-in who cannot go to the museum in person, can participate as a group member and remotely experience both the drama tour and what their family members are seeing and saying.

References

[1] Aoki, P., Grinter, R., Hurst, A., Szymanski, M., Thornton, J. and Woodruff, A. (2002) Sottovoce:
Exploring the interplay of conversation and mobile audio spaces. In *Proceedings of ACM SIGCHI*: 431–438.

[2] Baum, L., and Hughes, C. (2001) Ten Years of Evaluating Science Theater at the Museum of Science, Boston. *Curator: The Museum Journal*, **55**(4), 355–369.

[3] Callaway, C., Stock, O., DeKoven, E., Noy, K., Citron, Y., and Dobrin, Y. (2011) Mobile drama in an instrumented museum: Inducing group conversation via coordinated narratives. In *Proceedings of the 16th International Conference on Intelligent User Interfaces.* ACM, New York, NY, USA, 73–82.

[4] Callaway, C., Stock, O., DeKoven, E., Noy, K., Citron, Y., and Dobrin, Y. (2012) Mobile Drama in an Instrumented Museum: Inducing Group Conversation via Coordinated Narratives. *New Review of Hypermedia and Multimedia*, **18**(1–2), 37–61.

[5] Cheverst, K., Davies, N., Mitchell, K., Friday, A., and Efstratiou, C. (2000) Developing a context-aware tourist guide: some issues and experiences. In *Proceedings of the International Conference on Computer-Human Interaction*, ACM New York, NY, USA, The Hague, Netherlands, 17–24.

[6] Damiano, R., Gena, C., Lombardo, V., Nunnari, F. and Pizzo, A. (2008) A stroll with Carletto: adaptation in drama-based tours with virtual characters. *UMUAI* .

[7] Kim, T.J., Chang, A., Holland, L., and Pentland, A.S. (2008) Meeting Mediator: Enhancing Group Collaboration with Sociometric Feedback, In *Proceedings of the ACM Conference on Computer-Human Interaction*, Florence, 3183–3188.

[8] Kuflik, T., Stock, O., Zancanaro, M., Gorfinkel, A., Jbara, S., Kats, S., Sheidin, J. et al. (2011) A visitor's guide in an "active museum": Presentations, communications, and reflection. *Computing and Cultural Heritage of the ACM* **3**(3).

[9] Leinhardt, G. and Knutson, K. (2004) *Listening in on Museum Conversations* (Altamira Press).

[10] Petrelli, D. and Not, E. (2005) User-centred design of flexible hypermedia for a mobile guide: Reflections on the hyperaudio experience. *UMUAI* .

[11] Stock, O., Zancanaro, M., Busetta, P., Callaway, C., Krüger, A., Kruppa, M., Kuflik, T. et al. (2007) Adaptive, intelligent presentation of information for the museum visitor in PEACH. *UMUAI* .

[12] Zimmermann, A., and Lorenz, A. (2008) LISTEN: a user-adaptive audio-augmented museum guide. *User Modeling and User-Adapted Interaction*, **18**(5), 389–416.

12

Effective sensor positioning to localize target transmitters in a Cognitive Radio Network

Audri Biswas[1], Sam Reisenfeld[1,*], Mark Hedley, Zhuo Chen[2]

[1]Department of Engineering, Faculty of Science and Engineering, Macquarie University, NSW 2109, Australia
[2]Digital Productivity Flagship, CSIRO, NSW 2122, Australia

Abstract

A precise positioning of transmitting nodes enhances the performance of Cognitive Radio (CR), by enabling more efficient dynamic allocation of channels and transmit powers for unlicensed users. Most localization techniques rely on random positioning of sensor nodes where, few sensor nodes may have a small separation between adjacent nodes. Closely spaced nodes introduces correlated observations, effecting the performance of Compressive Sensing (CS) algorithm. This paper introduces a novel minimum distance separation aided compressive sensing algorithm (MDACS). The algorithm selectively eliminates Secondary User (SU) power observations from the set of SU receiving terminals such that pairs of the remaining SUs are separated by a minimum geographic distance. We have evaluated the detection of multiple sparse targets locations and error in l_2-norm of the recovery vector. The proposed method offers an improvement in detection ratio by 20% while reducing the error in l_2-norm by 57%.

Keywords: Cognitive Radio, Compressive Sensing, Radio Environment Map, Localization, Power Measurements.

1. Introduction

The spectrum scarcity along with inefficient spectrum usage has motivated the development of *Cognitive Radio* (CR). The increasing demand of high data rates due to large numbers of portable hand-held devices initiated significant research in the field of interference mitigation and effective spectral utilization. CR provides a promising solution to the existing problem by efficiently using the underutilized spectrum to facilitate services by *Dynamic Spectrum Sharing* (DSS) for both licensed and unlicensed users. CR technology is based on the concept of learning the state of channel use of *Primary Users* (PUs), and subsequent efficient allocation of channels and transmit parameters to *Secondary Users* (SUs). This allocation takes into account maximum acceptable interference levels to PUs and the throughput and performance requirements of SUs.

In a Cognitive Radio Network, both PUs and SUs share the same channels. Since SUs have lower priority, the channel use is constrained by a maximum acceptable level of interference to PUs. Many efforts have been made in previous literature [1][2] to tackle the issue of interference mitigation but only a few research papers have been published on channel collision avoidance based on the utilization of a *Radio Environment Map* (REM). To generate a REM, the locations of the transmitters and their transmit power levels need to be accurately estimated. From this estimation, the received power level throughout a two dimensional area may be estimated. For the REM, the received power levels interpolated over a two dimensional geographic area are obtained through the use of analytic equations for signal propagation.

In CR, the REM is extremely useful in secondary user channel and transmit parameter selection. This selection must be made with the dual requirements of SU communication effectiveness and bounded interference to PUs. The bounded interference to PUs can only be maintained if the PU locations and received power levels from other PUs, are known by SUs. Therefore an accurate REM is crucial for effective CR operation.

In [3], a cooperative algorithm is formulated that

*Corresponding author. Email: Audri.biswas,Sam.Reisenfeld@mq.edu.au takes the received signal strength at each SU to create a weighting function and uses it to compute the location of multiple PUs. Although it has relatively low computational complexity, it requires a high density of SUs, and the performance degrades with channel fading. The work in [4] and[5] is based on the concept of using sectorized antennas to detect Direction of Arrival (DOA) of a signal. The phase information of a received signal is exploited to estimate the position of PUs. However, this technique might not be feasible for a practical CRN implementation due to antenna requirements which may be impractical for portable devices.

In this paper we adopt a Compressive Sensing (CS) technique to retrieve the locations of multiple transmitting PUs in a CRN. The approach relies on a location fingerprinting approach, where a certain geographic area is discretised into equally spaced grid points. The PUs are assumed to be positioned at a subset of the grid points. The SUs are also assumed to be positioned at some known locations in the area of interest. Each SU measures Received Signal Strength (RSS) from target PUs. From this set of measurements, there is an attempt to recover the PU locations and transmit power levels. It is usually the case that the number of PUs is much smaller than the number of grid points. Consequently, the set of equations for power levels transmitted by PUs is underdetermined and there are many possible solutions. When the number of PUs is much smaller than the number of grid points, the sparsest solution for the set of equations yields accurate power levels at the correct grid points. Compressive sensing can be used to obtain the data required for the formulation of the REM. Similar techniques were used in [6], [7], [8] and [9].

In a physical system, some of the SUs will be closely geographically located. Having closely placed SUs introduces correlated observations which may increase the observation coherence. Performance of CS algorithms relies heavily on the coherence of the observations from SUs. High coherence among the power measurements makes it difficult for matrix inversion, which may cause inaccurate recovery of the sparse vector. To improve the performance of the CS algorithm, we propose a novel Min-dis-aided CS (MDACS) algorithm. The approach aims to improve the performance of CS algorithms by selectively removing measurements of closely spaced SUs from the set, such as to increase the minimum distance separation between adjacent SUs. The algorithm priorities the RSS of a SU before completely eliminating it from the set. The process generates a refined set of SUs with certain distance separation and high RSS. Our method achieved superior detection of multiple PUs with significantly fewer SU measurements, compared to random deployment of SUs.

In this paper, the locations of SUs are specified by two

dimensional vectors. Both the cases of uniform distribution and Gaussian distribution were considered for the random assignment of SU positions. Irrespective of distribution used, our novel approach of pre-selecting SU power measurements appears to achieve reliable detection ratio with fewer receiving nodes. Section II discusses the background of compressive sensing. Sections III-V describe the system model. Section VI-IX presents the simulation results which validate the effectiveness of our proposed method. The conclusion is given in Section VII.

2. Compressive Sensing

The CS technique is an approach for the solution of an under-determined set of equations for which the solution vector is known to be sparse. Some data vectors are sparse while others can be made more sparse by an appropriate basis transformation. A typical example would be the time frequency pair. A signal, which is a linear combination of several frequency components, can be easily retrieved by exploiting the sparsity in frequency domain. The complex Fourier Transform basis functions can be used to represent the time domain signal with few non-zero coefficients. In such case the CS algorithm can be used to obtain a sparsest solution vector to a set of underdetermined equations. The sparse vector, $x_{N \times 1}$ is the solution with the minimum number of non-zero elements. If $y_{M \times 1}$ is the raw observation vector obtained by the SU power measurments, there exist the following relationship,

$$y = \phi x, \tag{1}$$

where $\phi_{M \times N}$ is a measurement matrix, representing the power propagation losses from each grid point to each SU. In [7] it states that, a matrix ϕ satisfies *Restricted Isometry Property* (RIP) condition, when all subsets of S columns chosen from ϕ are nearly orthogonal. Once this is true, there is a high probability of completely recovering the sparse vector with at least $M = CK \times \log_e(N/K)$ measurements (where K is the number of PUs and C is a positive constant) using l_1-minimization algorithm [10]. This can be can be expressed as,

$$min \left\| \vec{x} \right\|_1 = min \sum_i |x_i|$$

subject to

$$\vec{y} = \phi \vec{x}. \tag{2}$$

This formulation is valid for a noiseless scenario but when external noise is considered the algorithm is modified to a *Second-Order Cone Program* for an optimized solution for a defined threshold [10]. This can be stated as,

$$min \left\| \vec{x} \right\|_1 = min \sum_i |x_i|$$

subject to

$$\left\| \vec{y} = \phi \vec{x} \right\|_2 \leq \varepsilon, \qquad (3)$$

where $\|\cdot\|_p$ is the l_p−norm and ε is the relaxation constraint for measurement errors. The sparest solution for $\vec{x}$ is the solution with minimum $\|\vec{x}\|_0$. However, the CS algorithm is effective because the same solution vector usually has minimum l_0 norm and minimum l_1 norm [10].

3. System Model

Let us consider a square area discretized into equally spaced $P \times P$ grid where, K PUs are randomly positioned at unique grid points. For simplicity of illustration, we assume that each PU is assigned a single dedicated sub-channel to carry out duplex communication with the base station. Now to observe radio environment and detect the free spectrum, M SUs are deployed randomly in the area of interest. Unlike [6] and [8] the SUs are not placed on the grid points. We adapted a more realistic approach of allowing the SUs to be placed at some known locations in the area. They have the added flexibility of being positioned at non-discretized points on the map. The SUs are controlled and managed by a central node called the *Fusion Centre* (FC). There exist a common control channel between central node and SUs for effective communication of RSS observations and channel allocation information. The FC processes the signal level measurements and manages SU channel allocation. The most crucial assumption in the model is that, spatial coordinates of both the grid points and SUs are known a priori by the FC which receives sensing information from each individual SU. The received power at a SU is a function of distance between the PU and SU as well as shadowing loss. The wireless channels are corrupted by noise and are also considered to be affected by lognormal shadowing. The simplified path-loss model as a function of distance may be described as,

$$Pathloss_{dB}(d) = K_1 + 10\eta log_{10}(\frac{d}{d_0}) + \alpha, \qquad (4)$$

where,

d is transmission distance in meters,

d_0 is the reference distance of the antenna far field,

K_1 is a dimensionless constant in dB,

η is the propagation loss exponent,

α is the shadowing loss in dB.

K_1 is a unit-less constant that relies on the antenna characteristics and average channel attenuation and $K_1 dB = 10log_{10}(K_1)$ [11]. α accounts for the random attenuation of signal strength due to shadowing where α in dB scale is a Gaussian random variable with

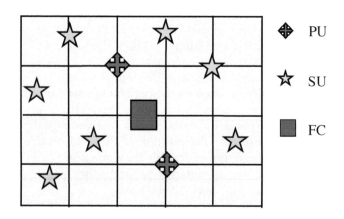

Figure 1. System model demonstrating the positioning of PU, SU and FC

zero mean and standard deviation $\sigma_{dB} = 5.5$dB [3]. This model was used in [3] for both multipath and shadowing characterization.

4. Localization using compresive sensing

This section combines the location dependent RSS information at each SU to formulate a sparse matrix problem, which can then be solved using the CS method to obtain the exact location of PUs in a CRN. Our grid layout consists of N grid points, with grid resolution w in both x-axis and y-axis. The N grid points are located at $\{V_n, 1 \leq n \leq N\}$, where V_n is a two dimensional position vector. The M SUs are located at $\{U_m, 1 \leq m \leq M\}$, where U_m is also a two dimensional position vector. Earlier in Section III we mentioned K PUs are positioned only at K discrete grids where $K < N$. The FC is assumed to have prior knowledge of V_n and U_m. Using the distance information and signal propagation model described in (4) a measurement matrix Φ is constructed. The entries of the matrix are the channel gain and are expressed using the following equations,

$$d_{mn} = \| U_m - V_n \|_2, \qquad (5)$$

$$\Phi_{mn} = 10^{\frac{-Pathloss_{dB}(d_{mn})}{10}}, \qquad (6)$$

where d_{mn} is the distance between m^{th} SU and n^{th} grid point and Φ_{mn} is the pathloss between m^{th} SU and n^{th} grid point. Let Y be a $M \times 1$ column vector where the mth element, Y_m, represents the summation of received power from K PUs on m^{th} SU.

$$Y_m = \sum_{k=1}^{K} Q_{m,k}, \qquad (7)$$

where,

$$Q_{m,k} = 10^{\frac{Q_{m,k,dB}}{10}}$$

and,

$$Q_{m,k,dB} = P_{k,t} - Pathloss_{dB}(d_{mk})$$

where, $Q_{m,k}$ is the power received at SU m which

was transmitted by PU k,

$P_{k,t}$ is the power transmitted by user k,

and, $d_{m,k}$ is the distance between SU m and

PU k.

Equation (6) and (7) may be combined to formulate a CS problem similar to (2). It is assumed that the FC has complete knowledge of Φ. Therefore,

$$Y = \Phi X \qquad (8)$$

with $X_{N \times 1}$ being a $N \times 1$ column vector, that is to be recovered using CS approach described in Section II. In a realistic scenario, the observations are corrupted with noise power vector P_n. The elements of P_n are statistically independent with variance σ_n^2, and are chi-square distributed with 1 degree of freedom. We can include the effect of additive noise by,

$$Y_n = \Phi X + P_n. \qquad (9)$$

Since the model assumes having only few PUs on a large grid size N, the vector $X_{N \times 1}$ satisfies the sparsity requirement for accurate recovery using a CS algorithm. Due to its sparse condition, the vector will have only few nonzero elements representing the transmit powers while the indices corresponding to non-zero elements indicate the grid points on which transmitting PUs are located. Hence using a single compressed sensing problem we can jointly estimate both the locations and transmit powers of multiple PUs by solving (3) described in Section II. From the estimation, FS can approximate the received power level throughout a two dimensional area, using the path loss model in (4).

5. Data Processing

Based on the problem formulation in Section IV, $Y_{M \times 1}$ is a power observation vector with each row representing sum of RSS received from K PUs on m^{th} SU, and $\Phi_{M \times N}$ is the measurement matrix with channel gain from each grid point. The small grid separation adds large coherence between the columns of the measurement matrix and this may violate the RIP condition[12]. A matrix transformation may be employed to increase the incoherence between the columns. We adopt a data processing technique described in [6] and [8] to decorrelate the rows which are the observation of signal strength from grid points on each SU. Let T be a

processing operator,

$$T = SR^+ \qquad (10)$$

where, $S = orth(\Phi^T)^T$. The built in function of Matlab, $orth(B)$ returns an orthonormal basis of the range of B, and B^T returns the transpose of B. R^+ is the Moore-Penrose pseudoinverse of a matrix R, where $R = \Phi$. Applying the operator T on both sides of (9) yields,

$$SR^+(Y_n) = SR^+\Phi X + SR^+P_n = S\Phi^+\Phi X$$
$$+ SR^+P_n = Ax + \omega$$

$$Y' = AX + \omega. \qquad (11)$$

Let Y' be $SR^+(Y_n)$, the noisy processed observation vector. $A = S\Phi^+\Phi$ be the processed measurement matrix and $\omega = SR^+P_n$ is the processed measurement noise. The row vectors are being orthogonalised by S while the columns are decorrelated by the influence of $\Phi^+\Phi$. Hence we can claim that matrix A satisfies the RIP condition. Note that [6] and [8] considered $\Phi^+\Phi = \mathbb{I}_N$, as a diagonal identity matrix. Although $\Phi^+\Phi$ acts like an identity on a portion of the space in the sense that it is symmetric. However it is not an identity matrix. After applying the processing operator, CS may be used to recover the sparse vector from processed observation Y', via l_1-minimization program [6].

6. Simulation And Results

The localization accuracy of the CS algorithm can be effected by certain external factors such as *Signal to Noise Ratio* (SNR), shadowing, density of SUs and distribution of SUs. This section analyses the dependency of these factors on the performance parameters of three l_1 constrained optimization algorithms (L1-Magic, OMP and CoSAMP) to produce an accurate result. L1 Magic, CoSAMP, and OMP are three numerical algorithms for constrained l_1 vector optimization [13], [14] and [15]. The performance parameters may be categorized as,

$$DetectionRatio = \left[\frac{PU_{Det}}{PU_{Total}} \right]$$

$$Normalized\ Error\ Per\ Grid\ Point = \frac{1}{N} \left\| X_{org} - X_{est} \right\|_2$$

where PU_{Det} is the number of detected PUs; PU_{Total} is the number of the PUs in the network; X_{org} is the original sparse vector; X_{est} the recovered vector using CS algorithms. The average absolute error between the vectors X_{org} and X_{est} is obtained by simulation. This is used to evaluate the accuracy of the algorithms to reconstruct a sparse vector with a minimum number of non-zero coefficients. Furthermore to study the impact of each factor, the simulation is analyzed independently to demonstrate the robustness and reliability of the algorithms.

6.1. Simulation Setup

The simulation is carried out on a 43×43 (i.e. $N = 1849$) square grid with a grid separation of 80m. Among the 1849 grid points, 10 PUs are uniformly distributed on the grid points. The transmit power is random and uniformly distributed over the range of 1 to 5 Watts. The scenario consists of 160 SUs with a two dimensional, zero mean, Gaussian spatial distribution with standard deviation σ_{sd}. The shadowing factor is log normal distributed.

Simulation (I) - Impact of SNR. Signal to noise ratio is one the crucial factors effecting the performance of each algorithm. SNR is calculated at the receiver as the ratio of average received powers at a SU to σ_n^2. Where,

σ_n^2 is the variance of the additive, zero mean, Gaussian nois

Then,

$$SNR(dB) = 10 \log_{10}(\frac{1}{M} \sum_{i=1}^{M} \frac{Y_i}{\sigma_n^2}).$$

Y_i is the received RSS from all transmitting PUs at i^{th} SU. As the received signal power is position dependent, SNR will vary with respect to the positioning of SUs. Such scenario prompted us to take the average SNR over M elements of the observation vector. Fig 2(a) and (b) shows the plots for detection ratio of PUs and normalized error per grid versus average received SNR in dB. As shown in Fig.2 (a) when SNR < 12dB, L1-Magic performs better than CoSAMP however when SNR > 15dB, CoSAMP outperforms L1-Magic and OMP. At a higher SNR = 25dB, both CoSAMP and L1-Magic achieved a detection ratio of 1 while OMP is at 0.6. Fig.2(b) shows that, with gradual increase in SNR, CoSAMP generates fewer normalized errors per grid compared to L1-Magic and OMP. Even at a low SNR = 15dB, CoSAMP produces 50% and 54% less errors compared to L1-Magic and OMP.

Similation (II) - Sampling Ratio. Sampling ratio $\frac{M}{N}$ is another major factor that has a significant impact on the performance of these algorithms. In this simulation we start with 200 SUs to detect the position of 10 PUs, where at each iteration 20 SUs are randomly removed to observe the effect of reduced sampling points. The SNR is kept constant at 25dB. The plots in Fig.3 follows a similar trend as in Fig.2. At very low sampling ratio of 0.05, almost all three algorithms fails to recover an accurate sparse solution as solving an undermined system with such small number of measurements is not feasible regardless of any methods used. However with increase in sampling ratio, CoSAMP achieves detection ratio of 1 using 10% less SUs compared to L1-Magic. OMP seems to require higher number of SUs to meet the accuracy of CoSAMP and L1-Magic. Similar conclusion

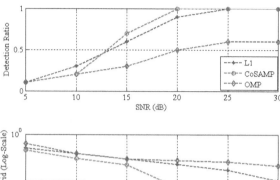
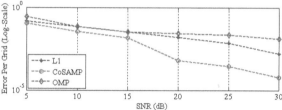

Figure 2. (a) Detection ratio for normal distribution (b) detection ratio for uniform distribution

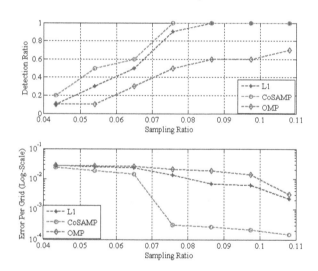

Figure 3. (a) Sampling ratio vs detection ratio (b) sampling ratio vs normalized error per grid

can be drawn from Fig. 3(b), where the graph of normalized error per grid for CoSAMP as a function of sampling ratio decreases much rapidly compared to the other two algorithms. Results from simulation (I) and (II) indicate that, CoSAMP is more robust and can perform with superior results compared to other two algorithms. The next set of simulations will be carried out using CoSAMP and L1-magic only.

7. Impact of SU Distribution

In the previous section, the simulations were carried out using SU positions, generated from a two dimensional, zero mean, Gaussian spatial distribution only. This section analyses the influence of the spread

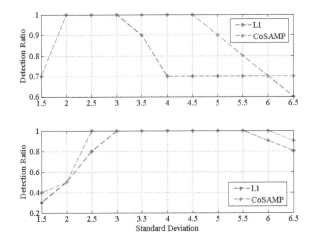

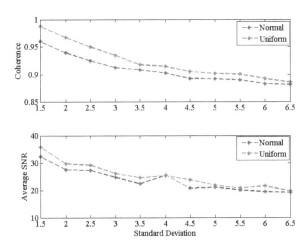

Figure 4. (a) Detection ratio for normal distribution (b) detection ratio for uniform distribution

Figure 5. (a) Spread of distribution vs coherence of measurement matrix (b) spread of distribution vs average received SNR.

of a particular spatial distribution, used to obtain location of SUs in a CRN. The two dimensional SU positions are two dimensional random vectors with statistically independent elements. Two cases were considered. In the first case each element is uniformly distributed over $[-X_{max}\sigma_{sd}, X_{max}\sigma_{sd}]$. In the second case, each element is zero mean Gaussian distributed with standard deviation $\{X_{max}\sigma_{sd}\}$. For each of the cases, simulations were carried out with 100 different scenarios. The PU positions are kept constant and the shadowing factor is log normal distributed. The first set of simulations shows the detection ratio of the optimization algorithms, where uniform distribution and Gaussian distribution were considered for the random assignment of SU positions. The second set aims to provide a deeper insight into the effect of the spread of a particular spatial distribution on the coherence of the measurement matrix Φ and average received SNR at each SU.

While keeping the SNR constant and the number of SUs and PUs constant, the σ_{sd} is varied in the range $[1.5, 6.5]$. Fig. 4 shows the results for the first set of simulations. The figure illustrates the ability to detect the presence of PUs, for a set of SUs drawn from (a) Gaussian normal distribution and (b) uniform distribution respectively. The results are averaged out over 100 scenarios. In Fig 4(a) the SU positions are extracted from a zero mean Gaussian normal distribution. As σ_{sd} is varied, the detection ratio increases from 0.7 to 1 and maintains the maximum, until $\sigma_{sd} = 4$ for L1-Magic and $\sigma_{sd} = 5$ for CoSAMP. When $\sigma_{sd} > 5$, the detection ratio has a downward slope irrespective of the algorithms used. And at $\sigma_{sd} = 6.5$ it reaches a minimum point. The set of SUs extracted from a Gaussian normal distribution have a significant proportion of the SUs

positioned around the origin. With the spread of the distribution gradually increasing, the SUs are pushed further away from the centre. The sharp tail of Gaussian distribution, extending towards infinity often forces some of the SUs to be positioned at a distance, where channel noise is large with respect to received signal strength. This may cause significant error in the construction of measurement matrix. This may also result in an incorrect recovery of the sparse vector. However due to large distance separation from the transmitting node, the observations at receiving nodes are mutually independent to each other. The independent observations reduces the coherence between the columns of the measurement matrix. Fig. 5(a) clearly shows the gradual reduction in coherence of the measurement matrix for normal distribution with an increase in σ_{sd}. But in Fig. 5(b) the average received SNR at SUs are also decreasing monotonically while reaching a minimum of less than 20dB. The received SNR is an average value, with some nodes having a received SNR of negative dB or close to 0dB. This explains the behaviour for normal distribution in terms of recovering the sparse vector. In Fig. 4(b), the uniform distribution have a slightly different trend. In case of normal distribution, the algorithms achieved detection ratio of 1 at $\sigma_{sd} = 2$. On the other hand uniform distribution requires $\sigma_{sd} = 2.5$, for at least one of the algorithms to hit a detection ratio of 1. This is solely due to higher coherence between the columns of measurement matrix as shown in Fig. 5(a). In spite of having relatively higher received SNR compared to normal distribution, a large coherence resulted in a poor detection ratio < 0.5. However uniform distribution achieved to maintain the maximum detection ratio for a larger range of σ_{sd} [3, 5.5] compared to [2, 3] in case of normal. This is due to higher received SNR as shown in Fig. 5(b). The working simulations clearly establishes a relationship between the geometry of SU positions and effectiveness of the CS algorithms. The plots also indicates that, with large σ_{sd}, CS fails to perform efficiently in spite of having lower coherence between the columns of Φ.

8. Minimum distance aided CS algorithm(MDACS)

The following section introduces the Minimum distance aided CS algorithm (MDACS). The proposed modification incorporates received SNR at each individual SUs to deduce the perfect set of measurement nodes. The output of the algorithm is a set of selected SUs, which helps to enhance the performance of CS algorithms. Prior to the improvements, the existing min-dist algorithm [16] relied on selecting a pair of SUs with a specific distance separation between adjacent SUs. The value of separation can be specified by the user. Once the pair is selected, the algorithm randomly removes a SU from the chosen pair. The method iterates through a loop and repeats the procedure until, a refined set is generated such that all SUs are separated from the adjacent SUs by the specified value. With incremental increase in distance separation, the algorithm sequentially eliminates SUs from a given set, until the l_2- norm error of the recovered sparse vector is greater than some predefined value. As the previous algorithm depends on random removal of SU nodes, there may be situations where SUs with higher RSS may be accidently eliminated. As a result corrupted measurement data may get included in the observation vector. Such scenarios may restrict CS algorithms from successfully retrieving the sparse vector. Considering the issues with the existing algorithm, the modification uses the RSS at each SU to produce a refined group of SUs with certain geometry. Algorithm 1, provides an informal high-level description of the modified method. The new set of SUs have the required minimum distance separation between each adjacent nodes and high RSS. The separation allows the observation to be independent reducing the coherence in the measurement matrix and high RSS reduces the chance of observations being corrupted by channel noise. Fig. 6 (a) and (b) evaluates the detection ratio of MDACS compared to the existing min-dist algorithm. In Fig. 6(a) the detection ratio has a consistent pattern compared to unusual pattern in Fig. 6(b). The inconsistency is due to random removal of SUs with higher RSS values. Simulation results in Fig. 7(b) shows that, in case of MDACS, the SUs have higher received SNR compared to min-dist. The number of SUs for both the modified and unmodified algorithms are almost identical. Fig. 7(a) indicates that modified algorithm can achieve maximum detection with slightly smaller number of SUs, while maintaining relatively higher SNR.

Algorithm 1: Minimum distance aided CS algorithm

Input: $\{su\_pos,\ mindist,\ snr\_dB,\ error\}$
Output: $Refined\ set\ of\ SU,\ X_{M \times 1}$
Method:
    $d \rightarrow mindist$;
    $snr \rightarrow snr\_dB$;
    $Q \rightarrow 0$;
    $min\_dist \rightarrow min\{pdist(SU\_POS)\}$;

    while (min_dist < d) **do**

        (i) Find SU pair with separation less than d;
        (ii) Extract the SU with higher SNR;
        (iii) Create new set with extracted SUs;
        (iv) Feed the refined set into CS algorithm;
        (v) $Q = (l_2$-norm of recovery vector) - Q;

        if ($Q > error$), **then**
            break;
        end

    end while

    Return $SU\_POS, X_{M \times 1}$

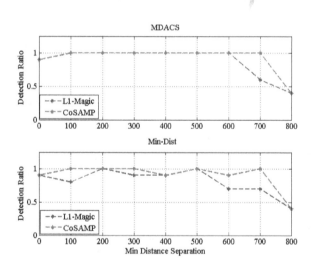

Figure 6. (a) Detection ratio of MDACS (b) detection ratio of existing algorithm.

8.1. Simulations

To verify the robustness of our proposed MDACS algorithm, the simulations were carried out for two different sets of distributions. First for Gaussian random distribution and second for uniform random distribution. In the previous section the simulations were conducted only with Gaussian random distribution. In Fig. 8 the effectiveness of our proposed MDACS algorithm is verified in order to successfully detect the presence of PUs

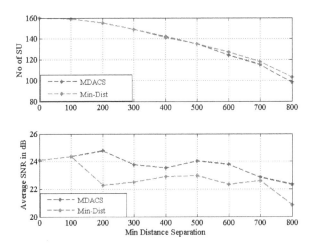

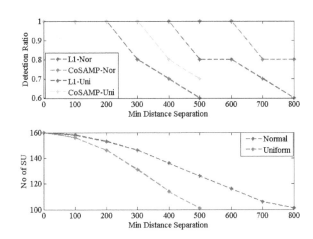

Figure 7. (a) No of SU vs minimum distance separation (b) Average received SNR vs minimum distance separation.

Figure 8. Evaluation of minimum distance algorithm for two different sets of distribution (a) Optimization algorithm for normal distribution (b) optimization algorithm for uniform distribution.

using L1-Magic and CoSAMP algorithms. For each distribution, σ_{sd} is kept constant at 2.5. Fig. 8(a), shows the detection ratio plots for each of the MDACS algorithms with respect to the different sets of distributions used for SU positioning. In x axis, we gradually increase the minimum distance separation between the SUs until the detection ratio drops below a certain threshold. Fig. 8(a) shows that for a set of SUs extracted from a uniform distribution, L1-magic and CoSAMP has a detection ratio < 0.8, when minimum distance separation is greater than 300m and 400m respectively. A similar trend can be observed in case of normal distribution, where the detection ratio drops below 0.8 at a distance separation of 500m and 700m. From the results, it can be seen that the CS algorithms can maintain a higher detection ratio for a larger distance separation in case of normal compared to uniform. Moreover as shown in Fig. 8(b), with systematic elimination of SUs from a random set, our MDACS algorithm achieved to reduce the number of measurements by 28% for normal distribution and 21% for uniform. In both cases CoSAMP outperformed L1-Magic in terms of achieving higher detection ratio.

8.2. Effect on Characteristics of Measurement Matrix

The systematic removal of measurement nodes, impacts the overall structure of the measurement matrix. Fig. 9 gives a deeper insight into the characteristics of each distribution by evaluating parameters, such as coherence of measurement matrix and average received SNR at SUs (observation vector). In previous simulation, with an incremental increase in distance separation, the number of SUs are decreasing. The reduction is due to elimination of SUs by the MDACS algorithm. This has a direct impact on the coherence of the measurement matrix as shown in Fig. 9(a). The measurement matrix is a rectangular matrix, where the

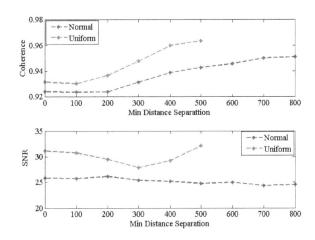

Figure 9. Impact of minimum distance separation on coherence, average received SNR and No of SU.

rows are the observations from each SU. A reduction in number of receiving nodes pushes the coherence of the measurement to a higher value, hence making it difficult for a matrix inversion. For uniform set, the matrix coherence reaches a maximum value of 0.9635 compared to 0.9510 for normal set. According to the theory of CS, a successful recovery of sparse vector is not feasible with matrix having high coherence between the columns. From the working simulations and results, we can clearly conclude that, SU positions extracted from a Gaussian distribution offers better recovery using MDACS algorithm compared to uniform.

8.3. Error in Recovery vector

On each iteration of the MDACS algorithm, it removes excess SUs until, the detection ratio or the l_2-norm of the recovered sparse vector drops below a certain

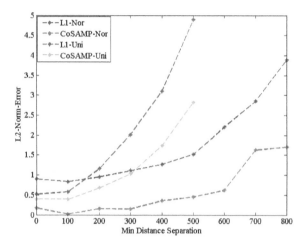

Figure 10. Difference in L2-norm of the recovery vector compared to original vector.

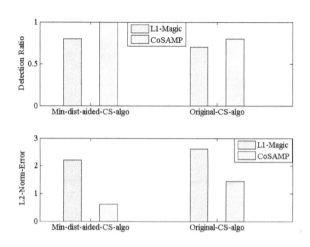

Figure 11. Detection ratio and Error comparison of proposed algorithm compared to original CS algorithm .

threshold. The stopping criteria can be a user defined threshold depending on the application. In scenarios where, localization of nodes have a higher priority, the error threshold can be raised to a higher value. In case of joint localization and exact transmit power reconstruction, error can be restricted to be less than 1. Irrespective of the CS algorithms used, the sparse vector should have the same $l_2 - norm$, as the positioning of PUs and their transmit power level is constant. In Fig. 10, the y-axis represents the difference is $l_2 - norm$ of the recovered vector compared to the original vector. As can be seen in the figure, all the four plots have a similar starting points with slight variations, mainly due to minor errors in accurately determining the transmit powers. Although the plots for uniform distribution have comparative small errors at the start, but with incremental distance separation, there is an exponential increase in the difference in l_2-norm. The plot of L1-Uni generates the maximum error with increasing distance separation followed by CoSAMP-Uni, L1-Nor and CoSAMP-Nor. The results indicates that CoSAMP-Nor have the least error while recovering the sparse vector, hence making it suitable for the generation of Radio Environment Map.

9. Proposed Algorithm Comparison

The working solutions and results from previous section, concludes that, CoSAMP-MDACS algorithm with SU positions extracted from a Gaussian random distribution generates maximum detection ratio with minimum error. The previous results (Fig. 8) also shows that, during our best case scenario CoSAMP-(MDACS)algorithm achieved a detection ratio of 1, with only 115 SUs. To validate the effectiveness of MDACS algorithm, we compared the performance with

original CoSAMP and L1-Magic CS algorithms. In both cases 115 SU positions were extracted from a Gaussian random distribution with $\sigma_{sd} = 2.5$. Fig. 11 illustrates the impact of our proposed method in enhancing the performance of the CS algorithms. Fig. 11(a) shows that, our method allows 20% and 10% more detection for CoSAMP and L1-Magic, compared to the original CS algorithms. Even in case of evaluating the difference in L2-norm-error, Fig. 11(b) indicates that, the proposed technique reduces the error by 57% in CoSAMP and 17% for L1-Magic. Moreover Fig. 12(b), shows that the set of SU generated from the refinement technique have 3% less coherence compared to a randomly deployed set of SUs. Less coherence between the columns allows better structure in the construction of measurement matrix and enables the refined set of SUs to operate at a lower received SNR of 24.95dB compared to 26.73dB as shown in Fig. 12(a).

10. Conclusion

The paper discusses the formulation of a novel algorithm to jointly deduce the location and transmit power of PUs in a cognitive radio network. The algorithm exploits the geographic location of the SUs to extract useful information about the positioning of PUs in a network. The proposed method introduces a refinement technique to selectively eliminate closely spaced SUs, in order to reduce the number of correlated observations. The novel method allows each adjacent SUs to have a minimum distance separation, such that the observations at each SUs are nearly independent. Simulation results shows that our novel MDACS algorithm achieved significant improvements in the overall performance of CS algorithms. Simulation results indicate that, our proposed approach has 20% higher detection ratio, while reducing the error by

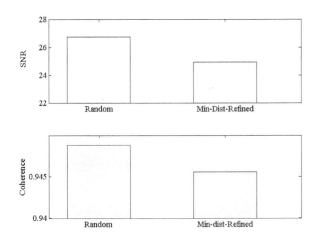

Figure 12. Impact of proposed algorithm on coherence and received SNR at SUs.

57%. Moreover the results also show that our approach generates a set of selective SUs with lower coherence compared to random positioning. This enables CS algorithms to offer perfect recovery at a comparatively lower received SNR. To verify the robustness of the algorithm, we tested our method for two spatial probability distributions for SU positions. In both cases, our algorithm achieved maximum detection ratio with fewer secondary user as receive power sensing. Future work will incorporate the construction of an efficient Radio Environment Map, to detect free spectrum in a geographic area.

References

[1] S. Wang, Q. Yang, W. Shi, and C. Wang. Interference mitigation and resource allocation in cognitive radio-enabled heterogeneous networks. In *Global Communications Conference (GLOBECOM), 2013 IEEE*, pages 4560–4565, Dec 2013.

[2] D. Hu and S. Mao. Co-channel and adjacent channel interference mitigation in cognitive radio networks. In *Military Communications Conference, 2011 - MILCOM 2011*, pages 13–18, Nov 2011.

[3] A. Mariani, S. Kandeepan, A. Giorgetti, and M. Chiani. Cooperative weighted centroid localization for cognitive radio networks. In *Communications and Information Technologies (ISCIT), 2012 International Symposium on Communication*, pages 459–464, Oct 2012.

[4] J. Werner, J. Wang, A. Hakkarainen, M. Valkama, and D. Cabric. Primary user localization in cognitive radio networks using sectorized antennas. In *Wireless On-demand Network Systems and Services (WONS), 2013 10th Annual Conference on*, pages 155–161, March 2013.

[5] I. Arambasic, J. Q. Casajus, I. Raos, M. Raspopoulos, and S. Stavrou. Anchor-less self-positioning in rectangular room based on sectorized narrowband antennas. In *Wireless Conference (EW), Proceedings of the 2013 19th European*, pages 1–6, April 2013.

[6] C. Feng, S. Valaee, and Z. Tan. Multiple target localization using compressive sensing. In *Global Telecommunications Conference, 2009. GLOBECOM 2009. IEEE*, pages 1–6, Nov 2009.

[7] X. Li, S. Hong, Z. Han, and Z. Wu. Bayesian compressed sensing based dynamic joint spectrum sensing and primary user localization for dynamic spectrum access. In *Global Telecommunications Conference (GLOBECOM 2011), 2011 IEEE*, pages 1–5, Dec 2011.

[8] B.A. Jayawickrama, E. Dutkiewicz, I. Oppermann, G. Fang, and J. Ding. Improved performance of spectrum cartography based on compressive sensing in cognitive radio networks. In *Communications (ICC), 2013 IEEE International Conference on*, pages 5657–5661, June 2013.

[9] H. Jamali-Rad, H. Ramezani, and G. Leus. Sparse multi-target localization using cooperative access points. In *Sensor Array and Multichannel Signal Processing Workshop (SAM), 2012 IEEE 7th*, pages 353–356, June 2012.

[10] E.J. Candes and M.B. Wakin. An introduction to compressive sampling. *Signal Processing Magazine, IEEE*, 25(2):21–30, March 2008.

[11] A. Goldsmith. *Wireless Communications*. Cambridge University Press, New York, NY, USA, 2005.

[12] S. Foucart and H. Rauhut. *A mathematical introduction to compressive sensing*. Springer, 2013.

[13] E.J. Candes and J. Romberg. l1-magic: Recovery of sparse signals via convex programming. *URL: www. acm. caltech. edu/l1magic/downloads/l1magic. pdf*, 4:14, 2005.

[14] J.A. Tropp and A.C. Gilbert. Signal recovery from random measurements via orthogonal matching pursuit. *Information Theory, IEEE Transactions on*, 53(12):4655–4666, Dec 2007.

[15] D. Needell and J. A. Tropp. Cosamp: Iterative signal recovery from incomplete and inaccurate samples. *Applied and Computational Harmonic Analysis*, 26(3):301–321, 2009.

[16] A. Biswas, S. Reisenfeld, M. Hedley, Z. Chen, and P Cheng. Localization of primary users by exploiting distance separation between secondary users. In *Cognitive Radio Oriented Wireless Networks - 10th International Conference, CROWNCOM 2015, Doha, Qatar, April 21-23, 2015, Revised Selected Papers*, pages 451–462, 2015.

13

Performance Analysis on the Coexistence of Multiple Cognitive Radio Networks

Lijun Qian[1,*], Oluwaseyi Omotere[1], Riku Jäntti[2]

[1]Department of Electrical and Computer Engineering, Prairie View A&M University, Texas A&M University System, Prairie View, Texas 77446, USA
[2]Department of Communications and Networking, Aalto University, P.O. Box 13000, 00076 Aalto, Finland

Abstract

The demand for wireless services is growing on a daily basis while spectral resources to support this growth are static. Therefore, there is need for the adoption of a new spectrum sharing paradigm. Cognitive Radio (CR) is a revolutionary technology aiming to increase spectrum utilization through dynamic spectrum access, as well as mitigating interference among multiple coexisting wireless networks. In many practical scenarios, multiple CR networks may coexist in the same geographical area, and they may interfere with each other and also have to yield to the primary user (PU). In this study, we investigate how much throughput a node in a CR network can achieve in the presence of another CR network and a PU. The results of this study illustrate how the transmission probability and sensing performance affect the achievable throughput of a node in coexisting CR networks. In addition, these results may serve as guidance for the deployment of multiple CR networks.

Keywords: Multiple cognitive radio networks, achievable rate

1. Introduction

The growth of wireless services in recent years is astronomical, this has lead to growing demand on the scarce spectrum resources. Cognitive radio is a key in minimizing the spectral congestion through its adaptability, where the radio parameters (such as frequency, power, modulation, bandwidth) can be changed depending on the radio environment, users situation, network condition, geolocation etc.

The regulation of wireless networks is done by government agencies through which spectrum is allocated to a particular application, this kind of static allocation of spectrum results in congestion in some parts of the spectrum and non use in some others, therefore, spectra utilization is very low over most of the bands. Cognitive radios are seen as a way to mitigate this low spectra usage. These radios sense the medium and dynamically adapt their waveforms to comply with the compliance policies fixed by the regulatory authorities and opportunistically access portions of the spectrum that are not used by the primary systems. A good example of this scenario is in the unlicensed bands such as the Industrial Scientific and Medical(ISM) band in 2.4 GHz where the Federal Communications Commission (FCC) [1]

rules if complied with by any technology is allowed to operate, there are multiple wireless technologies that are operating in these bands such as IEEE 802.11 Wireless Local Area Networks (WLAN), cordless phones and Bluetooth Wireless Personal Area Networks (WPAN). While unlicensed bands have opened up avenues for the advent of new technologies, their full potential is not realizable because of the presence of interference from other technologies operating in those bands. These unlicensed bands are overcrowded, while some licensed bands, such as the TV bands are not fully utilized. This results in poor spectrum utilization.

Multiple CR networks may coexist in the same geographical area, the cognitive capability of CR networks allows them to sense their communication environment and adapt the parameters of their communication scheme to maximize throughput, while minimizing the interference to the PU. One example is in disaster relief effort, where different organizations such as police, fire fighters, and emergency medical services are all deployed in the disaster area at the same time. All of these participating organizations use CRs to sweep a wide range of spectrum looking for suitable spectrum for communication. Another example is in battlefield communications, where multiple wireless networks may coexist. These networks may belong to different military branches or organizations such as the army and the air force. With the advancement of CR

*Corresponding author. Email: liqian@pvamu.edu

technology, it is expected that many of the network elements will have cognitive capability enabled by a software defined radio platform, such as the Joint Tactical Radio System (JTRS) program being a prime example.

In this study will consider two type of secondary access namely (1) Equal Secondary Access (2) Prioritized Secondary Access, their possible transmission scenarios, and their corresponding performance bound with the interference analysis over both Gaussian and Nakagami-m fading channels are considered. This bound determines whether it is feasible to deploy multiple CR networks in the same region with the required quality-of-service, say, the minimum throughput. We analyze the performance of a CR network in detail by considering the effects of various CR network parameters such as transmission probability and performance of spectrum sensing (false alarm and miss rate probabilities). The Complementary Cumulative Distribution Function (CCDF) and Moment Generating Function (MGF) of multiple interferers over Gaussian and Nakagami-m fading channels in a multiple coexisting CR networks are presented and the upper bound for the probability of false alarm, which is required to achieve a certain throughput is deduced.

2. Related Work

There are rich literatures on the coexistence of heterogeneous wireless networks in the ISM bands, such as the coexistence of WiFi (802.11) and Zigbee (802.15.4) radios [2]-[7]. IEEE 802.11 b/g networks may interfere with IEEE 802.15.4 sensor networks and thereby introduce significant coexistence problems for low-power sensor nodes [2] and [3]. In [4], a coexistence model of IEEE 802.15.4 and IEEE 802.11b/g, which exposes the interactive behavior between these two standards and therefore accurately explains their coexistence performance was proposed. The model focused on power and timing, and the concept of coexistence range was introduced. The authors of [5] used a multi-agent system based approach to achieve information sharing and decision distribution among multiple 802.11 networks deployed within small geographic vicinity. A multi-agent constraint optimization problem was formulated to solve the distributed resource management in multiple 802.11 networks. An experimental study was performed in [6], where the results raise important coexistence issues for 802.15.4 and 802.11 by showing that 802.15.4 significantly impacts 802.11 performance in many cases. The more recent study [7] proposed a novel MAC, Cooperative Busy Tone (CBT), that enables the reliable coexistence between WiFi and Zigbee. CBT allows a separate ZigBee node to schedule a busy tone concurrently with the desired transmission, thereby

improving the visibility of ZigBee devices to WiFi. In addition, a frequency flip scheme that prevents the mutual interference between cooperative ZigBee nodes, and a busy tone scheduler that minimizes the interference to WiFi are also designed in CBT. However, these works focus on the coexistence of heterogeneous wireless networks in the ISM bands. Furthermore, the analysis were mainly on the different PHY/MAC structures and standards of WiFi (802.11) and Zigbee (802.15.4) radios, rather than the coexistence of multiple homogeneous cognitive radio networks with PU network.

Although intensive research has been carried out on CR technology and single CR networks, only a few studies address the coexistence of multiple CR networks [8]-[11]. In [8], customer admission and eviction control was investigated using game theory for two co-located wireless service providers that temporarily lease a licensed spectrum band from the licensees and opportunistically utilize it during the absence of the legacy users. The goal is to provide WiFi-like Internet access in the spectrum whitespaces with better service quality than that of WiFi in the ISM band. The minimum blocking probabilities and maximum spectrum utilizations of three co-located systems with different bandwidth requirements were derived for one-channel band scenario in [9]. A channel packing scheme was then proposed for the multiple-channel band scenario to decrease the blocking probability and reduce the overall failure probability of the cognitive radio systems. A priority queue model was proposed for cognitive radio networks in [10], where the PU has preemptive priority while the cognitive users are further divided into different priority levels. A scheduling model was built based on the hybrid priority dynamic policy. In [11], three state sensing model was proposed to detect the PU active and idle states as well as the secondary user (SU) activities in multiple CR networks. It is shown that the scheduler provided much needed gain during congestions. However, none of the existing works discuss the fundamental per-node throughput of a cognitive radio user when multiple homogeneous cognitive radio networks coexist with PUs. Furthermore, we provide insights on the dominant factors of the per-link throughput and these were validated in the results.

The authors in [12] discussed the fundamental per-node throughput of a CR user when multiple CR networks coexist under simultaneous access with the PU but did not considered the performance under prioritized access and over Nakagami-m fading channels.

3. System Model

A model for the coexistence of multiple CR networks with a PU is illustrated in Figure 1 and Figure 2. These two figures show both the physical and logical representation of these networks under equal and prioritize access scheme. The two CR networks (CRN_1 and CRN_2) in Figure 1a and Figure 2a have equal access to spectrum, so they sense for spectrum availability in their surroundings ensuring interference to PU is avoided. Figure 1b and Figure 2b show Cognitive Gateway Network (CGN) and CR network (CRN) with different priority to access the spectrum whenever it is available, both CGN and CRN are in the same spatial domain and are using the same frequency opportunistically without causing interference to PU. Thus, both CGN and CRN need to perform spectrum sensing of the PU, and CRN need to perform additional spectrum sensing of the CGN because CRN has lower priority on spectrum. The main problem is that the CR networks under equal access will interfere with each other in such situations, in addition to yielding to the PUs, while under prioritize access, interference is avoided to the two CR networks since they both have different priority to spectrum utilization because the lower priority CRN will yield to the PU and CGN. We specifically study the impact of the interfering CR network on the performance of a given CR network under equal access and prioritize access.

3.1. Common Assumptions

We will focus on the case where two CR networks are uncoordinated and deployed in the same geographical area at the same time in addition to a PU. Each CR network performs its own spectrum sensing and the corresponding probabilities of detection and false alarm are taken into account. However, they do not coordinate their sensing nor share the sensing results. For example, although the organizations are collaborating on the disaster relief mission, each organization has its own CR network and these CR networks are not coordinated since the spectrum situation in the disaster area is not known a priori and each organization has its own administrative constraints such as security requirements.

Since CSMA/CA is a well-established Media Access Control (MAC) protocol and has been adopted by many practical wireless networks, we presume that the CR networks use CSMA/CA as the basis of their MAC protocol. It is also assumed that CR nodes can detect others' transmissions by using CSMA/CA, where the RTS/CTS message exchange is carried out before data transmission. The secondary CR networks are homogeneous in the sense that the nodes in the CR networks have similar capabilities and behaviors, such as the transmission power.

We assumed CR networks are located in an urban area. Since the CR nodes are typically less powerful than the primary nodes, they have smaller transmission ranges and are located closer to each other, we model the channel between CR nodes with Rayleigh fading. Noise is Additive White Gaussian Noise (AWGN). For the interference from CR nodes, we considered Gaussian and Nakagami-m distribution. A Gaussian distribution is mainly encountered when values of the quantity considered result from the additive effect of numerous random causes, each of them of relatively slight importance. In propagation, most of the physical quantities involved (power, voltage, fading time, etc.) are essentially positive quantities and cannot therefore be represented directly by a Gaussian distribution. On the other hand this distribution is used to represent the fluctuations of a quantity around its mean value (scintillation) and to represent the logarithm of a quantity. Nakagami-m is more flexible and it can model fading conditions from worst to moderate. The reason behind taking this distribution is its good fit to empirical fading data. Due to free parameter it provides more flexibility.

We focus on CR ad hoc networks instead of CR networks with infrastructure support such as the IEEE 802.22 systems [13]. There is a universal detector for PU signals in each CR network while each CR node uses CSMA/CA protocol by exploiting this detection result.

3.2. Equal Access Assumptions

The presence of the PU is defined using the following hypotheses. For equal access Hypothesis, H_0 denotes the case in which the PU is not present and H_1 stands for the case in which the PU is present.

3.3. Prioritized Access Assumptions

For the prioritized access, Hypothesis H_0^{PU} denotes the case in which the PU is idle and H_1^{PU} stands for the case in which the PU is active and because one of the CR networks has higher priority to access the spectrum, we denote this CR network has Cognitive Gateway Network (CGN) and its node as Cognitive Gateway (CG) and the lower priority CR network is denoted as CRN and its node as CR, therefore CR in CRN must sense for CG before transmitting data. H_0^{CG} denotes the case where CG is idle and H_1^{CG} stand for the case where CG is active. We assume a simplified frame structure with a sensing period τ and data period $T - \tau$ such that T is one frame duration. CRN may need a sensing period τ_2 longer than that of CGN (τ_1) to perform sensing of active CGs.

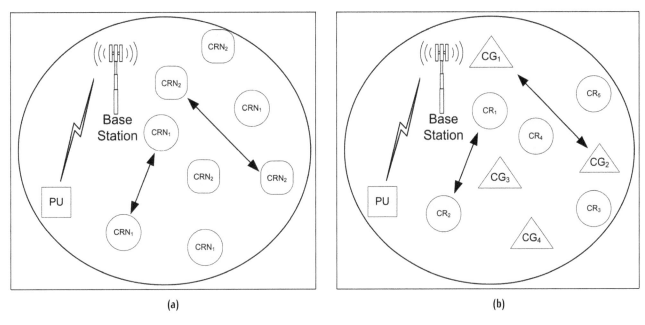

Figure 1. Physical network scenario, where two coexisting CR networks are within the range of a PU. (a) Equal Access (CRN1 and CRN2). (b) Prioritize Access (CGN and CRN).

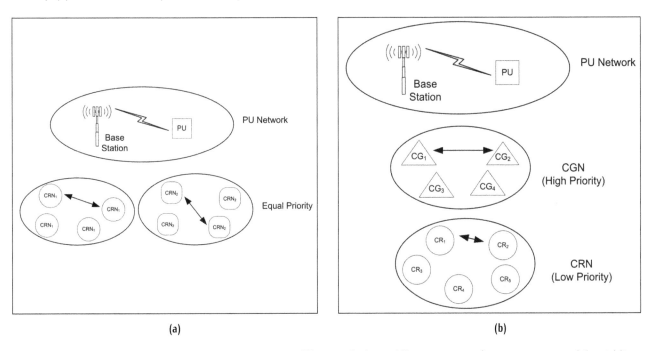

Figure 2. Logical network scenario, where two coexisting CR networks have different priority of spectrum access while yielding to a primary user. (a) Equal Access (CRN1 and CRN2). (b) Prioritize Access (CGN and CRN).

4. Theoretical Model

In this section we first derive the interference model for overlapping CR networks which is then exploited to deduce the per-node probabilistic throughput for such scenario. As discussed in the previous section, we consider both Gaussian and Nakagami-m distribution for the Interferer.

4.1. Probabilistic Throughput Per-node for Gaussian Interference

Both of the CR networks are uniformly random networks where nodes are independently distributed in an area according to a Poisson Point Process (PPP). Node densities of CRN_1 and CRN_2 are denoted by λ_1 and λ_2, respectively. We consider Rayleigh fading, x with $E\{x\} = 1$. The Cartesian coordinates of a node are denoted by X and Y. These random variables are independent of the other nodes' locations and uniformly distributed in $[-L, L]$. By setting the node density $\lambda = N/(4L^2)$, where N is the number of nodes, the probability of finding k nodes in an area A in the plane is given by

$$\Pr\{k \in A\} = \frac{e^{-\lambda A}(\lambda A)^k}{k!}. \tag{1}$$

With these assumption we can calculate the mean μ and variance σ^2 of interference I for a random Poisson network with density λ as follows [14]

$$\mu = \frac{2\lambda p \pi d_0^{(2-\alpha)}}{\alpha - 2} \tag{2}$$

$$\sigma^2 = \frac{2\lambda p \pi d_0^{2(1-\alpha)}}{\alpha - 1}, \tag{3}$$

where p is the transmission probability and d_0 the near field cut-off radius. The near field cut-off radius defines the distance in which other nodes in a network cannot transmit. For a large number of interferers, the interference can be modeled as Gaussian distributed due to the Central Limit Theorem, with parameters μ and σ^2 [15]. We call this as intra-network interference within one CR network.

In our case, the problem is that nodes in the other CR network may decide to transmit as well (depending on the sensing results) and thus, create inter-network interference. We can model inter-network interference similarly as before using Equations (2) and (3). The resulting interference $\mathcal{I}$ is Gaussian distributed $\mathcal{N}(\mu_1 + \mu_2, \sigma_1^2 + \sigma_2^2)$ which gives

$$\mu = \frac{2\lambda_1 p_1 \pi d_{0,1}^{(2-\alpha)}}{\alpha - 2} + \frac{2\lambda_2 p_2 \pi d_{0,2}^{(2-\alpha)}}{\alpha - 2} \tag{4}$$

$$\sigma^2 = \frac{2\lambda_1 p_1 \pi d_{0,1}^{2(1-\alpha)}}{\alpha - 1} + \frac{2\lambda_2 p_2 \pi d_{0,2}^{2(1-\alpha)}}{\alpha - 1}. \tag{5}$$

Furthermore, the received SINR γ is calculated as follows

$$\gamma = \frac{P x^2 R^{-\alpha}}{\mathcal{I} + \sigma_n^2}, \tag{6}$$

where P is the transmission power, R the distance between a transmitter and a receiver and σ_n^2 is the noise power. Then, we can calculate the probabilistic throughput

$$\Pr\{\gamma > \theta\} = \Pr\left\{\frac{x^2 P R^{-\alpha}}{\mathcal{I} + \sigma_n^2} > \theta\right\}$$

$$= \Pr\left\{x^2 > \frac{\theta(\mathcal{I} + \sigma_n^2)R^\alpha}{P}\right\}, \tag{7}$$

where θ is the required SINR for successful reception (threshold). By denoting $w = x^2$ this can be deduced to the following form

$$\Pr\{\gamma > \theta\} = E\left\{F_{c,w}\left(\frac{\theta(\mathcal{I} + \sigma_n^2)}{PR^{-\alpha}}\right)\right\}$$

$$= E\left\{\exp\left(\frac{-\theta(\mathcal{I} + \sigma_n^2)}{PR^{-\alpha}}\right)\right\}, \tag{8}$$

where $F_c(.)$ stands for the Complementary Cumulative Distribution Function (CCDF). Moreover, note that w is an exponential random variable and $F_{c,w}(w) = e^{-w}$. The expectation is taken over the Gaussian distribution which gives [15]

$$\Pr\{\gamma > \theta\} = \exp\left(-\frac{\theta(\mu + \sigma_n^2)}{PR^{-\alpha}}\right)\exp\left(\frac{\theta^2 \sigma^2}{2(PR^{-\alpha})^2}\right)$$

$$\times Q\left(\frac{\theta \sigma^2}{PR^{-\alpha}} - \frac{\mu}{\sigma}\right). \tag{9}$$

4.2. Probabilistic Throughput Per-node for Nakagami-m Interference

Both of the CR networks are uniformly random networks where nodes are independently distributed in an area according to a Poisson Point Process (PPP). Node densities of CRN_1 and CRN_2 and are denoted by λ_1 and λ_2, respectively. We consider Rayleigh fading, x_0 with $E\{x_0\} = 1$. The Cartesian coordinates of a node are denoted by X and Y. These random variables are independent of the other nodes' locations and uniformly distributed in $[-L, L]$. By setting the node density $\lambda = N/(4L^2)$, where N is the number of nodes, the probability of finding k nodes in an area A in the plane is given by

$$\Pr\{k \in A\} = \frac{e^{-\lambda A}(\lambda A)^k}{k!}. \tag{10}$$

Furthermore, the received SINR γ is calculated as follows

$$\gamma = \frac{x_0^2 R^{-\alpha} P_0}{\sum x_i^2 r_i^{-\alpha} P_i + \sigma_n^2} \tag{11}$$

where P_0 is the CR node transmission power, R the distance between a CR network transmitter and a receiver and σ_n^2 is the noise power. P_i is the transmission power of the interfering transmission. We use a deterministic distance-dependent path loss $r^{-\alpha}$ as a channel model, where r is the distance between the interfering transmitter and its victim receiver and α is the path loss exponent. x_i, $i = 1, 2, ..., K$ are independent gamma distributed RVs that represent the squared fading gains of the Nakagami-m fading. The Nakagami-m distribution, parameterized by fading severity parameter m, can model different flat fading environment, it reduces to Rayleigh fading model for $m = 1$ and describes less severe fading condition as m increases. γ is a ratio of mixture of large number of RVs, for which closed-form expression for its Complementary Cumulative Distribution Function (CCDF) is generally difficult to obtain, if not impossible. Therefore, we derived a closed form expression $\mathcal{M}(z) = \mathbb{E}[e^{-yz}]$ for the MGF of $\sum x_i^2 r_i^{-\alpha} \mathcal{P}_i$ expressed as

$$\mathcal{M}(z) = \mathbb{E}[e^{-z \sum_{i=1}^K x_i^2 r_i^{-\alpha} \mathcal{P}_i}] \tag{12}$$

Consider the interference generated in an area A around the victim receiver, where K is distributed as a Poisson RV with average $\lambda(L^2 - d_0^2)$. We define d_0 as the near field cut-off radius which defines the distance in which other devices in a network cannot transmit, r_i, $i = 1, 2, ..., K$ are independent and distributed according to the following pdf

$$f(r) = \begin{cases} \frac{2r}{(L^2 - d_0^2)}, & d_0 < r < L \\ 0, & \text{otherwise} \end{cases} \tag{13}$$

x_i, $i = 1, 2, ..., K$ are independent gamma distributed RVs that represent the squared fading gains of the Nakagami-m fading

$$f(x) = \frac{x^{m-1}}{\Gamma(m)} m^m e^{-mx} \tag{14}$$

We seek asymptotic $\mathcal{M}(z)$, therefore, we take the limit of (12) as $L \to \infty$

$$\mathcal{M}(z) = \lim_{L \to \infty} \mathbb{E}[e^{-z \sum_{i=1}^K x_i^2 r_i^{-\alpha} \mathcal{P}_i}] \tag{15}$$

we conditioned on K in order to compute (15) [16]

$$\mathcal{M}(z/K) = \lim_{L \to \infty} \prod_{i=1}^K \mathbb{E}[e^{-zx_i^2 r_i^{-\alpha} \mathcal{P}_i}]$$

$$= \lim_{L \to \infty} (\mathbb{E}[e^{-zx_1^2 r_1^{-\alpha} \mathcal{P}_1}])^K \tag{16}$$

on averaging out K, we obtain

$$\mathcal{M}(z) = \lim_{L \to \infty} \sum_{\kappa=0}^{\infty} \frac{e^{-\lambda(L^2 - d_0^2)}(\lambda(L^2 - d_0^2))^\kappa}{\kappa!}$$

$$\times \ (\mathbb{E}[e^{-zx_1^2 r_1^{-\alpha} \mathcal{P}_1}])^\kappa \tag{17}$$

Further simplification gives

$$\mathcal{M}(z) = \lim_{L \to \infty} e^{-\lambda(L^2 - d_0^2)(1 - (\mathbb{E}[e^{-zx_1^2 r_1^{-\alpha} \mathcal{P}_1}]))} \tag{18}$$

The exponent of (18) can be evaluated in the limit as $L \to \infty$

$$\lim_{L \to \infty} \lambda(L^2 - d_0^2)(1 - (\mathbb{E}[e^{-zx_1^2 r_1^{-\alpha} \mathcal{P}_1}]))$$

$$= \lambda \int_{d_0}^{\infty} [1 - e^{-zx_1^2 r_1^{-\alpha} \mathcal{P}_1}] 2r_1 dr_1$$

$$= \lambda[-d_0^2 + d_0^2 e^{-zx_1^2 \mathcal{P}_1 d_0^{-\alpha}} - (z\mathcal{P}_1)^{\frac{2}{\alpha}} \Gamma(1 - \frac{2}{\alpha}, zx_1^2 \mathcal{P}_1 d_0^{-\alpha})(x_1^{\frac{4}{\alpha}})] \tag{19}$$

From (19), and using eq.(3.381.9) of [17], viz.

$$\mathbb{E}[x_1^{\frac{2}{\alpha}}] = \int_{d_0}^{\infty} x^{\frac{2}{\alpha}} \frac{x^{m_1-1}}{\Gamma(m_1)} m_1^{m_1} e^{-m_1 x} dx = \frac{\Gamma(m + \frac{2}{\alpha}, md_0)}{m^{\frac{2}{\alpha}} \Gamma(m)} \tag{20}$$

$$\mathbb{E}[x_1^{\frac{4}{\alpha}}] = \int_{d_0}^{\infty} x^{\frac{4}{\alpha}} \frac{x^{m_1-1}}{\Gamma(m_1)} m_1^{m_1} e^{-m_1 x} dx = \frac{\Gamma(m + \frac{4}{\alpha}, md_0)}{m^{\frac{4}{\alpha}} \Gamma(m)} \tag{21}$$

We arrive at the following closed form expression for $\mathcal{M}(z)$

$$\begin{aligned} \mathcal{M}(z) &= \exp -\Bigg\{\lambda\Bigg(-d_0^2 + d_0^2 e^{-z\mathcal{P}_1 d_0^{-\alpha}\left(\frac{\Gamma(m+\frac{2}{\alpha}, md_0)}{m\Gamma(m)}\right)} \\ &\quad - (z\mathcal{P}_1)^{\frac{2}{\alpha}} \Gamma\left(1 - \frac{2}{\alpha}, z\mathcal{P}_1 d_0^{-\alpha}\left(\frac{\Gamma(m + \frac{2}{\alpha}, md_0)}{m^{\frac{4}{\alpha}} \Gamma(m)}\right)\right) \\ &\quad \times \left(\frac{\Gamma(m + \frac{4}{\alpha}, md_0)}{m^{\frac{4}{\alpha}} \Gamma(m)}\right)\Bigg)\Bigg\} \end{aligned} \tag{22}$$

From (11), we can calculate the probabilistic throughput

$$\begin{aligned} \Pr\{\gamma > \theta\} &= \Pr\left\{\frac{x_0^2 P_0 R^{-\alpha}}{\sum x_i r_i^{-\alpha} \mathcal{P}_i + \sigma_n^2} > \theta\right\} \\ &= \Pr\left\{x_0^2 > \frac{\theta(\sum x_i^2 r_i^{-\alpha} \mathcal{P}_i + \sigma_n^2)}{P_0 R^{-\alpha}}\right\} \end{aligned} \tag{23}$$

where θ is the required SINR for successful reception (threshold). By denoting $w = x^2$ and $y = \sum x_i^2 r_i^{-\alpha} \mathcal{P}_i$ this can be deduced to the following form

$$\begin{aligned} \Pr\{\gamma > \theta\} &= E\left\{F_{c,w}\left(\frac{\theta(y + \sigma_n^2)}{P_0 R^{-\alpha}}\right)\right\} \\ &= E\left\{\exp\left(\frac{-\theta(y + \sigma_n^2)}{P_0 R^{-\alpha}}\right)\right\} \end{aligned} \tag{24}$$

where $F_c(.)$ stands for the CCDF. Moreover, note that w is an exponential random variable and $F_{c,w}(w) = e^{-w}$. The expectation is taken over the Gamma distribution which gives

$$\Pr\{\gamma > \theta\} = \exp\left(\frac{\theta \sigma_n^2}{P_0 R^{-\alpha}}\right)\left(\mathcal{M}_y\left(\frac{\theta}{P_0 R^{-\alpha}}\right)\right) \tag{25}$$

5. Result for Equal Access CR Networks

This section gives the results on probabilistic throughput for coexisting CR networks with equal access. In CR networks, the received interference depends on the sensing results. Furthermore, in case of overlapping CR networks the operations of the other CR networks also affect the performance. Consequently, we have multiple scenarios listed in Table 1 depending on the PU's activities and spectrum sensing results of the CR networks. For instance, if the PU is idle (H_0), and only CRN_2 has a false alarm, then CRN_1 will be able to use that channel for transmission alone. We denote the probability of false alarm and probability of detection as $P_{f,i}$ and $P_{d,i}$ for CRN_i, the probability of this scenario is $(1 - P_{f,1})P_{f,2}P(H_0)$. Other cases are determined using similar reasoning. The probability of miss for CRN_i is defined as $P_{m,i} = 1 - P_{d,i}$.

Table 1. Possible transmission scenarios

Scenarios	H_0	H_1
Idle	$P_{f,1}P_{f,2}$	$P_{d,1}P_{d,2}$
CRN_1	$(1 - P_{f,1})P_{f,2}$	$P_{m,1}P_{d,2}$
CRN_2	$(1 - P_{f,2})P_{f,1}$	$P_{m,2}P_{d,1}$
CRN_1 & CRN_2	$(1 - P_{f,1})(1 - P_{f,2})$	$P_{m,1}P_{m,2}$

By using the scenarios defined in Table 1 we can derive the following equation for successful packet reception for a node in CRN_1 for both Gaussian and Nakagami-m interference in Equations (26) and (27), respectively.

$$
\begin{aligned}
\Pr\{\gamma > \theta\} &= (1 - P_{f,1})P_{f,2}P(H_0)\Pr\left\{\frac{x^2 P_1 R^{-\alpha}}{\mathcal{I}_1 + \sigma_n^2} > \theta\right\} \\
&+ P_{m,1}P_{d,2}P(H_1)\Pr\left\{\frac{x^2 P_1 R^{-\alpha}}{\mathcal{I}_1 + \mathcal{I}_{PU} + \sigma_n^2} > \theta\right\} \\
&+ (1 - P_{f,1})(1 - P_{f,2})P(H_0)\Pr\left\{\frac{x^2 P_1 R^{-\alpha}}{\mathcal{I}_1 + \mathcal{I}_2 + \sigma_n^2} > \theta\right\} \\
&+ P_{m,1}P_{m,2}P(H_1)\Pr\left\{\frac{x^2 P_1 R^{-\alpha}}{\mathcal{I}_1 + \mathcal{I}_2 + \mathcal{I}_{PU} + \sigma_n^2} > \theta\right\},
\end{aligned} \tag{26}
$$

where $\mathcal{I}_1$, $\mathcal{I}_2$, and $\mathcal{I}_{PU}$ denote the received intra-network, inter-network, and PU's interference, respectively.

$$
\begin{aligned}
\Pr\{\gamma > \theta\} &= (1 - P_{f,1})P_{f,2}P(H_0)\Pr\left\{\frac{x_0^2 P_0 R^{-\alpha}}{\sum x_{i1}^2 r_{i1}^{-\alpha}\mathcal{P}_{i1} + \sigma_n^2} > \theta\right\} \\
&+ P_{m,1}P_{d,2}P(H_1)\Pr\left\{\frac{x_0^2 P_0 R^{-\alpha}}{\sum x_{i1}^2 r_{i1}^{-\alpha}\mathcal{P}_{i1} + \mathcal{P}_{PU} + \sigma_n^2} > \theta\right\} \\
&+ (1 - P_{f,1})(1 - P_{f,2})P(H_0) \\
&\times \Pr\left\{\frac{x_0^2 P_0 R^{-\alpha}}{\sum x_{i1}^2 r_{i1}^{-\alpha}\mathcal{P}_{i1} + \sum x_{i2}^2 r_{i2}^{-\alpha}\mathcal{P}_{i2} + \sigma_n^2} > \theta\right\} \\
&+ P_{m,1}P_{m,2}P(H_1) \\
&\times \Pr\left\{\frac{x_0^2 P_0 R^{-\alpha}}{\sum x_{i1}^2 r_{i1}^{-\alpha}\mathcal{P}_{i1} + \sum x_{i2}^2 r_{i2}^{-\alpha}\mathcal{P}_{i2} + \mathcal{P}_{PU} + \sigma_n^2} > \theta\right\}
\end{aligned} \tag{27}
$$

where $\sum x_{i1}^2 r_{i1}^{-\alpha}\mathcal{P}_{i1}$, $\sum x_{i2}^2 r_{i2}^{-\alpha}\mathcal{P}_{i2}$ and $\mathcal{P}_{PU}$ denotes the sum of received intra-network, inter-network, and PU's interference respectively.

6. Result for Prioritized Access CR Networks

In this section, we derive the probabilistic throughput for coexisting CR networks with different priority. In a Prioritized access setup, one of the two CR networks has higher priority to access free spectrum and we denote this as Cognitive Gateway Network (CGN) and the one with lower priority we denote as CRN. Consequently, we have multiple transmission scenarios listed in Table 2 for CRN and Table 3 for CGN. In prioritized access, CGN can access the medium first if the channel is sensed as idle. CRN is slightly delayed to find out whether CGN started a transmission or not. After that, CRN can transmit if possible.

Table 2. Possible Transmission Probability for CRN under prioritized access

Scenarios	PU idle (H_0^{PU})	PU active (H_1^{PU})
CGN idle (H_0^{CG})	$(1 - P_{f,2}^{PU})(1 - P_{f,2}^{CG})$	$P_{m,2}^{PU}(1 - P_{f,2}^{CG})$
CGN active (H_1^{CG})	$(1 - P_{f,2}^{PU})P_{m,2}^{CG}$	$P_{m,2}^{PU}P_{m,2}^{CG}$

Table 3. Possible Transmission Probability for CGN under prioritized access

Scenarios	PU idle (H_0^{PU})	PU active (H_1^{PU})
	$(1 - P_{f,2}^{PU})(1 - P_{f,2}^{CG})$	$P_{m,2}^{PU}(1 - P_{f,2}^{CG})$

We denote the miss rate and false alarm probabilities of CGN at CRN by $P_{m,2}^{CG}$ and $P_{f,2}^{CG}$, and those of PU at CRN by $P_{m,2}^{PU}$ and $P_{f,2}^{PU}$, respectively. Similarly, the miss and false alarm probabilities of PU at CGN are denoted by $P_{m,1}^{PU}$ and $P_{f,1}^{PU}$. For successful packet reception of a node in CRN under Gaussian interference, we derived the following equation

$$
\begin{aligned}
\Pr\{\gamma > \theta\} &= (1 - P_{f,1}^{PU})(1 - P_{f,2}^{CG})P(H_0^{PU})P(H_0^{CG}) \\
&\times \Pr\left\{\frac{x^2 P_{CRN}R^{-\alpha}}{\mathcal{I}_{CRN} + \sigma_n^2} > \theta\right\} \\
&+ P_{m,2}^{PU}(1 - P_{f,2}^{CG})P(H_1^{PU})P(H_0^{CG}) \\
&\times \Pr\left\{\frac{x^2 P_{CRN}R^{-\alpha}}{\mathcal{I}_{CRN} + \mathcal{I}_{PU} + \sigma_n^2} > \theta\right\} \\
&+ (1 - P_{f,2}^{PU})P_{m,2}^{CG}P(H_0^{PU})P(H_1^{CG}) \\
&\times \Pr\left\{\frac{x^2 P_{CRN}R^{-\alpha}}{\mathcal{I}_{CRN} + \mathcal{I}_{CGN} + \sigma_n^2} > \theta\right\} \\
&+ P_{m,2}^{PU}P_{m,2}^{CG}P(H_1^{PU})P(H_1^{CG}) \\
&\times \Pr\left\{\frac{x^2 P_{CRN}R^{-\alpha}}{\mathcal{I}_{CRN} + \mathcal{I}_{CGN} + \mathcal{I}_{PU} + \sigma_n^2} > \theta\right\}
\end{aligned}
\tag{28}
$$

for CGN, we have

$$
\begin{aligned}
\Pr\{\gamma > \theta\} &= (1 - P_{f,1}^{PU})P(H_0^{PU})\Pr\left\{\frac{x^2 P_{CGN'}R^{-\alpha}}{\mathcal{I}_{CGN} + \sigma_n^2} > \theta\right\} \\
&+ P_{m,1}^{PU}P(H_1^{PU})\Pr\left\{\frac{x^2 P_{CRN}R^{-\alpha}}{\mathcal{I}_{CGN} + \mathcal{I}_{PU} + \sigma_n^2} > \theta\right\}
\end{aligned}
\tag{29}
$$

Successful packet reception for the case of Nakagami-m for CRN gives

$$
\begin{aligned}
\Pr\{\gamma > \theta\} &= (1 - P_{f,2}^{PU})(1 - P_{f,2}^{CG})P(H_0^{PU})P(H_0^{CG}) \\
&\times \Pr\left\{\frac{x_0^2 P_0 R^{-\alpha}}{\sum x_{iCR}^2 r_{iCR}^{-\alpha}\mathcal{P}_{iCR} + \sigma_n^2} > \theta\right\} \\
&+ P_{m,2}^{PU}(1 - P_{f,2}^{CG})P(H_1^{PU})P(H_0^{CG}) \\
&\times \Pr\left\{\frac{x_0^2 P_0 R^{-\alpha}}{\sum x_{iCR}^2 r_{iCR}^{-\alpha}\mathcal{P}_{iCR} + \mathcal{P}_{PU} + \sigma_n^2} > \theta\right\} \\
&+ (1 - P_{f,2}^{PU})P_{m,2}^{CG}P(H_0^{PU})P(H_1^{CG}) \\
&\times \Pr\left\{\frac{x_0^2 P_0 R^{-\alpha}}{\sum x_{iCR}^2 r_{iCR}^{-\alpha}\mathcal{P}_{iCR} + \sum x_{iCG}^2 r_{iCG}^{-\alpha}\mathcal{P}_{iCG} + \sigma_n^2} > \theta\right\} \\
&+ P_{m,2}^{PU}P_{m,2}^{CG}P(H_1^{PU})P(H_1^{CG}) \\
&\times \Pr\left\{\frac{x_0^2 P_0 R^{-\alpha}}{\sum x_{iCR}^2 r_{iCR}^{-\alpha}\mathcal{P}_{iCR} + \sum x_{iCG}^2 r_{iCG}^{-\alpha}\mathcal{P}_{iCG} + \mathcal{P}_{PU} + \sigma_n^2} > \theta\right\}
\end{aligned}
\tag{30}
$$

for CGN, we have

$$
\begin{aligned}
\Pr\{\gamma > \theta\} &= (1 - P_{f,1}^{PU})P(H_0^{PU}) \\
&\times \Pr\left\{\frac{x_0^2 P_0 R^{-\alpha}}{\sum x_{iCR}^2 r_{iCR}^{-\alpha}\mathcal{P}_{iCR} + \sigma_n^2} > \theta\right\} \\
&+ P_{m,1}^{PU}P(H_1^{PU}) \\
&\times \Pr\left\{\frac{x_0^2 P_0 R^{-\alpha}}{\sum x_{iCG}^2 r_{iCG}^{-\alpha}\mathcal{P}_{iCG} + \mathcal{P}_{PU} + \sigma_n^2} > \theta\right\}
\end{aligned}
\tag{31}
$$

The results from Section 5 and Section 6 are summarized in Table 4

Table 4. Summary of Results

	Equal Access	Prioritized Access
Gaussian	(26)	(28) (29)
Nakagami-m	(27)	(30) (31)

7. Performance Bound on Spectrum Sensing of CRN

In this section, the performance bounds on spectrum sensing and transmission probability are derived in order to satisfy certain quality-of-service requirements for coexisting CR networks. By formulating each term of Equation (26), (28) and (29) in the same way as in Equation (8) and solving that we can find an exact value for $\Pr\{\gamma > \theta\}$, similar to Equation (9) for the Gaussian interference. Similarly, formulating each term of Equation (27), (30) and (31) in the same way as in Equation (24) and solving that we can find an exact value for $\Pr\{\gamma > \theta\}$, similar to Equation (25) for the Nakagami-m interference. The main problem is that the performance of CRN_1 will be determined by the operations of CRN_2 and vice versa. By using these formulas we will analyze the throughput of overlapping CR networks to see what are the suitable bounds to guarantee reasonable performance.

We define the per-node throughput J such that the transmitter has a packet to transmit while a receiver is idle, i.e., the receiver does not have a packet to transmit. Moreover, the received SINR has to be larger than the threshold for successful packet reception. This can be mathematically formulated as follows

$$
J = p(1 - p)\Pr\{\gamma > \theta\}.
\tag{32}
$$

In practice CR users should achieve reasonable throughput to enable feasibility from the economic perspective. We denote this throughput threshold by

$\hat{J}$. Next, we derive the bound of the probability of false alarm that is required to achieve the desired throughput, $J \geq \hat{J}$. By analyzing Equation (26)-(31) also summarized in Table 4, we have concluded that in practice the second and the fourth term in Equation (26), (27), (28) and (30) and the second term in Equation (29) and (31) have negligible influence on the performance of CR users, since both the miss rate and the probability of the PU being active are small. In addition, it is not practical to design CR networks by assuming that their transmissions would overlap with the transmissions of the PU's.

As an example, let us consider Equation (27), an equal access with Nakagami-m interference, using the following approximation

$$J \geq \hat{J} \Rightarrow$$

$$\hat{J} \leq p(1-p)(1-P_{f,1})P_{f,2}P(H_0)\Pr\left\{\frac{x_0^2 P_0 R^{-\alpha}}{\sum x_{i1}^2 r_{i1}^{-\alpha}\mathcal{P}_{i1} + \sigma_n^2} > \theta\right\}$$

$$+ p(1-p)(1-P_{f,1})(1-P_{f,2})P(H_0)$$

$$\times \Pr\left\{\frac{x_0^2 P_0 R^{-\alpha}}{\sum x_{i1}^2 r_{i1}^{-\alpha}\mathcal{P}_{i1} + \sum x_{i2}^2 r_{i2}^{-\alpha}\mathcal{P}_{i2} + \sigma_n^2} > \theta\right\}$$

$$(33)$$

The above inequality shows the maximum achievable throughput for a node in CRN_1 given the PU's activity and the spectrum sensing performance of the two CR networks. Moreover, let us define

$$\xi_1 = P(H_0)\Pr\left\{\frac{x_0^2 P_0 R^{-\alpha}}{\sum x_{i1}^2 r_{i1}^{-\alpha}\mathcal{P}_{i1} + \sigma_n^2} > \theta\right\} \qquad (34)$$

$$\xi_2 = P(H_0)\Pr\left\{\frac{x_0^2 P_0 R^{-\alpha}}{\sum x_{i1}^2 r_{i1}^{-\alpha}\mathcal{P}_{i1} + \sum x_{i2} r_{i2}^{-\alpha}\mathcal{P}_{i2} + \sigma_n^2} > \theta\right\}$$

$$(35)$$

and assume that both CR networks have the same spectrum sensing performance, i.e., $P_{f,1} = P_{f,2} = P_f$.
Then,

$$\hat{J} \leq p(1-p)(1-P_f)[P_f\xi_1 + (1-P_f)\xi_2] \qquad (36)$$

It is observed that when the false alarm probability P_f is very small, the achievable throughput approaches $p(1-p)\xi_2$. It can be shown that as long as $\frac{\xi_1}{\xi_2} \leq \frac{2-P_f}{1-P_f}$, the achievable throughput will decrease when P_f increases.

If the spectrum sensing performance of CRN_2 is given a priori, then we can find out the maximum probability of false alarm of CRN_1 for achieving a certain throughput $\hat{J}$.

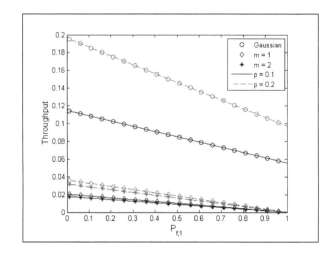

Figure 3. Per-node throughput in two coexisting CR networks with equal access. The throughput is a function of false alarm probability, the effect of Gaussian or Nakagami-m interference and transmission probability (p) on throughput of CRN_1

$$P_{f,1} \leq 1 - \frac{\hat{J}}{(P_{f,2}\xi_1 + (1 - P_{f,2})\xi_2)p(1-p)} \qquad (37)$$

In other words, Equation (37) defines the upper bound for the probability of false alarm of CRN_1.

Following similar derivation as Equation (37), upper bound for the probability of false alarm can be derived for Equation (26), (28) and (30). For prioritized access we further derived from Equation (29) the upper bound for the probability of false alarm for CGN under Gaussian interference below

$$J \geq \hat{J} \Rightarrow$$

$$\hat{J} \leq p(1-p)(1-P_{f,1}^{PU})P(H_0^{PU})\Pr\left\{\frac{x^2 P_{CGN'}R^{-\alpha}}{\mathcal{I}_{CGN} + \sigma_n^2} > \theta\right\}$$

$$(38)$$

The above inequality is the maximum achievable throughput for a node in CGN, the upper bound for the probability of false alarm of CGN is given by

$$P_{f,1} \leq 1 - \frac{\hat{J}}{P(H_0^{PU})\Pr\left\{\frac{x^2 P_{CGN'}R^{-\alpha}}{\mathcal{I}_{CGN}+\sigma_n^2} > \theta\right\}p(1-p)} \qquad (39)$$

Similar derivation is possible from Equation (31) for CGN under Nakagami-m interference.

8. Simulation Results

The performance of overlapping CR networks is studied by investigating the effects of different parameters on the throughput of CRN_1. Unless otherwise stated, the following practical values for network parameters

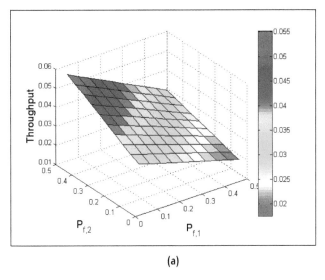
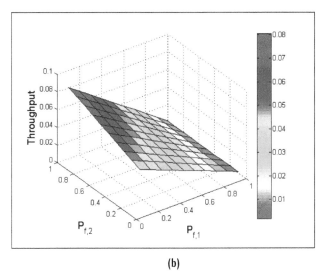

(a) (b)

Figure 4. Effect of false alarm probabilities on the throughput of CRN_1 for coexisting CR networks with equal access (a) Gaussian interference (b) Nakagami-m interference

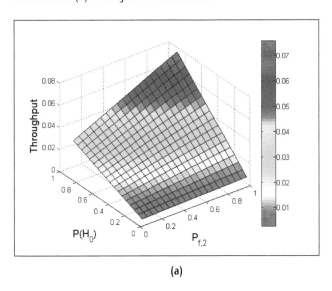
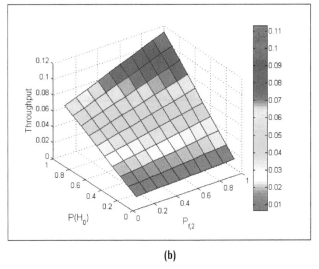

(a) (b)

Figure 5. Combined effect of primary user's activity and false alarm probability of CRN_2 on the performance of CRN_1 for coexisting CR networks with equal access (a) Gaussian interference (b) Nakagami-m interference

were used: $d_0 = 100m$, $R = 50$, $P = 30dBm$, $P_{PU} = 80dBm$, $\sigma_n = -70dBm$, $\theta = 10dB$, $L = 500m$, $\alpha = 4$, $p_1 = p_2 = 0.5$, and $N_1 = N_2 = 100$. Moreover, the used CR parameters are: $P_{f,1} = P_{f,2} = 0.1$, and $P(H_0) = 0.9$. For each result figure, we varied different parameters to demonstrate their impact.

8.1. Effect of Gaussian and Nakagami-m fading on Performance

We can determine the maximum value for the probability of false alarm that is required to achieve a certain throughput by exploiting Equation (37), this is shown in Figure 3. In Figure 3, we set $d_0 = 3m$, $R = 1m$, $P = 10nW$, $P_{PU} = 10\mu W$, $\sigma_n = 5fW$, and $L = 20m$, it

shows the effect of Gaussian, Nakagami parameter m and transmission probability p on the throughput of a node in CRN_1, the figure shows a higher throughput for the Gaussian interference because it does not consider details of the fading conditions as seen in Nakagami-m results, the results further shows that throughput reduces for higher m, but throughput increases as p increases until an optimal p is reached when further increase in p leads to decrease in throughput.

8.2. Effect of Sensing Performance on Throughput Under Equal Access

In this section, the effect of sensing performance on the throughput in case of overlapping CR networks is investigated, this is investigated for coexisting CR networks under equal access. Figure 4 shows the effect of sensing performance on the throughput, the figure captures the fundamental nature of overlapping CR networks. As expected, the sensing performance of both networks has an effect and it seems that both networks have equal and linear influence on the throughput of CRN_1. These results imply that CR users would like to have as low probability of false alarm as possible to achieve the best performance. Whereas, the false alarm probability of the interfering CR network should be high such that the CR network in question would be able to access and use the spectrum alone as often as possible. The activity of the interfering CR network has a significant impact on the performance in case of overlapping CR networks.

In case of secondary spectrum usage, the activity of the PU determines the amount of transmission opportunities for CR users. Even though there would be large portions of available spectrum in time, high false alarm probabilities of CR users will restrict the achievable throughput. This is shown in Figure 5 where the throughput of CRN_1 is plotted as a function of $P(H_0)$ and $P_{f,2}$. If the PU is active for the most of the time, high probabilities of false alarm have only a minor effect on the throughput. Nevertheless, if the PU is inactive often, the probability of false alarm affects the performance significantly. In any case it is beneficial for CRN_1 to have as high $P(H_0)$ and $P_{f,2}$ as possible for throughput maximization.

8.3. Effect of Sensing Performance on Throughput Under Prioritize Access

In this part of the simulations, the performance of a CR node in a CR network having low priority to spectrum access is examined. Figure 6 and Figure 7 show the effect of sensing performance (false alarm and miss rate probabilities) on throughput in case of overlapping CR networks under prioritize secondary access. These figures capture the fundamental nature of overlapping CR networks. As false alarm probability of CR network increase, the throughput decreases. Miss rate probability has the opposite effect on the throughput. These results imply that CR users would like to have as low probability of false alarm as possible when detecting both PU and CGN, while keeping the required miss rate probability (due to regulations) to achieve the best performance.

Also, the combined effect of primary user's activity $(P(H_0^{PU}))$ and false alarm probability of $CRN(P_{f,2}^{PU})$ and $CGN(P_{f,1}^{PU})$ at PU are shown in Figure 8 and Figure 9. In Figure 8, highest CRN throughput is achieved at highest $P(H_0^{PU})$ and lowest $P_{f,2}^{PU}$, while in Figure 9, the

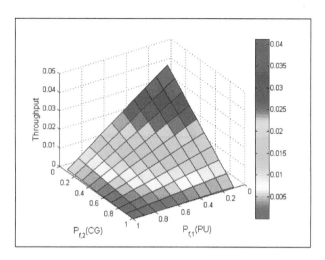

Figure 6. Effect of false alarm probability of CG and PU on the Throughput of CRN

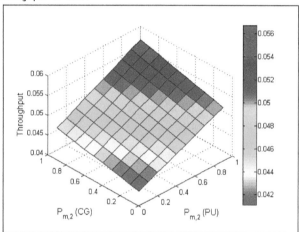

Figure 7. Effect of miss rate probability of CG and PU on the Throughput of CRN

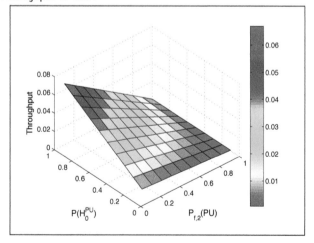

Figure 8. Combined effect of PU's activity and false alarm probability of CRN at PU on the Throughput of CRN

highest throughput is achieved at highest $P(H_0^{PU})$ with no visible effect of $P_{f,1}^{PU}$ on throughput.

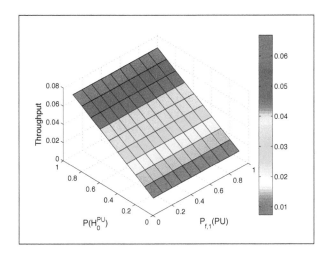

Figure 9. Combined effect of PU's activity and false alarm probability of *CGN* at PU on the Throughput of CRN

9. Discussions and Open Problems

The coexistence of wireless networks is unavoidable due to the current dilemma of spectrum scarcity. Advances in wireless communications and the introduction of concepts like cognitive radio and cognitive wireless networks, has turned the spectrum sharing among multiple systems from an idea into a possibility.

Our results are fundamental such that they can be applied to other types of wireless ad hoc networks. As an example, this framework finds application in Device-to-Device (D2D) communication [18]. The performance of ad hoc cognitive D2D systems sharing spectrum with cellular users in a macrocell can be investigated, the device throughput for multiple D2D systems in a cellular system can also be derived.

There also exist many challenges in the coexistence of multiple CR networks, these include spectrum availability detection, spectrum sharing, and interference mitigation [19]. Spectrum availability detection ensures identification of channels available for use without causing harmful interference to incumbents, achieved with high sensing performance. In addition, detection of coexisting secondary networks is also important, primarily to enable optimized decisions when selecting operating channels, this with spectrum sharing and interference mitigation ensure improve achievable throughput in CR network.

It will be more interesting to considered multiple CR ad hoc network from the network information theory point-of-view and derive the scaling law for this type of networks. The throughput scaling law for large-scale wireless networks initiated in [20], has been extensively studied [21]-[24]. They studied the random wireless network with static nodes randomly located in the unit area and grouped into source-destination (S-D) pairs for transmission. Under the multi-hop relay algorithm, the achievable per-node throughput in a

network was derived. In [25] and [26], the throughput scaling law was considered for a multihop CR network on top of a primary network, they showed that the two network can achieve the same throughput scaling law as a standalone wireless network, with finite outage probability for the secondary users in [25] and zero outage for the secondary users with high probability in [26]. It will be meaningful to compare the per-node throughput using the scaling laws for coexisting multiple CR networks, as this will afford the opportunity to investigate the achievable throughput scaling law promised in [20] for a node in a CR network even when the density is high.

10. Conclusions

In this study, the performance of overlapping CR networks which coexist together with a PU was investigated. We evaluated the performance of CR network over Gaussian and Nakagami-m fading channel by investigating the achievable per-node throughput. Specifically, we consider two cases: (1) equal access case where two CR networks have equal access to the spectrum; and (2) prioritized access case where one cognitive radio network, the cognitive gateway network (CGN), has higher priority to access the spectrum than the other cognitive radio network (CRN). Close form expressions for statistics, the Moment Generating Function (MGF) and Complementary Cumulative Distribution Function (CCDF) of multiple interferers in multiple coexisting CR networks are presented. By using these expressions, we derive the per-node throughput for multiple CR networks. Furthermore, the upper bound for the probability of false alarm during spectrum sensing that is required to achieve a certain throughput is deduced. The results illustrate how the transmission probability and spectrum sensing performance affect the achievable per-node throughput of overlapping CR networks. In addition, these results may serve as guidance for the deployment of multiple CR networks.

11. ACKNOWLEDGMENT

This research work is supported in part by the US Army Research Office under W911NF-12-1-0054 and W911NF-14-1-0044.

References

[1] "The fcc notice of proposed rulemaking and order et docket no. 03-108," *Facilitating opportunities for flexible, efficient, and reliable spectrum use emÂploying cognitive radio technologies*, Jun 2008..

[2] S. Shin, H. Park, and W. Kwon, "Mutual Interference Analysis of IEEE 802.15.4 and IEEE 802.11b," *Computer Networks*, vol. 51, no. 12, pp. 3338-3353, Aug 2007.

[3] J. Huang, G. Xing, G. Zhou, and R. Zhou, "Beyond Co-Existence: Exploiting WiFi White Space for Zigbee Performance Assurance," in *Proceedings of the 18th IEEE International Conference on Network Protocols*, Kyoto, Japan, pp. 305-314, Oct 2010.

[4] W. Yuan, X. Wang, and J.-P. Linnartz, "A coexistence model of ieee 802.15.4 and ieee 802.11b/g," in *14th IEEE Symposium on Communications and Vehicular Technology in the Benelux*, , pp. 1-5, Nov 2007.

[5] J. Xie, I. Howitt, and A. Raja, "Cognitive Radio Resource Management Using Multi-Agent Systems," in *Proceedings of the 4th IEEE Consumer Communications and Networking Conference*, Las Vegas, NV, USA, pp. 1123-1127, Jan 2007.

[6] S. Pollin, I. Tan, B. Hodge, C. Chun, and A. Bahai,"Harmful coexistence between 802.15.4 and 802.11: A measurement-based study," in *3rd International Conference on Cognitive Radio Oriented Wireless Networks and Communications (CrownCom)*,, pp. 1-6, May 2008.

[7] X. Zhang and K. G. Shin, "Enabling Coexistence of Heterogeneous Wireless Systems: Case for ZigBee and WiFi," in *Proceedings of the 12th ACM International Symposium on Mobile Ad Hoc Networking and Computing*, Paris, France, pp. 1-11, May 2011.

[8] H. Kim, J. Choi, and K. Shin, "Wi-Fi 2.0: Price and Quality Competitions of Duopoly Cognitive Radio Wireless Service Providers with Time-Varying Spectrum Availability," in *Proceedings of the 30th Annual IEEE International Conference on Computer Communications*, Shanghai, China, pp. 2453-2461, Apr 2011.

[9] L. Luo and S. Roy,"Analysis of Dynamic Spectrum Access with Heterogeneous Networks: Benefits of Channel Packing Scheme," in *Proceedings of the IEEE Global Telecommunications Conference*, Honolulu, HI, USA, pp. 1-7, Dec 2009.

[10] P. Zhu, J. Li, and X. Wang, "Scheduling Model for Cognitive Radio," in *Proceedings of the 3rd International Conference on Cognitive Radio Oriented Wireless Networks and Communications*, Singapore, Singapore, pp. 1-6, May 2008.

[11] Y. Zhao, M. Song, C. Xin, and M. Wadhwa, "Spectrum sensing based on three-state model to accomplish all-level fairness for co-existing multiple cognitive radio networks," in *2012 Proceedings of the IEEE INFOCOM*, pp. 1782-1790, 2012.

[12] J. Nieminen, L. Qian, and R. Jantti, "Per-node throughput performance of overlapping cognitive radio networks," in, *7th International ICST Conference on Cognitive Radio Oriented Wireless Networks and Communications (CROWNCOM)*, pp. 163-168, 2012.

[13] IEEE Std 802.22.1-2010, "IEEE Standard for Information Technology - Telecommunications and Information Exchange between Systems - Local and Metropolitan Area Networks - Specific Requirements - Part 22.1: Standard to Enhance Harmful Interference Protection for Low-Power Licensed Devices Operating in TV Broadcast Bands," Nov 2010.

[14] J. Venkataramam, M. Haenggi, and O. Collins, "Shot Noise Models for Outage and Throughput Analyses in Wireless Ad Hoc Networks," in *Proceedings of the IEEE Military Communications Conference*, Washington, D.C., USA, pp. 1-7, Oct 2006.

[15] J. Venkataraman and M. Haenggi, "Maximizing the Throughput in Random Wireless Ad Hoc Networks," in *Proceedings of the 42nd Annual Allerton Conference on Communication, Control, and Computing*, Monticello, IL, USA, pp. 1-9, Oct 2004.

[16] Y. Shobowale and K. Hamdi, "A unified model for interference analysis in unlicensed frequency bands," *IEEE Transactions on Wireless Communications*, vol. 8, no. 8, pp. 4004-4013, 2009.

[17] I. S. Gradshteyn and I. M. Ryzhik, *Table of Integrals, Series, and Products, Fifth Edition*, 7th ed., Academic Press, Jan. 2007.

[18] O. Omotere, L. Qian and X. Du, "Performance Bound of Ad Hoc Device-to-Device Communications using Cognitive Radio," *2013 IEEE Globecom Workshops*, 9-13 Dec. 2013.

[19] C. Ghosh, S. Roy, D. Cavalcanti, "Coexistence challenges for heterogeneous cognitive wireless networks in TV white spaces," *IEEE Wireless Communications*, vol.18, no.4, pp.22-31, Aug 2011.

[20] P. Gupta and P. R. Kumar, "The capacity of wireless networks," *IEEE Trans. Inf. Theory*, vol. 46, no. 2, pp. 388-404, Mar. 2000.

[21] F. Xue and P. R. Kumar, *Scaling Laws for Ad Hoc Wireless Networks: An Information Theoretic Approach*. Delft, The Netherlands: Now, 2006.

[22] S. R. Kullkarni and P. Viswanath, "A deterministic approach to throughput scaling in wireless networks," *IEEE Trans. Inf. Theory*, vol. 50, no. 6, pp. 1041-1049, Jun. 2004.

[23] L.-L. Xie and P. R. Kumar, "A network information theory for wireless communication: Scaling laws and optimal operation," *IEEE Trans. Inf. Theory*, vol. 50, no. 5, pp. 748-767, May 2004.

[24] A.Özgür, O. Lévêque, and D. N. C. Tse, "Hierarchical cooperation achieves optimal capacity scaling in ad hoc networks," *IEEE Trans. Inf. Theory*, vol. 53, no. 10, pp. 3549-3572, Oct. 2007.

[25] S.-W. Jeon, N. Devroye, M. Vu, S.-Y. Chung, and V. Tarokh, "Cognitive networks achieve throughput scaling of a homogeneous network," 2009 [Online]. Available: http://arxiv.org/pdf/0801.0938v2.

[26] Changchuan Yin; Long Gao; Shuguang Cui, "Scaling Laws for Overlaid Wireless Networks: A Cognitive Radio Network versus a Primary Network," *IEEE/ACM Transactions on Networking*, vol.18, no.4, pp.1317-1329, Aug. 2010.

14

Energy-Based Cooperative Spectrum Sensing of SC-FDMA Systems

Fucheng Yang and Lie-Liang Yang*

School of Electronics and Computer Science, University of Southampton, SO17 1BJ, UK

Abstract

In this paper, we propose a frequency-hopping M-ary frequency-shift keying spectrum sensing network (FH/MFSK SSN) for identifying the on/off states of the users supported by a single-carrier frequency-division multiple assess (SC-FDMA) primary radio (PR) system. Specifically, the spectrums of an uplink interleaved frequency-division multiple access (IFDMA) PR system are monitored by a number of cognitive radio sensing nodes (CRSNs). These CRSNs distributedly detect the on/off states of users based on one of the three energy detection schemes. After the local spectrum sensing, the CRSNs transmit their detected states to a fusion centre (FC) with the aid of FH/MFSK techniques. At the FC, the on/off states of the users supported the IFDMA PR system are finally classified according to either the conventional equal-gain combining (EGC) scheme or the novel erasure-supported EGC (ES-EGC) scheme. In this way, the on/off information about the spectrums occupied by an IFDMA PR system can be obtained, so that they can be exploited by a cognitive radio (CR) system. For local spectrum sensing, in this paper, we consider four synchronisation scenarios concerning the synchronisation between the received IFDMA signals and the CRSNs. The performance of the FH/MFSK SSN associated with various schemes is investigated by simulations. Our studies show that the FH/MFSK SSN constitutes one of the highly reliable spectrum sensing schemes, which are capable of exploiting both the space diversity provided by local CRSNs and the frequency diversity provided by the subcarriers of IFDMA system.

Keywords: Spectrum sensing, cognitive radio, cooperative, energy-based detection, frequency-hopping, M-ary frequency-shift keying, equal-gain combining, erasure-supported equal-gain combining, noncoherent detection, multiple-access.

1. Introduction

In wireless communications, the need for high data rate services is increasing as a result of the transition from voice-only communications to multimedia applications [1]. Given the limit of natural frequency spectrum, it has been recognised that the current static frequency allocation schemes are unable to accommodate the increasing number of high data rate devices. Cognitive radio with the capability to sense and exploit unoccupied channels or frequencies has therefore become a promising candidate for mitigating the problem of spectrum shortage [2]. According to Federal Communication Commission (FCC) [3], cognitive radio is defined

as a radio or system that can sense its operational electromagnetic environment and can dynamically and autonomously adjust its radio operating parameters to modify system operation, such as maximise throughput, mitigate interference, facilitate interoperability, access secondary markets.

In cognitive radio terminology, primary radios (PRs) have higher priority or legacy rights on the usage of specific parts of spectrum allocated to them, while cognitive radios (CRs) can access these spectrums in a way that they do not cause interference on the PRs or degrade the performance of the PRs. The studies show that the efficiency of CR systems depends mainly on the CRs' capability to sense the PR users' states (on/off) and to respond correspondingly and quickly. Hence, it

*Corresponding author. Email: lly@ecs.soton.ac.uk

is critical that CR systems can make quick and reliable decisions during spectrum sensing [4].

Depending on the knowledge available to the CRs, a range of spectrum sensing methods have been proposed and studied. As some examples, energy detection has been considered in [1, 5–7], matched filter (MF) detection in [5, 8], cyclostationary feature detection in [5, 8–10], etc. Each of these spectrum sensing techniques has some unique advantages and disadvantages, as detailed as follows. First, energy detection, also known as radiometry or periodogram, is the first way of spectrum sensing coming to our mind, owing to its low computation and implementation complexities [1]. In principle, an energy detector simply treats PR signals as noise and decides about their presence or absence based on the energy levels of the observed signals. Since it does not require any *a-priori* knowledge of PR signals, energy detection is viewed as a type of blind detection method. In energy detection, if the noise power is unable to be accurately estimated, its performance may significantly degrade. Furthermore, the noise-uncertainty in energy detection may lead to the so-called SNR wall phenomena [11]. Unlike the energy detector, MF detector and cyclostationary feature detector rely on the *a-priori* knowledge of PR signals' parameters, such as, waveforms, which is impractical for certain applications [4]. In a little more detail, MF detector makes coherent detection based on the *a-priori* knowledge of modulation type and carrier frequency of the PR signals. By contrast, cyclostationary feature detection belongs to a noncoherent spectrum sensing approach, which may distinguish various modulation signals. However, cyclostationary feature detector requires some parameters of PR signals, such as, symbol rate. In comparison with the above three types of spectrum sensing approaches, eigenvalue detection [2–4, 12–16] does not depend on the *a-priori* information as well as noise power, and it has the advantage of simultaneously achieving a high detection probability and a low false-alarm probability. However, the eigenvalue detection is highly dependent on the correlation of PR signals, it becomes less efficient when PR signals become less correlated.

In this paper, we propose and study a spectrum sensing network (SSN) for CR systems, where a number of cognitive radio sensing nodes (CRSNs) distributedly sense a PR system with multiple PR users. We assume that the PR system is the interleaved frequency-division multiple access (IFDMA) system for the LTE [17], which supports a number of synchronous PR users. To attain fast and low-complexity spectrum sensing, energy detection is employed by the CRSNs. Specifically, local decisions for the presence of multiple PR users are made by the CRSNs separately based on one of the *three types of energy detection schemes* considered, under the constraints of one of the *four synchronisation*

scenarios assumed between the PR signals and the CRSNs. By this way, every CRSN obtains a binary local decision vector, which is sent to the FC with the aid of frequency-hopping (FH) and M-ary frequency-shift keying (MFSK). Therefore, the SSN is referred to as the FH/MFSK SSN. Note that, in our SSN, we choose MFSK instead of other modulations, such as binary phase-shift keying (BPSK) and quadrature amplitude modulation (QAM), because of the following considerations. Firstly, it is well known that MFSK is an energy efficient modulation scheme, while the BPSK and QAM are bandwidth efficient, but not energy efficient modulation schemes. We prefer the energy-efficient scheme, in order to attain a low power spectral density, so that our SSN imposes little interference on the other wireless systems. Secondly, MFSK signals can be detected noncoherently without requiring channel estimation, which is suitable for operation in FH systems. By contrast, BPSK/QAM require the coherent detection that demands very accurate channel estimation. Explicitly, they are not suitable for operation in the FH systems, where the hopping rate is relatively high. In this paper, two types of noncoherent fusion detection rules are employed by the FC for making the final decision, which include a conventional equal-gain combining (EGC) fusion rule and a low-complexity erasure-supported EGC (ES-EGC) fusion rule [18]. The performance of the FH/MFSK SSN with EGC or ES-EGC fusion rule is investigated via simulation, under the assumptions that the channels from PR users to CRSNs and the channels from CRSNs to FC experience independent Rayleigh fading. Our studies and performance results show that our proposed FH/MFSK SSN constitutes a highly reliable spectrum sensing scheme, which is capable of exploiting the space diversity provided by CRSNs as well as the frequency diversity provided by the subcarriers of IFDMA system. Additionally, in comparison with the conventional EGC fusion rule, the novel ES-EGC fusion rule is robust to the errors made by CRSNs, yielding better detection performance.

The reminder of this paper is organised as follows. In Section 2, we provide the details of the proposed FH/MFSK SSN. Section 3 considers the fusion detection with either EGC or ES-EGC fusion rule. Section 4 demonstrates the simulation results for the detection performance. Finally, in Section 5, conclusions of this paper are derived.

2. System Model

The framework for our FH/MFSK SSN is shown as Fig. 1. We assume that the PR system is a LTE/LTE-A uplink SC-FDMA system, which supports K PR users. Each of the K PR users has two states: H_0 (off) and H_1 (on). We assume that the SC-FDMA system employs

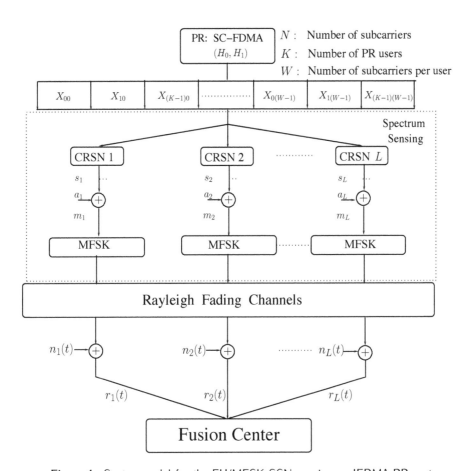

Figure 1. System model for the FH/MFSK SSN sensing an IFDMA PR system.

N subcarriers. As shown in reference [19], there are typically two strategies for allocation of N subcarriers to K users, yielding the so-called interleaved FDMA (IFDMA) and localised FDMA (LFDMA). In this paper, we consider only the IFDMA scheme. For convenience of our description, we assume that the N subcarriers are equally assigned to the K PR users. Hence, each of the K PR users occupies $W = N/K$ interleaved subcarriers. When the kth, $k = 1, 2, \ldots, K$, PR user is present to communicate, it occupies all the W subcarriers assigned to it. As the subcarriers are orthogonal with each other, we assume that every CRSN is capable of simultaneously sensing all the N subcarriers without inter-carrier interference. Furthermore, we assume that the CRSNs are operated in the strong SNR region and they are capable of acquiring some knowledge about the IFDMA PR system via its pilot signals.

In this contribution, energy sensing (detection) is employed by the L CRSNs, as seen in Fig. 1, to sense which PR user(s) is on/off or which subcarriers are available for the CR system. After the local sensing, each of the CRSNs obtains a binary vector of length K, indicating the on/off states of the K PR users. Then, the K-length binary vector is conveyed to an M-ary number and transmitted to the FC in the principles of

FH/MFSK. We assume that the number of frequency bands, expressed as M, used for FH/MFSK is equal to or larger than 2^K. Finally, at the FC, the on/off states of the K PR users are noncoherently classified based on the signals received from the L CRSNs. In this paper, two types of fusion detection schemes are considered, which are based on the conventional EGC [20] and the novel ES-EGC [18], respectively. Below, we provide the details about the operations carried out at the CRSNs and FC.

2.1. Spectrum Sensing at CRSNs

For convenience, the main parameters used in this paper are summarised as follows.

- N: number of subcarriers of SC-FDMA PR system;

- K: number of uplink PR users;

- $W = N/K$: number of subcarriers per PR user;

- L: number of CRSNs;

- M: number of frequency bands used by FH/MFSK;

- $U + 1$: number of multipaths of communications channels.

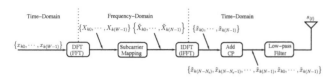

Figure 2. Transmitter schematic for the kth user supported by the SC-FDMA uplink.

The transmitter schematic of the SC-FDMA uplink is shown in Fig. 2. Let the W symbols transmitted by the kth PR user in time-domain be expressed as

$$\boldsymbol{x}_k = [x_{k0},\ x_{k1}, \cdots, x_{k(W-1)}]^T,$$
$$k = 0,\ 1, \cdots, K - 1 \qquad (1)$$

As shown in Fig. 2, first, $\boldsymbol{x}_k$ is transformed to the frequency-domain with the aid of the W-point DFT, yielding the W-length vector $\boldsymbol{X}_k$, which can be expressed as

$$\boldsymbol{X}_k = \mathcal{F}_W \boldsymbol{x}_k = [X_{k0},\ X_{k1}, \cdots, X_{k(W-1)}]^T \qquad (2)$$

where $\mathcal{F}_W$ denotes an W-point FFT matrix [19]. More specifically, the W entries in the vector $\boldsymbol{X}_k$ are given by

$$X_{kl} = \frac{1}{\sqrt{W}} \sum_{w=0}^{W-1} x_{kw} \exp\left(-j \frac{2\pi l w}{W}\right),$$
$$l = 0,\ 1, \cdots, W - 1 \qquad (3)$$

Following the DFT operation, the W elements in $\boldsymbol{X}_k$ are mapped to W out of the $N = WK$ subcarriers, according to the principles of IFDMA [19]. After the subcarrier mapping, the W-length vector $\boldsymbol{X}_k$ is extended to an N-length vector $\tilde{\boldsymbol{X}}_k$, which can be represented as

$$\tilde{\boldsymbol{X}}_k = [\tilde{X}_{k0},\ \tilde{X}_{k1}, \cdots, \tilde{X}_{k(N-1)}]^T \qquad (4)$$

In more detail, under the IFDMA strategy for mapping, the elements of $\tilde{\boldsymbol{X}}_k$ are given by

$$\tilde{X}_{kn} = X_{kw}, \text{ if } n = wK + k$$
$$\tilde{X}_{kv} = 0, \text{ otherwise} \qquad (5)$$

where $w = 0,\ 1, \cdots, W - 1;\ k = 0,\ 1, \cdots, K - 1$. After the subcarrier mapping, as shown in Fig. 2, $\tilde{\boldsymbol{X}}_k$ is transformed to the time-domain by carrying out the IDFT operation, yielding an N-length vector

$$\tilde{\boldsymbol{x}}_k = \mathcal{F}_N^H \tilde{\boldsymbol{X}}_k \qquad (6)$$

where $\mathcal{F}_N$ denotes the N-point FFT matrix.

According to [19], upon submitting (3) and (5) into (6), the vth, $v = 0,\ 1, \cdots, N - 1$, element of $\tilde{\boldsymbol{x}}_k$ can be expressed as

$$\tilde{x}_{k(v=qW+i)} = \frac{1}{\sqrt{N}} \sum_{n=0}^{N-1} \tilde{X}_{kn} \exp\left(j \frac{2\pi v n}{N}\right)$$
$$= \frac{1}{\sqrt{K}} \exp\left[j \frac{2\pi(qW+i)k}{N}\right] x_{ki} \qquad (7)$$

where the values of q, $q = 0,\ 1, \cdots, K - 1$, and i, $i = 0,\ 1, \cdots, W - 1$, are uniquely determined by the value of v. From (7) we can see that the W symbols of $\boldsymbol{x}_k$ of the kth PR user are repeatedly transmitted on the kth subcarrier, and all the W symbols are transmitted K times within one IFDMA symbol duration [19].

Following the N-point IDFT operation, as shown in Fig. 2, a cyclic prefix (CP) is added in the front of $\tilde{\boldsymbol{x}}_k$ in order to eliminate inter-symbol interference (ISI). Explicitly, the N_c-length CP for $\tilde{\boldsymbol{x}}_k$ is $\left[\tilde{x}_{k(-N_c)},\ \tilde{x}_{k(-N_c+1)}, \cdots \tilde{x}_{k(-1)}\right] = \left[\tilde{x}_{k(N-N_c)},\ \tilde{x}_{k(N-N_c-1)}, \cdots \tilde{x}_{k(N-1)}\right]$, which consists of the last N_c elements of vector $\tilde{\boldsymbol{x}}_k$. Let us express the time-domain vector after the CP as $\tilde{\boldsymbol{x}}_k'$, which is

$$\tilde{\boldsymbol{x}}_k' = \left[\tilde{x}_{k(-N_c)}, \cdots, \tilde{x}_{k(-1)}, \tilde{x}_{k0}, \cdots, \tilde{x}_{k(N-1)}\right]$$
$$= \left[\tilde{x}_{k(N-N_c)}, \cdots, \tilde{x}_{k(N-1)}, \tilde{x}_{k0}, \cdots, \tilde{x}_{k(N-1)}\right] \qquad (8)$$

Based on (8), finally, as shown in Fig. 2, we can form the complex baseband equivalent signal transmitted by the kth PR user, which is

$$s_k(t) = \sum_{v=0}^{N+N_c-1} \sqrt{2P} \tilde{x}_{kv}' \psi(t - vT_c) \qquad (9)$$

where P is the transmission power per dimension, $\tilde{x}_{kv}'$ is the vth element of $\tilde{\boldsymbol{x}}_k'$ and $\psi(t)$ is a unit-power chip-waveform impulse defined in $(0,\ T_c]$, where T_c is the chip duration, determined by the bandwidth used by the SC-FDMA system.

In our proposed SSN, each of the CRSNs is capable of simultaneously sensing all the K PR users. In this case, when the K uplink PR users' signals in the form of (9) are transmitted through wireless channels, the received complex baseband equivalent signal at the lth $(0 < l \le L)$ CRSN can be written as

$$R_l(t) = \sum_{k=0}^{K-1} s_k(t) * h_{kl}(t) + n_l(t) \qquad (10)$$

where $h_{kl}(t)$ denotes the channel impulse response (CIR) between the lth CRSN and the kth PR user, while $n_l(t)$ is the Gaussian noise process presenting at the lth CRSN, with zero mean and single-sided power-spectral density (PSD) of N_0 per dimension.

At the lth, $l = 1, \dots, L - 1$, CRSN, the received signal $R_l(t)$ is first sent to a filter matched to the chip waveform $\psi(t)$. Then, the filter's output signal is sampled at the chip rate of $1/T_c$. After the normalisation using $1/\sqrt{2P}T_c$, it can be shown that the vth, $(0 \le v \le$

$N + N_c - 1$), sample can be expressed as

$$
\begin{aligned}
\tilde{y}'_{l,v} &= \frac{1}{\sqrt{2P}T_c} \int_{vT_c}^{(v+1)T_c} R_l(t)\psi(t - vT_c)dt \\
&= \sum_{k=0}^{K-1} (h_{l,kv} * \tilde{x}'_{kv}) + \tilde{n}_{l,v} \\
&= \sum_{k=0}^{K-1} \sum_{u=0}^{U} h_{l,ku} \times \tilde{x}'_{k(v-N_c-u)} + \tilde{n}_{l,v}
\end{aligned}
\tag{11}
$$

where we assumed that the CIR has $(U+1)$ taps, i.e., $\boldsymbol{h}_{kl} = [h_{l,k0}, \cdots, h_{l,kU}]^T$. In the above equation, the Gaussian noise sample $\tilde{n}_{l,v}$ is expressed as

$$
\tilde{n}_{l,v} = \frac{1}{\sqrt{2P}T_c} \int_{vT_c}^{(v+1)T_c} n_l(t)\psi(t - vT_c)dt \tag{12}
$$

which has zero mean and a variance $2\sigma^2 = N_0/E_c$ with $E_c = PT_c$ representing the chip energy.

From the outputs of $\tilde{y}'_{l,v}$, we can form an N-length vector $\tilde{\boldsymbol{y}}_l$ at the lth CRSN. Furthermore, in the cases when the CRSNs do not know the beginning of an IFDMA symbol, they have to use an N-length vector having a random starting point. In this case, the N samples may span two consecutive IFDMA symbols. In order to consider this scenario, we use the superscript '0' to indicate the current IFDMA symbol, while the superscript '−1' to indicate the previous IFDMA symbol. In this contribution, four scenarios will be addressed. In the first scenario, namely, *synchronous sensing*, we consider the case of perfect synchronisation between the PR users and CRSNs. In the second and the third scenarios, we assume qusi-synchronisation between the PR users and the CRSNs, where the N samples used by a CRSN all come from one IFDMA symbol. However, we assume that there is no inter-(IFDMA) symbol interference in the second scenario, but there is in the third scenario. Correspondingly they are referred to as the *quai-synchronous sensing without ISI* and *quai-synchronous sensing with small ISI*, respectively. Finally, in the context of the fourth scenario, we assume that the N samples used by one CRSN are contributed by two consecutive IFDMA symbols, hence, it is an asynchronous scenario, giving the name of *asynchronous sensing*. Below we detail the representations corresponding to these operational scenarios.

Synchronous Sensing. When a CRSN perfectly synchronises with the incoming IFDMA signal, the CP added in the transmitted signals can be removed, yielding an N-length vector $\tilde{\boldsymbol{y}}_l$, as seen in Fig. 3. The value of the nth element of $\tilde{\boldsymbol{y}}_l$ is given by

$$
\tilde{y}_{l,n} = \tilde{y}'_{l,(n+N_c)}, \quad n = 0, 1, \cdots, N-1 \tag{13}
$$

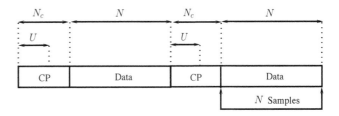

Figure 3. Illustration for the scenario of synchronous sensing.

Furthermore, it can be shown that $\tilde{\boldsymbol{y}}_l$ can be expressed based on matrix representation as

$$
\tilde{\boldsymbol{y}}_l = \begin{bmatrix} \tilde{y}_{l,0} \\ \tilde{y}_{l,1} \\ \vdots \\ \tilde{y}_{l,(N-1)} \end{bmatrix}
$$
$$
= \sum_{k=0}^{K-1} \begin{bmatrix} h^0_{l,kU} & h^0_{l,k(U-1)} & \cdots & h^0_{l,k0} & 0 & \cdots & 0 \\ 0 & h^0_{l,kU} & \cdots & h^0_{l,k1} & h^0_{l,k0} & \cdots & 0 \\ \vdots & \vdots & \ddots & \ddots & \ddots & \ddots & \vdots \\ 0 & \cdots & 0 & h^0_{l,kU} & \cdots & h^0_{l,k1} & h^0_{l,k0} \end{bmatrix}
$$
$$
\times \begin{bmatrix} \tilde{x}^0_{k,(-U)} \\ \vdots \\ \tilde{x}^0_{k,(-1)} \\ \tilde{x}^0_{k,0} \\ \vdots \\ \tilde{x}^0_{k,(N-1)} \end{bmatrix} + \begin{bmatrix} \tilde{n}_{l,N_c} \\ \tilde{n}_{l,(N_c+1)} \\ \vdots \\ \tilde{n}_{l,(N+N_c-1)} \end{bmatrix} \tag{14}
$$

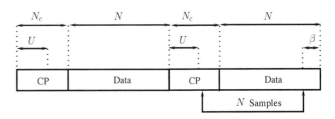

Figure 4. Illustration for the scenario of quai-synchronous sensing without ISI, where $0 \le \beta \le N_c - U$.

Quai-Synchronous Sensing without ISI. As an example, Fig. 4 shows a case corresponding to the scenario of quai-synchronous sensing without ISI. In this scenario, the sampling of a CRSN starts β chips before the first symbol $\tilde{x}^0_{k0}$, where $\beta \in (0, N_c - U)$. From Fig. 4 we can see that, when $\beta \in (0, N_c - U)$, there is no interference from the previous IFDMA symbol on the current IFDMA symbol. Furthermore, from Fig. 4, we can readily know that the nth element of $\tilde{\boldsymbol{y}}_l$ is given by

$$
\tilde{y}_{l,n} = \tilde{y}'_{l,(n+N_c-\beta)}, \quad n = 0, 1, \cdots, N-1 \tag{15}
$$

When expressed in matrix form, we have

$$
\tilde{\boldsymbol{y}}_l = \begin{bmatrix} \tilde{y}_{l,0} \\ \tilde{y}_{l,1} \\ \vdots \\ \tilde{y}_{l,(N-1)} \end{bmatrix}
$$
$$
= \sum_{k=0}^{K-1} \begin{bmatrix} h^0_{l,kU} & h^0_{l,k(U-1)} & \cdots & h^0_{l,k0} & 0 & \cdots & 0 \\ 0 & h^0_{l,kU} & \cdots & h^0_{l,k1} & h^0_{l,k0} & \cdots & 0 \\ \vdots & \vdots & \ddots & \ddots & \ddots & \ddots & \vdots \\ 0 & \cdots & 0 & h^0_{l,kU} & \cdots & h^0_{l,k1} & h^0_{l,k0} \end{bmatrix}
$$
$$
\times \begin{bmatrix} \tilde{x}^0_{k,(-U-\beta)} \\ \vdots \\ \tilde{x}^0_{k,(-1)} \\ \tilde{x}^0_{k,0} \\ \vdots \\ \tilde{x}^0_{k,(N-1-\beta)} \end{bmatrix} + \begin{bmatrix} \tilde{n}_{l,(N_c-\beta)} \\ \tilde{n}_{l,(N_c+1-\beta)} \\ \vdots \\ \tilde{n}_{l,(N+N_c-\beta-1)} \end{bmatrix} \quad (16)
$$

Furthermore, it can be shown that $\tilde{\boldsymbol{y}}_l$ can be expressed in matrix form as

$$
\tilde{\boldsymbol{y}}_l = \begin{bmatrix} \tilde{y}_{l,0} \\ \tilde{y}_{l,1} \\ \vdots \\ \tilde{y}_{l,(N-1)} \end{bmatrix}
$$
$$
= \sum_{k=0}^{K-1} \begin{bmatrix} h^{-1}_{l,kU} & h^{-1}_{l,k(U-1)} & \cdots & h^{-1}_{l,k0} & 0 & \cdots & 0 \\ 0 & h^{-1}_{l,kU} & \cdots & h^{-1}_{l,k1} & h^{-1}_{l,k0} & \cdots & 0 \\ \vdots & \vdots & \ddots & \ddots & \ddots & \ddots & \vdots \\ 0 & \cdots & 0 & h^0_{l,kU} & \cdots & h^0_{l,k1} & h^0_{l,k0} \end{bmatrix}
$$
$$
\times \begin{bmatrix} x^{-1}_{N+N_c-U-\beta} \\ \vdots \\ x^{-1}_{N-1} \\ x^0_{-N_c} \\ \vdots \\ x^0_0 \\ \vdots \\ x^0_{N-1-\beta} \end{bmatrix} + \begin{bmatrix} \tilde{n}_{l,(N_c-\beta)} \\ \tilde{n}_{l,(N_c+1-\beta)} \\ \vdots \\ \tilde{n}_{l,(N+N_c-\beta-1)} \end{bmatrix} \quad (18)
$$

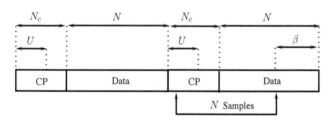

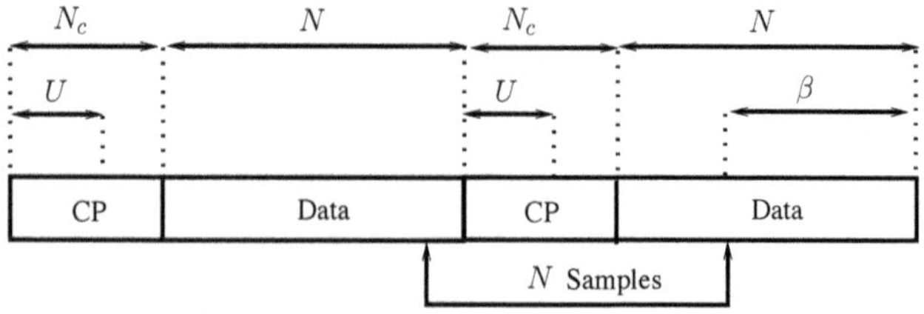

Figure 5. Illustration for the scenario of quai-synchronous sensing with small ISI, where $N_c - U \le \beta \le N_c$.

Figure 6. Illustration for the scenario of asynchronous sensing, where $N_c \le \beta < N$.

Quai-Synchronous Sensing with Small ISI. The scenario considered is similar as the one considered in Section 2.1, except that now $(N_c - U \le \beta \le N_c)$. In this case, the samples used for sensing are affected by both the -1st IFDMA symbol and the 0th IFDMA symbol, as seen in Fig. 5.

From Fig. 5, we can know that the nth element of $\tilde{\boldsymbol{y}}_l$ is given by

Asynchronous Sensing. Finally, for the scenario of asynchronous sensing, the situation can be seen in Fig. 6, where $N_c \le \beta < N$. Hence, the samples used for spectrum sensing depend on two consecutive IFDMA symbols. The nth entry of $\tilde{\boldsymbol{y}}_l$ can be expressed as

$$
\tilde{y}_{l,n} = \tilde{y}'_{l,(n+N_c-\beta)}, \quad n = 0, 1, \cdots, N-1 \quad (17)
$$

$$
\tilde{y}_{l,n} = \tilde{y}'_{l,(n+N_c-\beta)}, \quad n = 0, 1, \cdots, N-1 \quad (19)
$$

which, when in matrix form, can be represented as

$$
\tilde{\boldsymbol{y}}_l = \begin{bmatrix} \tilde{y}_{l,0} \\ \tilde{y}_{l,1} \\ \vdots \\ \tilde{y}_{l,(N-1)} \end{bmatrix}
$$

$$
= \sum_{k=0}^{K-1} \begin{bmatrix} h_{l,kU}^{-1} & h_{l,k(U-1)}^{-1} & \cdots & h_{l,k0}^{-1} & 0 & \cdots & 0 \\ 0 & h_{l,kU}^{-1} & \cdots & h_{l,k1}^{-1} & h_{l,k0}^{-1} & \cdots & 0 \\ \vdots & \vdots & \ddots & \ddots & \ddots & \ddots & \vdots \\ 0 & \cdots & 0 & h_{l,kU}^{0} & \cdots & h_{l,k1}^{0} & h_{l,k0}^{0} \end{bmatrix}
$$

$$
\times \begin{bmatrix} x_{N+N_c-U-\beta}^{-1} \\ \vdots \\ x_{N-1}^{-1} \\ x_{-N_c}^{0} \\ \vdots \\ x_0^0 \\ \vdots \\ x_{N-1-\beta}^0 \end{bmatrix} + \begin{bmatrix} \tilde{n}_{l,(N_c-\beta)} \\ \tilde{n}_{l,(N_c+1-\beta)} \\ \vdots \\ \tilde{n}_{l,(N+N_c-\beta-1)} \end{bmatrix} \quad (20)
$$

which has the same form as (18). However, we should note that in (18), $N_c - U \le \beta \le N_c$, while in (20) $N_c \le \beta < N$.

After obtaining the N observation samples, as shown in (14), (16), (18) or (20), the DFT operation is carried out to transform the time-domain observations $\tilde{\boldsymbol{y}}_l$ to the frequency-domain, yielding an N-length vector

$$
\tilde{\boldsymbol{Y}}_l = \mathcal{F}_N \tilde{\boldsymbol{y}}_l = [\tilde{Y}_{l,0}, \ \tilde{Y}_{l,1}, \cdots, \tilde{Y}_{l,(N-1)}],
$$
$$
l = 1, 2, \ldots, L \quad (21)
$$

where the vth $(0 \le v \le N-1)$ element of $\tilde{\boldsymbol{Y}}_l$ can be expressed as

$$
\tilde{Y}_{l,v} = \frac{1}{\sqrt{N}} \sum_{n=0}^{N-1} \tilde{y}_{l,n} \exp\left(-j\frac{2\pi v n}{N}\right)
$$
$$
= \frac{1}{\sqrt{N}} \sum_{n=0}^{N-1} \tilde{y}'_{l,(n+N_c)} \exp\left(-j\frac{2\pi v n}{N}\right) \quad (22)
$$

In correspondence to the subcarrier mapping operated at the transmitter side, at the CRSN, subcarrier demapping is carried out to execute the inverse operation of (5). The corresponding outputs for the kth PR user can be collected into an W-length vector as

$$
\tilde{\boldsymbol{Y}}_l^{(k)} = [\tilde{Y}_{l,0}^{(k)}, \ \tilde{Y}_{l,1}^{(k)}, \cdots, \tilde{Y}_{l,(W-1)}^{(k)}] \quad (23)
$$

in which the wth $(0 \le w \le W-1)$ element is

$$
\tilde{Y}_{l,w}^{(k)} = \tilde{Y}_{l,(wK+k)} \quad (24)
$$

With the aid of (23), a CRSN can now detect the on/off state of a PR user occupying a certain set of

subcarriers. As, for the purpose of CR sensing, a CR system only needs to know which subcarriers are active or inactive, low-complexity noncoherent detection can be employed. In this contribution, noncoherent energy detection is employed to detect the K PR users' states. Specifically, three types of local detection rules are investigated, which are referred to as the *average power assisted detection (APD)*, *majority vote assisted detection (MVD)* and the *maximum selection assisted detection (MSD)*. Their details are as follows.

In the context of the APD, the decision rule for detection of the kth PR user by the lth CRSN is given by

$$
\delta_{(l,k)} = \frac{1}{W} \sum_{w=0}^{W-1} |\tilde{Y}_{l,w}^{(k)}|^2 \underset{H_1}{\overset{H_0}{\lessgtr}} \lambda_{AP} \quad (25)
$$

where λ_{AP} is a preset threshold for the APD, which is chosen to satisfy a fixed false alarm probability of P_f.

When the MVD is employed, we first set a threshold $\lambda_{mv} > 0$. By comparing with this threshold, whenever an element $\tilde{Y}_{l,w}^{(k)}$ in $\tilde{\boldsymbol{Y}}_l^{(k)}$ exceeds λ_{mv}, the corresponding entry of a newly formed vector $\tilde{\boldsymbol{Y}}_l^{'(k)}$ is flagged by a logical one. Otherwise, it gives a logical zero. Based on $\tilde{\boldsymbol{Y}}_l^{'(k)}$, the local detection is made in the principles of MVD. Specifically, if the number of ones is equal to or more than λ_{MV} of the preset threshold, the CRSN renders that the corresponding PR user is on (H_1). Otherwise, it decides that the PR is off (H_0). In summary, the decision rule is described as

$$
\delta_{(l,k)} = \sum_{w=0}^{W-1} |\tilde{Y}_{l,w}^{'(k)}|^2 \underset{H_1}{\overset{H_0}{\lessgtr}} \lambda_{MV} \quad (26)
$$

where λ_{MV} is an integer threshold for the MVD.

Finally, when MSD is employed, the largest one of $\tilde{\boldsymbol{Y}}_l^{(k)}$ is chosen for making the local decision. The decision rule can be expressed as

$$
\delta_{(l,k)} = \max\{|\tilde{Y}_{l,0}^{(k)}|^2, \ |\tilde{Y}_{l,1}^{(k)}|^2, \cdots, |\tilde{Y}_{l,(W-1)}^{(k)}|^2\} \underset{H_1}{\overset{H_0}{\lessgtr}} \lambda_{MS} \quad (27)
$$

where λ_{MS} is the threshold for the MSD, which is chosen for satisfying a fixed false alarm probability P_f.

After the on/off states of all the K PR users are detected, the lth CRSN obtains an K-length binary vector holding the on/off states of the K PR users, which is expressed as $\boldsymbol{s}_l^{(B)} = [s_{l,0}^{(B)}, s_{l,1}^{(B)}, \cdots, s_{l,(K-1)}^{(B)}]$. This vector is then mapped to an M-ary number expressed as $s_l^{(M)}$, which is transmitted in the FH/MFSK principles, as shown in Fig. 1 and detailed in the next subsection.

2.2. Signal Processing and Transmission at CRSNs

Let the estimated states by the L CRSNs are collected into a vector $\boldsymbol{s}^{(M)} = [s_1^{(M)}, s_2^{(M)}, \cdots, s_L^{(M)}]$, where $s_l^{(M)} \in$

[0, M − 1]. Following the local spectrum sensing, the L CRSNs convey their local detected states to the FC with the aid of the FH/MFSK techniques. Let the total transmission time of $s^{(M)}$ to the FC be T_s seconds, which is referred to as the symbol duration. This symbol duration is equally divided into L potions referred to as *time-slots* having the duration $T_h = T_s/L$. Each CRSN uses one time-slot to send its detected states to the FC. As previously mentioned, the FH/MFSK scheme has M orthogonal sub-frequency bands, their centre frequencies are represented by $F = \{f_0, f_1, \ldots, f_{M-1}\}$. These M frequencies are used for both FH and MFSK modulation, which are implemented as follows. Let $a = [a_1, a_2, \cdots, a_L]$ be a FH address used for FH operation, where $a_l \in \{0, 1, \cdots, M − 1\}$, $l = 1, 2, \ldots, L$. With the aid the FH operation, different CRSNs may convey their signals on different sub-frequency bands. The operation enhances the diversity capability for final signal detection at the FC, expecially, when some of the CRSNs are close to each other, resulting in correlation in the space domain.

After processing $s^{(M)}$ using the FH address a, we obtain

$$m = [m_1, m_2, \cdots, m_L] = s^{(M)} \oplus a$$
$$= \left[s_1^{(M)} \oplus a_1, s_2^{(M)} \oplus a_2, \cdots, s_L^{(M)} \oplus a_L \right] \quad (28)$$

where $\oplus$ represents the addition operation in the Galois field of $GF(M)$. Therefore, the value of m_l ($l = 1, 2, \ldots, L$) is within $[0, M − 1]$ and is suitable for MFSK modulation. Following the FH operation, as shown in Fig. 1, the components of m are mapped to the MFSK's sub-frequencies $F_m = \{f_{m1}, f_{m2}, \ldots, f_{ml}\}$, where $f_{m_l} \in F$. Finally, the MFSK signals of the L CRSNs are transmitted one-by-one to the FC in a time-division fashion using L time-slots of duration T_h. Specifically, the signal transmitted by the lth CRSN during $iT_s < t \le (i + 1)T_s$ can be expressed in complex form as

$$s_l(t) = \sqrt{P} \psi_{T_h}[t − iT_s − (l − 1)T_h]$$
$$\times \exp[j2\pi(f_c + f_{m_l})t + j\phi_l], \quad l = 1, 2, \ldots, L \quad (29)$$

where P denotes the transmission power, which is assumed the same for all the L CRSNs, f_c is the main carrier frequency and ϕ_l is the initial phase introduced by carrier modulation. In (29), $\psi_{T_h}(t)$ is the pulse-shaped signalling waveform, which is defined over the interval $[0, T_h)$ and satisfies the normalisation of $\int_0^{T_h} \psi^2(t)dt = T_h$.

Assuming that the signals as shown in (29) are transmitted via flat Rayleigh fading channels to the FC, the received signal during $iT_s < t \le (i + 1)T_s$ can then be

expressed as

$$r_l(t) = h_l s_l(t) + n_l(t)$$
$$= \sqrt{P} h_l \psi_{T_h}[t − iT_s − (l − 1)T_h]$$
$$\times \exp[j2\pi(f_c + f_{m_l})t + j\phi_l] + n(t),$$
$$l = 1, 2, \ldots, L, \quad (30)$$

where $h_l = \alpha_l \exp(j\theta_l)$ denotes the channel gain with respect to the lth CRSN, which is assumed constant over one symbol-duration. In (29), $n(t)$ is the Gaussian noise process presenting at the FC, which has zero mean and single-sided power-spectral density (PSD) of N_0 per dimension.

3. Fusion Processing

When the FC receives the signal $r_l(t)$, $l = 1, 2, \cdots, L$, final decision is made with the aid of one of the two noncoherent fusion rules, namely the conventional EGC fusion rule and the ES-EGC fusion rules, which are detailed as follows.

First, for both the fusion rules, M decision variables are formed for every of the L CRSNs, which are

$$R_{ml} = \left| \frac{1}{\sqrt{\Omega P} T_h} \int_{iT_s+lT_h}^{iT_s+(l+1)T_h} r_l(t) \psi_{T_h}^*[t − iT_s − (l − 1)T_h] \right.$$
$$\left. \times \exp[−j2\pi(f_c + f_m)t]dt \right|^2,$$
$$m = 0, 1, \ldots, M − 1; \ l = 1, 2, \ldots, L \quad (31)$$

where $\Omega = E[|h_l|^2]$ denotes the average channel power. Since the M sub-frequency bands used for FH/MFSK are assumed to be orthogonal to each other, there is no interference between any two sub-frequency bands. Consequently, upon substituting (30) into (31) and absorbing the carrier phase ϕ_l into h_l, we obtain

$$R_{ml} = \left| \frac{\mu_{mm_l} h_l}{\sqrt{\Omega}} + N_{ml} \right|^2, \ m = 0, 1, \ldots, M − 1;$$
$$l = 1, 2, \ldots, L \quad (32)$$

where, by definition, $\mu_{mm} = 1$, while $\mu_{mm_l} = 0$, if $m \ne m_l$. In (32), N_{ml} is a complex Gaussian noise sample collected from the mth sub-frequency band during the lth time-slot, which is given by

$$N_{ml} = \frac{1}{\sqrt{\Omega P} T_h} \int_{iT_s+lT_h}^{iT_s+(l+1)T_h} n(t) \psi_{T_h}^*[t − iT_s − (l − 1)T_h]$$
$$\times \exp[−j2\pi(f_c + f_m)t]dt \quad (33)$$

It can be shown that N_{ml} has mean zero and a variance of $LN_0/(\Omega E_s) = L/\bar{\gamma}_s$, where $E_s = PT_s$ represents the total energy with each CRSN's transmitted energy per symbol being $E_h = E_s/L$, while $\bar{\gamma}_s = \Omega E_s/N_0$ denotes the average SNR per symbol.

Using the ML values shown in (32), we can form a time-frequency matrix R of $(M \times L)$, where each column holds M decision variables in the form of (32). Based on R, the FC carries out the final detection in the principles of EGC or ES-EGC fusion rule.

3.1. EGC Fusion Rule

In the context of the EGC fusion rule, the FC makes the final decision based on the time-frequency matrix as follows.

1. **Frequency de-hopping to form a detection matrix:**

$$D = R \boxminus (1 \otimes a^T) \qquad (34)$$

where 1 denotes an all-one column vector of M-length and $\otimes$ denotes the Kronecker product operation between two matrices [19]. In (34), the operation of $A \boxminus B$ shifts the elements in A based on the values provided by B[1]. Specifically, after the operation in (34), a detection matrix D is formed as

$$D_{(m\ominus a_l)l} = R_{ml}, \quad m = 0, 1, \dots, M - 1;$$
$$l = 1, 2, \dots, L \qquad (35)$$

where $\ominus$ denotes the subtraction operation in the Galois field of $GF(M)$. The operation in (35) means that the element indexed by m in R is changed to the one indexed by $m' = m \ominus a_l$ in D.

2. **EGC detection:** Based on the detection matrix D, M decision variables for final spectrum sensing are formed under the EGC principles [19] as

$$D_m = \sum_{l=1}^{L} D_{ml}, \quad m = 0, 1, \dots, M - 1 \qquad (36)$$

Finally, the largest one of $\{D_0, D_1, \cdots, D_{M-1}\}$ is selected and its index is mapped to an integer in the range $[0, M - 1]$, which represents the M-ary estimation of the K PR users' on/off states. Then, the M-ary integer is converted to a binary vector of K-length, whose K elements give the on/off states of the K PR users.

3.2. ES-EGC Fusion Rule

In our SSN, there are mainly two sources resulting in that the FC makes erroneous decisions. The first one is the incorrect detection made by the CRSNs. In this case,

the CRSNs directly send the FC incorrect information. Secondly, the wireless channels between CRSNs and FC are non-ideal, which also introduce errors. Statistically, when an element in the detection matrix D contains both signal and noise, its energy will be higher than that of the element containing only noise. This implies that, if an element in the undesired rows (the rows not matching to the states of the PR users) has high energy, it might be an erroneous element introduced by what the above-mentioned. Straightforwardly, this type of elements in the undesired rows may significantly degrade the detection performance of the FC.

Based on the above observation, in this contribution, the ES-EGC fusion rule is employed. When operated under this fusion rule, in each of the M rows of the detection matrix D, a given number of entries with the highest values are removed before forming the M decision variables based on the EGC principles. As a result, the errors transmitted by the CRSNs might be removed, especially when the signal-to-noise ratio (SNR) is relatively high. As our performance results in Section 4 show, this error-erasing process will significantly enhance the detection performance of the FC.

In detail, the ES-EGC fusion rule is operated as follows.

1. **Frequency de-hopping to form the detection matrix D**, which is the same as that done by the EGC fusion rule.

2. **Erasure operation:** After obtaining D, the ES-EGC fusion rule carries out the erasure operations. In each of the M rows of D, I $(0 \le I < L)$ elements corresponding to the I largest values are replaced by the value of zero, which results in a new matrix $\bar{D}$.

3. **EGC detection:** M decision variables are formed based on the matrix $\bar{D}$ in EGC principles [19] as

$$\bar{D}_m = \sum_{l=1}^{L} \bar{D}_{ml}, \quad m = 0, 1, \dots, M - 1 \qquad (37)$$

Finally, the largest of $\{\bar{D}_0, \bar{D}_1, \cdots, \bar{D}_{(M-1)}\}$ is selected and its index value in terms of m represents the M-ary estimation of value conveyed by the CRSNs. Furthermore, after mapping the M-ary value to the binary representation, the on/off states of the K PR users can be estimated.

4. Spectrum Sensing Performance

In this section, both the local spectrum sensing at CRSNs and the overall detection performance at the FC are investigated via simulations. Specifically, we consider the local missing probability, P_m, of the

---

[1] Note that, the element-shift operations do not change the values of the elements in A. Instead, the locations of the elements in matrix A are shifted to the other locations based on the values of the corresponding elements in B.

sensing at CRSNs and the overall missing probability, P_M, of the detection at the FC. At the CRSNs, we assume that the signals received from the PR users experience multipath Rayleigh fading. We compare the local missing probability of different detection approaches and show the influence of the thresholds applied for detection. At the FC, the overall spectrum sensing performance is investigated, when assuming that random FH addresses are used for transmitting the local decisions made by the CRSNs to the FC, and that the wireless channels from the CRSNs to the FC experience independent Rayleigh fading.

Note that, the parameters used in our simulations for each of the figures are detailed associated with the figure. In the figures, the 'Observation SNR at each CRSN' is the average SNR per PR user received at a CRSN. The false-alarm probability of all the CRSNs is assumed the same, which is expressed as P_f. The 'Channel SNR per bit' is the average received SNR at the FC per bit given by $\bar{\gamma}_b = \bar{\gamma}_s/b$, where $b = \log_2 M$ denotes the number of bits required to represent a M-ary number.

Fig. 7 shows the impacts of the four scenarios, as shown in Section 2.1, which address the synchronisation between the received signals from PR users and the sensing, on the PSDs of the received signals. As shown on the top of the figure, we consider an IFDMA PR system, which employs $N = 128$ subcarriers to support maximum $K = 16$ uplink users. Hence, each PR user occupies $W = 8$ subcarriers evenly distributed over the 128 subcarriers, as indicated by the eight dominant spectral lines in each of the four figures. We assume that, in the PR system, only user 1 is on, while all the other PR users are idle. Signals received by CRSNs from the PR users are assumed to experience multipath Rayleigh fading having $(U + 1) = 5$ time-domain resolvable paths. As shown in Section 2.1, the value of the parameter β reflects the synchronisation level between the PR signals and the local sensing. Specifically, we set $\beta = 0$, 2, 15 and 50, respectively, for the scenarios of synchronous sensing, qusi-synchronous sensing without ISI, qusi-synchronous sensing with small ISI and asynchronous sensing. From the results shown in the figures, we can clearly see that, when the sensing becomes more asynchronous with the arrival PR signals, inter-carrier interference increases, i.e., more power leaks from the activated subcarriers to their neighbouring subcarriers. However, at 5 dB of the SNR, the activated subcarriers stand out explicitly and have significantly higher power than the other idle subcarriers.

In Fig. 8, we investigate the performance of the three types of energy-based detection schemes, namely, the APD, MVD and the MSD, when the false-alarm probability of local CRSNs is set as $P_f = 0.05$. In the figure, $\beta = 0$ stands for the scenario of

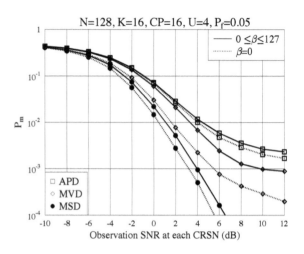

Figure 8. Missing probability of the local CRSNs sensing the spectrum of an IFDMA system using 128 subcarriers to support maximum 16 users, when communicating over multipath Rayleigh fading channels having 5 time-domain resolvable paths.

synchronous sensing. By contrast, $0 \leq \beta \leq 127$ means that β is a random variable taking integer values uniformly in $[0, 127]$, which provides the average performance achieved by the four synchronisation scenarios considered. From Fig. 8, first, we can see that the MVD outperforms the APD, and that the MSD achieves the best sensing performance among the three local detection schemes. Second, the synchronous sensing results in the best local sensing performance, as there is no inter-carrier interference.

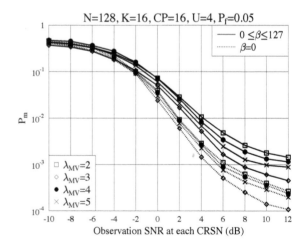

Figure 9. Missing probability of the local CRSNs sensing the spectrum of an IFDMA system with 128 subcarriers to support maximum 16 users, when the MVD associated with various values for λ_{MV} is employed.

In Fig. 9, we illustrate the local sensing performance of the CRSNs employing MVD, when the thresholds are $\lambda_{MV} = 2$, 3, 4 and 5. Similarly to Fig. 8, in Fig. 9

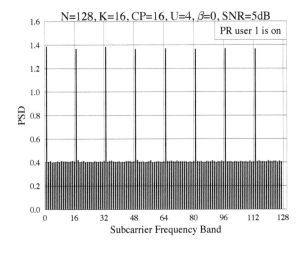

(a) Case 1: Synchronous sensing.

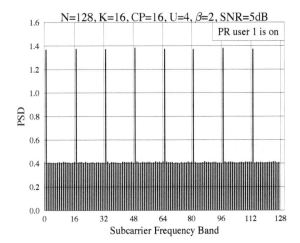

(b) Case 2: Qusi-synchronous sensing without ISI.

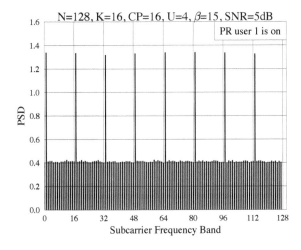

(c) Case 3: Qusi-synchronous sensing with small ISI.

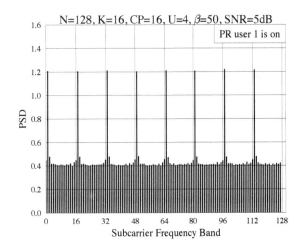

(d) Case 4: Asynchronous sensing.

Figure 7. Power spectral density presenting at the CRSNs in an IFDMA system using 128 subcarriers to support maximum 16 users, when communicating over multipath Rayleigh fading channels having 5 time-domain resolvable paths. The results were obtained from 10000 realisations.

both the synchronous sensing ($\beta = 0$) and the random asynchronous sensing ($0 \leq \beta \leq 127$) are considered. From the results of Fig. 9, again, we observe that the synchronous sensing outperforms the asynchronous sensing. For both the cases, we see that $\lambda_{mv} = 3$ results in the lowest missing probability, when the SNR is relatively high, which implies that there exists an optimal value for the threshold, resulting in that the MVD-assisted local sensing attains the lowest missing probability.

Fig. 10 portrays the sensing performance of the MSD detection scheme in the context of the four scenarios considered in Section 2.1. As our discussion in Section 2.1 shows, when the CRSNs are operated in the scenarios of synchronous sensing or quai-synchronous sensing without ISI, there is no interference from a

previous IFDMA symbol on the current IFDMA symbol. As shown in Fig. 10, we are unable to distinguish between the performance of these two scenarios. By contrast, when there is small or large ISI, corresponding to the scenarios of quai-synchronous sensing with small ISI and asynchronous sensing, the performance of local CRSNs degrades explicitly, in comparison with that of the scenarios of synchronous sensing and quai-synchronous sensing without ISI. Furthermore, the missing probability achieved under the scenario of asynchronous sensing is higher than that achieved under the scenario of quai-synchronous sensing with small ISI.

Fig. 11 shows the overall missing probability of the cognitive SSNs with various numbers of CRSNs, when the local CRSNs employs the MSD. In the studies,

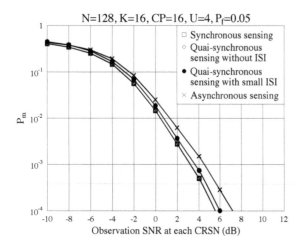

Figure 10. Missing probability of the MSD-assisted CRSNs sensing an IFDMA system using 128 subcarriers for supporting maximum 16 users, when four sensing scenarios are considered.

we assume an IFDMA system which has in total $N = 128$ subcarriers and supports maximum $K = 16$ users. Hence, each active user uses $W = 8$ subcarrier for uplink communications. At the FC, both the EGC fusion rule (Fig. 11(a)) and ES-EGC fusion rule (Fig. 11(b)) are considered. Furthermore, when the ES-EGC fusion rule is employed, we assume that an optimum number of entries per row are erased, which yields the best overall detection performance. From the results of Fig. 11(a) and Fig. 11(b), first, we can explicitly see that the overall missing probability decreases, as the number of CRSNs increases from $L = 10$ to $L = 15$ and to $L = 20$, owing to the improvement of spatial diversity. Second, similar as the detection at the CRSNs, the overall detection performance of the system with synchronous sensing corresponding to ($\beta = 0$) is better than that achieved by the systems using asynchronous sensing. Finally, when comparing Fig. 11(b) with Fig. 11(a), we can clearly see that the ES-EGC fusion rule outperforms the EGC fusion rule, which becomes more significant, when the channel SNR increases.

Finally, in Fig. 12, the overall missing probability performance of the cognitive SSN is investigated, when different observation SNR is assumed for the CRSNs. From Fig. 12, we can have similar observations as that from Fig. 11. Again, we can find that the ES-EGC fusion rule outperforms the EGC fusion rule, which becomes more explicit, as the SNR of the channels from CRSNs to FC increases.

5. Conclusion

A FH/MFSK SSN has been proposed for spectrum sensing of an uplink IFDMA PR system. In the FH/MFSK SSN, a number of CRSNs are employed for initial detection of the on/off states of the users

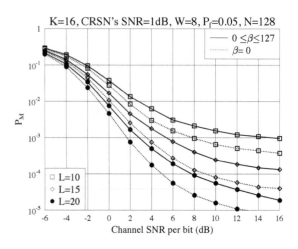

(a) Local detection: MSD; Fusion detection: EGC

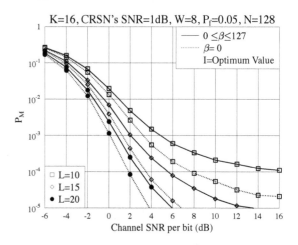

(b) Local detection: MSD; Fusion detection: ES-EGC

Figure 11. Overall missing probability of the cognitive spectrum sensing systems with different numbers of CRSNs, when the MSD local detection and the EGC or ES-EGC assisted fusion detection are employed.

supported the IFDMA PR system. At the CRSNs, four synchronisation scenarios have been assumed between received IFDMA signals and CRSN detectors, which are the synchronous sensing, quai-synchronous sensing without ISI, quai-synchronous sensing with small ISI and the asynchronous sensing. Our investigation shows that the sensing performance slightly degrades, as the received IFDMA signals and CRSN detectors become more asynchronised. However, the FH/MFSK SSN is usually capable of achieving reliable sending, even in the case of asynchronous sensing, owing to the space- and frequency-diversity provided by the FH/MFSK SSN and the IFDMA system, respectively. In this paper, three low-complexity energy detection schemes, namely, the APD, MVD and the MSD, have been studied in conjunction with the CRSN detection, showing that

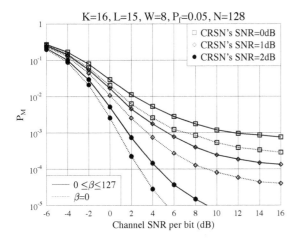

(a) Local detection: MSD; Fusion detection: EGC

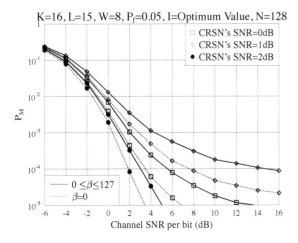

(b) Local detection: MSD; Fusion detection: ES-EGC

Figure 12. Overall missing probability of the cognitive SSN with the MSD for local detection and EGC or ES-EGC assisted fusion detection, when the CRSNs have various observation SNRs.

the MVD outperforms the APD and the MSD achieves the best sensing reliability among the three. At the FC, the states of the users supported by the IFDMA PR system are finally detected either by the EGC detection scheme or the ES-EGC detection scheme. Our studies demonstrate that the ES-EGC scheme is able to suppress the sensing errors made by CRSNs, and to achieve much higher sensing reliability than the EGC scheme, when the sensing at CRSNs is unreliable.

References

[1] T. Yucek and H. Arslan, "A survey of spectrum sensing algorithms for cognitive radio applications," *IEEE Communications Surveys Tutorials*, vol. 11, pp. 116 – 130, First Quarter 2009.

[2] A. Kortun, T. Ratnarajah, M. Sellathurai, C. Zhong, and C. B. Papadias, "On the performance of eigenvalue-based cooperative spectrum sensing for cognitive radio," *IEEE Journal of Selected Topics in Signal Processing*, vol. 5, pp. 49 – 55, February 2011.

[3] Y. Zeng and Y.-C. Liang, "Eigenvalue-based spectrum sensing algorithms for cognitive radio," *IEEE Transactions on Communications*, vol. 57, pp. 1784 – 1793, June 2009.

[4] L. Wei and O. Tirkkonen, "Cooperative spectrum sensing of OFDM signals using largest eigenvalue distributions," in *IEEE 20th International Symposium on Personal, Indoor and Mobile Radio Communications*, pp. 2295 – 2299, September 2009.

[5] E. Axell, G. Leus, and E. G. Larsson, "Overview of spectrum sensing for cognitive radio," in *2nd International Workshop on Cognitive Information Processing (CIP)*, pp. 322 – 327, June 2010.

[6] F. F. Digham, M.-S. Alouini, and M. K. Simon, "On the energy detection of unknown signals over fading channels," *IEEE Transactions on Communications*, vol. 55, pp. 21 – 24, January 2007.

[7] J. J. Lehtomaki, M. Juntti, H. Saarnisaari, and S. Koivu, "Threshold setting strategies for a quantized total power radiometer," *IEEE Signal Processing Letters*, vol. 12, pp. 796 – 799, November 2005.

[8] J. Ma, G. Y. Li, and B. H. Juang, "Signal processing in cognitive radio," *Proceedings of the IEEE*, vol. 97, pp. 805 – 823, May 2009.

[9] A. V. Dandawate and G. B. Giannakis, "Statistical tests for presence of cyclostationarity," *IEEE Transactions on Signal Processing*, vol. 42, pp. 2355 – 2369, September 1994.

[10] W. A. Gardner and C. M. Spooner, "Signal interception: performance advantages of cyclic-feature detectors," *IEEE Transactions on Communications*, vol. 40, pp. 149 – 159, January 1992.

[11] R. Tandra and A. Sahai, "SNR walls for signal detection," *IEEE Journal of Selected Topics in Signal Processing*, vol. 2, pp. 4 – 17, February 2008.

[12] T. J. Lim, R. Zhang, Y.-C. Liang, and Y. Zeng, "GLRT-based spectrum sensing for cognitive radio," in *IEEE Global Telecommunications Conference (GLOBECOM'08)*, pp. 1 – 5, November 2008.

[13] S. Wang and R. Nazanin, "Eigenvalue-based cooperative spectrum sensing with finite samples/sensors," in *46th Annual Conference on Information Sciences and Systems (CISS)*, pp. 1 – 5, March 2012.

[14] A. Kortun, M. Sellathurai, T. Ratnarajah, and C. Zhong, "Distribution of the ratio of the largest eigenvalue to the trace of complex Wishart matrices," *IEEE Transactions on Signal Processing*, vol. 60, pp. 5527 – 5532, October 2012.

[15] B. Nadler, F. Penna, and R.Garello, "Performance of eigenvalue-based signal detectors with known and unknown noise level," in *IEEE International Conference on Communications (ICC)*, pp. 1 – 5, June 2011.

[16] P. Bianchi, M. Debbah, M. Maida, and J. Najim, "Performance of statistical tests for single-source detection using random matrix theory," *IEEE Transactions on Information Theory*, vol. 57, pp. 2400 – 2419, April 2011.

[17] W. Zhang and Y. Sanada, "Cyclostationarity feature matched detection and application to IFDMA system,"

in *4th International Conference on Cognitive Radio Oriented Wireless Networks and Communications (CROWN-COM'09)*, pp. 1 – 5, 2009.

[18] F. Yang and L.-L. Yang, "Frequency-hopping/M-ary frequency-shift keying wireless sensor networks with soft-sensing," in *1st IEEE International Conference on Communications in China (ICCC'12)*, pp. 751 – 756, 2012.

[19] L.-L. Yang, *Multicarrier Communications*. United Kingdom: John Wiley, 2009.

[20] F. Yang and L.-L. Yang, "Frequency-hopping/M-ary frequency-shift keying wireless sensor network monitoring multiple source events," in *IEEE 75th Vehicular Technology Conference (VTC'12 Spring)*, pp. 1 – 5, 2012.

15

Mapping urban accessibility: gamifying the citizens' experience

Catia Prandi[1,*], Valentina Nisi[2], Paola Salomoni[1], Nuno Jardim Nunes[2], Marco Roccetti[1]

[1]Department of Computer Science and Engineering, University of Bologna, Bologna, Italy
[2]Madeira Interactive Technologies Institute, University of Madeira, Funchal, Madeira, Portugal

Abstract

In this paper we present the design process and some interesting field trial results of two different game applications, designed and developed in order to extend and motivate the community of mPASS. mPASS is an urban accessibility mapping system that allows citizens to collect reliable data about barriers and facilities via crowdsourcing and crowdsensing and it uses these data to calculate accessible paths. On the one hand mPASS needs to collect a sufficiently dense, detailed and trustworthy amount of data. On the other hand, the community interested in obtaining accessible paths is not big enough to reach the critical mass of information needed by the system in order to provide effective services. To overcome this problem, we investigated gamification strategies in designing two mobile applications targeting young adults walkers, aimed to enlarge the data contributors community. The design process and field trial results of both games are presented, highlighting the design decisions resulted from feedback sessions, focus groups and experience prototyping.

Keywords: urban accessibility, crowdsourcing, crowdsensing, gamification, pervasive game

1. Introduction

With an increasing number of people living in cities, urban mobility became one of the most important research fields in the so-called smart city environments. In fact, in [1], authors define a smart city as "a city well performing in a forward-looking way in economy, people, governance, mobility, environment, and living, built on the 'smart' combination of endowments and activities of self-decisive, independent and aware citizens". In this context, smart mobility is defined by four factors which reflect the most important aspects about urban mobility: (i) local accessibility; (ii) (inter)national accessibility; (iii) availability of ICT-infrastructure; and (iv) sustainable, innovative and safe transport systems [1]. From these definitions it is clear that smart mobility, and in particular urban accessibility, is a very important element that needs to be tackled in order to improve the quality of life in cities. This is especially relevant for people with disabilities and special needs, who frequently face barriers while moving in the urban environment. According to the World Report on disability [2] more than the 15% of the world's population is estimated to live with some form of disability. Moreover, the number of people with disabilities or reduced mobility is growing, due to ageing of populations. Improvement in urban accessibility can also benefit people who are not disabled but are "mobility impaired" by environmental barriers. For instance healthy elderly people, children, pregnant women or people with temporary health conditions. A UK based survey [3] reported that 8% of adults recorded having difficulties moving outdoors and carrying out normal day-to-day activities. Our work was inspired by the potential of pervasive computing and crowdsourcing to develop a system that provides citizens with customised accessible pedestrian paths. mPASS (mobile Pervasive Accessibility Social Sensing) [4] can be used to compute viable paths, not just for people with disabilities, but also for people experiencing mobility impairments, for instance, elderly people, people with temporary disabilities, mothers with baby strollers or tourists carrying heavy luggage [5]. In order to calculate these personalize paths mPASS needs an updated picture of the accessibility urban elements in the environment [6]. To gather these data mPASS uses georeferenced information collected by users via crowdsourcing and crowdsensing [7].

A key factor for the success of any crowdsourcing system is the recruitment of a sufficiently large group of users to reach critical mass engagement. This is especially hard in mPASS since the main target population (people with disabilities) represents a small group of citizens compared with other communities. In addition, in order to evaluate data trustworthiness our system requires multiple mapping of the same urban element.

These requirements motivated the research issues described in this paper: i) how can mPASS involve and motivate a wide variety of citizens in collecting data about urban accessibility during their daily routines?; ii) how can the system provide a constantly updated picture of the accessibility barriers and facilities in the urban environment?; iii) how can mPASS obtain multiple validation reports that ensure the trustworthiness of data?. All of these research questions suggested gamification as a potentially interesting strategy to adopt. In fact, gamification is the use of game elements and mechanics in order to increase motivation in performing certain tasks [8].

In particular, our intent was to use gamification to enlarge the community of mPASS users by recruiting people that are not directly interested or benefiting from the services provided by our system. We archived this goal by exploiting either intrinsic motivation (entertainment and/or social belonging) or extrinsic motivation (rewards) to engage a different target of citizens to map their surrounding location and report accessibility points such as zebra crossings, stairs, traffic lights, steps, disabled access ramps, etc..

In this paper we describe the concept, the design process and the development of two gamified location-based mobile applications (apps), designed to motivate and involve a wide variety of people in gathering data about urban accessibility. The two gamified apps have been designed expressly to increment the amount of data voluntarily collected and validated by citizens via crowdsourcing and crowdsensing. In particular we deployed two different strategies:

(i) Gamify the mPASS data gathering app, in order to engage people in mapping data exploiting extrinsic motivation, by means of explicit rewords.

(ii) Develop a georeferenced pervasive game, in order to involve people using intrinsic motivation associated with curiosity, exploration, spontaneity, interest and fun.

In order to conceive and design the games, we adopted an iterative design process. We started by sketching a number of possible game concepts that would involve citizens in reporting barriers and facilities. Then, we organized sessions of feedback with fellow researchers and students from our institution in order to validate refine and select the best game concepts. Out of several generated game concepts, we selected two to be developed further into experience prototyping sessions. The experience prototyping enabled the understanding of the flow of the game, and the engagement of users. The games experience allowed us to capture improvements and suggestions from the users and it also highlighted practical logistical problems. Moreover, an interesting and unexpected concept emerged from the sessions: users surprisingly noticed their lack of awareness about the surrounding urban environment. After the experience prototype sessions, we developed the resulted two games and we conducted a field trail with a target of young and avid walkers and players, showing interesting results that prove the feasibility of our approach in involving a different community in mapping urban accessibility.

The reminder of this paper is organized as follows. Section 2 presents background and related work, while Section 3 briefly introduces the mPASS system. Section 4 presents design of the two gamified apps, from ideation to the experience prototype. The development of both mobile apps and some interesting trial field results are described in Section 5 while Section 6 concludes the paper.

2. Backgroundand related work

Our research draws inspiration from a wide variety of projects focusing on gamification. These include alternate reality games, pervasive games, games with a purpose (GWAP), serious games, exergames and gameful design. In particular, we have investigated how gamification concepts can be exploited in crowdsourcing and crowdsensing systems. This section briefly describes the most significant research in these areas, which are related to:

(i) gamification in crowdsourcing systems that can benefit people with special needs;

(ii) crowdsourcing system to collect data in urban accessibility.

2.1. Gamification in crowdsourcing system

In recent years there was a proliferation of research projects and systems exploiting crowdsourcing as human-computation technique to perform distributed and collaborative tasks. Crowdsourcing is recognized to be very useful for solving tasks that are hard or impossible to be solved by a computer [9, 10]. The pioneering example was the EPS game [11] develop by von Ahn. Other interesting examples are often related to the annotation and tagging of images, videos or web content with the purpose of improving the accessibility of web pages. For example, in the ESP game the labelling of random web images with keywords is the basis of a simple online two-player game [11]. ESP is one of the first examples of a game with a purpose (GWAP), a game in which people, as a side effect of playing, perform some useful tasks through crowdsourcing [12, 13].

Another example is the Phetch game [14] that collects explanatory sentences (instead of keywords) for randomly chosen images. Phetch is a multiplayer game in which a player sees the image and helps other players to guess it giving a textual description of such image. The use of game mechanisms is a very important incentive to engage and motivate the crowd in performing voluntarily tasks of information retrieval [15]. In projects like ESP [11] or Phetch [14], the game is used to motivate and engage people in playing voluntarily, just for their entertainment. The real purpose of these games is hidden in the game mechanism and users don't need to know it for playing.

Some games with a purpose have deep social values. For example HearSay [16] is a non-visual web browser, where users collaboratively and voluntarily assign a label to each web page element using keyboard shortcuts or voice commands. These labels are stored in both local and remote repositories and shared with other users. The Social Accessibility project [17] also operates on a voluntary basis of users. It involves crowd workers to externally modify Web pages adding accessibility metadata in a collaborative environment. Similarly, reCAPTCHA [18] takes advantage of the people efforts in solving CAPTCHAs (Completely Automated Public Turing test to tell Computers and Humans Apart) to help to digitize books and newspapers. The Dotsub platform [19] offers the option to engage the crowd for captioning video. Instead, the DVX project [20] crowdsources the creation and distribution of amateur video description, allowing sighted video viewers to verbally describe DVD and Internet-based media.

2.2. Crowdsourcing systems to map urban accessibility

During the past few years, crowdsourcing has been exploited also in several projects related to real-word context [21]. In particular, different projects exploit accessibility issues. One example is the VizWiz smartphone application [20] where visually impaired people can take a picture using their smartphone, ask a question by speaking to the device, and then wait for a real-time spoken answers provided by paid workers on Amazon Mechanical Turk [22]. A similar approach is adopted in [23] where workers from Amazon Mechanical Turk have to find, label, and assess sidewalk accessibility problems or bus stop locations and surrounding landmarks in Google Street View imagery.

Several projects were developed with the aim of collaboratively collecting data about the indoor and/or outdoor urban accessibility environment, such as AccessToghether [24] and AXSmap [25]. These tools allow users to collect accessibility information about places and services and display them in a map of the neighbourhood, using a mobile phone or a computer. Another example is Human Access [26], a mobile application that allows users to select a place using Foursquare and then to rate some attributes related with its accessibility. In Wheelmap [27] users can search, find and mark wheelchair-accessible places by the mobile application or the online map. Wheelmap is based on OpenStreetMap [28], a collaborative and free editable map of the world created by users. In [29] the authors describe a platform that exploits crowdsourcing and crowdsensing to map outdoor accessibility elements in the urban environment. Another interesting work allows users to link accessibility annotations to geospatial data in order to compute a personalized route, considering the user's preferences and needs [30].

3. The mPASS system

The mPASS system [4, 6, 7] collects georeferenced data about aPOI (accessible Point of Interest). An aPOI is a accessibility urban barrier and facility or, more generally, a urban characteristics, which are relevant to pedestrians. This information is used in order to provide the community with personalized pedestrian paths, on the basis of preferences and needs expressed by each user.

The mPASS architecture and data flow are outlined in Fig. 1. Data are georeferenced trough OpenStreetMap and collected from 3 different sources: (i) authoritative data, by local authorities and disability organizations, including open data about the urban environment provided by municipalities; (ii) crowdsourced data by registered users, who contribute in reporting barriers and facilities both while moving and from home; (iii) data sensed by smartphones or tablets owned by the same community of users, while they are moving. The use of multiple data sources arises from the need to compute paths and maps on a complete and effective database of accessibility barriers and facilities. A partial mapping of the urban environment can induce the user to go through a (wrong) route without considering the presence of an undetected barrier. This can

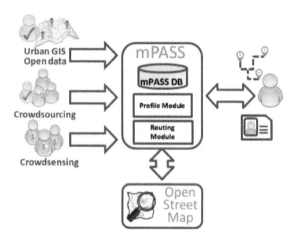

Figure 1. mPASS system

prevent the user from reaching his/her destination/goal compromising the effectiveness of mPASS services. For example if there is an undetected flight of stair on the path, a wheelchair user could be forced to stop and find an alternative route.

Collected data are provided to users on the basis of a user profile, which describes her/him in terms of barriers and facilities s/he likes, dislikes or wants to avoid. The routing algorithm removes all paths, which include barriers, to avoid and provides one to three possible solutions, where liked and disliked barriers and facility are weighted together with the total lengths of the path. All the solutions are summarized to the user who can select the more appropriate path on the basis of her/his actual preferences. A complete description of mPASS architecture can be found in [4], instead in [6, 7] we describe the personalized mobility service.

We evaluated the possible impact of mPASS on a 60 users group (26 female, 34 male), with ages ranged from 19 to 68 (with an average value of 44), including blind people and people with low vision (30), wheelchair users and users with physical impairments (5), deaf and hard of hearing users (1) and elderly people (15). The whole group has stated to be interested in personalized routing services while only the 50% was specifically interested in accessible paths. This research results confirm that only people with specific disabilities are concerned in collecting data related to barriers and facilities in urban environment.

4. From ideation to experience prototyping

Drawing on studies on urban mapping crowdsourcing systems and on the role of playful elements placed at the service of our society, we designed three main goals guided our game design concepts:

(i) social belonging focusing on disability;

(ii) location-based entertainment;

(iii) daily health and fitness activities in the urban environment.

We adopted an iterative design process in order to conceive, refine and prototype the games. In this section with describe the outcomes of each phases involved in the design and prototype process, from the ideation by sketching of some game concepts, to the refinement of the most suited games through a series of feedback and experience prototyping sessions, in order to capture users feedback and explore the game flow.

4.1. Ideation

The creative process of generating new game concepts was driven to the main idea to transform the process of collecting and sharing data about urban accessibility into an entertaining task for a wide variety of users, extending the mPASS direct beneficiaries.

We started the process by brainstorming a series of possible urban games to engage a wide variety of walkers in mapping urban elements. We then explored each game concept considering different strategies to validate the sensing activity and the collected urban data. The outcome of the ideation session was the design sketch of three games, designed on the three above mentioned strategies.

A Geo-minesweeper game (based on the traditional minesweeper game) was designed to appeal to people who love walking and with a strong social belonging. In fact, such game would push users to explore the city (the game grid is a area in the city map) and report accessibility barriers (that is the mines) in order to complete an urban path. If the player finds an aPOI and does not report it, he/she loses one game life and will have to start a new round of the game (like in the minesweeper traditional game). Our intent was to enhance feelings about social belonging, using the virtual mine as a metaphor: a mine, like an accessibility barrier for a person with disability, blocks the walker to reach his/her destination.

The second game concept was called HINT! (discovering your Hidden INTerest!). In this game the player has to guess the subject of the picture hidden under a specific area on the map. The more the player collects aPOIs via crowdsourcing and crowdsensing the more he/she obtains pieces of the puzzle in order to understand the subject of the pictures. The idea is to use different sets of pictures related to a specific topic (e.g. nature, animals, film, anime, culture, and so on) with the aim of enlarging the number of engaged player. When the user recognises the underlying picture, he/she obtains a voucher for the specific categories. We envisaged such game to appeal to the users who will strive to completed the puzzle and win the voucher, exploiting extrinsic motivation.

A third game concept generated was called KidCom! (Short for Kids Competition). This game was designed to stimulate a treasure hunt competition among children. The game involves answering question regarding general knowledge of the city or specific topics set by the teacher. Answering questions unlocks hints for the participants, that will lead them to find a secret place. This game is beneficial for children because by playing, they can improve their feeling of awareness with the urban environment and understand which urban elements can influence (in a positive or negative way) the pedestrian urban mobility.

The fourth game sketched was Geo-Zombie. The goal of the game is to stay alive, avoiding to be eaten by zombies. While trying to do that the user is exploring the surroundings while providing location of aPOI for the mPASS application in order to get weapons and ammunitions to shoot the zombies. We envisaged that such strategy could engage people by exploiting the feeling of positive fear and challenges evoked by the zombies apocalypse.

After conceiving the rules and designing possible scenarios for such games and their users by means of personas and storyboards, we presented the concepts to an audience of researchers and HCI students. We collected their feedback in order to refine and improve the games, before proceeding to a structured focus group.

4.2. Focus group

After ideation we organized an expert focus group in order to: (i) assess the pros and cons of each game strategy in relation to our goals; and (ii) narrow the selection to one or two games, to bring forward to the deployment stage. The focus group was organized at the Madeira Interactive Technologies Institute and lasted around two hours and involved seven participants (all researchers with familiarity with gameplay, game design and interactive technologies). The focus group started with the introduction to the four game concepts through a series of slides. The discussion was open after each game concept presented, taking notes about comments and issues came to notice.

During the focus group the Geo-Zombie and HINT! games emerged out as the most engaging yet feasible ones. The Geo-minesweeper can have the side effects to correlate, in a wrong way, the positive behaviour of mapping accessibility elements with the negative one to mine the city. Moreover, it needs a very accurate GPS localization to avoid inconsistent gameplay. Instead, the game revolving around the children's competition (KidCom!) was discarded because kids required more motivation than just finding a secret location and it needs people involved in the game coordination and organization (like teachers and parents), making the

game not suited to be played regularly. HINT! was criticized due the issues related to the copyright of the images but was appreciated the idea of using location-based voucher to motivate and engaged users.

We decided then to proceed with the experience prototyping of HINT! and Geo-Zombie, in order to assess if transferring the concept to a physical experience could reveal some unexpected findings.

4.3. Experience Prototyping

Experience prototyping is a technique borrowed from experience design and service design disciplines in order to test an experience or service in physical space and over time [31]. Such prototyping technique helps to refine the concept and the overall design of the experience before any investment is made in implementation details. Experience prototyping can be used in three critical design activities: understanding existing experience, exploring ideas, and communicating design concepts. We made use of the experience prototype to advance the design and understanding if the simulated game flow can motivate the walker in playing (and so, mapping aPOIs). By employing this method we were able to better understand the flow of the experience, the issues encountered by the participants as well as their feedback and desires regarding the game design.

In order to carry out an experience prototyping Geo-Zombie and HINT! we recruited four users who in turns tried both the games. For the Geo-Zombie, we prepared paper wireframes of the phone interface and physical zombies paper puppets to chase the users. To shoot the zombies we used a plastic gun recharge with water (ammunitions), see Fig. 2(a). For the Hint! game we prepared the paper wireframes of the screens and a puzzle final voucher for the players (Fig. 2(b)).

Subsequently we defined a series of tasks for the users to execute, and we tagged along them, taking notes and videos while they were playing the games. At the end of the experience a short interview was conducted with each participant. Our participants were all employees (faculty and staff) of the Madeira Interactive Technologies Institute, two female and two male, ranging from 25 to 45 years old, with some experiences in technology and gameplay. In particular, U1 a 45 years old Professor, U2 a 25 year old Master student, U3 a 30 year old PhD student and U4 a 33 year old accounting clerk and administrative manager.

We asked participants to carry out a ordinary task, something they could do in their daily live, where the gameplay would be an extra entertainment. In fact, we asked the users to compare the price of the coffee in the students canteen with the closest bar near the university. As suggested during the focus group, we asked users to report only one type of aPOI in each experience prototyping round, preventing users

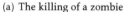 (a) The killing of a zombie 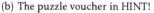 (b) The puzzle voucher in HINT! (c) The reporting of a zebra crossing

Figure 2. Pictures related to the experience prototyping

from being confused by paying attention to many different possible types of urban elements. In particular, during the Geo-Zombie experience prototyping, we asked users to report steps and stairs, while during the HINT! game experience prototyping, we asked for zebra crossings (see Fig. 2(c)).

4.4. Geo–Zombie experience

From our observations and interviews we can confidently affirm that during the experience prototyping of Geo-Zombie all the four users had a lot of fun. Two of them enjoyed the game so much that they continued to play after the task was completed reporting more aPOIs in order to acquire more points and ammunitions. Two of the users surprised us by entering in a building as an escape technique to hide from the zombies. That technique was successful for survival and for reaching faster some aPOIs, located close to the building. Another unexpected behaviour of one user was to switch strategy after some gameplay: instead of running away from zombies he preferred to chase them. At the end this user, U1, said:

> I found the game become too easy, it needs more zombies.

Such comment made us focus our attention on the number of zombies and on the level of difficulties that different players would enjoy. The same user also reported:

> After obtaining the gun, I changed my strategy: I really wanted to kill the zombie but I was still interested in finding zebra crossings because I was not aware that there are so many of them around this place.

Such comment made us realise that being engrossed in the game, may also distract players from reporting aPOIs.

Another consideration of the player U1 regarded the travelling speed of the Zombies.

> Maybe different speeds zombies can make the game more exciting

All of the Geo-Zombie players were so immerse in the game to incremented their walking speed to escape from the zombie. In some case they even started to run. A player explained:

> There was immediately a zombie there, and I had to kill him or I would die. The game made me feel different... excited!

4.5. HINT! experience

The second experience prototyping involved the same four players that had been involved with Geo-Zombie. The players seemed less excited to play HINT! than playing Geo-Zombie. This was somehow expected, since the HINT! game was designed to appeal to a different audience, motivated by the extrinsic motivation (the voucher) instead than by the game itself. The voucher was provided in pieces, making each single piece available to users for each aPOI reported. Getting the pieces of voucher seemed to be a strong motivator for three players out of four (U2, U3 and U4). Nevertheless, U2 was not interested in the voucher and U1 was disappointed by the type of voucher gift he received at the end. He clarified in the interview that it is important for the voucher to be personalized and connected with the user interests. On the other hand, two other players were excited to get some free voucher of any sort. U2 found particularly motivating the idea of using a voucher and confirmed:

> I prefer playing HINT!. It was kind of easy to do, without someone that was trying to catch me... and I like the voucher thing. Geo-Zombie was too much "of a game" to have in my daily routine.

Important to mention was a comment of player U1 that said:

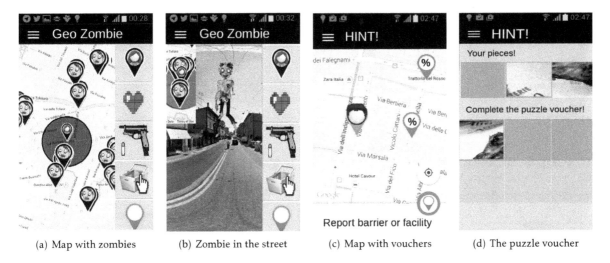

(a) Map with zombies   (b) Zombie in the street   (c) Map with vouchers   (d) The puzzle voucher

Figure 3. Screenshot of the developed prototype of Geo-Zombie and HINT!

I felt very motivated about reporting aPOIs just for the interest I had in exploring the area and discovering them. It is the space that I had around for ten years and I was surprised about how many zebra crossings there are besides zebra crossings are so big so I cannot imagine to look for another things!

U4 highlighted a similar thought:

Mapping in itself it is a strong motivation, more than the gameplay, because people become more aware about the space they are surrounded by and it is very important.

A final important finding was the importance of revealing the real purpose behind the game, to increment the intrinsic motivation in mapping.

5. Prototype development and preliminary fiel trial results

After integrating the feedback collected through the experience prototyping, we implemented both HINT! and Geo-Zombie. The games were developed using PhoneGap [32]. The gamified location-based apps uses the GPS position to locate the (marker of the) user in the map. We save all data (user details, configuration and reports) in a DB created using PostgreSQL [33] and PostGIS [34]. Each aPOI and its related data can be added to the DB by means of reports: a report is defined as a set of information about an aPOI (typology, description, photo, details about the user who sent it). HINT! exploits the GPS position and the user preferences to looking for close available voucher related to the user' interests (see Fig. 3(c) and 3(d)). In the Geo-Zombie game working prototype, we use

the camera and the direction of the phone, obtained through the gyroscope, to display the zombie in the real environment. This implementation allows us to considered Geo-Zombie a pervasive game in which the gaming experience comes into the real world [35] (see Fig. 3(a) and 3(b)).

In order to further gather users reaction to the games we tested mPASS (the basic app) and both games working prototypes with a group of third year graduate students in Cesena (University of Bologna). We asked to a class of 50 students to try using the mPASS mobile app on its own, the HINT! game and the Geo-Zombie game. Each game will be used by the students for a week.

Using mPASS, the results show that only 24 out of the 50 did more than one report, which was required to start the app the first time. When using HINT!, we asked the students to report at least 5 aPOIs, to get the voucher (a class assignment as done). 40 out of the 50 students finished the assignment (5 reports done), 22 of which did more reports than the 5 required. The total amount of reports done was 3.3 times the one obtained with the mPASS app. With Geo-Zombie, 34 out of the 50 did more than a report, which was required to start the app the first time, but the total amount of reports done was 3 times the one obtained with the mPASS app. The more interesting quantitative data are summarized in Table 1.

In summary, just using mPASS on its own we got to the lowest number or reports per person per week. While with HINT! we managed to significantly increase the number of reports: the voucher (extrinsic motivation) pushed a number of students to do at least 5 reports but, after obtaining the reward, they lost interest in mapping. We can assert this by observing the average number of reports for person that it is very close to the number of report required to obtain

Table 1. Quantitative results

Apps	N. of users	N. of report	N. of report per user (Average)	N. of report per user (Standard deviation)
mPASS	48/50	95	1.98	1.28
HINT!	47/50	311	6.62	3.56
Geo-Zombie	48/50	286	5.96	16.60

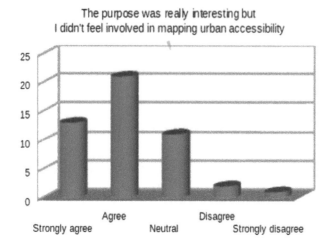

Figure 4. Answers to a item in the mPASS survey

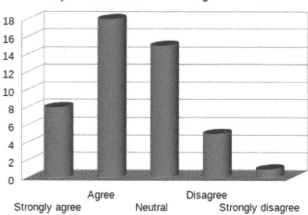

Figure 5. Answers to a item in the HINT! survey

a class assignment as done (the voucher). With the Geo-Zombie game, we had an valuable increase in the number of reports and a high standard deviation value: this can be explained by the fact that some students just tried the game whereas others really felt engaged in experiencing the zombies game (intrinsic motivation).

After each trial, we asked the students to fulfil a survey to better understand their feeling about the tried app. The questionnaire was composed by 5 items related to the goals of the system, 10 items connected to the specific tried app, and one open question for comments and hints. The questions was inspired by the comments and issues emerged in the design process.

The outcome confirms the assumptions we made analysing the quantitative data. Some examples of qualitative data are shown in Fig. 4, 5, 6: in the plots the value in y axis represents the number of users that given the answer reported on the x axis. Fig. 4 shows the students' answers to the question item "The purpose was really interesting but I didn't feel involved in mapping urban accessibility", related to the mPASS app. As expected, students understood the importance of mapping urban accessibility but they didn't feel motivated in contributing. Data in Fig. 5 validate our assumption about the power of extrinsic motivation exploited using the voucher (question item "I was just interested in obtaining the voucher"). In Fig. 6 it is possible to see how the question item "My goal was

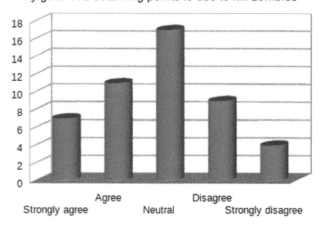

Figure 6. Answers to a item in the Geo-Zombie survey

obtaining points to use to kill zombies" reveals different reactions in students: some students loved the game flow and played a lot as effect of intrinsic motivation, and others didn't (in agreement with the hight value of standard deviation obtained by quantitative data).

6. Conclusion

mPASS (mobile Pervasive Accessibility Social Sensing) is a system that aims to collect data from citizens in order to map accessibility of the urban environment and calculate personalize accessible path taking into account users preferences and special needs. In providing effective services, mPASS needs an updated and reliable picture of the urban accessibility. The system makes this possible allowing users to collect, voluntarily, georeferenced data via crowdsourcing and via crowdsensing. Usually, in this kind of crowdsourcing system there are few users that collect most of the data. This is a problem for mPASS that needs a wide audience of users to validate the mapped elements and avoid errors, which cannot be limited to people who directly benefit from the mapping activity.

To support the effectiveness and the trustworthiness of the data collection, it is necessary to attract different targets and enlarge the system community. With this in mind, we adopted gamification strategies in order to conceive and design few location based games that would engage a wide variety of users in mapping urban accessibility, exploiting intrinsic and extrinsic motivation. Through a design process of ideation, concept validation, focus group and experience prototyping, we evaluated the game concepts, captured players reactions, comments and preferences before starting with the coding process.

The two best suited and well received games, HINT! and Geo-Zombie are being developed and tested. The results show the viability of our strategy in adopting gamification (and pervasive game) to enlarge the community of mPASS.

Acknowledgements. We thank all the participants (from the Madeira Interactive Technologies Institute and the University of Bologna) involved in this study. We would also like to thank Steven Dow and Jodi Forlizzi (Carnegie Mellon University) who provided us with precious suggestions, feedbacks and ideas.

References

[1] GIFFINGE, R. (2007), Smart cities: Ranking of european medium-sized cities. URL http://smart-cities.eu/download/smart_cities_final_report.pdf.

[2] (2011), World report on disability. URL http://www.who.int/disabilities/world_report/2011/accessible_en.pdf.

[3] WALKER, A., MAHER, J., COULTHARD, M., GODDARD, E. and THOMAS, M. (2001), Living in britain: Results from the 2001 general household survey. URL http://www.ons.gov.uk/ons/rel/ghs/general-household-survey/2001-edition/living-in-britain--full-report.pdf.

[4] PRANDI, C., SALOMONI, P. and MIRRI, S. (2014) mpass: Integrating people sensing and crowdsourcing to map urban accessibility. In Consumer Communications and Networking Conference (CCNC), 2014 IEEE 11th: 591–595. doi:10.1109/CCNC.2014.6940491.

[5] DEICHMANN, J. (2004) Accessible urban spaces âĂŞ a challenge for urban designers. In Walk21-V Citiesfor

People. URL http://www.walk21.com/papers/Copenhagen%2004%20Deichmann%20Accessible%20Urban%20Spaces.pdf.

[6] MIRRI, S., PRANDI, C., SALOMONI, P., CALLEGATI, F. and CAMPI, A. (2014) On combining crowdsourcing, sensing and open data for an accessible smart city. In Next Generation Mobile Apps, Services and Technologies (NGMAST), 2014 Eighth International Conference on: 294–299. doi:10.1109/NGMAST.2014.59.

[7] MIRRI, S., PRANDI, C. and SALOMONI, P. (2014) A context-aware system for personalized and accessible pedestrian paths. In High Performance Computing Simulation (HPCS), 2014 International Conference on: 833–840. doi:10.1109/HPCSim.2014.6903776.

[8] SEABORN, K. and FELS, D.I. (2015) Gamification in theory and action: A survey. International Journal of Human-Computer Studies 74: 14 – 31. doi:http://dx.doi.org/10.1016/j.ijhcs.2014.09.006, URL http://www.sciencedirect.com/science/article/pii/S1071581914001256.

[9] HOSSEINI, M., PHALP, K., TAYLOR, J. and ALI, R. (2014) The four pillars of crowdsourcing: A reference model. In Research Challenges in Information Science (RCIS), 2014 IEEE Eighth International Conference on: 1–12. doi:10.1109/RCIS.2014.6861072.

[10] PAN, Y. and BLEVIS, E. (2011) A survey of crowdsourcing as a means of collaboration and the implications of crowdsourcing for interaction design. In Collaboration Technologies and Systems (CTS), 2011 International Conference on: 397–403. doi:10.1109/CTS.2011.5928716.

[11] VON AHN, L. and DABBISH, L. (2004) Labeling images with a computer game. In Proceedings of the SIGCHI Conference on Human Factors in Computing Systems, CHI '04 (New York, NY, USA: ACM): 319–326. doi:10.1145/985692.985733, URL http://doi.acm.org/10.1145/985692.985733.

[12] VON AHN, L. (2006) Games with a purpose. Computer 39(6): 92–94. doi:10.1109/MC.2006.196.

[13] VON AHN, L. and DABBISH, L. (2008) Designing games with a purpose. Commun. ACM 51(8): 58–67. doi:10.1145/1378704.1378719, URL http://doi.acm.org/10.1145/1378704.1378719.

[14] VON AHN, L., GINOSAR, S., KEDIA, M., LIU, R. and BLUM, M. (2006) Improving accessibility of the web with a computer game. In Proceedings of the SIGCHI Conference on Human Factors in Computing Systems, CHI '06 (New York, NY, USA: ACM): 79–82. doi:10.1145/1124772.1124785, URL http://doi.acm.org/10.1145/1124772.1124785.

[15] HARRIS, C.G. (2012) The application of crowdsourcing and games to information retrieval. Bulletin of IEEE Technical Committee on Digital Libraries 8(2).

[16] BORODIN, Y., BIGHAM, J.P., STENT, A. and RAMAKRISHNAN, I.V. (2008) Towards one world web with hearsay3. In Proceedings of the 2008 International Cross-disciplinary Conference on Web Accessibility (W4A), W4A '08 (New York, NY, USA: ACM): 130–131. doi:10.1145/1368044.1368074, URL http://doi.acm.org/10.1145/1368044.1368074.

[17] Takagi, H., Kawanaka, S., Kobayashi, M., Itoh, T. and Asakawa, C. (2008) Social accessibility: Achieving accessibility through collaborative metadata authoring. In *Proceedings of the 10th International ACM SIGACCESS Conference on Computers and Accessibility*, Assets '08 (New York, NY, USA: ACM): 193–200. doi:10.1145/1414471.1414507, URL http://doi.acm.org/10.1145/1414471.1414507.

[18] von Ahn, L., Maurer, B., McMillen, C., Abraham, D. and Blum, M. (2008) recaptcha: Human-based character recognition via web security measures. *Science* **321**(5895): 1465–1468. doi:10.1126/science.1160379, URL http://www.sciencemag.org/content/321/5895/1465.abstract. http://www.sciencemag.org/content/321/5895/1465.full.pdf.

[19] Dotsub. URL https://dotsub.com/. Retrieved: September, 2015.

[20] Miele, J. (2012) The descriptive video exchange: the technology and implications of crowd-sourced description. In *CSUN 2012*.

[21] Alt, F., Shirazi, A.S., Schmidt, A., Kramer, U. and Nawaz, Z. (2010) Location-based crowdsourcing: Extending crowdsourcing to the real world. In *Proceedings of the 6th Nordic Conference on Human-Computer Interaction: Extending Boundaries*, NordiCHI '10 (New York, NY, USA: ACM): 13–22. doi:10.1145/1868914.1868921, URL http://doi.acm.org/10.1145/1868914.1868921.

[22] Amazon mechanical turk. URL https://www.mturk.com/mturk/welcome. Retrieved: Obtober, 2015.

[23] Hara, K., Le, V. and Froehlich, J. (2013) Combining crowdsourcing and google street view to identify street-level accessibility problems. In *Proceedings of the SIGCHI Conference on Human Factors in Computing Systems*, CHI '13 (New York, NY, USA: ACM): 631–640. doi:10.1145/2470654.2470744, URL http://doi.acm.org/10.1145/2470654.2470744.

[24] Access together. URL http://www.accesstogether.org/. Retrieved: Obtober, 2015.

[25] Axsmap. URL http://www.axsmap.com/. Retrieved: Obtober, 2015.

[26] Kouroupetroglou, C. and Koumpis, A. (2014), Human access: evolution of a crowdsourcing accessibility evaluations mobile ap. URL http://www.w3.org/WAI/RD/2014/way-finding/paper4/. Extended Abstract for the RDWG Symposium on Accessible Way-Finding Using Web Technologies.

[27] Wheelmap. URL http://wheelmap.org/en/. Retrieved: Obtober, 2015.

[28] Open street map. URL http://www.openstreetmap.org/. Retrieved: Obtober, 2015.

[29] Cardonha, C., Gallo, D., Avegliano, P., Herrmann, R., Koch, F. and Borger, S. (2013) A crowdsourcing platform for the construction of accessibility maps. In *Proceedings of the 10th International Cross-Disciplinary Conference on Web Accessibility*, W4A '13 (New York, NY, USA: ACM): 26:1–26:4. doi:10.1145/2461121.2461129, URL http://doi.acm.org/10.1145/2461121.2461129.

[30] Holone, H. and Misund, G. (2008) People helping computers helping people: Navigation for people with mobility problems by sharing accessibility annotations. In *Proceedings of the 11th International Conference on Computers Helping People with Special Needs*, ICCHP '08 (Berlin, Heidelberg: Springer-Verlag): 1093–1100. doi:10.1007/978-3-540-70540-6_164, URL http://dx.doi.org/10.1007/978-3-540-70540-6_164.

[31] Kean, K. and Nisi, V. (2014) *Experience Prototyping: Gathering Rich Understandings to Guide Design* (The name of the publisher), 224–237. doi:10.4018/978-1-4666-4623-0.ch011.

[32] Phonegap. URL http://phonegap.com/. Retrieved: Obtober, 2015.

[33] Postgresql. URL http://www.postgresql.org/. Retrieved: Obtober, 2015.

[34] Postgis. URL http://postgis.net/. Retrieved: Obtober, 2015.

[35] Benford, S., Magerkurth, C. and Ljungstrand, P. (2005) Bridging the physical and digital in pervasive gaming. *Commun. ACM* **48**(3): 54–57. doi:10.1145/1047671.1047704, URL http://doi.acm.org/10.1145/1047671.1047704.

Optimal Random Access and Random Spectrum Sensing for an Energy Harvesting Cognitive Radio with and without Primary Feedback Leveraging

Ahmed El Shafie*

Wireless Intelligent Networks Center (WINC), Nile University, Giza, Egypt.

Abstract

We consider a secondary user (SU) with energy harvesting capability. We design access schemes for the SU which incorporate random spectrum sensing and random access, and which make use of the primary automatic repeat request (ARQ) feedback. We study two problem-formulations. In the first problem-formulation, we characterize the stability region of the proposed schemes. The sensing and access probabilities are obtained such that the secondary throughput is maximized under the constraints that both the primary and secondary queues are stable. Whereas in the second problem-formulation, the sensing and access probabilities are obtained such that the secondary throughput is maximized under the stability of the primary queue and that the primary queueing delay is kept lower than a specified value needed to guarantee a certain quality of service (QoS) for the primary user (PU). We consider spectrum sensing errors and assume multipacket reception (MPR) capabilities. Numerical results show the enhanced performance of our proposed systems.

Keywords: Cognitive radio, energy harvesting, queues, stability, dominant system, queueing delay.

1. Introduction

Cognitive radio technology provides an efficient means of utilizing the radio spectrum [2]. The basic idea is to allow secondary users to access the spectrum while providing certain guaranteed quality of service (QoS) performance measures for the primary users (PUs). The secondary user (SU) is a battery-powered device in many practical situations and its operation, which involves spectrum sensing and access, is accompanied by energy consumption. Consequently an energy-constrained SU must optimize its sensing and access decisions to efficiently utilize the energy at its disposal. An emerging technology for energy-constrained terminals is energy harvesting which allows the terminal to gather energy from its environment. An overview of the different energy harvesting technologies is provided in [3] and the references therein.

Data transmission by an energy harvester with a rechargeable battery has got a lot of attention recently [4–13]. The optimal online policy for controlling admissions into the data buffer is derived in [4] using a dynamic programming framework. In [5], energy management policies which stabilize the data queue are proposed for single-user communication and some delay-optimal properties are derived. Throughput optimal energy allocation is investigated in [6] for energy harvesting systems in a time-constrained slotted setting. In [7, 8], minimization of the transmission completion time is considered in an energy harvesting system and the optimal solution is obtained using a geometric framework. In [9], energy harvesting transmitters with batteries of finite energy storage capacity are considered and the problem of throughput maximization by a deadline is solved for a static channel.

The authors of [10] consider the scenario in which a set of nodes shares a common channel. The PU has a rechargeable battery and the SU is plugged to a reliable power supply. They obtain the maximum stable throughput region which describes the maximum arrival rates that maintain the stability of the network queues. In [11], the authors investigate the effects of network layer cooperation in a wireless three-node network with energy harvesting nodes and bursty traffic. In [12], Sultan investigated the optimal cognitive sensing and access policies for an SU with an energy

★Part of this work has been presented in the 8th International Conference on Wireless and Mobile Computing, Networking and Communications (WiMob), 2012 [1]

*Corresponding author. Email: ahmed.salahelshafie@gmail.com

queue. The analysis is based on Markov-decision process (MDP). In [13], the authors investigated the maximum stable throughput of a backlogged secondary terminal with energy harvesting capability. The SU randomly accesses the channel at the beginning of the time slot without employing any channel sensing. The secondary terminal can leverage the availability of primary feedback and exploit the multipacket reception (MPR) capability of the receivers to enhance its throughput.

In this paper, we develop spectrum sensing and transmission methods for an energy harvesting SU. We leverage the primary automatic repeat request (ARQ) feedback for secondary access. Due to the broadcast nature of the wireless channel, this feedback can be overheard and utilized by the secondary node assuming that it is unencrypted. The proposed protocols can alleviate the negative impact of channel sensing because the secondary access is on basis of the sensed primary state as well as the overheard primary feedback. The problem with depending on spectrum sensing only is that sensing does not inform the secondary terminal about its impact on the primary receiver. This issue has induced interest in utilizing the feedback from the primary receiver to the primary transmitter to optimize the secondary transmission strategies. For instance, in [14], the SU observes the ARQ feedback from the primary receiver as it reflects the PU's achieved packet rate. The SU's objective is to maximize its throughput while guaranteeing a certain packet rate for the PU. In [15], the authors use a partially observable Markov decision process (POMDP) to optimize the secondary action on the basis of the spectrum sensing outcome and primary ARQ feedback. Secondary power control based on primary feedback is investigated in [16]. In [17] and [18], the optimal transmission policy for the SU when the PU adopts a retransmission based error control scheme is investigated. The policy of the SU determines how often it transmits according to the retransmission state of the packet being served by the PU.

The contributions of this paper can be summarized as follows.

- We investigate the case of an SU equipped with an energy harvesting mechanism and a rechargeable battery.

- We propose a novel access and sensing schemes where the SU possibly senses the channel for a certain fraction of the time slot duration and accesses the channel with some access probability that depends on the sensing outcome. The SU may access the channel probabilistically without sensing in order to utilize the whole slot duration for transmission. Furthermore, it leverages the primary feedback signals.

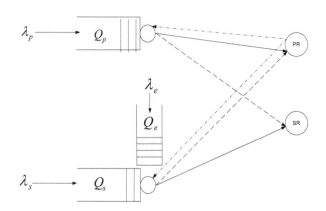

Figure 1. Primary and secondary queues and links. The PU has data queue Q_p, whereas the secondary terminal has data queue Q_s and energy queue Q_e. There is a feedback channel between the primary receiver (PR) and the PU to acknowledge the reception of data packets. This feedback channel is overheard by the secondary transmitter. Both the PR and the secondary receiver (SR) may suffer interference from the other link.

- Instead of the collision channel model, we assume a generalized channel model in which the receiving nodes have MPR capability.

- We propose two problem-formulations. In the first problem-formulation, we characterize the stability region of the proposed schemes. The sensing and access probabilities are obtained such that the secondary throughput is maximized under the constraints that both the primary and secondary queues are stable. Whereas in the second problem-formulation, we include a constraint on the primary queueing delay to the optimization problem for delay-aware PUs. The sensing and access probabilities are obtained such that the secondary throughput is maximized under the stability of the primary queue and that the primary queueing delay is kept lower than a specified value needed to guarantee a certain QoS for the PU.

- We compare our systems with the conventional access system in which the SU senses the channel and accesses unconditionally if the PU is sensed to be inactive. The numerical results show the gains of our proposed systems in terms of the secondary throughput.

The rest of the paper is organized as follows. In the next section, we discuss the system model adopted in this paper. The secondary access without incorporating the primary feedback is investigated in Section 3. In

Section 4, we discuss the feedback-based scheme. The case of delay-aware PUs is investigated in Section 5. We provide numerical results and conclusions in Section 6.

2. System Model

We consider the system model shown in Fig. 1. The model consists of one PU and one SU. The channel is slotted in time and a slot duration equals the packet transmission time. The PU and the SU have infinite buffer queues, Q_p and Q_s, respectively, to store fixed-length data packets. If a terminal transmits during a time slot, it sends exactly one packet to its receiver. The arrivals at Q_p and Q_s are independent and identically distributed (i.i.d.) Bernoulli random variables from slot to slot with means λ_p and λ_s, respectively.

The SU has an additional energy queue, Q_e, to store harvested energy from the environment. The arrival at the energy queue is also Bernoulli with mean λ_e and is independent from arrivals at the other queues. The Bernoulli model is simple, but it captures the random availability of ambient energy sources. More importantly, in the analysis of discrete-time queues, Bernoulli arrivals see time averages (BASTA). This is the BASTA property equivalent to the Poisson arrivals see time averages (PASTA) property in continuous-time systems [19]. It is assumed that the transmission of one data packet consumes one packet of energy.

We adopt a late arrival model as in [10, 11, 13, 20] where an arrived packet at a certain time slot cannot be served at the arriving slot even if the queue is empty. Denote by $\mathcal{V}^t$ the number of arrivals to queue Q at time slot t, and $\mathcal{Z}^t$ the number of departures from queue Q at time slot t. The queue length evolves according to the following form:

$$Q^{t+1} = (Q^t - \mathcal{Z}^t)^+ + \mathcal{V}^t \qquad (1)$$

where $(z)^+$ denotes $\max(z, 0)$.

Adequate system operation requires that all the queues are stable. We employ the standard definition of stability for queue as in [20, 21], that is, a queue is stable if and only if its probability of being empty does not vanish as time progresses. Precisely, $\lim_{t\to\infty} \Pr\{Q^t = \tilde{0}\} > 0$. If the arrival and service processes are strictly stationary, then we can apply Loynes theorem to check for stability conditions [22]. This theorem states that if the arrival process and the service process of a queue are strictly stationary processes, and the average service rate is greater than the average arrival rate of the queue, then the queue is stable. If the average service rate is lower than the average arrival rate, the queue is unstable [20].

Instead of the collision channel model where simultaneous transmission by different terminals leads to sure packet loss, we assume that the receivers have MPR capability as in [23–25]. This means that transmitted data packets can survive the interference caused by concurrent transmissions if the received signal to interference and noise ratio (SINR) exceeds the threshold required for successful decoding at the receiver. With MPR capability, the SU may use the channel simultaneously with the PU.

3. Secondary Access Without Employing Primary Feedback

The first proposed system is denoted by Φ_{NF}. Under this protocol, the PU accesses the channel whenever it has a packet to send. The secondary transmitter, given that it has energy, senses the channel or possibly transmits the packet at the head of its queue immediately at the beginning of the time slot without sensing the channel. We explain below why direct transmission can be beneficial for system performance.

The SU operation can be summarized as follows.

- If the secondary terminal's energy and data queues are not empty, it senses the channel with probability p_s from the beginning of the time slot for a duration of τ seconds to detect the possible activity of the PU. If the slot duration is T, $\tau < T$.

- If the channel is sensed to be free, the secondary transmitter accesses the channel with probability p_f. If the PU is detected to be active, it accesses the channel with probability p_b.

- If at the beginning of the time slot the SU decides not to sense the spectrum (which happens with probability $1 - p_s$), it immediately decides whether to transmit with probability p_t or to remain idle for the rest of the time slot with probability $\overline{p_t} = 1 - p_t$.[1]

This means that the transmission duration is T seconds if the SU accesses the channel without spectrum sensing and $T - \tau$ seconds if transmission is preceded by a sensing phase. We assume that the energy consumed in spectrum sensing is negligible, whereas data transmission dissipates exactly one unit of energy from Q_e.

We study now secondary access in detail to obtain the mean service rates of queues Q_s, Q_e and Q_p. The meaning of the various relevant symbols are provided in Table 1. For the secondary terminal to be served, its energy queue must be nonempty. If the SU does not sense the channel, which happens with probability $1 - p_s$, it transmits with probability p_t. If the PU's queue is empty and, hence, the PU is inactive, secondary transmission is successful with probability $\overline{P}_{0s}$, whose expression as a function of

---

[1]Throughout the paper $\overline{\mathcal{X}} = 1 - \mathcal{X}$.

τ	Sensing duration
T	Slot duration
p_s	Probability of sensing the channel
P_{MD}	Misdetection probability
P_{FA}	False alarm probability
p_t	Probability of direct channel access if the channel is not sensed
p_f	Probability of channel access if the channel is sensed to be free
p_b	Probability of channel access if the channel is sensed to be busy
$\overline{P}_p$	Probability of successful primary transmission to the primary receiver if the secondary terminal is silent
$\overline{P_p^{(c)}}$	Probability of successful primary transmission to the primary receiver with concurrent secondary transmission
$\overline{P}_{0s}$	Probability of successful secondary transmission if the PU is silent and transmission occurs over T seconds
$\overline{P}_{1s}$	Probability of successful secondary transmission if the PU is silent and transmission occurs over $T - \tau$ seconds
$\overline{P_{0s}^{(c)}}$	Probability of successful secondary transmission if the PU is active and transmission occurs over T seconds
$\overline{P_{1s}^{(c)}}$	Probability of successful secondary transmission if the PU is active and transmission occurs over $T - \tau$ seconds

Table 1. List of symbols involved in the queues' mean service rates.

the secondary link parameters, transmission time T, and the data packet size is provided in Appendix A. If $Q_p \neq 0$, secondary transmission is successful with probability $\overline{P_{0s}^{(c)}}$ (see Appendix A). If the SU decides to sense the channel, there are four possibilities depending on the sensing outcome and the state of the primary queue. If the PU is sensed to be free, secondary transmission takes place with probability p_f. This takes place with probability $1 - P_{\mathrm{FA}}$ if the PU is actually silent. In this case, the probability of successful secondary transmission is $\overline{P}_{1s}$, which is lower than $\overline{P}_{0s}$ (for proof, see [1]). On the other hand, if the PU

is on, the probability of detecting the channel to be free is P_{MD} and the probability of successful secondary transmission is $\overline{P_{1s}^{(c)}}$. If the channel is sensed to be busy, the secondary terminal transmits with probability p_b. Sensing the PU to be active occurs with probability P_{FA} if the PU is actually inactive, or with probability $1 - P_{\mathrm{MD}}$ if the PU is actively transmitting. The probability of successful secondary transmission is $\overline{P}_{1s}$ when the PU is silent and $\overline{P_{1s}^{(c)}}$ when the PU is active. Given these possibilities, we can write the following expression for the mean secondary service rate.

$$
\begin{aligned}
\mu_s = {} & (1 - p_s)\, p_t \mathrm{Pr}\{Q_p = 0, Q_e \neq 0\}\overline{P}_{0s} \\
& + (1 - p_s)\, p_t \mathrm{Pr}\{Q_p \neq 0, Q_e \neq 0\}\overline{P_{0s}^{(c)}} \\
& + p_s p_f \mathrm{Pr}\{Q_p = 0, Q_e \neq 0\} (1 - P_{\mathrm{FA}})\, \overline{P}_{1s} \\
& + p_s p_f \mathrm{Pr}\{Q_p \neq 0, Q_e \neq 0\} P_{\mathrm{MD}}\overline{P_{1s}^{(c)}} \\
& + p_s p_b \mathrm{Pr}\{Q_p = 0, Q_e \neq 0\} P_{\mathrm{FA}}\overline{P}_{1s} \\
& + p_s p_b \mathrm{Pr}\{Q_p \neq 0, Q_e \neq 0\} (1 - P_{\mathrm{MD}})\, \overline{P_{1s}^{(c)}}
\end{aligned} \tag{2}
$$

Based on the above analysis, it can be shown that the mean service rate of the energy queue is

$$
\begin{aligned}
\mu_e = {} & (1 - p_s)\, p_t \mathrm{Pr}\{Q_s \neq 0\} \\
& + p_s p_f \Big(P_{\mathrm{MD}}\mathrm{Pr}\{Q_s \neq 0, Q_p \neq 0\} \\
& \qquad + (1 - P_{\mathrm{FA}})\mathrm{Pr}\{Q_s \neq 0, Q_p = 0\} \Big) \\
& + p_s p_b \Big(P_{\mathrm{FA}}\mathrm{Pr}\{Q_s \neq 0, Q_p = 0\} \\
& \qquad + (1 - P_{\mathrm{MD}})\mathrm{Pr}\{Q_s \neq 0, Q_p \neq 0\} \Big)
\end{aligned} \tag{3}
$$

A packet from the primary queue can be served in either one of the following events. If the SU is silent because either of its data queue or energy queue is empty, the primary transmission is successful with probability $\overline{P}_p$. If both secondary queues are nonempty, secondary operation proceeds as explained above. In all cases, if the SU does not access the channel, the probability of successful primary transmission is $\overline{P}_p$, else it is $\overline{P_p^{(c)}}$.[2] Therefore,

$$
\begin{aligned}
\mu_p = & \left(1 - \Pr\{Q_s \neq 0, Q_e \neq 0\}\right)\overline{P}_p \\
& + \Pr\{Q_s \neq 0, Q_e \neq 0\} \\
& \times \Bigg[(1 - p_s)\left(p_t \overline{P_p^{(c)}} + (1 - p_t)\overline{P}_p\right) \\
& \quad + p_s P_{\mathrm{MD}}\left(p_f \overline{P_p^{(c)}} + \left(1 - p_f\right)\overline{P}_p\right) \\
& \quad + p_s (1 - P_{\mathrm{MD}})\left(p_b \overline{P_p^{(c)}} + (1 - p_b)\overline{P}_p\right)\Bigg]
\end{aligned}
\tag{4}
$$

The maximum primary throughput is $\overline{P}_p$, i.e., $\mu_p \leq \overline{P}_p$, which occurs when the PU operates alone, i.e., when the SU is always inactive.

Following are some important **remarks** on the proposed access and sensing scheme. Firstly, the proposed access and sensing scheme can mitigate the negative impact of sensing errors. Specifically, the SU under the proposed protocol randomly accesses the channel if the PU is either sensed to be active or inactive. Hence, the false alarm probability and the misdetection probability are controllable using the spectrum access probabilities. These access probabilities can take any value between zero and one. Hence, the SU can mitigate the impact of the sensing errors via adjusting the values of the access probabilities. Accordingly, this would enhance the secondary throughput and prevent the violation of the PU's QoS.

Secondly, when the MPR capabilities of the receivers are strong (which means $\overline{P_p^{(c)}} \approx \overline{P}_p$ and $\overline{P_{is}^{(c)}} \approx \overline{P}_{is}$ for $i = 0, 1$), the SU does not need to sense the channel at all, i.e., $p_s = 0$. This is due to the fact that the SU does not need to employ channel sensing as it can transmit each time slot simultaneously with the PU without violating the primary QoS because the receivers can decode packets under interference with a probability almost equal to the decoding probability when nodes transmit alone.

As in [1, 10, 13], we assume that the energy queue is modeled as M/D/1 queue with mean service and arrival rates $\mu_e = 1$ and λ_e, respectively. Hence, the probability that the secondary energy queue being nonempty is $\lambda_e/\mu_e = \lambda_e$ [26]. Based on this assumption, the energy queue in the approximated system empties faster than in the actual system, thereby lowering the probability that the queue is nonempty. This reduces the secondary throughput by increasing the probability that the

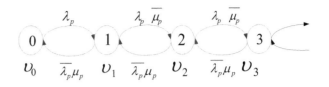

Figure 2. Markov chain of the PU under dominant system $\mathcal{S}_1$. State self-transitions are omitted for visual clarity. Probabilities $\overline{\mu_p} = 1 - \mu_p$ and $\overline{\lambda_p} = 1 - \lambda_p$.

secondary node does not have energy. Therefore, our approximation result in a lower bound on the secondary service rate or throughput [1, 13]. We denote the system under the approximation of one packet consumption from the energy queue each time slot as $\mathcal{S}$.

Since the queues in the approximated system, $\mathcal{S}$, are interacting with each other, we resort to the concept of the dominant system to obtain the stability region of system $\mathcal{S}$. The dominant system approach is first introduced in [27]. The basic idea is that we construct an appropriate dominant system, which is a modification of system $\mathcal{S}$ with the queues decoupled, hence we can compute the departure processes of all queues. The modified system ensures that the queue sizes in the dominant system are, at all times, at least as large as those of system $\mathcal{S}$ provided that the queues in both systems have the same initial sizes. Thus, the stability region of the new system is an **inner bound** of system $\mathcal{S}$. At the boundary points of the stability region, both the dominant system and system $\mathcal{S}$ coincide. This is the essence of the indistinguishability argument presented in many papers such as [10, 20, 25, 27]. Next, we construct two dominant systems and the stability region of approximated system $\mathcal{S}$ is the union of the stability region of the dominant systems. We would like to emphasize here that system $\mathcal{S}$ is an **inner bound** on the original system, Φ_{NF}.

3.1. First Dominant System

In the first dominant system queue, denoted by $\mathcal{S}_1$, Q_s transmits dummy packets when it is empty and the PU behaves as it would in the original system. Under this dominant system, we have $\Pr\{Q_s = 0\} = 0$. Substituting by $\Pr\{Q_s = 0\} = 0$ into (4), the average primary service rate after some simplifications can be given by

$$
\mu_p = \overline{P}_p - \lambda_e \Delta_p \left(\overline{p_s} p_t + p_s P_{\mathrm{MD}} p_f + p_s \overline{P_{\mathrm{MD}}} p_b\right)
\tag{5}
$$

where $\Delta_p = \overline{P}_p - \overline{P_p^{(c)}} \geq 0$. The Markov chain modeling the primary queue under this dominant system is provided in Fig. 2. Solving the state balance equations, it is straightforward to show that the probability that the

---

[2]We assume that the access delay of the SU does not affect the primary outage probability. This is valid as far as $(1 - \frac{\tau}{T})e \approx e$, which is true here as $\tau \ll T$. For details, see Appendix A.

primary queue has k packets is

$$\nu_k = \nu_0 \frac{1}{\overline{\mu_p}} \left[\frac{\lambda_p \overline{\mu_p}}{\overline{\lambda_p} \mu_p} \right]^k \tag{6}$$

where $\overline{\lambda_p} = 1 - \lambda_p$ and $\overline{\mu_p} = 1 - \mu_p$. Using the condition $\sum_{k=0}^{\infty} \nu_k = 1$,

$$\nu_0 = 1 - \frac{\lambda_p}{\mu_p} \tag{7}$$

For the sum $\sum_{k=0}^{\infty} \nu_k$ to exist, we should have $\lambda_p < \mu_p$. This is equivalent to Loynes' theorem. Since $\Pr\{Q_p = 0\} = 1 - \frac{\lambda_p}{\mu_p}$,

$$\mu_s = \lambda_e \left[\left(1 - \frac{\lambda_p}{\mu_p}\right) \left(\overline{p_s} p_t \overline{P_{0s}} + p_s p_b P_{\mathrm{FA}} \overline{P_{1s}} + p_s p_f \overline{P_{\mathrm{FA}}} \ \overline{P_{1s}} \right) \right.$$
$$\left. + \frac{\lambda_p}{\mu_p} \left(\overline{p_s} p_t \overline{P_{0s}^{(c)}} + p_s p_f P_{\mathrm{MD}} \overline{P_{1s}^{(c)}} + p_s p_b \overline{P_{\mathrm{MD}}} \ \overline{P_{1s}^{(c)}} \right) \right] \tag{8}$$

Let

$$\mu_p = \overline{P_p} + \mathcal{D}^{\dagger} \mathcal{P} \tag{9}$$

where $(\bullet)^{\dagger}$ denotes vector transposition, $\mathcal{P} = [p_t, p_b, p_f]^{\dagger}$ and $\mathcal{D} = -\Delta_p \lambda_e \left[\overline{p_s}, p_s \overline{P_{\mathrm{MD}}}, p_s P_{\mathrm{MD}} \right]^{\dagger}$. Substituting from (9) into (8),

$$\mu_s = \left(1 - \frac{\lambda_p}{\overline{P_p} + \mathcal{D}^{\dagger} \mathcal{P}}\right) \mathcal{A}^{\dagger} \mathcal{P} + \frac{\lambda_p}{\overline{P_p} + \mathcal{D}^{\dagger} \mathcal{P}} \mathcal{G}^{\dagger} \mathcal{P} \tag{10}$$

where $\mathcal{G} = \left[\overline{p_s} p_t \overline{P_{0s}^{(c)}}, p_s \overline{P_{\mathrm{MD}}} \ \overline{P_{1s}^{(c)}}, p_s P_{\mathrm{MD}} \overline{P_{1s}^{(c)}} \right]$ and $\mathcal{A} = \left[\overline{p_s} \overline{P_{0s}}, p_s P_{\mathrm{FA}} \overline{P_{1s}}, p_s \overline{P_{\mathrm{FA}}} \ \overline{P_{1s}} \right]^{\dagger}$. After some mathematical manipulations, we get

$$\mu_s = \frac{(\overline{P_p} - \lambda_p) \mathcal{A}^{\dagger} \mathcal{P} + \mathcal{P}^{\dagger} \mathcal{D} \mathcal{A}^{\dagger} \mathcal{P} + \lambda_p \mathcal{G}^{\dagger} \mathcal{P}}{\overline{P_p} + \mathcal{D}^{\dagger} \mathcal{P}} \tag{11}$$

The portion of the stability region based on the first dominant system is characterized by the closure of the rate pairs (λ_p, λ_s). One method to obtain this closure is to solve a constrained optimization problem such that λ_s is maximized for each λ_p under the stability of the primary and the secondary queues. The optimization problem is given by

$$\max_{p_s, \mathcal{P} = [p_t, p_b, p_f]^{\dagger}} \mu_s, \ \text{s.t.} \ \ 0 \le p_t, p_s, p_f, p_b \le 1, \ \lambda_p \le \mu_p \tag{12}$$

For a fixed p_s, the optimization problem (12) can be shown to be a quasiconcave program over $\mathcal{P}$. We need to show that the objective function is quasiconcave over

convex set and under convex constraints. From (9), μ_p is affine and hence convex over $\mathcal{P}$ for a fixed p_s. The Hessian of the numerator of μ_s is given by $H = \mathcal{A}\mathcal{D}^{\dagger} + \mathcal{D}\mathcal{A}^{\dagger}$. Let y be an arbitrary 3×1 vector. The matrix H is negative semidefinite if $y^{\dagger} H y \le 0$. Since the matrices $\mathcal{A}\mathcal{D}^{\dagger}$ and $\mathcal{D}\mathcal{A}^{\dagger}$ are generated using a linear combination of a single vector, the rank of each is 1 and therefore each of them has at least two zero eigenvalues. The trace of each is negative and equal to $\Lambda = -\Delta_p \lambda_e (\overline{p_s}^2 \overline{P_{0s}} + p_s^2 P_{\mathrm{FA}} \overline{P_{1s}} \overline{P_{\mathrm{MD}}} + p_s^2 P_{\mathrm{MD}} \overline{P_{\mathrm{FA}}} \overline{P_{1s}}) \le 0$. Hence, $\mathcal{A}\mathcal{D}^{\dagger}$ and $\mathcal{D}\mathcal{A}^{\dagger}$ are negative semidefinite with eigenvalues $(0, 0, \Lambda)$. Accordingly, $y^{\dagger} \mathcal{A}\mathcal{D}^{\dagger} y \le 0$, $y^{\dagger} \mathcal{D}\mathcal{A}^{\dagger} y \le 0$ and their sum is also negative. Based on these observations for a fixed p_s, the numerator of (11) is nonnegative[3] and concave over $\mathcal{P}$ and the denominator is positive and affine over $\mathcal{P}$; hence, μ_s is quasiconcave, as is derived in Appendix B. Since the objective function of the optimization problem is quasiconcave and the constraints are convex for a fixed p_s, the problem is a quasiconcave program for each p_s. We solve a family of quasiconcave programs parameterized by p_s. The optimal p_s is chosen as the one which yields the highest objective function in (12).

The problem of maximizing a quasiconcave function over a convex set under convex constraints can be efficiently and reliably solved by using the bisection method [28].

Based on the construction of the dominant system $\mathcal{S}_1$ of system $\mathcal{S}$, it can be noted that the queues of the dominant system are never less than those of system $\mathcal{S}$, provided that they are both initialized identically. This is because the SU transmits dummy packets even if it does not have any packets of its own, and therefore it always interferes with PU even if it is empty. The mean service rate of primary queue is thus reduced in the dominant system and Q_p is emptied less frequently, thereby reducing also the mean service rate of the secondary queue. Given this, if the queues are stable in the dominant system, then they are stable in system $\mathcal{S}$. That is, the stability conditions of the dominant system are **sufficient** for the stability of system $\mathcal{S}$. Now if Q_s saturates in the dominant system, the SU will not transmit dummy packets as it always has its own packets to send. For $\lambda_p < \mu_p$, this makes the behavior of the dominant system identical to that of system $\mathcal{S}$ and both systems are **indistinguishable** at the boundary points. The stability conditions of the dominant system are thus both sufficient and **necessary** for the stability of system $\mathcal{S}$ given that $\lambda_p < \mu_p$.

To get some insights for this system under the first dominant system, we consider the problem when $\lambda_p/\overline{P_p}$

---

[3] The non-negativity of the numerator and the denominator of μ_s follow from the definition of the service rate.

is close to unity and with significant MPR capabilities,[4] which means that the primary queue is nonempty most of the time and therefore the optimal sensing decision is $p_s^* = 0$. Note that, in general, this case provides a lower bound performance on what can be obtained in S_1. When $p_s = 0$, the maximum secondary stable throughput is given by solving the following optimization problem:

$$\max_{0 \leq p_t \leq 1} \lambda_e p_t \left[\left(1 - \frac{\lambda_p}{\mu_p} \right) \overline{P}_{0s} + \overline{P_{0s}^{(c)}} \frac{\lambda_p}{\mu_p} \right], \text{ s.t. } \lambda_p \leq \mu_p \quad (13)$$

The problem is **convex** and can be solved using the Lagrangian formulation. The access probability p_t is upperbounded by $\mathcal{F}$

$$\mathcal{F} = \min \left\{ 1, \frac{\overline{P}_p - \lambda_p}{\lambda_e \Delta_p} \right\} \quad (14)$$

The second term in $\mathcal{F}$ must be nonnegative for the problem to be feasible. The optimal access probability is thus given by

$$p_t^* = \min \left\{ \mathcal{F}, \max \left\{ \frac{\overline{P}_p - \sqrt{\overline{P}_p \lambda_p \left(1 - \overline{P_{0s}^{(c)}} / \overline{P}_{0s} \right)}}{\lambda_e \Delta_p}, 0 \right\} \right\} \quad (15)$$

with $0 \leq \lambda_p \leq \mu_p$. From the optimal solution, we notice the following remarks. As λ_p increases, the secondary access probability, p_t, decreases as well. This is because the possibility of collisions increases with increasing the access probability (or increasing the secondary access to the channel) and since the PU is busy most of the time, the possibility of collisions and packet loss increase as well. In addition, by observing the optimal solution in (15), we notice that as the secondary energy arrival, λ_e, increases, the access probability decreases. This is because accessing the channel most of the time with the availability of energy may cause high average packet loss for the PU. We note that as the capability of MPR of the primary receiver, i.e., $\overline{P_p^{(c)}}$, increases, the access probability of the secondary queue increases. This occurs because the possibility of decoding the primary packet under interference is almost equal to the probability of decoding without interference when the MPR capability of the primary receiver is high. Therefore, the secondary throughput increases. In addition, as the ability of the secondary receiver of decoding the secondary packets under interference, which is represented by $\overline{P_{0s}^{(c)}} / \overline{P}_{0s}$, increases, the access probability of the secondary terminal increases as far as the primary queue stability condition is satisfied.

3.2. Second Dominant System

In the second dominant system, denoted by S_2, queue Q_p transmits dummy packets when it is empty and the SU behaves as it would in system S. By substituting with $\Pr\{Q_p = 0\} = 0$ into (2), the average secondary service rate is given by

$$\mu_s = \left[\overline{p_s} p_t \overline{P_{0s}^{(c)}} + p_s p_f P_{\text{MD}} \overline{P_{1s}^{(c)}} + p_s p_b \overline{P_{\text{MD}}} \; \overline{P_{1s}^{(c)}} \right] \Pr\{Q_e \neq 0\} \quad (16)$$

where $\Pr\{Q_e \neq 0\} = \lambda_e$. Under this dominant system, the SU optimal sensing decision is $p_s^* = 0$. This is because the PU is always nonempty. Hence, Q_s mean service rate in (16) is rewritten as

$$\mu_s = p_t \lambda_e \overline{P_{0s}^{(c)}} \quad (17)$$

The probability of Q_s being nonempty is λ_s / μ_s. Hence, the primary queue mean service rate is given by

$$\mu_p = \left(1 - \frac{\lambda_s}{\mu_s} \lambda_e \right) \overline{P}_p + \frac{\lambda_s}{\mu_s} \lambda_e \left[p_t \overline{P_p^{(c)}} + (1 - p_t) \overline{P}_p \right] \quad (18)$$

After some simplifications, the primary mean service rate is given by

$$\mu_p = \overline{P}_p - \frac{\lambda_s}{\overline{P_{0s}^{(c)}}} \Delta_p \quad (19)$$

Note that μ_p is independent of p_t. The portion of the stability region of S based on S_2 is obtained by solving a constrained optimization problem in which μ_p is maximized under the stability of the primary and the secondary queues. Since the primary mean service rate is independent of p_t, the stability region of the second dominant system is given by solving the following optimization feasibility problem

$$\max_{0 \leq p_t \leq 1} \overline{P}_p - \frac{\lambda_s}{\overline{P_{0s}^{(c)}}} \Delta_p, \\ \text{s.t. } \lambda_s \leq p_t \lambda_e \overline{P_{0s}^{(c)}} \quad (20)$$

Hence, the optimal access probability is

$$p_t \geq \frac{\lambda_s}{\lambda_e \overline{P_{0s}^{(c)}}} \quad (21)$$

with $\lambda_s \leq \lambda_e \overline{P_{0s}^{(c)}}$. Based on (21), the solution of the problem is a set of values which satisfies the secondary queue stability constraint. We note that as the secondary mean arrival rate, λ_s, increases, the lower limit of p_t increases as well. This is because the SU must increase its service rate, which increases with

---

[4]As proposed in [13], the primary parameters λ_p, $\overline{P}_p$ and $\lambda_p / \overline{P}_p$ can be efficiently estimated by overhearing the primary feedback channel.

the increasing of the access probability, to maintain its queue stability. We also note that one of the feasible points is $\lambda_s = \mu_s$, which means a saturated SU (since the arrival rate is equal to the service rate, $\Pr\{Q_s \neq 0\} = \lambda_s/\mu_s = 1$). This system is equivalent to a system with random access without employing any channel sensing with backlogged (saturated) primary and secondary transmitters.

Since the stability region of system S is the union of both dominant systems, the stability region of the proposed protocol always contains that of the random access without employing any spectrum sensing. Based on this observation, we can say that at high primary arrival rate, or at high probability of nonempty primary queue, the random access without employing any sensing scheme is optimal, i.e., the SU should not employ channel sensing in such case. This is because the PU is always active and therefore there is no need to sense the channel and waste τ seconds of the data transmission time.

4. Feedback-based Access

In this section, we analyze the use of the primary feedback messages by the cognitive terminal. This system is denoted by Φ_F. In the feedback-based access scheme, the SU utilizes the available primary feedback information for accessing the channel in addition to spectrum sensing. Leveraging the primary feedback is valid when it is available and unencrypted.

In the proposed scheme, the SU monitors the PU feedback channel. It may overhear an acknowledgment (ACK) if the primary receiver correctly decodes the primary transmission, a negative acknowledgment (NACK) if decoding fails, or nothing if there is no primary transmission. We introduce the following modification to the protocol introduced earlier in the paper. If a NACK is overheard by the SU, it assumes that the PU will retransmit the lost packet during the next time slot [29]. Being sure that the PU will be active, the secondary terminal does not need to sense the channel to ascertain the state of primary activity. Therefore, it just accesses the channel with some probability p_r. If an ACK is observed on the feedback channel or no primary feedback is overheard, the SU proceeds to operate as explained earlier in Section 3. We assume the feedback packets are very short compared to T and are always received correctly by both the primary and secondary terminals due to the use of strong channel codes.

It is important to emphasize here the benefit of employing primary feedback. By avoiding spectrum sensing, the secondary terminal does not have to waste τ seconds for channel sensing. It can use the whole slot duration for data transmission. As proven in [1, 30], this reduces the outage probability of the secondary link. Therefore, by differentiating between the primary

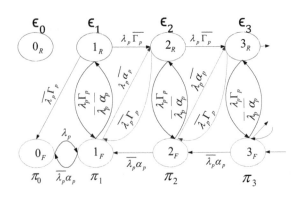

Figure 3. Markov chain of the PU for the feedback-based access scheme under dominant system S_1^f. Probabilities $\overline{\Gamma_p} = 1 - \Gamma_p$ and $\overline{\alpha_p} = 1 - \alpha_p$. State self-transitions are not depicted for visual clarity.

states of transmission, i.e., whether they are following the reception of an ACK or not, the SU can potentially enhance its throughput by eliminating the need for spectrum sensing when the PU is about to retransmit a previously lost packet. Note that we denote the system operating exactly as system S with primary feedback leveraging as S_f.

4.1. First dominant system

As in the previous section, under the first dominant system, denoted by S_1^f, Q_s transmits dummy packets when it is empty and the PU behaves as it would in system S_f.

The PU's queue evolution Markov chain under the first dominant system of this protocol is shown in Fig. 3. The probability of the queue having k packets and transmitting for the first time is π_k, where F in Fig. 3 denotes first transmission. The probability of the queue having k packets and retransmitting is ϵ_k, where R in Fig. 3 denotes retransmission. Define α_p as the probability of successful transmission of the PU's packet in case of first transmission and Γ_p is the probability of successful transmission of the PU's packet in case of retransmission. It can be shown that both probabilities are given by:

$$\alpha_p = \overline{P}_p - \lambda_e \Delta_p \left(\overline{p_s} p_t + p_s P_{\text{MD}} p_f + p_s \overline{P_{\text{MD}}} p_b \right) \quad (22)$$

$$\Gamma_p = \overline{P}_p - \lambda_e \Delta_p p_r \quad (23)$$

Solving the state balance equations, we can obtain the state probabilities which are provided in Table 2. The probability π_0 is obtained using the normalization condition $\sum_{k=0}^{\infty}(\pi_k + \epsilon_k) = 1$.

η	$\lambda_p \alpha_p + \left(1 - \lambda_p\right)\Gamma_p$
$\pi_\circ$	$\dfrac{\eta - \lambda_p}{\Gamma_p}$
$\epsilon_\circ$	0
π_1	$\pi_\circ \dfrac{\lambda_p}{1 - \lambda_p} \dfrac{\lambda_p + \left(1 - \lambda_p\right)\Gamma_p}{\eta}$
ϵ_1	$\pi_\circ \dfrac{\lambda_p}{\eta}\left(1 - \alpha_p\right)$
$\pi_k, k \geq 2$	$\pi_\circ \dfrac{\lambda_p\left(1 - \alpha_p\right)}{\left(1 - \eta\right)^2}\left[\dfrac{\lambda_p\left(1 - \eta\right)}{\left(1 - \lambda_p\right)\eta}\right]^k$
$\epsilon_k, k \geq 2$	$\pi_\circ \dfrac{\left(1 - \lambda_p\right)\left(1 - \alpha_p\right)}{\left(1 - \eta\right)^2}\left[\dfrac{\lambda_p\left(1 - \eta\right)}{\left(1 - \lambda_p\right)\eta}\right]^k$
$\sum_{k=1}^\infty \pi_k$	$\pi_\circ \dfrac{\lambda_p \Gamma_p}{\eta - \lambda_p} = \lambda_p$
$\sum_{k=1}^\infty \epsilon_k$	$\pi_\circ \dfrac{\lambda_p}{\eta - \lambda_p}\left(1 - \alpha_p\right) = \dfrac{\lambda_p}{\Gamma_p}\left(1 - \alpha_p\right)$

Table 2. State probabilities for the feedback-based access scheme.

It should be noticed that $\lambda_p < \eta$, where η is defined in Table 2, is a condition for the sum $\sum_{k=0}^\infty (\pi_k + \epsilon_k)$ to exist. This condition ensures the existence of a stationary distribution for the Markov chain and guarantees the stability of the primary queue. The service rate of the SU is given by:

$$\mu_s = \lambda_e \left[\pi_0 \left(\overline{p_s} p_t \overline{P}_{0s} + p_s p_b P_{FA} \overline{P}_{1s} + p_s p_f \overline{P_{FA}}\ \overline{P}_{1s} \right) \right.$$
$$+ \left(\sum_{k=1}^\infty \pi_k \right) \left(\overline{p_s} p_t \overline{P_{0s}^{(c)}} + p_s p_f P_{MD} \overline{P_{1s}^{(c)}} \right.$$
$$\left. + p_s p_b \overline{P_{MD}}\ \overline{P_{1s}^{(c)}} \right) + \left. \left(\sum_{k=1}^\infty \epsilon_k \right) p_r \overline{P_{0s}^{(c)}} \right]$$
$$(24)$$

Let $\mathcal{I} = [0, 0, 0, 1]^\dagger$, $\mathcal{H} = -\lambda_e \Delta_p \mathcal{I}$, $\mathcal{J} = [\mathcal{D}^\dagger, 0]^\dagger$, $\hat{\mathcal{U}} = -\lambda_p \mathcal{J} + \overline{\lambda_p} \mathcal{H}$, $\eta = \overline{P}_p + \hat{P}^\dagger \hat{\mathcal{U}}$, $\hat{P} = [p_t, p_f, p_b, p_r]^\dagger$, $\Gamma_p = \overline{P}_p + \mathcal{H}^\dagger \hat{P}$, $\alpha_p = \overline{P}_p - \hat{P}^\dagger \mathcal{J}$, and $p_r = \mathcal{I}^\dagger \hat{P}$. After some algebra, and substituting by the state probabilities in Table 2, the secondary data queue mean service rate in (24) can be rewritten as

$$\mu_s = \frac{\left[(\overline{P}_p - \lambda_p)\mathcal{K}^\dagger + \tilde{\delta} P_p \mathcal{I}^\dagger + \lambda_p \overline{P}_p \mathcal{C}^\dagger\right]\hat{P} + \hat{P}^\dagger \Psi \hat{P}}{\overline{P}_p + \mathcal{H}^\dagger \hat{P}} \quad (25)$$

where $\mathcal{K} = \left[\overline{p}_s \overline{P}_{0s}, p_s P_{FA} \overline{P}_{1s}, p_s \overline{P_{FA}}\ \overline{P}_{1s}, 0\right]^\dagger$, $\Psi = (\hat{\mathcal{U}} \mathcal{K}^\dagger + \lambda_p \mathcal{C} \mathcal{H}^\dagger - \tilde{\delta} \mathcal{J} \mathcal{I}^\dagger)$, $\mathcal{C} = \left[\overline{p}_s\ \overline{P_{0s}^{(c)}}, p_s P_{MD} \overline{P_{1s}^{(c)}}, p_s \overline{P_{MD}}\ \overline{P_{1s}^{(c)}}, 0\right]^\dagger$, and $\tilde{\delta} = \lambda_p \overline{P_{0s}^{(c)}}$. It is straightforward to show that the Hessian matrix of the numerator of (25) is $\nabla_{\hat{P}}^2 \hat{P}^\dagger \Psi \hat{P} = \Psi + \Psi^\dagger$ which is a negative semidefinite matrix and therefore the numerator is concave.[5] The denominator is affine over $\hat{P}$. Since for a given p_s the denominator is affine and the numerator is concave over $\hat{P}$, (25) is quasiconcave over $\hat{P}$ for each p_s.

For a fixed λ_p, the maximum mean service rate for the SU is given by solving the following optimization problem using expression (24) for μ_s

$$\max_{p_s, p_f, p_t, p_b, p_r} \quad \mu_s$$
$$\text{s.t.} \quad 0 \leq p_s, p_f, p_t, p_b, p_r \leq 1 \quad (26)$$
$$\lambda_p \leq \eta$$

The optimization problem is a quasiconcave optimization problem given p_s which can be solved efficiently using the bisection method [28]. For proof of quasiconcavity of the objective function, the reader is referred to Appendix B. The constraint $\lambda_p \leq \eta$ is affine over $\hat{P}$ for a fixed p_s. Since the objective function is quasiconcave given p_s and the constraint is convex given p_s, (26) is quasiconcave program for a fixed p_s.

Based on the construction of the dominant system $\mathcal{S}_1^f$, the queues of the dominant system are never less than those of system $\mathcal{S}_f$, provided that they are both initialized identically. This is because the SU transmits dummy packets even if it does not have any packets of its own, and therefore it always interferes with PU even if it is empty. The mean service rate of primary queue is thus reduced in the dominant system and Q_p is emptied less frequently, thereby reducing also the mean service rate of the secondary queue. Given this, if the queues are stable in the dominant system, then they are stable in system $\mathcal{S}_f$. That is, the stability conditions of the dominant system are **sufficient** for the stability of system $\mathcal{S}_f$. Now if Q_s saturates in the dominant system, the SU will not transmit dummy packets as it always has its own packets to send. For $\lambda_p < \eta$, this makes the behavior of the dominant system identical to that of system $\mathcal{S}_f$ and both systems are **indistinguishable** at the boundary points. The stability conditions of the dominant system are thus both sufficient and **necessary** for the stability of system $\mathcal{S}_f$ given that $\lambda_p < \eta$.

---

[5] Ψ is a negative semidefinite because it composes of three matrices $\hat{\mathcal{U}} \mathcal{K}^\dagger$, $\lambda_p \mathcal{C} \mathcal{H}^\dagger$ and $-\tilde{\delta} \mathcal{J} \mathcal{I}^\dagger$ each of which is a negative semidefinite matrix. These matrices are negative semidefinite because each of them is a nonpositive matrix (all elements are nonpositive) with rank 1.

4.2. Second dominant system

The second dominant system of $\mathcal{S}^f$ is denoted by $\mathcal{S}_2^f$. Under $\mathcal{S}_2^f$, the PU sends dummy packets when it is empty. This system reduces to a random access scheme without employing any spectrum sensing and without leveraging the primary feedback. This is because the PU is always nonempty and the optimal sensing decision is not to sense the channel at all. Moreover, the access probability of the SU is fixed over all primary states. Hence, $p_s^* = 0$ and $p_r^* = p_t^*$. Accordingly, the second dominant system of $\mathcal{S}^f$ is exactly the second dominant system of $\mathcal{S}$. The stability region of system $\mathcal{S}_f$ is the union of both dominant systems.

Following are some important notes. First, the stability region of the first dominant system of $\mathcal{S}$ or $\mathcal{S}^f$ always contains that of the second dominant system. This can be easily shown by comparing the mean service rate of nodes in each dominant system. Second, the stability region of systems $\mathcal{S}$ and $\mathcal{S}^f$ are inner bounds for the original systems Φ_{NF} and Φ_{F}, respectively, where the energy queue is operating normally without the assumption of one packet consumption per time slot. Third, when the SU is plugged to a reliable power source, the average arrival rate is $\lambda_e = 1$ packets per time slot. Under this case, the stability region of systems $\mathcal{S}$ and $\mathcal{S}^f$ coincide with their corresponding original systems Φ_{NF} and Φ_{F}, respectively. This is because the energy queue in this case is always backlogged and never being empty regardless of the value of μ_e. Hence, in general, the case of $\lambda_e = 1$ energy packets per time slot is an **outer bound** for the proposed systems, Φ_{NF} and Φ_{F}, as the SU can always send data whenever its data queue is nonempty.

Next, we analyze the case of spectrum access without employing any sensing scheme to give some insights for system $\mathcal{S}^f$. Note that the results obtained for this case are tight when $\lambda_p/\overline{P_p}$ is close to unity and the MPR capabilities are strong. This is because, under this condition, the probability of the primary queue being empty at a given time slot is almost zero and therefore the optimal sensing decision which avoids wasting τ seconds of the transmission time is $p_s^* = 0$.

4.3. The case of $p_s = 0$

Under this case, the mean service rate of the SU is given by

$$\mu_s = \lambda_e \left[\pi_0 p_t \overline{P_{0s}} + \left(\sum_{k=1}^{\infty} \pi_k \right) p_t \overline{P_{0s}^{(c)}} + \left(\sum_{k=1}^{\infty} \epsilon_k \right) p_r \overline{P_{0s}^{(c)}} \right] \quad (27)$$

Substituting with probability of summations in Table 2, the secondary mean service rate is given by

$$\mu_s = \lambda_e \left[\pi_0 p_t \overline{P_{0s}} + \lambda_p p_t \overline{P_{0s}^{(c)}} + \frac{\Gamma_p - \alpha_p}{\Gamma_p} p_r \overline{P_{0s}^{(c)}} \right] \quad (28)$$

For a fixed λ_p, the maximum service rate for the SU is given by solving the following optimization problem:

$$\max_{p_t, p_r} \mu_s \text{ s.t. } 0 \le p_t, p_r \le 1, \lambda_p \le \eta \quad (29)$$

The optimization problem is quasiconcave (quasiconcave objective with a linear constraint) and can be solved using bisection method [28]. Fixing p_r makes the optimization problem a convex program parameterized by p_r. The optimal p_r is taken as that which yields the highest value of the objective function. Let $\ell = \lambda_e \Delta_p$. We obtain the following optimization problem for a given p_r:

$$\max_{0 \le p_t \le 1} \left(\frac{\overline{P_p} - \lambda_p \ell p_r - \lambda_p + \lambda_p \frac{\overline{P_{0s}^{(c)}}}{\overline{P_{0s}}} \overline{P_p}}{\Gamma_p} \right) p_t - \frac{\lambda_p \ell}{\Gamma_p} p_t^2 \quad (30)$$

$$\text{s.t.} \quad \lambda_p \le \eta$$

The objective function of (30) is concave over convex set under linear constraints and therefore a concave program. It can be solved using the Lagrangian formulation. Setting the first derivative of the objective function to zero, the root of the first derivative is given by

$$p_t = \frac{\overline{P_p} - \lambda_p \ell p_r - \lambda_p + \lambda_p \frac{\overline{P_{0s}^{(c)}}}{\overline{P_{0s}}} \overline{P_p}}{2\lambda_p \ell} \quad (31)$$

Since $\lambda_p \le \eta = \lambda_p \alpha_p + \overline{\lambda_p} \Gamma_p$ and using (22), the access probability is upperbounded as

$$p_t \le \frac{\overline{P_p} - \overline{\lambda_p} \ell p_r - \lambda_p}{\lambda_p \ell} \quad (32)$$

The optimal solution is then given by

$$p_t^* = \min \left\{ \frac{\overline{P_p} - \overline{\lambda_p} \ell p_r - \lambda_p}{\lambda_p \ell}, \frac{\overline{P_p} - \overline{\lambda_p} \ell p_r - \lambda_p + \lambda_p \frac{\overline{P_{0s}^{(c)}}}{\overline{P_{0s}}} \overline{P_p}}{2\lambda_p \ell} \right\} \quad (33)$$

5. Delay–Aware Primary Users

In this section, we investigate the primary queueing delay and plug a constraint on the primary queueing delay to the optimization problems. That is, we maximize μ_s under the constraints that the primary queue is stable and that the primary packet delay is smaller than or equal a specified value $D \ge 1$.[6] The value of $D \ge 1$ is application-dependent and is related

---

[6]Note that based on the adopted arrival model, the minimum primary queueing delay is 1 time slot, i.e., $D = 1$ time slot.

to the required QoS for the PU. Delay analysis for interacting queues is a notoriously hard problem [20]. To bypass this difficulty, we consider the special case where the secondary data queue is always backlogged (or saturated)[7] while the primary queue behaves exactly as it would in the original systems Φ_{NF} and Φ_F. This represents a lower bound (or worst-case scenario) on performance for the PU compared with the original systems in which the secondary data queue is not backlogged all the time. Next, we compute the primary queueing delay under each system.

5.1. Primary Queueing Delay for System $\mathcal{S}$ with Saturated SU

Let D_p be the average delay of the primary queue. Using Little's law and (6),

$$D_p = \frac{1}{\lambda_p} \sum_{k=1}^{\infty} k v_k = \frac{1 - \lambda_p}{\mu_p - \lambda_p} \quad (34)$$

For the optimal random access and sensing, we solve the following constrained optimization problem. We maximize the mean secondary service rate under the constraints that the primary queue is stable and that the primary packet delay is smaller than or equal a specified value D. The optimization problem with μ_p given in (5) and μ_s in (8) can be written as

$$\max_{p_s, p_f, p_b, p_t} \mu_s$$

$$\text{s.t.} \quad 0 \leq p_s, p_f, p_b, p_t \leq 1 \quad (35)$$
$$\lambda_p \leq \mu_p$$
$$D_p \leq D$$

The delay constraint in case of system $\mathcal{S}$ with backlogged SU can be converted to a constraint on the primary mean service rate. That is, $D_p = \frac{1-\lambda_p}{\mu_p-\lambda_p} \leq D$ can be rewritten as $\mu_p \geq \lambda_p + \frac{1-\lambda_p}{D}$. The intersection of the stability constraint and the delay constraint is the delay constraint. That is, the set of λ_p which satisfies the delay constraint is $\{\lambda_p : \lambda_p \leq \mu_p - \frac{1-\lambda_p}{D}\} = \{\lambda_p \leq \frac{\mu_p - 1/D}{(1-1/D)} \leq \mu_p\}$, whereas the set of λ_p which satisfies the stability constraint is $\{\lambda_p : \lambda_p \leq \mu_p\}$. The intersection of both sets is given by $\{\lambda_p \leq \frac{\mu_p-1/D}{(1-1/D)}\} \cap \{\lambda_p : \lambda_p \leq \mu_p\} = \{\lambda_p : \lambda_p \leq \frac{\mu_p-1/D}{(1-1/D)}\}$, both sets are equal when the delay constraint approaches ∞, i.e., $D \rightarrow \infty$. Hence, the delay constraint subsumes the stability constraint.

The optimization problem is quasiconcave given p_s because μ_s is quasiconcave (the proof is in Appendix B)

and the delay constraint is linear on the optimization parameters.

At high $\lambda_p/\overline{P_p}$ and strong MPR capabilities, the probability of the primary queue being empty at a given time slot is almost zero and therefore the optimal sensing decision is $p_s^* = 0$. In this case, we can get the optimal solution of the optimization problem. The optimization problem can be stated as

$$\max_{0 \leq p_t \leq 1} \lambda_e p_t \left[\left(1 - \frac{\lambda_p}{\mu_p} \right) \overline{P}_{0s} + \overline{P_{0s}^{(c)}} \frac{\lambda_p}{\mu_p} \right], \text{ s.t. } \lambda_p \leq \mu_p, \ D_p \leq D \quad (36)$$

where

$$\mu_p = \overline{P}_p - \lambda_e \Delta_p p_t \quad (37)$$

The optimization problem (36) is **convex** and can be solved using the Lagrangian formulation. The delay constraint subsumes the stability constraint, $\lambda_p < \mu_p$, and p_t is upperbounded by $\mathcal{U}$

$$\mathcal{U} = \min \left\{ 1, \frac{\overline{P}_p - \left(\frac{1-\lambda_p}{D} + \lambda_p \right)}{\lambda_e \Delta_p} \right\} \quad (38)$$

The second term in $\mathcal{U}$ must be nonnegative for the problem to be feasible. The optimal access probability is thus given by

$$p_t^* = \min \left\{ \mathcal{U}, \max \left\{ \frac{\overline{P}_p - \sqrt{\overline{P}_p \lambda_p \left(1 - \overline{P_{0s}^{(c)}} / \overline{P}_{0s} \right)}}{\lambda_e \Delta_p}, 0 \right\} \right\} \quad (39)$$

From the optimal solution (39), we can establish here a similar argument about the impact of each parameter on the secondary access probability as the one beneath (33). However, the difference here is that we have the impact of the delay constraint which has the following affect on the secondary access probability. As the delay constraint, D, increases, the access probability of the SU decreases to avoid increasing collisions with the PU which causes primary throughput loss. If the amount of collisions is high, the delay constraint may be violated if the SU accesses with an access probability higher than p_t^*.

5.2. Primary Queueing Delay for System $\mathcal{S}^f$ with Saturated SU

Applying Little's law, the primary queueing delay is given by

$$D_p = \frac{1}{\lambda_p} \sum_{k=1}^{\infty} k \left(\pi_k + \epsilon_k \right) \quad (40)$$

Using the state probabilities provided in Table 2,

$$D_p = \frac{(\alpha_p - \eta)(\eta - \lambda_p)^2 + \left(1 - \lambda_p \right)^2 \left(1 - \alpha_p \right) \eta}{(\eta - \lambda_p) \left(1 - \lambda_p \right) (1 - \eta) \Gamma_p} \quad (41)$$

---

[7]This case equivalent to the first dominant systems of $\mathcal{S}$ and $\mathcal{S}^f$.

For a fixed λ_p, the maximum mean service rate for the SU is given by solving the following optimization problem using expression (24) for μ_s

$$\begin{aligned}
\max_{p_s,p_f,p_t,p_b,p_r} \quad & \mu_s \\
\text{s.t.} \quad & 0 \leq p_s, p_f, p_t, p_b, p_r \leq 1 \\
& \lambda_p \leq \eta \\
& D_p \leq D
\end{aligned} \tag{42}$$

Note that μ_s is given in Eqn. (25). The optimization problem can be shown to be a concave program for a given p_s and p_r. More Specifically, for a fixed p_r, the denominator in (25) becomes a constant. Since the numerator is concave for a given p_s as shown beneath (25), the objective function of (42) is concave. The delay constraint can be rewritten as

$$\mathcal{E} = \frac{(\eta - \Gamma_p)(\eta - \lambda_p)^2}{\eta} + \overline{\lambda_p}(W - \eta) + \frac{D(\eta - \lambda_p)(\eta - 1)\Gamma_p \lambda_p}{\eta} \leq 0 \tag{43}$$

where $W = \lambda_p + \overline{\lambda_p}\Gamma_p$ and $D \geq 1$. The second derivative of $\mathcal{E}$ for a given p_r with respect to η is given by

$$\nabla_\eta^2 \mathcal{E} = \frac{2(\Gamma_p(D-1)\lambda_p^2 + \eta^3)}{\eta^3} \geq 0 \tag{44}$$

$\nabla_\eta^2 \mathcal{E}$ is always nonnegative. Hence, $\mathcal{E}$ is convex over η for a fixed p_r. Since η is affine over $\hat{\mathcal{P}}$ for a fixed p_s, $\mathcal{E}$ is then convex over $\hat{\mathcal{P}}$. This completes the proof of concavity of the optimization problem (42) for a given p_s and p_r. Note that we solve a family of concave problems parameterized by p_s and p_r. The optimal pair (p_r, p_s) is taken as the pair which yields the highest objective function in (42).

6. Numerical Results and Conclusions

In this section, we provide some numerical results for the optimization problems presented in this paper. A random access without employing spectrum sensing is simply obtained from system S by setting p_s to zero. Let S_R and S_R^f denote the random access system without employing any spectrum sensing without and with feedback leveraging, respectively. We also introduce the conventional scheme of spectrum access, denoted by S^c. In this system, the SU senses the channel each time slot for τ seconds. If the PU is sensed to be inactive, the SU accesses with probability 1. If the PU is sensed to be active, the SU remains silent. The mean service rates for this case are obtained from Section 3 with $p_t = 0$, $p_s = 1$, $p_f = 1$ and $p_b = 0$. We define here two variables $\delta_{0s} = \frac{\overline{P}_{0s}^{(c)}}{\overline{P}_{0s}}$ and $\delta_{1s} = \frac{\overline{P}_{1s}^{(c)}}{\overline{P}_{1s}}$, both of them are

less than 1 as shown in Appendix A. Fig. 4 shows the stability region of the proposed protocols. Systems S_R and S_R^f are also plotted. The parameters used to generate the figure are: $\lambda_e = 1$ energy packets/slot, $\overline{P}_p = 0.7$, $\overline{P}_p^{(c)} = 0.1$, $\overline{P}_{0s} = 0.8$, $\overline{P}_{0s}^{(c)} = 0.1$, $\overline{P}_{1s} = 0.6$, $\overline{P}_{1s}^{(c)} = 0.3$, $P_{FA} = 0.01$, and $P_{MD} = 0.02$. We can note that primary feedback leveraging expands the stability region. It is also noted that randomly accessing the channel without channel sensing and with primary feedback leveraging can outperform system S for some λ_p. This is because in system S_R^f the SU does not sense the channel at the following time slot to primary packet decoding failure at the primary destination. Therefore, the SU does not waste τ seconds in channel sensing and it is sure of the activity of the PU.

Fig. 5 provides a comparison between the maximum secondary stable throughput for the proposed systems and the conventional system. The parameters used to generate the figure are: $\lambda_e = 0.4$ energy packets/slot, $\overline{P}_p = 0.7$, $\overline{P}_p^{(c)} = 0.1$, $\overline{P}_{0s} = 0.8$, $\overline{P}_{0s}^{(c)} = 0.1$, $\overline{P}_{1s} = 0.6$, $\overline{P}_{1s}^{(c)} = 0.075$, $P_{FA} = 0.05$, and $P_{MD} = 0.01$. For the investigated parameters, over $\lambda_p < 0.475$ packets/slot, the proposed protocols outperform the conventional system. Whereas over $\lambda_p \geq 0.475$ packets/slot, all systems provide the same performance. This is because at high primary arrival rate, the probability of the primary queue being empty is very low and the PU will be active most of the time slots. Hence, the SU senses the channel each time slot and avoids accessing the channel when the PU is sensed to be active and at retransmission states. That is, $p_t = 0$, $p_s = 1$, $p_r = 0$, $p_b = 0$ and $p_f = 1$. We note that feedback leveraging always enhances the secondary throughput.

Figs. 6 and 7 show the impact of the MPR capability at the receiving nodes on the stable throughput region. Without MPR capability, collisions are assumed to lead to sure packet loss. Therefore, a collision model without MPR corresponds to the case of the probabilities of correct reception being zero when there are simultaneous transmissions. As shown in Fig. 6, the secondary service rate is reduced when there is no MPR capability. As the strength of MPR capability increases, the stability regions expand significantly. It can be noted that the performance of S and S^f are equal when the MPR capability is high. This is due to the fact that the SU does not need to employ channel sensing or feedback leveraging as it can transmit each time slot simultaneously with the PU because the secondary receiver can decode packets under interference with a probability almost equal to the probability when it transmits alone. The figure is plotted for different MPR strength of the secondary receiver, namely, for $P_1 = \delta_{0s} = \delta_{1s} = 0$, $P_2 = \delta_{0s} = \delta_{1s} = 1/8$, $P_3 = \delta_{0s} = \delta_{1s} = 1/4$ and

$P_4 = \delta_{0s} = \delta_{1s} = 1/2$. The parameters used to generate the figure are: $\lambda_e = 0.4$ energy packets/slot, $\overline{P}_p = 0.7$, $\overline{P_p^{(c)}} = 0.1$, $\overline{P}_{0s} = 0.8$, $\overline{P}_{1s} = 0.6$, $P_{FA} = 0.05$, and $P_{MD} = 0.01$. Fig. 7 demonstrates the impact of the MRR capability of the primary receiver on the stability region of system $\mathcal{S}$. As can be seen, the increases of $\overline{P_p^{(c)}}$ increases the secondary stable throughput for each λ_p. The parameters used to generate the figure are: $\lambda_e = 0.8$ energy packets/slot, $\overline{P}_p = 0.7$, $\overline{P}_{0s} = 0.8$, $\overline{P_{0s}^{(c)}} = 0.1$, $\overline{P}_{1s} = 0.6$, $\overline{P_{1s}^{(c)}} = 0.075$, $P_{FA} = 0.05$, and $P_{MD} = 0.01$ and for different values of $\overline{P_p^{(c)}}$.

Fig. 8 shows the impact of the energy arrival rate on the secondary stable throughput for the considered systems. The parameters used to generate the figure are: $\lambda_p = 0.4$ packets/slot, $\overline{P}_p = 0.7$, $\overline{P_p^{(c)}} = 0.1$, $\overline{P}_{0s} = 0.8$, $\overline{P_{0s}^{(c)}} = 0.1$, $\overline{P}_{1s} = 0.6$, $\overline{P_{1s}^{(c)}} = 0.075$, $P_{FA} = 0.05$, and $P_{MD} = 0.01$. As expected, the secondary service rate increasing with increasing λ_e. We note that there are some constant parts in systems $\mathcal{S}_R$ and $\mathcal{S}_R^f$ at high λ_e. This is due to the fact that increasing the energy arrivals at the energy queue may not boost the secondary throughput because the SU even if it has a lot of energy packets it cannot violate the primary QoS. The violation of the primary QoS may occur due to the presence of sensing errors. We also note that at low energy arrival rate, all systems have the same performance. This is because the secondary access probabilities and the rate in each system are limited by the mean arrival rate of the secondary energy arrival rate. Fig. 9 demonstrates the impact of varying the primary queueing delay constraint, D, on the secondary service rate. The parameters used to generate the figure are: $\lambda_e = 0.4$ energy packets/slot, $\overline{P}_p = 0.7$, $\overline{P_p^{(c)}} = 0.1$, $\overline{P}_{0s} = 0.8$, $\overline{P_{0s}^{(c)}} = 0.1$, $\overline{P}_{1s} = 0.6$, $\overline{P_{1s}^{(c)}} = 0.075$, $P_{FA} = 0.05$, and $P_{MD} = 0.01$ and two different values of the primary queueing delay constraint. As is clear from the figure, the secondary service rate is reduced when the primary queueing delay constraint is more strict.

Appendix A

We adopt a flat fading channel model and assume that the channel gains remain constant over the duration of the time slot. We do not assume the availability of transmit channel state information (CSI) at the transmitters. Each receiver is modeled as zero mean additive white Gaussian noise (AWGN). We derive here a generic expression for the outage probability at the receiver of transmitter j (node k) when there is concurrent transmission from the transmitter v. Assume that node j starts transmission at $i\tau$ and node v starts transmission at $n\tau$. Outage occurs when the

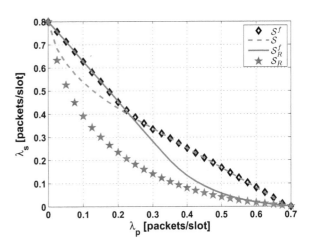

Figure 4. Stability region of the proposed systems.

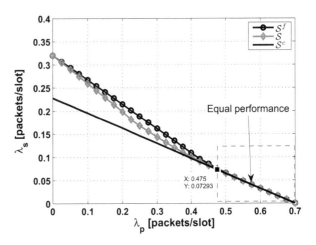

Figure 5. Stability region of the proposed systems. The conventional system, $\mathcal{S}^c$, is also plotted for comparison purposes.

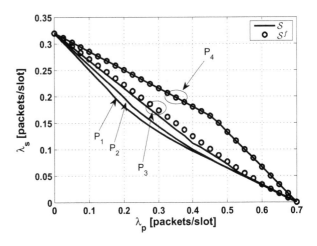

Figure 6. Stability region of the proposed systems.

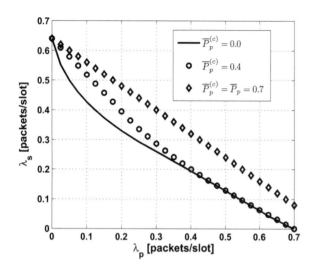

Figure 7. Stability region of system $\mathcal{S}$ for different values of the primary receiver MPR capability.

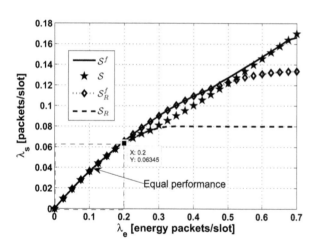

Figure 8. Maximum secondary throughput versus energy arrival rate.

spectral efficiency $R_j^{(i)} = \frac{b}{W T_j^{(i)}}$, where W is the channel bandwidth, $T_j^{(i)}$ is the transmission time of node j and b is number of bits per data packet, exceeds the channel capacity

$$P_{jk,in}^{(c)} = \Pr\left\{ R_j^{(i)} > \log_2\left(1 + \frac{\gamma_{jk,i}\beta_{jk}}{\gamma_{vk,n}\beta_{vk} + 1}\right)\right\} \quad (45)$$

where the superscript c denotes concurrent transmission, $\Pr\{.\}$ denotes the probability of the argument, β_{jk} is the channel gain of link $j \to k$, $\mathcal{N}_k$ is the noise variance at receiver k in Watts, $\gamma_{jk,i} = \mathbb{P}_j^{(i)}/\mathcal{N}_k$, $\mathbb{P}_j^{(i)}$ Watts is the transmit power employed by node j when it starts transmission at $t = i\tau$, $\gamma_{vk,n} = \mathbb{P}_v^{(n)}/\mathcal{N}_k$, and $\mathbb{P}_v^{(n)}$ is the used

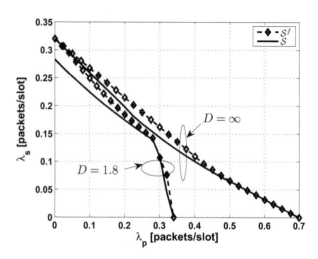

Figure 9. Maximum secondary throughput versus λ_p for specific primary queueing delay.

transmit power by node v when it starts transmission at $t = n\tau$. The outage probability can be written as

$$P_{jk,in}^{(c)} = \Pr\left\{ \frac{\gamma_{jk,i}\beta_{jk}}{\gamma_{vk,n}\beta_{vk} + 1} < 2^{R_j^{(i)}} - 1\right\} \quad (46)$$

Since β_{jk} and β_{vk} are independent and exponentially distributed (Rayleigh fading channel gains) with means σ_{jk} and σ_{vk}, respectively, we can use the probability density functions of these two random variables to obtain the outage probability of link $j \to k$ as

$$P_{jk,in}^{(c)} = 1 - \frac{1}{1 + \left(2^{R_j^{(i)}} - 1\right)\frac{\gamma_{vk,n}\sigma_{vk}}{\gamma_{jk,i}\sigma_{jk}}}\exp\left(-\frac{2^{R_j^{(i)}} - 1}{\gamma_{jk,i}\sigma_{jk}}\right) \quad (47)$$

We note that from the outage probability (47), the numerator is increasing function of $R_j^{(i)}$ and the denominator is a decreasing function of $R_j^{(i)}$. Hence, the outage probability $P_{jk,in}^{(c)}$ increases with $R_j^{(i)}$. The probability of correct reception $\overline{P_{jk,i}^{(c)}} = 1 - P_{jk,i}^{(c)}$ is thus given by

$$\overline{P_{jk,in}^{(c)}} = \frac{\overline{P}_{jk,i}}{1 + \left(2^{\frac{b}{TW\left(1 - \frac{i\tau}{T}\right)}} - 1\right)\frac{\gamma_{vk,n}\sigma_{vk}}{\gamma_{jk,i}\sigma_{jk}}} \leq \overline{P}_{jk,i} \quad (48)$$

where $\overline{P}_{jk,i} = \exp\left(-\frac{2^{R_j^{(i)}} - 1}{\gamma_{jk,i}\sigma_{jk}}\right)$ is the probability of packet correct decoding at receiver k when node j transmits alone (without interference). As is obvious, the probability of correct reception is lowered in the case of interference.

Following are some important notes. Firstly, note that if the PU's queue is nonempty, the PU transmits the packet at the head of its queue at the beginning of the time slot with a fixed transmit power $\mathbb{P}_p$ and data transmission time $T_p = T$. Accordingly, the superscript i which represents the instant that a transmitting node starts transmission in is removed in case of PU.

Secondly, for the SU, the formula of probability of complement outage of link s $\rightarrow$ sd when the PU is active is given by

$$\overline{P^{(c)}_{s,i0}} = \frac{\exp\left(-\frac{2^{\frac{b}{TW\left(1-\frac{i\tau}{T}\right)}}-1}{\gamma_{ssd,i}\sigma_{ssd}}\right)}{1+\left(2^{\frac{b}{TW\left(1-\frac{i\tau}{T}\right)}}-1\right)\frac{\gamma_{psd,0}\sigma_{psd}}{\gamma_{ssd,i}\sigma_{ssd}}} \tag{49}$$

where $n = 0$ because the PU always transmits at the beginning of the time slot and $\gamma_{ssd,i} = e/(T(1 - i\tau/T)\mathcal{N}_{sd}) = \gamma_{ssd,0}/(1 - i\tau/T)$. The denominator of (49) is proportional to $\left(2^{\frac{b}{TW\left(1-\frac{i\tau}{T}\right)}} - 1\right)\left(1 - i\frac{\tau}{T}\right)$, which in turn is monotonically decreasing with $i\tau$. Using the first derivative with respect to $i\tau$, the numerator of (49), $\overline{P_{s,i0}} = \exp\left(-\frac{2^{\frac{b}{TW\left(1-\frac{i\tau}{T}\right)}}-1}{\frac{e}{T\left(1-i\frac{\tau}{T}\right)}\sigma_{ssd}}\right)$, can be easily shown to be decreasing with $i\tau$ as in [1, 30]. Since the numerator of (49) is monotonically decreasing with $i\tau$ and the denominator is monotonically increasing with i, $\overline{P^{(c)}_{s,i0}}$ is monotonically decreasing with $i\tau$. Therefore, the secondary access delay causes reduction in probability of secondary packets correct reception at the secondary destinations.

Thirdly, for the PU, $i = 0$, $j = p$ and $k = pd$, the formula of probability of complement outage of link p $\rightarrow$ pd when the SU transmits at $n\tau$ is given by

$$\overline{P^{(c)}_{p,0n}} = \frac{\overline{P_{p,0}}}{1+\left(2^{\frac{b}{TW}}-1\right)\frac{\gamma_{spd,n}\sigma_{spd}}{\gamma_{ppd,0}\sigma_{ppd}}} \tag{50}$$

Since $\tau/T \ll 1$, $\gamma_{spd,n} = \frac{e}{T(1-n\tau/T)\mathcal{N}_{pd}}$ for $n \in \{0, 1\}$ is then approximately given by $\gamma_{spd,n} = \gamma_{spd} = \frac{e}{T\mathcal{N}_{pd}}$. Hence, the impact of τ or secondary access delay on the primary outage probability is insignificant and it can be eliminated. That is,

$$\overline{P^{(c)}_{p,0n}} \approx \frac{\overline{P_{p,0}}}{1+\left(2^{\frac{b}{TW}}-1\right)\frac{\gamma_{spd}\sigma_{spd}}{\gamma_{ppd,0}\sigma_{ppd}}} = \overline{P^{(c)}_p} \tag{51}$$

Based on the above, we simply denote the probability of correct reception for the PU without and with interference as $\overline{P_p}$ and $\overline{P^{(c)}_p}$, respectively. The probability

of correct reception for the SU without and with interference when it starts transmission from $i\tau$ seconds relative to the beginning of the time slot are denoted by $\overline{P_{is}}$ and $\overline{P^{(c)}_{is}}$, respectively.

Appendix B

In this Appendix, we prove the quasiconcavity of $V(\rho) = \theta(\rho)/w(\rho)$, where $\theta(\rho)$ is nonnegative and concave, $w(\rho)$ is positive and affine, and $\rho = [\rho_1, \rho_2, \ldots, \rho_M]^\dagger$, M is a positive integer, belongs to the compact set $\mathbf{dom}\,V(\rho) = [0, 1]^M$ which is a convex set. Let S_ζ to be the ζ-superlevel set of $V(\rho)$ which is given by $S_\zeta = \{\rho \in \mathbf{dom}\,V(\rho)|V(\rho) \geq \zeta\}$. The quasiconcavity of $V(\rho)$ is proved as follows. Since $\theta(\rho) \geq 0$ and $w(\rho) > 0$, it suffices to show that S_ζ are convex sets for all $\zeta \in \mathbb{R}$, $\mathbb{R}$ is the set of real numbers [28]. If $\zeta < 0$, then by the non-negativity of $V(\rho)$, we have $S_\zeta = \{\rho \in \mathbf{dom}\,V(\rho)|V(\rho) \geq \zeta\} = \mathbf{dom}\,V(\rho)$ which is a convex set. If $\zeta \geq 0$, then $\theta(\rho) - \zeta w(\rho)$ is a concave function and hence, $S_\zeta = \{\rho \in \mathbf{dom}\,V(\rho)|V(\rho) \geq \zeta\} = \{\rho \in \mathbf{dom}\,V(\rho)|\theta(\rho) - \zeta w(\rho) \geq 0\}$ is a convex set since the superlevel sets of concave functions are convex.

References

[1] A. El Shafie and A. Sultan, "Optimal random access and random spectrum sensing for an energy harvesting cognitive radio," in *IEEE 8th International Conference on Wireless and Mobile Computing, Networking and Communications (WiMob)*, 2012, pp. 403–410.

[2] Q. Zhao and B. Sadler, "A survey of dynamic spectrum access," *IEEE Signal Processing Magazine*, vol. 24, no. 3, pp. 79–89, 2007.

[3] S. Sudevalayam and P. Kulkarni, "Energy harvesting sensor nodes: Survey and implications," *IEEE Communications Surveys and Tutorials*, vol. 13, no. 3, pp. 443–461, 2011.

[4] J. Lei, R. Yates, and L. Greenstein, "A generic model for optimizing single-hop transmission policy of replenishable sensors," *IEEE Transactions on Wireless Communications*, vol. 8, no. 2, pp. 547–551, 2009.

[5] V. Sharma, U. Mukherji, V. Joseph, and S. Gupta, "Optimal energy management policies for energy harvesting sensor nodes," *IEEE Transactions on Wireless Communications*, vol. 9, no. 4, pp. 1326–1336, 2010.

[6] C. Ho and R. Zhang, "Optimal energy allocation for wireless communications powered by energy harvesters," in *Proceedings IEEE International Symposium on Information Theory (ISIT)*, Jun. 2010, pp. 2368–2372.

[7] J. Yang and S. Ulukus, "Transmission completion time minimization in an energy harvesting system," in *44th Annual Conference on Information Sciences and Systems (CISS)*, March 2010, pp. 1–6.

[8] ——, "Optimal packet scheduling in an energy harvesting communication system," *IEEE Transactions on Communications*, vol. 60, no. 1, pp. 220–230, Jan. 2012.

[9] K. Tutuncuoglu and A. Yener, "Optimum transmission policies for battery limited energy harvesting nodes,"

IEEE Transactions on Wireless Communications, vol. 11, no. 3, pp. 1180–1189, March 2012.

[10] N. Pappas, J. Jeon, A. Ephremides, and A. Traganitis, "Optimal utilization of a cognitive shared channel with a rechargeable primary source node," in *Journal of Communications and Networks (JCN)*, vol. 14, no. 2, Apr. 2012, pp. 162–168.

[11] I. Krikidis, T. Charalambous, and J. Thompson, "Stability analysis and power optimization for energy harvesting cooperative networks," *IEEE Signal Processing Letters*, vol. 19, no. 1, pp. 20–23, January 2012.

[12] A. Sultan, "Sensing and transmit energy optimization for an energy harvesting cognitive radio," *IEEE Wireless Communications Letters*, vol. 1, no. 5, pp. 500–503, Oct. 2012.

[13] A. El Shafie and A. Sultan, "Optimal random access for a cognitive radio terminal with energy harvesting capability," *IEEE Communications Letters*, vol. 17, no. 6, pp. 1128–1131, 2013.

[14] K. Eswaran, M. Gastpar, and K. Ramchandran, "Bits through ARQs: Spectrum sharing with a primary packet system," in *Proceedings IEEE International Symposium on Information Theory (ISIT)*, June 2007, pp. 2171–2175.

[15] F. Lapiccirella, Z. Ding, and X. Liu, "Cognitive spectrum access control based on intrinsic primary ARQ information," in *Proceedings IEEE International Conference on Communications (ICC)*, May 2010.

[16] S. Huang, X. Liu, and Z. Ding, "Distributed power control for cognitive user access based on primary link control feedback," in *IEEE INFOCOM*, March 2010.

[17] M. Levorato, U. Mitra, and M. Zorzi, "Cognitive interference management in retransmission-based wireless networks," in *47th Annual Allerton Conference on Communication, Control, and Computing*, oct. 2009, pp. 94–101.

[18] ——, "Cognitive interference management in retransmission-based wireless networks," in *IEEE Transactions on Information Theory*, vol. 58, no. 5, May 2012, pp. 3023–3046.

[19] B. Kim, Y. Chang, Y. C. Kim, and B. D. Choi, "A queueing system with discrete autoregressive arrivals," *Performance Evaluation*, vol. 64, no. 2, pp. 148–161, 2007.

[20] A. Sadek, K. Liu, and A. Ephremides, "Cognitive multiple access via cooperation: protocol design and performance analysis," *IEEE Transactions on Information Theory*, vol. 53, no. 10, pp. 3677–3696, Oct. 2007.

[21] W. Luo and A. Ephremides, "Stability of N interacting queues in random-access systems," *IEEE Transactions on Information Theory*, vol. 45, no. 5, pp. 1579–1587, July 1999.

[22] R. Loynes, "The stability of a queue with non-independent inter-arrival and service times," in *Proc. Cambridge Philos. Soc*, vol. 58, no. 3. Cambridge University Press, 1962, pp. 497–520.

[23] S. Ghez, S. Verdu, and S. Schwartz, "Stability properties of slotted aloha with multipacket reception capability," *IEEE Transactions on Automatic Control*, vol. 33, no. 7, pp. 640–649, 1988.

[24] S. Ghez, S. Verdú, and S. Schwartz, "Optimal decentralized control in the random access multipacket channel," *IEEE Transactions on Automatic Control*, vol. 34, no. 11, pp. 1153–1163, 1989.

[25] V. Naware, G. Mergen, and L. Tong, "Stability and delay of finite-user slotted ALOHA with multipacket reception," *IEEE Transactions on Information Theory*, vol. 51, no. 7, pp. 2636–2656, July 2005.

[26] L. Kleinrock, "Queueing systems. volume I: Theory," 1975.

[27] R. Rao and A. Ephremides, "On the stability of interacting queues in a multiple-access system," *IEEE Transactions on Information Theory*, vol. 34, no. 5, pp. 918–930, Sep. 1988.

[28] S. Boyd and L. Vandenberghe, *Convex optimization*. Cambridge University Press, 2004.

[29] K. Seddik, A. Sultan, A. El-Sherif, and A. Arafa, "A feedback-based access scheme for cognitive radio systems," *Proceedings IEEE 12th International Workshop on Signal Processing Advances in Wireless Communications (SPAWC)*, pp. 91–95, June 2011.

[30] A. El Shafie and A. Sultan, "Optimal selection of spectrum sensing duration for an energy harvesting cognitive radio," in *Proceedings IEEE Global Communications Conference (Globecom)- Cognitive Radio and Networks Symposium (GC13 CogRN)*, 2013, pp. 1020–1025.

17

Spectrum Sensing For Cognitive Radios Through Differential Entropy

Sanjeev Gurugopinath[1], R. Muralishankar[2,*] and H. N. Shankar[3]
Emails: sanjeevg@pes.edu, {muralishankar, hnshankar}@cmrit.ac.in

[1]Department of Electronics and Communication Engineering, PES University, Bengaluru 560085.
[2]Department of Electronics and Communication Engineering, CMR Institute of Technology, Bengaluru 560037.
[3]Department of Electrical and Electronics Engineering, CMR Institute of Technology, Bengaluru 560037.

Abstract

In this work, we present a novel Goodness-of-Fit Test driven by differential entropy for spectrum sensing in cognitive radios, under three different noise models – Gaussian, Laplacian and mixture of Gaussians. We analyze the proposed detector under Gaussian noise which models the worst-case. We then analyze by considering the Laplacian noise process which has tails heavier than that of the Gaussian. We generalize the analysis considering the noise to be a mixture of Gaussians, which is often the case with noise and interference in communication systems. We analyze the performance under each of these cases for a large class of practically relevant fading channel models and primary signal models, with emphasis on low Signal-to-Noise ratio regimes. Towards this end, we derive closed form expressions for the distribution of the test statistic under the null hypothesis and the detection threshold that satisfies a constraint on the probability of false-alarm. Through Monte Carlo simulations, we demonstrate that our detection strategy outperforms an existing spectrum sensing technique based on order statistics.

Keywords: Spectrum sensing, goodness-of-fit, differential entropy, maximum entropy principle, non-Gaussian noise.

1. Introduction

Goodness-of-Fit Tests (GoFT) for Spectrum Sensing (SS) has received considerable attention in the recent past [2–6]. This approach may be gainfully employed in Cognitive Radio (CR) when a proper knowledge of the primary signal and the fading models is far from complete. In its general form, the GoFT for SS compares a decision statistic to a threshold and rejects the null-hypothesis when the statistic exceeds the threshold. The detection threshold is chosen so as to satisfy a constraint on the probability of false-alarm.

The authors in [2] present a GoFT based on the Anderson-Darling statistic (which we term here as the Anderson-Darling statistic based Detector (ADD)). This is shown to outperform the well-known radiometer or Energy Detector (ED) under low SNR regime with

Rayleigh fading and constant primary signal. Later, it is shown that a combination of the Student's-t Test and the ADD, called the Blind Detector (BD) [3], is robust to noise variance uncertainty. The major infirmities of these works are as follows: (i) The underlying Anderson-Darling statistic is known to perform well only against another Gaussian with a shift in mean. ADD does not perform well in many other relevant SS contexts as, for example, when the primary signal follows other signal models [7]. (ii) The ADD is useful only where the observations under $\mathcal{H}_0$ are i.i.d. (iii) ADD is effective only with small number of observations. Thus, the utility of ADD and BD in SS is diminished.

In [4], the authors propose an Order Statistic based Detector (OSD) and show that it improves upon ADD under conditions discussed in the foregoing. Here, the performance of OSD detector is studied only for a constant primary model. Further, the threshold is set empirically. A Higher Order statistics based Detector [6] is shown to provide good performance under low SNR. Recently, a zero-crossings based GoFT [5] is shown to be robust to uncertainties of the noise model and the parameters; its computational complexity matches that of the GoFT based on ED.

In this work, we propose a novel GoFT based on an estimate of the differential entropy in the received observations. We bring out the many advantages of this technique: (i) relative ease in computing the detection threshold; (ii) relaxation of the restriction of a constant primary signal; and (iii) enhanced performance relative to OSD in several situations which are practically realistic. Additionally, we study the performance of the detector for the Laplacian noise model and a bimodal, two parameter mixed Gaussian noise model. In fact, the mixed Gaussian noise is used, inter alia, to model a combination of Gaussian and Middleton's class A noise components [5] and co-channel interference (CCI) [8]. Further, we obtain a closed-form expression for the optimal detection thresholds for spectrum sensing, considering Gaussian and Laplacian noise models and the near-optimal detection threshold for the mixed Gaussian.

The system model is described in § 2. Differential entropy estimate based detection is introduced and analyzed in § 3. In particular, the cases where the noise process is purely Gaussian, is Laplacian and follows a bimodal Gaussian are studied in § 3.1-3.3 successively. Simulation results are presented and discussed in § 4. Concluding remarks comprise § 5.

2. System Model

Consider a CR node collecting M observations from a primary transmitter operating in a particular frequency band. Based thereon, it decides whether the band is occupied or vacant. The GoFT based SS problem is essentially a detection problem which rejects the noise-only hypothesis given by

$$\mathcal{H}_0 : Y_i \sim f_{\mathbb{N}}, \ i \in \mathcal{M} \triangleq \{1, \cdots, M\},$$

with the probability of false alarm given by

$$p_f \triangleq \mathcal{P}\{\text{reject } \mathcal{H}_0 | \mathcal{H}_0\} \leq \alpha_f,$$

where $\alpha_f \in (0, 1)$ is a fixed constant. The noise distribution $f_{\mathbb{N}}$ for SS can be modeled by various distributions [5]. In this paper, we consider the following: Gaussian, Laplacian and mixture of Gaussians. First, for the sake of simplicity and to study the baseline, we consider the Gaussian, which is adopted in many spectrum sensing approaches. Second, we look at the Laplacian noise having tail heavier than Gaussian. Finally, we take up the bimodal Gaussian distribution, known to be useful in some applications in communication domains [8].

We develop a detector based on the following assumptions:

(a) Noise variance is known perfectly;
(b) The statistics of the primary signal model and the fading channel between the primary transmitter and CR node can be arbitrary.

2.1. Effect of Noise Variance Uncertainty

In practice, the estimate of the noise variance can deviate significantly from its true value, leading to a poor performance of the detector, especially under low SNR regime [3]. Note that our detector can be made robust to the noise variance uncertainty by considering the technique followed in [3]. The detector proposed in this work can be combined with the Student's t-test, similar to the combination of the Anderson-Darling statistic based test with the Student's t-test, discussed in [3]. A detailed study of the performance of the combined detector is currently work in progress.

We present the Order Statistic-based Detector (OSD) [4], known to be the best GoFT detector for testing $f_{\mathbb{N}}$ against a mean-change model, and its implementation in the following subsection.

2.2. The Order Statistic-Based Detector (OSD) [4]

We outline the key steps involved in the construction of the OSD.

1. Let $F_{\mathbb{N}}$ be the Cumulative Distribution Function (CDF) of the noise process. Obtain a transformation on the received observations, Y_i, as

$$z_i = F_{\mathbb{N}}(Y_i), \ i \in \mathcal{M}.$$

2. Sort the variables z_i as

$$z_{(1)} \leq z_{(2)} \leq \cdots \leq z_{(M)}.$$

3. Obtain the beta transformation on $z_{(i)}$ as

$$\rho_i \triangleq \sum_{j=i}^{M} \frac{M!}{(M-j)!j!} z_{(i)}^j [1 - z_{(i)}]^{M-j}, \ i \in \mathcal{M}$$

and then, sort as

$$\rho_{(1)} \leq \rho_{(2)} \leq \cdots \leq \rho_{(M)}.$$

4. The OSD is devised thus:

$$\sum_{i=1}^{M} \left| \rho_{(i)} - \frac{i}{(M+1)^2} \right| \underset{\sim\mathcal{H}_0}{\overset{\sim\mathcal{H}_0}{\gtrless}} \tau_{\text{os}}.$$

Here, for some fixed false-alarm $\alpha_f \in (0, 1)$, the optimal threshold, τ_{os}, is given by [4]

$$\tau_{\text{os}} = 2.599 + 0.8228M - 30.79\alpha_f + 73.75\alpha_f^2$$
$$- 49.08\alpha_f^3 - 0.6466\alpha_f M.$$

The proposed differential entropy estimate based GoFT is discussed in the following section.

3. Differential Entropy Estimate-based GoFT

The differential entropy, denoted by $h(X)$, for a continuous random variable X is defined as [9]

$$h(X) \triangleq -\int_{-\infty}^{\infty} f_X(x) \log(f_X(x)) dx$$

where $f_X(\cdot)$ is the probability density function of X.

In this technique, we estimate the differential entropy in the observations and use it as a test statistic to carry out spectrum sensing. We derive the distribution of the statistic and the value of the optimal detection threshold next, which depend on the noise statistics.

3.1. Detection Under Gaussian Noise

Let $f_{\mathbb{N}} \sim \mathcal{N}(0, \sigma_n^2)$, where $\mathcal{N}(\mu, \sigma^2)$ represents the Gaussian distribution with mean μ and variance σ^2. The detection strategy proposed in this work exploits the fact that among all continuous distributions with finite mean and variance, and with support $(-\infty, \infty)$, the Gaussian yields maximum differential entropy. For this detector, the entropy when $Y_i \sim f_{\mathbb{N}}, i \in \mathcal{M}$ (i.e., for observations under $\mathcal{H}_0$), is less than the entropy if the primary is present, i.e., $Y_i \nsim f_{\mathbb{N}}$. It is known that under $\mathcal{H}_0$, i.e., when $Y_i \sim \mathcal{N}(0, \sigma_n^2)$ [9],

$$h(Y|\mathcal{H}_0) = \frac{1}{2} \log(2\pi e \sigma_n^2).$$

Now, the Differential Entropy estimate-based Detector (DED) is constructed for a given set of observations with sample mean and variance

$$\widehat{Y} \triangleq \frac{1}{M} \sum_{i=1}^{M} Y_i \quad \text{and} \quad \frac{1}{M-1} \sum_{i=1}^{M} (Y_i - \widehat{Y})^2$$

respectively. Then,

$$\widehat{h}(Y) \triangleq \frac{1}{2} \log \left\{ \frac{2\pi e}{M-1} \sum_{i=1}^{M} (Y_i - \widehat{Y})^2 \right\}$$

represents the maximum likelihood estimate of differential entropy in the observations. The test is of the form

$$\widehat{h}(Y) \underset{\sim \mathcal{H}_0}{\overset{\nsim \mathcal{H}_0}{\gtrless}} \tau_{\mathrm{G}},$$

where τ_{G} is set such that a constraint on the probability of false-alarm, α_f, is satisfied. See Appendix A for a procedure to find the optimal τ_{G} given α_f.

3.2. Detection Under Laplacian Noise

It is known that for the Laplacian distribution, $\mathcal{L}(\lambda)$, with parameter λ, the differential entropy is given by

$$h(Y|\mathcal{H}_0) = \log_2(2e\lambda),$$

where $\lambda \triangleq \sqrt{\sigma_n^2/2}$. An unbiased estimate of λ is given by

$$\widehat{\lambda} = \frac{1}{M} \sum_{i=1}^{M} |Y_i - \widehat{Y}|,$$

where $\widehat{Y}$ denotes the estimate of the $\frac{1}{2}$-median. Therefore, an estimate of $h(\cdot)$ is obtained as

$$\widehat{h}(Y) \triangleq \log_2 \left(\frac{2e}{M} \sum_{i=1}^{M} |Y_i - \widehat{Y}| \right),$$

and hence, the test is

$$\widehat{h}(Y) \underset{\sim \mathcal{H}_0}{\overset{\nsim \mathcal{H}_0}{\gtrless}} \tau_{\mathrm{L}}.$$

Here, τ_{L} is set such that a constraint on the probability of false-alarm, α_f, is satisfied. See Appendix B for computing τ_{L} given α_f.

3.3. Detection Under Mixed Gaussian Model

The mixed Gaussian noise model is considered in a variety of signal processing applications for communications. For instance, it is used to model a combination of thermal noise and man-made clutter noise [5], and the Co-Channel Interference (CCI) [8]. Some non-Gaussian noise processes can also be modeled as mixtures of Gaussians [10]. The PDF of the mixture Gaussian noise is [11]

$$f_{\mathbb{N}}(x) = \frac{1}{\sqrt{2\pi \sigma_n^2}} e^{-(x^2 + \mu^2)/(2\sigma_n^2)} \cosh\left(\frac{\mu x}{\sigma_n^2} \right). \quad (1)$$

In general, the differential entropy of this two-component mixture-Gaussian model is expressed implicitly as

$$h(Y|\mathcal{H}_0) = \frac{1}{2} \log(2\pi e \sigma_n^2) + \left(\frac{\mu}{\sigma_n} \right)^2 - \mathcal{I}.$$

$\mathcal{I}$ for different μ and σ_n are tabulated [11]. Also, expressions for tight upper and lower bounds on the entropy are reported [11]. Thus, under $\mathcal{H}_0$,

$$h_{UB}(Y|\mathcal{H}_0) \leq \frac{1}{2} \log(2\pi e \sigma_n) + \left(\frac{\mu}{\sigma_n} \right)^2 \left\{ 1 - \mathrm{erf}\left(\frac{\mu}{\sqrt{(2\sigma_n^2)}} \right) \right\}$$

$$- \sqrt{\frac{2\mu^2}{\pi \sigma_n^2}} e^{-\mu^2/(2\sigma_n^2)} + \log 2,$$

$$h_{LB}(Y|\mathcal{H}_0) \geq \frac{1}{2} \log(2\pi e \sigma_n) + \left(\frac{\mu}{\sigma_n} \right)^2 \left\{ 1 - \mathrm{erf}\left(\frac{\mu}{\sqrt{2\sigma_n^2}} \right) \right\}$$

$$- \sqrt{\frac{2\mu^2}{\pi \sigma_n^2}} e^{-\mu^2/(2\sigma_n^2)}.$$

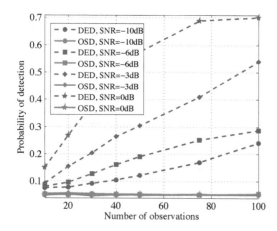

Figure 1. Probability of detection: DED and OSD for different M and SNRs | Gaussian primary signal | Nakagami-m fading: Shape parameter = 1, Scale parameter = 0.5.

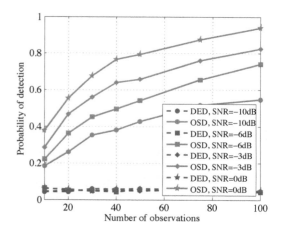

Figure 2. Probability of detection: DED and OSD vs. M for different SNRs | Constant primary signal | Nakagami-m fading: Shape parameter = 1, Scale parameter = 0.5.

We choose the upper bound as a test statistic for SS against the PDF of (1). Based on the estimates, the test is

$$\widehat{h}_{UB}(Y) \underset{\sim \mathcal{H}_0}{\overset{\nsim \mathcal{H}_0}{\gtrless}} \tau_{\mathrm{MG}}.$$

Note that the above test is pessimistic, i.e., it follows the worst-case design. Obtaining the exact PDF of the test statistic in this case is difficult. Therefore, we estimate the PDF of the test statistic and set the threshold through Monte Carlo simulations. Further, we provide the asymptotically optimal threshold for this setting (vide Appendix C).

4. Simulation Results

We evaluate the SS performance of DED and OSD through extensive simulations under various primary signal models, noise models and fading. The primary signal models chosen are constant and Gaussian, while the noise models are Gaussian, Laplacian and mixture of Gaussians. We employ fading models such as Nakagami-m, Weibull and Rayleigh. Nakagami-m (and as its special case, Rayleigh) fading is favored for several indoor wireless communication without line of sight [12]. For some applications in communication with frequency in excess of 900MHz, Weibull fading is found to be a good fit [12]. We set the false-alarm, α_f, to 0.05 and vary the SNR from −10dB to 0dB.

The performance of DED and OSD under the Gaussian noise (vide Fig. 1) shows the probability of detection (p_d) using DED and OSD for M observations and for different values of SNR under Nakagami-m fading with shape and scale parameters 1 and 0.5 respectively. These fading parameters are chosen arbitrarily. The primary signal is taken to be Gaussian [5]. Such an assumption is practically relevant in CR context owing to the errors due to synchronization

and timing offsets. As can be seen, DED outperforms OSD. The performance of OSD is non-trivial, i.e., it operates on the chance line in the receiver operating characteristics.

Fig. 2 presents p_d when the primary signal is constant. We observe that the OSD fares better than DED. Under a constant primary, such performance benefits of the OSD have been observed earlier [4]. A point to note is that the constant primary assumption is largely of theoretical interest as it is highly constrained [13]. Further, the deteriorated performance of DED is due to invariance of entropy to scaling [9].

Fig. 3 presents p_d under Weibull fading, with shape and scale parameters 1 and 2 respectively. The fading parameters are set arbitrarily. The primary signal is Gaussian. Evidently, DED is better than OSD across all M and SNRs. For a constant primary signal with the Weibull fading and with the same parameters as before, OSD is seen to outperform DED (vide Fig. 4). When the primary signal is not constant, the pattern shows DED better than OSD. Similar conclusions can be drawn from Fig. 5 which presents p_d for varying SNRs under Rayleigh fading with parameter 1 and Gaussian primary signal.

Next, we evaluate DED and OSD under Laplacian noise model with the primary being Gaussian and Rayleigh fading. Fig. 6 and Fig. 7 show p_d vs. M and p_d vs. average primary SNR respectively. The noise variance is assumed to be unity. Yet again, OSD proves to perform only trivially in both cases due to primary variation. However, the performance of DED improves significantly with an increase in M and SNR. Additionally, comparing Fig. 5 and Fig. 6, we can see that the p_d with Gaussian noise is higher than p_d with Laplacian noise. This effect is due to the heavy-tailed nature of the Laplacian distribution, i.e., owing to elevated tail probabilities, the detection threshold that

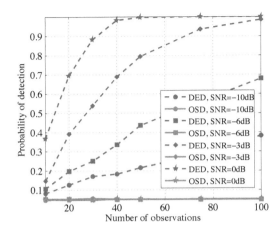

Figure 3. Probability of detection: DED and OSD vs. M for different SNRs | Gaussian primary signal | Weibull fading: Shape parameter = 1, Scale parameter = 2.

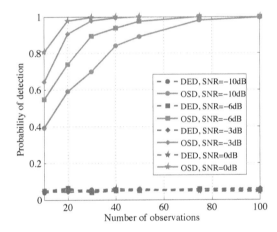

Figure 4. Probability of detection: DED and OSD vs. M for different SNRs | Constant primary signal | Weibull fading: Shape parameter = 1, Scale parameter = 2.

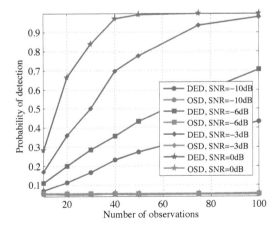

Figure 5. Probability of detection: DED and OSD vs. M for different SNRs | Gaussian primary signal | Rayleigh fading: Parameter = 1.

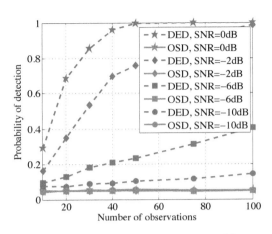

Figure 6. Probability of detection: DED and OSD vs. M for different primary SNRs | Rayleigh fading | Laplacian noise | Gaussian primary signal.

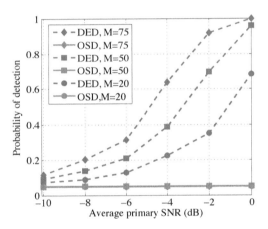

Figure 7. Probability of detection: DED and OSD vs. M for different SNRs | Rayleigh fading | Laplacian noise | Gaussian primary signal.

satisfies the given false-alarm increases, which in turn pulls down p_d.

We now move from a unimodal probability density assumption for the noise to a bimodal Gaussian (mixture of two Gaussians) [8] to evaluate DED and OSD. We present p_d with DED and OSD taking the primary signal as Gaussian and the fading as Rayleigh. Fig. 8 and Fig. 9 show p_d vs. average primary SNR and p_d vs. M respectively. We set $\mu = 2$ and the mixing parameter as 0.5. We note that the the performance of OSD is trivial, whereas DED outperforms OSD. As expected, the performance of DED improves with increase in SNR and M. The shortcomings of OSD lends credence to the proposition that its usefulness is restricted to the case of Gaussian noise and constant primary signal.

We present the utility of Gaussian mixture assumption for noise, by comparing the performance of DED

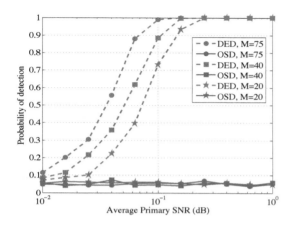

Figure 8. Probability of detection: DED and OSD vs. average primary SNR for different M | Rayleigh fading | Mixture Gaussian noises | Gaussian primary signal.

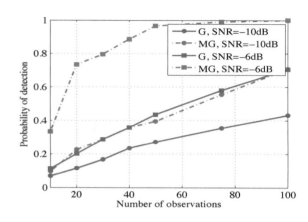

Figure 10. Probability of detection: DED and OSD vs. M for different primary SNRs | Rayleigh fading | Gaussian and mixture Gaussian noises | Gaussian primary signal.

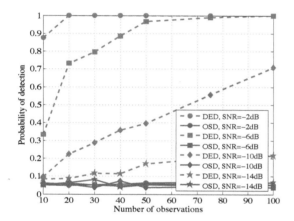

Figure 9. Probability of detection: DED and OSD vs. M for different average primary SNRs | Rayleigh fading | Mixture Gaussian noises | Gaussian primary signal.

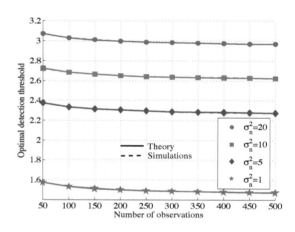

Figure 11. Optimal threshold τ_G using (A.3) and from simulations vs. M for different σ_n^2.

under both Gaussian and bimodal mixture Gaussians, with Gaussian distributed primary and with the Rayleigh fading (vide Fig. 10) for different SNRs. We can see that DED under the bimodal Gaussian noise performs better than unimodal Gaussian counterpart. In particular, the performance of DED under bimodal Gaussian noise for −10dB SNR close to that under the unimodal Gaussian for −6dB SNR. Therefore, for a given p_d, the bimodal Gaussian model accommodates an additional 4dB decrease in SNR.

We present the behaviour of optimal detection threshold under different noise conditions, such as, Gaussian, Laplacian and mixture of Gaussians. Fig. 11 shows the optimal detection threshold of (A.3) vs. M, varying over σ_n^2. Clearly, the simulation results are in excellent agreement with the analytically derived results. Further, the detection threshold is independent of the average primary SNR, as we employ a GoFT approach.

Next, Fig. 12 shows the agreement between the expressions derived in Appendix B and the corresponding Monte Carlo simulations. The closeness of the curves validates our claim. On the other hand, not surprisingly, comparing Fig. 11 and Fig. 12 for the same vales of M and σ_n^2 clearly indicates that the detection threshold for the Laplacian case is higher for the same false alarm constraint, which is due to the fact that the Laplace distribution is heavy-tailed. This also explains the deterioration in performance for the same set of parameters under Laplacian noise which was observed earlier.

Finally, the results shown in Fig. 13 validate our analysis of Appendix C. That the analysis holds for large M and $\mu(\geq 3)$ is borne out by the fact that the disparity between the simulations and theory reduces progressively.

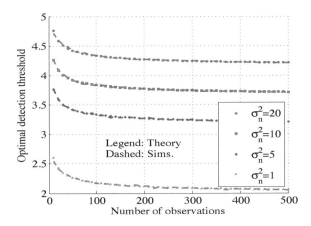

Figure 12. Optimal threshold τ_L using (B.4) and from simulations vs. M for different λ.

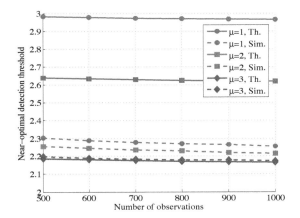

Figure 13. Near-optimal threshold τ_G^{MG} using (C.7) and from simulations vs. M and for different μ.

5. Concluding Remarks

We proposed a novel spectrum sensing technique based on differential entropy estimate with the goodness-of-fit formulation. The distribution of the test statistic under the null hypothesis and the detection threshold that satisfies a constraint on the probability of false-alarm were obtained in closed form. Through Monte Carlo simulations, it was shown that the proposed detector significantly outperforms the order statistics based detector in the low SNR regime, under various fading and primary signal models. The results with unimodal Gaussian vis-à-vis bimodal Gaussian noise process were compared. For a given probability of detection, this mixture model was shown to provide an additional leeway to the tune of 4dB in SNR over the corresponding unimodal Gaussian.

Appendix A. Calculation of τ_G

We adopt one of the many ways to arrive at the result here. Under $\mathcal{H}_0$, since $Y_i \sim \mathcal{N}(0, \sigma_n^2)$, it follows from

Cochran's Theorem that the unbiased estimate, $\mathcal{V}$, of the variance of Y_i follows a scaled, central χ^2 distribution with $M-1$ degrees-of-freedom. Thus,

$$\mathcal{V} \triangleq \frac{1}{M-1} \sum_{i=1}^{M} (Y_i - \widehat{Y})^2 \sim \frac{\sigma_n^2}{M-1} \chi_{M-1}^2,$$

which implies that the statistic $\widehat{h}(Y)$ can be written as

$$\widehat{h}(Y|\mathcal{H}_0) = \frac{1}{2} \log(2\pi e) + \frac{1}{2} \log \mathcal{V}. \tag{A.1}$$

Under $\mathcal{H}_0$, the statistic $\log \mathcal{V}$ follows a log-scaled, central χ^2 distribution with $M-1$ degrees-of-freedom, represented by $\log \chi_{M-1}^2$. It is easy to show that the CDF, $F_X(\cdot)$, of the random variable $X \sim \log \chi_n^2$, is given by

$$F_X(a) \triangleq \int_{-\infty}^{a} f_X(x)dx = \frac{\gamma_{inc}\left(\frac{n}{2}, e^{(a - \log 2)}\right)}{\Gamma\left(\frac{n}{2}\right)},$$

where $\gamma_{inc}(\cdot, \cdot)$, and $\Gamma(\cdot)$ are the lower incomplete gamma function and the standard gamma function, respectively [14]. The proof of this result is straightforward and is omitted for brevity. Therefore, the probability of false-alarm, p_f, is given by

$$p_f = \mathcal{P}\{\widehat{h}(Y|\mathcal{H}_0) \geq \tau_G\}$$
$$= 1 - \frac{\gamma_{inc}\left(\frac{M-1}{2}, \exp\left\{2\tau_G - \log\left(\frac{4\pi e \sigma_n^2}{M-1}\right)\right\}\right)}{\Gamma\left(\frac{M-1}{2}\right)}. \tag{A.2}$$

Now, by simple transformations on (A.1), using (A.2), it is straightforward to show that, for $\alpha_f \in (0,1)$, the threshold, τ_G, should be chosen to satisfy

$$1 - \frac{\gamma_{inc}\left(\frac{M-1}{2}, \exp\left\{2\tau_G - \log\left(\frac{4\pi e \sigma_n^2}{M-1}\right)\right\}\right)}{\Gamma\left(\frac{M-1}{2}\right)} = \alpha_f. \tag{A.3}$$

Appendix B. Calculation of τ_L

On lines similar to those in Appendix A, for a Laplacian, it can be shown that

$$\frac{2}{\lambda} \sum_{i=1}^{M} |Y_i - \widehat{Y}| \sim \chi_{2M}^2.$$

Therefore, it is easily seen that

$$\widehat{h}(Y|\mathcal{H}_0) = \log_2\left(\frac{2e}{M} \sum_{i=1}^{M} |Y_i - \widehat{Y}|\right)$$

follows a $\log-\chi^2$ distribution. Again, following an approach similar to that in Appendix A, it can be shown that for a given $\alpha_f \in (0,1)$, the optimal threshold, τ_L, is required to satisfy

$$1 - \frac{\gamma_{inc}\left(M, \exp\left[\log(2)\left\{\tau_L - \log_2\left(\frac{\lambda e}{M}\right) - 1\right\}\right]\right)}{\Gamma(M)} = \alpha_f. \tag{B.4}$$

Appendix C. Computing the Near–Optimal τ_G^{MG}

It is known that if $\{Y_i, i \in \mathcal{M}\}$ represent a set of i.i.d. random variables from any distribution, not necessarily unimodal, and with finite variance σ^2, then the random variable defined by

$$Y_s^2 \triangleq \frac{1}{M-1} \sum_{i=1}^{M} \left(Y_i - \widehat{Y}\right)^2,$$

has mean and variance in an asymptotic sense (as $M \to \infty$) respectively given by [15]

$$\mathbb{E}Y_s^2 = \sigma^2 \quad \text{and} \quad \text{var}(Y_s^2) = \sigma^4 \left[\frac{2}{M-1} + \frac{\kappa}{M}\right], \quad (C.5)$$

where κ is the excess kurtosis and μ_4 is the fourth central moment, i.e., about the mean of the parent distribution. Therefore, for the bimodal Gaussian,

$$\mathbb{E}Y_s^2 = \sigma_n^2 + \mu^2 \quad \text{and}$$
$$\text{var}(Y_s^2) = (\sigma_n^2 + \mu^2)^2 \left[\frac{2}{M-1} + \frac{\kappa}{M}\right]. \quad (C.6)$$

A closed form expression for the distribution of Y_s^2 for the bimodal Gaussian distribution is hard to obtain. However, it can be well approximated in the asymptotic sense by a Gaussian distribution with moments in (C.5) and (C.6).

For large values of μ (≥ 3), $h(Y|\mathcal{H}_0)$ can be approximated as [11]

$$h(Y|\mathcal{H}_0) \approx \frac{1}{2} \log(2\pi e \sigma_n^2) + \log 2.$$

Hence, an estimate of the above entropy is given by

$$\widehat{h}(Y|\mathcal{H}_0) = \frac{1}{2} \log\left(\frac{2\pi e}{M-1} \sum_{i=1}^{M} (Y_i - \widehat{Y}_i)^2\right) + \log 2$$
$$= \frac{1}{2} \log(4\pi e Y_s^2).$$

Therefore, the probability of false-alarm, p_f, becomes

$$p_f = \mathcal{P}\left\{\widehat{h}(Y) \geq \tau_G^{MG} | \mathcal{H}_0\right\}$$
$$\overset{(a)}{=} \mathcal{P}\left\{Y_s^2 \geq \frac{\exp(2\tau_G^{MG} - 1)}{4\pi}\right\}$$
$$= \mathcal{Q}\left[\frac{\frac{\exp(2\tau_G^{MG}-1)}{4\pi} - \mathbb{E}Y_s^2}{\sqrt{\text{var}(Y_s^2)}}\right],$$

where $\overset{(a)}{=}$ denotes that the equality holds due to the fact that $\log(\cdot)$ is monotone, and $\mathcal{Q}(\cdot)$ denotes the Q-function. Now, it is straightforward to show that, given $\alpha_f \in (0, 1)$,

the near-optimal threshold, τ_G^{MG}, is

$$\tau_G^{MG} = 0.5 \log\left(4\pi e \left\{(\sigma_n^2 + \mu^2)\left[\mathcal{Q}^{-1}(\alpha_f)\sqrt{\left(\frac{2}{M-1} + \frac{\kappa}{M}\right)} + 1\right]\right\}\right). \quad (C.7)$$

Acknowledgement. This work was supported and funded by CMR Institute of Technology, 132, AECS Layout, ITPL Road, Bengaluru 560037, INDIA. Weblink: www.cmrit.ac.in

References

[1] Gurugopinath, S., Muralishankar, R., Shankar, H. N.: Differential Entropy Driven Goodness-of-Fit Test For Spectrum Sensing. Proc. CROWNCOM 2015, (2015)

[2] Wang, H., Yang, E.-H., Zhao, Z., Zhang, W.: Spectrum Sensing in Cognitive Radio Using Goodness of Fit Testing. IEEE Trans. Wireless Commun., vol. 8, no. 11, 5427-5430, (2009)

[3] Shen, L., Wang, H., Zhang, W., Zhao, Z.: Blind Spectrum Sensing for Cognitive Radio Channels with Noise Uncertainty. IEEE Trans. Wireless Commun., vol. 10, no. 6, 1721-1724, (2011)

[4] Rostami, S., Arshad, K., Moessner, K.: Order-Statistic Based Spectrum Sensing for Cognitive Radio. IEEE Commun. Lett., vol. 16, no. 5, 592-595, (2012)

[5] Gurugopinath, S., Murthy, C. R., Seelamantula, C. S.: Zero Crossings Based Spectrum Sensing Under Noise Uncertainties. Proc. NCC, (2014)

[6] Denkovski, D., Atanasovski, V., Gavrilovska, L.: HOS Based Goodness-of-Fit Testing Signal Detection. IEEE Commun. Lett., vol. 16, no. 3, 310-313, (2012)

[7] Nguyen-Thanh, N., Kieu-Xuan, T., Koo, I.: Comments and Corrections on "Spectrum Sensing in Cognitive Radio using Goodness-of-Fit Testing". IEEE Trans. Wireless Commun., vol. 11, no. 10, 3409-3411, (2012)

[8] Rohde, G., Nichols, J., Bucholtz, F., Michalowicz, J.: Signal Estimation Based on Mutual Information Maximization. Proc. ACSSC, 597-600, (2007)

[9] Cover, T. M., Thomas, J. M.: Elements of Information Theory. 2nd ed. John Wiley and Sons, Inc., (2005)

[10] Wang, Y., Wu, L.: Nonlinear Signal Detection From an Array of Threshold Devices for Non-Gaussian Noise. Digit. Signal Process., vol. 17, no. 1, 76-89, (2007)

[11] Michalowicz, J. V., Nichols, J. M., Bucholtz, F.: Calculation of Differential Entropy for a Mixed Gaussian Distribution. Entropy, vol. 10, no. 3, 200-206, (2008)

[12] Hashemi, H.: The Indoor Radio Propagation Channel. Proceedings of the IEEE, vol. 81, no. 7, 943-968, (1993)

[13] Axell, E., Leus, G., Larsson, E., Poor, H. V.: Spectrum Sensing for Cognitive Radio: State-of-the-Art and Recent Advances. IEEE Signal Process. Mag., vol. 29, no. 3, 101-116, (2012)

[14] Gradshteyn, I., Ryzhik, I.: Tables of integrals, series and products. 7th ed. Academic Press, (2007)

[15] Mood, A. M., Graybill, F. A., Boes, D. C.: Introduction to the Theory of Statistics, 3rd ed. McGraw-Hill, (1974)

18

FM-CW radar sensors for vital signs and motor activity monitoring

Octavian Adrian Postolache[1,*], Pedro Manuel Brito da Silva Girão[2],
José Miguel Costa Dias Pereira[1], Gabriela Postolache[3]

[1]Instituto de Telecomunicações/LabIM/EST/IPS, Portugal; [2]Instituto de Telecomunicações/DEEC/IST/UTL, Av. Rovisco Pais, Lisbon, Portugal; [3]Escola Superior de Saúde, Universidade Atlântica, Oeiras, Portugal

Abstract

The article summarizes on-going research on vital signs and motor activity monitoring based on radar sensors embedded in wheelchairs, walkers and crutches for in home rehabilitation. Embedded sensors, conditioning circuits, real-time platforms that perform data acquisition, auto-identification, primary data processing and data communication contribute to convert daily used objects in home rehabilitation into smart objects that can be accessed by caregivers during the training sessions through human–machine interfaces expressed by the new generation of smart phones or tablet computers running Android OS or iOS operating systems. The system enables the management of patients in home rehabilitation by providing more accurate and up-to-date information using pervasive computing of vital signs and motor activity records.

Keywords: FM-CW Doppler radar, smart phone, smart walker, smart wheelchair

1. Introduction

The health system all over the world has been drastically changing moving from acute health delivery to prevention, from secondary healthcare delivery to primary care and to home care, from patient healthcare delivery to wellness. Nowadays, one of the major directives in HealthCare systems is the involvement of the patient and the family environment in the management of his/her own disease or health problem. The changes are radical and have repercussions on new institutional and state planning, on new technologies, on consumption behaviours and on continuing medical education.

Many R&D projects and public administrative reforms are being conducted worldwide in order to identify issues related with the caregivers' concerns, the requirements for the efficient home telecare as well as to implement telecare around the recipient's care plan. For instance, preliminary results of European Project—Collaborative evaluation of rehabilitation in stroke across Europe—have shown large discrepancies in recovery pattern and organization of the rehabilitation centres [1]. Furthermore, recently review of randomized clinical stroke rehabilitation trials revealed that most of the studies on effectiveness of interventions for motor recovery after stroke enrolled small numbers of patients, which precluded their clinical applicability (limited external validity) [2]. These data suggest the necessity of large randomized trials for rehabilitation assessment based on information technologies approach, for technology assessment deployment and medical liability. Adding telecommunication tools to the practice of rehabilitation, especially if integrated with home rehabilitation, may provide researchers with timely access to adaptive rehabilitative processes and to design large studies with better ecological validity, lowering key constraints to timely assessment [3]. Large-scale telemedicine reports have shown good functional outcome and mortality comparable to other case series and trials of conventionally treated patients [4, 5].

One of the aims of our working group is to design and to develop a contextual-aware system that continuously assesses physiological signs and motor activity and stimulate the users to take actions that contribute to improve their health. Our team is currently exploring the viability of a system for in home rehabilitation combining low-cost smart sensors installed in a wheelchair, walker, bed or chair and a wearable device attached to the wrist of the patient. They are parts of a pervasive computation architecture that delivers diagnostics and decisions in autonomous form based on performance measures (process and outcomes measures) conducted with well-established instruments (questionnaire, physical examination) used in rehabilitation and also integrated with new methods and technologies that produce data on physiological and motor activity in an unobtrusive way.

The article reports on the design and implementation of smart sensors based on microwave Doppler radar technology with availability to sense subjects' vital signs and motor activity during in home rehabilitation sessions. In Section 2, we discuss the pervasive healthcare requirements, mainly for in home rehabilitation. In Section 3, we present the design of proposed smart wheelchair, smart walker and crutches for physiological and motor activity monitoring with the environment we are deploying. In Section 4 the software developed for a smart phone is described. Finally, we present conclusions and address further work in Section 5.

2. Pervasive healthcare requirements

Pervasive healthcare may be defined from two perspectives: (i) as the application of pervasive computing technologies for healthcare and (ii) as making healthcare available everywhere, anytime and to anyone [6]. It is a main tool on effort to change the healthcare delivery model: from doctor-centric to patient-centric, from acute reactive to continuous preventive, from sampling to monitoring. Pervasive healthcare applications include pervasive health monitoring, intelligent emergency management system, pervasive healthcare data access and ubiquitous mobile telemedicine. The term 'pervasive' stands for the tendency to expand or permeate, while 'ubiquity' is the property of being omnipresent. A main objective of Ubiquitous Computing (UbiComp) is physical integration and embedding of computing and communication technology into environments. In this sense, the ultimate goal of pervasive healthcare is to become a means for achieving ubiquitous health.

Pervasive healthcare systems for in home rehabilitation require sensing and computing systems that permit long-term subjects' health assessment, health critical events signalling, motor activity and activities of daily living monitoring. Also, an optimal setting of pervasive healthcare should allow biofeedback therapy. This can be accomplished by using new devices that can unobtrusively monitor physiological signals and motor activity and can be easily adapted to the user's house reality and

commonly used objects. Many research projects and implemented healthcare systems have shown that vital signs and other health parameters can be autonomously measured by embedding monitoring sensors in clothes, chairs, beds, toilets, bathtubs and kitchen appliances among others [7]. In addition to the information on vital signs, activities of daily living, current location, fall detection, gait and balance, and skin breakdowns, sensors and sensors networks can generate a significant amount of information and/or services to the user. What is also needed in an optimal setting of UbiComp is that technology 'disappears' so that the 'computer' and the 'human–computer interface' are hidden at least in the perception of the human. This implies that the user doing a task is not aware of operating a computer system. This scenario should be realized through non-invasive/unobtrusive sensors, identification tagging, actuators, tracking and positioning and sensors network. There are several methodologies used in monitoring motor activities such as electrical potentials from muscles, magnetic and optical motion capture systems, video recordings and questionnaires. For instance, a common way for motion sensing is the use of Passive Infrared (PIR) sensors [8]. These sensors detect changes in the heat flow in the environment and can therefore detect humans and animals moving in the sensing region of the sensor. Motion detection using PIR sensors compared to video analysis is less powerful, but by far cheaper and simpler to implement. These sensors always have a directed input and are available with different lenses offering observation angles of 30° and 180°, and ranges of 2–15 m. Inter-daily gait velocity and daily activity metrics of eight elderly living independently, monitored using a PIR sensing system, showed no correlation to clinical or daily ethnographic data [9]. The team of Walsh et al. [9] suggested that a clinical assessment does not always provide an adequate estimate of the degree of diurnal and daily variation in gait speed. The clinical measurement of gait speed may suffer from the white coat effect (i.e. the patient may walk faster in the clinic as he is being watched by a healthcare professional). Similarly, other inter- and intra-variations were found, such as deviations in the minimum and maximum number of hits per day, in activity monitoring and in the distribution of the activity [9]. However, precise measurement of motion using PIR sensing system requires advanced calibration methods that may be unsuitable for mass deployment. As an alternative for PIR sensors for motion detection can be used sensors networks based on accelerometers and gyroscopes. Accelerometers are available as integrated micro-machined devices combined with driving electronics in an IC, e.g. the ADXL202E. These sensors are fairly easy to interface to a microcontroller and their power consumption is rather small (e.g. ADXL202E 0.6 mA at 3 V). Also the device size is minimal. The changes in acceleration are reflected quickly in the sensors output, of the order of milliseconds. In the past many accelerometer-based systems for the recognition of human activity have been developed. They differ in the number of acceleration sensors used, the way sensor information is processed and the usage scenario [10]. Gyroscopes give information on angular velocity. These devices are generally more expensive, bigger in size and also need more power. They usually supply an analogue signal that represents the angular velocity in volt per degree per second. For many applications, especially when no prior knowledge about the orientation of the device is available, it can be very useful to combine three accelerometers or three gyroscopes to gain information about acceleration/motion in all dimensions. Inertial measurement units contain one or more sensors to detect motion or orientation i.e. accelerometers, gyroscopes and magnetometers. When combined with suitable RF hardware they are termed wireless inertial measurement units [11]. Such inertial measurement units can be used to efficiently record motion data [11, 12].

In areas where people object to the presence of video cameras the option of using PIR sensors, accelerometers or gyroscopes is an alternative for activities of daily living monitoring. However, the multiple capabilities of microwave radar sensors and the potential low cost of the full integration in home telecare make their use an attractive target for unobtrusive motion detection as well as for non-contact physiological parameter assessment. We designed and developed a smart sensor based on microwave radar technology for motion and health monitoring. Using radar sensors embedded on smart objects, vital signs information (for instance from the radar sensors implemented on a wheelchair) or information on gait, activities of daily living and falls (i.e. from the radar sensor embedded on a wheelchair, walker or crutches) are obtained. There is an advantage of sensing RF energy as opposed to light, infrared or thermal energy when attempting to infer people's physiological signals or movements. Visible light cameras largely depend on daylight; light and infrared do not penetrate smoke or solid non-transparent walls. Radio-frequency waves can penetrate smoke and various non-metal walls or materials, unlike light, thermal or millimetre-wave energy. We believe that by embedding low-cost, small microwave radar sensors into clothes, beds, chairs and everyday living spaces ubiquitous health monitoring can be possible.

Another requirement in pervasive healthcare is control of the smart devices, either locally by the resident or remotely by friends/family/care professionals (Figure 1). Many research laboratories are recently working on the design, development and implementation of smart sensors and multimodal interfaces related to motions/voices/image analysis and comprehension that allow residents, friends and family and/or care professionals to view the current state of the monitored person and the connected devices within the home. Also, it is very useful to automate particular tasks for the resident through

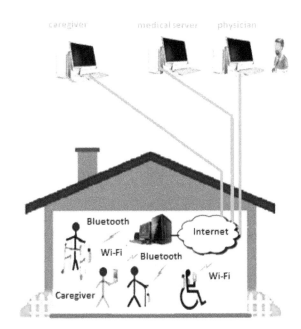

Figure 1. Diagram of patient-centred health monitoring for 'at home' rehabilitation.

context models, mixed reality systems, coordination models and proactive environments (see Figure 1).

A comprehensive health monitoring system should also be context-aware where the system adapts to the changing contexts, allowing better decision on person's current conditions and health. Incorporating affective reasoning into the decision-making capabilities of interactive environments can enable them to create customized experiences that dynamically are tailored to individual users, ever-changing levels of engagement, interest and emotional state.

3. Smart wheelchair, smart walker and crutches for in home rehabilitation

To transform objects used in rehabilitation into smart objects, embedded processing and communication devices must be added. Considering the necessity to sense the motor activity of a patient during the training session, we propose the use of a FSK/FM-CW Doppler radar (IVS-162 from InnoSenT) as one of the main components of smart objects that integrate an assistive environment for the people with less mobility or people with long-term health condition. The range and the velocity of the moving target, that is to say, the patient during the rehabilitation using walkers or crutches, can be achieved using the features of this radar.

Additionally, the respiration and cardiac activity monitoring of a patient resting on a wheelchair is achieved through the use of the 24GHz FM-CW radar sensor. Since the change of the displacement is small compared to the wavelength (12.5 mm at 24 GHz), the demodulated signal is proportional to the periodic displacement of the target, allowing accurate detection of respiratory and cardiac motion. We achieved good Heart Rate (HR) information even with signals passing through the wheelchair backrest (polyester material) and through wheelchair user's clothes. Depending on the direction of the motion, the polarized electromagnetic waves from the radar sensor are 'compressed' or 'diluted' producing frequency variation called the Doppler frequency. According to Doppler theory, a target with a time-varying position, but no constant velocity, will modulate the reflected signal's phase in proportion to the target's position. For instance, a stationary person's chest has a periodic movement with no constant velocity, and a Continuous Wave (CW) radar with the chest as the target will receive a signal similar to the signal it transmits, but with its phase modulated by the time-varying chest position. The received signal has a time-varying phase. In other words, the reflected signal is modulated by the periodic displacement of the heart and the respiration. The displacements by the heart beat and the respiration are assumed to be 0.05–0.15 mm and 1–2 mm, respectively.

The used FM-CW Doppler radar sensor architecture includes two antennas: Transmit Antenna (TX), that is associated to the body incident microwave signal; Receive Antenna (RX), that is associated to microwave signal reflected by the body. The received signal coming from RX is amplified by a low-noise amplifier and applied to two mixers M1 and M2 together with the transmitted signal, provided by splitter devices connected to a Voltage-Controlled Oscillator (VCO) through a preamplifier circuit. The VCO signal frequency depends on the value of the tuning voltage (Vtune) (Figure 2).

The M1 and M2 mixer outputs expressed by intermediate frequency IF1 and IF2 signals, correspond to signal in Phase I and signal in quadrature Q. We used IF1 and IF2 to extract by appropriate signal processing not only the velocity (v) of the user, but also the motion direction that can be useful to estimate the posture and physical activity of the wheelchair, walker or crutches user. Particularly for the walker and crutches, the radar sensor is used to estimate the gait type and also the rehabilitation evolution during the training period [13, 14].

Embedding a radar sensor on the backrest of the wheelchair (DRS1) (Figure 3) the information on respiration and cardiac activity was obtained. Although the sensor has a reduced sensing range, this is not critical considering that the sensor antennas are located at 5–15 cm from the target.

Experimental work regarding wheelchair user's clothes—materials such as 100% cotton, 100% polyester and even E-textile—was carried out showing good sensitivity of the implemented device for non-contact heart and respiratory rate estimation.

The wheelchair backrest radar sensor can also be used to obtain the information on low amplitude motion of the wheelchair user when the wheelchair is stopped, when the user controls the wheelchair motion himself or when a caregiver manually operates the wheelchair. Complete information about the motion of the wheelchair is obtained mounting a second radar sensor (DRS2) near the wheel that can obtain the information of the travelling distance through the detection of a conductive tape on the spoke wheel.

Referring to the respiratory and cardiac information, an analogue processing scheme, expressed by active filters and amplifiers, was associated to DRS1. Thus, a second-order active low-pass filter, characterized by a cutoff frequency f_c = 0.3 Hz, was designed and implemented to extract the respiratory wave, while a second-order active

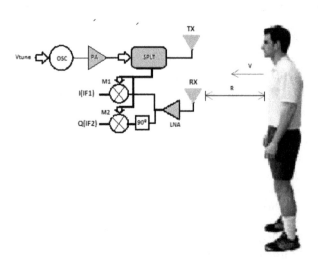

Figure 2. FM CW Doppler radar block diagram (Vtune = tuning voltage; OSC = voltage-controlled oscillator; M1, M2 = analogue mixers; I(IF1) = in phase intermediary frequency signal output; Q(IF2) = in quadrature intermediary frequency signal output; PA = preamplifier; SPLT = signal splitter; TX-transmit antenna; RX-receive antenna; LNA = low-noise amplifier.

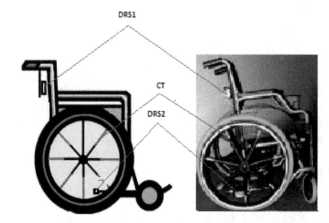

Figure 3. The architecture of a smart wheelchair with Doppler radar for vital signs and motor activity monitoring: (DRS1, DRS2 = Doppler radar sensors; CT = conductive tape).

high-pass filter, f_c = 0.9 Hz, was designed and implemented to extract the cardiac wave, denominated ballistocardiography wave. Additionally, two programmable gain amplifiers (PGA1 and PGA2) based on INA122 and CD4052 were implemented to assure the gain necessary to provide Acquisition and Communication Module (ACM) input signals in the 0–5 V range. The ACM was designed to be used with all smart objects (wheelchair, walker and crutches).

To improve the gait recovery assessment, we designed and implemented a smart walker and smart crutches that

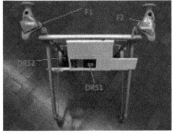

Figure 4. Smart walker architecture and prototype (DRS1, DRS2 = Doppler radar sensors; F1, F2 = piezoresistive force sensors).

include the Doppler radar sensor for motion sensing. The smart walker and smart crutches prototypes are presented in Figures 4 and 5.

As the conditioning circuit for Doppler radar signal are mentioned a second-order low-pass filter, f_c = 0.5 Hz, and an instrumentation amplifier INA122 that permits one to filter the noise, including the power line signal interference, but also to amplify the signal considering the dependence of the DRS1 output signal on the distance between the radar antenna and the target (the walker's user legs) during the rehabilitation training. Considering the analogue 0–5 V input range of the used ACM, an auxiliary DC voltage is applied to the inverter input of the instrumentation amplifier and adjusted in order to obtain values of the filtered and amplified Doppler radar signal in the range of 0–5 V range for different kinds of gaits.

To provide a general solution for all implemented smart objects, a data acquisition and Bluetooth data communication module was considered. It performs an analogue-to-digital conversion using a 16-bit ADC (ADS8344) that communicates through the SPI bus with a 16F673 PIC microcontroller. Figure 6 presents the ACM block diagram for the particular case of smart walker setup. Figure 6 shows that no conditioning circuit follows DRS2. However, several tests were done using a comparator and a Schmidt trigger to assure a rectangular-shaped signal characterized by TTL level according to the wheel position.

Referring to the force conditioning circuit, it includes a reference voltage (Vref = 1VDC) and a two-channel non-inverter amplifier scheme whose input resistances are the force sensors resistance. The signals from the aX, aY and aZ channels of the 3D accelerometer are analogue filtered

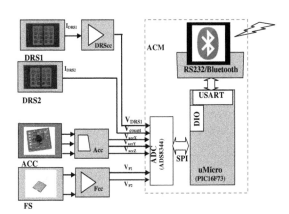

Figure 5. Smart crutches architecture and prototype (DRS = Doppler radar sensor; FS = piezoresistive force sensor).

Figure 6. Sensing, acquisition and communication block diagram (DRS1, DRS2 = Doppler radar sensors; FS = piezoresistive force sensors; DRScc = Doppler radar sensor conditioning circuit; Fcc = force conditioning circuit; ACC = accelerometer ADXL335; ACM = acquisition and data communication module.

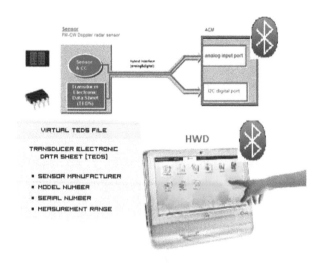

Figure 7. Smart sensor IEEE1451.4 compatible architecture (ACM = acquisition and data communication module; HWD = healthcare window device).

using a set of first-order, Butterworth low-pass filters, f_c = 45 Hz, used to remove the power line interference.

After signal acquisition and data coding by the ACM, the data are wireless transmitted through Bluetooth connection to a smart phone or tablet computer that runs Android OS software developed to assure the acquisition control, data storage, data synchronization and Graphical User Interface (GUI).

Regarding the ACM architecture, an advanced solution that includes a sensor identification reader was developed. This solution assures the IEEE1451.4 compatibility [15] for the measurement channel characterized by analogue input and embedded in the smart objects. For each of the sensing channels (e.g. DRS1 channel) attached to the daily used object is associated two-wire serial communication (I2C) EEPROM (24LC256) where specific information about the sensor is stored (Figure 7).

According to the above-mentioned standard, the main information about the sensor is materialized by the BASIC TEDS (TEDS, Transducer Electronic Data Sheet), whose components, bit length and allowable range are expressed in Table 1 [16].

In order to extend the information about the sensor, a combination between the hardware TEDS (the sensor characteristics are stored in the EEPROM memory) and Virtual TEDS (the sensor characteristics are stored in a database) represents an interesting solution.

Table 1. Basic TEDS content.

	Bit length	Allowable range
Manufacturer ID	14	17–16381
Model number	15	0–32767
Version letter	5	A–Z (data type Chr5)
Version number	6	0–63
Serial number	24	0–16777215

One of the healthcare LabVIEW software implementations developed by the authors includes a Virtual TEDS database and is installed in a touch panel compact computer (Eee Top from Asus) that was denominated Healthcare Window Device (HWD) in the present defined architecture. The application is accessed by the accompanying person and/or caregiver and performs the following tasks: (i) control of Bluetooth data communication between the HWD and ACM associated with the smart sensors embedded in the daily used objects (e.g. walker, wheelchair), (ii) smart sensor identification through Bluetooth MAC stored in the Virtual TEDS database, (iii) data logging and signal processing of the signals acquired from the sensor and (iv) GUI, including personalized front panels based on user's identification through a password or through the use of RFID tags. In the case of RFID technology use, an additional low-cost RFID reader from Phidget is attached to the HWD using the USB communication interface.

Referring to the signal processing, analogue filtering, amplification and digital signal processing algorithms implemented on the HWD were considered to extract the vital signs and motor activity information. Several results concerning the cardiac activity detected by radar sensors after analogue and signal processing based on active high-pass filtering are presented in Figure 8. Additionally, a reference ECG signal obtained from Medlab P-OX 100 is included in order to highlight the cardiac detection capability of the implemented measurement channel. Thus the baseline wandering and artefact removal based on DWT and ICA [17], adaptive peak detection for heart rate (HR) and respiration rate (Resp) calculation, and DWT for heart rate variability estimation [18, 19] can be mentioned.

The radar output signal is highly dependent on the position of the user body and on its involuntary motion on the wheelchair. Using appropriate adaptive filtering techniques [20, 21] the low amplitude artefacts that characterize the low amplitude involuntary motion of the wheelchair user can be removed. However, during high amplitude motions of the user sitting on the wheelchair the acquired radar signal can be used exclusively to estimate the user motor activity.

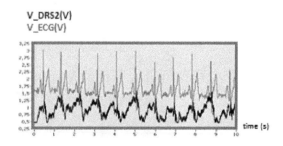

Figure 8. The evolution of the DRS2 and ECG voltage signals, after analogue and digital signal processing.

Considering the mobility requirements, the caregiver or physiotherapist is planned to interact with the smart objects used for rehabilitation using mobile devices such as smart phones or tablet computers.

The motor activity, mainly sensed by the Doppler radar sensors mounted on the walker or crutch, is monitored through the evolution of the acquired signal by ACM but also through the values of statistical parameters (e.g. variance, kurtosis) used as input features for gait recognition algorithms [22–24].

In the walker and crutches case a study concerning the correlation between the measured forces by embedded piezoresistive sensors, the body posture and radar wave pattern is underway. The cross-correlation between the piezoresistive sensors signal and the signal from radar sensors can give important information on the rehabilitation progress. The signals acquired from the radar sensors attached to the wheelchair wheel or walker can be processed to extract the information on the distance and the average velocity associated with the user motion during the rehabilitation session. Some results obtained on the wheelchair case, where the signals associated to the wheel motion are acquired using the Doppler radar sensor and processed and visualized at the HWD level, are presented in Figure 9.

Regarding the objects used in the rehabilitation tasks, some tests were done with people using the smart crutches that include the microwave Doppler radar sensor to extract information about the leg motion during the crutches usage. In order to highlight the relation between the signal associated with the leg motion and the crutches acceleration, a MEMS acceleration sensor (ADXL335) was mounted on the crutches. In Figure 10 is presented the evolution of intermediary frequency radar signal (Vrad_n) and the acceleration (AX_n) in normalized values.

Taking into account the future work of gait recognition during the rehabilitation session, several statistical parameters, such as variance and kurtosis, were calculated. For the particular case of kurtosis evolution during two particular tests (2 crutches—2 points (2c2p) and 2 crutches—3 points (2c3p)) are presented in Figure 11.

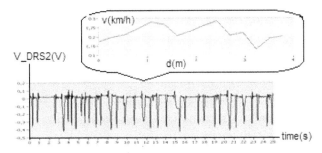

Figure 9. The evolution of the normalized voltage signal acquired from DRS2 measuring channel of the wheelchair and the corresponding velocity variation.

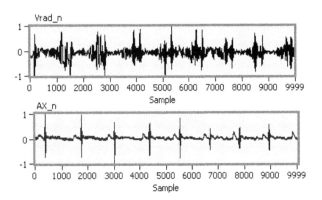

Figure 10. The correspondence between the Vrad_n and AX_n during 2 point gait with two crutches.

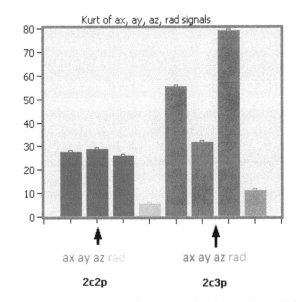

Figure 11. Radar and accelerometer signal kurtosis evolution for 2c2p and 2c3p gait tests.

It can be observed that the Kurt parameter associated with the radar signal is different from one type to another gait type, a characteristic that can be used as a feature for gait recognition [25] after a validation for an extended number of tests will include also 2 crutches—4 point gait tests.

4. Mobile software

Mobile solutions, such as smart phones and tablet computers, were considered appropriate as interfaces between physiotherapist, caregiver or even patient and the smart objects equipped with FM-CW Doppler radars. One of the implementations developed by the team was targeted on the use of a HTC Desire smart phone that runs the Android 2.2 mobile OS. Android SDK and Java [26, 27] were used to develop a general application related to smart object monitoring during the utilization by the users with motor disabilities. The main tasks implemented

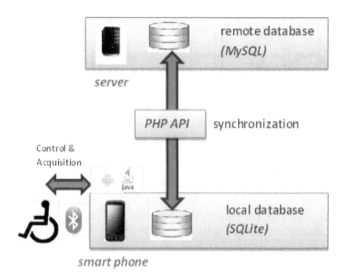

Figure 12. System physical architecture.

by the mobile application are: Bluetooth communication between the mobile device and the smart object, embedded data processing and graphical representation as well as data management including data storage and synchronization between a smart phone local database and a remote database associated with a web-based server application. The system physical architecture is presented in Figure 12.

To develop the present mobile software prototype, a set of activity classes were implemented: *ServerSync.java* that permits one to manage all the information regarding the application; *SingleChannel.java* that assures the graphical representation of individual waves associated with vital signs or motor activity measurement channels (e.g. gait wave from radar channel); *MultipleChannel.java* that assures multiple graphical representation of clinical status. A flowchart associated to the *SingleChannel.java* and *MultipleChannel.java* activities classes' interaction with Java methods of Bluetooth service is presented in Figure 13.

The GUI for mobile applications corresponding to force and radar response during the training session is presented in Figure 14(a).

The application permits one to visualize the motion pattern detected using the Doppler radar sensor during the physiotherapy training session using smart objects such as walkers or crutches. At the same time, the caregiver or physiotherapist can visualize the evolution of the force applied on the walker or crutch hand support (when F1 or F2 button is selected) for a specific gait during the rehabilitation session.

The mobile interface can also provide information concerning the motion of the wheelchair or walker. For the particular case of the particular case of walker, the detected motion of the wheels is sensed by (DRS2) mounted in the wheel and pressing the *Count* button, the number of turns performed by the wheel for a given

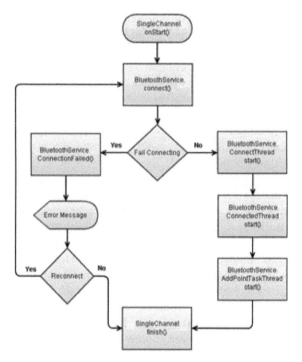

Figure 13. Flowchart associated with mobile GUI.

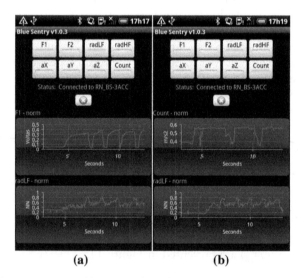

(a)   **(b)**

Figure 14. Graphical user interface of the application for force and radar response during physiotherapy training session.

period of time is presented (e.g. Figure 14(b)). At the same time, in Figure 14(b) is presented the Doppler radar signal after low-pass filtering for specific gait during the physiotherapy training session.

Additional functionalities characterize the developed mobile application. Thus, the user of mobile device can perform the data synchronization between the local database and the remote database manually or automatically from time to time according to the selected time intervals between two synchronizations.

5. Conclusion

This paper describes a prototype implementation of a mobile healthcare information management system for in home rehabilitation based on pervasive computing and Android OS operating system. The prototype can improve the management of patients in home rehabilitation by providing more accurate and up-to-date information using pervasive computing of vital signs and motor activity records. It is a promising patient-centred management approach that can provide accurate and reliable data, empowers the patients, influences their behaviour and potentially improves their medical condition. It also has potential to save time and cost by reducing the visits and travel of physiotherapists or occupational therapists, and reducing hospital admission in health hazardous situations. Future research will be carried out in order to establish the relations between data from sensors used in our prototype and rehabilitation progress assessment.

Acknowledgement. The work was supported by Fundação para a Ciência e Tecnologia project RIPD/APD/109639/2009.

References

[1] Collaborative evaluation of rehabilitation in stroke across Europe, http://www.ist-world.org/ProjectDetails.aspx?ProjectId=82a07b52f7f74bdfbfb6a9fd7dcbaa86&SourceDatabaseId=9cd97ac2e51045e39c2ad6b86dce1ac2.

[2] RABADI, M.H. (2011) Review of the randomized clinical stroke rehabilitation trials in 2009. *Med. Sci. Monit.* **17**(2): RA25–RA43.

[3] WINTERS, J.M. (2002) Telerehabilitation research: emerging possibilities. *Annu. Rev. Biomed. Eng.* **4**: 287–320.

[4] AUDEBERT, H.J., KUKLA, C., VATANKHAH, B., GOTZLER, B., SCHENKEL, J., HOFER, S., FURST, A. *et al.* (2006) Comparison of tissue plasminogen activator administration management between Telestroke Network hospitals and academic stroke centers: the Telemedical Pilot Project for Integrative Stroke Care in Bavaria/Germany. *Stroke* **37**: 1822–1827.

[5] SCHWAB, S., VATANKHAH, B., KUKLA, C., HAUCHWITZ, M., BOGDAHN, U., FURST, A., AUDEBERT, H.J. *et al.* (2007) Long-term outcome after thrombolysis in telemedical stroke care. *Neurology* **69**: 898–903.

[6] KORHONEN, I. and BARDRAM, J.E. (2004) Guest editorial introduction to the special section on pervasive healthcare. *IEEE Trans. Inf. Technol. Biomed.* **8**(3): 229–234.

[7] POSTOLACHE, O., GIRÃO, P., PINHEIRO, E. and POSTOLACHE, G. (2010) Unobtrusive and non-invasive sensing solution for on-line physiological parameters monitoring. In LAY-EKUAKILLE, A. and CHANDRA MUKHOPADHYA, S. [eds.] *Wearable and Autonomous Biomedical Devices and Systems for Smart Environment: Issues and Characterization* **75**: 277–314.

[8] HAYLER, S., AUSTIN, D., HAYES, T.L., KAYE, J. and PAVEL, M. (2010) Unobtrusive and ubiquitous in-home monitoring: a methodology for continuous assessment of gait velocity in elders. *IEEE Trans. Biomed. Eng.* **57**(4): 813–820.

[9] WALSH, L., GREENE, B.R., BURS, A. and SCANAILL, C.N. (2011) Ambient assessment of daily activity and gait velocity. In *Proceedings of the 5th ICST Conference on Pervasive Computing Technologies for Health Care*, Dublin, Ireland, May, 1–8.

[10] CZABKE, A., MARSCH, S. and LUETH, T.C. (2011) Accelerometer based real-time activity analysis on a microcontroller. In *Proceedings of the 5th ICST Conference on Pervasive Computing Technologies for Health Care*, Dublin, Ireland, 1–7.

[11] GAFFNEY, M., WALSH, M., O'CONNELL, S., WANG, B., O'FLYNN, O. and MATHUNA, C.O. (2011) A smart wireless inertial measurement unit system. Simplifying and encouraging usage of WIMU technology. In *Proceedings of the 5th ICST Conference on Pervasive Computing Technologies for Health Care*, Dublin, Ireland, May, 1–2.

[12] ZHANG, J., MARKOVIC, S., SAPIR, J. and WAGENAAR, R.C. (2011) Continuous functional activity monitoring based on wearable tri-axial accelerometer and gyroscope. In *Proceedings of the 5th ICST Conference on Pervasive Computing Technologies for Health Care*, Dublin, Ireland, May 2011, 1–4.

[13] POSTOLACHE, O.A., GIRÃO, S.P.M., PINHEIRO, E.C., PEREIRA, J.M., MADEIRA, R., POSTOLACHE, G., MENDES, J.G. *et al.* (2011) Multi-usage of microwave Doppler radar in pervasive healthcare systems for elderly. In *IEEE International Instrumentation and Measurement Technology Conference, IMTC 2011*, Hangzhou, China, May, 1–5.

[14] POSTOLACHE, O., MADEIRA, R., GIRÃO, S.P. and POSTOLACHE, G. (2010) Microwave FMCW Doppler radar implementation for in-house pervasive health care system. In *IEEE Workshop on Medical Measurements and Applications Proceedings (MeMeA)*, Ottawa, Canada, May 2010, 47–52.

[15] ULIVIERI, N., DISTANTE, C., LUCA, T., ROCCHI, S. and SICILIANO, P. (2006) IEEE1451.4: a way to standardize gas sensor. *Sens. Actuators, B* **114**(1): 141–151.

[16] WOBSCHALL, D. (2008) Networked sensor monitoring using the universal IEEE 1451 Standard. *IEEE Instrum. Meas. Mag.* **11**(2): 18–22.

[17] PINHEIRO, E.C., POSTOLACHE, O.A. and GIRÃO, S.P. (2011) Cardiopulmonary signal processing of users of wheelchairs with embedded sensors. In *IEEE Workshop on Medical Measurements and Applications (MeMeA 2011)*, Bari, Italy, 1–6.

[18] POSTOLACHE, O., GIRÃO, S.P., JOAQUIM MENDES, G. and POSTOLACHE, G. (2009) Unobtrusive heart rate and respiratory rate monitor. In *IEEE Workshop on Medical Measurements and Applications (MeMeA 2009)*, Cetraro, Italy, May 2009, 83–88.

[19] POSTOLACHE, O., GIRÃO, P.M., POSTOLACHE, G. and DIAS PEREIRA, J.M. (2007) Vital signs monitoring system based on EMFi sensors and wavelet analysis. In *Proceedings of IEEE Instrumentation and Measurement Technology Conference (IMTC 2007)*, Warsaw, Poland, May 2007, 1: 1–4.

[20] MYUNG, H.I., SOO, Y.L., TAE, S.P., TAE, S.K., MIN, H.C. and YOUNG, B.A. (2006) Ballistocardiogram artifact removal from EEG signals using adaptive filtering of EOG signals. *Physiol. Meas.* **27**: 1227–1240.

[21] CHAN, K.W. and ZHANG, Y.T. (2002) Adaptive reduction of motion artifact from photoplethysmographic recordings using a variable step sze LMS filter. In *Proceedings of IEEE Sensors*, **2**: 1343–1346.

[22] MOUSTAKAS, K., TZOVARAS, D. and STAVROPOULOS, G. (2010) Gait recognition using geometric features and soft biometrics. *IEEE Signal Processing Letters* **17**(4): 367–370.

[23] YANMEI, C., QING, W., JINGPING, J. and RONGCHUN, Z. (2006) A novel human gait recognition method by segmenting and extracting the region variance feature. In *ICPR 2006 Proceedings of International Conference on Pattern Recognition*, **4**: 425–428.

[24] JUNPING, Z., JIAN, P., CHANGYOU, C. and FLEISCHER, R. (2010) Low-resolution gait recognition. *IEEE Transactions on Systems, Man, and Cybernetics, Part B: Cybernetics* **40**(4): 986–996.

[25] SPRAGER, S. (2009) A cumulant-based method for gait identification using accelerometer data with principal component analysis and support vector machine. In *Proceedings of the 2nd WSEAS International Conference on Sensors, and Signals and Visualization, Imaging and Simulation and Materials Science*, 94–99.

[26] BURNETTE, E. (2009) Hello, Android: Introducing Google's Mobile Development Platform. In *Pragmatic Bookshelf (Pragmatic Programmers)*, November, 3rd ed.

[27] MEIER, R. (2010) Professional Android 2 Application Development. *Wrox Ed.*

19

The homes of tomorrow: service composition and advanced user interfaces

Claudio Di Ciccio[1], Massimo Mecella[1,*], Mario Caruso[1], Vincenzo Forte[1], Ettore Iacomussi[1], Katharina Rasch[2], Leonardo Querzoni[1], Giuseppe Santucci[1], Giuseppe Tino[1]

[1]Dipartimento di Informatica e Sistemistica, University of Rome "La Sapienza", via Ariosto 25, I-00185 Rome, Italy; [2]KTH Royal Institute of Technology, School of Information and Communication Technology Forum 120, 16440 Kista, Sweden

Abstract

Home automation represents a growing market in the industrialized world. Today's systems are mainly based on *ad hoc* and proprietary solutions, with little to no interoperability and smart integration. However, in a not so distant future, our homes will be equipped with many sensors, actuators and devices, which will collectively expose services, able to smartly interact and integrate, in order to offer complex services providing even richer functionalities. In this paper we present the approach and results of SM4ALL- Smart hoMes for All, a project investigating automatic service composition and advanced user interfaces applied to domotics.

Keywords: advanced user interfaces, domotics, smart devices, smart homes, service composition, SM4ALL

1. Introduction

Embedded systems, i.e. specialized computers used in larger systems in order to control the bundled equipments, are nowadays pervasive in immersive realities. For instance, they are widely adopted in those scenarios where both explicit and implicit interactions with human users are needed, in order to (i) provide continuous sensed information and (ii) react to service requests from the users themselves. Examples are digital libraries, eTourism applications, automotive appliances, next-generation buildings and domotics. Sensors/devices/appliances/actuators offering services are no more static, as in classical networks (e.g. for environmental monitoring and management or surveillance), but they form an overall distributed system that needs

to continuously adapt instead. Such a task can be achieved by adding, removing and composing basic elements, i.e. the offered services.

This paper intends to outline some insights stemming from the European-funded project SM4ALL (Smart hoMes for All—http://www.sm4all-project.eu/), started on 1 September 2008 and finished on 31 August 2011. SM4ALL aims at studying and developing an innovative platform for software smart embedded services in immersive environments, based on a service-oriented approach and composition techniques. This is applied to the challenging scenario of private homes in the presence of users with different abilities and needs (e.g. young, elderly or disabled people).

In order to introduce the novel idea of services underlying SM4ALL, the reader should consider the following scenario: a person is at home and decides to take a bath. He/she would like to simply express this to the house; then, the available services should collaborate in order to move the house itself to a new state in which the desired situation holds. The temperature in the bathroom should be raised through the heating service, the

☆This work has been partly supported by the EU project FP7-224332 SM4ALL (http://www.sm4all-project.eu/).
*Corresponding author. Email: mecella@dis.uniroma1.it

wardrobe in the sleeping room opened in order to offer the bathrobe, the bath filled up with 37 °C water, etc. Some services, nonetheless, cannot be directly automated. If we consider a disabled user, the act of helping her to get to the bath can be considered an action offered by a service, though implemented, so to speak, by a human being, such as the nurse. We might suppose that she is notified (e.g. through her smartphone/tablet, while doing her job in another room) to go into the bath and help the patient at the right moment. This service could also be realized by the son of the patient (or any other person), living in a nearby house: thus, if the nurse is not at home, he is in turn asked to help the patient. The scenario draws the idea of a system of services, some of which are offered by completely automated systems (such as sensors, appliances or actuators), while the others are realized through the collaboration of other humans. Clearly, as in all the complex systems, there are tradeoffs to be considered: for instance, the goal of the person willing a relaxing bath could be in contrast with the availability of the nurse/son offering the 'help' service.

The rest of the paper is organized as follows: Section 2 provides a background on the current state of the art for home automation systems and other relevant techniques adopted in our approach, e.g. service composition, Section 3 gives the reader an overview of the SM4ALL system architecture. For sake of space, the remainder of the paper focuses only on some components, namely (i) the Pervasive Layer (Section 4), (ii) the Service Repository and the common service and data models used by all the components (Section 5), (iii) the Composition Layer (Section 6) and (iv) the User Interface (Section 7), which are among the most innovative ones produced by the project. Finally, Section 8 draws some conclusions.

2. Relevant work

Presently, we are assisting at a blooming of research projects on the usage of smart services at home and domotics, in particular for assisting people with physical or mental disabilities.

For instance, at Georgia Tech, a domotic home has been built for the elder adult with the goals of compensating physical decline, memory loss and supporting communication with relatives [1]. This work also considers issues of acceptability of domotics identifying key issues for the adoption of the technology by the end user. Acceptability, dangers and opportunities are also surveyed in [2]. Having a reliable system is a primary concern for all users.

At Carnegie Mellon, people's behavior is studied by automatic analysis of video images [3]. This is fundamental in detecting anomalies and pathologies in a nursing home where many patients live. Pervading the environment with active landmarks, called Cyber Crumbs, aims at guiding the blind by equipping him/her with a smart badge [4]. A number of projects to give virtual companions to people, to monitor people's health and behavioral patterns, and to help Alzheimer patients are presented in [5]. The Gator Tech Smart House [6] is a programmable approach to smart homes targeting the elder citizen. The idea is to have a service layer based on Open Services Gateway Initiative, in order to enable service discovery and composition. This work is close to what we propose as for the service-based approach, though it does not commit to any open standard or XML-based technology; no reference is made to the communication model adopted in the home and, most notably, there is no specific attention toward user interfaces.

Finally, in [7], the current adoption of service technologies for smart energy systems, including domotic ones, is discussed.

As far as service composition is concerned, there have been in the last years several works addressing it from different points of view. So far, the work on services has largely resolved the basic interoperability problems for service composition (e.g. standards such as WS-BPEL and WS-CDL exist and are widely supported in order to compose services, even if their applicability in embedded systems is still to be demonstrated), and designing programs, called orchestrators, that execute compositions by coordinating available services according to their exported description is the bread and butter of the service programmer [8, 9].

The availability of abstract descriptions of services has been instrumental in devising automatic techniques for synthesizing service compositions and orchestrators. Some works have concentrated on data-oriented services, by binding service composition to the work on data integration [10]. Other works have looked at process-oriented services, in which operations executed by the service have explicit effects on the system. Among these approaches, several consider *stateless* (also known as atomic) services, in which the operations that can be invoked by the client do not depend on the history of interactions, as services do not retain any information about the state of such interactions. Much of this work relies on the literature on Planning in AI [11–13]. Others consider *stateful* services which impose some constraints on the possible sequences of operations (also known as conversations) that a client can engage with the service. Composing stateful services poses additional challenges, as the composite service should be correct with regard to the possible conversations allowed by the component ones. Relevant approaches span over different areas, including research on Reasoning about Actions and Planning in AI, and research about Verification and Synthesis in Computer Science [14–17].

In this paper, we focus on composition of process-oriented stateful services. In particular, we have considered, extended and realized the framework for service composition adopted in [18–23], sometimes referred to as the

'Roman Model' [24, 25]. In the Roman Model, services are represented as transition systems (i.e. focusing on their dynamic behavior) and the composition aims at obtaining an actual composite service that preserves such an interaction. The composite service is expressed as a (virtual) target service specifying a desired interaction with the client.

Several research activities dealt with the idea of automatically generating different interfaces according to different variables, i.e. users, context and devices. The problem of generating different interfaces for different devices, having a single common application, is often indicated as the problem of creating *plastic interfaces* [26], i.e. creating user interfaces that adapt to devices characteristics.

Many ideas come from past research in *model-based* user interface design [27], where the designer is supposed to design an interactive system by editing and manipulating abstract models (e.g. task models) that describe the system's behavior and where the system is supposed to automatically generate the final application code.

The same idea of heavily exploiting formal models to design interactive applications comes from research on data-intensive web design, as illustrated in [28], that stems from past research on model-based hypermedia design, like RMM [29], and that has a major focus on data modeling.

The Abstract Adaptive Interface of SM4ALL diverges from these approaches because it does not have the goal of generating directly an interface. Instead, it provides all the pieces of information needed to design an interface that is suitable for the actual home status and for user preferences, in a parametric way. In particular, looking at the status of the available services, it provides the list of possible user actions together with associated icons and textual commands; the list is then ordered according to the home status and user preferences (cf. Section 7). Once such information is provided, it is possible to implement interfaces targeting different hardware platforms (e.g. smartphones or laptops) and interaction styles (e.g. icon based or menu based).

Finally, we would like to point out that some projects (e.g. EU-PUBLI.com [30] in an e-Government context and WORKPAD [31] in the field of emergency management) considered the issue of collaborating services, when some of which are not actually classical software applications, but human operators executing actions. As assumed in this work as well, they were all abstracted by the system as services and therefore seamlessly integrated into a general architecture.

3. The SM4ALL architecture

The goal of the SM4ALL architecture, shown in Figure 1, is to seamlessly integrate devices, in order to simplify the access to the services that they expose, and dynamically compose such services in order to offer the end users more complex functionalities and a richer experience with the domotic environment. There is an ever-increasing variety of devices, such as controlling parts of the home (doors, lights), media devices, etc. Sensors are devices for measuring physical quantities, ranging from simple thermometers to self-calibrating satellite-carried radiometers. Sensors and devices have an inherent connection, e.g. a device for opening the window blinds can change the luminosity value detected by a sensor. In SM4ALL, all the devices make their functionalities available according to the service-oriented paradigm. Due to the different technologies employed by the devices that are expected to interact within SM4ALL, the architecture relies on abstracting them as SOAP-based services, according to a riche service model (cf. Section 5.2) consisting not only of the service interface specification, but also of its conversational description, of the related graphical widgets (i.e. icons) to be presented in the user layer (by means of graphical interfaces, BCIs,...), etc. *Proxies* are indeed the software components offering such services by 'wrapping' and abstracting the real devices offering the functionalities. Services are not necessarily offered by hardware devices, but could also be realized through a human intervention; in this case, the proxy exposes a SOAP-based service to the platform above, whereas it interacts with the service provider (i.e. the human) by means of a dedicated graphical user interface, when executing the requested operations.

One particular service is the Localization Service, built on top of a subsystem for localizing persons[1] inside the home. It is in charge of tracking users in order to provide the location of each. The granularity of the provided information is at the level of presence inside a room (i.e. the service is able to state, e.g. whether 'Massimo is in the kitchen', though it cannot recognize his position within, e.g. in front of the oven, rather than on the chair nearby the table). Because of (i) the current advancements of indoor localization technologies, (ii) the requirements of the project and (iii) the consideration that indoor localization is a subject worthy of a research project *per se* (therefore, the research on this topic is out of the scope of SM4ALL), it is a sufficient and viable solution for the project.

During their run time, services continuously change their status, both in terms of values of sensed/actuating variables (e.g. a service wrapping a temperature sensor reports the current detected temperature, a service wrapping windows blinds report whether the blinds are open, closed, half-way, etc.) and in terms of their conversational state. The definition of the sensed/actuating variables, representing the 'state' of the domotic environment, is

---

[1]This subsystem is realized by adapting a commercial tool, namely the Ekahau Real-Time Location System (RTLS)— http://www.ekahau.com/.

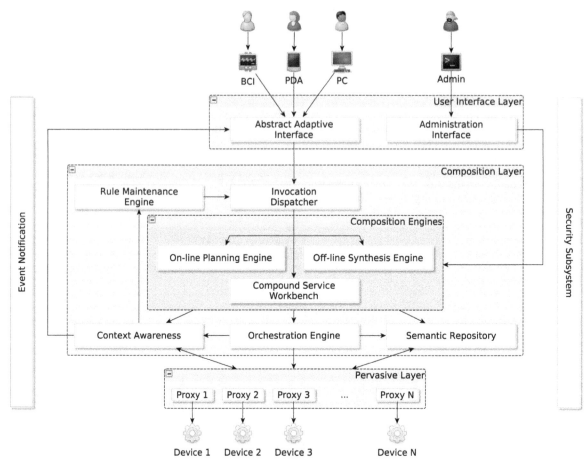

Figure 1. The SM4ALL Architecture.

performed in accordance with the *data model*. The data model, as well the service model, is designed to be 'additive', i.e. each new domotic device, plugged in the home, is expected to add new pieces to these models in order to register itself to the system.

A *Pervasive Controller* and a *Discovery Framework* are in charge, when a new device joins the system, to dynamically load and deploy the appropriate service, and to register all the relevant information into the *Service Semantic Repository*. All of the status information, both in terms of (i) service conversational states and (ii) values of the environmental variables, are kept available in the *Context Awareness Manager*, through a publish and subscribe mechanism.

Proxies, Pervasive Controller and Discovery Framework, together with the data and service models, constitute the *Pervasive Layer* of the SM4ALL architecture.

On the basis of the service descriptions, *Composition Engines* are in charge of providing complex services by suitably composing the available ones. In SM4ALL, three different types of approaches are provided, each providing different functionalities and therefore complementing one another, in order to provide a rich and novel environment to the users:

Off-line synthesis (provided through the Off-line Synthesis Engine). In the off-line mode, at design/deployment time of the house, a desiderata (i.e. not really existing) target service is defined, as a kind of complex routine, and the synthesis engine synthesizes a suitable orchestration of the available services realizing the target one. Such an orchestration specification is used at execution time (i.e. when the user chooses to invoke the composite/desiderata service) by the Orchestration Engine in order to coordinate the available services (i.e. to interact with the user on one hand and to schedule service invocations on the other hand). In this approach, the orchestration specification is synthesized off-line (i.e. not triggered by user requests, at run time) and executed on-line as if it were a real service of the home. The off-line mode is based on the Roman Model: it will be further detailed in Section 6. The Off-line Synthesis Engine produces what in SM4ALL is referred to as a *routine*.

On-line planning (provided through the On-line Planning Engine). The user, during its interaction with the home, may decide not to invoke a specific service (either available/real or composite), but rather to ask the home to realize a *goal*; in such a case, the engine, on the basis of specific planning techniques [32], synthesizes and executes available service invocations in order to reach such a goal.

Visual design of complex services (provided through the Compound Service Workbench). A skilled user may want to define a *compound service*, by visually composing services offered by proxies, in a way similar to what currently happens in technologies like WS-BPEL. The compound service offers an aggregated operation, which is the result of the proper orchestration of operations offered by other services. Also in this case, the synthesis is performed off-line, but differently from the previous case, it is not supported by automatic techniques, but by a visual workbench. Both routines and compound services fall under the category of 'composite services'.

The *Orchestration Engine* interprets the specification of a composite service (either synthesized automatically, through the Off-line Synthesis Engine, or visually by the user, through the Compound Service Workbench) and consequently orchestrates the set of component services. In the case of the On-line Planning Engine, due to the need of continuously planning and monitoring services during plan executions, the Orchestration Engine is bypassed and services are directly invoked by the planner itself.

The *Rule Maintenance Engine* manages the automatic firing of actions when a predetermined situation occurs, i.e. the rules activated when given conditions hold. Rules can be defined by administrators through the User Layer. The triggering of rules to be applied, since they are automatic, is caused by changes in the environment and is therefore indirectly caused by the Context Awareness Manager when the predefined conditions are verified. Its output is the request to fulfill a (simple/composite) service or goal, as if the requests were generated by a user.

The *Invocation Dispatcher* is in charge of concretely invoking services (both simple or composite) and plans. All service invocations go through the Invocation Dispatcher. For example, if the Orchestration Engine, or the On-line Planning Engine, needs to invoke a service, the request is forwarded to the proper component through the Invocation Dispatcher. This is needed in order to differently manage requests for plans, basic and composite services, and allows a simple form of concurrency control (as it will be further clarified in the following).

Composition Engines, Invocation Dispatcher, Rule Maintenance Engine, Orchestration Engine, Context Awareness Manager and Semantic Service Repository constitute altogether the *Composition Layer* of the SM4ALL architecture.

Users are able to interact with the home and the platform through different kinds of user interfaces, e.g. a home control station accessible through a touchscreen in the living room. In particular, Brain–Computer Interfaces (BCIs) [33] allow also people with disabilities to interact with the system [34]. Of course, users can still control the home equipment as if there were not the SM4ALL platform. For example, a user is obviously allowed to switch the living room light on directly from the manual switcher on the wall, without using any BCI and/or touchscreen; in such a case, the platform, through the specific proxy wrapping the light/switcher as a service, is notified of the specific variable value change. Therefore, all needed actions are undertaken. De facto, the event is equivalent, due to the engineering of the platform, to the one of clicking a specific button on the touchscreen and/or selecting the icon on the BCI.

Users are able, through the interfaces, to invoke actions offered by services (either simple of composite) and to achieve goals, in order to reach specific situations that they would like to be realized in the home. Moreover, through the interfaces, they receive the feedback about state changes in the home, as well as requests for further inputs (in case additional parameters are needed for some actions to be executed), notifications about action/service completions, etc.

In order to abstract over the specific interfaces, the platform provides a unique façade component, namely the *Abstract Adaptive Interface*, which is in charge of (i) forwarding requests to the underlying layers and (ii) receiving messages from the latter, to be dispatched further to the proper interface. In such a way, the whole platform is unaware of the specific interfaces adopted by real users: particular implementation details are thus hidden. Indeed, there are specific algorithms needed to properly arrange icons on a BCI screen, while others are used for touch devices, and so forth.

Aside from the user interfaces, which are used by inhabitants to control and interact with their home, a specific *Administration Interface* is provided, in order to execute complex tasks, including (but not limited to):

- the definition of a target composite service to be synthesized off-line; this is performed by the domotic engineer at design/deployment time of the home, when her work is to define routines the users would like to run afterwards;

- the definition of rules;

- the definition, by a very skilled user, of a compound service trough the Compound Service Workbench.

As a rule of thumb, whichever task requiring the interaction with a user interface, though not strictly related to the direct control of the home, appears in the Administration Interface control panel.

Abstract Adaptive Interface and the various user interface modules are collected in the *User Layer* of the SM4ALL architecture.

Finally, an underlying *Event Notification Service* (e.g. for publishing updates of environmental variables) and a *Security Subsystem* (e.g. for AAA of users) complete the architecture.

3.1. Dealing with concurrency

Systems like SM4ALL are meant to be part of the environment where humans live, and are thus designed to allow interaction with multiple users at the same time. Moreover, the actions users can fulfill with these systems can be both limited in time or last for several tenths of minutes. As a consequence, several actions involving different devices can be in execution at the same time and this can easily lead to concurrency issues. As an example, suppose that Alice wants to bake a cake and this requires four eggs from the refrigerator. At the same time Bob wants to prepare fresh pasta that requires two eggs. However, the refrigerator currently contains a total of five eggs. There is clearly a contention among a set of limited resources (the eggs) that are needed to fulfill some goals. At the lower level physical devices part of the system can be used with different purposes by several actors at the same time. The SM4ALL typical scenario assumes that several humans act in the house together with the system. The system cannot take complete control of the house (as users should be free to act without necessarily interacting with the system), thus it can happen that a device involved in the execution of a specific procedure by the system is also maneuvered directly by a user.

At a higher level it can happen that a single specific device is considered part of the execution of several different procedures enacted by the SM4ALL system. These procedures can interact in different ways with the device, but nevertheless require exclusive access to it in order to avoid possible inconsistencies due to the interleaving among atomic actions pertaining to the executions of concurrent procedures. At an even more abstract level, but with strong practical implications in the system execution, is concurrency taking place in the physical environment where SM4ALL is deployed. Some devices, in fact, act by changing some aspects of the house global status (think about a heater that, when turned on, increases the temperature of the room where it is installed). These changes can negatively impact the execution of actions by other devices or change the way other concurrent procedures should be enacted. The possibilities seem to be infinite. Controlling concurrency at all the levels in order to prevent unexpected behaviors represents thus an extremely ambitious goal whose attainment appears far beyond the objectives of the SM4ALL project.

While a complete solution of the aforementioned issues goes beyond the scope of this project, nevertheless, we were faced with their practical implications during the design of the SM4ALL architecture. We decided to provide a practical solution that, even if far from being optimal from the performance and resource utilization point of view, is able to reduce the implications of concurrency issues during system usage.

At first level concurrency is handled directly on the device. Given the one-to-one mapping between each hardware device and a corresponding proxy deployed in the Pervasive Layer, the proxy handles concurrent request by serializing them. Concurrency can also be limited at the User Layer by enforcing single-action interactions with users: each user is allowed to issue a single command at a time to the system. If the execution of the issued command takes time, the user will not be able to issue other commands. This kind of interaction is enforced through visual elements in the user interface. Concurrent commands issued by independent users are allowed. A third point of synchronization is realized within the Composition Layer. Each command issued at the User Layer is passed down for plan execution (here we refer to 'plan execution' both in the case of direct invocation of a service and in the case of invocation of a routine or complex service, as well as of a goal). Two different paths are followed in this phase: either the command is related to a a simple action or an action previously synthesized (i.e. an action for which an orchestration exists), or the action is passed to the On-line Planning Engine to prepare a plan for it. Whichever the case is, the resulting invocations are passed to the Invocation Dispatcher. It checks if another execution plan is currently in execution. If this is the case, the Dispatcher checks if the plan that must be executed includes calls to services that are already considered by the plan currently in execution. If both checks are true, the Dispatcher enqueues the plan for later execution in order to avoid any possible clash with other concurrent executions.

4. The Pervasive Layer

The Pervasive Layer is in charge of communicating with home devices. It is able to manage the invocations coming from the upper layers, on one hand, and notify about the events which are generated by sensors, on the other hand. Nowadays, many home automation systems are commercially available, e.g. KNX, LonWorks and X10 are among the most common. Each is based on its own communication protocol, thus making it very difficult for them to be integrated inside a unique domotic system. However, the functionalities offered by the different home automation systems and their interworking models are basically the same. The Pervasive Layer is the middleware in charge of offering the home devices functionalities to the upper layers through a common standardized way. Every physical device installed in the house is managed by a specific software module, which is responsible for interacting with it and keeping track of its current state; this module contains all of the logic needed to communicate with the device. It is named *proxy* in the SM4ALL architecture: in the SM4ALL context, it acts like a driver for an operating system. In order to provide high modularity and dynamicity, proxies are implemented as OSGi bundles; each bundle has its own life cycle which is completely independent from the others. Therefore, each proxy can be installed, started, stopped or removed from the system at run time: no system reboot or temporary stop is needed.

The skeleton of a proxy, with its SOAP-based communication stack, is generated automatically from the service interface. The developer of the proxy is in charge of implementing service details, according to the specific automation protocol. Every proxy exposes not only the interface descriptors and the related data types in use, but also behavioral descriptors (see Section 5.2) and user interface configuration details. When a proxy is started and plugged in the system, it registers itself to the Service Repository by means of a package containing all of the aforementioned details. From then on, the service offered by the proxy can be invoked from the upper layers and the current conversational state, as well as the controlled environmental variables values, can be retrieved at any point in time. At the beginning of its life cycle, the proxy also registers itself to the Context Awareness Manager as a publisher, so that SM4ALL components can be notified of the changes of states in an asynchronous way. In the current SM4ALL prototype, proxies are based on KNX.

The approach described above, which basically virtualizes devices, can potentially present some performance issues; hence, we conducted several tests, aiming at measuring the Total Round Trip Time (TOT RTT) of service/proxy invocations by a client (e.g. the user layer). The Total Round Trip Time includes (i) Proxy/KNX Round Trip Time (PK RTT), i.e. the time needed by the proxy for sending the command to the KNX bus and receiving the acknowledgment message back and (ii) proxy processing time (PPT), i.e. the time needed by the proxy to compute and refresh its own data structures.

Three main cases were identified and tested:

1. the client establishes its first connection to the proxy, does its first invocation and the proxy serves its first request (case 1 in Figure 2, right bars);

2. the client establishes its first connection to the proxy, does its first invocation served by a proxy which has already responded to some previous requests (case 2 in Figure 2, central bars);

3. the client invokes an operation offered by a proxy which has previously served some other request, on top of an already established connection between the two (case 3 in Figure 2, left bars).

We executed the tests on a local area network, in which the Pervasive Layer (i.e. the proxies and the KNX software

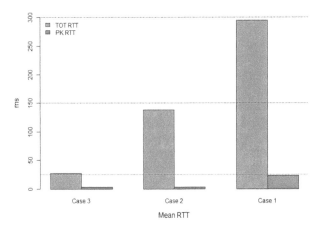

Figure 2. Performance tests.

layer used by all of them) is deployed on a EEE Box with an Intel Atom N330 dual core processor, 2 GB RAM and an Ubuntu distribution with the EIB/KNX demon. Each case was executed 100 times, and the average TOT RTTs and PK RTTs (over the 100 executions) for each case are depicted in Figure 2.

As the reader can appreciate, in the typical scenario (case 3) the overall overhead due to the approach is about 25 ms, mostly due to internetworking time, which is absolutely not perceivable by a human (with respect to the case in which she switches on the light through a standard switcher on the wall, instead of using the SM4ALL system). In the worst case (case 3, which happens only after a full reset and restart of the system) the delay is of 300 ms, still acceptable.

5. The Service Repository and the models

5.1. Service Repository

The main functionality of the Service Repository is to manage the available services in the smart home, i.e. to register new services, unregister removed services and provide an interface for service retrieval. The Service Repository also serves additional information necessary for reasoning over the service descriptions, such as the data model which is used for describing environment variables.

When a new device is inserted into the system and the corresponding proxy is deployed into the Pervasive Layer, the proxy registers a template service description, which details the functionalities of the service, but is not yet fitted to the smart home it is installed in. Specifically, the template may refer to variables that only exist in the scope of the template and may not yet have been set up in the house. During service registration, the Service Repository therefore adapts the template description to reflect the actual house set-up. This includes registering new variables published by a service, e.g. the conversational status, with the Context Awareness Manager, thereby making them available. The instantiated service description is from then on available for retrieval by other components. They are in particular the Composition Engines which need to query the Service Repository for services that can be used in compositions/plans. Typical queries for service matching concern the effects of the services, i.e. are aimed at finding those services which can change the user context in the desired way. Especially for the On-line Planning Engine, it is crucial that these requests are executed as fast as possible, so that planning can be performed without long waiting times for the user. In order to fulfill these requirements, the Service Repository uses a novel service indexing method and query algorithm, which was developed for SM4ALL and is described in detail in [35]. The basic idea of the indexing structure is to model context as a multi-dimensional space, where each environment variable corresponds to one context dimension. Service effects are described using projections of this space into a lower-dimensional space, which assigns value ranges to those context dimensions which are changed by the service.

During the registration of a new service, the service's effects are added to the in-memory index. Service matching requests are similarly transformed into low-dimensional projections representing the desired service effect. In the matching algorithm, first all services whose effects have no dimensions in common with the desired effect are filtered out using a fast bit-set operation. Only for the remaining services, it is then checked if the service effects conform to the desired effects and the matching services are returned. Using the described mechanisms, we have found that matching requests can be executed in less than 100 ms even for 1000 available services and 100 different context dimensions.

5.2. Service and data models

Service and composition models. The service model focuses on the behavior of services, in terms of conversational states that they traverse during the execution of the exposed actions, as well as on the way they (i) affect the environment and (ii) are inhibited (allowed) in the execution by the environment (respectively, by the expression of post-conditions and pre-conditions on top of the variables—see Section 5.2).

The smart home environment is populated by many deployed *service instance*s, which are actual occurrences of given *service types* (also *service*s for sake of brevity). Indeed, a developer can produce many instances showing the same behavior: e.g. many lamps of the same product series, installed in different rooms, are different instances of the same service type. Every service instance can be identified by one or more *properties,* which are deployment characteristics (such as the location in the house, the power consumption, etc.). Figures 3 and 4 show an

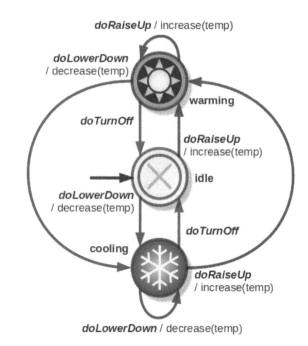

Figure 3. The `airConditionerService` transition system.

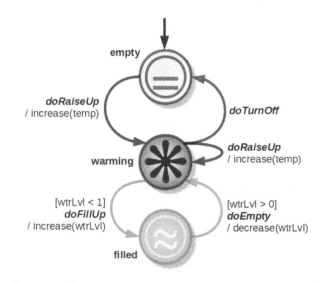

Figure 4. The `bathroomManagementService` transition system.

example with two service types: `airConditionerService` is supposed to be an air conditioner, while `bathroomManagementService` is a software manager of the bathroom.

Each service is represented by a *transition system,* which is a behavioral representation consisting in *state*s connected by *transition*s. The state is a break-point in the execution of a service (depicted as a node in the graphs of Figures 3 and 4), which new transitions (the arcs) can be fired from, through the invocation of an *action* (the emphasized part of the label). Action names are intended to correspond to the operation names offered by the service interfaces (i.e. to the 'name' attribute in 'operation' nodes of WSDL files).

Transitions can be constrained by *pre-conditions* and *post-conditions* (effects) to verify, respectively, before and after the related action is executed. Such pre- and post-conditions are written as logic formulae over the set of home variables. In Figures 3 and 4, pre-conditions are written, when expressed, before the action name, between square brackets; post-conditions are put after the slash following the action name. The meaning of increase and decrease is graphically represented by Figures 5 and 6.

As further explained in the following, a user can ask the system to realize a given behavior, specified by a *target service* (or simply, target), as the one depicted in Figure 7. In particular, the Off-line Synthesis Engine returns a *composition,* i.e. an imperative program which, given the current target state and its next action to invoke, specifies which is the service instance to call the next action on, according to any possible coherent environmental status (in terms of both variables and service instances' states). Hence, it verifies the realizability of the target service by analyzing the actions, i.e. whether the paths admitted by transitions lead to consistent states with respect to the available services and the constraints set by pre- and post-conditions. Target services are described through the same syntax and semantics of any other service type.

The Compound Service Workbench works off-line as well. It allows the construction of new services (namely compound services), by means of a graphical toolkit. Whereas the target service must be specified as a transition system where each action corresponds to one of the actions that some available service offers, each compound service action can be a new action, defined as a structured sequence of the ones exposed by services. Its main utility is the gained ease in composing new target services:

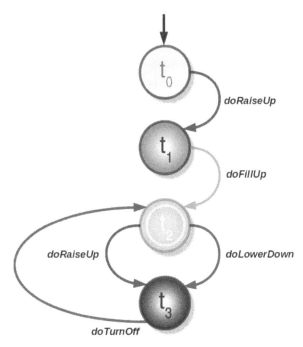

Figure 7. A target service, based on the component services of Figures 3 and 4.

indeed, the outcome of a synthesis can be wrapped in a single action and made part of another complex structure of automated invocations.

In case the user requires a goal to be immediately fulfilled, she can express the desired objective by means of formulae over the variables, and the On-line Planning Engine returns a plan, in terms of a structured path of invocations over actions, able to lead the environment to the desired status. Hence, being a planner, it builds the solution by considering the chain of effects and pre conditions (respectively, post- and pre-conditions) and thus establishing the actions to invoke in the proper order.

The service model is an XML standard for service descriptors. More than reported here, the XML Schemata which this model is built upon are published on-line at http://www.dis.uniroma1.it/~cdc/sm4all/proposals/servicemodel/latest, so to publicly show it as up to date with the latest version. Pre- and post-conditions are the natural link to the data model, described in Section 5.2.

Data model. The *data model* is an extensible framework of variable types. It concerns the specific environmental information used by reasoning engines only. That is, free parameters such as, e.g. name in an operation cheers (name: string): string may not adhere to the data model. Nevertheless, in case the developer wants (i) to describe the effects on the environment once a service action is invoked (post-condition), or (ii) to express the conditions that must hold in the context for an action to take place (pre-condition), she has to write statements

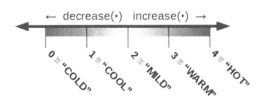

Figure 5. temperatureLevel.

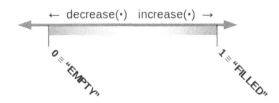

Figure 6. waterLevelInTub.

formulated on top of variables whose type is coherent with the data model.

This is due to the fact that both the Composition Layer and the User Layer must be able to cope with a predefined uniform set of common data types, so that the interaction with the environment is clear, despite the service developer. We call *variable types* (or simply *types*) the types, and *variables* are the entities whose type is a *variable type*. The data model is an XML standard, i.e. it is based on XML Schemata to define value spaces. Each service developer can define her own types, provided (i) they are described in XML Schema documents identified by a unique *namespace* and (ii) they extend, directly or indirectly, the SM4ALL *base types*.

The base types are identified by the http://www.sm4all-project.eu/datamodel/base namespace. They are published and kept up to date with the evolution of the standard on a public URL, namely http://www.dis.uniroma1.it/~cdc/sm4all/proposals/datamodel/latest. Indeed, types in the data model are derived by XML Schema native ones, and are designed to be extended by SM4ALL system service designers. The data model allows XML Schema simple types only as SM4ALL variable types, according to the XML Schema definition: complex types are not considered.

Common variable types are enumerations on top of the `numeric` type. This allows the ordering over the possible values, as inherited from the basic integer type (see Figures 5 and 6 for a visual representation of it). In such cases, the insertion of a `documentation` tag for each enumerated value provides also a human-readable form. The `documentation` node is intended to contain the information to show the users through the User Layer. That is to say: if, e.g. a variable of type `temperature-Level` reaches the value 3, the reasoning engines are informed of it, whereas the users are notified of a new 'warm' status. Having enumerations over variables with finite sets of possible values makes feasible and effective the reasoning tasks of the composition engines.

6. Composition

The On-line Planning Engine performs service compositions at run time, i.e. as the user asks for a new plan it must return an orchestration to be invoked immediately after. As previously introduced, the representation of services is based upon their pre and post-conditions, i.e. logic formulae on top of environmental variables; goals as well are logic formulae on top of the same environmental variables, which the user expects to become true due to the enactment of the synthesized plan. The reasoning core is a planner that, as described in [32, 36], solves the underlying planning problem through the reduction of it into a CSP (Constraint Satisfaction Problem—see [37]).

In the Off-line Synthesis Engines, services are described as Transition Systems (TSs). Goals are in this case target TSs which the engine must realize by simulation, on top of the set of available services. Pre- and post-conditions are expressed as constraints over the TS transitions (see [38, 39]), on top of environmental variables. Once the orchestration is computed, the target itself is stored into the Service Repository: it can be invoked at any time in the future, like any other service. The returned orchestration is different from the On-line Planning Engine output. Indeed, it is a relation that, given the current target state and the next action to be fired, indicates which services can be invoked in order to enact it, according to any of the possible (i.e. coherent with the realizability of the goal) services' and environmental variables states. The solution approach is based on reducing the problem to the synthesis of Linear-time Temporal Logic formulae (see [40]) by Model Checking over Game Structures.

7. The User Layer

The home can be controlled from the user through different kinds of interfaces (BCIs, remote controls, touchscreens, keyboards, voice recognition, etc.). The *AAI* (Abstract Adaptive Interface) represents the core of the SM4ALL User Layer. It retrieves status information from the Context Awareness Manager and service descriptions from the Service Repository. It organizes the whole in order to correctly show the available actions to the user, depending on the interaction mode she is currently making use of (i.e. visual, aural, BCI, etc.). Indeed, the AAI is intended to be put as an abstraction layer among the multiple user interface devices and the underlying composition layer.

Its main novelty is represented by the ability to manage many different user interface models with a unique adaptable algorithm, able to change itself on the basis of the interaction device characteristics (speech/aural, visual/touch, handheld, brain-controlled ...) and on the basis of the user preferences, automatically gathered, analyzed and synthesized on top of the previous interactions with the system.

Through a message screen the user can see notifications coming from the system. The room actions' screen shows the list of actions that can be invoked, gathered up by groups which are built according to the rooms where the services offering the actions are actually located. The number of available services in the home can be very high, and a service can offer many actions; on the other hand, the icons that can be shown on a screen are limited. A pagination of the information, though useful and indeed exploited in many prototypes, is not sufficient to provide an effective interaction, since it would introduce a huge effort for the user to find the desired element among the big amount of items, navigating back and forth. Hence, in SM4ALL, the AAI integrates a mechanism for grouping and smartly ordering the icons in order to improve the ease of interaction. An icon may represent either a service or an action. Sometimes, only a few actions, among the ones offered by a given service, are available, e.g. a 'bedroom light' service offers a 'turn off' and a 'turn on' action, but only the first (or the second, conversely) can be triggered when the lamp is switched on (off). In such a case, there is no need to show the service icon, as the only available action is enough.

When the user can fire more than one action, related to a single service, a clustering is needed. It is realized by initially showing the service icon; once activated, all of the other items are hidden and only the available related actions are displayed.

Another way to reduce the number of displayed icons is to divide services themselves into groups represented by a given type (e.g. 'Multimedia' for televisions, MP3 players, etc.). The idea is almost the same: at first, the menu shows only a type which many services belong to, and then, after the type is selected, all of the other items are hidden and the only related services are displayed (see Figures 8 and 9).

Beyond grouping, the AAI exploits the possibility to order the items according to their importance, with respect to the preferences of each user. This way, the actions which are known to be more relevant for the user will be displayed on the first screen, in order to appear at a first glimpse, while the others are going to be shown next. Two algorithms are offered: a *static* one and a *dynamic* one. The user can select which one she prefers through

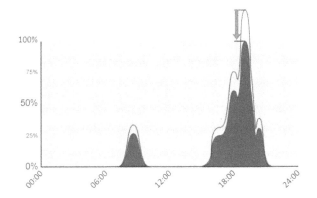

Figure 10. An example of automatic normalization of the parametric score.

an administration menu. The static algorithm makes use of explicitly defined user settings to identify her preferences. Each preference is constituted by (i) a set of conditions, representing the state of the environment which enables the action, (ii) a time frame in which the preference has to be considered (Always, Morning, Afternoon, Evening, Night) and (iii) a usage expectation degree (certain, highly probable, very probable, probable). The dynamic algorithm orders the actions according to the probability that each one is going to be executed, on the basis of the current environment status and previous invocations: the higher the probability, the higher the priority of the associated icon in the list (*partial order*). The home environment status consists of several parametric values related to the execution (e.g. the time of invocation). Each parameter is associated to a *relevance* (*weight*), manually tunable by administrators. At every call, the parametric value is computed and its *incidence* (*score*) re-calculated. Indeed, it is taken from a run-time updated graph, i.e. a normalized sum of Gaussian curves: at each execution, a new Gaussian centered in the parameter value which is associated to the call (e.g. the time of invocation) is added to the previous graph. In order to tune the evolution of the curve, norm and variance of the Gaussians are both customizable. If the global peak overcomes the maximum admissible value (100%), a normalization is automatically performed (see Figure 10). The probability is thus the *sum* of the *weighted scores* (Σ_i *relevance$_i$* $\times$ *incidence$_i$*) of all the parameters, related to the current home environment status.

8. Concluding remarks

Throughout this paper, we presented the pervasive intelligent home system SM4ALL, and we focused, among the others, on the service composition techniques and on the self-adapting ones of the User Layer: they are the most involved in the challenge of hiding the heterogeneity of used hardware devices to the other software modules, which is a very important requirement in the field of dom-

Figure 8. An example of the user interface grouping services by the type they belong to (here, before activating the 'Multimedia' services type selector—first icon, on the left of the horizontal list).

Figure 9. An example of the user interface grouping services by the type they belong to (here, after the 'Multimedia' services type selector is activated).

otics, where a lack of standardization still holds. Currently, we have developed a running prototype interfaced with real KNX devices actually installed in a house set up on purpose in Rome, hosted by Fondazione Santa Lucia. A showcase has been demonstrated in October 2011; this has shown the wide acceptability of the system by both normal-bodied users and disabled ones. However, here we showed some performance tests demonstrating the feasibility of the approach.

References

[1] MYNATT, E., MELENHORST, A., FISK, A. and ROGERS, W. (2004) Understanding user needs and attitudes. *IEEE Pervasive Comput.* **3**(2): 36–41.

[2] ROBERTS, J. (2006) Pervasive health management and health management utilizing pervasive technologies: synergy and issues. *J. UCS* **12**(1): 6–14.

[3] HAUPTMANN, A., GAO, J., YAN, R., QI, Y., YANG, J. and WACTLAR, H. (2004) Automatic analysis of nursing home observations. *IEEE Pervasive Comput.* **3**(2): 15–21.

[4] ROSS, D. (2004) Cyber crumbs for successful aging with vision loss. *IEEE Pervasive Comput.* **3**(2): 30–35.

[5] JOSEPH, A. (2004) Successful aging. *IEEE Pervasive Comput.* **3**(2): 36–41.

[6] HELAL, S., MANN, W.C., EL-ZABADANI, H., KING, J., KADDOURA, Y. and JANSEN, E. (2005) The Gator Tech Smart House: a programmable pervasive space. *IEEE Comput.* **38**(3): 50–60.

[7] PARADISO, J., DUTTA, P., GELLERSEN, H. and SCHOOLER, E. (2011) Smart energy systems. Special issue. *IEEE Pervasive Comput.* **10**.

[8] ALONSO, G., CASATI, F., KUNO, H. and MACHIRAJU, V. (2004) *Web Services. Concepts, Architectures and Applications* (Springer).

[9] PAPAZOGLOU, M. (2008) *Web Services: Principles and Technology* (Pearson Education).

[10] MICHALOWSKI, M., AMBITE, J.L., KNOBLOCK, C.A., MINTON, S., THAKKAR, S. and TUCHINDA, R. (2004) Retrieving and semantically integrating heterogeneous data from the Web. *IEEE Intell. Syst.* **19**(3): 72–79.

[11] BLYTHE, J. and AMBITE, J.L. [eds.] (2004) In *Proceedings of ICAPS 2004 Workshop on Planning and Scheduling for Web and Grid Services*.

[12] CARDOSO, J. and SHETH, A. (2004) Introduction to semantic Web services and Web process composition. In *Proceedings of SWSWPC 2004* .

[13] WU, D., PARSIA, B., SIRIN, E., HENDLER, J.A. and NAU, D.S. (2003) Automating DAML-S Web services composition using SHOP2. In *Proceedings of ISWC 2003*.

[14] BULTAN, T., FU, X., HULL, R. and SU, J. (2003) Conversation specification: a new approach to design and analysis of eService composition. In *Proceedings of WWW 2003*.

[15] GEREDE, C.E., HULL, R., IBARRA, O.H. and SU, J. (2004) Automated composition of eServices: lookaheads. In *Proceedings of ICSOC 2004*.

[16] MCILRAITH, S.A. and SON, T.C. (2002) Adapting GOLOG for composition of semantic Web services. In *Proceedings of KR 2002*.

[17] PISTORE, M., TRAVERSO, P. and BERTOLI, P. (2005) Automated composition of Web services by planning in asynchronous domains. In *Proceedings of ICAPS 2005*.

[18] BERARDI, D., CALVANESE, D., DE GIACOMO, G., LENZERINI, M. and MECELLA, M. (2003) Automatic composition of eServices that export their behavior. In *Proceedings of ICSOC 2003*.

[19] BERARDI, D., CALVANESE, D., DE GIACOMO, G., LENZERINI, M. and MECELLA, M. (2005) Automatic service composition based on behavioral descriptions. *Int. J. Coop. Inf. Syst.* **14**(4): 333–376.

[20] BERARDI, D., CALVANESE, D., DE GIACOMO, G. and MECELLA, M. (2005) Composition of services with non-deterministic observable behavior. In *Proceedings of IC-SOC 2005*.

[21] BERARDI, D., CHEIKH, F., DE GIACOMO, G. and PATRIZI, F. (2008) Automatic service composition via simulation. *Int. J. Found. Comput. Sci.* **19**(2): 429–451.

[22] MUSCHOLL, A. and WALUKIEWICZ, I. (2007) A lower bound on Web services composition. In *Proceedings of FOSSACS 2007*.

[23] SARDINA, S., PATRIZI, F. and DE GIACOMO, G. (2008) Behavior composition in the presence of failure. In *Proceedings of KR'08*.

[24] CALVANESE, D., DE GIACOMO, G., LENZERINI, M., MECELLA, M. and PATRIZI, F. (2008) Automatic service composition and synthesis: the Roman model. *IEEE Data Eng. Bull.* **31**(3): 18–22.

[25] HULL, R. (2005) Web services composition: a story of models, automata, and logics. In *Proceedings of IEEE ICWS*.

[26] THEVENIN, D. and COUTAZ, J. (1999) Plasticity of user interfaces: framework and research agenda. In *Proceedings of Interact'99*.

[27] PUERTA, A. and EISENSTEIN, J. (1999) Towards a general computational framework for model-based interface development systems. In *Proceedings of 4th International Conference on Intelligent User Interfaces*.

[28] FRATERNALI, P. (1999) Tools and approaches for developing data-intensive Web applications: a survey. *ACM Comput. Surv.* **31**(3): 227–263.

[29] ISAKOWITZ, T., STOHR, E. and BALASUBRAMANIAN, P. (1995) RMM: a methodology for structured hypermedia design. *Commun. ACM* **38**(8): 34–44.

[30] CONTENTI, M., MECELLA, M., TERMINI, A. and BALDONI, R. (2005) A distributed architecture for supporting e-Government cooperative processes. In *Proceedings of TCGOV 2005*.

[31] CATARCI, T., DE LEONI, M., MARRELLA, A., MECELLA, M., SALVATORE, B., VETERE, G., DUSTDAR, S. *et al.* (2008) Pervasive software environments for supporting disaster responses. *IEEE Internet Comput.* **12**: 26–37.

[32] KALDELI, E., LAZOVIK, A. and AIELLO, M. (2009) Extended goals for composing services. In *Proceedings of ICAPS 2009*.

[33] MCFARLAND, D. and WOLPAW, J. (2011) Brain–computer interfaces for communication and control. *Commun. ACM* **54**(5): 60–66.

[34] ALOISE, F., SCHETTINI, F., ARICÒ, P., BIANCHI, L., RICCIO, A., MECELLA, M., BABILONI, F. *et al.* (2010) Advanced brain–computer interface for communication and control. In *Proceedings of AVI 2010.*

[35] RASCH, K., LI, F., SEHIC, S., AYANI, R. and DUSTDAR, S. (2011) Context-driven personalized service discovery in pervasive environments. *World Wide Web*: http://dx.doi.org/10.1007/s11280-011-0112-x.

[36] KALDELI, E. (2009) Using CSP for adaptable Web service composition. Tech. Rep. 2009-7-01, University of Groningen. www.cs.rug.nl/~eirini/tech_rep_09-7-01.pdf.

[37] DO, M. and KAMBHAMPATI, S. (2000) Solving planning-graph by compiling it into CSP. In *Proceedings of AIPS'00.*

[38] DE MASELLIS, R., DI CICCIO, C., MECELLA, M. and PATRIZI, F. (2010) Smart home planning programs. In *Proceedings of ICSSSM 2010.*

[39] PATRIZI, F. (2009) *Simulation-based techniques for automated service composition.* Ph.D. thesis, Department of Systems and Computer Science and Engineering, SAPIENZA—Università di Roma, Rome, Italy.

[40] PNUELI, A. and ROSNER, R. (1989) On the synthesis of a reactive module. In *Proceedings of POPL'89.*

20

Design and deployment of a new wireless sensor node platform for building environmental monitoring and control

Essa Jafer[1,*], Rostislav Spinar[2], Paul Stack[3], Cian O'Mathuna[1], Dirk Pesch[2]

[1]Tyndall National Institute, University College Cork (UCC), Cork, Ireland; [2]Cork Institute of Technology (CIT), Cork, Ireland; [3]Department of Civil and Environmental Engineering, University College Cork (UCC), Cork, Ireland

Abstract

It is commonly agreed that a 15–40% reduction of building energy consumption is achievable by efficiently operated buildings when compared with typical practice. Existing research has identified that the level of information available to Building Managers with existing Building Management Systems and Environmental Monitoring Systems is insufficient to perform the required performance-based building assessment. The majority of today's buildings are insufficiently sensored to obtain an unambiguous understanding of performance. The cost of installing additional sensors and meters is extremely high, primarily due to the estimated cost of wiring and the needed labour. From these perspectives wireless sensors technology proves to have a greater cost-efficiency while maintaining high levels of functionality and reliability. In this paper, a wireless sensor network mote hardware design and implementation are introduced particularly for building deployment application. The core of the mote design is based on the 8-bit AVR microcontroller, Atmega1281 and 2.4 GHz wireless communication chip, CC2420. The sensors were selected carefully to meet both the building monitoring and design requirements. Beside the sensing capability, actuation and interfacing to external meters/sensors are provided to perform different management control and data recording tasks.

Keywords: building automation systems, sensors interfacing and motes deployment, wireless sensor network

1. Introduction

A deeper understanding of system operation is possible if more detailed information is made available to Building Managers. This information must recognize the education and background of Building Managers if they are to fulfil their role with respect to organizational objectives and legislative compliance. Efficiency cannot be determined from displayed sensor readings without data access, storage and post-processing. Scheduling information must be displayed concurrently with Building Management System (BMS) data. All information used is dependent on accurate, robust and structured data.

Traditionally building automation systems are realized through wired communications. However, the wired automation systems require expensive communication cables to be installed and regularly maintained and thus they are not widely implemented in industrial plants because of their high cost [1, 2].

In recent years, wireless technologies have become very popular in both home and commercial networking applications. The use of wireless technologies offers distinctive advantages in the field of home and building automation [3–5]. First, installation costs are significantly reduced since no cabling is necessary. Neither conduits nor cable trays are required. Wireless technology also allows placing sensors where cabling is not appropriate for aesthetic, conservatory or safety reasons [4, 5]. With current

*Corresponding author. Email: essajh@Campus.ie

wireless technology, a great challenge arises because of the level of expertise needed to fully make use of the sensors. The most sophisticated hardware often requires advanced knowledge of embedded programming to achieve the level of performance desired. A second issue is about the need for high active lifetime of the wireless installation which means the need for low-power design starts with the obligatory use of energy-efficient hardware (e.g. low supply voltages and sleep modes support in microcontrollers) [6].

Environmental monitoring and devices control of intelligent building based on Wireless Sensor Network (WSN) is considered as one of the most crucial applications. In the past, WSN has been used to measure number of signals within building environment like ambient light and temperature [7–11] to control and enhance the building energy performance. The initial target of the work in this paper is to deploy an efficient WSN capable of measuring wider range of vital signals inside the building and provide new methodologies for establishing reliable RF link and interactive user control.

In addition, this paper is focusing on the development of a miniaturized Wireless Sensor platform that is intended to be used for building sensing, meters interfacing and actuation. Next the deployment of large scale (around 60 nodes) of this platform is described in terms of network structure, topology and data presentation. The Environmental Research Institute (ERI) building, located at University College Cork (UCC), Ireland, was designed as a green flagship building and a low-energy research facility [12]. This building was chosen as the test bench for our large-scale deployment because it is the most densely measured building on the UCC campus.

The paper is structured as follows: Section 2 will be dealing with design aspects of the Wireless Sensor Node and the selection of the different sensors used for the target applications. The adopted WSN is described in Section 3. The data storage and representation techniques are given in Section 4. Number of Surveillance and Security concerns is discussed in Section 5. A newly developed tool for occupant interaction is presented in Section 6. Finally conclusions and future work plans are drawn in Section 7.

2. WSN node design

2.1. System architecture and functional units

The mote is designed in a modular three-layer mode. As Figure 1(a) shows, the overview system contains four main units, these are data processing unit, RF communication unit, sensors/meters and actuation (multi-sensor) unit and power supply management unit. The data processing unit can make valid control for other units. To have deeper look into the developed system, the block

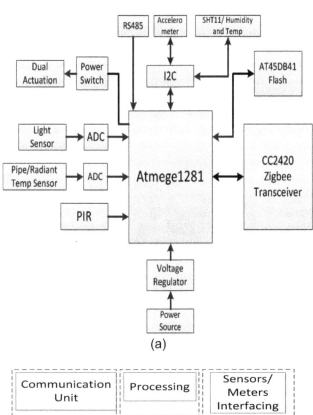

(a)

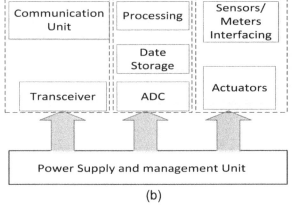

(b)

Figure 1. (a) System block diagram of the WSN mote and (b) block diagram of the mote functional units.

diagram of the mote functional units is shown in Figure 1(b).

The multi-sensor layer was designed to interface with number of selected sensors as well as to incorporate additional capability for use within the building environment. This includes dual actuation capabilities for any AC/DC system using an external high-power relay-based system for devices that consume up to 280 V and 25 A (to turn on and off appliances) as well as an on-board low-power switch to enable the actuation facility. The type of on-board sensor is either digital communicating with the microcontroller through serial bus interface like I2C or analogue connected with any of the ADC channels.

The two external sensors/meters interfaces are dedicated to any meter using MODBUS protocol [13] and variable resistance temperature sensors. The MODBUS

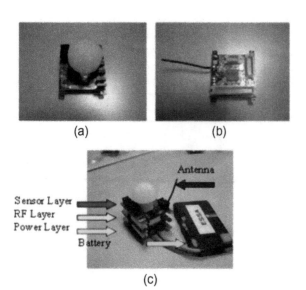

Figure 2. Photographs of the (a) sensor layer, (b) Zigbee and processor (RF) layer, and (c) 25 mm² mote.

meter exchanges data/commands through RS485 serial communications. This interface layer is also designed to incorporate external flash memory (Atmel AT45DB041). The layer features a 4-Mbit serial flash for storing data, measurements and remote re-programming. The photographs of both the RF and sensor layers are shown in Figure 2. The complete three-layer stackable 25 mm mote is also shown.

The processor and RF parts are located on the two sides of one layer called RF layer, while the third (power) layer contains the battery interfacing and voltage regulator.

2.2. Sensors selection

In this section, the different types of sensors and interface design options selected for the building monitoring application are illustrated.

Occupation sensor (passive infrared). Detecting the occupancy of the rooms inside the building was one of the essential requirements to be monitored, and there was need to find a suitable passive infrared (PIR) sensor module. The Panasonic AMN44122 [14] was selected for this purpose since it provides the required functionality in a module that is smaller, more convenient and of lower-energy consumption than the custom circuitry used in the prototype. Furthermore, the module provides a digital detection output that is used to trigger an interrupt on the processor when activity registers on the sensor. According to the datasheet of the PIR sensor, it has a detection distance of maximum 10 m (32.808 ft) and a detection range of 110° in horizontal and 93° in vertical. A simple laboratory test has been performed to verify the actual performance of the PIR sensor leading to results similar to those in the datasheet as in Table 1. However,

Table 1. The comparison of the AMN44122 PIR sensor with reference to datasheet.

Items		Data sheet	Laboratory test
Detection distance		10 m (32.808 ft)	9 m (29.528 ft)
Detection range	Horizontal	110°	90°
	Vertical	93°	90°

it was found that the actual detection region with high reliability is a little smaller than the detection region specified in the datasheet.

Humidity/temperature/light sensor. Relative humidity (RH) is an important indicator of air quality in buildings. Extremely low or high humidity levels (the comfort range is 30–70% RH) can cause discomfort to workers and can reduce building longevity. The temperature and humidity sensor SHT11 [15] shown in Figure 3 was used on the sensor board that integrates signal processing, tiny footprint and provides a fully calibrated digital output.

It uses I2C serial interface to communicate with the microcontroller and provide either the humidity or temperature data based on the received commands.

An ambient miniaturized photo diode with output current was used to measure the amount of light in LUX at room disc level.

Windows/doors status monitoring. The detection of the windows/doors status was one of the building parameters required to be monitored by the WSN node. Three-axis accelerometer was selected for this application since it can provide useful angle information which helps one to know how wide door/window is opened or closed. The LIS302DL is an ultra-compact low-power three-axis linear accelerometer that is integrated in the node design [16].

The main design challenge with using the accelerometer is that the microcontroller has to be continuously in active mode to record sensor data which means high current consumption and short battery lifetime. In order to overcome this problem, a mechanical vibration sensor with a very small package was used in this design to provide an external interrupt to the Atmel microcontroller when there is any kind of motion at any direction as

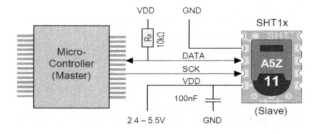

Figure 3. Typical application circuit of the SHT11.

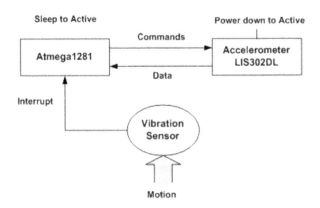

Figure 4. Functional block diagram of the motion sensor design.

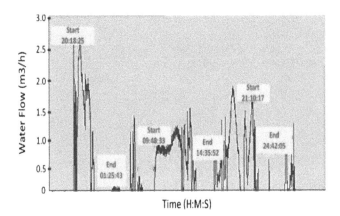

Figure 5. Water flow rate measurements.

presented by Figure 4. The selected accelerometer can be in power down mode with the lowest current consumption when there is no activity operating fully under the control of the microcontroller commands through serial bus interface. From the obtained power measurements for a fixed run time and duty cycle, a gain value of 3.5–4 was observed in the current consumption using the selected vibration switch.

Water flow/electricity meter interfacing using RS485 and MODBUS handshaking. It is required to get the flow rate measurements from different locations inside the building where pipes are made from different materials and have wide scale diameter size. The ultrasonic non-introductive unit was found to be the optimal solution for measuring the water flow rate of the water on building pipes since it is not disturbing the existing pipes installation and gives flexible testing option. Half-duplex RS485/RS232 IC was used to interface the water flow meter with the Universal Asynchronous Receiver Transmitter of microcontroller using the standard industrial MODBUS protocol [13].

The STUF-300EB flow meter from Shenitech [17] was used for this application. It provides excellent capabilities for accurate liquid flow measurement from outside of a pipe. The device is main powered and can be easily mounted on different pipe sizes.

To verify the performance of the meter interfacing, first the ultrasonic device was deployed in a chosen site inside the building. Figure 5 shows the water flow readings obtained from running the meter for almost 2 days.

The start and end times of each flow activity are marked. A MODBUS message is placed by the transmitting device into a frame with start and end headers. The receiver will be used to identify the beginning and end of the message using the two headers and will apply error checking using the Longitudinal Redundancy Checking algorithm.

The RS485 interface using MODBUS protocol will be used in later stage to interface both single-three-phase

electricity meters and measure the lighting and zones energy consumptions.

Water pipe/radiant temperature sensor interfacing. The monitoring of the water temperature that is passing in the building pipes was needed as part of the wireless sensor system. Surface Mount Temperature Sensor from SIEMENS [18] was selected for this application as a non-introductive unit and can be mounted directly on a pipe inlet to sense the temperature of water passing through. The sensor performance was compared with those of the existing wired sensors read by the BMS as shown in Table 2.

It is very clear that the wireless sensor displays a comparative performance to the wired one and can provide useful data from number of pipe sites inside the building. It has to be mentioned that the temperature of the pipe surface is always higher than that of water by a few degrees. This will be taken into account in the calibration process by the mote to get accurate readings. The same interface was used to measure the room radiant temperature as the device manufactured using the same sensing material.

Actuation capability. The wireless control of switching on/off different types of AC loads in the building is meant to be the second application for the node beside the data monitoring. The base station presented by embedded PC and another node will be responsible for collecting and processing the different types of sensors data and send the commands to some of the designated

Table 2. Verifying the readings of the sensor with the existence of BMS.

Temp °C (BMS)	Temp °C (sensor)	Temp °C (calibrated sensor)
20.25	19.01	20.01
23.12	21.03	22.03
30.45	29.50	30.50
45.21	43.20	44.20
48.87	47.62	48.62

Figure 6. Wireless actuation for heat radiators.

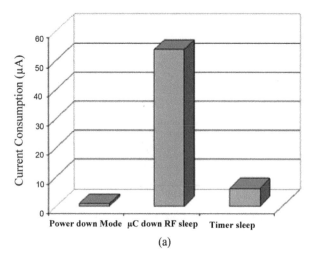

(a)

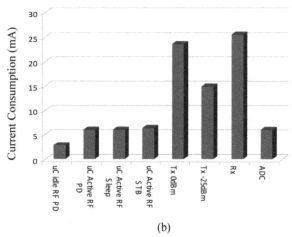

(b)

Figure 7. Current consumption at different power modes of both microcontroller (uC) and transceiver (RF) units. PD and STB refer to Power Down and Standby modes.

nodes to perform actuation like switching on/off light, heat pumps, water valves or radiators. To achieve this goal on a miniaturized node, number of design options were taken into consideration with many aspects like the effect of AC high voltage on the low-power circuitry of the node and also the possible ways to interconnect with different types of single-/three-phase loads. The current design provides two options, first controlling small current, up to 2 Amps, AC loads like PCs using on-board PHOTOMOS relay which is an optoelectronic device that drives a power MOSFET [19]. The second option is providing the ability to connect an external relay that derives higher current loads through one of the on-board connectors.

To examine the actuation capability of the node, a small demonstration was set up inside one of the building rooms to control the operation of heat radiators as shown in Figure 6. Another node was deployed in the same room to monitor the room temperature/humidity and send the readings to the base station which will take an action and send the appropriate command to the actuator to either switch off or on the radiator.

Node power consumption. The power consumption of the node was critical issue for the design to make it reliable for long-term deployment. Primarily the mote will be powered from a 3.3 V lithium coin cell rechargeable battery with limited current capacity. In order to increase the operation lifetime of the mote, a number of SW/HW techniques were employed. At the HW level, the sensor layer has the ability to shut down the power from the unused sensors. Low current voltage regulator was integrated in the RF layer to provide stable voltage level. Also we focused on how to employ efficiently the different power-saving modes of both the microcontroller and transceiver units that are measured and presented by Figure 7.

From the previous figure number of power down options are available to reduce the overall node current consumption. The best scenario is to put both the microcontroller and transceiver in deep power down mode when there is no data transmission which brings

down the total current to nearly 6 µA. Here the duty cycle has to be carefully considered for all the sensors to provide frequent useful data and at the same time guarantee low-power operation when there is no activity. In order to demonstrate such behaviour, the node has been programmed to send the sensors data every 15 s and go to power down after. The obtained current consumption measurements are given in Figure 8. Experimentally the lifetime of the different deployed nodes was found to be in the range of 4–10 weeks based on the type of the used sensors and desired duty cycle.

3. Adopted WSN

3.1. WSN system architecture

The adopted WSN architecture is based on recently released IETF IPv6 over low-power WPAN (6LoWPAN) (RFC 4944) open standard for IP communication over low-power radio devices—IEEE 802.15.4 represents one such link. WSN LoWPAN networks are connected

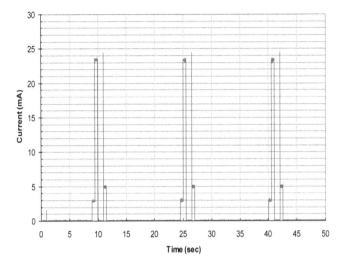

Figure 8. Node current consumption behaviour at fixed duty cycle.

to other IP networks through one or more border routers forwarding packets between different media including Ethernet, Wi-Fi or GPRS as shown in Figure 9 [20]. The IETF 6LoWPAN standard extends the same communication capabilities to low-power devices whose battery power must last for months or even years.

The 6LoWPAN utilizes a pay-only-for-what-you-use header-compression scheme. Through direct integration with IP routers, it can take advantage of advanced network security schemes rather than depending on those provided by *ad hoc* gateways.

The IP above offers widespread commercial adoption and broad interoperability due to its attributes such as openness, flexibility, scalability and manageability. Many industrial standards, including BACNet, LonTalk, CIP and SCADA, introduced an IP using either TCP/IP or UDP/IP over Ethernet [12]. The final topology of the

nodes deployed in the building is mesh network based on the 6LoWPAN protocol communication to meet the low-power and connectivity requirements of the used nodes platforms.

In this desired topology, the data nodes are deployed over three floors. The border router in Figure 9 at each floor is acting as a gateway to gather the data from the nodes in each floor and send them to the main server for further processing. In addition, a number of repeaters were used to deliver the data packets at the weak RF covered places between the adjacent sensor nodes.

3.2. ERI WSN topology design for reliable communications

While sensor positions were predefined within the ERI space to ensure appropriate sensed data are collected from the correct areas of the building, the positioning of gateways and repeaters to ensure a reliable communications network was supported through the design of the WSN topology using a dedicated WSN tool [21]. To assess the RF link quality for reliable communications, a temporary wireless sensor communications network was deployed in buildings spaces that were to be augmented with wireless sensing infrastructure. The RF link RSSI measurements were used for tuning the radio propagation model that is used by the design tool for infrastructure positioning. This propagation model is used to accurately predict the received signal strength between transmitters and receivers by considering the impact of the environment, such as wall type, on the signal level. Using this propagation model the design tool specifies the appropriate positions for gateway nodes, based on fixed sensor node positions, to provide a reliable communication backbone for all sensors. To develop an accurate propagation model, measurements are taken throughout the environment across all building floors focusing on the areas of interest.

The RF characterization is used to create a communications coverage map that is used for signal level prediction when assessing the suitability of candidate infrastructure position points during the topology design process.

The sequence of steps for the network topology design can be summarized as:

1. Floor plans of the building are input into a software site survey measurement tool. This allows the user to define the location of sensors and the measurement path. This tool stores the measurement data and visualizes the RF coverage map overlaid on the building layout.

2. Sensor nodes are deployed in areas of interest from a sensing point of view to establish a temporary broadcast-based communications network. The sensor nodes broadcast a dummy packet of data at set time intervals.

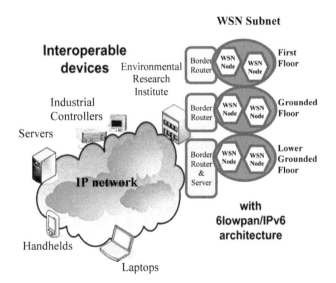

Figure 9. WSN in the broader view.

3. The measurement tool scans for sensors broadcasting and when it receives a packet it stores the received signal strength in a database for processing later.

4. Steps 2 and 3 are repeated in different areas of the building until a complete RF coverage map of the environment is built.

5. Based on the RF coverage map the Design tool suggests the number and positions of gateways and repeaters that are required for reliable communications.

Shown in Figure 10(a) are the measurements recorded with three nodes being used to establish a temporary communications network. These temporary nodes were deployed in the areas of interest on the ground floor of the ERI building.

The objectives of these measurements were to establish the position of gateways and repeaters to support reliable communications, the topology design decision was whether to place a gateway per floor or to use a single gateway to collect all data (with repeaters where necessary on each floor). Figure 10(b) shows measurements recorded on the first floor of the ERI building from nodes deployed on ground floor (with the strongest signal being from node 0004). Signal level was received from node 0004, which is due to an open stair well, but the signal level is very low and cannot be relied upon for guaranteed communications. Consequently, the topology design decision is that it is not feasible to have nodes on the ground floor send data to a gateway positioned on or near the first floor; the material type on the floor is extra heavily poured concrete that attenuates the signal greatly.

Again to establish reliable communications on the first floor, measurements were recorded with temporary nodes

being deployed in the areas of interest across this floor, as shown in Figure 10(c). The design decision for the position of the gateway on this floor is restricted to placing the gateway in the stairwell because of the availability of power sockets and also the gateway must interface with the *ad hoc* WiFi backbone back to the BMS server. To have reliable communications between the nodes on this floor and the gateway, a repeater node must be positioned in the corridor marked with X in Figure 10(c) map below to ensure connectivity.

4. ERI data storage and representation

To provide sensed data to the end user (or other software components) for the purpose of Building Performance Monitoring (BPM), there are a number of conceptual and practical challenges that need to be overcome. The conceptual challenges can be the definition of BPM to different stakeholders of a building [22]. Practical challenges include data quality, availability and consistency, and benchmarking. A Data Warehouse (DW) implementation was created to store large data sets provided by the data streams of the WSN in ERI [23, 24]. In Figure 10, the staging area was designed to support data from multiple sensor, meter and actuator types. These data are processed to form data cubes that support the presentation of relevant building performance measures to stakeholders. To extract the environment information from the WSN deployment in the ERI, a Service-Orientated Architecture (SOA) was used [25]. The different building blocks of this SOA were developed and validated by our research team. The Service Orchestration ensures that separate and independent services interact in a way that a larger application's goals are met. As an architectural concept SOA abstracts from any particular operating system and any implementation details. It does not matter which

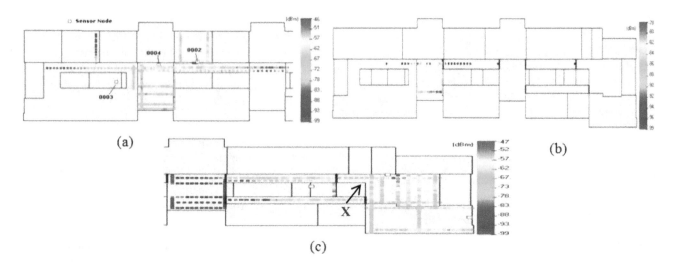

Figure 10. (a) Measurement data path recorded in the ERI ground floor, (b) first floor measurements from nodes deployed on ground floor and (C) first floor measurements.

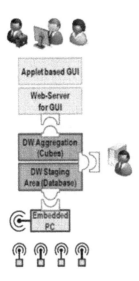

Figure 11. SOA for WSN to DW and DW to GUI.

platform and which language are used to implement some service. The functionality of a service is entirely defined by the service interface.

For the ERI deployment, the data are gathered from the first and ground floors and sent through the wireless backbone to the embedded PC (gateway) in the basement of the building. From embedded PC, a SOA connection is maintained to a DW. Figure 11 shows the architecture used to gather data from the sensors and present data through a Graphical User Interface (GUI) to the end user.

A sample of the obtained results using a building operator GUI is displayed in Figure 12 showing 1 day data from light (Immunology Lab), radiant (Immunology Lab), occupancy (Seminar Room) and door status (the Lobby). Figure 13 shows samples of the selected deployment sites.

In total (60) nodes were deployed in the selected three main zones within the ERI building to perform various functions of sensing and monitoring. Although each node has the same sensor layer, the types/number of sensors/meters interfaces used with each are different depending on the required parameters to be measured and their desired physical locations.

These building performance data will be used to support decision making for facility manager and building operators to optimize maintenance activities [21] and assist in fault detection and diagnosis.

5. Surveillance, security and climate change matters

With the development of novel BMS, the border between environmental monitoring and surveillance of an individual may need to be examined more closely. From a technical standpoint sensing technology to monitor the environment [26, 27] is similar to sensing technology to evaluate individuals' performance at various tasks [28]. Ubiquitous wireless sensors are a relatively recent technology and when we work/live in environments with novel sensors, acknowledgement of people's concerns about surveillance, privacy and autonomy is a must.

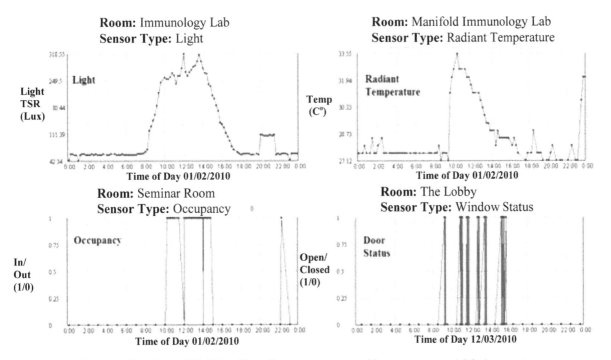

Figure 12. GUI 1-day recorded data of (a) light, (b) radiant temperature, (C) occupancy and (D) door status.

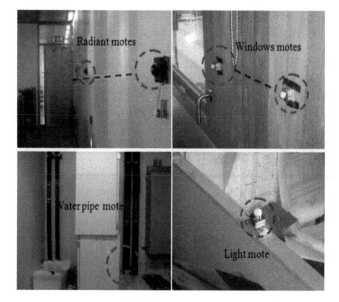

Figure 13. Number of deployment sites for (window, radiant, light and water pipe) sensors.

Clearly new sensing technology, where the boundaries between environmental monitoring and person monitoring are fuzzy, has the potential to turn work/home life into life of surveillance, where the system administrator can omnisciently monitor the activity of tenants.

Considering the apparent or real threats to privacy and autonomy there is a need to establish ethical guidelines for the appropriate deployment of BMS.

The field of Human–Computer Interaction (HCI) has established guidelines on how to evaluate the working systems that operate via the keyboard, mouse, and VDU, or even the mobile technologies of the 2000s. One set of guidelines, heuristic evaluation [29], emphasizes that the system status should be visible to the user and keep the user informed about what is going on.

The technical advance of wireless environmental monitoring [26, 27] is rapid, so rapid that appropriate design guidelines acknowledging the autonomy and privacy of the individual have yet to be established. Contemporary design guidelines from HCI are informative. However, these guidelines are based on the idea of a user actively controlling the user interface and so still fall short of addressing issues specific to environmental monitoring, such as threats to autonomy and privacy via the surveillance of real-world activities [30]. The need for appropriate design guidelines that respects individuals' rights is made even more acute by the inevitable convergence of environmental monitoring with other fields such as, for example, applied biometrics, i.e. user authentication via image recognition or biological signals [31]. Issues of network security are also important when designing novel sensing technologies. The lesson learned from the internet infrastructure, where there are daily security concerns/breaches, is that incorporating security into the system from the start is critical. The consequence of a breach in security with a BMS could mean that the water and electricity supply is controlled by a remote attacker, or that a remote attacker could learn private information. It is imperative to protect the infrastructure from synthetic, or natural, attacks. The next section will be addressing a newly developed user interface tool to monitor and interact with the building performance data recorded by the deployed wireless sensor nodes.

6. Mobile tool for occupant interaction

Access from mobile devices and desktop applications enables the stakeholders to interact with the system. Figure 14 is a prototypical view to provide a Building Operator view of building performance data. The view is divided into logical sections for graphically visualizing the data, locations or zones in the site they maintain the sensors and actuators in that zone and date selection. The data presented in the graph represent the gas boiler curve on 1 May 2009. The Maintenance and Monitoring Tools access the DW Web services and the data received are displayed in a cognitive format to the end user.

Figure 15 is a view of a Monitoring Tool to interact with the tenant in a building. The objective is to collect user's preferences through feedback on their current environmental conditions. Based on analysis of the user responses, actuation commands can be initiated. For example, if the user is extremely cold and the system finds that the room heating conditions are below normal, then the service in the WSN is called to turn on the heater in the user's room.

Through our Web services implementation, a middleware was created to integrate various components to improve the provision of building information to end users and with improved data analysis techniques, it supports more accessible and easier understood information to support stakeholders' decision-making processes.

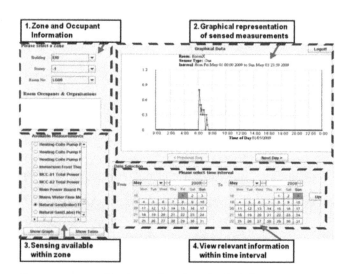

Figure 14. Graphical user interface for building operator.

Figure 15. Thermal comfort feedback from tenant.

7. Conclusions and future work

This paper presents the design, development and deployment of a miniaturized WSN mote based on Zigbee technology for building monitoring, exploring its system control management and technology characters. The stackable technique was adopted in this work to manufacture efficiently the mote layers within small cubic size. The node can implement wide scale of stable sensors/meters data acquisition to provide the needed functions. In addition to the building monitoring, it has the capability to act as an actuator using on-board or interfaced external relay. As an advance step before installing the WSN, an RF characterization study of the building was implemented to establish the position of gateways and repeaters to support reliable communications. An efficient BPM was developed to maintain the data streams from all wireless sensors to the DW and at the same time provide the end user with useful information.

As novel sensor technologies become ubiquitous the convergence of environmental monitoring with individual monitoring becomes a source of worry for building tenants. There is a need to establish ground rules about how building tenants can access the data gathered by the BMS. How to design a system that is safe from outside attack is also imperative.

In the future, a number of ideas can be considered for implementation to tackle the issues of keeping the network secure from any unauthorized parties. One of these standard approaches for keeping sensitive data secret is to encrypt the data with a secret key that only intended receivers possess, hence achieving confidentiality. Data authenticity will be considered as well in the future so that the receiver needs to make sure that the data used in any decision-making process or HCI originate from the correct source. Data authentication prevents unauthorized parties from participating in the network and legitimate nodes should be able to detect messages from unauthorized nodes and reject them. In the two-party communication case, data authentication can be achieved through a purely symmetric mechanism: the sender and the receiver share a secret key to compute a Message Authentication Code (MAC) of all communicated data. When a message with a correct MAC arrives, the receiver knows that it must have been sent by the sender. However, authentication for broadcast messages requires stronger trust assumptions on the network nodes.

Data integrity and freshness are two issues that can be dealt with within the scope of the above.

On the plus side and despite the security risks associated with deploying ubiquitous sensors, the more efficient use of natural resources brought about by environmental monitoring mitigates the effects of climate change. Therefore, the more efficient use of energy and water resources through the wide-scale deployment of smart building sensors is a proactive step in lessening the risks associated with climate change. Even in residential homes, sensors can identify ways for the occupant to use heating and lighting more ecologically thus saving the homeowner money.

The experiments in this paper demonstrate the capabilities and reliability of the proposed mote platform and adopted WSN topology to perform the desired tasks and extend the current BMS sensing parameters.

A number of plans are adapted for future work improvement. This includes extending the number of deployed nodes to cover other zones inside the ERI building. A flat version of the current stackable miniaturized nodes is under development to have more enhanced features like multi-antenna tuning, better external interfacing and USB programming capability. It is planned to use another type of rechargeable batteries like AA that have a bigger capacity with version to significantly increase the node lifetime.

The energy harvesting techniques will be investigated through a number of solutions available in building environment like light, heat and surface vibration to provide efficient alternate power sources for the embedded systems.

Acknowledgements. The authors would like to acknowledge the support of Science Foundation Ireland (SFI) and the funding provided to the National Access Program (NAP) at the Tyndall National Institute, and Enterprise Ireland, all of which have contributed to this work.

References

[1] GUTIÉRREZ, J.A. (2007) On the IEEE Std. 802.15.4 to enable wireless sensor networks in building automation. *Int. J. Wireless Inf. Networks* **14**: 295–301.

[2] ÖSTERLIND, F., PRAMSTEN, E., ROBERTHSON, D., ERIKSSON, J., FINNE, N. and VOIGT, T. (2007) Integration building automation systems and wireless sensor networks. In *Proceedings of IEEE Symposium on Emerging Technologies and Factory Automation*, Patras, Greece, 25–28 September, 1376–1379.

[3] KELLER, M., O'DONNELL, J., KEANE, M., MENZEL, K., BARTON, J., Ó'MATHÚNA, C., KLEPAL, K. *et al.* (2007) Buildwise: building a sustainable future, wireless sensor networks for energy and environment management in buildings. D1 Specification Report University College Cork.

[4] JANG, W.S., HEALY, W.M. and SKIBNIEWSKI, M.J. (2008) Wireless sensor networks as part of a Web-based building environmental monitoring system. *J. Autom. Construction* 17: 729–736.

[5] REINISCH, C., KASTNER, W., NEUGSCHWANDTNER, G. and GRANZER, W. (2007) Wireless Technologies in Home and Building Automation. In *Proceedings of IEEE International Conference on Industrial Informatics (INDIN)*, Vienna, Austria, 23–27 July.

[6] XU, J., YOU, B., CUI, J., MA, J. and LI, X. (2009) Design nodes for embedded and ultra-low power wireless sensor networks. In *Proceedings of SPIE—5th International Symposium on Instrumentation Science and Technology 7133*.

[7] YUAN, J., WANG, Y.S., ZHANG, X.L., ZHAO, L.J. and HUANG, L.J. (2011) Automatic lighting control system for teaching building based on wireless sensor network. *Appl. Mech. Mater.* **43**: 93–96.

[8] GALETZKA, M., HAUFE, J., LINDIG, M., EICHLER, U. and SCHNEIDER, P. (2010) Challenges of simulating robust wireless sensor network applications in building automation environments. In *Proceedings of the 15th IEEE International Conference on Emerging Technologies and Factory Automation*, Bilbao, Spain, 13–16 September.

[9] NGUYEN, N.-H., TRAN, Q.-T., LEGER, J.-M. and VUONG, T.-P. (2010) A real-time control using wireless sensor network for intelligent energy management system in buildings. In *Proceedings of IEEE Worskshop on Environmental, Energy, and Structural Monitoring Systems*, Taranto, Italy, September, 87–92.

[10] ZHENG, T., QIN, Y., GAO, D., DUAN, J. and ZHANG, H. (2010) A practical deployment of intelligent building wireless sensor network for environmental monitoring and air-conditioning control. In *Proceedings of 2nd IEEE International Conference on Network Infrastructure and Digital Content*, Beijing, China, 24–26 September, 624–628.

[11] YUEN HUI CHEE J.A., KOPLOW, M., MARK, M., PLETCHER, N., SEEMAN, M., BURGHARDT, F., STEINGART, D. *et al.* (2008) PicoCube: A 1 cm³ sensor node powered by harvested energy. In *Proceedings of IEEE Conference on Design Automation Conference*, 114–119.

[12] SPINAR, R., DIRK, P., SREENAN, C.J., JAFER, E., O'DONNELL, J., and KEANE, M. (2009) Management with IP-based Wireless Sensor Network. In *Proceedings of European Conference on Wireless Sensor Networks (EWSN09)*, Cork, Ireland, 11–13 February.

[13] MODBUS Industrial Protocol, www.modbus.org.

[14] AMN44122 Passive Infrared (PIR) Motion Sensor, Passive, http://pewa.panasonic.com/.

[15] SHT11 Digital humidity and temperature sensor, http://www.sensirion.com.

[16] LIS302DL, 3-axis smart digital output accelerometer, http://www.st.com.

[17] STUF-300EB Ultrasonic Water Flowmeter, from Shenitech, http://www.shenitech.com.

[18] Surface mount pipes temperature sensor, http://www.buildingtechnologies.siemens.com.

[19] Panasonic PHOTOMOS optically isolated relays, http://pewa.panasonic.com.

[20] BLUMENTHAL, J., GROSSMANN, R., GOLATOWSKI, F. and TIMMERMANN, D. (2007) Weighted centroid localization in Zigbee-based sensor networks. In *Proceedings of IEEE International Symposium on Intelligent Signal Processing (WISP)*, Madrid Spain, 3–7 October, 1–6.

[21] GUINARD, A., MC GIBNEY, A. and PESCH, D. (2009) A wireless sensor network design tool to support building energy management. In *Proceedings of Workshop on Embedded Sensing Systems For Energy-Efficiency In Buildings (BuildSys'09)*.

[22] WANG, Y., STACK, P., TUMWESIGYE, E. and MENZEL, K. (2009) Aspects of interface design for energy management in buildings. In PETRA VON BOTH, and VOLKER KOCH, [eds.] *Proceedings of Forum Bauinformatik, ISBN 978-3-86644-396-9*, University Karlsruhe, Karlsruhe, Germany, 359–370.

[23] AHMED, A., MENZEL, K., PLOENNIGS, J. and CAHILL, B. (2009) Aspects of multi-dimensional building performance data management. In WOFGANG HUHNT, [ed.] "Computation in Civil Engineering", *Proceedings of Computing in Civil Engineering EG-ICE Conference, ISBN 978-3-8322-8287-5*, TU, Berlin, Germany, 9–16.

[24] GÖKÇE, H.U., WANG, Y., GÖKÇE, K.U. and MENZEL, K. (2009) A data-warehouse architecture supporting energy management of buildings. In DIKBAS, A., ERGEN, E. and GIRITLI, H. [eds.] *Proceedings of 26th W78 Conference on Information Technology in Construction, ISBN 978-0-415-56744-2 (hbk), ISBN 978-0-203-85978-0 (eBook)*, ITU, Istanbul, Turkey, 287–292.

[25] STACK, P., MANZOOR, F., CAHILL, B. and MENZEL, K. (2009) A service oriented architecture (SOA) for building performance monitoring. In GÜRLEBECK, K. and KÖNKE, C. [eds.] *International Conference on Applications of Computer Science and Mathematics in Architecture and Civil Engineering*.

[26] JAFER, E., O'FLYNN, B., O'MATHUNA, C. and WANG, W. (2010) Design of miniaturized wireless sensor mote and actuator for building monitoring and control. In *The 17th International Conference on Telecommunications—Signal Processing and Applications Track (ICT 2010)*, Doha, Qatar, 4–7 April, 887–892.

[27] JAFER, E., SPINAR, R., STACK, P., O'MATHUNA, C. and PESCH, D. (2011) Wireless sensor network deployment for building environmental monitoring and control. In *2nd International ICST Conference on Ambient Media and Systems (Ambi-Sys)*, Porto, Portugal, 24–25 March.

[28] LEE, M. (2010) Creating salient summaries of home activity lifelog data. In *Proceedings of 28th CHI Conference, ISBN 978-1-60558-930-5*, Atlanta, GA, USA, 10–15 April, 2919–2922.

[29] LEVENTHAL, L. and BARNES, J. (2007) *Usability Engineering Process Products and Examples* (London: Wiley).

[30] TESSA, D., GAURA, E. and BRUSEY, J. (2009) Wireless sensor networks to enable the passive house-deployment experiences. In BANARGHI, P. *et al.* [eds.] "Smart Sensing and Context", *Proceedings of 4th European Conference on Smart Sensing and Context (EuroSSC) Conference, ISBN 978-3-642-04470-0*, University of Surrey, Guildford, UK, 177–192.

[31] REVETT, K. (2008) *A Remote Access Approach: Behavioral Biometrics* (London: Wiley).

21

Wildfire safety with wireless sensor networks

Andrey Somov

CREATE-NET, via alla Cascata 56/D, 38123 Trento, Italy

Abstract

Nowadays, the Wireless Sensor Network (WSN) paradigm is extensively used for the environmental monitoring including wildfires. Like other disasters, this phenomenon, if not detected early, may have grave consequences, e.g. a significant pecuniary loss, or even lead to human victims. This paper surveys the approaches to early wildfire detection using WSN facilities with a special focus on real deployments and hardware prototypes. In our work we propose not merely a description, but a classification of the fire detection methods which are divided into three groups: *gas sensing*, *sensing of environmental parameters*, and *video monitoring*. Then the methods are comparatively analyzed from the viewpoints of the cost, power consumption, and implementation complexity. Finally, we summarize our vision of the prospects of resolving the wildfire detection problem using WSNs.

Keywords: environmental monitoring, remote sensing, sensor node, wildfire, wireless sensor network

1. Introduction

The use of sensor networks covering large territories to ensure the effective monitoring of such phenomena as wildfires remains to be a problem of particular interest and significance [1]. Wildfire (see Figure 1), being an *uncontrolled* fire, destroys vegetation (forests, bushes, grass), animal species and *spreads quickly* over *large areas*, therefore posing a threat to human health, lives, and livelihoods (see Table 1). Wildfire can be defined as both a natural disaster resultant from the hot weather conditions or, for example, lightning and a man-caused phenomenon.

There are currently a number of approaches to address this problem. However, from a technical point of view, it has not been completely and effectively resolved as yet [2].

Traditionally, the monitoring task was performed by a specially trained team in a lookout tower located at a high point [3]. This method of monitoring is still applicable in some countries, such as the US, Canada, and Australia. Due to unreliability of human observations, some vision techniques have been proposed to monitor small forests from the tower [4].

Satellite imaging, for example, though able to ensure sensing of vast areas, has, as a method, considerable restraints in terms of real-time spatial resolution and sensitivity. In addition, it is associated with the exceptionally high deployment and operational costs, which make it difficult to use in all cases [5, 6].

Another widely applied method of monitoring wildfires or gas leakages is based on getting data on the emissions source. The ultrasensitive devices installed aboard the airplanes, trailers, and other vehicles enable the acquisition of data in cross patterns [2]. This approach requires the availability of operators and maintenance personnel. Its main shortcoming, however, is that spatial and time resolution is limited to a point measurement at the vehicle current location. Apart from that, in the case of using airborne platforms their ultrahigh sensitivity should be provided to detect ground emissions after the gases have propagated to a considerable distance from the sources.

In order to simplify and reduce the costs of fire monitoring, the concept of Wireless Sensor Networks (WSNs) [7] has been recently proposed. Cheap and compact wireless sensor devices deployed over a large territory and operating both jointly and autonomously may be effectively used to detect hazardous gases and monitor wildfires [8].

Email: andrey.somov@create-net.org

Figure 1. Fire in the Everglades National Park, USA (photograph: Flip Schulke).

In the context of wildfire, WSN should satisfy the following requirements:

- **Low cost**. The monitoring of wild lands suggests the availability of many nodes spread over the surveyed area. As there always is a risk of losing the nodes during the fire, the cost of a sensor node should be minimal.

- **WSN lifetime**. Since the WSNs for wildfire monitoring are deployed in difficult-to-access areas, the power source has to support the long-term operation of a sensor node.

- **Early fire detection**. Since the wildfire spreads quickly, the WSN has to fast and accurately detect or predict the fire and send an alarm signal to the firefighters as soon as possible.

The current advances in ICT successfully address the *Low-cost* and *WSN lifetime* requirements. The typical off-the-shelf electronic components available on the market are cheap. The lifetime problem in the WSN domain is addressed from several viewpoints, i.e. duty-cycle adjustment [9], power management [10], WSN synchronization [11], and energy scavenging [12]. The *Early fire*

detection requirement makes us carefully consider the fire phenomena and their progress in time. Figure 2 shows a generic diagram of the fire formation. We shall see later how important this diagram is for the fire detection and WSN development.

As it was mentioned above, the fire starts with overheating, as a result of hot weather conditions or lightning. Due to overheating or smouldering of wood materials, the pyrolysis products, primarily carbon oxide (CO) and hydrogen (H_2), evolve in the atmosphere. Finally, smoke and flame appear.

The present paper aims at surveying the existing approaches to and sensor systems for the wildfire monitoring and detection. We classify these systems into three groups based on the wildfire detection approach used and offer a comparative analysis of the systems.

The paper is organized as follows: Section 2 will briefly introduce the reader to the WSN architecture and then will overview the related environmental applications of WSNs. A survey of existing sensor systems for wildfire detection and their classification are presented in Section 3. Section 4 provides the comparative analysis of these systems. Finally, in Conclusion we summarize our vision of the prospects of resolving the problem.

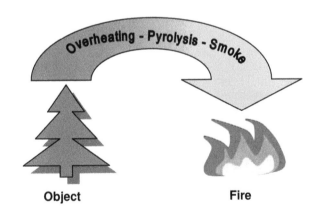

Figure 2. Generic fire formation diagram.

Table 1. Average area of forest annually affected by fire by region, 2005 [35].

Region	Information availability		Area of forest affected by fire (% of forest area)
	Number of countries	% of total forest area	
Africa	21	22.4	5.4
Asia	29	87.9	0.5
Europe	42	99.4	0.1
North and Central America	15	98.9	0.5
Oceania	6	82.5	2.4
South America	5	14.0	0.3
World	118	65.2	0.7

2. Environmental WSN

The history of the environmental monitoring is long enough [13]. The WSNs used for this application are deployed in potentially harsh and remote environments where the inevitable node and communication failures have to be tolerated. It means that apart from the *WSN lifetime* requirement presented in the Introduction, there are two other significant challenges associated with the environmental monitoring application:

- **Radio communication**. Radio chip is generally the most 'hungry' component on board [14]. The energy spent for communication and used to set up *ad hoc* networks and clusters should therefore be minimized. Besides, radio communication in remote areas is characterized by unpredictability in wet and windy conditions.

- **Remote management**. The impossibility of a regular examination of systems in isolated regions makes remote access a mandatory requirement. Bugs are to be fixed, subsystems might need to be shut down, and schedules changed.

A sensor network (see Figure 3) is designed to ensure data transmission from an array of sensors to a user's data repository on a server. They do not necessarily use a simple one-way data stream over a communications network. The system components are able to make decisions as to what data are to be transmitted in order to minimize power use while maximizing the information content.

Proceeding from sensor nodes toward the user the systems, e.g. sink, gate, usually build up the computer power, data storage, and power availability. If a large number of sensor nodes are available for one gate (network coordinator), they are normally arranged as an *ad hoc* set of clusters with representative nodes (sinks) communicating a group's data to the gate.

A WSN consists of wireless nodes which measure physical conditions (i.e. temperature, humidity, pressure) using sensors, digitize the measurements, and store or distribute the measured data over the network. The sensor nodes are connected by a radio channel. A typical wireless sensor node block diagram is presented in Figure 4.

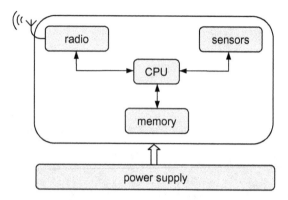

Figure 4. Architecture of a typical wireless sensor node.

A typical wireless sensor node has five main blocks: (i) Central Processing Unit (CPU), (ii) memory chip, (iii) radio transceiver, (iv) one or more sensors, and (v) power supply.

Due to low power consumption and good performance, a Microcontroller Unit (MCU) typically serves as CPU in a sensor node. It controls the data acquisition process, synchronizes the components on board and communication with other nodes. Communication within the network is usually organized using the IEEE 802.15.4 standard [15], while data are transmitted over the ZigBee protocol stack [16]. Among the known data wireless transmission standards, such as Bluetooth, WiFi, etc., ZigBee appears to be the most acceptable in terms of the trade-off between the bandwidth and power consumption. Depending on the application, a sensor node may have various extra hardware components on board. Power supply of a sensor node is implemented as a (rechargeable) battery. However, in order to ensure long autonomous operation, some sensor node platforms also adapt super capacitors [17] and/or energy scavenging technology [18].

The following examples show the WSN application in environmental monitoring.

ZebraNet [19] is a GPS-based WSN to track the animal migration with sensors built in collars on the necks of zebras. The wireless sensor node has the following HW features: a single energy buffer as a lithium-ion battery, a dual-clock microcontroller, separate power supplies for each device to lower energy consumption, and an on-chip memory since the system has to generate detailed logs. The middleware of the system has GPS sensing and radio communication as priority events, and the remaining events could be regarded as a combination of scheduled and unplanned events. In order to reduce power consumption, the developers have carried out three low-level techniques: the timely use of components, the on-the-fly processing, and the dual-clock scheme which helps consume twice less energy using a slow clock. Therefore, two main technical problems tackled in this scenario are lifetime and localization of sensor nodes.

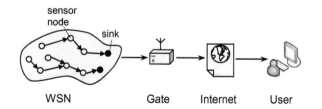

Figure 3. Typical sensor network architecture.

A study of an active volcano is presented in [20]. The WSN consisting of 16 Tmote Sky sensor nodes was deployed on the Reventador volcano in Northern Ecuador. The study required high data rates and high data fidelity. The nodes were equipped with a microphone and a seismometer to collect the seismic and acoustic data on volcanic activity. These sensors were hosted on a separate acquisition board. Two D-type batteries powered each sensor node. The batteries within the entire network were changed twice during its 3-week deployment. The radio link between the sensor network and the observatory point was supported by three modems. Batteries and photovoltaic cells powered the modems.

The glacier dynamics in Iceland is analyzed in [21]. This deployment aims to develop the improved models of the glacier behavior. The network is of a star configuration. The PIC18 MCU-based sensor nodes are supplied by three 3.6 V batteries wired in parallel. The custom design of the antenna allows transmission through the ice. Some of the probes are placed within the ice, while most of them are located 10–30 cm below. The probes collected data once per hour. The gateway is an ARM-based platform. In order to decrease the high sleep current of the CPU, the MSP430 MCU was used which put ARM to the power-off mode and upon request powered it up. For the long-term operation the gateway supports solar and wind energy harvesting. The gateway is also equipped with a GPS antenna for logging the glacier dynamics and a GPRS antenna to transmit the collected data.

A global shift of flora from the grass to tree vegetation is addressed in [22]. Light Under Shrub Thicket for Environmental Research (LUSTER) system deployed under the shrubs in Hog Island, USA, studies the effects of sunlight to evaluate the light dynamics in the context of ecological research. LUSTER's architecture is composed of a sensor node layer, a storage layer, and a delay-tolerant networking layer. The custom design of the sensor node is compatible with Mica2 and MicaZ motes. In fact, two versions of the node were developed. The first one, called 'Medusa', is the eight-channel node with light sensors. 'Solar Dust' has solar cells instead. This approach allows the harvesting of solar energy which is stored either in the super capacitor or in the battery. Voltage generated by solar cells is also assessed in terms of light intensity.

The present paper does not aim at describing all the available environmental applications of WSN. More detailed information on the subject can be found in [23, 24]. However, it should be noted that all these systems have encountered the challenges of being deployed in remote areas with limited access and power resources. The lifetime challenge appears to be a common problem associated with all the environmental WSNs listed above.

In the next section we are focusing our attention on wildfire monitoring using WSN.

3. Wildfire monitoring with WSN

The wildfire detection WSN should detect the fire at an early stage (see diagram in Figure 2). In this section we classify the currently available fire detection approaches into three groups:

(i) **Gas sensing**. This approach helps detect the fire at the pyrolysis phase. Wood pyrolysis is accompanied by the H_2 and CO emission in the atmosphere. For the atmosphere analysis a wireless node with a specific sensor on board is applied.

(ii) **Environmental parameters' sensing**. The sensor nodes measure the ambient temperature, humidity, light, and barometric pressure to detect the fire.

(iii) **Video monitoring**. In this case the WSN is a mix of sensor nodes and video cameras which are used to verify an alarm received from the sensor nodes.

The more detailed analysis of the three approaches is presented below.

3.1. Gas sensing

This approach is based on the periodical sensing of the atmosphere with the purpose of discovering a specific gas which precedes the smoke and inflammation. This strategy helps predict the fire at an early stage. However, the sensor nodes which adapt this technology are power 'hungry' devices and they are quite expensive. Besides, the presented platforms of sensor nodes have not been deployed in real conditions as yet.

Semiconductor sensor. An autonomous wireless sensor system for early fire detection is presented in [17]. This system consists of sensing and power management modules. The sensing module has an on-board semiconductor sensor which can detect the pyrolysis products (H_2, CO) and, therefore, detect the fire before inflammation. The principle of its operation is based on changing the sensor's sensitive layer conductivity in response to gas absorption (the conductivity increases as the gas concentration gets higher). The physical and chemical processes on the sensitive layer's surface are activated by heating, which increases its sensitivity to certain gases.

The power management module is a device which supports the energy scavenging technology. It can accumulate energy both from alternating and direct current based harvesters, though not at the same time. The harvested energy is stored in a battery and/or two super capacitors wired in series. The experimental system deployment shows that it takes around 6 s for the environment sensing and data communication (issuing an alarm signal) to the host node. The alarm signal is being generated upon exceeding the pyrolysis density threshold in the atmosphere. The application of the energy scavenging

Table 2. Power consumption for some off-the-shelf sensors used for fire detection.

Sensor (manufacturer)	Sensing parameter	Power consumption, mW
MS5540B (Intersema)	Barometric pressure	0.012
STDS75 (STM)	Temperature	0.5
HIH-4000-001 (Honeywell)	Humidity	10
EC-5 (Decagon)	Soil moisture	30
SGS-2140, semiconductor (Delta-S)	CO, H_2	215 (pulse heating)
MQ-4 semiconductor (Hanwei Electronics)	Smoke	750
GGS-2000T (UST)	CO, H_2	800 (constant heating)
Spectroscopy sensor [25]	Dangerous gases	800 mA

technology based on photovoltaic harvesting supports the stable operation of the system. However, the power consumption of the semiconductor sensor SGS-2140 (see Table 2) can be a limiting factor for the network deployment in sunless areas due to unavailability of other energy scavenging technologies providing a sufficient amount of energy for the network operation [18].

Spectroscopy sensor. The LaserSPECks sensor node platform [25] is developed for gas sensing applications using quartz-enhanced photoacoustic spectroscopy. This method operates as follows: the sensor checks whether an air sample is optically clear. If not, it means that the sample contains any other contaminant material. Due to specific molecular structures, each contaminant has the exact amount of light absorption associated with it. As compared to semiconductor sensors, the optical approach is much more reliable for detecting a specific gas.

The hardware architecture of LaserSPECks v1.0 includes two MCUs. The first one performs either measurements or communication while the other one calculates the sampled data. However, the sensor consumes up to 800 mA, which is a significant disadvantage of the system. The platform is implemented using off-the-shelf components and is based on the Generalized Network of Miniature Environmental Sensors (GNOMES) 3.0 platform [26]. The LaserSPECks's developers claim that the second version of the platform will consume less power to simplify its deployments in remote areas.

3.2. Sensing of environmental parameters

A WSN which supports multiple sensors for measuring the environmental conditions is the most popular approach to fire detection. This is primarily due to the fact that the temperature, humidity, barometric pressure, and soil moisture sensors have low power consumption (see Table 2). This feature, along with an appropriate duty cycle, may provide an opportunity for the WSN of this kind to operate for several years.

While monitoring almost the same environmental parameters, these WSNs alarm their users following different techniques which are described below.

Calculation of 'forest-fire risk-level' index. The Forest-Fire Surveillance System (FFSS) performs the real-time moni-

toring of the mountains in South Korea [27]. The FFSS uses TIP50CM off-the-shelf motes [28] which integrate the temperature, humidity, and light sensors. The nodes support the TinyOS operating system. The data collected by the sensor nodes are then transmitted to the gateway through the sink nodes. The gateway, connected to Internet, performs the preliminary verification and analysis of the received packets and in the case of their correctness forwards the data to FFSS. Upon receiving the data, a middleware program calculates the *forest-fire risk-level* index defined by the Office of Forestry. If the index corresponds to the fire danger level, the FFSS automatically alarms the user and the system administrator.

Threshold rule. A WSN system for the early forest fire detection with special focus on low power consumption is proposed in [29]. The designed system measures different ambient parameters at different heights of the trees. To ensure the early fire detection, the environmental temperature, relative humidity, barometric pressure, light intensity, smoke, and soil moisture are measured and processed by the sensor node. All the sensors except for the smoke one are off-the-shelf components. The fire alarm process starts with the detection of smoke. Other sensors on the node keep monitoring the environment. As soon as the risk threshold for each of the sensors is exceeded, the node generates a warning message.

Each custom sensor node is powered by two AA batteries. The authors claim at least 1 year of the system operation, which is achieved by the energy-efficient hardware, data acquisition, signal processing, and communication. This system has not been deployed in real conditions as yet. It is supposed, however, that its user will be able to remotely update the status of the ambient conditions. Besides, with the GSM/GPRS technology on a network coordinator, the response can be received by mobile communications.

Another example of using the 'threshold rule' to warn the user is the 'FireBug' WSN described in [1]. The WSN based on Mica2 motes with the independently mounted MTS420CA sensor board was deployed in California, USA. The sensor board hosts the temperature, relative humidity, barometric pressure, acceleration, light intensity, and GPS location sensors. The light intensity and acceleration sensors were not used during the field testing. The GPS unit was only needed for an accurate location of the mote. Once it has been defined, the GPS unit is turned off. The main purpose of this WSN is to investigate the system's ability to detect the fire and the robustness of the hardware in wildfire conditions. The WSN managed to record the flame passage. The nodes within this deployment were scorched and the fire was put out at the final stage. However, before being destroyed, the nodes reported the temperature increase and the barometric pressure and humidity decrease as the flame front advanced.

The forest fires on the Eastern hills in Bogota, Columbia, happen frequently. In order to address this problem, the forest fire early detection system using WSN is proposed in [30]. The WSN is deployed using off-the-shelf devices from Crossbow: MDA300 acquisition board, Mica2 mote, MIB520 gateway. The MoteView software helps in the WSN configuration and capturing of temperature and humidity. Besides, the software allows a user to define the thresholds for both environmental parameters. The system, however, generates an alarm signal after the temperature threshold has been exceeded.

A WSN for wildfire monitoring with the capability of adjusting the sensing parameters in accordance with the weather conditions is presented in [31]. Similar to the sensor nodes presented in [1] and [30], this WSN adopts off-the-shelf sensor node and acquisition sensor board (Mica2 and MTS400, respectively). The acquisition board hosts typical sensors, i.e. temperature, relative humidity, light intensity, barometric pressure, acceleration, and GPS location. The collected data are forwarded from the sensor node to the base station through the routing nodes. The base station processes the data and stores them in the database connected to the web server. The client's PC queries the web server and provides the user with the latest information and location on the captured data. In order to ensure the long-term operation of the WSN, the nodes perform sensing in the sunny and dry weather conditions (when the fire probability is higher) with a high duty cycle. On the contrary, at night time or when raining the nodes collect the data with a low duty cycle. If the fire is detected by one of the nodes, the adjacent nodes start sensing the environment with the increased duty cycle.

3.3. Video monitoring

Apart from the sensor nodes with typical sensors for monitoring the environmental conditions, a WSN may include some video cameras which ensure the exact location of the (potential) fire.

The fires destroy large areas of wild lands in Spain. To ensure the fire early detection and verification, the WSN deployment which contains multi-sensor nodes and video cameras is proposed in [32]. The authors use Linksys WRT54GL router as a sensor node supporting the IEEE 802.11 b/g wireless interface. The fire infrared and smoke detectors are connected through serial ports. These detectors are used for the environment sensing and fire alarming. In fact, an alarm message is only generated when both sensors have values higher than a threshold. Upon receiving an alarm message, the central server selects the appropriate video camera and transmits video information to the firefighters in order to verify the alarm signal. In order to support the WSN long-term operation, the energy scavenging technology is applied. A large number of sunny days in Spain allow using the photovoltaic cells. The preliminary calculations show that the photovoltaic system can support the stable operation of the WSN without any difficulties.

The WSN developed in [33] deals with the monitoring of weather conditions, e.g. temperature, humidity, thermal belts, and temperature inversions, in the wildland fire environments. This deployment consists of three WSNs and two video cameras. The cameras were set up at Hells Half Acre and Spot Mountain. The WSNs were set up at Hells Half Acre (six nodes), Kit Carson (five nodes), and Spot Mountain (two nodes) in the USA. The deployment is a multi-tiered portable system called 'FireWxNet' which comprises two parts. The aim of the first part is to bring communications to the remote areas where sensing will be performed. The second part is a multi-hop WSN which includes two video cameras with an autonomous power source. The sensor nodes in the network are made of a modified off-the-shelf Mica2 platform [34]. Each node is equipped with a temperature sensor, an accurate relative humidity sensor, and an anemometer for the wind direction and speed measurement. In the daytime the WSN operates using solar energy, at night it uses batteries. The main purpose of this system, however, is studying the fire behavior to give the firefighting community the opportunity of measuring and viewing the fire and weather conditions easily and safely.

4. Comparative analysis

Table 3 summarizes the available approaches to wildfire monitoring and sensor node platforms used for this application. However, only three out of nine WSNs were deployed in real conditions.

Gas sensing approach seems the most reliable and accurate since it predicts the fire before inflammation by detecting the pyrolysis products in the atmosphere. However, each platform hosts the sensors which consume too much power: semiconductor and spectroscopy ones. Besides, the cost of the semiconductor sensor used in [17] is of the order of $30 (US); LaserSPECks node costs around $2k (US). The developers of LaserSPECks node claim that the price per node can be less than $100 (US) with suitable advances in laser manufacturing and increase in the application demand. The developers of the system based on the semiconductor sensor are intending to

Table 3. WSN platforms for wildfire monitoring.

	System	Application	Sensor node platform	Real deployment	Advantages	Drawbacks
Gas sensing	Autonomous system for early fire detection [17]	Pyrolysis detection	Custom node Sensor: semiconductor (CO, H_2)	No (only test deployment)	- the system uses PV energy - fire prediction before inflammation	- high price per sensor
	LaserSPECks [25]	Dangerous gas detection	GNOMES platform	No	- accurate and early fire prediction	- high power consumption
Sensing of environmental parameters	FFSS [27]	Forest fire monitoring in South Korea	TIP50CM mote from Maxfor	No	- calculates the forest-fire risk-level index for alarming	N/A
	WSN for early forest fire detection [29]	Forest fire detection	Custom node Sensors: temperature, humidity, barometric pressure, light intensity, smoke, soil moisture	No	- monitors environmental parameters at free heights - low power consumption	N/A
	FireBug [1]	Wildfire monitoring in California, USA	Mica2 mote and MTS420CA sensor board Sensors: temperature, relative humidity, barometric pressure	Yes	- the research community gained the experience in real deployment	- did not really help the firefighters
	System for early forest fire detection [30]	Fire monitoring at the Eastern hills in Bogota, Columbia	Mica2 mote and MDA300 sensor board Sensors: temperature, humidity	No	- the system is based on hardware and software from a single vendor	- alarming when the temperature threshold is exceeded
	WSN for wildfire monitoring [31]	Wildfire monitoring	Mica2 mote and MDA400 sensor board Sensors: temperature, humidity, barometric pressure, light intensity	No	- the system adjusts sensing duty cycle in accordance with the weather conditions	N/A

(continued on next page)

Table 3. (Continued).

	System	Application	Sensor node platform	Real deployment	Advantages	Drawbacks
Video monitoring	WSN for rural and forest fire detection and verification [32]	Rural and forest fire detection and verification	Linksys WRT54GL router and custom sensor board. Sensors: infrared, smoke, video cameras	Yes	– the system uses PV energy – support of video cameras – verification of alarm	– high power consumption
	FireWxNet [33]	Fire behavior investigation and weather monitoring in Hells Half Acre, Kit Carson, Spot Mountain, USA	Mica2 mote and MTS101 sensor board	Yes	– the system uses PV energy – support of video cameras – the system monitors specific environmental conditions: thermal belts and temperature inversions	– high power consumption

deploy the network in real conditions by applying the energy scavenging technology and thanks to lower price in comparison with the LaserSPECks platform. In fact, the high price and power consumption can be the limiting factors for the LaserSPECks network experimentation in the field.

Among the three approaches analyzed in the present work the technique based on sensing the environmental parameters appears to be the simplest, cheapest, and most energy efficient. The sensor nodes currently available on the market [34] either have some typical (temperature, humidity) sensors on board or can easily expand their sensing capabilities by using a sensor acquisition board [34]. Besides, these sensors, except for the smoke one, consume a negligible amount of power (see Table 1), which allows the nodes to operate for more than 1 year [29]. However, this approach can detect (not predict like gas sensing platforms) the fire at an early stage, i.e. when the direct flame has already appeared. Since the wildfire spreads quickly, the WSN of this kind cannot really help to put out the fire [1], but can be useful for research purposes to analyze the fire behavior and environment during the fire.

Video monitoring seems to be a trade-off between the two previous approaches. It is a power 'hungry' approach, but the application of the energy scavenging technology (PV energy) can help to resolve this problem. Smoke and infrared sensors are used for fire alarming [32], while video cameras are to verify the alarm signal. The video facilities, however, can be used for time-to-time monitoring [33]. It should also be noted that one camera can cooperate with several sensor nodes.

The experience gained during the WSN deployment in real conditions [1, 32, 33] shows that the user must be alarmed very quickly, i.e. potential fire should be detected at an early stage. The network topology therefore should be simple and reliable enough so as not to add any delays in the alarm signal propagation. The network topologies proposed in [27] and [31], for example, do not meet this requirement having two 'mediator' tiers between the sensor node and the user.

Figure 5 presents a typical network communication scheme for the wildfire monitoring applications.

The sensor nodes usually support IEEE 802.15.4 standard and transmit data using ZigBee protocol stack (see Section 2). It is obvious that the network coordinator should support two communication technologies (which do not interfere with each other): one to communicate with the nodes and the other one to forward data from the nodes to the user. The system described in [29] proposes a combination of ZigBee and GSM/GPRS communications. These communication facilities do not interfere and allow the receiving of an alarm by mobile communication.

In our vision the prospects of using WSN for wildfire monitoring are in adopting useful features of all applicable

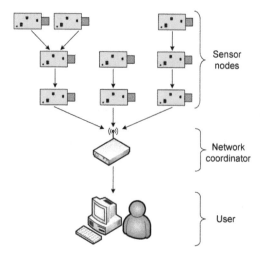

Figure 5. WSN communication scheme for wildfire monitoring application.

approaches, i.e. early fire formation prediction (*gas sensing*), low cost and fast prototyping of the WSN (*sensing of environmental parameters*), and fire verification (*video monitoring*). However, from the viewpoint of power consumption such an integration remains to be problematic.

4.1. Comparison of deployed WSNs

We start the comparison of deployed WSNs by defining their objectives which, in fact, are different. FireBug [1] (classified as *sensing of environmental parameters*) is mainly focused on engineering aspects of deployment and deployed by the specialists with technical background. In contrast, FireWxNet [33] and WSN for rural and forest fire detection [32] (classified as *video monitoring*) are deployed by the specialists with different research background. It should be noted, however, that *video monitoring* networks have different objectives. FireWxNet is focused on fire behavior investigation and weather monitoring. WSN for rural fire detection aims at fire detection and verification.

The networks we compare are designed using off-the-shelf sensor nodes and base stations/routers. Due to the application of video cameras both *video monitoring* WSNs are characterized by high power consumption. In order to address the problem of long-term operation, both networks apply the energy scavenging technology. FireBug is powered by the batteries only.

The communication scheme (from the sensors to the user) in FireBug is organized with the following principles. The data from motes (operate on 433 MHz frequency) are first collected by base station and then forwarded to the user through a server. This WSN communication scheme is both simple and reliable.

Due to its deployment features, FireWxNet uses more complicated data delivery to the user. A number of sensor

nodes are wirelessly connected to the base station (IEEE802.11) through the sensor gate. The sensor gate is the sensor node connected to the base station using USB cable. The video camera can also be connected to the base station by wired means. The base stations with the directional antennas form the network *backhaul* tier. A satellite dish (connected to one of the base stations by wires) located in the researchers' camp provides the backhaul with the Internet access. Upon receiving an alert message a network operator in the camp can easily forward it to a special rescue service.

WSN for rural fire detection uses similar to FireBug's communication scheme: the sensor nodes and video cameras are connected to the access points (IEEE802.11g) which forward the data to the user. However, the video cameras are used for the verification of alert message from the sensor node. As soon as the possibility of fire is detected by the sensors, the network operator turns on the respective video camera which covers this 'alert' zone and checks if the received alert is true.

The WSN for rural fire detection seems the most successful system out of totally three deployments presented in this survey. This network provides secure fire monitoring with the *fire verification* option which can help to avoid false detections. Besides, the rare usage of the video cameras (for verification purposes) as well as photovoltaic system for the battery replenishment provides potentially long lifetime cycle for the system.

5. Conclusion

In this paper we have provided a survey on the problem of the early wildfire detection overviewing a number of approaches with the application of WSN.

The existing methods are surveyed and classified into three groups: *gas sensing*, *sensing of environmental parameters*, and *video monitoring*. The analysis of the classification has been aimed at demonstrating the advantages and drawbacks of each of the groups. The *gas sensing* approach can predict the fire at the stage of pyrolysis emission in the atmosphere. However, due to the high cost and power consumption of these sensor nodes, the WSN deployment on large territories seems unaffordable. The low cost and power consumption along with the simple implementation of the nodes supporting the approach classified as *sensing of environmental parameters* make the WSN application attractive. Unfortunately, this approach is generally applicable at the open fire stage, which cannot be really helpful for putting out the fire. *Video monitoring* is useful for the verification of fire detected by conventional temperature and humidity sensors. Video cameras are power 'hungry' devices and without a proper energy scavenging technology application they cannot be used for continuous monitoring purposes.

Summing up we may point out that the *gas sensing* and *video monitoring* approaches provide the really early fire detection capability. The major restraints for their extensive use remain high power consumption and implementation costs.

Besides, it should be mentioned that only three out of nine WSN platforms presented in this work have been deployed in real conditions. It testifies to the fact that the use of WSNs for wildfire monitoring is still at its initial phase. For a thorough analysis and evaluation of the WSN application, more deployments are required.

Acknowledgement. The author would like to acknowledge Dr Yuliya Verkhovskaya (VNIIEM, Russia) for valuable comments.

References

[1] DOOLIN, D.M. and SITAR, N. (2005) Wireless sensors for wildfire monitoring. In *Proceedings of Conference on Sensors and Smart Structures Technologies for Civil, Mechanical, and Aerospace Systems*, San Diego, CA, USA, 7–10 March 2005, 477–484.

[2] VOLOKITINA, A., SOFRONOV, M. and SOFRONOVA, T. (2008) Topical scientific and practical issues of wildland fire problem. *Mitig. Adapt. Strateg. Glob. Chang.* 13(7): 661–674.

[3] FLEMING, J. and ROBERTSON, R.G. (2003) The Osborne firefinder. In *Fire Management TechTips*, October 2003, 1–2.

[4] DEN BREEJEN, E., BREUERS, M., CREMER, F., KEMP, R., ROOS, M., SCHUTTE, K. and DE VRIES, J.S. (1998) Autonomous forest fire detection. In *Proceedings of the Third International Conference on Forest Fire Research and the Fourteenth Conference on Fire and Forest Meteorology*, Luso, Portugal, 16–20 November 1998, 2003–2012.

[5] LEBLON, B. (2005) Monitoring forest fire danger with remote sensing. *Nat. Hazards* 35(3): 343–359.

[6] BURGAN, R., KLAVER, R. and KLAVER, J. (1998) Fuel models and fire potential from satellite and surface observations. *Int. J. Wildland Fire* 8(3): 159–170.

[7] CHONG, C.Y. and KUMAR, S.P. (2003) Sensor networks: evolution, opportunities, and challenges. In *Proceedings of IEEE* 91(8): 1247–1256.

[8] ANTOINE-SANTONI, T., SANTUCCI, J.F., DE GENTILI, E. and COSTA, B. (2008) Wildfire impact on deterministic deployment of a wireless sensor network by a discrete event simulation. In *Proceedings of the Fourteenth Mediterranean Electrotechnical Conference*, Ajaccio, France, 5–7 May 2008, 204–209.

[9] MOSER, C., THIELE, L., BRUNELLI, D. and BENINI, L. (2007) Adaptive power management in energy harvesting systems. In *Proceedings of Design, Automation and Test in Europe Conference and Exhibition*, Nice, France, 16–20 April, 1–6.

[10] JIANG, X., TANEJA, J., ORTIZ, J., TAVAKOLI, A., DUTTA, P., JEONG, J., CULLER, D. *et al.* (2007) An architecture for energy management in wireless sensor networks. *ACM Sigbed Rev.* 4(3): 31–36.

[11] MACII, D., AGEEV, A. and SOMOV, A. (2009) Power consumption reduction in wireless sensor networks through optimal synchronization. In *Proceedings of Instrumentation and Measurement Technology Conference (I2MTC'09)*, Singapore, 5–7 May 2009, 1346–1351.

[12] JIANG, X., POLASTRE, J. and CULLER, D. (2005) Perpetual environmentally powered sensor networks. In *Proceedings of the Fourth International Symposium on Information Processing in Sensor Networks (IPSN'05)*, Los Angeles, CA, USA, 25–27 April, 463–468.

[13] MARTINEZ, K., HART, J.K. and ONG, R. (2004) Environmental sensor networks. *IEEE Comput.* 37(8): 50–56.

[14] CHAO, C.M. and CHANG, Y.C. (2007) A power-efficient timing synchronization protocol for wireless sensor networks. *J. Inf. Sci. Eng.* 23(4): 985–997.

[15] IEEE Standards Association (2011), http://standards.ieee.org/about/get/802/802.15.html.

[16] ZigBee specification (2011), www.zigbee.org/Products/DownloadZigBeeTechnicalDocuments.aspx.

[17] SOMOV, A., SPIRJAKIN, D., IVANOV, M., KHROMUSHIN, I., PASSERONE, R., BARANOV, A. and SAVKIN, A. (2010) Combustible gases and early fire detection: an autonomous system for wireless sensor networks. In *Proceedings of the First International Conference on Energy-Efficient Computing and Networking (e-Energy'10)*, Passau, Germany, 13–15 April 2010, 85–93.

[18] ROUNDY, S., WRIGHT, P.K. and RABAEY, J.M. (2004) *Energy Scavenging for Wireless Sensor Networks with Special Focus on Vibrations* (USA: Kluwer Academic Publishers).

[19] ZHANG, P., SADLER, C.M., LYON, S.A. and MARTONOSI, M. (2004) Hardware design experience in zebranet. In *Proceedings of the Second International Conference on Embedded Networked Sensor Systems (SenSys'04)*, Baltimore, Maryland, USA, 3–5 November 2004, 227–238.

[20] WERNER-ALLEN, G., LORINCZ, K., WELSH, M., MARCILLO, O., JOHNSON, J., RUIZ, M. and LEES, J. (2006) Deploying a wireless sensor network on an active volcano. *IEEE Internet Comput.* 10(2): 18–25.

[21] MARTINEZ, K., HART, J.K. and ONG, R. (2009) Deploying a wireless sensor network in Iceland. In *Proceedings of the Third International Conference on Geo Sensor Networks (GSN'09)*, Oxford, UK, 13–14 July 2009, 131–137.

[22] SELAVO, L., WOOD, A., CAO, Q., SOOKOOR, T., LIU, H., SRINIVASAN, A., WU, Y. *et al.* (2007) LUSTER: Wireless sensor network for environmental research. In *Proceedings of the Fifth Conference on Embedded Networked Sensor Systems (SenSys'07)*, Sydney, Australia, 6–9 November 2007, 103–116.

[23] MAINWARING, A., POLASTRE, J., SZEWCZYK, R., CULLER, D. and ANDERSON, J. (2002) Wireless sensor networks for habitat monitoring. In *proceedings of the First International Workshop on Wireless Sensor Networks and Applications (WSNA'02)*, Atlanta, GA, USA, 28 September 2002, 88–97.

[24] TOLLE, G., POLASTRE, J., SZEWCZYK, R., CULLER, D., TURNER, N., TU, K., BURGESS, S. *et al.* (2005) A macroscope in the redwoods. In *Proceedings of the Third Conference on Embedded Networked Sensor Systems (SenSys'05)*, San Diego, CA, USA, 2–4 November 2005, 51–63.

[25] HO, S., KOUSHANFAR, F., KOSTEREV, A. and TITTEL, F. (2007) LaserSPECks: laser spectroscopic trace-gas sensor

networks—sensor integration and application. In *Proceedings of Sixth International Symposium on Information Processing in Sensor Networks (IPSN'07)*, Cambridge, MA, USA, 25–27 April 2007, 226–235.

[26] WELSH, E., FISH, W. and FRANTZ, J. (2003) GNOMES: a testbed for low-power heterogeneous wireless sensor networks. In *Proceedings of International Symposium on Circuits and Systems (ISCAS'03)*, Bangkok, Thailand, 25–28 May 2003, 836–839.

[27] SON, B., HER, Y.-S. and KIM, J.-G. (2006) A design and implementation of forest-fires surveillance system based on wireless sensor networks for South Korea mountains. *Int. J. Comput. Sci. Netw. Secur.* 6(9): 124–130.

[28] TIP50CM mote, MAXFOR Technology (2011), www.maxfor.co.kr.

[29] BAYO, A., ANTOLIN, D., MEDRANO, N., CALVO, B. and CELMA, S. (2010) Development of a wireless sensor network system for early forest fire detection. In *Proceedings of European Workshop on Smart Objects: Systems, Technologies and Applications (RFID SysTech'10)*, Ciudad, Spain, 15–16 June 2010, 1–7.

[30] LOZANO, C. and RODRIGUEZ, O. (2011) Design of forest fire early detection system using wireless sensor networks. *J. Electron. Electr. Eng.* 3(2): 402–405.

[31] LI, Y., WANG, Z. and SONG, Y. (2006) Wireless sensor network design for wildfire monitoring. In *Proceedings of the Sixth World Congress on Intelligent Control and Automation*, Dalian, China, 21–23 June 2006, 109–113.

[32] LLORET, J., GARCIA, M., BRI, D. and SENDRA, S. (2009) A wireless sensor network deployment for rural and forest detection and verification. *Sensors* 9(11): 8722–8747.

[33] HARTUNG, C., HAN, R., SAIELSTAD, C. and HOLBROOK, S. (2006) FireWxNet: A multi-tiered portable wireless system for monitoring weather conditions in wildland fire environments. In *Proceedings of the Fourth International Conference on Mobile Systems, Applications and services (MobiSys'06)*, Uppsala, Sweden, 19–22 June 2006, 28–41.

[34] Crossbow Technology (2011), www.xbow.com.

[35] Food and Agriculture Organization of the United Nations (2010) Global forest resources assessment 2010. *FAO Forestry Paper 163*.

22

Managing Data in Help4Mood

Maria K. Wolters[1,*], Juan Martínez-Miranda[2], Soraya Estevez[3], Helen F. Hastie[4], Colin Matheson[1]

[1]School of Informatics, 10 Crichton Street, Edinburgh EH8 9aB, University of Edinburgh Edinburgh, UK
[2]IBIME, Universitat Politécnica de Valencia, Valencia, Spain
[3]Fundaciò i2CAT, Barcelona, Spain
[4]School of Mathematical and Computer Sciences, Heriot-Watt University, Edinburgh, UK

Abstract

Help4Mood is a system that supports the treatment of people with depression in the community. It collects rich cognitive, psychomotor, and motor data through a Personal Monitoring System and a Virtual Agent, which is then analysed by a Decision Support System; analysis results are fed back to patients and their treating clinicians. In this paper, we describe how the complex data is managed and discuss ethical issues. Data is stored in functional units that correspond to treatment relevant entities. Custom XML DTDs are defined for each unit, which are used to exchange information between system components. As far as possible, observations and findings are coded using SNOMED CT to ensure interoperability with other applications such as Electronic Health Records.

Keywords: XML, depression, SNOMED CT, decision support

1. Help4Mood—Supporting People with Depression

Depression is the main cause of disability worldwide [1]. It is characterised by a persistent and intense change of mood which affects behaviour, cognition, and physiology. Two types of depression can be distinguished, a melancholic form where patients' movements are significantly slowed down, and a non-melancholic form, where movements are not affected or agitated. Slowed movements are reflected in both gross motor function, such as gait, and fine motor function, such as movement initiation and reaction times [2, 3]. They also contribute to slowed speech and a flat intonation [4, 5]. Sleep duration can be either severely reduced (insomnia) or significantly increased (hypersomnia).

At the moment, recovery is monitored infrequently through self-reported patient questionnaires that require the person with depression to remember their symptoms over a period of time that can be as long as two weeks (e.g., PHQ-9 [6]). Those self-reports can be unreliable, especially if the patient is not keeping regular notes or a diary.

Help4Mood enables patients to monitor selected cognitive, behavioural, and physiological aspects of their depression. Patients interact with the system every day to share how they are feeling and complete a few tasks that are informed by cognitive behaviour therapy, such as tracking and challenging negative thoughts. Help4Mood also collects activity and sleep data through a personal monitoring system.

Once every 1–2 weeks, Help4Mood generates a summary of the data that patients will then discuss with the clinician who treats them. This can be a family physician, a psychologist, a psychiatrist, or another health professional with mental health training. The summary includes overall mood, sleep and activity trends, and a list of frequent intrusive negative thoughts, which can be treated using cognitive behaviour therapy. The data generated by Help4Mood will also be useful for reviewing the effectiveness of medication. This design is based on extensive consultation with clinicians and patients in Spain, Romania, and the UK [7]

*Corresponding author. Email: maria.wolters@ed.ac.uk

In this paper, we describe our approach to data management in Help4Mood. We focus on the high-level data structures that form the basis for communicating with clinicians, patients, and other stakeholders.

In Section 2, we give an overview of the Help4Mood system. The basic high-level Help4Mood data structures are described in Section 3. Ethical issues are discussed in Section 4, and provisions for interoperability with Electronic Health Records are outlined in Section 5. Future work plans are summarised in Section 6.

2. Overview of Help4Mood

Help4Mood consists of a *Personal Monitoring System*, a *Virtual agent*, and a *Decision Support System*. Help4Mood is structured around patients' sessions with the Virtual Agent. Ideally, patients interact with their Virtual Agent daily. The Virtual Agent asks questions, sets tasks, and summarises the results of each session. Sessions can include summaries of activity and sleep patterns. Some of these tasks will yield cognitive data, such as relevant negative automatic thoughts, others are designed to capture relevant neuropsychomotor symptoms of depression.

The sensors of the *Personal Monitoring System* assess sleep and activity patterns using sleep sensors and a wrist actigraph. While sleep data is collected every night, the wrist actigraph will only be worn for 72 hours at a time. Sessions with the Virtual Agent can include summaries of activity and sleep patterns.

The *Decision Support System* plans and controls sessions with the Virtual Agent and converts data about the patient's sleep, motor, speech, and other psychomotor patterns into graphical, textual, and conceptual summaries that can be communicated to clinicians, patients, and electronic health records. As yet, there are very few rules for adjusting medications and interpreting data that could be implemented in a traditional decision support framework [7, 8]. Therefore, the decision support system focuses on trend analysis and planning the interactions between Help4Mood and the patient.

Figure 1 shows the internal structure of Help4Mood. On the left of the graph, we see the sensing / monitoring components, the Virtual Agent and the Monitoring System. The (Personal) Monitoring System includes the sensors and wireless communication infrastructure.

The structure of the Virtual Agent is more complex. The Virtual Agent consists of a Graphical User Interface (GUI) and a talking head (the "Agent"). Verbal messages are generated by the Natural Language Generation (NLG) component. These messages are displayed by the GUI and spoken by the Agent. Spoken messages are passed to a text-to-speech synthesis engine (TTS) that creates speech with annotations that help synchronise the Virtual Agent's head and facial movements. The

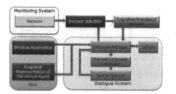

Figure 1. System Structure

Dialogue System controls the flow of messages, using scripts to ensure the correct wording where clinically relevant.

Data collected via the Virtual Agent and the Personal Monitoring System is processed by the Knowledge Engine. The Knowledge Engine creates summary reports and detects relevant trends about the patient's mood and behaviour. This information is passed on to the Cognitive/Emotional Model. This component is crucial for planning the interaction between Virtual Agent and user; it passes session plans and information about the intended affective behaviour of the agent on to the Dialogue System, which performs the low-level control.

Communication between the system's components is implemented using ICE (Internet Communication Engine) as middleware [9]. ICE, which is covered by the GNU public license, has several key advantages. It is independent of programming language and operating system, which is important on a project where components are developed by partners with different IT infrastructures. Since clients do not need to be aware of how the server implements their objects, the server implementation can be changed even after clients have been deployed. Communications between client and server are protected by using SSL (Secure Socket Layer). Last, but not least, ICE produces little overhead.

3. Core Data Structures

All data structures are described using XML. We chose this solution over a relational database, because Help4Mood has a highly modular architecture, and almost all inter- and intra-module communication is based on the exchange of XML messages. Elements are extensively cross-indexed to ensure flexible access to data. Individual components such as the Decision Support System may store data in an internal data base.

The XML elements that are used to capture relevant data are summarised in Table 1. They fall into four main categories, high-level tracking of patient and Help4Mood use, storing monitoring results, managing the interaction between patient and Virtual Agent, and storing the data collected during the interaction. Each set of elements is briefly explained below.

Table 1. Basic Elements of the Help4Mood data structure. Each one is defined using XML.

Element	Description
High-Level Tracking of Patient and Help4Mood Usage	
User Model	high-level summary of information about the patient
Adherence	adherence of patient to Help4Mood; can refer to sessions, tasks, and monitoring
Report	summary report for clinician
Managing the Results of Monitoring	
Monitor. Data	set of data points
Measure	high-level measure computed from monitoring data
Score	score on stand. questionnaire
Managing the Interaction with the Virtual Agent	
Session	content and results of a session with the Virtual Agent
Event	event triggered by the Decision Support System during a session
Task	task that is performed by the patient during a specific session
Emotion	emotion used by Virtual Agent during interaction with patient
Storing Information Collected During Interaction	
Diary	information on diary entries
Speech	changes in speech
Neg. Thought	frequency of negative automatic thoughts
Self-Report	results of self-report questions
Exercise	completion of exercise

3.1. High Level Tracking

The three high-level tracking elements in Table 1 summarise relevant information about the patient and system usage and store the regular reports generated by the system. Patient information, which is stored in the user model, includes basic demographics (occupation, gender, age) as well as current depression scores. The user model also includes information about the background photo chosen by the user, the avatar the user has chosen, and their preferred interaction style and personality (friendly or formal). As for reports, only official reports that are sent to the clinicians and can be discussed in patient/clinician meetings are stored. The feedback given to the patient at the end of each session is not saved, because it can be reconstructed easily.

3.2. Monitoring

The next two elements in Table 1 are used to describe high-level monitoring data. While the measure element covers specific analysis results, the monitoringdata element contains the measures obtained during a session.

The information contained in these elements is passed onto the Decision Support System, which processes them further. Sensor data are timestamped. Time stamp information is not just used to interpret the data, it is also used to prompt the patient to start a new round of data collection. Specific dialogues are encoded in the VA that tell patients when to put on the actigraph and when to take it off for data collection.

3.3. Managing the Interaction with the Virtual Agent

Sessions typically start with a daily mood check, followed by a diary task. Patients reflect on a specific prompt and write their thoughts into a text field. These entries are stored, but not analysed. Next, patients document negative thoughts relating to this entry, and Help4Mood provides guidance for challenging them. Other activities, such as speech tasks, relaxation exercises, or self-report questions, follow. Finally, the Virtual Agent bids the patient goodbye.

Interactive sessions in Help4Mood need to satisfy four constraints:

Minimum Requirements: Patients should complete a *daily mood check*, which is a validated four-item questionnaire, the CES-VAS-VA [10]. Every fortnight, patients also fill in a formal screening questionnaire, the PHQ-9 [6].

Sustaining Interest: Session structure should be varied, with some different tasks each time.

Adapting To Stamina: Patient state can vary greatly; on some days, all patients can do is a brief mood check, on other days, they are able to complete a session with four tasks.

Ensuring Sufficient Data: Subjective data about the patient such as self-reports and additional psychomotor data such as speech should be collected at least twice a week.

The Decision Support System controls the Virtual Agent's interaction with the user through events. Events are triggered when their preconditions are fulfilled. They are implemented as interaction tasks. Each task is associated with an emotion that controls the affective behaviour of the Virtual Agent [11] (c.f. Table 1).

The sequence of events and task/emotion pairs that occurred during a session and the data that was generated during a session is stored in a session element for easy reference. This data is used by the Decision Support System to plan further sessions and ensure regular coverage of relevant data.

Table 2 shows the structure of an event element. Each event is linked to a session, a patient, and a specific time within the session. A range of auxiliary elements

Table 2. The *Event* class

Attribute	Value	Description
⟨Type⟩	{1,2,3,4}	Event type as classified by data source
⟨Session⟩	timestamp	Session ID
⟨Patient⟩	alphanumerical code	Patient ID
⟨Description⟩	descriptor	Formal description of the event
⟨Generated⟩	timestamp	time at which the event was generated
⟨Preconditions⟩	list of conditions	pre-conditions that trigger the event.
⟨Postconditions⟩	list of conditions	findings or observable entities

is used to specify events. Descriptors link Events to a formal code that describes the underlying procedure and can be exported to external systems. Preconditions and postconditions are described using `condition` elements that consist of ⟨Property, Operator, Value⟩-tuples. Preconditions trigger events, postconditions describe the outcomes of an event.

During most tasks, the system collects rich information about the patient's cognition and current psychomotor functioning. Relevant high-level data is encoded in the `diary`, `speech`, `selfreport` and `negative thought` elements.

4. Privacy, Security, and Ethical Considerations

The data that Help4Mood logs about a person's activity and mood is private and confidential. It is therefore imperative that it is stored securely. Since we do not assume that Help4Mood's users have a broadband internet connection, all data is initially stored in a single encrypted partition on a dedicated laptop, which can only be used to run the Help4Mood application. Raw data can only be accessed by the clinicians and technical support personnel that give out the Help4Mood kit, which consists of sensors and laptop.

The baseline solution for transmitting data to the relevant health care professionals is to send an encoded PDF with a summary of relevant trends via e-mail. This is the most portable solution, and it does not require the clinician-side Electronic Health Record / Electronic Medical Record system to support standards such as HL7. For systems that do support HL7, the PDF will be embedded in a HL7 CDA record.

The ethical considerations around the data that is collected can be summarised by one question: Will the system be able to pick up indications of suicide or self-harm, and if yes, what should the reaction be? Since the cost of failing to detect suicidal or self-harm tendencies far outweighs the cost of false alerts, it is highly likely

that many false alarms would be generated, which would increase the burden on the treating clinical team. Therefore, we decided to analyse only data that does not contain any unambiguous pointers to self-harm or suicide. This means that diary data is excluded from analysis, because people can explicitly describe suicidal ideation there. There is one exception: The PHQ-9 questionnaire, which is administered every fortnight, includes a question on self-harm or suicidal ideation; if the answer indicates cause for concern, users will be taken off the Help4Mood intervention immediately because they will need closer supervision.

5. Electronic Health Record Integration

In order to foster interoperability with IT systems across the European Union, it is important to use a standard vocabulary to describe findings, procedures, and actions. For Help4Mood, we chose the international Core Release of SNOMED CT [12]. SNOMED CT is a highly complex, extendable clinical vocabulary that can be integrated with standards such as HL7 [13], which Help4Mood will support.

Most of the SNOMED-CT concepts used in Help4Mood come from the *Clinical Finding* hierarchy. Clinical findings are the outcome of assessments, observations, or judgements. For example, if the sleep sensor data indicate that the patient tossed and turned frequently at night, this can be encoded as the Clinical Finding "restless sleep".

Another class of concepts that are relevant to Help4Mood are *Procedures*. In SNOMED-CT, procedures are activities that occur at a specific time and involve the patient and include education and administration. Examples of procedures are guiding the patient through a relaxation exercise or showing the patient a list of activities that were identified as comforting.

A question or a procedure that produces a result is an *Observable Entity*. For example, "gender" is an observable entity, while "female gender" is a finding. While many demographic characteristics of patients are covered by Observable Entities, other information such as occupation is encoded using concepts from the *Social Context* hierarchy.

Modelling questionnaires in SNOMED-CT requires concepts from three different hierarchies. The questionnaires as measurement instruments are part of the *Staging and Scales* hierarchy. Questionnaire scores are modelled as observable entities, and the interpretation of questionnaire scores is encoded as a clinical finding.

For example, assessing a patient using the Beck Depression Inventory (BDI, [14]) is a procedure that has the Concept ID 446765009. The patient's score on the BDI is an observable entity with the Concept ID 446053003, and the BDI itself is an assessment scale with the Concept ID 273306008. The finding that

Table 3. Anchoring New Concepts in SNOMED-CT. H4M: Help4Mood concept, is-a: linked SNOMED-CT concept

Procedure	H4M	999991021	Assessment using PHQ-9
	is-a	445536008	Assessment using assessment scale
Observable Entity	H4M	999991022	PHQ-9 score
	is-a	363870007	Mental state, behavior / psychosocial function observable
Finding		999992011	Change of Score on Cognitive Game SIMON
	is-a	248536006	Finding of functional performance and activity

is associated with a patient's score is encoded using one of the subtypes of the clinical finding "Depressive Disorder" (Concept ID 35489007).

We defined our own codes only if the relevant findings, observable entities, or procedures were not included in SNOMED-CT. In all cases, these codes are linked to a parent concept in SNOMED-CT. For example, unlike the Beck Depression Inventory, none of our depression measures are modelled explicitly in SNOMED-CT, although they are well-known and validated. Therefore, we assigned system-specific codes to the resulting scores and linked them to relevant parent concepts. For example, the PHQ-9 score is an Observable Entity which is in an is-a relation with the SNOMED CT concept *Mental state, behaviour / psychosocial function observable*. The interpretation of cognitive games is also not covered. While the scores themselves are observable entities, changes in scores as well as relevant trends are modelled as findings. Table 3 summarises the implementation of these examples.

While information such as questionnaire scores can be stored more or less directly, concepts such as "restless sleep" require interpretations of sensor data. The Decision Support System will implement algorithms for mapping raw sensor data to these categories, which will be refined as data is collected in user studies and trials.

6. Taking Help4Mood Further

The data management approach outlined here provides a detailed, systematic representation of all of the relevant high-level information that Help4Mood collects about a patient with depression. It was designed for easy maintenance and maximum interoperability with Electronic Health Records. New sensors and interaction modules can be integrated easily. No new elements are required for additional sensor data, and we anticipate that for most exercises, we will only track completion.

We are planning three trials of the Help4Mood system. These will be iterative, starting with a bare-bones system and progressively adding functionality. At this stage, the most important function of the data structures is to make data readily accessible for future analysis. Given the relative lack of information on the sleep and activity patterns of people with depression in the community [8], one of the key important contribution of Help4Mood will be clean, usable data. Data will be summarised using visualisations and natural language summaries.

In future iterations of Help4Mood, the DSS will be extended to suggest activities or provide brief psychoeducation that reinforces the "homework" that clinicians often give to patients. We also plan to add HL7 integration, and refine the elements and clinical vocabulary described here to provide a more detailed ontology for interoperability.

References

[1] US DEPARTMENT OF HEALTH & HUMAN SERVICES (1999) *Mental health: A report of the Surgeon General. Executive summary* (Rockville, MD).

[2] SCHRIJVERS, D., HULSTIJN, W. and SABBE, B.G. (2008) Psychomotor symptoms in depression: a diagnostic, pathophysiological and therapeutic tool. *J Affect Disord* **109**(1-2): 1–20.

[3] BUYUKDURA, J.S., MCCLINTOCK, S.M. and CROARKIN, P.E. (2011) Psychomotor retardation in depression: Biological underpinnings, measurement, and treatment. *Progr Neuro-Psychopharmacol Biol Psych* **35**(2): 395–409.

[4] ALPERT, M., POUGET, E.R. and SILVA, R.R. (2001) Reflections of depression in acoustic measures of the patient's speech. *J Affect Disord* **66**(1): 59–69.

[5] STASSEN, H.H., KUNY, S. and HELL, D. (1998) The speech analysis approach to determining onset of improvement under antidepressants. *Eur Neuropsychopharmacol* **8**(4): 303–310.

[6] KROENKE, K., SPITZER, R.L. and WILLIAMS, J.B. (2001) The PHQ-9: validity of a brief depression severity measure. *Journal of general internal medicine* **16**(9): 606–13.

[7] WOLTERS, M., ALBERTINI, S., BURTON, C., HASTIE, H., MARTINEZ-MIRANDA, J., ROSELL, J., SERRANO-BLANCO, A. *et al.* (2011) *User and Clinical Requirements for Help4Mood*. Tech. rep., The Help4Mood consortium.

[8] BURTON, C., MCKINSTRY, B., TATAR, A.S., SERRANO-BLANCO, A., PAGLIARI, C. and WOLTERS, M. (in press) Activity monitoring in patients with depression: A systematic review. *Journal of Affective Disorders* **141**.

[9] ZERO C *Manual for ICE 3.4.* URL http://doc.zeroc.com/display/Ice/Ice+Manual.

[10] MOULLEC, G., MAÏANO, C., MORIN, A.J.S., MONTHUY-BLANC, J., ROSELLO, L. and NINOT, G. (2010) A very short visual analog form of the Center for Epidemiologic Studies Depression Scale (CES-D) for the idiographic measurement of depression. *J Affect Disord* .

[11] MARTÍNEZ-MIRANDA, J., BRESÓ, A. and GARCÍA-GOMEZ, J.M. (2012) Modelling therepautic empathy in a virtual agent to support the remote treatment of major

depression. In *Proceedings of ICAART 2012* (Vilamoura, Portugal), 2: 264–269.

[12] THE INTERNATIONAL HEALTH TERMINOLOGY STANDARDS DEVELOPMENT ORGANISATION (2009) *SNOMED Clinical Terms User Guide*. Tech. Rep. July.

[13] BENSON, T. (2009) *Principles of Health Interoperability - HL7 and SNOMED* (New York, NY: Springer).

[14] BECK, A.T., WARD, C.H., MENDELSON, M., MOCK, J. and ERBAUGH, J. (1961) An inventory for measuring depression. *Archives of general psychiatry* 4: 561–71.

23

Living without a safety net in an Intelligent Environment

Juan Carlos Augusto[1,*], Paul J. McCullagh[1], Julie-Ann Augusto-Walkden[2]

[1]University of Ulster, School of Computing and Mathematics, Jordanstown, UK; [2]South Eastern Health and Social Care Trust, Newtownards, UK

Abstract

Computing systems comprise a surreptitious and intrinsic part of our daily life activities. Applications that support humans in daily life facilitate the development of the so-called Intelligent Environments. Like any technology Intelligent Environments can fail. This paper examines potential negative consequences of such systems if they are too naively or optimistically developed and used. The aim of this work is to encourage those contributing to the technical area to reflect on these issues and to provide symbiotic solutions which make such a powerful technical development safer for humans so that it can unfold all its potential to empower future citizens, especially the vulnerable.

Keywords: Ambient Intelligence, Intelligent Environments, safety critical

1. Introduction

Building computing systems that operate safely in the real world is very difficult. Compounded by commercial pressure unreliable systems are sometimes expedited and deployed in the marketplace. Even with the best intentions and state-of-the-art resources it is almost unavoidable that systems contain weaknesses that will lead to failure; evidence has demonstrated that it is not a matter of 'if' but 'when'.

Intelligent Environment systems [1, 2] are inherently complex, because of the need for a symbiotic interaction of hardware, software, human processes. Here we use the term Intelligent Environment to refer as a whole to the infrastructure (Smart Environments [3]) and the software that governs their behaviour (Ambient Intelligence [4]). By their very definition, '... digital environments that proactively, but sensibly, support people in their daily lives'. [5], these systems are conceived to be deployed in the real world to support humans in a variety of supervisory contexts. Some examples of such systems are 'smart' homes, classrooms, cars, offices, manufacturing

plants, etc. In some of those applications the artificial system is given an enormous responsibility (e.g. related to safety or well-being).

The magnitude of practical problems to be solved has often concentrated designers' efforts on what to do to get these systems working. Little or no attention is paid to what happens when systems do not behave as anticipated. Nobody wants to announce that their system at some point will fail to deliver as expected, but it is an unavoidable circumstance that will eventually happen. Power cuts occur, sensors sometimes malfunction, sensors can be displaced and hence the quality of the input to the software taking decisions is degraded. Software can contain bugs, software and hardware updates can introduce errors, or rare, unanticipated and potentially unsafe scenarios can occur. Interoperability issues in complex computing and communication environments can lead to unintended consequences. As humans start to experience and benefit from the first successful Ambient Intelligence (AmI) systems supporting their daily activities, it may be unavoidable that the human (traditional) circle of care (family, friends, healthcare professionals) relaxes, invests trust in the system and may not be there when the artificial system fails.

*Corresponding author. Email: jc.augusto@ulster.ac.uk

Consider the requirement of the role of AmI in smart homes [6], in particular providing care for vulnerable people [7]. In the UK for the first time there are more people over the age of 65 years than are under the age of 18 years. More elders have care and support needs, which highlight the need for an affordable system. In England in 2010 £80m was invested in technologies to support preventative care and assist older people to remain in their own homes. In 2011, the Scottish government also has invested significantly in home care. It will spend £10m on a 4-year scheme designed to deploy telehealth systems, which aid treatment of health conditions within patients' homes. The Scottish Assisted Living Demonstrator programme will involve about 10000 people, both the elderly and those with disabilities[1]. This is in spite of a lack of agreement for the cost-effectiveness of such an intervention [8]. However, Gaikwad and Warren [9] demonstrated that home-based interventions applied to chronic disease management improved functional and cognitive patient outcomes and reduced healthcare spending.

Local authorities work with partners in housing, health, voluntary and independent sectors, and with service users and carers, to implement a telecare-based approach. However, technology-based intervention should not be seen as a substitute for meaningful human interactions and interventions, but as a means of enhancing them. Fisk [10] points out that technology is a tool and on its own is neither empowering nor disabling.

Researchers involved in the development of Intelligent Environments have a responsibility to start the discussion on how to design holistically safer systems. Systems (in the broader sense, i.e. the combination of hardware, software, humans and procedures being introduced) should have a responsible attitude towards the environment they serve when they cannot deliver appropriately, and disclose such information in a timely fashion. The AmI community cannot adopt the concept of an 'accident waiting to happen'. A thread of discussion should be opened within our community on the different ways this can be achieved.

However, we begin this debate from a far from perfect human-centric baseline. In the US it has been estimated that up to 98000 people currently die in hospitals each year as a result of preventable medical errors. This exceeds deaths caused by motor-vehicle accidents, breast cancer and AIDS. It is not acceptable for patients to be harmed by the healthcare system whose overarching goal is, 'First, do no harm'. [11]. In the UK approximately 20000–30000 people die as a result of medical errors every year, according to Dr Richard Smith, editor of the British Medical Journal[2]. A rethink of healthcare systems is required to cut the number of mistakes made by medical personnel [12] to the low levels of errors among other safety critical industries such as pilots or nuclear plant workers. According to the chief medical officer, Sir Liam Donaldson, clinical misjudgements or mistakes mean that the odds of dying as a result of being treated in hospital are 33000 times higher than those of dying in an air crash [13]. 'In an airline industry, the evidence . . . from scheduled airlines is the risk of death is one in 10 million. If you go into a hospital in the developed world, the risk of death from a medical error is one in 300', he said.

Home healthcare is not without risk, of course. Roback and Herzog [14] considered risks that are encountered when placing electronic equipment in this environment. They found that adverse events could stem from technology itself, from human–technology interaction or from the environment in which the technology is placed. Guidelines aimed at performance improvement complement the more general guidelines on tele-homecare adopted by the American Telemedicine Association. Concerns on the safe development and deployment of these technologies were also clearly raised in [15].

Thus a major new question arises: Will AmI systems make this form of care safer or potentially dangerous?

2. The argument

This section explains why systems can and will most probably fail at some point and exposes the potential negative consequences for the people these systems are supposed to help.

2.1. Hypothesis 1: 'Computing systems DO fail!'

As software practitioners and consumers, we all experience minor faults on a daily basis, due to faulty or poorly developed software. However, the history of Software Engineering is plagued with examples of catastrophic failure made by organizations that have exceptional resources and powerful development teams. For example:

- A Computer-Aided Despatch system for London's Ambulance Service was introduced in 1992. It handled approximately 5000 patients, with over a thousand '999' emergency calls per day. If the position of vehicles was incorrectly recorded, multiple vehicles were sent to the same location; it has been claimed that the occurrence of such an error leads to the death of between 20 and 30 people.

- Intel Pentium processor, released in 1994, was designed to be three times faster for floating point computation than the 486DX chip. However, an error in the lookup table resulted in a component, which was not fit for the purpose. For example, the calculation of ratio 4195835/3145727 yielded 1.3337 and not 1.3338, an error in the 5th significant digit.

---

[1]www.guardian.co.uk/healthcare-network/2011/mar/16/scotland-spends-10m-transfer-telehealth-techology (accessed September 2011).

[2]http://news.bbc.co.uk/1/hi/uk/682000.stm (accessed September 2011).

- The Ariane 5 rocket, ESA (European Space Agency) was launched on 4 June 1996. Thirty-seven seconds later it self-destructed. An uncaught exception: numerical overflow in a conversion routine resulted in incorrect altitude computed by the on-board computer.

- The Mars Polar Lander was launched 3 January 1999 and lost 3 December 1999. Engine shutdown due to spurious signals gave false indication that spacecraft had landed. Subsequently NASA's Mars Rover freezes (21 January 2004) due to too many open files in flash memory.

- The BMW 3 Series, with 100s of embedded components, was extensively tested but in 1999 a safety recall of over 16000 cars was required due to faults with airbag control unit—in certain conditions the airbag inflated for no reason. More recently Toyota was forced to recall 180000 vehicles in the UK, due to a failure of the controlled servo braking mechanism. Toyota reported that its biggest-ever safety scare cost the company $2bn worldwide. Honda and Renault also issued recalls recently due to software failures.

The list, of course, is not exhaustive. An open approach where legitimate safety concerns can be raised is required. There is evidence that this is beginning to happen [16] in the health system, allowing safety concerns to be raised by humans. AmI systems require a similar culture of transparency.

2.2. Hypothesis 2: 'The more complex the system the more prone to failure'

Modern computer systems are built as a complex interconnection of specialized modules (Figure 1). As systems become more complex, the potential for failure increases [17]. Therefore Software Engineering has provided important methods and tools in an attempt to increase the reliability in software and computing systems. These include testing, verification and validation as steps that can help developers and users ensure that the right system has been built in the right way. The reader can find a good summary on these approaches in [18, 19]. Even when big companies have specialized teams this is still insufficient to provide 'bullet proof' systems.

The impact of complexity on reliability can be recognized in all fields. For example, Richard Cook [20] cites 18 reasons why complexity in the medical system can lead to failure. He discusses: '*How failure is evaluated; how failure is attributed to proximate cause; and the resulting new understanding of patient safety*'.

A complex system of relevance is The UK's National Programme for Information Technology, described as 'The Biggest Computer Programme in the World … Ever!'. Brennan [21] points out that '*apart from the spine, the central repository of electronic health records, there is no single deadline or point of failure, just thousands of local implementations of systems of a type that we really should have got the hang of by now*'. An audit by the House of Commons Public Accounts Committee (14 January 2009) concluded [22]: '*Some systems are being deployed across the NHS. The Care Records Service, however, is at least four years behind schedule, with the Department's latest forecasts putting completion at 2014–15. At 31 August 2008, new care records systems had been deployed in 133 of the 380 Trusts*'. … '*The estimated cost of the Programme is £12.7 billion, including £3.6 billion of local costs, although this figure remains uncertain*'. By 18 July 2011, a further report from Public Accounts Committee recommended that the DoH consider scrapping the project altogether, rather than continue with the remaining multi-billion pound investment. 'The [DoH] should review whether to continue the programme and consider whether the remaining £4.3bn would be better spent elsewhere'. The complexity of systems that work well in isolation caused delay and uncertainty. The interaction and acceptance of new systems with the people intended to use them was also underestimated.

2.3. Hypothesis 3: Intelligent Environment systems are inherently complex

Intelligent Environments can be developed in any environment where technology can be deployed to assist humans. That infrastructure is supported by a so-called Ambient Intelligence that relates software specifically designed to make decisions based on a sensed reality to the technical infrastructure. This creates a complex interdependence and a reliance on several well-established areas (Figure 2). For example, the system needs *sensors* to gather information from the monitored environment and *actuators* to intervene upon that environment. These sensors are interconnected through a (wired or wireless) network that provides information flows. For an environment to be useful to humans as they move along different

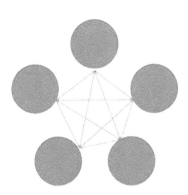

Figure 1. Modern computing systems are constructed as a set of autonomous modules that can interact with each other in various sophisticated ways.

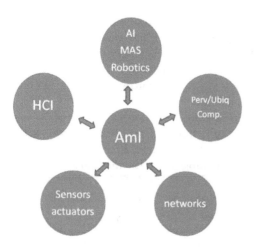

Figure 2. AmI is a multidisciplinary area, each of them highly complex in itself.

areas in their daily living routines, services have to be ubiquitous, i.e. be accessible everywhere and provide services transparently and according to the place and circumstance. These systems require sophisticated algorithms which can adapt to the user and provide appropriate interventions consistent with the user needs and preferences. For a system of this type to be successful it has to provide a subtle interaction with the user so that all the complexity is hidden within the system and the users enjoy the benefits with minimal effort, thanks to a natural interaction (e.g. everyday natural language).

Sensors and actuators can sometimes be occluded, transmit noisy signals or be moved (intentionally or by accident). Networks can sometimes be unreliable and are vulnerable to changes in the infrastructure and to security attacks. Ubiquitous systems can be altered according to changes in the infrastructure or in the tasks the user performs in different places. Artificial Intelligence software can sometimes fail to provide an acceptable answer to some of the difficult problems that it faces. Different users interact differently with machines due to cultural, physical or intellectual differences, therefore there is no 'size that fit all' and it is also very difficult to have very flexible and human-level intelligent interfaces.

2.4. Hypothesis 4: AmI systems support people. Some of this support is critical (there is a potential for human harm or life loss if the AmI system fails)

We can potentially consider a wide range of Intelligent Environments. Some that have been started to be explored are: Smart Homes, Smart Classrooms, Smart Cars, health-related applications in hospitals, public transportation in cities, emergency services, industry, decision support for business and public surveillance. Let us exemplify this step with the first three as exemplars.

Smart Homes. A prominent example of an environment enriched with AmI is a Smart Home; that is a house equipped to bring advanced services to its users. Examples of such technology include movement sensors (Passive Infrared detectors), pull chord switch, thermostat, smoke detector, doorbell indicator, pressure pads, on-off switch detectors, phone and medical devices (e.g. blood pressure monitor, heart monitor, etc.). Examples of enriched devices are electro-domestics (e.g. cooker and refrigerator), household items (e.g. taps, bed and sofa) and temperature handling devices (e.g. air conditioning and radiators). Expected benefits of the application of this technology can be: (a) increased safety (e.g. by monitoring lifestyle patterns or the latest activities and providing assistance when a potentially harmful situation is developing), (b) enhanced comfort (e.g. by adjusting temperature automatically) and (c) better economy (e.g. controlling the use of lights). There is a plethora of sensing/acting technology: stand-alone devices (e.g. smoke or movement detectors), sensors embedded in household objects (e.g. a microwave controller or a bed occupancy sensor) and body-worn devices (e.g. shirts manufactured with electrodes that monitor heart beat, and potentially unsafe conditions). Figure 3(a) illustrates a plan of a house with a typical distribution of sensors.

Recent applications include the use of Smart Homes to provide a safe environment where people with special needs can enjoy a better quality of life. For example, in the case of people at early stages of dementia (the most frequent case being elderly people suffering from Alzheimer's disease) the system can be tailored to mini-

 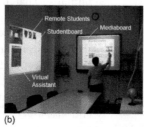 

(a)   (b)   (c)

Figure 3. Intelligent Environments, from left to right: (a) Smart Homes [23], (b) Smart Classrooms [24], (c) Smart Cars (Courtesy of Siemens).

mize risks and ensure appropriate care at critical times by monitoring activities, diagnosing interesting situations and possibly advising the carer when intervention is required. This is a further example of AmI, whereby a message can be generated automatically and sent to carer (who may live remotely) by appropriate technology, such as mobile phone or digital television; the carer's environment of course having sensed the most appropriate delivery channel. Failing to detect an unsafe situation or to deliver a call for help through an appropriate channel at the right time can be critical for the person being cared by the system.

Education services. Universities and higher education institutions are starting to consider the concept of Smart Classrooms [25] where technology such as smart boards, smart sound system capable to recognize and process verbal instructions, and smart cameras which can capture images autonomously are to be shown to students attending a lecture remotely (Figure 3(b)). Twenty years ago lecturers went to the classroom to write the content of the lecture on a board and to explain it. Nowadays lecturers deliver a lecture with the help of slides, the Internet and simulation software. Students can actively participate using interactive boards, and express their response to queries by "voting" on an answer, hence empowering the lecturer and student with information on whether the knowledge has been transferred as intended, all in near real time. If the technology fails then the lecturer will strive to achieve the objectives of that lecture but students may lose significant content (e.g. for those attending remotely it may simply mean they do not have a class that day).

Intelligent cars. Modern cars have dozens of sensors to provide fuel efficiency, improved stability in the vehicle (e.g. better grip at high speed or in difficult weather conditions). More recently some manufacturers started to use sensors that can assist the driver in parking the vehicle by detecting proximity to cars at the front and back of the parking vehicle (Figure 3(c)). These sensors are starting to be used to prevent collisions. A more sophisticated recent development [26] has built a system that allows the car to 'observe' the driver, continuously estimating the driver's internal state and responding appropriately. Observations are focused on hand and leg motions and associated actions (e.g. passing, turning, stopping, car following, lane change or speeding up). This allowed the car to recognize and warn the driver about possible dangers. Other systems are under study that will recognize from the facial gestures and body movements of potentially dangerous situations, for example, the driver falling asleep while driving. Microsoft, among others, employ AmI technologies for driver assistance by providing route planners and customized dynamic route suggestions to bypass congestion [27, 28]. As one of the authors of this article

Figure 4. Current state of the art highlights success while often denying problems.

painfully experienced, a damaged car can easily be the direct result of a malfunctioning sensor during parking. Other failures can have severe consequences (e.g. injury or death).

Having explored the broader scope of AmI in an Intelligent Environment, we will emphasize health–social care applications like the use of Smart Homes for care of the elderly (Ambient Assisted Living).

2.5. Hypothesis 5: The current state of the art on developing AmI systems is not well organized. In particular, it does not contemplate as a standard that the system may/will fail

Marketing focuses on what an intelligent system can do and not so much on its limitations and never on its pitfalls (Figure 4). It is not good advertisement for a company to highlight the potential faults systems may have. Still companies should face this topic unashamedly and show genuine interest on offering good and reliable service. Hence, the concepts of 'mean time before failure' and 'service level agreement' should be considered mandatory for AmI components and systems.

2.6. Hypothesis 6: As humans start to experience the first successful AmI systems supporting their lives the human caring circle relaxes and is not there when the artificial system fails

Current caring systems are human based and rely on professionals from the health system, relatives and friends to care for another human being (Figure 5(a)). Imagine the scenario where an Ambient Assisted Living system is deployed and it works acceptably most of the time to the point that the human carers accept the system and get used to it. As this happens they will feel confident enough to be absent more often (Figure 5(b)); in some extreme cases they may withdraw completely (Figure 5(c)). However, people with dementia, for example, will continue to deteriorate, often challenging the requirements of the original system. This provides the ethical dilemma—living without a safety net in an Intelligent Environment.

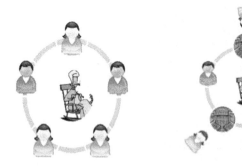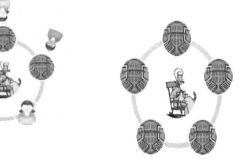

Figure 5. Potential deterioration of human circle of care.

3. Proposed solutions

The obvious and easy thing to say in these circumstances is: '*Systems should not be built to operate alone*', a sort of 'bury your head in the sand' strategy. The problem is people do not necessarily use systems in the ideal form. If a system has been designed to monitor whether an elderly person may have fallen and the system does not work properly, failing to detect or alert to such an occurrence then regardless of the fact that other carers may or not be available is irrelevant and does not exculpate the responsibility of the system; it is still failing to detect or achieve its main objective.

We have already experienced examples from other areas. McLaren recalled baby push chairs in the US during 2009 as some children had their fingers injured in the folding mechanism. McLaren could have claimed that it was not an intended use or they could have applied a warning sticker in an attempt to absolve themselves of responsibility. This solution would not have ameliorated the problem, reduced litigation or built a credible public reputation. For the same reasons car manufacturers (Toyota, Honda and Renault) recalled cars during 2010 because of the suspicion of faulty mechanisms.

There is a need for the community developing Intelligent Environments to adopt a more mature approach to the problem than simply passing the responsibility of problems to the final user. Below there are some suggestions which may be helpful to initiate a much needed discussion on this topic. We recognize that this is not a definitive solution but a starting point for further debate.

3.1. A formal software engineering approach to AmI systems design

Software Engineering uses systematic methods to increase reliability of software. 'Testing' has been used, but testing is limited to probing a system on a few of the many possible situations that can face. Research conducted for decades has matured to produce efficient tools based on Formal Methods which allow the automated analysis of the behaviour of a system in a more rigorous way.

These methods and tools allow for the Verification of Software and Hardware Systems. The most common strategy used is Model Checking which provides tools that development teams can use to increase the reliability and robustness of their software system [17, 18, 29]. This process is time consuming and therefore is mostly applied in the development of high-integrity systems where safety or security is important. Formal methods have been used in industrial applications to address the following:

- Safety, which is a measure of the continuous delivery of service free from occurrences of catastrophic failures.

- Reliability, which is a measure of the continuous delivery of proper service (where service is delivered according to specified conditions) or equivalently of the time to failure.

- Availability, which is a measure of the delivery of proper service with respect to the alternation of proper and improper service.

These criteria are equally relevant to AmI in healthcare. For example, Somerville [19] provides a formal specification to provide a state schema for an insulin pump, which is a safety critical application. Software Engineering Methods used for verification of Intelligent Environments are described in [23, 30, 31].

3.2. The need for enhanced understanding of human–computer (AmI) interaction

Further ethnographic research is required to understand how people interact with these systems and use the information they provide, particularly with regard to safety issues. This is required for the person being monitored, the carer and the healthcare professional. Data may be collected through participant observation, interviews and questionnaires. Human–computer interaction experts can contribute to the knowledge base. For previous work that has highlighted the need for methods of validation by users that combine scientific objectiveness with the need of allowing the subjective opinion of the final user of AmI systems, see [32].

3.3. A partnership between AmI and human

In a systematic review of the benefits of home telecare for elderly people and those with long-term conditions, James Barlow *et al.* [8] concluded that, the most effective interventions appear to be automated vital signs monitoring (for reducing health service use) and telephone follow-up by nurses (for improving clinical indicators and reducing health service use). There was insufficient evidence about the effects of home safety and security alert systems. However, Barlow concluded that because there was insufficient evidence, this did not mean that those interventions have no effect. However, a key point is the relationship between systems and humans.

Hardware and software should have monitors and reporting built-in. A system of triage may be appropriate. For the most serious errors, the system should conclude that it could cause more harm than good and remove the appearance of a safety net. However for minor errors, it may be possible for the system to work safely with reduced sensors or a faulty software process and continue to work with a reduced capacity. This should be clearly signalled to the users (cared for person, carer and healthcare professional). Where a clean bill of health is given, the system must still monitor the occurrence of unanticipated event that could jeopardize safety.

3.4. The ethical dimension

The British Computer Society (BCS) has drawn up seven general principles of informatics ethics [33], which we

Table 1. Informatics ethics and AmI [33].

Ethical principles	Definition (BCS)	Factors relating to AmI Systems
Information privacy and disposition	All persons have a fundamental right to privacy, and hence to control over the collection, storage, access, use, communication, manipulation and disposition of data about themselves.	The cared for person, where appropriate, should have control over the information that is collected and made available to carers and relatives. Otherwise, a carer should have appropriate access.
Openness	The collection, storage, access, use, communication, manipulation and disposition of personal data must be disclosed in an appropriate and timely fashion to the subject of those data.	The AmI system must be open (so that its decisions can be evaluated), and the information must be made available to the cared for person or their carer.
Security	Data that have been legitimately collected about a person should be protected by all reasonable and appropriate measures against loss, degradation, unauthorized destruction, access, use, manipulation, modification or communication.	Data must be kept securely, particularly as they may be stored for trend analysis and communicated to remote locations.
Access	The subject of an electronic record has the right of access to that record and the right to correct the record with respect to its accurateness, completeness and relevance.	The data collected should be considered no different to other information in the electronic health record.
Legitimate infringement	The fundamental right of control over the collection, storage, access, use, manipulation, communication and disposition of personal data is conditioned only by the legitimate, appropriate and relevant data needs of a free, responsible and democratic society, and by the equal and competing rights of other persons.	Competing rights of other persons must be respected in AmI systems.
Least intrusive alternative	Any infringement of the privacy rights of the individual person, and of the individual's right to control over person-relative data as mandated under Principle 1, may only occur in the least intrusive fashion and with a minimum of interference with the rights of the affected person.	The least intrusive principle applies in AmI systems. This may have particular relevance to the recording (and communication) of images and multimedia data within an Intelligent Environment.
Accountability	Any infringement of the privacy rights of the individual person, and of the right to control over person-relative data, must be justified to the affected person in good time and in an appropriate fashion.	AmI system must be open and accountable for any infringement of the privacy rights of the individual person, e.g. alerting a call centre to wandering behaviour.

believe should be tested in any AmI system. These fundamental principles are evaluated in Table 1 and have added relevance where data are collected and processed by complex algorithms; on vulnerable people, some of whom may be dependent on carers or relatives. In particular, AmI systems should also be accountable for any infringement of the privacy rights of the individual person.

4. Conclusions

AmI researchers have a responsibility to design safer systems, with a high level of transparency. This includes systems that have a responsible attitude towards the environment they serve when they cannot deliver appropriately. Formal specification may provide a means of designing many unsafe conditions out of software. This is time consuming and expensive for normal software, but is important for safety critical AmI applications, and should not be discounted.

It is evident that the hardware and software should be reliable in an AmI system. Thus monitoring is a requirement that is self-testing, periodic checking processes with self-report of possible underperformance, e.g. due to a faulty, misplaced sensor or sensor whose battery may need replacement. It may be possible to provide a system which can continue to reason under uncertainty, but this condition must be identified so that periodic human triage can attend to maintenance issues.

We should strive to ensure that AmI used within an assistive environment should *improve* quality of life. Hence AmI can not only detect alarms, but can become proactive, for example to anticipate abnormal situations and provide guidance for a person under its care. For example, the AmI system could be used to guide a person with dementia back to bed during the night-time, if inappropriate or frequent wandering was detected by location sensors. Context, of course, is important to ensure a proper and sensible decision is made. However, built into this service model, there should always be a human backup. If the AmI system fails to achieve its objective, then a human carer or friend can be alerted (e.g. via a call centre), and appropriate care restored. This means we should not design a system equivalent to Figure 5(c), where the human 'safety net' is eliminated, even by stealth or overconfidence in the system.

The sensitivity and specificity of the AmI system then is a key quality metric. If the number of alerts to the users is reduced then the AmI system will add value. However, they should not be reduced to a point where external human help is needed and not signalled by the system, or beyond which the humans become disengaged.

As the capacity of AmI systems increases, and they become interconnected then Web 2.0 technologies (and beyond) may provide human contact with virtual neighbours, and contact with other AmI systems, to build a community feeling and thus enhance the safety net. This of course raises many societal questions with an ethical dimension. What information should be shared and with whom, and will this always benefit the individual being cared for? AmI, like other services, must adhere to the highest ethical principles in support of the human.

References

[1] NAKASHIMA, H., AGHAJAN, H. and AUGUSTO, J.C. [eds.] (2009) *Handbook on Ambient Intelligence and Smart Environments* (Springer Verlag).

[2] COOK, D.J., AUGUSTO, J.C. and JAKKULA, V.R. (2009) Ambient Intelligence: applications in society and opportunities for AI. *Pervasive Mob. Comput.* **5**: 277–298.

[3] COOK, D.J. and DAS, S.K. (2004) *Smart Environments: Technology, Protocols, and Applications* (Wiley).

[4] IST Advisory Group (2001) *The european union report, scenarios for ambient intelligence in 2010*, ftp://ftp.cordis.lu/pub/ist/docs/istagscenarios2010.pdf.

[5] AUGUSTO, J.C. (2007) Ambient Intelligence: the confluence of pervasive computing and artificial intelligence. In SCHUSTER, A. [ed.] *Intelligent Computing Everywhere* (Springer Verlag), 213–234.

[6] FRIEDEWALD, M., DA COSTA, O., PUNIE, Y., ALAHUHTA, P. and HEINONEN, S. (August2005) Perspectives of ambient intelligence in the home environment. *Telematics and Informatics* **22**(3): 221–238.

[7] ORPWOOD, R., GIBBS, C., ADLAM, T., FAULKNER, R. and MEEGAHAWATTE, D. (2005) The design of smart homes for people with dementia—user interface aspects. *Univ. Access Inf. Soc.* **4**: 156–164.

[8] BARLOW, J., SINGH, D., BAYER, S. and CURRY, R. (2007) A systematic review of the benefits of home telecare for frail elderly people and those with long-term conditions. *J. Telemed. Telecare* **13**(4): 172–179.

[9] GAIKWAD, R. and WARREN, J. (June 2009) The role of home-based information and communications technology interventions in chronic disease management: a systematic literature review. *Health Inf. J.* **15**(2): 122–146.

[10] FISK, M. Elderly people and independent living: the implications of SMART house technologies. In *Proceedings of British Society of Gerontology Annual Conference.*

[11] KOHN, L.T., CORRIGAN, J.M. and DONALDSON, M.S. [eds.] (2000) *To Err Is Human: Building a Safer Health System.* Published by the Committee on Quality of Health Care in America, Institute of Medicine.

[12] LEAPE, L., LAWTHERS, A.G. and BRENNAN, T.A. (1993) Preventing medical injury. *Qual Rev Bull.* **19**(5): 144–149.

[13] HALL, S. (November 2006) Medical error death risk 1 in 300. *The Guardian*, www.guardian.co.uk/society/2006/nov/07/health.lifeandhealth.

[14] ROBACK, K. and HERZOG, A. (2003) Home informatics in healthcare: Assessment guidelines to keep up quality of care and avoid adverse effects. *Technol. Health Care* **11**: 195–206.

[15] ROBERTS, J. (2006) Pervasive health management and health management utilizing pervasive technologies: synergy and issues. *J. Universal Comput. Sci.* **12**(1): 4–15.

[16] DYER, C. (2010) Doctor who was excluded for raising patient safety concerns is entitled to substantial damages. *BMJ* **340**: c739.

[17] HOLZMANN, G. (2003) *The Spin Model Checker—Primer and Reference Manual* (Addison-Wesley Publishing).

[18] BERARD, B., BIDOIT, M., FINKEL, A., LAROUSSINIE, F., PETIT, A., PETRUCCI, L., SCHNOEBELEN, PH. *et al. Systems and Software Verification* (Springer Verlag).

[19] SOMERVILLE, I. (2007) *Software Engineering* (Addison Wesley).

[20] COOK, R.I. *How Complex Systems Fail* (Cognitive technologies Laboratory, University of Chicago), www.ctlab.org/documents/How%20Complex%20Systems%20Fail.pdf.

[21] BRENNAN, S. (2005) *The NHS IT Project: The Biggest Computer Programme in the World—Ever!* (Radcliffe Publishing).

[22] House of Commons Public Accounts Committee *The National Programme for IT in the NHS: Progress since 2006. 2nd Report of Session 2008–09 HC 153.* Published by authority of House of Commons: Stationery Office Ltd.

[23] AUGUSTO, J.C. and MCCULLAGH, P. (2007) Ambient Intelligence: Concepts and Applications. *Int. J. Comput. Sci. Inf. Syst.* **4**(1): 1–28.

[24] SHI, Y., XIE, W., XU, G., XIANG, P. and ZHANG, B. (July–September 2003) Project smart remote classroom—providing novel real-time interactive distance learning technologies. *J. Distance Edu. Technol.* **1**(3): 28–45.

[25] AUGUSTO, J.C. (June 2009) Ambient Intelligence: opportunities and consequences of its use in smart classrooms. *Italics* **8**(2): 53–63.

[26] PENTLAND, A. (2005) Perceptual environments. In COOK, D. and DAS, S. [eds.] *Smart Environments: Technologies, Protocols and Applications* (Wiley).

[27] KRUMM, J. and HORVITZ, E. (2006) Predestination: inferring destinations from partial trajectories. In *Proceedings of 8th International Conference on Ubiquitous Computing*, 243–260.

[28] LETCHNER, J., KRUMM, J. and HORVITZ, E. (2006) Trip router with individualized preferences: incorporating personalization into route planning. In *Proceedings of IAAT 06*, 1795–1800.

[29] ABDALLAH, A.E., BOWEN, J.P. and NISSANKE, N. (2005) Dependable computing systems: paradigms, performance issues, and applications, part I: models and paradigms, Chapter 9. In DIAB, H.B. and ZOMAYA, A.Y. [eds.] *Wiley Series on Parallel and Distributed Computing* (Chichester: John Wiley & Sons).

[30] AUGUSTO, J.C. Increasing reliability in the development of intelligent environments. In *Proceedings of 5th International Conference on Intelligent Environments (IE09)*, Barcelona, Spain, 20–21 July 2009, 134–141.

[31] AUGUSTO, J.C., ZHENG, H., MULVENNA, M., WANG, H., CARSWELL, W. and JEFFERS, P. Design and Modelling of the Nocturnal AAL Care System. In *Proceedings of 2nd Int. Symposium on Ambient Intelligence (ISAmI 2011)*, Springer Verlag, 109–116.

[32] AUGUSTO, J.C., BOHLEN, M., COOK, D., FLENTGE, F., MARREIROS, G., RAMOS, C., QIN, W. *et al.* (2009) The Darmstadt Challenge (the Turing Test Revisited). In *Proceedings of the 1st International Conference on Agents and Artificial Intelligence (ICAART)*, Porto, Portugal.

[33] BCS Health Informatics Committee *A Handbook of Ethics for Health Informatics Professionals*, http://www.bcs.org/upload/pdf/handbookethics.pdf (accessed September 2011).

Permissions

List of Contributors

Tiago Gomes, Tiago Abade and José Creissac Campos
Departamento de Informática/Universidade do Minho & HASLab/INESC TEC, Braga, Portugal

Michael D. Harrison
Newcastle University & Queen Mary University of London, UK

José Luís Silva
Madeira-ITI, Universidade da Madeira, Funchal, Portugal

Manoj Bode, Shashi Shekhar Jha and Shivashankar B. Nair
Department of Computer Science & Engineering, Indian Institute of Technology Guwahati, Guwahati-781039, Assam, INDIA

Dan Shan, Kai Zeng, Weidong Xiang and Paul Richardson
4901 Evergreen Rd, Dearborn, MI, USA, 48092

D. Borra and F. Fagnani
Dipartimento di Scienze Matematiche, Politecnico di Torino, Italy

M. Iori and C. Borean
Swarm Joint Open Lab, Telecom Italia, Italy

Sal vatore Gaglio
ICAR CNR, Viale delle Scienze, Ed. 11, 90128 Palermo, Italy

DICGIM Univ ersity of Palermo,V iale delle Scienze, Ed. 6, 90128 Palermo, Italy

Giuseppe Lo Re, Gloria Martorella and Daniele Peri
DICGIM Univ ersity of Palermo,V iale delle Scienze, Ed. 6, 90128 Palermo, Italy

Simon Wells, Michael Schlafli, Judith Masthoff and Paula Forbes
University of Aberdeen, Computing Science, Meston building, Meston Walk, Aberdeen, AB24 3UE, UK

Henri Kotkanen and Antti Jylhä
University of Helsinki, Department of Computer Science, P.O. 68 (Gustaf HÃdllstrÃumin katu 2b), FI-00014 University of Helsinki, Finland

Silvia Gabrielli
CREATE-NET - Via alla Cascata 56/D Povo - 38123 Trento – Italy

Ahmed Elsokary, Peter Lohmiller, Václav Valenta and Hermann Schumacher
Ulm University, Institute of Electron Devices and Circuits, Albert-Einstein-Allee 45, 89081 Ulm, Germany

Shah Nawaz Khan amd Andreas Mitschele-Thiel
Integrated Communication Systems Group, Technische Universität Ilmenau, P.O. Box 100 565, Ilmenau 98693, Thüringen, Germany

Amr Y. Elnakeeb, Hany M. Elsayed and Mohamed M. Khairy
Department of Electronics and Electrical Communications, Faculty of Engineering, Cairo University, Egypt

Ming-Tuo Zhou
Smart Wireless Laboratory, NICT Singapore Representative Office, 20 Science Park Road, #01-09A/10 TeleTech Park, Singapore 117674

Chunyi Song
Institute of Marine Information Science and Engineering, Zhejiang University, China

Chin Sean Sum
Wi-SUN Alliance

Hiroshi Harada
Graduate School of Informatics, Kyoto University, Japan

Charles Callaway
TrentoRISE, via Sommarive, 20, Povo (TN) 38100, Italy

Oliviero Stock
FBK-irst, via Sommarive, 18, Povo (TN) 38100, Italy

Audri Biswas and Sam Reisenfeld
Department of Engineering, Faculty of Science and Engineering, Macquarie University, NSW 2109, Australia

Mark Hedley
Zhuo Chen
Digital Productivity Flagship, CSIRO, NSW 2122, Australia

Lijun Qian and Oluwaseyi Omotere
Department of Electrical and Computer Engineering, Prairie View A&M University, Texas A&M University System, Prairie View, Texas 77446, USA

Riku Jäntti
Department of Communications and Networking, Aalto University, P.O. Box 13000, 00076 Aalto, Finland

Fucheng Yang and Lie-Liang Yang
School of Electronics and Computer Science, University of Southampton, SO17 1BJ, UK

Catia Prandi, Paola Salomoni and Marco Roccetti
Department of Computer Science and Engineering, University of Bologna, Bologna, Italy

Valentina Nisi and Nuno Jardim Nunes
Madeira Interactive Technologies Institute, University of Madeira, Funchal, Madeira, Portugal

Ahmed El Shafie
Wireless Intelligent Networks Center (WINC), Nile University, Giza, Egypt

Sanjeev Gurugopinath
Department of Electronics and Communication Engineering, PES University, Bengaluru 560085

R. Muralishankar
Department of Electronics and Communication Engineering, CMR Institute of Technology, Bengaluru 560037

H. N. Shankar
Department of Electrical and Electronics Engineering, CMR Institute of Technology, Bengaluru 560037

Octavian Adrian Postolache and José Miguel Costa Dias Pereira
Instituto de Telecomunicações/LabIM/EST/IPS, Portugal

Pedro Manuel Brito da Silva Girão
Instituto de Telecomunicações/DEEC/IST/UTL, Av. Rovisco Pais, Lisbon, Portugal

Gabriela Postolache
Escola Superior de Saúde, Universidade Atlântica, Oeiras, Portugal

Claudio Di Ciccio, Massimo Mecella, Mario Caruso, Vincenzo Forte, Ettore Iacomussi, Leonardo Querzoni, Giuseppe Santucci and Giuseppe Tino
Dipartimento di Informatica e Sistemistica, University of Rome "La Sapienza", via Ariosto 25, I-00185 Rome, Italy

Katharina Rasch
KTH Royal Institute of Technology, School of Information and Communication Technology Forum 120, 16440 Kista, Sweden

Essa Jafer and Cian O'Mathuna
Tyndall National Institute, University College Cork (UCC), Cork, Ireland

Rostislav Spinar and Dirk Pesch
Cork Institute of Technology (CIT), Cork, Ireland

Paul Stack
Department of Civil and Environmental Engineering, University College Cork (UCC), Cork, Ireland

Andrey Somov
CREATE-NET, via alla Cascata 56/D, 38123 Trento, Italy

Maria K. Wolters and Colin Matheson
School of Informatics, 10 Crichton Street, Edinburgh EH8 9aB, University of Edinburgh Edinburgh, UK

Juan Martínez-Miranda
IBIME, Universitat Politécnica de Valencia, Valencia, Spain

Soraya Estevez
Fundaciò i2CAT, Barcelona, Spain

Helen F. Hastie
School of Mathematical and Computer Sciences, Heriot-Watt University, Edinburgh, UK

Juan Carlos Augusto and Paul J. McCullagh
University of Ulster, School of Computing and Mathematics, Jordanstown, UK

Julie-Ann Augusto-Walkden
South Eastern Health and Social Care Trust, Newtownards, UK

Index

Printed in the USA
CPSIA information can be obtained
at www.ICGtesting.com
JSHW051432221024
72173JS00006B/1447

9 781682 853405